The International Business Environment

Fourth Edition

Leslie Hamilton and

Philip Webster

OXFORD
UNIVERSITY PRESS

OXFORD
UNIVERSITY PRESS

Great Clarendon Street, Oxford, OX2 6DP,
United Kingdom

Oxford University Press is a department of the University of Oxford.
It furthers the University's objective of excellence in research, scholarship,
and education by publishing worldwide. Oxford is a registered trade mark of
Oxford University Press in the UK and in certain other countries

First edition 2009
Second edition 2012
Third edition 2015

Impression: 1

Published in the United States of America by Oxford University Press
198 Madison Avenue, New York, NY 10016, United States of America

British Library Cataloguing in Publication Data
Data available

Library of Congress Control Number: 2018959889

ISBN 978–0–19–880429–1

Printed in Great Britain by
Bell & Bain Ltd., Glasgow

New to this edition

This fourth edition has been revised and updated throughout. The changes include new material on Brexit, the election of Donald Trump, and more material on Africa, Latin America, and the Middle East. This edition incorporates new case studies, mini case studies, and learning tasks. The case studies are drawn from a wide range of geographical areas with a particular emphasis on emerging markets. We have also included cases on some of the giant MNCs—Google, Apple, and Facebook—that are such important actors in the international business environment.

We are indebted to all of the Oxford editorial team for their terrific support throughout, especially Angela Adams (Commissioning Editor) for encouraging us to develop the idea for the book, Helen Adams, Gina Policelli, and Kirsten Shankland (Development Editors on the first, second, and third editions), and Kate Gilks (Publishing Editor for this fourth edition) for her constant support and guidance.

Over the years spent teaching at Leeds Met (now Leeds Beckett University), we have been grateful for the comments and reflections of our domestic and foreign students who have taken the International Business Environment module. We hope that we have learned from these to produce a book that meets the needs of the intended wider audience of future students.

Oxford University Press acknowledgements

In listing those whom OUP would like to thank, we include the many reviewers who made a direct contribution to the way this book was put together. We express our gratitude to all who helped us. The authors and publisher are grateful to those who granted permission to reproduce copyright material. Every effort has been made to trace and contact copyright holders. If notified, the publisher will undertake to rectify any errors or omissions at the earliest opportunity.

The authors and publishers would like to extend thanks to the following for use of images in the book:

World map

iStock.com/ dikobraziy

Part opening images

Part I: © Antun Hirsman/Shutterstock.com; Part II: © Shutterstock.com/Chintung Lee

Chapter opening images

Chapter 1: © iStock.com/ralfgosch; Chapter 2: © iStock.com/matejmo; Chapter 3: © Shutterstock.com/Slavko Sereda; Chapter 4: © Getty Images; Chapter 5: © 123RF.com/frankljunior; Chapter 6: © Shutterstock/John Carnemolla; Chapter 7: © Shutterstock.com/Simon Poon; Chapter 8: © Shutterstock.com/Cornfield; Chapter 9: © Shutterstock.com/Markus Pfaff; Chapter 10: © Shutterstock.com/antb; Chapter 11: © Shutterstock.com/isak55; Chapter 12: © Shutterstock.com/canadastock

Brief contents

PART ONE Global Context   1

PART TWO Global Issues   215

Detailed contents

List of figures

List of tables

List of cases

Guide to the book

This book is aimed at undergraduate students and Masters-level students taking an introductory module on either the Business Environment or International Business Environment on business or related courses. It will provide a thorough underpinning for those modules which deal with International Business Management or Strategy.

The International Business Environment takes, as its starting point, a global perspective with a focus on understanding the global economy, the globalization process, and its impact on international business organizations. It examines the institutions and processes of the global economy and the economic, political, technological, and socio-cultural environment within which business organizations operate.

The International Business Environment is based on a module that the authors have successfully taught for a number of years. The authors have combined experience in academia of module development and delivery at undergraduate and postgraduate level, and this has provided the foundation for this text. Les and Phil have vast experience of teaching the International Business Environment and Business Strategy, and the text benefits from this experience and the feedback from students, including many international students, on these modules.

Why use this book?

This book is aimed at undergraduate students studying the International Business Environment as part of a Business or International Business degree. It also offers an essential knowledge base for postgraduate students in Business, especially those specializing in the International Business Environment.

The text provides comprehensive coverage of the core topics that are central to the International Business Environment. Each topic is presented with a balance of theory, case studies, and exercises aimed to develop the reader's ability to understand and analyse the internal and external environmental factors affecting the business environment.

The case studies and examples used throughout the text identify the opportunities and threats to business organizations arising from changes in the global business environment. Detailed case studies, highlighting key concepts and issues from the chapter, are provided at the start and end of each chapter.

Structure of the book

The book is divided into two parts. The first section, The Global Context, comprises Chapters 1–6 and sets the context for the international business environment, while in the second section, Global Issues, Chapters 7–12 deal with a range of global issues.

The first chapter of the book describes the process of the globalization of markets and production, and examines the key drivers and barriers to that process. It emphasizes the increasing complexity and interdependence of the world economy, concluding that the opportunities and threats arising from the global business environment can have consequences for all business organizations. Chapter 2 examines in more detail some of the more important features of the world economy. It identifies the pattern of global wealth and inequality, and the pattern of international trade. Chapters 3, 4, and 6 include detailed analytical frameworks that provide the tools to enable students to undertake an analysis of external environmental issues and how these impact on business organizations. Chapter 3 looks at the analysis of industries while Chapter 4 places this analysis within an examination of the global macro-environment using the familiar PESTLE framework. These frameworks are then used in Chapter 6 to assess country attractiveness as markets or locations for production. Chapter 5 raises, as part of the context of international business, some of the important issues which arise in the field of corporate social responsibility. Chapters 7–12 analyse in detail the issues in the socio-cultural, technological, political, legal, financial, and ecological environments.

How to use this book

Identify and review with Learning Outcomes

Introducing you to every chapter, learning outcomes outline the main concepts and themes that the chapter covers to clearly identify what you can expect to learn. They can also be used to review your learning and effectively plan your revision.

Contextualize and explore with Case Studies

Topical, diverse case studies at the beginnings and ends of chapters contextualize key ideas and explore real-life examples from the business world.

Case Study Brexit—Reconfiguring cross-border li

Table

Evaluate and challenge with Counterpoint Boxes

Develop your critical thinking skills by evaluating alternative viewpoints and challenging key ideas, either through class discussion or your own reading.

Analyse and apply with Mini Case Studies

Distributed across chapters, these shorter cases illustrate theories and concepts discussed in the chapter, prompting you to analyse how organizations actually apply these ideas in practice.

Mini Case Study 1.1 One belt one road

For several decades, the Chinese economy has been growing and industrializing very rapidly. It has had a major impact on international trade and investment. It is the world's largest exporter of goods and a major source of foreign direct investment (FDI). To feed the rapid expansion of Chinese industry, it

Persia
Ocean
of inte
tive co
cantly

Practise and learn with Learning Tasks

Put your knowledge into practice with a range of learning tasks designed to test and develop your understanding.

Recap and consolidate with Chapter Summaries

Finish every chapter by recapping key themes and consolidating your understanding with these easy-to-digest summaries.

● CHAPTER SUMMARY

In this chapter, we have explained the nature of globalization as a proc nations are reduced. Nations thereby become increasingly interdepende of this interdependence is between members of the NAFTA, Western Eu the rest of the world playing a minor role. Their dominance is under so South Korea. Increased interdependence is indicated by increases in exp

● REVIEW QUESTIONS

1. What is globalization?
2. Where is globalization mainly taking place? Why should that be th
3. Identify the main:
   a. indicators of globalization;

Test and revise with Review Questions

Check your progress and test your knowledge with these end-of-chapter questions, designed to help you revise the coverage of each chapter.

Research and problem-solve with Assignment Tasks

What would you do if you were a business manager? What solutions would you suggest as a researcher? Use these scenario-type questions to develop your research, reasoning, and problem-solving skills.

● ASSIGNMENT TASKS

1. You are a reporter for a quality business newspaper. The editor asks whether globalization is faltering. In the article you should:
   a. analyse and illustrate the growth in trade and FDI; and
   b. assess the challenge to globalization posed by President Trump'
2. CityUK, the body representing UK financial services, aims to persua unrestricted access to the Single Market, allowing them to operate

● FURTHER READING

For a discussion of the discussion and debates around globalization, see

● Baldwin, R. (2016) *The Great Convergence: Information Technology a* Harvard University Press.

Develop and advance with Further Reading

Advance your learning and further develop your understanding with relevant and recommended supplementary reading.

Define and check with the Glossary

Key terms are highlighted in the book and then defined in this end-of-book glossary, helping you to check your understanding and usage of terminology.

Absolute cost barriers obstacles deterring entry of new firms because the capital costs of entering are huge or where the existing firms control a vital resource, e.g. oil reserves—the company Aramco controls 98 per cent of Saudi Arabian oil reserves

Accountability the idea that organizations and people

How to use the online resources

Supporting content for both students and registered lecturers of the book is available in the online resources. Students can test themselves with multiple-choice questions and web exercises, or explore the subject further via web and video links. Lecturers can download PowerPoint slides, answer guidance to the book's review questions, and extended case studies.

Visit www.oup.com/uk/hamilton-webster4e/ to find out more.

About the authors

Leslie Hamilton is currently an associate member of staff at Leeds Beckett University (formerly Leeds Metropolitan University) and holds an MSc in Economics from the University of Hull. He has more than 30 years' experience of teaching at both undergraduate and postgraduate levels, mostly in the areas of the International Business Environment and the European Union. At Leeds Business School, Les was responsible for developing and leading a large module on the Global Business Context. He has taught in France, Germany, Hong Kong, Russia, and Spain. Les worked for two years in the Netherlands researching the economic and social implications of EU policies towards the regions, and examining issues around migration. His other publications cover a variety of topics including the EU, international business, and the business environment.

Philip Webster is an associate member of staff at Leeds Beckett University (formerly Leeds Metropolitan University). He was formerly Director for Undergraduate Studies at Leeds Business School and Principal Lecturer in Business Strategy and International Business. He graduated from the University of Leeds with an MA in Economic Development, and worked in financial services and the computing industry before moving into education. Phil has over 30 years' experience of teaching International Business Environment, Business Strategy and Business Ethics, and Corporate Social Responsibility. He has taught mainly in the UK, but also in India, Sabah, and Hong Kong. Phil has also worked and lived in Malaysia and Cambodia.

Contributors

Neil Barnett is a Senior Associate Professor in Public Policy at Leeds Beckett University, moving there from a career in local government and the NHS. He holds a Masters degree in Public Management from Aston University, and teaches at undergraduate and postgraduate level on a range of modules covering public management and global business environment. He has developed, taught on, and been course leader for a range of executive programmes for public sector managers. Neil has also published in a range of academic journals including *Public Policy and Administration and Local Government Studies*.

John Bratton is Visiting Professor at Edinburgh Napier University, Edinburgh, and Visiting Professor at Strathclyde University, Glasgow, UK. He holds a BSc in Economics from the University of Hull and a PhD in sociology of work from the University of Manchester. He has more than 30 years' experience of teaching at both undergraduate and postgraduate levels in the UK and Canada. His research interests traverse the sociology of work, and he is author of *Japanization at Work: Managerial Studies in the 1990s* (1992) and co-author of *New Technology and Employment* (1981), *Capitalism and Classical Social Theory* (2014), now in its second edition, and author of *Work and Organizational Behaviour* (2015), now in its third edition.

Kirsteen Grant is Associate Professor of Human Resource Management at Edinburgh Napier University. Kirsteen draws on complementary backgrounds in organizational practice and academia. Her practitioner experience lies in supporting strategic organizational change, and people management and development in public sector organizations. She has worked extensively in the areas of professional development, engagement, leadership, learning, and talent development. Her research interests centre on professional, responsible, and precarious work; the (changing) nature and expectations of work; talent management; workplace skills utilization; and high-performance working. She is a Fellow of the Higher Education Academy and Chartered Fellow of the Chartered Institute of Personnel and Development.

Steven Gregory is a Senior Lecturer in Economics, Analytics and International Business at Leeds Beckett University. He is Course Leader for the university's MSc in International Trade and Finance and also leads final year undergraduate modules on International Business and Multinational Enterprises. In addition to teaching, Steven is actively engaged in course and learning development, and was for many years also an Associate Lecturer with the Open University Business School. His research interests are in the political economy of international business and the impact of transnational corporations.

Dorron Otter studied PPE at the University of Oxford and then worked in a variety of different occupations including youth and community work, retailing, tourism, and finance. After undertaking teacher training at the University of York, he spent five years teaching Economics at Queen Mary's College in Basingstoke. Dorron's postgraduate studies took him to the University of Leeds, where he studied the political economy of global development and then became the first BP Fellow in Economic Awareness at the University of Durham. From 1991 to 2017, Dorron worked at Leeds Beckett University combining an active teaching profile with a range of senior management academic roles. He is the co-editor of Wetherly and Otter, *The Business Environment: Themes and issues in a globalizing world*, which is also published by Oxford University Press. Although retired from a full-time academic post, he remains active in academic consultancy and writing.

PART ONE
Global Context

CHAPTER ONE

Globalization

LEARNING OUTCOMES

This chapter will enable you to:

- explain the nature of globalization;

- assess the pace and extent of globalization;

- analyse the factors driving and facilitating globalization;

- explain the importance of globalization for organizations and countries; and

- analyse the factors inhibiting globalization.

Case Study Brexit—Reconfiguring cross-border links

© iStock.com/andrej_k

Table 1.1 Share of UK trade 2015

	Share of UK exports		Share of all UK exports	Share of UK imports	
	Goods	Services		Goods	Services
EU	47%	39%	44%	54%	49%
Rest of world	53%	61%	56%	46%	51%
Total	100%	100%	100%	100%	100%

Source: House of Lords European Union Committee (2016). Parliamentary information licensed under the Open Parliament Licence v3.0

Globalization creates commercial, financial, social, cultural, political, and technological cross-border interconnections through trade, investment, migration, and technology.

The UK joined the European Economic Community in 1973; over the following four decades, it became increasingly integrated with the Community. This was brought about by the reduction in barriers to the free movement of goods, services, capital, and people, leading to growth in exports and imports of goods and services, foreign investment, and the cross-border movement of people.

This case examines different aspects of economic, social, and legal interconnections developed between the UK and the EU in the period up to June 2016, when the UK voted to leave the EU.

Integration through Exports and Imports of Goods and Services

The extent of integration through trade is reflected in Table 1.1, which shows that, in 2015, almost half of the total £222 billion of UK exports went to other EU member states. The UK Office for National Statistics (ONS) reported that over £10 billion of UK exports took the form of passenger cars while financial services exports totalled just over £22 billion (ONS 2017 and 2016). At 47 per cent, the degree of degree of dependence of UK goods exporters on EU markets was greater than that of services at 39 per cent. More than half of UK imports of goods and nearly half of service imports were provided by the EU.

Table 1.2 shows that the 27 EU member states ran a trade surplus with the UK, but at 6–7 per cent, they were not so dependent on the UK market for their exports.

Table 1.2 Comparison of UK and EU Trade

	£ (billion)	Share of total exports
UK exports to EU countries (2016)	222	44%
EU countries' exports to the UK (2015)	291	6–7%

Source: House of Lords European Union Committee (2016). Parliamentary information licensed under the Open Parliament Licence v3.0

Integration through Investment

According to the ONS, the EU as a single region is the largest source of UK inward investment, with a value of £495.8 billion; this is equivalent to 47.9 per cent of total UK inward investment (see Figure 1.1). The UK services sector is the most important area for foreign investors, with a large proportion of that investment taking place in financial services. Manufacturing is well behind in second position, followed by mining and quarrying (ONS 2016a).

As regards outward investment, the EU was the most important destination for UK investment abroad, with a value in 2014 of £404.2 billion, or 39.8 per cent of total UK outward investment with the Netherlands being by far the largest host in the EU (see Figure 1.2). The services sector is by far the most favoured area for UK investors abroad far outstripping mining and quarrying and manufacturing (ONS 2016a).   ➜

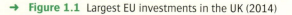

Figure 1.1 Largest EU investments in the UK (2014)

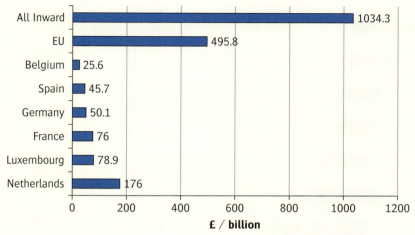

Source: ONS (2016a)

In terms of UK direct investment abroad, the largest destinations for UK overseas direct investment in 2014 were the USA (£239.8 billion), the Netherlands (£118.8 billion), Luxembourg (£108.1 billion), and Hong Kong (£52.3 billion). However, the EU, as a single region, is the largest destination for UK investment, with a value of £404.2 billion, or 39.8 per cent of total UK outward investment (ONS 2016a).

Integration through Cross-border Movement of People

In 2015, according to the United Nations, the number of British people living in the EU was 1.2 million; the largest numbers of

Figure 1.2 Largest outward investment in the EU from the UK (2014)

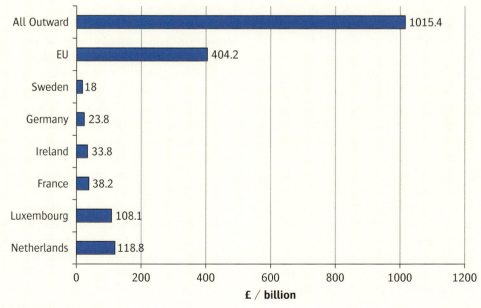

Source: ONS (2016a)

→ **Figure 1.3** UK nationals living in other EU countries (2015)

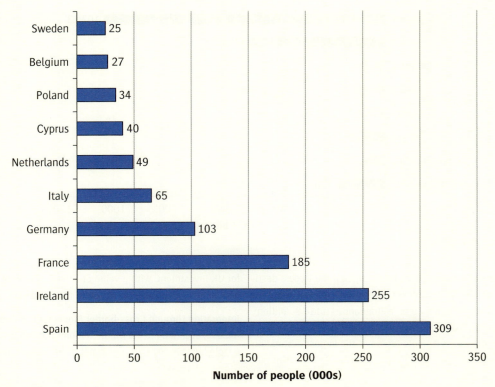

Source: UN Trends in International Migrant Stock (2015)

these were in Spain (309,000), Ireland (255,000), France (185,000), and Germany (103,000) (see Figure 1.3).

The ONS (2015; 2016b) estimated that about 3 million EU nationals were living in the UK, which was equivalent to around 5 per cent of the UK population. The main source of EU migrants to the UK was Poland, with 916,000. The Irish were the second-largest group, with 332,000 residing here. Next in line was Romania at 233,000 followed by Portugal with 219,000 (see Figure 1.4).

There was a marked difference in the age distribution between UK and EU migrants. There were around 106,000 UK nationals in Spain and more than 133,000 living in Ireland claiming the UK state pension (BBC News, 8 July 2016). By comparison, over 2 million EU migrants in the UK were working. In the year ending September 2015, a majority (71 per cent) of EU citizens coming to the UK reported that had travelled there for work and a majority (57 per cent) of those people already had a job lined up (ONS 2016b).

Legal Integration

Integration of the UK into the EU has also occurred through the application of many EU laws to the UK. Between 1993 and 2014, according to the House of Commons Library, 231 Acts and 4,283 statutory instruments implementing EU obligations went through the UK parliament (BBC 2016). EU law applies in areas such as mergers and acquisitions, the right of airlines to access routes and to overfly member states, protection of intellectual property such as inventions, designs, and brand names, work-ers' rights regarding working time and holiday pay, for example, and environmental policies.

The UK government initiated the undoing of nearly 45 years of integration by triggering article 50 of the Lisbon Treaty in March 2017. Leaving the European Union means that the UK and the EU have to undertake very complicated and long-drawn out negotiations reconfiguring the long-term political, legal, economic, technological, and social relation-ships with the EU. The opening negotiations dealt with →

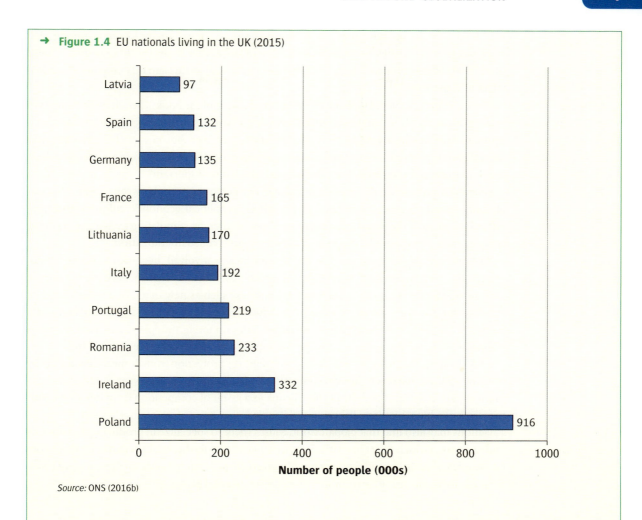

→ **Figure 1.4** EU nationals living in the UK (2015)

Source: ONS (2016b)

the rights that EU citizens would have in the UK and of UK nationals in other EU member states, and the status of the border between Northern Ireland and the Irish Republic. The terms of EU membership preclude the UK from negotiating trade deals with non-member countries before secession from the EU is completed in 2019. The UK government has stated an intention to take legal control by transferring the panoply of EU laws into UK law.

Sources: House of Lords European Union Committee (2016); ONS (2015; 2016; 2016a; 2016b; 2017); United Nations (2015); BBC, bbc.co.uk 8 July 2016

The Process of Globalization

How is it that a teenager in the UK can press a key on his computer and immediately bring chaos to Houston, the biggest US seaport? Why is it that a collapse in the US housing market causes banks to be nationalized in the UK? Why should a demand for democracy in the Middle East be bad news for Egypt's tourist industry but good news for Shell? Why does an earthquake in Japan cause an increase in the price of computer chips and a fall in stock markets worldwide, or the expansion of the Chinese economy cause unemployment among Dell employees in the USA? How can a court decision in Holland ordering the Russian government to pay $50 billion compensation to shareholders in a defunct Russian oil company result in a fall in BP's share price?

These are all examples of globalization—a major theme of the book. They show that events in one corner of the globe can have a major impact on others, sometimes good, sometimes bad. Business operates in a world where globalization confronts business with significant new **threats** and **opportunities** in its external environment to which it has to respond. So globalization is important for business, but what is it and why is it so important?

Globalization involves the creation of linkages or interconnections between nations. It is usually understood as a process in which barriers (physical, political, economic, cultural) separating different regions of the world are reduced or removed, thereby stimulating exchanges in goods, services, money, and people. Removal of these barriers is called **liberalization**.

As these exchanges grow, nations, and the businesses involved, become increasingly integrated and interdependent. Globalization promotes mutual reliance between countries. Globalization can have many advantages for business such as new markets, a wider choice of suppliers for goods and services, lower prices, cheaper locations for investment, and less costly labour. It can also carry dangers because dependence on foreign suppliers and markets leaves businesses vulnerable to events in foreign economies and markets outside their control.

Globalization also poses a threat insofar as it removes protection from domestic producers by opening up their markets to foreign competitors. Manufacturing in footwear, textile and clothing, and toys in the USA and the EU has shrunk as a result of competition from low-cost countries such as China, Vietnam, Pakistan, and Bangladesh.

Nations may also find that globalization causes them to specialize in producing those goods and services in which they are relatively more efficient. While this could generate benefits from **economies of scale** in production, it could also create dependence on a smaller range of products, and leave their economies more vulnerable to external events.

Globalization is Not Global (Yet)

Globalization is something of a misnomer because most foreign trade and investment takes place within and between four economic blocs:

- Western Europe, dominated by EU member states;
- **North Atlantic Free Trade Area (NAFTA)** comprising the USA, Canada, and Mexico;
- Japan; and
- China.

A significant proportion of world trade takes place either within Western Europe and NAFTA or between the blocs. However, much of this trade is internal: just over half of trade in NAFTA is between the member states (globalEDGE n.d.) while 60 per cent of EU trade in goods takes place between the member states (Eurostat 2016).

This situation is reflected in the strategies pursued by big Western and Japanese multinational companies. These organizations focus their strategies on the bloc where they produce.

Figure 1.5 World merchandise export share (%)

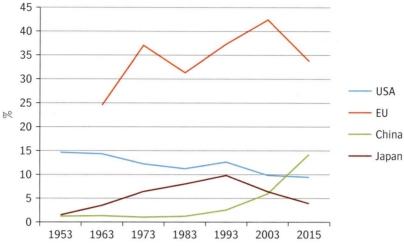

Source: WTO (2016)

This concentration of trade in their own bloc is largely due to the size of their markets. Globally, rich countries make up less than a fifth of the world population but dominate in terms of the consumption of goods and services.

For a long time, NAFTA, the EU, and Japan dominated world trade. However, their predominance came under threat from the 1990s from China whose share of world trade in manufacturing has grown very rapidly. China has joined Germany and the USA among the leading traders. In 2015, China's share of merchandise exports was just over 14 per cent compared to 9.4 per cent for the USA, 8.3 per cent for Germany, and 2.9 per cent for the UK (WTO 2016) (Figure 1.5).

Mini Case Study 1.1 One belt one road

For several decades, the Chinese economy has been growing and industrializing very rapidly. It has had a major impact on international trade and investment. It is the world's largest exporter of goods and a major source of foreign direct investment (FDI). To feed the rapid expansion of Chinese industry, it has invested heavily in commodity producing countries in Africa and Latin America and has become an increasingly important trading partner, investor, and source of finance in them.

In 2013 it set up the Silk Road Belt and the twenty-first-century Maritime Silk Road initiative, which together are called One Belt One Road (OBOR). The Silk Road Belt will establish three routes connecting China to Europe through Central Asia, the Persian Gulf, the Mediterranean via West Asia, and the Indian Ocean though South Asia. The Maritime Silk Road will be a series of interconnections by sea, river, and canal (Figure 1.6). The initiative covers more than 60 countries, and aims to increase significantly technical cooperation and infrastructure investment in sectors such as power generation, transport facilities, and telecommunications, and to develop trade routes among the participating countries and particularly with China. It will connect cities in more than 65 countries across Europe, Asia, and Africa, representing more than 4 billion people (over 60 per cent of the world's population and nearly 30 per cent of global GDP).

Finance of $1.1 trillion has been agreed provided by, among others, the Silk Road Fund and the Asia Infrastructure Bank →

→ set up by China. More than 50 agreements have been signed with countries such as Hungary, Mongolia, Russia, Tajikistan, and Turkey. More than 200 firms have also signed up. Examples of projects include the China–Pakistan Economic Corridor where large investments were made in infrastructure such as electricity generation and transport. Egypt will receive $15 billion of Chinese investment to set up an Economic Zone in the Suez Canal area and for investment in land and maritime transport facilities. Other projects under way include a train connection between Eastern China and Iran that may be expanded to Europe, new rail links with Laos and Thailand, and high-speed-rail projects in Indonesia. Within a decade, trade between China and countries on the Silk Road is expected to exceed $2.5 trillion (HSBC 2017).

Questions

1. Advance commercial and political reasons why China has established the One Belt One Road initiative.
2. Discuss the impact of OBOR on the degree of internationalization of the Chinese economy
3. What are the implications of the initiative for firms:
   - producing materials used in the construction industry?
   - making transport equipment?
   - providing financial services?

Figure 1.6 Routes, one belt one road

Source: © McKinsey & Company. Reproduced with kind permission.

The Indicators of Globalization

There are three main economic and financial indicators of globalization. These are:

- international trade in goods and services;
- the transfer of **money** capital from one country to another; and
- the movement of people across national borders.

Of the three, international trade and foreign investment are the most important. Each of the three indicators will be examined in turn.

International Trade

International trade means that countries become more interconnected through the exchange of goods and services; that is, through imports and exports. Between 1950 and 2006, world trade grew 27-fold in volume terms, three times faster than world output growth (WTO 2007). We can conclude from this that importing and exporting were becoming an ever more crucial component of global and national economic activity. From 2005 to 2015, trade in goods and services almost doubled (Figure 1.7).

As can be seen from 1.8, up to 2012 export growth exceeded that of world output (GDP), the total value of the world's output of goods and services. Both went into hard reverse in 2009 due to the global recession with trade in intermediate goods, such as semi-finished products, and capital goods, like machinery, much more badly affected than consumption goods. World trade suffered its sharpest decline in 70 years, but recovered strongly in 2010. However, from 2012 growth faltered due to a weak global economy, before picking up somewhat at the end of 2016.

Trade in services is around one-third of that in goods. Service exports grew exceptionally fast in the period between 2000 and 2008, at an average rate of 14 per cent per annum. However, like merchandise trade, they suffered a setback with the global crisis. Subsequently, growth resumed but turned negative in 2014 (Figure 1.9).

Figure 1.7 Trade in merchandise and commercial services

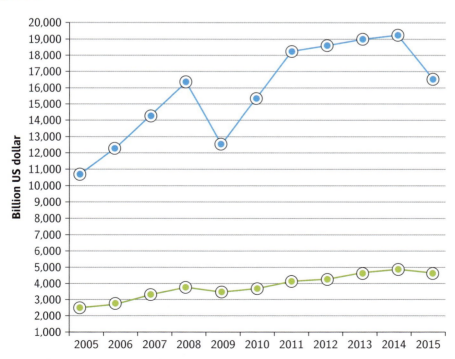

● Merchandise trade   ● Trade in commercial services

Source: WTO (2016)

Figure 1.8 Growth in world goods exports by volume and real GDP growth (%)

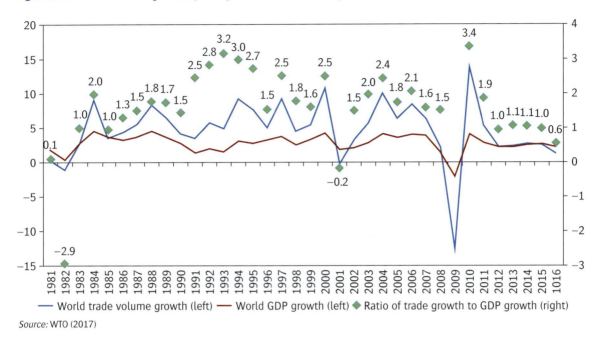

— World trade volume growth (left) — World GDP growth (left) ◆ Ratio of trade growth to GDP growth (right)

Source: WTO (2017)

Figure 1.9 Growth in volume of merchandise exports by region (Index 2012 = 100)

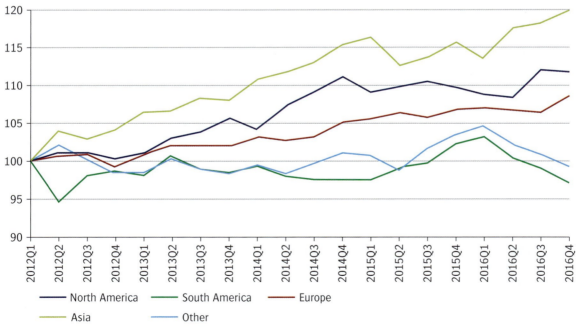

— North America — South America — Europe

— Asia — Other

Source: WTO (2017)

In 2016, four countries—China, the USA, Germany, and Japan—were the largest traders of goods, with a share of around 36 per cent. The USA, the UK, and Germany are the major exporters of commercial services, with China ranking fifth in service exports (WTO 2017).

Learning Task

Examine Figures 1.8, 1.9, and 1.10.

1. Describe the growth path of merchandise exports over the period.
2. Which regions have benefited most/least from export growth?
3. Comment on the growth of commercial services exports.

Come up with some explanations for your findings.

Some economies like Germany are particularly dependent on international trade. According to the **World Trade Organization** (WTO Trade Profiles), Germany's exports and imports of goods and services equate to around 85 per cent of its GDP compared with more than two-fifths for China, 57 per cent for the UK, but only about 28 per cent in the USA. Furthermore, the UK is heavily dependent on customers in the USA and the EU for sales of goods and services. Events in those regions are outside the control of UK business, but could have a major impact on it. For example, a rapid and simultaneous expansion of those economies would be very good news for sales of British manufactures, but a **recession**, as occurred in 2008/09, could mean a significant fall in turnover and profits.

Figure 1.10 Growth in the value of commercial services exports by category (%)

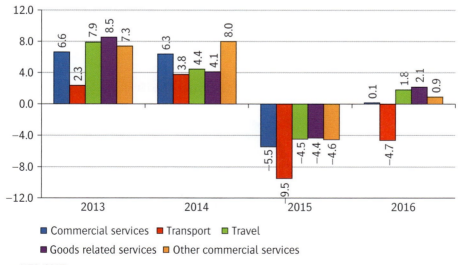

Source: WTO (2017)

Multinational companies (MNCs) are major traders and account for a large proportion of international trade, with significant proportions accounted for by trade between subsidiaries within the same company—this is called intra-firm trade. So, for example, Ford makes gearboxes in its factory in Bordeaux and exports them to its assembly plants in other European countries. Almost one-third of world trade is intra-firm according to UNCTAD (2016). Trade relies on, and generates, cross-border financial links through the need for services such as trade financing and insurance against currency risks. Banks often follow their customers into foreign markets.

Financial Flows

Foreign Indirect Investment

The second main driver is the transfer of money capital across borders.

This can take two forms. The first, **foreign indirect investment** (FII, or portfolio investment), occurs where money is used to purchase financial assets in another country. These assets can comprise foreign stocks, bonds issued by governments or companies, or even currency. Thus, UK financial institutions such as HSBC and Barclays often purchase bonds or company shares quoted on foreign stock exchanges such as New York or Tokyo. Purchasers buy them for the financial return they generate. This activity has been increasing very rapidly—in the 1990s, such trading was expanding at more than 20 per cent per annum, helping to bring about an increased integration of **financial markets**. Growth faltered after the East Asian financial crisis of the late 1990s, but picked up again in the new century. The interlinkages created by FII were demonstrated in 2006 when it was estimated that foreign financial institutions held more than 10 per cent of the US$8 **trillion** in outstanding US residential mortgages in the form of mortgage-related securities. This left them vulnerable to the downturn in the US housing market which started in 2007, and led to a worldwide **credit crunch** (see Chapter 11). The International Monetary Fund (2017) estimated that the stock of cross-border portfolio investment amounted to around US$45 trillion. Figure 1.11 shows that developed countries like the USA and Eurozone members are by far the most popular sources of portfolio investments. They are also the largest hosts for this investment.

Figure 1.11 Top ten economies—portfolio investment assets 2016 ($trn)

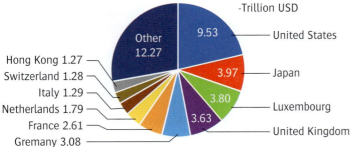

Source: IMF (2017)

Activity on the foreign exchange market is enormous. The average daily turnover worldwide in 2001 was US$1.4 trillion. By 2016, turnover had almost trebled to US$5 trillion, with most business taking place in the main financial centres: New York, London, Singapore, and Tokyo. Only a very small proportion of currency trading is associated with the financing of trade in goods and services—most goes on the buying and selling of financial assets (Bank for International Settlements 2016).

Another example of cross-border flows of money is migrant remittances. Migrants often send money to their home countries, and the total amount has grown over time. This reached $601 billion in 2016, the big recipients being India and China with $72 billion and $64 billion respectively, while the Philippines received $30 billion. The USA was the biggest source, sending some US$56 billion in 2015 (World Bank 2016). Remittances are a vital source of foreign currency for some poor countries—Tajikistan, the Kyrgyz Republic, Nepal, Tonga, and Moldova are countries whose remittances from abroad equate to more than 25 per cent of GDP (World Bank 2016).

Foreign Direct Investment

The second form of capital movement is FDI. This occurs when a firm establishes, acquires, or increases production facilities in a foreign country. Multinational corporations (MNCs) are responsible for FDI and the massive increase that has occurred in FDI in the last 50 years. The distinguishing feature between FII and FDI is that MNCs not only own the assets but also exercise managerial control over them.

FDI grew spectacularly in the 1990s, but fluctuated widely in the opening decade of the century. It declined steeply after 2000 due to weak growth of the world economy. Following a five-year upward trend from 2003, FDI inflows declined dramatically as a result of the global financial crisis—by 16 per cent in 2008 and 37 per cent in 2009 to $1.1 trillion. Outflows from rich countries fell much more steeply than those from developing economies. Since the global crisis, the recovery in FDI has been bumpy. FDI inflows rose to $1.75 trillion in 2016 still below the peak of 2007 (Figure 1.12).

Countries can receive inflows of investment, but they can also be sources of investment. Until recently, the major recipients of FDI were developed countries, mainly because of their large and affluent markets. In 2006, they received around 60 per cent of FDI inflows while accounting for the vast majority (more than four-fifths) of the outflows. In the aftermath of the global crisis, rich countries' share of inflows fell but then increased to 60 per cent in 2016. Developed economies continued to dominate outflows (Figure 1.13). The USA heads the league of FDI recipients, followed a long way behind by the UK, China, and Hong Kong. Brazil ranked seventh and India ninth. The USA is also, by far, the biggest source of FDI followed by China, the Netherlands, and Japan (Figures 1.13 and 1.14).

Until 2010, FDI largely involved MNCs in rich countries investing in production facilities in other rich countries, with developing countries and Eastern Europe, having smaller and less lucrative markets, playing only a minor part. Where FDI did take place in poor countries, it was often to exploit natural resources such as oil or other minerals, to take advantage of cheap labour, or, sometimes, to penetrate a market. China was favoured by foreign multinationals because labour was cheap and there was great market potential. Firms like Volkswagen, Toyota, Caterpillar, and Tesco invested there to take advantage of cheap resources or to exploit the market.

The top 100 MNCs hold over $13 trillion of assets, have sales of more than $7 trillion, and employ some 16 million workers (UNCTAD 2017). While the vast majority are based in rich countries,

Figure 1.12 FDI inflows 2005–18 ($bn)—pie chart includes percentages

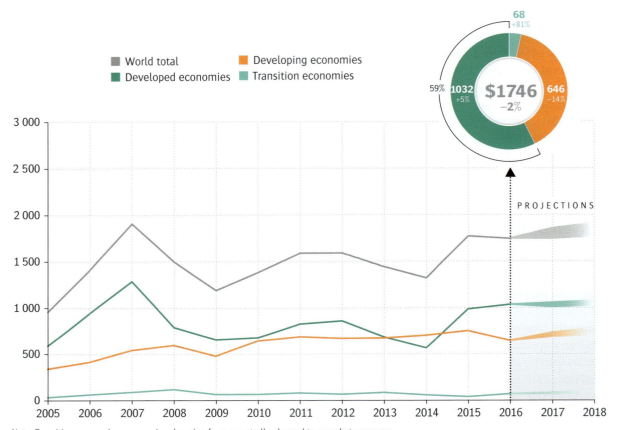

Note: Transition economies: economies changing from a centrally planned to a market economy.
Source: UNCTAD (2017)

an increasing number of MNCs are found in developing economies such as Tata of India, Hong Kong's CK Hutchison, China's Lenovo, Vale of Brazil, and Russia's Gazprom. Most MNCs are privately owned, but there are some 1,500 state-owned MNCs from both rich and poor countries with more than 86,000 foreign affiliates. Fifteen of the top 100 MNCs are state-owned; one example is China's Cosco Shipping (UNCTAD 2017).

Learning Task

Referring to Figures 1.13 and 1.14, advance reasons why:

1. the USA and China are the biggest foreign direct investors; and

2. the USA and UK are the receivers of most FDI.

Big MNCs are the most important foreign direct investors. Table 1.3 shows the 20 biggest global companies ranked by the value of their foreign assets.

Figure 1.13 FDI inflows—the top 20 host economies 2015 and 2016 (US$bn)

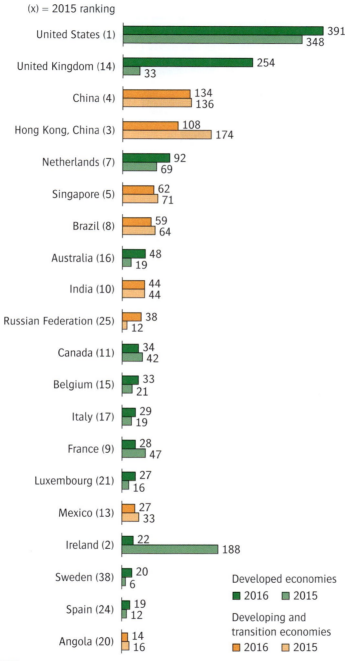

(x) = 2015 ranking

United States (1): 391 / 348
United Kingdom (14): 254 / 33
China (4): 134 / 136
Hong Kong, China (3): 108 / 174
Netherlands (7): 92 / 69
Singapore (5): 62 / 71
Brazil (8): 59 / 64
Australia (16): 48 / 19
India (10): 44 / 44
Russian Federation (25): 38 / 12
Canada (11): 34 / 42
Belgium (15): 33 / 21
Italy (17): 29 / 19
France (9): 28 / 47
Luxembourg (21): 27 / 16
Mexico (13): 27 / 33
Ireland (2): 22 / 188
Sweden (38): 20 / 6
Spain (24): 19 / 12
Angola (20): 14 / 16

Developed economies
■ 2016   ■ 2015
Developing and transition economies
■ 2016   ■ 2015

Source: UNCTAD (2017)

However, only a few of the 500 MNCs that dominate international business have a genuinely global presence. US MNCs concentrate on North America, European companies on Western Europe, and Japanese MNCs on Asia. However, FDI statistics show that the growth of developing economies such as China, India, and Brazil has caused many MNCs to invest there.

Figure 1.14 FDI outflows—the top 20 source economies 2015 and 2016 (US$bn)

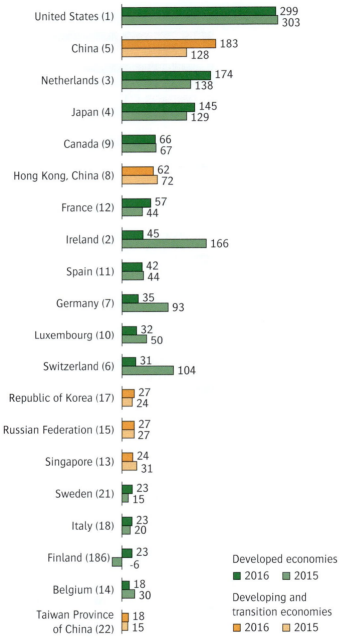

Source: UNCTAD (2017)

Table 1.3 The world's top 20 non-financial MNCs, ranked by foreign assets $bn, 2016

Ranking by:					Assets $bn		Sales $bn		Employment 000s		TNI (%)
Foreign assets	TNI	Corporation	Home economy	Industry	Foreign	Total	Foreign	Total	Foreign	Total	
1	38	Royal Dutch Shell	UK	Mining, quarrying, and petroleum	350	411	152	234	67	92	74
2	63	Toyota Motor	Japan	Motor vehicles	304	436	174	255	149	349	60
3	36	BP plc	UK	Petroleum refining and related industries	235	263	141	183	44	75	75
4	24	Total SA	France	Petroleum refining and related industries	233	243	110	142	70	102	81
5	20	Anheuser-Busch InBev	Belgium	Food and beverage	208	258	40	46	163	207	82
6	61	Volkswagen Group	Germany	Motor vehicles	197	432	192	240	347	627	60
7	67	Chevron	US	Petroleum refining and related industries	189	260	54	110	29	55	58
8	68	General Electric	US	Industrial and commercial machinery	179	365	70	124	191	295	57
9	79	Exxon Mobil	US	Petroleum refining and related industries	166	330	122	219	36	71	52
10	58	Softbank	Japan	Telecommunications	146	220	45	82	42	64	62
11	23	Vodafone	UK	Telecommunications	144	165	45	52	76	105	82
12	64	Daimler AG	Germany	Motor vehicles	139	256	144	170	112	282	60
13	32	Honda	Japan	Motor vehicles	130	170	113	129	143	208	78
14	86	Apple	US	Computer equipment	127	321	140	216	46	116	48
15	26	BHP Billiton	Australia	Mining, quarrying, and petroleum	119	119	30	31	11	27	79
16	42	Nissan	Japan	Motor vehicles	117	165	89	108	88	152	70
17	51	Siemens	Germany	Industrial and commercial machinery	115	140	68	88	137	351	66
18	71	Enel SpA	Italy	Electricity, gas, and water	111	134	38	76	30	62	55
19	17	CK Hutchinson Holdings	Hong Kong, China	Retail trade	111	131	26	33	264	290	85
20	57	Mitsubishi	Japan	Wholesale trade	108	141	20	59	52	68	62

Source: UNCTAD (2017)

Learning Task

Examine Table 1.3.

1. In which type of economy are these companies based?

2. Which companies are most/least international?

3. Identify two sectors appearing most frequently and advance explanations for this.

Counterpoint Box 1.1 Google—'Don't be evil'

The founders of Google claimed that the company was 'not a conventional company. We do not intend to become one' (SEC 10-K filing 2016). The brand is one of the world's most recognized and generates revenues through online advertising. Its core products such as Search, Android, Maps, Chrome, YouTube, Google Play, and Gmail each have over 1 billion monthly active users and the company thinks that these numbers are only 'scratching the surface' (SEC 10-K filing 2016). The company is ambitious, aiming to extend internet access to a further 5 billion people. The company sees itself as a benefactor of mankind:

> Those people will be able to learn and start businesses, to grow and prosper in ways they simply could not without an Internet connection. Creating platforms for other people's success is a huge part of who we are. We want the world to join us online and to be greeted with the best possible experience once they get there . . . The opportunities to improve lives on a grand scale are endless. And there are people around the world whose lives we can improve every day by bringing information into their homes, into their schools, and into their pockets—showing them just how powerful the simple idea of 'getting online' can be. (SEC Filing 10-K 2016)

The organization even sees itself as helping get rid of undemocratic regimes:

> the presence of communication technologies will chip away at most autocratic governments, since . . . the odds against a restrictive, information-shy regime dealing with an empowered citizenry armed with personal fact-checking devices get progressively worse . . . (Eric Schmidt Google executive chairman, cited in *The Observer* 2 July 2017)

The company slogan in the first decade of the millennium was 'Don't be evil'.

Google has been very successful in terms of:

- number of users worldwide;

- revenues and profits which more than doubled between 2011 and 2016, with profit margins on turnover of 25 per cent or more (Figure 1.15); and

- market share—its share of search activity in the EU, Brazil, and India is 90 per cent or more, and 80 per cent in the USA (Statista 2018).

On the other hand, Google has encountered fierce criticism from the European Commission, national governments, and customers.

In 2017, the European Commission fined Google €2.4 billion for illegally abusing its dominant position as a search engine by giving prominence to its own shopping-comparison site over rivals. The company was using its monopoly position in one market to gain power in another. Google had 90 days to stop the abuse, or would face penalty payments of up to 5 per cent of daily worldwide turnover. The organization has also clashed with the Commission over privacy and the protection of personal data (see European Commission Memo 17/17; *The Guardian* 10 January 2017).

Google has been accused of tax avoidance in Europe by shifting profits to low tax countries such as Ireland. Allegedly Google was billing 92 per cent of its non-US sales to Ireland (Public Accounts Committee 2012). The chair of the UK Parliamentary Public Accounts Select Committee said that the company was 'devious, calculated and, in my view, unethical' (BBC News 16 May) and 'You are a company that says you "do no evil". And I think that you do do evil' (YouTube 16 May 2016).

Publishers have problems with Google. *The Guardian* withdrew ads when it found them on YouTube videos posted by extremists (also see Counterpoint Box 3.2 Online advertising: the latest shining object?). Axel Springer, the German publishing company, a Google customer, supported the EU action ➡

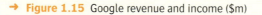

→ **Figure 1.15** Google revenue and income ($m)

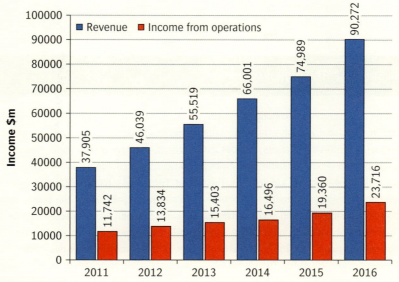

Source: Alphabet SEC 10-K filing 2016; http://www.google.com/finance?fstype=ii&q=NASDAQ: GOOG. Accessed 1 August 2017.

against it. Its chief executive spoke of Google's market power and publishers' increasing dependence on it for online advertising and the traffic generated by it. He saw the company as a threat to 'our values, our understanding of the nature of humanity, our worldwide social order and, from our own perspective, the future of Europe . . . We are afraid of Google' (Schmidt 2017).

Sources: European Commission IP17/1784 and Memo 17/1785; *The Observer* 2 July 2017; *Financial Times* 1 July 2017; *New York Times* 26 March 2017; Public Accounts Committee (2012)

Questions

1. Explain:
   a. why the EU is unhappy with Google;
   b. why publishers feel intimidated by Google.
2. Construct a defence for Google in the face of the attacks it faces.

See García Martínez (2017) and Google's response to the EU fine in Walker (2017).

Greenfield and Brownfield Investment

MNC investment overseas can be broken down into **greenfield** and **brownfield investment**. Greenfield investment involves the establishment of completely new production facilities, such as Ford setting up its new car factory near St Petersburg in Russia. Brownfield investment entails the purchase of already existing production facilities—the **acquisition** of UK-based brewer SABMiller by Belgium's Anheuser-Busch InBev is an example of this. MNCs have undertaken massive brownfield investment. In 2000 they were involved in around 11,000 **cross-border mergers** and acquisitions (M&As) to a value of more than US$1.1 trillion, two to three times greater than the figures for 1995. However, after 2000 there was a significant drop in **merger** activity to around US$380 billion by 2004; it then started to pick up so that by 2007, the total had again reached US$1 trillion. The recovery was curtailed by the global crisis so much so that even by 2016 the total value at $737 billion was significantly below the 2007 figure (UNCTAD 2017).

The top purchasers were rich country MNCs from the USA, Western Europe, and Japan, but companies from China and Hong Kong also played a prominent role. Just over 40 per cent of cross-border M&As by value take place between rich countries. UNCTAD (2017) found significant rises in cross-border mergers in the oil and gas, beverages, and electronics sectors.

Mini Case Study 1.2 The digital connectors

UNCTAD (2017) noted that digitization is becoming an increasingly important factor in the global economy, fundamentally changing the ways business produces and markets its goods and services. MNCs like Google, Facebook, LinkedIn, and Twitter have been major players in creating global connectivity. Their digital platforms allow firms to promote themselves internationally to billions of potential customers using social networks. Facebook in 2017 had nearly 2 billion monthly active users (MAUs) (*Zephoria Digital Marketing* 6 July 2017). Its platforms include Instagram, Messenger, and WhatsApp. There were 1 billion users for Google Maps, YouTube, Chrome, Google Maps, Gmail, Search, and Google Play—in 2016, 82 billion apps were downloaded, and 1 billion hours of YouTube videos viewed each day (*The Verge* 17 May 2017). Twitter lagged behind Facebook and Google with 328 MAUs (Twitter n.d.). MAUs for Microsoft's LinkedIn, which provides a social network for business professionals, totalled 106 million (LinkedIn n.d.) (Table 1.4).

While MNCs providing social networks often claim that their reach is global, UNCTAD (2017) found a significant digital divide between developed and developing economies. In developed economies, more than 80 per cent of the population and businesses used the internet. In Africa one-fifth of the population and less than half of businesses did so. The figures for Asia and Latin America fell in between those for developed and developing economies.

Facebook, Google, and Twitter have all experienced problems in China, running up against attempts by the Chinese authorities to control information flows to their citizens. Google pulled its search engine out of China, Facebook was banned, and Twitter was blocked. Despite mission statements from Facebook 'to give people the power to share and make the world more open and connected' and Google 'to organise the world's information and make it universally accessible', the size of the Chinese market has made both of these organizations amenable to negotiations with the Chinese government over censorship (Facebook SEC 10-K filling 2016;Google n.d.).

Other countries blocking social networks include Turkey, Iran, Pakistan, North Korea, Vietnam, and Eritrea.

Sources: Facebook Sec 10-K filing 2016; *The Guardian* 30 November 2016; *Mother Jones* 28 March 2014; *South China Morning Post* 12 March 2017; Twitter SEC 10-K Filing 2016; UNCTAD (2017)

Questions
1. Explain how Google and Facebook contribute to globalization.
2. How globalized are these MNCs in terms of sales and assets?
3. What is the digital divide?
4. Discuss how the divide can be seen by digital MNCs as:
    a. a challenge;
    b. an opportunity.

Table 1.4 The big digital connectors 2016/17

	Sales $bn	Assets $bn	Foreign Sales as % of Total	Foreign Assets as % of Total	MAUs million
Google	75	147	54	24	1000
Facebook	18	49	53	21	2000
LinkedIn	3	6	38	18	106
Twitter	2	7	35	7	328

Sources: UNCTAD (2017); *Zephoria Digital Marketing* 6 July 2017; *The Verge* 17 May 2017; http://www.linkedin.com; http://about.twitter.com

Migration

The globalization of markets has not been paralleled by the liberalization of labour flows. While globalization has led to the dismantling of barriers to trade in goods, services, and capital, barriers to cross-border labour movements are not falling as fast. Nevertheless, migration between developing and developed countries has risen. Flows of migrants are greatest to North America and Europe, while Asia, Latin America, and Africa are major sources.

According to the OECD (2016), the number of migrants (people residing for more than a year in a country other than where they were born) was 243 million—just over 3 per cent of the world's population. This means that the migrant population more than doubled in 25 years. Europe has most migrants with 76 million (around 10 per cent of the population), Asia has 75 million (about 2 per cent), and North America 54 million (15 per cent) (UN 2016). This increase in numbers has occurred despite the fact that, during the last 30 years of the twentieth century, migration had become steadily more difficult—particularly for people in developing countries wanting to enter Europe. Migrants constitute a significant proportion of the population in some countries. In Australia, Canada, New Zealand, Luxembourg, and Switzerland, this proportion exceeds 20 per cent. The USA, along with certain European countries such as the UK, France, Germany, the Netherlands, and Sweden, has a between 10 and 15 per cent of immigrants. None of these compare with the Middle Eastern state of Qatar where more than four-fifths of the population are migrants. Care needs to be taken regarding the accuracy of migration statistics, because countries differ in their definition of 'migrant' and clandestine migrants are unlikely to be picked up by official statistics. The official immigrant population in the USA for 2015 is 47 million, with the number of unauthorized migrants estimated at over 11 million (Baker and Rytina 2013). The OECD (2016) reported that migration comprised equal shares of men and women, most of whom were of working age, and increasingly educated.

People move for a variety of economic, social, and political reasons. They may move voluntarily to find work, to earn higher wages, to study, or to reunite with their families. Widening inequalities in income and job opportunities increase the pressures to move. Movement may also be stimulated by employers in developed countries actively recruiting labour from abroad. At the start of the new century, the attitudes of certain governments towards migration changed as shortages of skilled workers emerged. For example, the USA, the UK, and Germany started to look much more favourably on the entry of workers with high levels of education and skills in areas such as IT. The 2007/08 global crisis caused a hardening of attitudes to migration in rich countries.

Migration may also be involuntary where people, often in large numbers, are forced to migrate by political instability and violations of human rights—as we have seen, for example, in civil unrest in North Africa and the conflicts in Syria and Iraq. Natural disasters, such as hurricanes, earthquakes, and floods, can also force people to move. The UNHCR (2015) noted an unprecedented increase in numbers of refugees and asylum seekers mainly from Syria, Afghanistan and Somalia moving mostly to neighbouring countries, but also to Europe.

Large short-term movements of people also occur as a result of executives going on foreign business trips, students involved in study abroad, and tourism. The UNWTO (2017) recorded over 1.2 billion international tourists in 2016. France, the most popular tourist destination, receives 85 million tourists annually, the USA around 78 million, Spain 69 million, and China 57 million. Some small countries, for example, in the Caribbean where St Lucia, Antigua and Barbuda, and the Bahamas are heavily dependent on tourism for their income.

Learning Task

In 2016, almost 1 million illegal migrants were apprehended in the EU (Eurostat 2017).
   Examine Figure 1.16.

1. In which countries were the highest number of illegal migrants present?

2. Why are these countries attractive to migrants?

Figure 1.16 Number of illegal migrants in EU and EFTA 2016

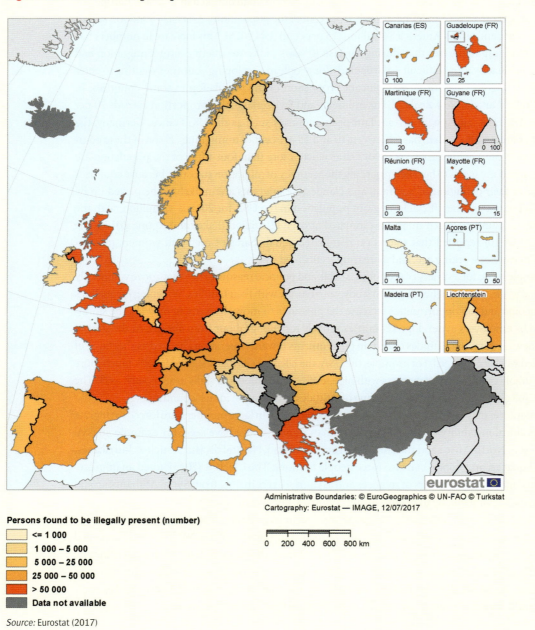

Persons found to be illegally present (number)

- <= 1 000
- 1 000 – 5 000
- 5 000 – 25 000
- 25 000 – 50 000
- > 50 000
- Data not available

Source: Eurostat (2017)

Globalization is All-pervasive

Although globalization is often seen as an economic phenomenon involving trade and investment, it also has many other cultural and social dimensions. Held et al. (1999) argue that globalization is all-pervasive. They define globalization as:

> the widening, deepening and speeding up of worldwide interconnectedness in all aspects of contemporary social life, from the cultural to the criminal, the financial to the spiritual. (1999: 2)

As Held et al. (1999) observe, globalization is not confined to economic life, but influences many other areas of society. They contend that each of these areas is becoming more deeply affected by the phenomenon. Cultural life involving the attitudes, behaviour, and values that are characteristic of a society can be influenced by the process. Globalization can influence **culture** through the transfer of knowledge, ideas, and beliefs across national borders.

Mass media, such as television and film, illustrate how culture has been influenced by globalization. American programmes such as *The Simpsons* and *Breaking Bad* are watched worldwide. While the USA is by far the major exporter of TV programmes, countries with large internal markets, such as Brazil, Japan, and the UK, are also active exporters. Similarly, US films like *Guardians of the Galaxy* and *Wonder Woman* are widely shown around the world. The collapse of communism in Eastern Europe and the arrival of cable and satellite systems opened up more markets to US media companies like Netflix and Amazon Prime. Diet is another area influenced by globalization. In France, the consumption of fast food such as hamburgers and soft drinks like Coca-Cola has increased, and this is attributed by some commentators to the globalization of fast food chains like McDonald's, Subway, and Burger King. The movement of people can also have an impact on diet. In the second half of the twentieth century, many migrants came to the UK from South East Asia. Thousands of Indian, Chinese, and Thai restaurants are spread across UK towns and cities. Another obvious route for transfer of culture across borders is through education. Universities in the USA, Western Europe, and Australia have enthusiastically embarked on campaigns to recruit students from abroad. Some have also gone in for FDI by setting up education facilities in other countries or have established partnerships with foreign colleges. The EU, through its Erasmus and Socrates programmes, has led to large numbers of students studying in other member states. In a further move to facilitate the movement of students and workers across borders, more than 40 European countries have initiated a programme of reform of their university systems. The idea is to standardize the structure of university studies with degrees taking three or four years and the introduction of a common system of assessment, the European Credit and Transfer System.

Another conduit for such transfers is through the world of work. For example, the UK and the USA have been favoured locations for Japanese car companies, meaning that capital has been moved to these countries from Japan. The movement of capital across national borders brings with it different ways of working, such as Just-in-Time, where suppliers deliver raw materials and components immediately before they are needed in the manufacturing process, or quality circles, where small groups of employees meet together to identify how production could be improved. In turn, domestic firms have been influenced by new methods. For example, Nissan has persuaded suppliers to alter their production methods, and Toyota's rivals, such as General Motors and Ford, on finding their market shares slipping because of their inability to compete with the Japanese, have responded to the threat by introducing some of their working methods. As a result, in the UK and the USA, car industry working methods have become similar to those in Japan. Another example concerns McDonald's setting up in Moscow in partnership with the City Council. The company had to devise a strategy for dealing with a Russian workforce that had a reputation for being surly and slovenly. McDonald's introduced expatriate managers and training programmes to show the Russian staff how they wanted things to be done. Moscow City Council officials could not believe that the employees in the fast food outlet were Russian, because they were so friendly.

The globalization process can also be seen in sport, where football players like Lionel Messi and Cristiano Ronaldo cross borders to play abroad. There has been a rush of FDI into the English premier football league. Chelsea is owned by a Russian businessman, while Liverpool and Manchester United were acquired by US tycoons. Manchester United is promoted and known worldwide; it is marketed as an international brand and there is a lucrative trade in Manchester United team kit and other products outside the UK. Furthermore, many top teams in England are now managed by foreigners.

A further impact of globalization is on health. A new treatment for disease, discovered in one country, can be quickly transferred to others, helping to limit the spread of disease and improve the quality of health care. On the other hand, diseases may also spread more quickly as people move across borders; for example, the outbreak of the Ebola virus in 2014 spread across several West African countries. Illness can also be spread through trade. The avian flu virus was first contracted by Vietnamese and Thai poultry farmers. The infection spread to other countries through cross-border trade in poultry and the movement of migratory birds.

With regard to crime, globalization, by removing barriers to movement, can make it easier for criminals to operate in other countries. Criminals can move more easily across borders, as can pornography, prostitution, and illegal substances such as drugs. Large amounts of cocaine are produced in Colombia, and gangs there ensure that the drug finds its way to users in the USA. The Russian mafia is involved in trafficking women for the vice trade in Amsterdam. Communications technology facilitates the electronic movement across borders of money generated by these illegal activities into countries where criminals can portray it as being derived from a legitimate source. Alternatively, they may move the money to countries where the laws regulating such **money laundering** activities are deficient. The internet makes it easier for criminals in one country to commit crimes in another, whether selling pornography or stealing money from bank accounts.

Religion, or the spiritual dimension as Held et al. (1999) call it, is another globalized area. Major religions, such as the Catholic, Anglican, Muslim, and Jewish faiths, all operate multinationally and have been spreading their values over large parts of the world for the last few centuries. In the UK, the established churches, such as the Church of England, are in decline in contrast to evangelical churches, which have their roots in the USA and, ironically, have their origin in English Puritanism. Evangelical churches are also expanding rapidly in parts of Africa and Latin America.

Mini Case Study 1.3 Globalization—divergence and convergence

Baldwin (2016) identifies waves of globalization which he calls accelerations. The first acceleration occurred in the nineteenth century, when technical advance improved the methods and reduced the costs of transporting goods, particularly by rail and steamship. This facilitated an explosion of global trade. This allowed countries to specialize in what they were relatively good at producing. However, Baldwin points out that while the costs of moving goods fell, the costs of moving technical knowledge and people over long distances did not reduce significantly. The result was that 'markets expanded globally but industries clustered locally', leading to what he called the Great Divergence between rich and poor countries (Baldwin 2016: 5). Countries such as the industrializing UK, part of what became known as the North, had the capital to make higher technology goods and export them. The North focused increasingly on large-scale manufacturing where productivity and wages were high, whereas the South, containing poor countries such as India, concentrated on low-wage, low-productivity agriculture and small-scale manufacturing. As a result, between 1820 and 1990, the gap between rich and poor countries expanded rapidly, with the share of world income for rich economies soaring from 20 per cent to around 70 per cent.

The second acceleration, which according to Baldwin caused a Great Convergence, started in the 1990s when China and other developing countries started to emerge as important global players. Baldwin attributes this to the IT revolution and the resulting improvements in, and falling costs of, telecommunications. Advances in technology allowed MNCs to take advantage of the wage gap created by the Great Divergence by splitting up production processes and transferring the labour intensive operations to developing countries through FDI or by outsourcing it to independent suppliers. Digitization made it profitable for MNCs to establish, coordinate, and control complex global supply chains over long distances. According to Baldwin, the IT revolution not only made feasible the offshoring of production, but also significantly lowered the cost of transferring managerial, marketing, and technical knowledge. The information revolution caused a major shift of production from rich to poor countries, allowing a few developing countries, like China and India, to industrialize at a 'dizzying pace' (Baldwin 2016: 8). This process resulted in developed countries' share of world income reverting back to where it was in 1900.

Source: Baldwin (2016)

Questions

1. How did technical advances in transport facilitate the first acceleration of globalization?
2. Advance reasons for the North benefiting most from the first acceleration.
3. Explain how the IT revolution in the second acceleration benefited:
   a. MNCs;
   b. the South.

The Drivers of Globalization

In 1983, Theodore Levitt claimed:

> Gone are accustomed differences in national or regional preferences. Gone are the days when a company could sell last year's model—or lesser versions of advanced products—in the less developed world. Gone are the days when prices, margins and profits were generally higher than at home.

Although Levitt was overstating the case, he was making the point that technology, through communication, transport, and travel, was driving the world towards convergence. In the business world the process of competition would drive firms to seek out these markets and force down prices by standardizing what was sold and how it was made in an effort to cut costs and to maintain profit. International competition is not a new business phenomenon, nor is FDI or international trade. As we have seen in the first section, the process of globalization is ongoing. The organization of trade is also different, with much of it taking place between and within large multinational organizations across borders that are increasingly irrelevant. It is supported by international organizations such as the WTO and agreements that did not exist a century ago.

The process has also embraced an increasing number of countries, as free **market ideology** was accepted as the dominant economic philosophy. The countries of South East Asia, Latin America, India, Central and Eastern Europe, and even China have one by one bowed to the power of market forces. However, the global financial crisis of 2007/08 did raise questions about giving markets free rein and led to calls for more government intervention (see Chapter 5 for discussion of this).

The big MNCs have not been passive participants in the liberalization process. They are usually to be found at the forefront, pushing governments to open up their economies by removing barriers to trade and investment. Indeed, Rugman and Hodgetts (2002) argue that their managers are the real drivers of globalization. MNCs encourage governments through pressure groups such as the European Round Table (ERT), set up by MNCs from 17 countries. It brings together leaders of around 50 of the biggest MNCs with a combined turnover exceeding US$2 trillion, supporting nearly 7 million jobs in Europe. It was instrumental in promoting the idea of a single market for the EU and keen to integrate the former **communist** countries and the developing nations into a global-ized system. Similarly, the National Association of Manufacturers in the USA has pressed for markets to be opened up from Cape Horn, the southernmost tip in South America, to Alaska.

Competition is one of the dominant drivers in the process of globalization of the world economy. If your competitors are globalizing and capturing new growth opportunities, scale efficiencies, and gaining invaluable knowledge of global operations, then you may cease to exist or be forced into small domestic market niches unless you follow suit.

There are other drivers, although some might be more correctly labelled as 'facilitators'. In the next sections, we look at the factors facilitating the globalization of business and the barriers that help keep business 'local'.

Political/Regulatory

Governments have taken steps to remove barriers to trade and the movement of capital through international organizations such as the General Agreement on Tariffs and Trade (**GATT**) and its successor organization, the World Trade Organization (WTO), and they have also set up **free trade** areas, customs unions, and common markets.

- **Free trade area**—member states agree to remove tariffs and **quotas** on goods from other members of the area. Members have the freedom to set the level of tariff imposed on imports of goods from non-members of the area.

- **Customs union**—this is a free trade area for goods, but with the addition that members agree to levy a common tariff on imports of goods from non-members.

- **Common market**—this is a customs union, but with the addition that member states agree to allow free movement of goods, services, capital, and labour.

There have been major reductions in the barriers to movement, particularly for goods and capital, brought about by liberalization. These have been achieved multilaterally through negotiations in GATT and the WTO, or bilaterally between individual governments.

Governments help bring about increased economic and political interlinkage by signing treaties setting up **regional trade areas** (RTAs), such as NAFTA with the involvement of the USA, Canada, and Mexico, where barriers to movement, such as tariffs and quotas, are abolished among the members. Other examples are the Association of Southeast Asian Nations (ASEAN), incorporating ten countries in South East Asia, and Mercosur, comprising four countries in South America. The number of RTAs rose dramatically from about 30 in 1990 to 279 in 2017 (WTO n.d.); the vast majority were free trade areas and a much smaller number were customs unions. While such bodies do promote integration among the members, they often limit integration with non-members by maintaining barriers against imports from them.

Sometimes, governments push integration further by agreeing to the establishment of customs unions that comprise a free trade area plus a common import tariff against non-members. Alternatively, they may set up a common market like the EU where there is complete freedom of movement for goods, services, capital, and people. One result of this removal of barriers to the movement of people in the EU is that someone in Southern Spain could drive to Lapland without necessarily having to stop at a single border. Nineteen members of the EU have taken the integration process even further by removing currency as a barrier through agreement on the introduction of a common currency, the euro. Economic integration often leads to political integration. Therefore, EU member states are subject not only to EU laws but also to common policies in areas such as agriculture, the regions in the EU, and environmental policy.

Changes in political regimes have also helped reduce barriers; for example, the collapse of communism in the late 1980s and early 1990s led to Eastern European countries becoming more interconnected economically, politically, and militarily, particularly with Western Europe and the USA. Many of the former communist countries joined the North Atlantic Treaty Organization (NATO) and the EU. China opened up its economy to foreign investors and joined the WTO.

Governments, particularly in poorer countries in Asia, Africa, and Latin America, anxious to promote economic development, facilitate the movement of capital into their countries by setting up **export processing zones** (EPZs) where MNCs can invest, produce, and trade under favourable conditions. In countries such as China, Mexico, and Sri Lanka, the largest share of exports comes from EPZs (Yücer and Siroën 2017). MNCs are usually given financial incentives to invest and often they are allowed to import goods and produce output free of tax. Yücer and Siroën (2017) found that 62 mainly developing countries had an active EPZ programme. There are also many tax-free free trade zones, or freeports, which are supposed to act as entrepots and be used for storage purposes.

Technological

Improvements in communications, and reductions in transport costs, have facilitated the movement of goods, services, capital, and people. Modern communications technology makes it easier for businesses to control far-flung empires. It further allows people to connect and interact over long distances, and, with transport becoming easier and cheaper, goods and people are able to travel long distances quickly and at a relatively low cost.

The internet and cheaper telephony make it easier not only for MNCs to control their foreign operations, but also for migrants to maintain links with their countries of origin. Furthermore, these technologies have been a major force in integrating the world's financial markets. A trader in a bank in New York can use the computer to monitor movements in share prices, **interest rates**, and currency rates in all the major financial markets, and can respond by buying and selling almost simultaneously. Vast amounts of money can be transferred across borders at the press of a button.

In 1930, it cost more than a week's average wage in the UK for a three-minute telephone call from London to New York. Now it costs a fraction of the average hourly wage. Demand for telecommunications has increased very rapidly. The number of mobile phone subscribers worldwide more than doubled between 2005 and 2010, and in 2018 numbered around 5 billion. Access to a mobile network is available to over 98 per cent of the world population (Statista n.d.; World Bank Open Data n.d.).

The growth in demand for telecommunications services has been driven by the development of the cellular technology associated with mobile phones. Another factor, the internet, has revolutionized telecommunications. It has become a very cheap and reliable method of communicating text, data, and images; it is also being increasingly used for voice communication. The number of people in the world with internet access grew more than tenfold from less than 100 million in the mid-1990s to around 4 billion in 2017. Access to the net is highest in the developed world, with a penetration level of 88 per cent in North America compared to 45 per cent in Asia and 28 per cent in Africa. India is a good example of a country that has benefited from the impact of advances in communications technology. It has a ready supply of relatively cheap, educated labour and has become an increasingly popular location for call centre jobs. This has come about as a result of the advances in communication technology, which have significantly reduced the costs and improved the quality and reliability of telephony. Consequently, there has been a movement of IT and other business processes jobs from the UK and the USA to South East Asia, with India a particularly favoured location.

Technology can also reduce movements of people. Improvements in the costs and quality of video links may mean that business executives do not need to attend meetings abroad. They can be virtual travellers, interacting electronically through teleconferencing with fellow managers in other countries.

Economic

In many modern industries, the scale of investment needed for R&D and production facilities can mean that the size of a single domestic market is insufficient to support that industry. The production of electronic components requires high levels of investment in both R&D and the manufacturing process, and this drives firms to go global. This is especially so when **product life cycles** are shortening, increasing the pressure to recover investment quickly. Competitive pressures on costs also push firms to reduce product lines and to expand globally to seek every possible saving from economies of scale in R&D, manufacturing, and marketing.

The desire to cut costs can be seen in the aluminium industry. Aluminium is a relatively expensive metal to produce, as it takes a lot of electricity to turn ore into metal. This is why aluminium firms locate their smelters in locations with access to cheap energy. Other industries will seek out cheap sources of labour. In the footwear industry, which uses relatively simple technology and is therefore **labour intensive**, labour costs represent about 40 per cent of total costs. Hourly wages in some countries are very low; for example, in manufacturing wage rates in Mexico and Turkey are around one-sixth, and in Brazil just over one-fifth less than in the USA (Conference Board n.d.). As a result, manufacturing has been relocating to countries with low labour costs.

Firms may globalize because they have outgrown their domestic market. Furthermore, the pace of growth in mature, developed economies for many industries is relatively modest. To maintain a rate of growth required by capital markets will mean for most of the world's leading companies that they must seek opportunities beyond their domestic borders. IKEA, based in Sweden and the world's largest furniture retailer, is an example of this. The Swedish market is relatively small; therefore, in order to grow, IKEA had to go abroad. In the new century it rapidly expanded to 411 stores in 49 countries in North America, Europe, Asia, and Australasia (IKEA n.d.).

The rapid improvements in technology, and the consequent reduction in communication and transport costs, have enabled people to experience other societies' lifestyles first hand or through the medium of TV and film or the internet. This has led to a convergence in tastes, which MNCs have been quick to exploit by creating global brands such as Coca-Cola, Levi, Sony, Nike, and McDonald's. This has been called the 'Californiazation' or 'McDonaldization' of society (Ohmae 1985; Ritzer 2004, respectively).

Global companies mean global customers. Global customers require basic supplies of input materials, global financial and accounting services, and global hotel chains to house travelling executives. Dealing with one supplier of a standard product or service has many advantages for the global buyer: lower purchase costs, a standard product of consistent quality, lower administration costs, and more opportunities for cooperation with suppliers. For example, Japanese banks became more global following the globalization of Japanese car manufacturers.

 Counterpoint Box 1.2 Globalization: the free market

Supporters of globalization claim that free movement of goods, services, and capital increases economic growth and prosperity, and leads to a more efficient allocation of resources with benefits to all countries involved. It results in more competition, lower prices, more employment, higher output, and higher standards of living. Countries, therefore, should open up their economies to free movement by removing barriers such as tariffs, quotas, laws and regulations, subsidies, and the purchase by public bodies of goods and services on nationalist grounds. It is also argued that a liberalized world economy would eradicate global poverty.

Critics see an element of hypocrisy when rich countries use the arguments above to persuade poor countries to open up their economies to imports and inward investment. Historically, almost all rich countries, including the USA and the UK, protected domestic industries from foreign competition with subsidies, tariffs, quotas, and regulation, and through state-owned enterprises. Many, such as Japan, Finland, and South Korea, controlled foreign investment tightly while France,

Austria, Finland, Singapore, and Taiwan developed key industries through state-owned enterprises. However, despite this, they grew rich. Critics also point to the period after 1980 when developing countries liberalized their economies and their economic growth rates fell compared with the 1960s and 1970s when they protected their domestic industries from foreign competition. Opponents claim that globalization increases inequality between countries and also results in economic instability, citing the 2007–09 financial crisis which spread rapidly from the USA around the world.

Sources: Sachs (2005); Bhagwati (2004); Wolf (2005; 2010); Stiglitz (2002); Chang (2008; 2010); Chua (2003)

Question

Milanovic (2017) identifies the middle class in fast-growing Asian economies and the global super rich as being the major beneficiaries of globalization leading to increased inequality within nations, but reduced inequality between them. Discuss.

Barriers to Globalization

Despite the fast pace of globalization, it remains the case that goods, services, capital, and people move more easily within nations than across borders. Trade between regions within nations is generally much higher than trade across borders, even when adjusted for income and distance levels. This occurs even when trading restrictions appear to be low—for example, between Canada and the USA.

Government Policies

Governments pursue policies that can hinder the flow of goods and services and the movement of capital and people across borders. According to the head of the WTO, the global economic crisis did not lead governments to resort to protectionism, describing it as 'the dog that hasn't barked' (*The Guardian* 27 January 2011). This claim was contradicted by Evenett and Fritz (2017) who identified over 11,000 crisis era protectionist measures by governments, including tax breaks and soft loans for exporters and restrictions on the ability of foreign firms to win public contracts. They claim that these have a greater effect on trade than tariffs.

Mini Case Study 1.4 President Trump and globalization

Donald Trump's election as US President could put a brake on globalization if he implements his campaign pledges. He came into power with the slogan 'America First'. In his inaugural presidential address, he said:

> From this moment on, it's going to be America First . . . We must protect our borders from the ravages of other countries making our products, stealing our companies, and destroying our jobs. Protection will lead to great prosperity and strength . . . We will follow two simple rules: Buy American and Hire American. (http://www.whitehouse.gov/inaugural-address)

He does not view the world as a global community where countries share certain values and interests and strive together for the common good. It is seen as an arena where countries and businesses compete for advantage in pursuit of their own interests.

The US President dislikes multilateral agreements, preferring to negotiate bilateral deals with allies. It was therefore no surprise that, on his first day in office, he withdrew the USA from the Trans-Pacific Partnership involving the USA and 11 countries, mainly around the Pacific Rim, which aimed to create a single market similar to that in the EU. The USA also withdrew from the 2015 Paris climate change agreement. Stiglitz (2017) claimed that Donald Trump had 'thrown a hand grenade into the global economic architecture that was so painstakingly constructed in the years after World War II's end'.

In the presidential campaign, Mr Trump declared that the NAFTA free trade agreement with Canada and Mexico was the worst trade deal ever signed by the USA and had destroyed manufacturing jobs. He set about renegotiating it. He threatened to impose a 35 per cent import levy on companies firing US workers and moving operations abroad (PBS 4 December 2016). The President said:

> . . . you (manufacturers) want to go to Mexico or some other country, good luck. We wish you a lot of luck. But if you think you're going to make your air conditioners or your cars or your cookies or whatever you make and bring them into our country without a tax, you're wrong. (First Presidential debate, http://www.ontheissues.org)

The President's ire was directed at big employers such as Boeing and Lockheed Martin and the car makers. He tweeted:

> General Motors is sending Mexican-made model of Chevy Cruze to US car dealers-tax free across border. Make in USA or pay big border tax!
>
> Toyota Motor said will build a new plant in Baja, Mexico, to build Corolla cars for US. NO WAY! Build plant in US or pay big border tax. (*The Observer* 7 January 2017)   →

→ Table 1.5 US world ranking trade and investment

Merchandise exports[a]	2
Merchandise imports[a]	1
Service exports[a]	1
Service imports[a]	1
FDI outflows[b]	1
FDI inflows[b]	1

[a]2015; [b]2016
Sources: WTO Trade Profiles, accessed 4 July 2017; UNCTAD (2017)

Ford responded by cancelling plans to open a new plant in Mexico and announcing new jobs at its Michigan factory. Because China was their largest market, automobile makers were concerned by President Trump's accusations that China, their largest market, was 'stealing US jobs and raping the American economy' (BBC News 27 April 2016).

Germany's large trade surplus with the USA was also the focus of an angry Presidential tweet (@realDonaldTrump 30 May 2017).

The President announced plans to clamp down hard on immigration. Giant tech companies such as Google and Netflix reacted with dismay, fearing restrictions on their ability to recruit the best talent.

Because the USA is a major player in the world economy, the President's decisions on trade, investment, and migration have major implications for the world economy (Table 1.5).

Sources: Gvosdev (2017); npr (2017); Solis (2016); Stiglitz (2017); *The Verge* 28 January 2017; Bloomberg 28 January 2017

Questions

1. President Trump's rhetoric raised concerns among business. Explain the concerns of:
   - US car manufacturers;
   - non-US car manufacturers;
   - giant tech companies.
2. Car manufacturers apparently hoped that Donald Trump's anti-globalization rhetoric would be softened after taking power. Assess the extent to which their hopes have been met.
3. What are the implications of President Trump's policies for world trade, investment, and migration?

Tariffs and Subsidies

Numerous tariffs remain on imports of goods. Rich countries impose particularly high tariffs on goods coming from poor countries. The USA, the EU, and Japan levy high tariffs on imports of agricultural products that are important to developing economies while tariffs imposed on manufactured goods from other rich countries are lower. Such differences in tariffs help to explain why trade tends to take place within and between rich countries. Poor countries also impose tariffs. India imposes a tariff of 40 per cent on vehicles able to carry ten or more people (WTO n.d.).

Rich countries subsidize their farmers, with the EU, Japan, Norway, Switzerland, and South Korea contributing large proportions of their farmers' incomes. Subsidies can also be used to promote globalization. In EPZs, they are often used to attract foreign investors.

Foreign Aid

Rich countries usually give financial assistance to poor countries. Frequently, such aid (for example, from the USA and Japan) is used to promote the interests of domestic firms by requiring the recipients to buy goods and services produced by firms in the donor country irrespective of whether they give best value for money.

Controls on Capital

Controls on capital can take the form of either controls on inflows or on outflows of foreign direct and indirect investment.

Although big steps had been made in liberalizing the movements of capital, these stalled in the wake of the global financial crisis with a general acceptance that capital inflows could cause cycles of economic boom and bust. Developed countries have generally been more amenable to free movement of capital. Countries such as China, Indonesia, and India have been reluctant to remove restrictions on capital inflows (OECD 2017). In 2016, China introduced controls on outward FDI, fearing large falls in its foreign exchange reserves (*Forbes* 29 November 2016). Previously, Brazil introduced controls on inflows of portfolio investment because they were driving up the value of the currency and affecting the country's international competitiveness. Countries are often reluctant to accept inflows of FDI where it involves sectors they regard as strategically important, such as the basic utilities of gas, electricity, and water. The USA and the EU are not prepared to cede control of their airline companies to foreign organizations. US law prevents foreign firms from buying more than 24.9 per cent of an American airline (the corresponding figure for the EU is 49 per cent).

Public Procurement

Government departments, nationalized industries, public utilities in telecommunications, gas, and water often spend large amounts of public money purchasing goods and services. **Public procurement** worldwide accounts for between 10 per cent and 15 per cent of GDP. In the EU it equates to 14 per cent of GDP (WTO n.d.; European Commission n.d.). Governments are very important customers for firms, particularly those producing goods and services for the defence, health, and education sectors. When issuing contracts, governments will often favour domestic producers over their foreign rivals, even when domestic firms are more expensive.

Border and Immigration Controls

Border controls affect trade in goods. They can require the filling in of export/import forms and also customs officers stopping vehicles and checking goods at the frontier. This can take time, add to traders' transport costs, and make goods less competitive in the foreign market.

Many barriers remain to the movement of people. These include stringent visa requirements, quotas requiring employers to search for a national employee before employing a foreign one, and refusal by the authorities to accredit foreign educational and vocational qualifications.

Technical Standards

Technical standards and regulations can be formidable barriers. There are thousands of different technical specifications relating to goods and services which can effectively protect domestic markets from foreign competition and consequently restrict trade. The EU has tried to deal with this through its Single Market Programme. It uses the principle of mutual recognition whereby countries accept products from other member states as long as they do not constitute a danger to the consumer.

Companies in the service sector can be hampered by the myriad of technical standards and requirements. Financial institutions such as banks may find it difficult to use the internet to sell their services in foreign markets because countries may lay down different solvency require-ments, or different levels of liquidity for financial institutions operating in their territory.

In addition, new barriers can appear: where several companies are competing to develop a new product, the first to do so may establish its technical specifications as a standard for the new product, which then acts as a barrier to trade for competitors.

Protection of Intellectual Property Rights

Different national policies towards what are called intellectual property rights (IPRs) could consti-tute barriers as well. IPRs relate to new products and production processes, brand names, and logos, as well as books and films. Their owners argue that they should have the legal right to prevent others from commercially exploiting them. However, the extent of protection and enforcement of these rights varies widely around the world. Some countries, such as China and Malaysia, do not offer the firms creating the ideas and knowledge much protection against counterfeiting. Firms contend that the lack of protection of IPRs stunts their trade and FDI in those countries.

Cultural and Geographical Distance
Culture

Cultural distance can constitute an important barrier. Differences in language, religious beliefs, race, national and regional tastes, social norms and values, and business practices, which regu-late what is regarded as acceptable behaviour and attitudes, can constitute major impediments to globalization. Culture can be an important influence on consumer behaviour, work culture, and business practices. Thus, McDonald's cannot sell Big Macs in India because to Hindus the cow is sacred, nor can it assume that staff in Eastern Europe will have the same attitudes to work as its workers in the USA. Another example concerned Tyrrells, the UK crisp company: the founder described how it encountered difficulties when trying to sell parsnip crisps in France, not realizing that the French saw parsnips as pig feed (*Financial Times* 21 March 2011).

Some goods and services are more sensitive than others to cultural differences. Ghemawat (2001) researched the impact of culture and found that products such as meat, cereals, tobacco, and office machines had to be adapted to local cultures, whereas firms producing cameras, road vehicles, cork and wood, and electricity did not need to adapt their products—or were under less compulsion to do so.

Corruption

Another area where cultural distance can cause problems for firms is corruption. In some coun-tries, such as in Africa and the Middle East, it is the norm for firms to reward individuals who help them get business. However, in other countries, such behaviour would be deemed corrupt and illegal. The prospect of prosecution in their home countries might deter firms from trading with, and investing in, countries where such behaviour is the norm.

Learning Task

Tourism accounts for 10 per cent of global income and is growing rapidly.

1. Identify the economic benefits of tourism.
2. a) Discuss possible impacts of tourism on local cultures.

   See   http://www.wttc.org/-/media/files/reports/economic-impact-research/regions-2017/
   world2017.pdf,   http://www.wttc.org/-/media/files/reports/economic-impact-research/2017-
   documents/global-economic-impact-and-issues-2017.pdf,

   http://geographyfieldwork.com/GeographyCulture.htm, and http://geographyfieldwork.com/
   MachuTourismImpact.htm.

   b) Analyse the impact on the pattern of demand for goods and services in countries experiencing
   high levels of tourism.

Geography

Geographical distance can also be a barrier. It has been shown that the more distance there is
between countries, the less trade there will be between them (Ghemawat 2001). Geographical
distance can make trade difficult, particularly for firms producing goods that are low in value but
high in bulk, such as cement or beer. The cost of transporting cement or beer over long distances
would be prohibitive. Fragile or highly perishable products such as glass and fruit may suffer
similar problems. Firms respond to the barrier posed by geographical distance in various ways.
Brewers have responded either by taking over a foreign brewer or by granting a licence to firms
in foreign markets to brew their beer. Thus, barriers to one aspect of globalization, trade, result
in globalization in another form, investment or licensing. Historically, geographical distance is
likely to have declined in importance as transport has become cheaper and techniques for carrying fragile or perishable products more effective.

The Benefits and Costs of Globalization for Business

Globalization can comprise major changes in the external environment of business. It creates
opportunities for business, particularly for the big MNCs who are in the best position to take
advantage. However, it can pose threats as well. We examine the benefits and costs in turn.

The Benefits for Business

Removal of barriers to trade or investment can:

- open up markets to businesses that were previously excluded, giving them the possibility of
  higher revenues and growth. The activities of car producers and tobacco firms in South East
  Asia illustrate this. As their traditional markets in North America and Western Europe have
  matured, General Motors, Ford, Volkswagen, Toyota, and Philip Morris have all looked to the

fast-expanding markets of South East Asia as a source of growth. China, with its rapidly growing car market, has been a particularly favoured location for car industry investment. Similarly, the fall of communism gave banks from the USA and Western Europe the opportunity to move into the former communist bloc countries and in many countries, such as the Czech Republic, Bulgaria, and Croatia, they have ended up controlling a majority of banking assets;

- give business access to cheaper supplies of final products, components, raw materials, or to other **factors of production**, such as labour, which lowers their costs and makes them more competitive. It is hardly surprising that firms such as HSBC, Tesco, ebookers, and BT have been relocating activities to India where graduates can be employed for a fraction of the corresponding salaries in the USA or the UK. The relatively low cost of IT professionals has also resulted in the biggest computer firms establishing operations in India. Similarly, China is not seen by Western MNCs simply in terms of its market potential but also as a very cheap source of supply. Many MNCs relocated manufacturing production to China where there was an abundant supply of cheap labour;

- allow firms to obtain previously denied natural resources. For many years, Saudi Arabia was unwilling to give foreign firms access to its energy deposits. The Saudi authorities had a change of heart in the 1990s, allowing Shell to explore for gas.

The Costs for Business

Globalization can also have costs for business.

- The environment is likely to become more complex and risky. Business is confronted by new sets of factors in the form of different political regimes, laws and regulations, tax systems, competition policies, and cultures. In extreme cases, they may find that the host government seizes their investment or takes discriminatory action against them. For example, Bolivia nationalized natural gas production and took four electricity generating companies, including power stations owned by France's GDF Suez and UK's Rurelec, into public ownership (PRS Group 2010).

- Inefficient firms may find that it removes the barriers protecting them from foreign competitors. National airlines such as Lufthansa, or telecommunications companies such as France Telecom, found it difficult to face up to the more intense competition engendered by the liberalization of civil aviation and telecommunications in the EU. Often, the endangered businesses will pressurize governments to leave the protective barriers in place or to reintroduce the barriers previously removed. Removal of the barriers may allow the entry of new competitors from abroad or it may permit existing customers to switch their custom to foreign suppliers who are cheaper or who can offer better product quality. Weaker domestic firms may find that their access to factors of production is threatened.

- Globalization can raise the dependence of plants and firms on foreign markets and suppliers. As a result of NAFTA, more than 3,000 plants (called **maquiladoras**) were set up along the Mexico/USA border employing some 1.3 million workers, producing goods for the North American market. They accounted for half of Mexico's exports. When the US economy went into recession in 2008, the maquiladoras began shedding workers. By 2009, nearly 30 per cent of jobs had disappeared and exports had fallen by more than one-third (Muñoz Martinez 2010). In the Mexican border towns, they say that when the US economy catches cold, Mexico gets pneumonia (Rosen 2003).

• Globalization can cause the environment to become more volatile. Firms generally prefer to operate in an environment where the financial and macroeconomic systems are stable and predictable. However, there is evidence from global financial crises, for example, in the late 1990s and in 2007/08, that the economies of developing economies, whose financial systems have integrated most with the rest of the world, are more subject to greater instability than other developing countries (Prasad et al. 2003; Green et al. 2010). Increasing integration of financial markets allows enormous sums of money to be moved effortlessly across borders, leaving financial markets more vulnerable to instability and the world financial system more prone to violent fluctuations in **exchange rates** and interest rates. Such fluctuations can pose a major risk to business costs, revenues, and profits.

● CHAPTER SUMMARY

In this chapter, we have explained the nature of globalization as a process through which barriers between nations are reduced. Nations thereby become increasingly interdependent, although we point out that most of this interdependence is between members of the NAFTA, Western Europe, the EU, Japan, and China, with the rest of the world playing a minor role. Their dominance is under some challenge from India, Brazil, and South Korea. Increased interdependence is indicated by increases in exchanges across borders of goods and services, financial capital, and people.

We also make the point that globalization is not just about economic exchanges, but also has a cultural and social dimension. The media, our diet, education, work practices, sport, health, crime, and religion all demonstrate the impact of globalization.

The main drivers of globalization are identified as competition, reduction in regulatory barriers, improvements in technology, saturated domestic markets, the desire to cut costs, and the growth of global customers. There still remain important barriers to the process, including regulation, technology, and cultural and geographic distance.

Globalization presents both opportunities and threats to business. On the one hand, it presents access to new and bigger markets and to different and cheaper sources of raw materials, components, and labour. On the other hand, the environment is more complex and less stable.

This book will explore this environment and the implications for business. In Chapter 2 we shall look at the global economy and explain in more depth some of the topics discussed in this chapter.

● REVIEW QUESTIONS

1. What is globalization?

2. Where is globalization mainly taking place? Why should that be the case?

3. Identify the main:

   a. indicators of globalization;

   b. drivers of globalization;

   c. facilitators of globalization;

   d. barriers to globalization.

● ASSIGNMENT TASKS

1. You are a reporter for a quality business newspaper. The editor asks you to write an article analysing whether globalization is faltering. In the article you should:

   a. analyse and illustrate the growth in trade and FDI; and

   b. assess the challenge to globalization posed by President Trump's policies and Brexit.

2. CityUK, the body representing UK financial services, aims to persuade the UK parliament to negotiate unrestricted access to the Single Market, allowing them to operate freely across the EU and to recruit and transfer staff anywhere in the Union.

   a. You, as a CityUK researcher, are required to make the case in a draft pamphlet which will be sent to all MPs.

   b. Advise CityUK on how best to transmit the pamphlet to MPs.

You should refer to: the House of Commons Library 'The financial sector's contribution to the UK economy' 4 April 2017 and CityUK website, the ONS Pink Book, Letter from Financial Conduct Authority to Treasury Committee Chair regarding passports', UK Parliament, August 2016. Google 'Sallie Newell' for advice on writing pamphlets.

Case Study Brexit and the car industry

© Usoltceva Anastasiia/Shutterstock

In 2016, the UK voted to exit the EU, with withdrawal to be completed by March 2019. This caused great uncertainty and consternation in the UK car industry, which feared major adverse changes to its external environment.

UK membership of the single market led foreign MNCs to use it as a platform for exporting barrier-free to other EU markets. Following the vote to withdraw, the car industry demanded unrestricted access to the single market with no new barriers to trade or restrictions in the free movement of workers. The possible introduction of tariff and non-tariff barriers created great concern in the car industry because the EU took 57 per cent of UK car exports. The body representing the industry, the Society of Motor Manufacturers and Traders (SMMT) (2016), warned that, after withdrawal from the EU, the introduction of tariffs on exports of cars and imports of components would cause a fall in sales and employment in the industry and could add £1,500 to the cost of cars sold in the UK (*The Guardian* 26 January 2017). If withdrawal were to lead to car firms operating on WTO trading arrangements, a 10 per cent tariff would be imposed on automotive exports and imports at a cost of £1.8 billion on the former and £2.7 billion on the latter. The UK economy could be badly affected, given that the industry was a major contributor to the UK with an annual turnover of around £72 billion and investment of £2.5 billion (SMMT 2017, Brexit Position Paper). As can be seen from Figure 1.17, the automotive sector is a major source of export earnings for the UK.

Big MNCs such as Nissan, Ford, Peugeot, and BMW had complex supply chains across the EU. For example, components from BMW's Mini travel thousands of miles, criss-crossing EU borders. The crankshaft is cast in France, milled into shape in the UK, inserted into the engine in Germany, and finally →

installed in the car back in the UK. The car can then be exported to the continent. Annually, Ford make 2 million engines in the UK, exports them to its plants in the EU, installs them, and then imports the cars back to the UK. Less than half of car components are made in the UK. Nissan claims to import 5 million parts per day from Japan, China, and Europe. Dhingra et al. (n.d.) point out that withdrawal from the single market would make it more difficult and costly to manage what were already complex supply chains. The UK chancellor of the exchequer tried to reassure the car industry:

... we should take particular note of those sectors with complex pan-European supply chains where often components and self-assemblies move backwards and forwards across European borders several times before they get incorporated into a final product ... (Reuters 19 October 2016)

Car firms were also concerned that withdrawal would make it more difficult to recruit staff in the EU and transfer them across borders. Some 10 per cent of employees in the UK industry are EU nationals (SMMT 2017).

In 2016, the Japanese company Nissan was choosing a production location for the new Qashqai model. The company, fearing the imposition of tariffs on its exports to the EU, demanded compensation from the UK government, threatening that the new model would be made elsewhere if that did not happen. The Japanese government waded in by sending a 15-page list of demands on behalf of Japanese business operating in the UK warning of 'great turmoil' and of Japanese companies exiting the UK (*The Telegraph* 13 November 2016). In response, Nissan's CEO was invited to see the UK Prime Minister while the UK Business Secretary went to

Figure 1.17 UK exports of products to the EU, 2015

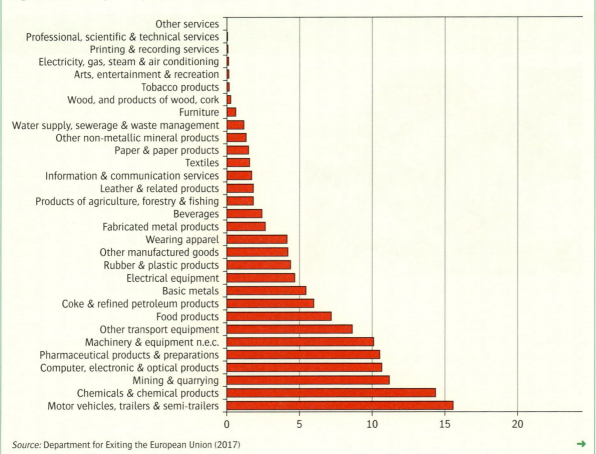

Source: Department for Exiting the European Union (2017)

→ Japan to meet car company executives from Nissan, Toyota, and Honda to reassure them about Brexit. Nissan subsequently announced that the new model would be built in the UK. The UK government refused to make public the terms of the deal with Nissan. Subsequently, when the UK announced that it would leave the single market, the CEO of Nissan stated that the competitiveness of its UK plant would be under review when the new trade deal with the EU was struck. While Nissan adopted an aggressive approach, Toyota's was very different. It pledged to continue operating in the UK and announced £240 million of investment supported by £21.3 million of government support. However, Japanese companies' continuing concerns were expressed by the Japanese ambassador in 2018. He stated that Japanese firms companies had invested in the UK to gain free access to EU markets, and that they could therefore be closed if market access were to be restricted and profitability reduced (*Financial Times* 8 February 2018).

Other car firms were concerned that Nissan was being given favourable treatment. Ford, the giant US-based car maker with extensive operations in the EU, pointed out that with 15,000 UK employees, it employed more workers than Nissan.

PA (2016), the consultancy firm, suggested that car companies would respond differently to the prospect of the UK exit from the EU. It divided the industry into three categories:

- firms likely to leave after UK withdrawal from the EU because of their dependence on relatively low profit exports to the EU—these included Toyota and Honda;

- those who might, or might not, move out of the UK— BMW's Mini production, Nissan and Peugeot's subsidiary, Vauxhall who were well established in the UK but could move operations to the EU; and
- Tata's Jaguar Land Rover and VW's Bentley, whose well-known British brands sold well in the EU and in global markets.

Sources: Department for Exiting the European Union (2017); Dhingra et al (n.d.); *Financial Times* 16 March 2017; *The Guardian* 30 September, 8 November 2016, 26 January, 28 February, 4 March 2017; Sky News 19 October 2016 @news.sky.com; *The Observer* 22 January 2017; PA (2016); SMMT (2016); *The Telegraph* 13 November 2016; Today programme BBC Radio 4, 27 January 2017.

Questions

1. Why would car firms locate production in the UK?
2. Discuss the uncertainties for car firms caused by Brexit.
3. Why is the car industry particularly concerned about the imposition of tariffs on automotive exports and imports?
4. a. What non-tariff barriers (NTBs) could be introduced after Brexit?
   b. What impact could NTBs have on car makers?
5. a. How did the UK government respond to pressure from Nissan and the Japanese authorities?
   b. Give reasons for the UK government responses.
6. Justify car industry claims that unrestricted access to the single market is in the best interest of the UK economy.

FURTHER READING

For a discussion of the discussion and debates around globalization, see:

- Baldwin, R. (2016) *The Great Convergence: Information Technology and the New Globalization* London: Harvard University Press.

- King, S.D. (2017) *Grave New World: The End of Globalization, The Return of History* London: Yale University Press.

For an examination of the various theories around globalization and how the world economy has been transformed by MNCs, states, and interest groups, see:

- Dicken, P. (2015) *Global Shift: Mapping the Changing Contours of the World Economy*. 7th edn. London: Guildford Publications.

For changes in the extent and depth of globalizations, see:

- Ghemawat, P. and Altman, S.A. (2016) 'DHL Connectedness Index: The State of Globalization in an Age of Ambiguity'. Available at http://www.dhl.com.

- KOF Index of Globalization. Available at http://globalization.kof.ethz.ch.

● REFERENCES

Baker, B. and Ryina, N. (2013) 'Estimates of the Unauthorized Immigrant Population Residing in the United States: January 2012'. Office of Immigration Statistics, March.

Baldwin, R. (2016) *The Great Convergence: Information Technology and the New Globalization*. London: Harvard University Press.

Bank for International Settlements (2016) 'Triennial Central Bank Survey of foreign exchange and OTC derivatives markets in 2016', December. Available at http://www.bis.org/publ/rpfx16.htm.

BBC (2016) http://www.bbc.co.uk/news/uk-politics-eu-referendum-36473105, 8 June.

Bhagwati, J.N. (2004) *In Defence of Globalization*. Oxford: Oxford University Press.

Chang, H.-J. (2008) *The Myth of Free Trade and the Secret History of Capitalism*. New York: Bloomsbury Press.

Chang, H.-J. (2010) *23 Things They Don't Tell You About Capitalism*. London: Allen Lane.

Chua, A. (2003) *World on Fire: How Exporting Free Market Democracy Breeds Ethnic Hatred and Global Instability*. New York: Doubleday.

Conference Board (n.d.) http://www.conferenceboard.org.

Department for Exiting the European Union (2017) 'The United Kingdom's Exit from, and New Partnership with, the European Union', 15 May.

Dhingra, S., Ottaviano, G., Sampson, T., and Van Reenen, J. (n.d.) 'The impact of Brexit on foreign investment in the UK, CEP Brexit Analysis No. 3'.

European Commission (n.d.) http://ec.europa.eu.

Eurostat (2016) 'Intra-EU trade of the most traded goods' *Statistics Explained.*

Eurostat (2017) 'Statistics on enforcement of immigration legislation', May.

Evenett, S.J. and Fritz, J. (2017) *The 21st Global Trade Alert Report*. London: CEPR Press.

García Martínez, A. (2017) 'Google's fine shows Europe is a brake on US tech innovation', *The Guardian*, 2 July. Available at http://www.theguardian.com/commentisfree/2017/jul/01/

google-fine-european-commission-brussels-bureaucrats-absurd.

Ghemawat, P. (2001) 'Distance Still Matters: The Hard Reality of Global Expansion'. *Harvard Business Review* September: 137–47.

globalEDGE (n.d.) http://globaledge.msu.edu/trade-blocs/nafta/statistics.

Google (n.d.) http://www.google.co.uk/about.

Green, D., King, R., and Miller-Dawkins, M. (2010) 'The Global Economic Crisis and Developing Countries: Impact and Response'. *Oxfam Research Report*, January.

Gvosdev, N. (2017) 'The Implications of "The World is Not a Global Community"'. *Ethics and International Affairs*, 31 May.

Held, D., McGrew, G., Goldbatt, D., and Perraton, J. (1999) *Global Transformations*. Stanford: Stanford University Press.

House of Lords European Union Committee (2016), 'Brexit: the options for trade', December.

HSBC (2017) 'Reshaping the Future World Economy', 15 May.

IKEA (n.d.) http://franchisor.ikea.com.

IMF (2017) 'Coordinated Portfolio Investment Survey', 15 March.

Levitt, T. (1983) 'The Globalization of Markets'. *Harvard Business Review* May–June: 91–102.

LinkedIn (n.d.) http://www.linkedin.com.

Milanovic, B. (2017) *Global Inequality: A New Approach for the Age of Globalization*. Cambridge: Harvard University Press.

Muñoz Martinez, H. (2010) 'The Double Burden on Maquila Workers: Violence and Crisis in Northern Mexico'. Available at http://www.global-labour-university.org.

npr (2017) http://www.npr.org/2017/04/07/522879370/trump-can-t-bring-all-those-jobs-back-from-china-here-s-what-he-can-do, 7 April.

OECD (2016) 'Perspectives on Global Development 2017'.

OECD (2017) 'FDI Regulatory Restrictiveness Index', 27 March.

Ohmae, K. (1985) *Triad Power: The Coming Shape of Global Competition*. New York: Free Press.

ONS (2015) 'Population of the United Kingdom by Country of Birth and Nationality Report: August 2015'.

ONS (2016) 'UK-EU and UK-non-EU Trade in Financial Services, FISIM and non-FISIM, 2015'.

ONS (2016a) 'International perspective on UK foreign direct investment (FDI): 2014'.

ONS (2016b) 'Statistical bulletin: Migration Statistics Quarterly Report: December 2016'.

ONS (2017) 'UK Trade', April.

PA (2016) 'Brexit: The Impact on Automotive manufacturing in the UK' July

PRS Group (2010) 'Bolivia: Country Report', 1 May. Available at https://www.prsgroup.com.

Prasad, E., Rogoff, K., Wei S.-J., and Kose, M.A. (2003) 'Effects of Financial Globalization on Developing Countries: Some Empirical Evidence'. IMF Occasional Paper No. 220, 3 September.

Public Accounts Committee (2012) 'Minutes of Evidence', HC 716, 12 November 2012.

Ritzer, G. (2004) *The McDonaldization of Society*. London: Pine Forge Press.

Rosen, D.H. (2003) 'How China Is Eating Mexico's Lunch'. *The International Economy* Spring, 78.

Rugman, A. and Hodgetts, R.M. (2002) *International Business*. London: Prentice Hall.

Sachs, J. (2005) *The End of Poverty*. New York: Penguin Press.

Schmidt, E. (2017) http://www.axelspringer.co.uk/dl/433625/LetterMathiasDoepfnerEricSchmidt.pdf.

SMMT (2016) http://www.smmt.co.uk/industry-topics/europe.SMMT (2017) 'SMMT Access to Talent Position Paper 1 September 2017'

Solis, M. (2016) 'Trump withdrawing from the Trans-Pacific Partnership'. Available at https://www.brookings.edu/blog/unpacked/2017/03/24/trump-withdrawing-from-the-trans-pacific-partnership.

Statista (2018) https://www.statista.com/statistics/220534/googles-share-of-search-market-in-selected-countries.

Statista (n.d.) http://www.statista.com.

Stiglitz, J. (2002) *Globalization and its Discontents*. London: Penguin.

Stiglitz, J. 'Trump's Rogue America', Project Syndicate, 2 June 2017. Available at http://www.project-syndicate.org/commentary/trump-rogue-america-by-joseph-e--stiglitz-2017-06.

Twitter (n.d.) http://about.twitter.com.

UN (2016) 'International Migration Report 2015'.

United Nations (2015) 'UN Trends in International Migrant Stock 2015'.

UNCTAD (2016) 'World Investment Report 2016'.

UNCTAD (2017) 'World Investment Report 2017'.

UNHCR (2015) *Global Trends: Forced Displacement in 2015*.

UNWTO (2017) '2016 Annual Report'.

Walker, K. (2017) 'The European Commission decision on online shopping: the other side of the story', *The Keyword*, 27 June. Available at http://www.blog.google/topics/google-europe/european-commission-decision-shopping-google-story.

Wolf, M. (2005) *Why Globalization Works*. Yale: Yale University Press.

Wolf, M. (2010) *Fixing Global Finance*. Baltimore: Johns Hopkins University Press.

World Bank (2016) 'Migration and Remittances Factbook 2016', 3rd edn.

World Bank Open Data (n.d.) http://www.data.worldbank.org.

WTO (2007) 'World Trade Report 2007'.

WTO (2016) 'World Trade Statistical Review 2016'.

WTO (2017) 'Trade recovery expected in 2017 and 2018, amid policy uncertainty', Press/793 Trade Statistics and Outlook.

WTO (n.d.) http://www.wto.org.

WTO Statistics Database (n.d.) http://stat.wto.org.

WTTC (2017) 'Travel & Tourism: Economic Impact 2017 World', March. Available at https://www.wttc.org/-/media/files/reports/economic-impact-research/regions-2017/world2017.pdf.

Yücer, A. and Siroën, J-M. (2017) 'Trade Performance of Export Processing Zones'. *The World Economy* May, Vol 40 Issue 5.

CHAPTER TWO

The Global Economy

LEARNING OUTCOMES

This chapter will enable you to:

- identify the global pattern of wealth and inequality;

- analyse the pattern of international trade and investment;

- explain why countries trade with each other;

- identify the controls and impediments to trade; and

- assess the significance of exchange rates for the business environment.

Case Study China and the global economy

© iStock.com/Easyturn

Almost 200 years ago, in 1820, China was the world's largest economy with almost twice the GDP of the second largest, India, six times that of the UK and almost 20 times greater than the USA.

China's economy declined sharply during the second half of the nineteenth century, largely as a result of war and internal rebellion, while in the West, the Industrial Revolution saw many countries increase their productivity and wealth. However, after three decades of globalization, China is once again a major force in the world economy.

This case illustrates China's re-emergence as an economic power. It shows how China transformed itself from a centralized, closed economy into a much more open one and how growth has raised the living standards of some sectors of the economy but not all, and that rapid growth can also have its costs.

China joined the World Trade Organization (WTO) on 11 December 2001 but the country's re-emergence as a major world player really began around 1978. At this time, the government started a process of moving from a centrally planned economy, highly dependent on collectivized agriculture to a more market oriented economy. Liberalization measures in relation to state-owned enterprises, prices, domestic labour mobility, external trade, and foreign direct investment (FDI) have been progressively implemented since, and growth has been rapid. Between 1979 and 2012, economic growth averaged 10 per cent (with some significant variations); while it has recently slowed considerably, it was still close to 7 per cent in 2016, almost three times that of the USA and many other developed economies.

The result of this growth is that China, with a population of 1.4 billion, is now the world's second largest economy in nominal terms with an estimated gross domestic product (GDP) of over US$11 trillion or 14 per cent of the world economy at the end of 2016. However, using PPP (purchasing power parity, a measure that takes into account the relative cost of living), both the World Bank and the International Monetary Fund (IMF) suggest that China is now the world's largest economy, with US$21.4 trillion PPP compared to the USA's estimated US$18.5 trillion PPP.

China's growth has been largely export led with exports growing at over 30 per cent per year for five years up to 2007 and 15 per cent from 2005 to 2012. It is also a very open economy with trade (imports plus exports) as a percentage of GDP measuring 53.6 per cent between 2010 and 2012, up from 44 per cent in 2001 before falling back in more recent years to 37 per cent at the end of 2016, still well above the USA with a figure of around 28 per cent.

The country currently runs a large trade surplus ($509 billion in 2016), exporting considerably more than it imports. This has led to large trade imbalances with some other countries and allegations that the Chinese Central Bank has, by buying foreign assets (mostly US dollars) unfairly manipulated the currency (yuan), to keep it low against other currencies and make Chinese exports more competitive.

While foreign direct investment (FDI) has played an important part in economic development ($134 million in 2016), much of it has been into low-cost processing sectors. The country has lagged behind the USA ($391 million in 2016) and other countries in terms of attracting foreign direct investment into advanced manufacturing and other key areas of high value adding business. This too seems to be changing, and the authorities are revising guidance for foreign entry to markets and cutting the number of restrictive measures.

The government's 13th Five-Year Plan (2016–20) suggests a commitment to changing the balance of the economy, reducing the reliance on exports and increasing domestic demand. The plan highlights the need for the development of services and measures to address social and environmental issues including setting targets to reduce pollution, invest further in the education of the workforce and improve access to health care.

The rapid changes already achieved have created many challenges for the country, including high inequality, rapid urbanization, and challenges to environmental sustainability. →

→ The country remains the second largest oil consumer, using around 11.3 million barrels per day (bpd) in 2016. It is also the top consumer of steel, copper, and aluminium, accounting for around 40 per cent of global consumption for each.

China also faces demographic pressures related to an aging population and the internal migration of labour to the urban areas of Beijing and other mostly coastal areas where over 55 per cent of the population now live.

For 2017, the Chinese government expects the economy to grow by around 6.5 per cent, compared to a 6.7 per cent expansion in 2016, which was the slowest growth in 26 years. However, a leading rating agency has recently downgraded China's credit rating amidst concerns that slowing growth, rising debt, and slower structural reforms will weaken the economy further.

While the country has undoubtedly changed significantly, the future is by no means certain. With a population of 1.4 billion, the average income is still only $8,216 (2016) and the economy has slowed and market reforms are incomplete. The current US president, Trump, has repeatedly blamed China for the loss of American jobs and accused leaders of currency manipulation, threatening to impose taxes on Chinese imports and asking US firms to move manufacturing bases back home. China could respond to such measures by cutting US imports and imposing sanctions on US firms, leaving the prospect of an all-out 'trade war' between the two countries a distinct possibility.

Interesting times lie ahead both for China and for the world economy.

Sources: WTO, IMF, WHO

Introduction

The global economy is large, complex, and volatile; therefore, predicting what is going to happen over the next few years is not an exact science. Geo-political tensions, continuing debates over economic governance at global, regional, and national levels, growing controversy over tax avoidance strategies by transnational firms, unemployment, inequality, poverty, and environmental issues all continue to help to shape the global economic map. At the end of 2016, the World Bank estimated the size of the global economy to be $US 76.5 trillion, and forecasts suggest that global economic activity in investment, manufacturing, and trade will rise modestly during 2017 and continue throughout 2018. However, any growth resulting from this stronger activity is unlikely to be evenly spread, and not all economies or all groups within individual countries are likely to benefit. Which economies will grow the fastest? Which are the richest? Which are the poorest? Where are the new markets of the world? What sort of goods and services do they require? Who trades with whom? What trade restrictions are in place? What is happening to exchange rates?

These are just a few of the many questions international businesses will be asking as globalization spurs the search for new markets and new locations to site increasingly global activities. This chapter seeks to answer some of these questions. It looks at the incidence of global wealth and poverty, and how this is likely to change in the future. It examines the pattern of international trade, why countries trade, regulation of trade, and exchange rates.

Measuring the Size of the Global Economy

The most common method of measuring the size of an economy is by calculating GDP. This is the market value of total output of goods and services produced within a nation, by both residents and non-residents, over a period of time, usually a year.

In comparing the relative size of different economies, one obvious problem is that the calculation of GDP is in a country's national currency. A common currency is required and this is normally the

US$, using foreign exchange rates to convert. This is not without its problems, as foreign exchange rates reflect only internationally traded goods and services and are subject to short-term speculation and government intervention. For example, in the 1940s, £1 sterling bought US$4. This rate was fixed as part of an international regime, which considered that it was best for business if there was certainty about future exchange rates. In 1949, the UK government, for domestic reasons, decided to devalue sterling to US$2.80. It remained at this rate until 1967 when it was further devalued to US$2.41. In 1971, the USA moved to a **floating exchange rate** and other currencies followed suit. In the 1970s, sterling was floated and has varied from US$2.50 in the early 1970s to almost parity (US$1=£1) in 1984, back to about US$2 in 2007 and around US$1.70 in 2014. Following the UK referendum vote to leave the European Union on 23 June 2016, the rate again fell sharply by more than 10 per cent to a 31-year low of US$1.33; it continues to trade at under US$1.3 in the early months of 2017. So measuring and comparing the wealth of the UK with the USA using foreign exchange rates would have indicated sudden changes in wealth, which is clearly not the case as the wealth of a mature economy such as the UK tends to change slowly, and fairly smoothly, over time.

This way of measuring GDP may indicate a country's international purchasing power, but does not reflect living standards adequately. Most things, especially the basics of food, transport, and housing tend to be much cheaper in low-income countries than in high-income countries. A Western European travelling in much of Asia or Africa will find hotels, food, and drinks a lot cheaper than at home, on average. The opposite, of course, is also true; people from those countries will find that their money does not go very far in Western Europe. A better indicator of living standards can be achieved by calculating GDP using what is known as the purchasing power parity (PPP) method. This calculates GDP on the basis of purchasing power within the respective domestic market—that is, what you can buy with a unit of a country's currency. The **International Comparison Program**, carried out periodically by the World Bank, collects information from 199 countries to establish PPP estimates. When these rates are used, the relative size of developed economies is very much reduced and that of lower income countries much increased, as indicated in Table 2.1. This table compares GDP and GDP **per capita**, at both current prices and PPP, of some of the richest and the poorest countries of the world. The data is derived from the International Monetary Fund's World Economic Outlook database.

Learning Task

The World Bank, using a slightly different measure (Gross National Income which is GDP plus net income flows from abroad), classifies countries for 2017 into four different per capita income groups: low income, US$1,025 or less in 2015; lower middle income, US$1,026–US$4,035; upper middle income, US$4,036–US$12,475; and high income, US$12,475 or more (World Bank n.d.).

From the information in Table 2.1, complete the following tasks:

1. Explain why, if countries were ranked according to their nominal GDP or their PPP GDP, the rankings vary depending on which measure of income is used.

2. Use your answer to question 1 to explain why the USA is more than seven times richer than China according to GDP per capita but just over three and a half times richer using the PPP figures.

3. Group the countries according to the World Bank classification of different income groups. Comment on their regional spread.

GDP as an Indicator of the Standard of Living

GDP tells us the absolute size of an economy and will indicate that, in nominal terms, according to Table 2.1, India is almost twice as large as Australia. However, if we look at their respective GDPs using PPP, we can see that India's GDP is more than seven times that of Australia. What does this tell us about the standard of living? Not a lot, because India has a very big population, over 53 times more people than Australia. When we take this into account to calculate on average how much of that GDP accrues to each person then, using PPP we can see that Australia has a per capita income of US$50,817—over seven times that of India's US$7,153. Does this mean that Australian citizens are seven times as well off as Indian citizens? They might be, and some might be many more times better off than some Indian citizens, but not all, because many Indian citizens are also very wealthy. These figures are averages and say nothing about the distribution of wealth. According to some (see Piketty 2014), wealth in capitalist economies is becoming increasingly unequal and will continue to do so. Piketty's argument is that the return on wealth is higher than the rate of economic growth; therefore, those with wealth will see income and wealth grow more quickly than those without (visit the **online resources** for a video of Piketty discussing his work at Parliament in the UK). It should also be noted that GDP only measures goods that pass through official markets, so does not capture home production or any illicit, black-market trade and takes no account of the relative costs of pollution caused by generating the GDP in various countries. Even the economist Simon Kuznets, who developed the concept in the 1930s, pointed out that GDP was not a welfare measure. He realized that while it counts what is bought and sold, it was quite possible for GDP to rise and welfare to decrease.

GDP also only measures activity that takes place in the formal, officially recorded, economy. If an electrician does jobs for cash and does not declare the income to the tax authorities, then there is additional output in the economy but it is not recorded. This is an example of activity in the so-called 'shadow economy'. This would include all activities (legal and illegal) that produce an output but do not get recorded in official statistics. Most studies, including that of the Institute for Economic Affairs in the UK, use a narrower definition than this to include 'all market-based legal production of goods and services that are deliberately concealed from public authorities'. They found that the shadow economy was about 10 per cent of GDP in the UK, about 14 per cent in Nordic countries, and 20–30 per cent in many Southern European countries (Schneider and Williams 2013). Schneider et al. (2010), using the same narrower definition, in a survey of the shadow economies of 162 countries from 1999 to 2007 found that the unweighted average size of the shadow economy was 31 per cent in 2007 (down from 34 per cent in 1999).

The countries with the largest average size of shadow economy over the period were Zimbabwe (61.8 per cent), Georgia (65.8 per cent), and Bolivia (66.1 per cent). The lowest were Switzerland (8.5 per cent), the USA (8.6 per cent), and Luxembourg (9.7 per cent). By region, sub-Saharan Africa has the highest estimate with a mean of 40.8 per cent, followed by Latin America and the Caribbean (38.7 per cent). The lowest is the OECD (Organization for Economic Co-operation and Development—33 of the most developed economies) at 16.8 per cent. Within the last group, Greece had an average of 27.5 per cent and Italy 27.0 per cent.

Table 2.1 Gross domestic product, 2017 (IMF estimates)

	GDP current prices (US$ million)	GDP PPP (US$ million)	Population (000s)	GDP per capita current prices (US$)	GDP per capita US$ (PPP)
Afghanistan	20,570	67,462	36,800	558	1,833
Australia	1,359.723	1,251.461	24,626	55,215	50,817
Benin	8,792	25,407	11,395	771	2,229
Bolivia	39,267	83,608	11,071	3,546	7,552
Botswana	15,564	39,054	2,108	7,140	17,918
Brazil	2,140,940	3,216,031	207,681	10,308	15,485
Bulgaria	52,291	152,079	7,074	7,392	21,498
China	11,795,297	23,194,411	1390,848	8,480	16,676
Colombia	306,493	720,151	49,294	6,216	14,609
France	2,420,440	2,833,064	64,900	37,294	43,652
Germany	3,423,287	4,134,668	83,001	41,230	49,814
Ghana	42,753	131,498	28,278	1,511	4,650
Haiti	7,897	19,979	10,983	719	1,819
India	2,454,458	9,489,302	1326,572	1,850	7,153
Indonesia	1,020,515	3,257,123	261,989	3,895	12,432
Italy	1,807,425	2,303,108	60,760	29,747	37,905
Japan	4,841,221	5,420,228	126,463	38,281	42,860
Malaysia	9623,282	922,057	32,199	9,623	28,636
Oman	1,7485,182	189,582	4,079	17,485	46,475
Pakistan (2016)	284,185	988,239	193,560	1,468	5,105
Poland	1,2721,758	1,114,105	37,960	12,721	29,349
Russia	1,0885,484	3,938,001	143,375	10,885	27,466
Rwanda	8,918	24,717	11,825	754	2,090
South Africa	317,568	761,296	56,821	5,589	13,409
Spain	1,232,440	1,768,816	46,257	26,643	38,238
Sweden	507,046	522,849	10,177	49,824	51,377
Turkey	793,698	2,082,079	80,773	9,826	25,776
UK	2,496,757	2,905,392	66,030	37,812	44,001
USA	19,417,144	19,417,144	325,741	59,609	59,609
Venezuela	251,589	404,109	31,431	8,004	12,856
Vietnam	215,589	648,243	93,607	2,305	6,925

Source: IMF, World Economic Outlook Database (April 2017)

 Learning Task

Explain why countries in sub-Saharan Africa have the highest average shadow economies.

Another problem is that GDP figures do not take into account environmental degradation and the depletion of natural resources. When oil is taken from the ground, it is irreplaceable. The value of that oil is added to GDP, but the depletion of reserves is not accounted for, even though it will affect the welfare of future generations. When the oil is turned into petrol, that again adds to GDP, but the damage done to the atmosphere when we use it in our cars is not deducted (see Chapter 12 for more discussion on the environment). GDP simply measures the additions to output without taking into account the negative effects of pollution, congestion, and resource depletion.

Counterpoint Box 2.1 GDP and the quality of life

GDP per person is often used as an indicator of human progress, welfare, and happiness; however, it tells us only about income. It does not tell us if GDP is spent on health and education projects or on armaments or on space projects or on clearing up after natural disasters. To emphasize that development is about people, the United Nations Development Programme (UNDP) has developed a set of measures which capture some other elements of development, the **Human Development Index** (HDI). This is an aggregate measure of three features of development: life expectancy, education, and standard of living (PPP per capita income). Its purpose is to emphasize those other elements of development not captured by GDP. The top two countries in the 2016 HDI rankings were Norway and Australia. The latter would rank only nineteenth in a table ranked in order of GDP per capita PPP, but does very well on the other measures of welfare. On the other hand, Qatar and Kuwait, with high per capita incomes, are thirty-third and fifty-first, respectively, in HDI terms (see for more information and the full tables, or visit the **online resources** for a video of an interview with Amartya Sen).

Does more money make people happier? In the 1970s, Richard Easterlin (1974) drew attention to the fact that, within a society, rich people seemed to be happier than poor people,

but that rich societies seemed no happier than poor societies, and getting richer did not necessarily make people happier. It became known as the Easterlin paradox. Others have claimed the evidence is not so clear, although Proto and Rustichini (2013) found that in rich countries, life satisfaction peaked at an income somewhere between $26,000 and $30,000 per year (2005 USD in PPP) (visit the **online resources** for a video link on this topic). The New Economics Foundation has established the Happy Planet Index, which measures which countries deliver long, happy, sustainable lives using data on life expectancy, experienced well-being, and ecological footprint (see http://www.happyplanetindex.org for a video on this).

Nicolas Sarkozy (then President of France), at the time unhappy with current measures of economic performance (i.e. GDP), set up a commission in 2008, chaired by Joseph Stiglitz, to see if the present measures properly reflected societal well-being as well as economic, environmental, and social sustainability. A link to this report can be found in the supporting **online resources**.

Question

Access the resources mentioned above and advance reasons why more money might not make people happier.

Mini Case Study 2.1 Illegal and illicit trades, tax havens, and the global economy

While globalization has clearly increased the total legal output of the world's economy, it has also significantly increased the business opportunities for criminal entrepreneurs. Criminal networks have acquired a global outlook for new illicit markets, which includes

not only goods that are generally deemed illegal, but also the illicit trade in normally legal goods. These trades take many forms, the most lucrative being the trafficking of drugs, arms and people, illegal wildlife trade, and various forms of counterfeiting.   ➜

→ Estimates of the total revenue from these activities vary considerably, as the definition of 'illicit' also varies and by their very nature the activities are hidden as much as possible from regulatory authorities. A 2017 report from Global Financial Integrity, 'Transnational Crime and the Developing World,' evaluated the overall size of criminal markets in 11 categories: the trafficking of drugs, arms, humans, human organs, and cultural property, counterfeiting, illegal wildlife crime, illegal fishing, illegal logging, illegal mining, and crude oil theft. The study suggests that the annual value of transnational crime averages between $1.6 trillion and $2.2 trillion globally. However, using a broader measure, the World Economic Forum put the figure as high as $12 trillion in 2014, about 15 per cent of global GDP, which is similar to China's total economic output.

It seems clear that transnational criminal networks generate huge sums of money, and like any other business they require access to the international financial system in order to conduct their increasingly complex operations. Offshore tax havens, also called 'secrecy jurisdictions', are often cited for their role in tax evasion and avoidance by wealthy individuals and profit shifting by something of the world's largest transnational corporations leading to tax 'base erosion'. However these same locations also act as the conduit through which the funds from illicit trades pass.

The tax havens offer a wide range of facilities and many specialize in certain services such as lax regulation for incorporating offshore companies, secret banking or low or non-existent tax rates. The term 'offshore' can be misleading, because while some tax havens are indeed islands like Jersey, Bermuda, and the Seychelles, others are larger OECD countries providing the same secrecy and tax advantages such as Switzerland, Lichtenstein, and Holland, while US states including Delaware also operate an opaque system where **shell companies** with no employees are easy to establish. Whatever their specialism, by various means tax havens provide facilities that enable people or entities to escape the more stringent laws, rules, and regulations imposed by other jurisdictions.

Secrecy is a defining characteristic of tax havens, and the deliberate lack of transparency and disclosure rules makes it almost impossible to find out who is the true beneficiary of the vast funds that are held and flow through them each year. While many of the structures set up by these jurisdictions are complex, the basic model is quite straightforward. Banks, companies, or other institutions are able to accept money from anywhere in the world without reporting it to the authorities in the country of origin. Under such circumstances, the laundering of criminal proceeds is simply a matter of depositing money in an institution that does not ask questions before moving it on undetected through other parts of the financial system, where it will remain free from tax or be used to finance further criminal activities including international terrorism.

Illegal and illicit trade has a negative impact on the world economy far beyond the estimated turnover figures. Drug trafficking and counterfeit medicines damage public health and increase the financial burden on governments. In other cases, legitimate trade is often displaced, reducing the potential tax revenues, and many activities that target wildlife and natural resources cause incalculable cost to the environmental ecosystems.

While some economists and politicians argue that the existence of tax havens can actually enhance the efficiency of global financial flows and reduce tax competition, others see them as harmful systems that lower global welfare in various ways. Either way, despite some efforts by global organizations, governments and companies in controlling illicit trade, the facilities provided by tax havens ensure that these activities continue to be a significant threat to the global economy.

Sources: http://www.oecd.org/gov/risk/oecdtaskforceon-counteringillicittrade.htm, http://www.gfintegrity.org/press-release/transnational-crime-is-a-1-6-trillion-to-2-2-trillion-annual-business-finds-new-gfi-report, https://www.oecd.org/cleangovbiz/toolkit/moneylaundering.htm, http://www.gfintegrity.org/issue/tax-havens-bank-secrecy, http://www.taxjustice.net/wp-content/Price_of_Offshore_Revisited_120722.pdf, and https://www.transparency.org.

Questions

Access the materials in the **online resources** and consider the following:

1. Why do tax havens exist?
2. Who are the main beneficiaries of tax havens and secrecy jurisdictions?
3. What measures can be taken to mitigate the worst effects of the 'offshore' financial system?

Economic Growth

Despite concerns about how it is measured, growth in national output (**economic growth**) is seen as a key objective for all national governments, as they believe it is fundamental to raising standards of living. It is measured by the annual percentage change in a nation's gross domestic product at constant prices, as GDP can grow through the effects of inflation. Quite modest rates of growth can have a significant effect on living standards if they are maintained. A growth rate of 2 per cent could double real incomes every 36 years. We saw in the opening case study that China's GDP had increased six-fold in just 20 years from 1984.

According to the **International Monetary Fund** (IMF), world GDP between 2009 and 2017 grew on average by 3.3 per cent per year. However, as shown in Table 2.2, growth rates for individual countries can vary quite markedly, from country to country and year to year. Growth in the most

Table 2.2 Economic growth (annual percentage change in GDP)

	2009	2010	2011	2012	2013	2014	2015	2016	2017
World	−0.1	5.4	4.2	3.5	3.4	3.5	3.4	3.1	3.5
G7	−3.8	2.8	1.6	1.4	1.4	1.8	2.0	1.5	1.9
EU	−4.3	2.1	1.7	−0.4	0.3	1.7	2.4	2.0	2.0
Developing economies	2.9	7.4	6.3	5.4	5.1	4.7	4.2	4.1	4.5
Sub-Saharan Africa	3.9	7.0	5.0	4.3	5.3	5.1	3.4	1.4	2.6
Afghanistan	20.6	8.4	6.5	14.0	3.9	1.3	0.8	2.0	3.0
Australia	1.7	2.3	2.7	3.6	2.1	2.8	2.4	2.5	3.1
Brazil	−0.1	7.5	4.0	1.9	3.0	0.5	−3.8	−3.6	0.2
China	9.2	10.6	9.5	7.9	7.8	7.3	6.9	6.7	6.6
Colombia	1.7	4.0	6.6	4.0	4.9	4.4	3.1	2.0	2.3
Germany	−5.6	4.0	3.7	0.7	0.6	1.6	1.5	1.8	1.6
India	8.5	10.3	6.6	5.5	6.5	7.2	7.9	6.8	7.2
Indonesia	4.7	6.4	6.2	6.0	5.6	5.0	4.9	5.0	5.1
Japan	−5.4	4.2	−0.1	1.5	2.0	0.3	1.2	1.0	1.2
Kenya	3.3	8.4	6.1	4.6	5.7	5.3	5.6	6.0	5.3
Mexico	−4.7	5.1	4.0	4.0	1.4	2.3	2.6	2.3	1.7
Nigeria	8.4	11.3	4.9	4.3	5.4	6.3	2.7	−1.5	0.8
Russia	−7.8	4.5	4.0	3.5	1.3	0.7	−2.8	−0.2	1.4
South Africa	−1.5	3.0	3.3	2.2	2.5	1.7	1.3	0.3	0.8
Tanzania	5.4	6.4	7.9	5.1	7.3	7.0	7.0	6.6	6.8
Thailand	−0.7	7.5	0.8	7.2	2.7	0.9	2.9	3.2	3.0
Turkey	−4.7	8.5	11.1	4.8	8.5	5.2	6.1	2.9	2.5
UK	−4.3	1.9	1.5	1.3	1.9	3.1	2.2	1.8	2.0
USA	−2.8	2.5	1.6	2.2	1.7	2.4	2.6	1.6	2.3
Vietnam	5.4	6.4	6.2	5.2	5.4	6.0	6.7	6.2	6.5

Source: IMF, World Economic Outlook Database (2017)

advanced and mature economies of the developed world tend to be much lower than in the developing economies of the world. Table 2.2 shows that world growth rates since 2006 have varied from -0.38 per cent to 5.3 per cent, but for the G7 (the most advanced economies of the world) the corresponding figures are -3.7 per cent and 2.8 per cent, and for developing economies 3.1 per cent and 8.7 per cent. In late 2008 and 2009, after the financial crisis (see Chapter 11), the world economy went into recession. World output shrank in a recession which lasted longer and was deeper (the fall in output from its peak to its trough was about 4 per cent) than any other post-war recession.

This affected some economies more than others. The developed economies suffered worst, with Japan, Germany, and the UK contracting by over 5 per cent. At the same time, China continued to grow at a slightly slower rate than hitherto, 9.2 per cent, India by 8.5 per cent, and Nigeria by 7 per cent. In 2010, the world economy began to recover and world growth rates rose above 3 per cent until 2012 and have since averaged around 2.5 per cent. The European debt crisis still threatened, meaning that recovery and growth rates in the EU have been lower than for other advanced economies. Rates of growth in developing economies and sub-Saharan Africa have generally been lower than pre-crisis rates, but still well above advanced economy rates of growth. The World Bank now expects another modest recovery with growth projected to reach 2.7 per cent in 2017 and further strengthen to around 2.9 per cent in 2018–19. Once again the emerging and developing economies (EMDE's) are expected to grow faster at around 4.1 per cent in 2017 and 4.5 in 2018 by comparison to 1.9 per cent in the advanced economies. Visit the **online resources** for a link to the Global Economic Prospects Report on the World Bank's website.

Counterpoint Box 2.2 Is economic growth a good thing?

Not everybody agrees that the pursuit of economic growth is necessarily a good thing. Edward Mishan, in his book *The Costs of Economic Growth* (1967), pointed out that economic growth brought with it social costs such as pollution, traffic congestion, and 'the frantic pace of life'. In a later book (Meadows et al. 1972), *The Limits to Growth*, the authors explored the relationship between growth and resources. They concluded that, if growth continued at its present pace, then the limits to growth would be reached sometime in the twenty-first century.

The World Economic Forum has also developed a broader measure of national performance called the Inclusive Development Index that places greater emphasis on standard of living and social needs (WEF 2018).

Visit the link on our **online resources** for an interview in January 2010 with Dennis Meadows, one of the authors (see Chapter 12 for a fuller discussion of these issues).

Nor is everybody agreed that growth is necessarily the solution for poverty as the benefits of growth can be highly unbalanced. For a recent discussion of this, and the problems of climate change and resource depletion, see Simms et al. (2010). You can find the link on the supporting **online resources**.

Question

Explain why economic growth is not necessarily the solution to poverty. How else could poverty be addressed?

The Changing World Economy

Predicting the longer-term direction of the global economy is fraught with difficulty, and major institutions such as the World Bank and the IMF have become more cautious about issuing estimates beyond the next couple of years. However, a recent report by PwC suggests that the world economy will roughly double in size by 2042, growing at an annual average rate of around 2.6 per cent between 2016 and 2050 due largely to continued technology driven improvements in productivity.

The growth is expected to be driven largely by emerging market and developing countries, with the E7 economies of Brazil, China, India, Indonesia, Mexico, Russia, and Turkey growing at an annual average rate of almost 3.5 per cent over the next 34 years, compared to just 1.6 per cent for the advanced G7 nations of Canada, France, Germany, Italy, Japan, the UK, and the USA. If these projections are correct, then by 2030, the E7's purchasing power will be greater than that of the G7. By 2050, six of the seven largest economies will be the emerging economies of China, India, Indonesia, Brazil, Russia, and Mexico, with the USA in third place. The report also suggests that by then, the E7's share of GDP would be 50 per cent, while that of the G7 countries falls to just over 20 per cent and the EU 27 could fall below 10 per cent.

The output of the current developing world will be bigger (57.7 per cent) than the current developed world (42.3 per cent). China alone will account for 28 per cent of GDP, and India 18 per cent, while the share of the USA will fall to 16 per cent and the Eurozone to 9 per cent (see Figure 2.1). Per capita GDP will increase fourfold in developing economies and only double in advanced economies, so there will be some convergence of per capita GDP; however, there will still be a substantial gap between advanced and developing economies (IMF 2018; PwC 2017).

For China and India, this would be more like their positions in the nineteenth century when they were the world's two biggest economies. In that century, together they accounted for around 30 per cent of world GDP (Maddison 2003). Their populations were large then, as now, so per capita incomes were lower than Western Europe. In fact, China remained the largest economy until 1890 when the lead was lost to Western Europe and the USA following the Industrial Revolution, which originated in the mid-eighteenth century in Britain. This transformed Western society from an agricultural economy with small-scale cottage industries to an industrialized economy with mass production carried out in factories in towns. There was mass migration from the countryside to the cities as a result.

Figure 2.1 Percentage of world GDP

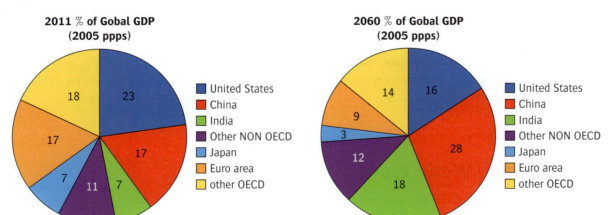

Source: Data from OECD (2012)

The driver for all of this was the application of steam power, not just in factories but also for transport, allowing the movement of relatively low value goods across large distances over both land and water. The benefits of this transformation were confined to the industrialized nations of the time largely because they held the advantage in technological progress, but also because many of the countries of Africa, Asia, and Latin America were the colonies of the Western powers supplying primary products to the industrialized nations. In the case of Africa, they also supplied young men and women as unpaid, slave labour.

In the nineteenth century, the UK was the dominant power producing 30 per cent of total world industrial output, but this position was changing as the USA and other Western European powers developed. By 1913, the USA was producing 36 per cent of world industrial output and the UK only 14 per cent (Dicken 2004). This pattern continued until World War II, when the world divided into three different spheres.

The first sphere was the Western world, led by the USA and organized along capitalist lines. It set up world institutions such as the World Bank, the IMF, and the General Agreement on Tariffs and Trade (GATT) (later WTO) in order to aid recovery of the war-torn Western European economies and to establish a 'world system' to combat the power of the Soviet bloc. The 1950s also saw the emergence of Japan as a new competitor for the developed Western world so that the bi-polar world of trade in manufactures became a tri-polar world.

The second sphere to emerge after World War II was the Eastern communist bloc led by Russia. Russia had become a communist state after the 1917 revolution, but it was after World War II that communism took hold in other countries. Some Eastern and Central European countries were invaded by Russia and others, Cuba and China, experienced revolutions. The Soviet Union was a centrally planned economy and this system was imposed on the satellite states of Eastern and Central Europe so that trade and investment between the two spheres was minimal. China became the People's Republic of China in 1949 and for the next 30 years had little to do with the world economy, following a policy of self-reliance. The Soviet bloc ushered in some political and economic reforms in the 1980s in a move towards becoming a democratic market economy, and this was a prelude to popular revolutions which swept across Eastern Europe following the withdrawal of Soviet Union support for the communist regimes. In 1991, the Baltic States declared themselves independent and by the end of that year the whole Soviet sphere unravelled, with the Soviet Union itself ceasing to exist. China had started its move towards becoming a market economy in 1979, but, unlike the Soviet bloc, communism still prevails there.

The world is now less divided along political lines, but there is still an enormous gap between those who have and those who have not. In East Asia, a number of newly industrialized economies have emerged (initially South Korea, Taiwan, Singapore, and Hong Kong, and later Malaysia, Thailand, and Indonesia) to become global players, but, for much of the rest of the world, poverty remains a major problem and narrowing this gap will be a major challenge.

For business, business analysts, and fund managers, these changes are of great interest as they seek new markets and investment opportunities. The growth and potential of Brazil, Russia, India, and China has been well documented, so much so that they are now well known by the acronym 'BRIC', a label given to them in 2001 by Jim O'Neill, former chief economist of Goldman Sachs (2003). Various other groupings have been identified as the next great wave of emerging markets. Goldman Sachs (2007) identified what they called the N11 (next 11) economies with strong market growth potential. These countries were Bangladesh, Mexico, South Korea,

Vietnam, Pakistan, Egypt, the Philippines, Nigeria, Indonesia, Turkey, and Iran. Next came the Economic Intelligence Unit's CIVETS, Colombia, Indonesia, Vietnam, Egypt, Turkey, and South Africa, and now we have MINTs, Mexico, Indonesia, Nigeria, and Turkey. What all these countries have in common is a large, youthful population in contrast to the ageing populations of the more advanced economies. Some, such as Mexico, Indonesia, and Turkey, are close to large markets, in the form of the USA, China, and the EU. Some have abundant natural resources, but none have the potential to be the next BRICs. Critics of these new acronyms say that they are no more than marketing ploys by fund managers to attract new investment funds. Although they form convenient groupings, they are all very diverse economies and tend to be much less stable than more advanced economies, often with weak governance and high levels of corruption (see Chapter 5). While they all, no doubt, have potential for business, further research needs to be undertaken before committing resources, as we shall see in Chapter 6.

In 2010, the BRICs became BRICS with the inclusion of South Africa, conveniently maintaining the acronym. This was not because of South Africa's prospects, as had been the case with the original members, but was a reflection of the rise of a new political grouping representing the emerging market countries of the world. The original members had begun meeting annually in 2006, but one problem was that Africa was not represented, hence the invitation to South Africa to join the original BRICs.

In the years since 2012, the prospect of rapid and sustainable growth for the BRIC countries has stalled and a number have severe economic and political problems. Mounting debt burdens and falling global commodity prices have affected these emerging markets, which rely heavily on export-led growth, and recently the economies of both Russia and Brazil have experienced periods of recession.

Structural transformation in China, as it attempts to move from an export-driven economy to one relying on domestic consumption is one issue and among the other members of the group only India has recently shown signs of strong potential for growth. The country has largely benefited from being a net importer of crude oil, and is also less susceptible to market volatility as it is less dependent on exports than, for example, Russia and South Africa. While India has the lowest per capita GDP among the other members of the bloc and is also lagging behind others in terms of quality of life, recent economic reforms have led to greater foreign investments and improved economic competitiveness. India's ranking in the World Economic Forum's Global Competitiveness Report improved from 71 in 2014 to 55 in 2015.

Similar to the OECD study, Goldman Sachs (2011) estimated that by 2050, China and India will be the first and third largest economies, with Brazil and Russia taking fifth and sixth places. China's economy will be some 30 per cent bigger than the US economy and India's about 12 per cent smaller. Brazil, Russia, Indonesia, and Mexico will all be bigger than any of the European economies, with Turkey not far behind. These economies will provide opportunities for outsourcing manufacturing activities, opening new offices, mergers, acquisitions, and alliances; however, of major significance will be the emergence of a global middle class. In 2050 Russia, Mexico, Brazil, Turkey, China, Indonesia, and India will still have per capita incomes less than the USA, Japan, and Western Europe, but they will be very much greater than today (see Figures 2.2 and 2.3).

Estimating the growth of the middle class is fraught with problems of definition, but what business is mainly interested in is 'spending power'. For this, per capita GDP is a good proxy measure of 'middle class'. The World Bank, as we saw above, separates the 'middle class' into

Figure 2.2 GDP level, 2010 ($USbn)

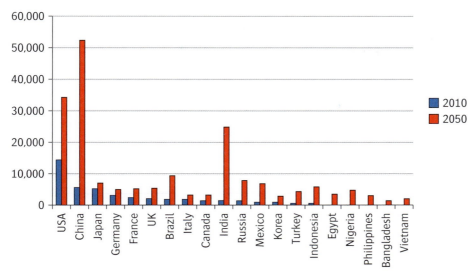

Source: Goldman Sachs (2011)

'lower middle' and 'upper middle' with a cut-off point at about $4,000 dollars per year or about $11 per day. The lower cut-off point of about $2.80 dollars per day is useful in terms of a measurement that takes people out of extreme poverty, but not very useful to businesses wanting to sell cars, washing machines, health care, and financial services. Kharas and Gertz (2010), using a measure of $10–100 per day, estimated that by 2015 the number of Asian middle class consumers will equal the number in Europe and North America, and that by 2021 there could be more

Figure 2.3 GDP per capita level, 2010 ($US)

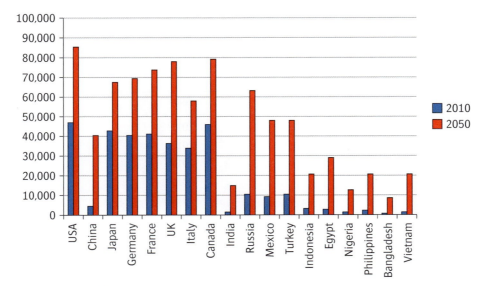

Source: Goldman Sachs (2011)

Table 2.3 The middle class: size and distribution

	2009		2020		2030	
	millions	%	millions	%	millions	%
North America	338	18	333	10	322	7
Europe	664	36	703	22	680	14
Central and South America	181	10	251	8	313	6
Asia Pacific	525	28	1,740	54	3,228	66
sub-Saharan Africa	32	2	57	2	107	2
Middle East and N. Africa	105	6	165	5	234	5
World	1,845	100	3,249	100	4,884	100

Source: Kharas and Gertz (2010)

than 2 billion Asians in middle class households. By 2030, they project that two-thirds of the global middle class will be in the Asia Pacific region (see Table 2.3).

This will mean that by 2030 there will be 5 billion members of the global middle class, of whom only 21 per cent will be resident in North America and Europe. These new consumers in developing countries will have spending patterns similar to current residents of high-income countries, providing enormous opportunities to international business in the form of new markets. According to Ernst and Young (2013), countries hit a 'sweet spot' of interest to businesses when per capita incomes move beyond, on average, about $6,000 per annum, although different industries have different 'sweet spots' and therefore need more specific information. They give, as an example, the automobile market in China; in 2001, this was tiny, but once per capita incomes hit $6,000 in 2008 it grew very quickly. General Motors in 2004 sold one car in China for every 10 sold in the USA. By 2009, this had reached parity. The estimated 'sweet spots' for various countries are shown in Table 2.4.

Table 2.4 When will the emerging markets countries hit their sweet spots? (projected)

Country	Year
Egypt	2011
Indonesia	2015
India	2017
Philippines	2019
Vietnam	2019
Pakistan	2024
Nigeria	2025
Bangladesh	2029

Source: Economist Intelligence Unit quoted in Ernst and Young (2013)

In the next section, we go on to look at two other aspects of international business: trade flows and exchange rates.

Learning Task

1. Explain what is meant by the 'sweet spot' of per capita income.
2. Why might different industries have different sweet spots?
3. Why is the growth of a global middle class of such interest to international business?

Counterpoint Box 2.3 Increasing global inequality

It is claimed that the middle class is growing and that progress has been made in reducing global poverty. However, recent research suggests that the real incomes of the world's very poorest have gone up by just $3 a year over the last 25 years.

The scale of inequality between the rich and poor is staggering. According to the latest annual statistics from Oxfam, the eight richest people in the world now have the same wealth as the poorest half of the population or approximately, 3.6 billion people. In 2016 it was thought that 62 people owned the same as the poorest 50 per cent on the planet; however, new information has shown that poor people for example in China and India owned even fewer assets than previously thought, making the wealth gap more even pronounced.

Research also highlights other indicators that inequality is growing. Between 1988 and 2011, the incomes of the poorest 10 per cent increased by just $65, while the incomes of the richest 1 per cent grew by $11,800 or 182 times as much. This has led to a situation where since 2015, over 50 per cent of the world's wealth has been in the hands of just 1 per cent of the population. Oxfam claim that over the next 20 years, 500 people will hand over $2.1tn to their heirs—a sum larger than the annual GDP of India, a country with 1.3 billion people.

At the same time, in a world where we produce enough food to feed everyone, the World Food Programme estimate that around 800 million people or one in nine of the global population still go to bed hungry each night, and one in three will suffer from some form of malnutrition.

The causes and scale of inequality are disputed, but many argue that the current situation is not only economically inefficient but also politically corrosive, and undermines collective progress.

Questions

1. What are the likely reasons for growing inequality?
2. Is a more equal distribution of wealth necessary, and if so, why?
3. What policies are needed to reverse or slow the current trends?

Sources: Oxfam (2018) 'An economy for the 1%' January at https://d1tn3vj7xz9fdh.cloudfront.net/s3fs-public/file_attachments/bp210-economy-one-percent-tax-havens-180116-en_0.pdf, *Guardian* (2017) 'Eight men own more than 3.6 billion' 16 January at https://www.theguardian.com/commentisfree/2017/jan/16/eight-people-earn-more-billion-economics-broken, http://www.pwc.com

International Trade

One of the key drivers of globalization is international trade, the exchange of goods and services between nations. In this section we shall look in more detail at the pattern of global trade and put forward several theories to answer the question of why countries trade. We shall also look at the regulation of trade through the WTO.

The Pattern of Trade

International trade grew very quickly in the second half of the twentieth century and more quickly than global output, which had been rising at 3 per cent per annum. In the second half of the twentieth century, merchandise trade grew almost 20-fold while world merchandise output only increased six-fold. Trade has grown especially quickly in the last 30 years at about 7.3 per cent per annum. In 1950, world exports were approximately US$0.5 trillion, rising to US$2.03 trillion dollars in 1980, and about US$22 trillion in 2012. Of this US$22 trillion, most (US$17.9 trillion) was in merchandise trade, and the rest (US$4.4 trillion) was in services. World commodity prices had a significant impact on the value of merchandise trade in 2015, and following modest growth between 2012 and 2014 the total value fell back to $US 16.2 trillion. Generally, service trade has grown more quickly than merchandise trade, but this also declined a little in 2015 to $US 4.6 trillion. Exports as a percentage of world output were about 13 per cent in 1970, 25 per cent in 2005, and after declining by 12 per cent in 2009, were back to around 30 per cent by 2015 (World Bank 2016, World Trade Organization 2017).

The main contributors to this growth are the reduction of trade barriers, and continuing liberalization of markets following the adoption by many countries of free trade ideology as the dominant economic philosophy since the late 1970s (see Chapter 1 for further discussion). The continuing reduction in transport and communications costs, and, not least, the growth in vertical specialization in production and the establishment of MNC **global supply chains**, are also major drivers. The growth in foreign direct investment has been faster than growth in both global output as measured by GDP and the growth in trade, reaching $1.76 trillion dollars in 2016, the highest level since the financial crisis of 2008. The corresponding increase in the numbers and activities of multinational enterprises or transnational corporations and their ever-increasing number of subsidiaries and affiliates that form modern global supply chains is also notable. This growing 'internationalization' of production involves vertical specialization, with firms locating different parts of an increasingly fragmented production process in different countries based on a number of factors including not only access to raw materials and nearness to markets but also the attractiveness of taxation regimes, other regulatory controls, and, of course, the level of wages. Horizontal integration is also a feature of MNE activity as the firms acquire additional business entities at the same level in the value chain, often by merger or acquisition to capture a larger share of a particular market. The cross-border trade between the multinational firms and their affiliates accounts for a large share of international trade in both goods and services, and while precise measurements are difficult to establish, some estimates put the total at around one-third of all trade. It should be noted that while the trends described all show long-term increases, they are also increasingly volatile; this makes future predictions difficult and subject to regular revision. What the trends do point to is an ever-greater interconnectedness in the global economy, with multinational enterprises playing a central role.

MNEs have increasingly complex internal ownership structures. The top 100 MNEs in UNCTAD's Transnationality Index have on average more than 500 affiliates each, across more than 50 countries. The ownership structures typically have about 20 holding companies owning affiliates across multiple jurisdictions, and numerous entities located in offshore investment hubs. (See Chapter 1 for the latest FDI data.)

Merchandise trade comprises three categories: manufactured goods, mining, and agricultural products. The share of primary commodities in total world exports of merchandise trade has fallen dramatically. In 1960, primary commodities (excluding fuels) accounted for 38 per cent of world exports, but by 2012 it had fallen to only 9 per cent. Over the same period, the share of manufactured goods has increased from 51 per cent to 64 per cent. Developing countries have increased their share of world trade in manufactured goods from less than 25 per cent in 1960 to about 42 per cent in 2015, with South East Asian countries being the main contributors to this growth. Other developing regions' exports did not see the same growth. African states' exports have averaged only 2 per cent growth since 1980, while world exports have grown at 6 per cent per annum. Developed economies still account for the majority of traffic—see Tables 2.5, 2.6, and 2.7. The World Trade Organization (2013) estimates that developing countries will see their share of world exports rise from 41 per cent in 2010 to 57 per cent in 2030, with developed economies dropping from 59 per cent to 43 per cent. China's share of world exports will increase from 9 per cent to 15 per cent over the same time period.

Table 2.5 World exports of merchandise and commercial services 2010–16 (billion dollars and percentage)

	Value 2016	Annual percentage change			
		2010–16	2014	2015	2016
Merchandise	15955	1	2.5	−14	−3
Commercial services	4808	4	5	−6	0

Source: WTO (2017)

Table 2.6 Leading exporters and importers in world merchandise trade 2016 (billion dollars and percentage)

Rank	Exporters	Value	Share	Rank	Importers	Value	Share
1	China	2098	13.2	1	USA	2251	13.9
2	USA	1455	9.1	2	China	1587	9.8
3	Germany	1340	8.4	3	Germany	1055	6.5
4	Japan	645	4.0	4	UK	636	3.9
5	Netherlands	570	3.6	5	Japan	607	3.7
6	Korea	495	3.1	6	France	573	3.4
7	Hong Kong, China	517	3.2	7	Hong Kong, China	547	3.4
	Domestic exports	26	0.2		Retained imports	121	0.7
	Re-exports	491	3.1				
8	France	501	3.1	8	Netherlands	503	3.1
9	UK	409	2.6	9	Canada	417	2.6
10	Italy	462	2.9	10	Korea	406	2.5

Note: Hong Kong imports includes re-exports.
Source: WTO Statistical Review (2017)

Table 2.7 Leading exporters and importers in world service trade 2016 (billion dollars and percentage)

Rank	Exporters	Value	Share	Rank	Importers	Value	Share
1	USA	733	15.2	1	USA	482	10.3
2	UK	324	6.7	2	China	450	9.6
3	Germany	268	5.6	3	Germany	311	6.6
4	France	236	4.9	4	France	236	5.0
5	China	307	4.3	5	UK	195	4.1
6	Netherlands	177	3.7	6	Ireland	192	4.1
7	Japan	169	3.5	7	Japan	183	3.9
8	India	161	3.5	8	Netherlands	169	3.6
9	Singapore	149	3.1	9	Singapore	155	3.3
10	Ireland	146	3.0	10	India	133	2.8

Source: WTO Statistical Review (2017)

Table 2.8 Intra- and inter-regional merchandise trade 2015 (billion dollars)

Origin	Destination							
	North America	S & C America	Europe	CIS	Africa	Middle East	Asia	World
North America	1251	214	379	17	43	79	504	2,493
South and Central America	173	179	114	9	18	17	170	695
Europe	540	119	4,665	218	221	229	738	6,810
CIS	28	7	385	131	16	22	134	735
Africa	39	29	201	2	98	18	152	555
Middle East	99	11	148	7	36	113	694	1,288
Asia	1065	185	900	127	207	302	3,093	5,917
World	3195	744	6,792	512	639	780	5,485	18,494

Source: WTO

 Learning Task

Use the information in Table 2.8 to answer the following questions.

1. For each region, calculate its share of world merchandise trade.

2. What proportion of world trade is accounted for by North America and Europe?

3. For each region, calculate the share of intra-regional trade. For example, what proportion of Europe's trade is within Europe?

4. What conclusions can you draw from these and any other calculations in terms of the economic self-reliance of different regions?

Why do Countries Trade?

The earliest theory (seventeenth and eighteenth centuries) in relation to international trade was that of mercantilism, which held that countries should maximize exports and try to limit imports as much as possible. Generating a trade surplus (when the value of exports exceeds the value of imports) was the aim of governments, as this would result in an inflow of gold and silver. The governments of mercantilist nations, such as Britain, the Netherlands, France, Spain, and Portugal, restricted or banned imports with tariffs and quotas and subsidized domestic industries to encourage exports.

Mercantilists viewed exports as a good thing, as they stimulated industry and increased the number of jobs at home, and considered imports as bad, since these meant a loss of demand and jobs. The current problems besetting the world economy are threatening a new wave of mercantilist policies as countries look to exports of goods to deliver economic growth. Whereas mercantilists viewed trade as a zero sum game (i.e. one country could only gain if another lost), Adam Smith (1776) set out to prove that all could gain by engaging in free trade. Smith demonstrated that if countries specialized in producing the goods in which they were most efficient (i.e. in which they had an absolute advantage), then world output would be increased and the surpluses could be traded.

David Ricardo (1817) extended this theory to show that even when a country had an absolute advantage in the production of all goods, total output could still be increased if countries specialized in the production of a good in which they had a comparative advantage. A country has a comparative advantage over another country if it can produce at a lower opportunity cost. In other words, it has to forgo fewer resources than the other in order to produce it.

These theories help to explain the pattern of trade, but do not tell us why one country should be more efficient than another and therefore what that country should specialize in. The factor proportions theory (or factor endowment theory), developed by Eli Heckscher (1919) and Bertil Ohlin (1924), explains that countries will produce and export products that utilize resources which they have in abundance, and import products that utilize resources that are relatively scarce.

For much of the less developed world, the pattern of trade predicted by these theories holds true, but this pattern has tended to favour the richer nations at the expense of the poor. This is especially the case for sub-Saharan Africa. These countries produce and export primary products (other than oil for most) for which they have a comparative advantage, and they import manufactured goods for which they are at a comparative disadvantage. The problem is that the theories predict that total output is increased, but say nothing about how that increase will be shared between countries. History shows that the demand for primary products does not rise as quickly as the total rise in demand for all goods and services, so there tends to be long-run deterioration in the terms at which primary products exchange for manufactured goods. In other words, the price of manufactured goods tends to rise more quickly than the price of primary products. This, together with a very narrow range of products, probably goes a long way to explaining the low levels of income in those countries.

What none of this explained was that most trade takes place not between nations which are very different, but between similar, developed nations and that it is trade in similar goods—so-called intra-industry trade. New trade theory in the 1980s explained that there were gains to be made from **specialization** and economies of scale and that those who were first to enter the market could erect entry barriers to other firms and become the dominant firm. As output increases, the unit costs of production fall and new entrants are forced to produce at similar levels. Without a large domestic market to justify producing on that scale, cost then becomes a major barrier to entry (see Chapter 3 for a discussion of entry barriers). The end result can be a global market supporting very few competitors, and thus new trade theory becomes a major factor in explaining the growth of globalization.

A feature of intra-industry trade is **product differentiation**. Much international trade theory regards products as homogeneous, but modern manufacturing firms produce a range of similar products appealing to different consumer preferences. For example, a few car producers based in a few developed economies each manufacture a range of models and most of the trade in those products takes place between those countries.

 Mini Case Study 2.2 Intra-firm trade and transfer pricing—is this really trade?

Most trade theory pays little specific attention to the role of multinational or transnational corporations. Intra-firm trade is international trade that takes place between units of the same corporate entity. This deviates from the basic ideals of a market economy where transactions take place between independent buyers and sellers, and price is determined by supply and demand. Some question as to whether this is trade at all in any meaningful sense.

If a firm transfers intermediate goods it has produced from a factory in one US state to its own factory in another state, the movement is not recorded as trade. However, if the same goods cross a national border, it is counted in global trade statistics.

It is estimated that around 60 per cent of international trade happens within, rather than between, multinationals although few countries collect reliable data and firms are reluctant to reveal what they claim to be commercially sensitive information. These estimates suggest that a significant part of the world trade is based on non-market pricing planned in corporate headquarters.

One of the major concerns about this form of trade is that while the prices used are supposed to reflect market-based prices (referred to as the 'arm's length principle'), these can be difficult to determine. In reality, 'transfer pricing' (administered prices set by the firms) may allow for profit shifting and cross subsidization to achieve lower tax rates, avoid regulation, or hide risks.

For example, if a subsidiary of a firm located in a low tax (or even zero 'tax haven') sells goods or services to another part of the enterprise in a higher tax jurisdiction at a price above true market level, this will transfer profit to the lower rate area and cause a corresponding loss of tax revenue for the higher taxing country.

Although transfer pricing is not illegal, mispricing is and estimates vary as to how much tax revenue is lost by governments around the world as a result of this practice. Washington-based Global Financial Integrity estimates the amount at several hundred billion dollars annually. The UN Conference on Trade and Development (UNCTAD 2015) also points to significant loss of tax revenue in developing countries, and suggests that governments lost around $100 billion per year in revenues due to tax avoidance by multinational enterprises (MNEs), and as much as $300 billion in total lost development finance as investment is increasingly channelled offshore low tax hubs.

Sources: UNCTAD (2015), Tax Justice Network, Global Integrity International

Questions

1. What policy implications does intra-firm trade pose for national governments?

2. How might transfer pricing be effectively monitored? Visit the Tax Justice Network website to read about unitary taxation.

Trade Intervention

All of the theories and models make the assumption that trade takes place freely between nations. However, as noted in Chapter 1, this is far from the case. Every nation imposes trade restrictions of some description. Generally, their purpose is to limit imports by imposing tariff or non-tariff barriers, or to encourage exports by subsidizing exporting firms.

A tariff is a tax or duty placed on an imported good by a domestic government. Tariffs are usually levied as a percentage of the declared value of the good, similar to a sales tax. Unlike a sales tax, tariff rates are often different for every good and tariffs do not apply to domestically produced goods.

Non-tariff barriers can take a number of forms: quotas, licences, rules of origin, product requirements (standards, packaging, labelling and markings, product specifications), customs procedures and documentation requirements, local content rules, and exchange rate manipulation.

Subsidies can take many forms, and can be difficult to identify and calculate. Financial assistance of any sort, including cash payments, low interest loans, tax breaks, export credits and export guarantees, export promotion agencies, and free trade and export processing zones, all distort trade in favour of domestic producers. According to the OECD, 52 countries accounting for approximately two-thirds of global agricultural output provided an average of $519 billion or EUR 442 billion to support individual farmers between 2014 and 2016. The report shows that across countries, subsidies varied considerably, ranging from negative support to 50 per cent or higher of gross farm receipts.

Why Intervene?

National defence—it is argued that certain industries need defending from imports because they are vital in times of war. Weapons, transport, utilities, and food would probably fall into this category, but where would the line be drawn? Similar arguments have been put forward to ban exports of technically advanced, especially military, products. The USA banned exports of satellites to China because this would have given the Chinese access to US military technology. It resulted in a fall in the American share of world satellite sales.

When US firms sell high-tech products and military equipment to allies, the US government tries to prevent the selling-on of such technology to countries such as China and Venezuela. In July 2007, Saab withdrew from an international trade deal with Venezuela because of an arms ban imposed by the USA on Venezuela. Bofors, a subsidiary of Saab, had supplied Venezuela with weapons for 20 years, but the ban meant they could not sell any weapons with US-made parts.

To protect fledgling domestic industries from foreign competition—it is argued that industries in their infancy may need protection until they can compete internationally. This gives them time to grow to a size where they can gain economies of scale, learn from doing business, and develop the supporting infrastructure discussed above. Some of the Asian economies, Japan, South Korea, and Taiwan, have successfully protected infant industries until they have grown to compete internationally and the barriers have been removed. On the other hand, some Japanese industries, such as banking, construction, and retailing, have remained protected and inefficient.

To protect domestic industries from foreign competition and thereby save jobs—governments often come under pressure to support industries in decline because the human cost involved in the event of sudden closure can be very high. Protection may be justified to delay the closure and allow time for adjustment.

To protect against over dependence on a narrow base of products—the law of comparative advantage tells us that countries should specialize in the production of goods in which they have a comparative advantage. For some countries, this will result in a range of primary products for which demand is **income inelastic**. This could condemn these countries to persistent poverty, so protection to expand the industrial base may be the only way to escape from poverty.

Political motives—the USA, for example, has an embargo on trade with Cuba because it disagrees with Cuba's politics.

To protect domestic producers from dumping by foreign companies or governments—dumping occurs when a foreign company charges a price in the domestic market which is 'too low'. In most instances, 'too low' is generally understood to be a price which is lower in a foreign market than the price in the domestic market. In other instances, 'too low' means a price which is below cost, so the producer is losing money. Vietnam took its first case to the WTO in 2010 (having joined in 2006), accusing the USA of unfair duties on frozen shrimp imported from Vietnam. The USA has charged duties ranging from 2.5 per cent to 25.76 per cent because it fears **dumping** by the Vietnamese. The case was completed in April 2011, with the WTO finding that the USA had acted inconsistently with the provisions of the Anti-Dumping Agreement and the GATT (key WTO accords). Firms in the USA have accused China of dumping by keeping the value of the Renminbi low (see 'Exchange Rates', page 70).

Retaliation—to respond to another country's imposition of tariffs or some other restriction or against 'dumping'.

To prevent the import of undesirable products—drugs, live or endangered animals, and certain foodstuffs may be deemed undesirable.

To resist cultural imperialism and/or maintain a particular lifestyle—that is, the imposition of one country's culture, politics, systems of governance, and/or language on another. Quite often, the West, and in particular the USA, is accused of cultural imperialism. As we noted in Chapter 1, American films and television programmes are watched worldwide, and most of these promote American values and beliefs.

 Learning Task

1. Which of the above reasons for trade intervention do you think is justified and which is not?
2. For each, identify the costs and the benefits of the policy for domestic consumers and producers and foreign producers and workers.

Control of Trade

The World Trade Organization (WTO), an intergovernmental organization that seeks to regulate world trade, officially came into being on 1 January 1995 with 123 member nations. This organization was the successor to the GATT established in 1947 with just 23 members. In the depression of the 1930s, many countries had suffered from falling exports and had tried to solve their problems by restricting imports. Others retaliated and the net effect was a reduction, by one-third, of world trade in manufactured goods. These beggar-my-neighbour trade policies were in part responsible for World War II, so there was a determination to devise a system in which there was much more economic cooperation. A much more ambitious scheme, the International Trade Organization, was proposed—covering not only trading relations but also financial arrangements. However, this was blocked by the USA. This left the GATT as the only mechanism for regulating trade until the establishment of the WTO. The aim of the GATT was the reduction of tariffs and liberalizing trade giving countries access to each other's markets.

The GATT's, and now the WTO's, principles are as follows:

- **Non-discrimination**: a country should not discriminate between trading parties. Under the 'most favoured nation' rule, a member has to grant to all members the most favourable conditions it allows trade in a particular product. Once goods have entered a country, the 'national treatment rule applies' in that they should be treated exactly the same as domestic goods.

- **Reciprocity**: if a member benefits from access and tariff reductions made by another member, it must reciprocate by making similar access and tariff reductions to that member.

- **Transparency**: members' trade regulations have to be published so all restrictions can be identified.

- **Predictability and stability**: members cannot raise existing tariffs without negotiation, so everyone can be confident there will be no sudden changes.

- **Freeing of trade**: general reduction of all barriers.

- **Special assistance and trade concessions for developing countries**.

 Mini Case Study 2.3 **Afghanistan's entry to the WTO**

On 29 July 2016, Afghanistan became the 164th member of the World Trade Organization. Located in South Asia, Afghanistan is a land-locked country sharing borders with larger neighbours Pakistan and Iran and the smaller countries of Turkmenistan, Uzbekistan, and Tajikistan.

It is one of the poorest countries in the world, classified by the UNCTAD as one of the 'least developed countries (LDCs)', which are defined as 'low income countries suffering from structural impediments to sustainable development'. Afghanistan has a population of 32.53 million, a GPD of $19.33 billion at current prices ($62.32 billion PPP), and a per capita GDP of $610 ($1,900 PPP) (2015 est.).

The country has been embroiled in conflict for more than three decades, having been invaded by the Soviet Union in 1979 and more recently by joint US and British forces in 2001, with a period of civil war between the two events. In 2016, the security situation in Afghanistan was still volatile, with NATO-led American and allied troops still in the country providing training and anti-terrorism support. Fighting has continued between the Taliban insurgents who control large parts of the country and the Afghan National Security Forces.

Numerous civilian casualties have resulted from the fighting and there has been a significant slowdown of the National Unity Government's reform agenda aimed at wide-ranging ➜

→ legislative and constitutional change, establishing rights for women, greater freedom of speech, and developing much-needed trade and investment for a very weak economy. In addition to the ongoing violence, the country suffers from pervasive corruption, weak economic governance, and a corrosive shadow opium economy.

Much of Afghanistan's fragile economy is based on the export of textiles and agricultural products such as carpets, wool, raisins, pistachios, and almonds. However, a significant part of the economy remains illicit and in Afghanistan the cultivation and distribution of opiates is a valuable industry. According to a recent United Nations report, the country is responsible for approximately 70 per cent of the world's opium production, with opium grown in 21 of the country's 34 provinces. In 2016 the total area under cultivation was estimated at 201,000 hectares, an increase of 10 per cent from the previous year, and the farm gate value was up 57 per cent at $0.9 billion, representing roughly 5 per cent of Afghanistan's estimated GDP.

However, as with many illicit trades, the citizens of the country receive little economic benefit and the report suggests that the poppy farmers receive less than 1 per cent of the revenues generated from the sale of heroin produced and trafficked around the world (United Nations Office on Drugs and Crime, World Drug Report 2017).

WTO membership is, of course, not exclusively reserved for upper or middle-income countries. The economic benefits of free trade appeal to countries of all income levels, particularly to developing nations looking to boost growth through exports.

As a WTO member, Afghanistan can in theory benefit from access to new legal markets, inclusion in global supply chains, and lower tariffs that may ultimately lead to more competitive industries and higher wages. Free trade can also allow local businesses to purchase inputs at lower costs, leading to more competitive prices for manufactured goods. However, Afghanistan's biggest economic challenge remains finding sustainable sources of growth.

Accession to the WTO was and remains a controversial issue for many in the country, as local producers fear that they may lose out to a flood of low-priced imports if all trade barriers are removed. As in many developing countries, the WTO negotiators have offered a package of time limited tariff rates that provides a degree of protection to local businesses although in the view of some, they do not go far enough in protecting the weak economy. For example, tariffs on agricultural imports are capped at certain levels, which can threaten the market share of local food producers. Given Afghanistan's development status, questions remain as to whether the terms negotiated with the WTO will provide sufficient protection for other local industries.

Afghanistan does have future potential, as the country is reportedly rich in natural resources including gemstones, copper, and iron ore, as well as valuable oil and gas deposits that could be used to transform the country's economy. However, investment is needed to exploit these resources, and while most of the foreign aid money received is used to fund internal security measures, the pervasive corruption and weak economic governance makes it difficult for the country to attract FDI. Indeed, in 2016, Transparency International's Corruption Perceptions Index 2016 ranked Afghanistan 169th most corrupt country out of 176 surveyed.

As one of the poorest countries ever to join the WTO, Afghanistan's accession raises many questions about how the organization can support a trade-led economic growth strategy.

Sources: WTO Accession Documents; UNCTAD World Investment Report 2016; UNOCD World Drug Report 2017; World Bank: Afghanistan Development Update 2017; Transparency International Corruption Perception Index 2016

Questions

1. Explain why Afghanistan might benefit from accession to the WTO.
2. Identify the possible effects of membership on domestic producers.
3. What measures will the government need to take to develop long-term sustainable growth?

Under the GATT, these principles were applied only to merchandise trade, and then some sectors, such as agriculture and textiles, were ignored. These have now begun to be addressed under the WTO. Another weakness with the GATT was the lack of any effective process for settling disagreements and a deterrent against offenders. The WTO now has a dispute resolution process and is able to take sanctions against offenders, as it did against the USA in 2002. Under pressure

Table 2.9 GATT/WTO rounds

Period	Round	Countries	Subjects
1947	Geneva	23	Tariffs
1949	Annecy	13	Tariffs
1950–51	Torquay	38	Tariffs
1955–56	Geneva	26	Tariffs
1960–61	Dillon	26	Tariffs
1964–67	Kennedy	62	Tariffs, anti-dumping measures
1973–79	Tokyo	102	Tariffs, non-tariff measures, and framework agreements
1986–94	Uruguay	123	Tariffs, agriculture, textiles, and clothing brought into GATT Agreement on Services (GATS) Intellectual property (TRIPS) Trade-Related Investment (TRIMS) Creation of WTO and dispute settlement
2001–	Doha	141	'Bali Package' accepted in December 2013 but possibly blocked by India in August 2014 Nairobi Package accepted in December 2015. Effectively the end of the Doha round with limited agreement and outcomes.

Source: WTO

from domestic steel producers, the American administration imposed tariffs on steel imports. WTO members reported this and the WTO allowed other members to impose retaliatory tariffs. The US tariffs were removed in 2004. In early 2018, the USA again imposed import tariffs on steel and aluminium, this time from China, the European Union, Canada, Mexico, and Turkey. As a result, retaliatory tariffs on steel were imposed by the countries affected and the USA launched five separate WTO dispute actions, claiming that their tariffs were justified on the grounds of a national security exemption.

Trade negotiations have taken place in a series of 'rounds'. There have been nine of these rounds if we include the current and incomplete Doha round. These are summarized in Table 2.9.

The GATT was a fairly loose arrangement, but the WTO is a permanent organization dealing with a much wider range of issues. About three-quarters of its members are less developed countries. Its top-level decision-making body is the Ministerial Conference, which meets at least every two years. Below this are other committees, which meet on a regular basis. The WTO has permanent offices in Geneva.

The GATT/WTO has been successful in reducing tariffs on industrial products from an average of about 40 per cent in 1947 to something like 4 per cent today, but whether it increases trade is the subject of debate. Trade has increased faster than world GDP, as we have seen—but is this because of the measures taken by the GATT/WTO? Not according to Rose (2004), who found that trade had increased for members and non-members alike. On the other hand, Subramanian and Wei (2005) found that GATT/WTO had served to increase trade substantially (possibly by US$8 trillion in 2000 alone), but that the increase had been uneven. Industrial countries witnessed a larger increase in trade than did developing countries, bilateral trade was greater when both partners undertook liberalization, and those sectors that did not liberalize did not see an increase in trade.

The WTO is not without its critics, as we have witnessed with the demonstrations by anti-globalization protestors at the Ministerial Council meetings from Seattle in 1999 to Hong Kong in 2005. The major criticism is that it is a club favouring the developed countries, at the expense of the less developed countries. Decision-making is by consensus, often following many rounds of meetings most often attended by those countries with the resources to have representatives present at these meetings. Many of the less developed countries are excluded from this process. Other arguments against are that: market access in industry is still a problem for less developed countries; anti-dumping measures have increased; there are still enormous agricultural subsidies in the developed world; and labour standards and the environment are ignored.

Some of these problems have meant that the current round of negotiations has been difficult, with the talks suspended on more than one occasion. The previous round of talks in Seattle had ended in failure and a major disagreement between developed and developing countries—the latter accused the WTO of being for free trade whatever the cost, a charge that the WTO contests. Whatever their protestations, the package for discussion at the Doha round has been called the Doha Development Agenda. The concern is to ensure that developing economies benefit from the growth of trade by improving market access to developed economies for developing countries. The most significant differences are between developed countries, led by the EU, the USA, and Japan, and the major developing countries, led and represented mainly by China, Brazil, India, South Korea, and South Africa. There is also considerable contention against and between the EU and the USA over their maintenance of agricultural subsidies. Thirteen years after the talks started, agreement was reached in a deal in Bali in December 2013. However, just before the treaty was due to be signed, India, who had since elected a new government, blocked the deal. This is a crucial stage in the life of the WTO. Up to 60 countries are ready to implement the 'Bali Package' outside the WTO. Many countries, such the USA, the EU, and Japan, frustrated with the lack of any progress, are organizing their own regional trade initiatives covering more complex, non-tariff barriers to trade. If talks at the WTO make no further progress, then the WTO could be increasingly side-lined as an effective world organization (*Financial Times* 2 August 2014).

The Doha round of negotiations effectively came to an end with the adoption of the 'Nairobi Package' following a five-day conference in Kenya, in December 2015. It contains a series of six Ministerial Decisions on agriculture, cotton, and issues related to least-developed countries (LDCs). There were also some limited outcomes on agriculture trade, trade facilitation, and information technology products, but major issues from the original Doha Agenda including domestic agricultural subsidies were not resolved. The future for multilateralism in trade negotiations is unclear and it may be that the focus is shifting more towards a bilateral and regional trade agenda (World Trade Organization 2016).

Exchange Rates

An exchange rate is the price of one currency as expressed in another or, to put it another way, the rate at which one currency is exchanged for another. The way in which the value of a currency is determined is dependent upon the exchange rate regime in place. In a floating exchange rate system, the market value of a currency is determined by the demand for and the supply of a currency. Most of this supply and demand comes from speculators (see Chapter 11) with trade and investment flows having a minor role. Nevertheless, countries with trade surpluses, and those who attract inflows of capital, will see demand for their currency rise and therefore an appreciation in the value of the currency. The reverse is also true. According to the International Monetary Fund (2013), 30 countries have a freely floating exchange rate. In this system, the rate could be very volatile and this could create problems for firms that are heavily involved in international trade and investment. They could face wild fluctuations in import prices and in the value of export earnings and foreign assets.

Countries may adopt a **fixed exchange rate** policy where they peg the value of their currency against another. Fixed rates give a degree of stability to business whether it is an importer, exporter, or investor wishing to move capital in or out of the country.

There are also a number of systems which try to capture the benefits of both systems by allowing currencies to float within a pre-set band and/or where governments actively manage the exchange rate. It may be that the authorities decide that they are prepared to see the value of the currency fluctuate within prescribed bands against another currency. When the currency looks as if it is going to break through the bands, the authorities intervene to buy the domestic currency when it is sinking too low or to sell it when it is threatening to rise too high in value. This gives business less certainty than the fixed rate regime, but more certainty than a floating regime.

According to the IMF (2014), 13 countries, including El Salvador and Panama, use the US dollar as their domestic currency and 44 others peg their currency against it, while 26 countries peg theirs against the euro. Movements in exchange rates can be an important influence on the business environment—good news for some, bad for others. A rise in the exchange rate can make imports cheaper, which is good news for those firms buying a lot of goods and services from abroad. On the other hand, it is likely to be bad news for exporters as it could make them less competitive in foreign markets. Requena-Silvente and Walker (2007) found that car exporters to the UK reduced their mark-up to keep prices stable and maintain market share when their currencies rose against sterling.

Similarly, for businesses producing abroad, a rise in the exchange rate could reduce the value of their foreign sales and assets when translated back into their domestic currency.

Adverse long-lasting realignments of exchange rates can have a major impact on business strategy. They may cause firms to:

- relocate production;
- change the source of supply;
- look for new product markets or strong currency markets;
- make products having a more global appeal to facilitate the switch from weak to strong currency markets; and
- look for ways of increasing productivity.

A way of affecting both imports and exports is by exchange rate manipulation by governments. When two firms in different countries do business, the prices they quote will be determined by a combination of their domestic price converted to the other's currency using foreign exchange rates. If £1 exchanges for US$2, then a UK exporter with a domestic price of £100 will quote US$200 to an American buyer. Any change in the exchange rate will affect the foreign exchange price. If the £ strengthens to £1 = US$2.5, then the US price will be US$250. In a competitive market, a price rise might not be possible, which would then mean that if the UK firm could only charge US$200, it would only receive £80 of revenue. One way of maintaining the competitiveness of a country's exports would be to keep the value of its currency low in relation to others. Being a member of a currency union (i.e. sharing a common currency), such as the EU, not only eliminates transaction costs when exchanging currency but also reduces the risks associated with changes in exchange rates. It is also claimed that this reduction in uncertainty can promote investment (see text of a speech by Mark Carney, Governor of the Bank of England, on the economics of currency unions, available on the **online resources**).

● CHAPTER SUMMARY

In this chapter, we have looked at the global pattern of wealth, international trade, and exchange rates. One way of comparing countries is to compare their respective GDP. This can be adjusted for purchasing power parity (PPP), which narrows the gap between rich and poor. The richest economy is still the USA, in absolute terms, but China has now surpassed it in PPP.

GDP indicates the different sizes of economies, but does not say much about the standard of living; population has to be taken into account to give income per capita. Even then, GDP per capita says nothing about the quality of life. In determining the degree of development, the UNDP also looks at other indicators such as income inequality, life expectancy, literacy rates, and school enrolments. On any of these measures, the world is still a very divided place when comparing the rich with the poor. Economic growth is seen as the key to raising standards of living. The world is changing and, by 2060 or before China will be the biggest economy, followed by India, with the USA in third place. Many current emerging nations will be as big as current advanced economies, but per capita incomes in those countries will still be lower. There will be an enormous global middle class by 2030, with two-thirds of it in the Asia Pacific region.

International trade has increased, with exports in 1970 just 13 per cent of world output, whereas they are predicted to be 34 per cent by 2030. Developing countries are increasing their share of trade in manufactures, but this is still dominated by the developed nations. Countries trade with each other and world output increases, but history shows that the rich nations tend to benefit at the expense of the poor. There have been a number of theories put forward to explain the pattern of trade; however, many do not fully take account of the role and activities of multinational corporations and their affiliates across the world Many countries impose restrictions, but the WTO works to liberalize trade. It has faced criticism because it is seen as a club that helps to maintain the established patterns of trade, which favour the rich.

An exchange rate is the price of one currency expressed in another. Fluctuations in exchange rates can have a major impact on business. Some countries have been accused of manipulating the exchange of their currencies in order to make their goods more competitive in overseas markets.

● REVIEW QUESTIONS

1. Why would it be useful for business to build up knowledge of the global distribution of income and wealth, and how it is changing over time?

2. Discuss the proposition that happiness does not necessarily increase with increased wealth.

3. Analyse and explain the major trends in international trade and foreign direct investment. Discuss links between these trends and the changing distribution of world income.

4. What are the advantages and disadvantages to countries of foreign trade?

5. Discuss why the level of exchange rates is important for international business.

● ASSIGNMENT TASKS

1. It is often quoted that widening inequality is a fundamental issue facing the global economy. Prepare a paper that:

   a. explains what is meant by 'inequality';

   b. investigates the extent of this inequality and the underlying causes;

   c. discusses whether inequality is a problem or a benefit; and

   d. identifies the risks to international business of inequality.

2. You are working for a pharmaceutical business that currently only exports to Europe. It is looking to expand its export destinations and you are asked to prepare a report which selects three countries as suitable destinations. You should concentrate on:

   a. economic growth prospects and associated risks; and

   b. any trade restrictions such as tariffs, non-tariff barriers, and domestic subsidies.

3. In the last 40 years, trade has grown faster than total global output as measured by GDP, and foreign direct investment has grown faster than both. Write a paper to discuss the importance of the activities of multinational enterprises or transnational corporations in the global economy. In particular, consider the effects of:

   a. increasing internationalization and fragmentation of production on trade volumes and labour markets;

   b. vertical and horizontal integration on market concentration and competitiveness; and

   c. increasingly complex internal ownership structure of multinational firms on 'profit shifting', tax base erosion, and other regulatory issues.

🔍 Case Study Middle East and North African economies

© iStock.com/imagean

Plagued by war, violence and currently low oil prices, the countries in the Middle East and North Africa (MENA) region are an important if disparate group of economies that exert influence over political and business decisions on a truly global scale.

MENA is a large area located in South West Asia and North East Africa with a total population of close to 440 million. The richest countries are the oil-rich Gulf states; Saudi Arabia has the largest economy in nominal terms, although it is behind the sparsely populated countries of Qatar, United Arab Emirates, and Kuwait in terms of GDP per capita. The poorest countries are Djibouti, Mauritania, and Yemen, with current figures for Syria not available (see Table 2.10 for country ranking in the region).

In 2016, the region (MENA) had a combined GDP at current prices of around $2.8 trillion (just over $8 trillion PPP) or about 6.7 per cent of the world total. The GDP per capita of $8,229 ($18,400 PPP) is misleading in a region characterized by relatively small, wealthy elites and widespread poverty. For many countries, a high birth rate in excess of 3 per cent also places additional strain on resources.

During the first decade of this century, the region experienced some reasonable economic growth and increased →

→ investment. However, despite some reforms by a number of governments aimed at increasing economic openness, diversification, and building stronger institutions, political instability and security issues have slowed economic progress. Economic growth in the MENA region was 2.3 per cent in 2015 against an overall average of 4.0 per cent for emerging and developing countries. Some analysts suggest that the current GDP figures may now only represent only around 40 per cent of the region's true potential output.

MENA's main significance and source of influence is related to the very large fossil fuel reserves in a number of countries further aided by helpful geological factors that can make extraction cheaper than in many other parts of the world. While a number of governments are not entirely open regarding their levels of production or the size of their reserves, estimates at the end of 2015 suggest that the MENA grouping of countries held around 802,846 billion of barrels of crude oil or 52 per cent of the world's oil reserves. In addition, estimates also suggest that the region holds 79,198 billion cubic metres of natural gas, or around 40 per cent of known world reserves. Saudi Arabia alone is believed to hold around 270 billion barrels of crude oil, making it second only to Venezuela in proven reserves. In total, six countries in the region are in the top ten reserve holders worldwide.

With such potential riches, the region should be wealthy and prosperous; indeed, there have been a number of periods of rapid economic growth particularly when oil prices have risen sharply on world markets. At such times, oil-producing states— in particular, Saudi Arabia, Kuwait, Qatar, and the United Arab Emirates—have benefited directly from exports and oil revenues

Table 2.10 The MENA countries

Country	GDP current prices ($US millions)	Population (000)	GDP per capita current prices ($US)
Saudi Arabia	639.617	31.743	20,150.13
Islamic Republic of Iran	376.755	80.46	4,682.51
United Arab Emirates	371.353	9.856	37,677.91
Egypt	332.349	90.2	3,684.57
Iraq	167.026	36.067	4,630.96
Algeria	160.784	40.762	3,944.43
Qatar	156.734	2.578	60,786.72
Kuwait	109.859	4.225	26,004.71
Morocco	103.615	33.827	3,063.07
Sudan	94.421	39.599	2,384.45
Oman	63.171	3.957	15,963.98
Lebanon	51.991	4.597	11,308.91
Tunisia	41.869	11.224	3,730.42
Jordan	38.743	6.976	5,553.97
Libya	33.157	6.385	5,193.24
Bahrain	31.907	1.319	24,182.90
Yemen	27.318	29.132	937.712
Mauritania	4.714	3.794	1,242.58
Djibouti	1.894	0.993	1,908.31
Syria	n/a	n/a	n/a

Source: IMF World Economic Outlook Database (April 2017)   →

➡ have been used to develop modern infrastructure and create jobs. A number of social indicators including literacy rates and life expectancy have also increased, and some states have accumulated significant official currency reserves. Such booms have also provided opportunities for migrant workers from nearby non-oil producing countries such as Jordan, Egypt, and Yemen who have found employment in the oil industry, construction, and teaching. Remittances sent home by these workers have helped to boost their own economies, although many of the countries remain extremely poor. The richer countries of the region remain important trading partners with countries in the West; for example, Saudi Arabia, the largest economy in the Middle East, has enormous net foreign assets, amounting to over $700 billion.

Three of the world's major religions (Judaism, Christianity, and Islam) originated in the region, and religious identity remains a major factor in a part of the world where a number of countries have theocratic governments. Religion is also a fault line for both intra-national and cross-border hostilities, and many tensions and conflicts in the region have ancient religious roots. Within various states, groupings of religious conservatives resist change to the political status quo or advocate forms of political Islam and often oppose politically progressive groups and policies.

Overall the region remains plagued by uneven development, a turbulent socio-political environment with ongoing conflicts in Syria, Iraq, Libya, and Yemen, and high levels of corruption. All of these factors hinder further development and discourage investment.

Foreign direct investment inflows have always been unevenly spread across the MENA countries. The richer countries have been and remain the main destinations, but FDI has fallen precipitously in recent years from a high of almost $127 billion in 2007 to $25 billion in 2016, an all-time low of only 1 per cent of GDP. Regulatory/administrative and regional instability and insecurity are deterrents to inward investment. Some non-oil related industries including tourism have dropped sharply in countries such as Tunisia and Egypt, and intra-regional trading has also reduced, with only 10 per cent of the region's trade taking place between MENA countries.

Private business is seen as essential for economic recovery and diversification, yet the private sector accounts for only 40 per cent of GDP in the MENA region against an OECD average of 59 per cent. In some countries, such as Libya, the share is just 5 per cent.

For the future, governments in the region face serious policy challenges. As the world oil price has fallen in recent years, the non-oil exporting countries in the region have fared slightly better in growth terms. They are forecast to continue to do so in 2017 and 2018, although many of them remain poorer than their oil-rich neighbours. The oil-exporting countries in particular need diversification strategies to reduce their reliance on oil revenues, and long-term solutions to the numerous conflicts will significantly encourage foreign investment.

The outlook for the Middle East region continues to be uncertain, particularly if the oil price remains depressed and conflict continues to impede economic activity and inward investment. Governments will need to find policies that stimulate investment confidence and growth, reduce public discontent, and respect religious differences.

Note: **MENA** comprises Algeria, Bahrain, Djibouti, Egypt, Iran, Iraq, Jordan, Kuwait, Lebanon, Libya, Mauritania, Morocco, Oman, Qatar, Saudi Arabia, Somalia, Sudan, Syria, Tunisia, the United Arab Emirates, and Yemen.

The region does not have one single grouping for statistical purposes so while the World Bank uses the acronym MENA. The International Monetary Fund (IMF) produces statistics that add in the countries of Afghanistan and Pakistan to form MENAP, and other estimates and projections often include Israel, Turkey, and Cyprus.

Sources: World Economic Forum; OECD: Recent FDI trends in MENA region; World Bank: MENA Economic Monitor

Questions

1. Summarize the significance of the MENA region to the world economy.
2. Analyse the factors that have led to the growth and uneven development in the region.
3. Why might the region's non-oil producing countries see stronger growth?
4. What are the main priorities for governments in the region in the medium term?
5. Prepare a report on the future prospects for the region focusing on:
   a. regional stability and security;
   b. economic diversification and productivity;
   c. attracting foreign direct investment; and
   d. addressing inequality.

● FURTHER READING

For a book that challenges the idea that the best way of improving the quality of human lives is to raise material living standards, see:

- Wilkinson, R. and Pickett, K. (2010) *The Spirit Level: Why Equality is Better for Everyone*. London: Penguin Books.

For a book that says that, under capitalism, inequality is inevitable, see:

- Piketty, T. (2014) *Capitalism in the Twenty-First Century*. Cambridge, MA: Harvard University Press.

For an illuminating account of the role played by tax havens in the global economy recently updated to include revelations from the Panama Papers, see:

- Shaxson, N. (2016) *Treasure Islands: Tax Havens and the Men Who Stole the World*. Vintage Press, London.

For a historical account of the evolution of world trade up to the twenty-first century, see:

- Findlay, R. and O'Rourke, K.H. (2007) *Power and Plenty: Trade, War, and the World Economy*. Princeton, NJ: Princeton University Press.

- VanGrasstek, C. (2013) *The History and Future of the World Trade Organization*. Geneva: WTO.

For an in-depth analysis of the Chinese economy, its relationship with global trade, and emerging economies and global trade, see:

- Eichengreen, B., Chui, Y., and Wyplosz, C. (eds) (2008) *China, Asia, and the New World Economy*. Oxford: Oxford University Press.

- Hanson, G.H. (2012) *The Rise of Middle Kingdoms: Emerging Economies in Global Trade*. NBER Working Paper No. 17961. March 2012. JEL No. F10.

For an application and extension of the Porter diamond to national competitiveness, see:

- Özlem, Ö. (2002) The Case of Turkey: National Advantage'. *Journal of Business Research* 55(6).

- Stone, H.B. and Ranchhod, A. (2006) 'Competitive Advantage of a Nation in the Global Arena: A Quantitative Advancement to Porter's Diamond Applied to the UK, USA and BRIC Nations'. *Strategic Change* 5(6).

Rugman et al. have been one of the main critics of the Porter diamond. See:

- Rugman, A., Verbeke, A., and Van Den Broeck, J. (eds) (1995) *Research in Global Strategic Management: Volume V Beyond the Diamond*. Greenwich, CT: JAI Press.

● REFERENCES

Dicken, P. (2004) *Global Shift: Reshaping the Global Economic Map in the 21st Century*. London: SAGE Publications.

Easterlin. R. (1974) *'Does Economic Growth Improve the Human Lot? Some Empirical Evidence'*. In Paul A. David and Melvin W. Reder (eds) Nations and Households in

Economic Growth: Essays in Honor of Moses Abramovitz. New York: Academic Press, Inc.

Ernst and Young (2013) 'Hitting the Sweet Spot: The Growth of the Middle Class in Emerging Markets'. Available at http://www.ey.com/Publication/vwLUAssets/Hitting_the_sweet_spot/$File/Hitting_the_sweet_spot.pdf.

Goldman Sachs (2003) 'Dreaming with BRICS: The Path to 2050'. Global Economics Paper No. 99. Available at http://www.goldmansachs.com/korea/ideas/brics/99-dreaming.pdf.

Goldman Sachs (2007) 'The N-11: More than an Acronym'. Global Economics Paper No. 153. Available at http://www.chicagobooth.edu/~/media/E60BDCEB6C5245E59B7ADA7C6B1B6F2B.pdf.

Goldman Sachs (2011) 'The BRICs 10 Years On: Halfway Through the Great Transformation'. Global Economics Paper No. 208. Available at http://blogs.univ-poitiers.fr/o-bouba-olga/files/2012/11/Goldman-Sachs-Global-Economics-Paper-208.pdf.

Heckscher, E.F. (1919 [1991]) 'The Effect of Foreign Trade on the Distribution of Income. Economisk Tidsckrift'. In Heckscher E.F. and Ohlin, B., *Heckscher-Ohlin Trade Theory*. Cambridge, MA: The MIT Press (translated, edited, and introduced by Harry Flam and M. June Flanders).

International Monetary Fund (2013) 'De Facto Classification of Exchange Rate Regimes and Monetary Policy Frameworks'. Available at https://www.imf.org/external/np/mfd/er/2008/eng/0408.htm.

International Monetary Fund (2014) World Economic Outlook Database, April 2014. Available at http://www.imf.org/external/pubs/ft/weo/2014/01/weodata/index.aspx.

International Monetary Fund (2018) World Economic Outlook Update, January 2018. Available at https://www.imf.org/en/Publications/WEO/Issues/2018/01/11/world-economic-outlook-update-january-2018.

Kharas, H. and Gertz, G. (2010) *The New Global Middle Class: A Cross-Over from West to East*. Wolfensohn Center for Development at Brookings. Available at https://www.brookings.edu/wp-content/uploads/2016/06/03_china_middle_class_kharas.pdf.

Maddison, A. (2003) *The World Economy: Historical Statistics*. Paris: Development Centre Studies, OECD.

Meadows, D.H., Randers, J., and Behrens, William W. III (1972) *The Limits to Growth*. New York: Universe Books.

Mishan, E. (1967) *The Costs of Economic Growth*. London: Staples Press.

OECD (2010) 'Agricultural Policies in OECD Countries at a Glance'. Available at http://www.oecd.org/tad/agricultural-policies/45539870.pdf.

OECD (2012) 'Looking to 2060: Long-term Global Growth Prospects, A Going for Growth Report', November 2012, OECD Publishing, Paris. Available at http://www.oecd.org/eco/outlook/2060%20policy%20paper%20FINAL.pdf.

Ohlin, B. (1924 [1991]) 'The Theory of Trade'. In Heckscher E.F. and Ohlin, B., *Heckscher-Ohlin Trade Theory*. Cambridge, MA: The MIT Press (translated, edited, and introduced by Harry Flam and M. June Flanders).

Piketty, T. (2014) *Capitalism in the Twenty-First Century*. Cambridge, MA: Harvard University Press.

Proto, E. and Rustichini, A. (2013) 'A Reassessment of the Relationship between GDP and Life Satisfaction'. *PLOS ONE* 8(11): e79358. doi:10.1371/journal.pone.0079358.

PwC (2017) 'The Long View: How Will the Global Economic Order Change by 2050?' February. Available at https://www.pwc.com/gx/en/world-2050/assets/pwc-world-in-2050-summary-report-feb-2017.pdf.

Ricardo, D. (1817) *On the Principles of Political Economy and Taxation*. London: John Murray.

Requena-Silvente, F. and Walker, J. (2007) 'The Impact of Exchange Rate Fluctuations on Profit Margins: The UK Car Market, 1971–2002'. *Journal of Applied Economics* X(1) May.

Rose, A. (2004) 'Do WTO Members have More Liberal Trade Policy?'. *Journal of International Economics* 63(2).

Schneider, F. and Williams C.C. (2013) *The Shadow Economy*. London: Institute of Economic Affairs.

Schneider, F., Buehn, A., and Montenegro, C.E. (2010) 'Shadow Economies All Over the World, New Estimates for 162 Countries from 1999 to 2007'. World Bank Working Paper WPS5356. Available at http://documents.worldbank.org/curated/en/311991468037132740/pdf/WPS5356.pdf

Simms, A., Johnson, V., and Chowla, K. (2010) *Growth Isn't Possible*. London: New Economics Foundation.

Smith, A. (1776) *An Inquiry into the Nature and Causes of the Wealth of Nations*. Oxford: Clarendon Press.

Subramanian, A. and Wei, S.-J. (2005) 'The WTO Promotes Trade, Strongly But Unevenly'. CEPR Discussion Papers 5122. Available at http://www.cepr.org/content/discussion-papers.

UNCTAD (2015) 'World Investment Report 2015' (Chapter 5). Available at http://unctad.org/en/PublicationChapters/wir2015ch5_en.pdf.

WEF (2018) http://www3.weforum.org/docs/WEF_AM18_ Report.pdf.

World Bank (2016) *Africa's Pulse, An Analysis of Issues Shaping Africa's Future,* Volume 9, April 2014. Available at http://www.worldbank.org/content/dam/ Worldbank/document/Africa/Report/Africas-Pulse-brochure_Vol9.pdf.

World Bank (n.d.) http://data.worldbank.org/about/ country-classifications.

World Investment Report (2015) (Ch. 5). Available at http://unctad.org/en/PublicationChapters/ wir2015ch5_en.pdf.

World Trade Organization (2013) *World Trade Report 2013. Factors Shaping the Future of World Trade.* Available at http://www.wto.org/english/res_e/publications_e/ wtr13_e.htm.

World Trade Organization (2017) 'World Trade Statistical Review 2017'. Available at https://www.wto.org/ english/res_e/statis_e/wts2017_e/wts17_toc_e.htm.

CHAPTER THREE

Analysing Global Industries

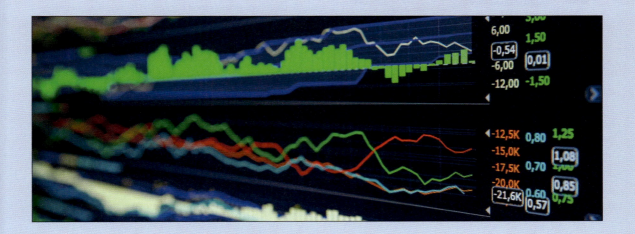

LEARNING OUTCOMES

This chapter will enable you to:

- distinguish between the concept of market and industry;

- identify various market structures and their implications for competition and performance;

- measure market concentration, analyse it, and explain the link with market power; and

- explain and use the Porter Five Forces model for industry analysis.

Case Study Food Industry restructuring

© iStock.com/skodonnell

The global packaged food industry contains some very large multinational firms like Nestlé based in Switzerland; Unilever jointly based in the UK and the Netherlands; PepsiCo, Kraft Heinz, Mars, Mondelez, General Mills, and Kelloggs all based in the USA; and the French companies Lactalis and Danone. Historically the big food firms have been based in West Europe or the USA, but Euromonitor (2017) points to the steady rise of the two largest Chinese food manufacturers, China Mengniu Dairy and Inner Mongolia Yili, in the world rankings. The sales

value of packaged food worldwide was estimated to be around $2.5 trillion in 2016, and was forecast to grow very slowly to $2.6 trillion by 2019 (Statista n.d.).

These giant companies produce a wide range of food products such as coffee, ice cream, chocolate, confectionery, bottled water, food seasoning and spreads, frozen food, baby food, and pet food. But big as they are, these food companies together only account for a small share of the world market; there are also thousands of smaller food packaging companies operating nationally or regionally (see Figure 3.1).

The industry faces sclerotic growth in the mature markets of North America and West Europe but also a slowdown of growth in previously fast-growing emerging markets such as Brazil, Russia, China, and India. Market growth is being driven by countries in the Asia-Pacific, the Middle East, and Africa. Furthermore, it finds consumers in its traditional markets moving away from processed foods to fresh and organic foods seen as heathier alternatives. These developments have driven firms to look for growth through mergers and acquisitions.

Kraft has been an active player in the acquisition of rivals and the restructuring of the industry. It merged with Heinz in 2015

Figure 3.1 Food—top ten global firms market share (%)

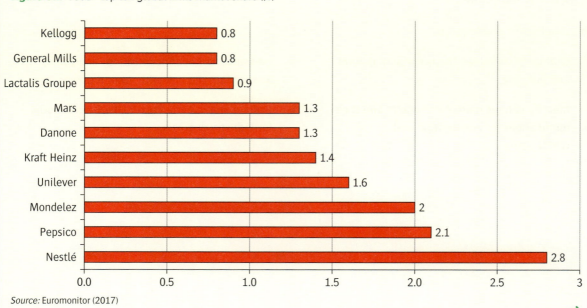

Source: Euromonitor (2017)

→ and took over Cadbury, the UK confectionery producer, in 2010. With the Cadbury takeover, Kraft aimed to cut unit costs through economies of scale in its snack business in emerging markets like India. Kraft then went on in 2012 to restructure the business by spinning off its Kraft Foods operations, including Cadbury, with the new business renamed as Mondelez International.

In 2017 Kraft Heinz made a hostile bid of $143 billion for Unilever, the producer of food, beverages, and personal products such as shampoo and deodorants. The merger would have brought together well-known brands such as Heinz tomato ketchup and Magnum ice cream.

The merger of the world's fourth and fifth largest food manufacturers would have made them number one globally in packaged food ahead of Nestlé. The combined company would also have been number one in West Europe and Australasia (*Financial Times* 18 February 2017). Kraft was strong in North America and therefore reliant on mature markets while Unilever's strength lay in Europe, Latin America, the Middle East, and parts of Asia (*New York Times* 17 February 2017). Kraft earned 75 per cent of its revenues in the USA, whereas 58 per cent of Unilever sales were made in emerging markets. Kraft's reliance on stagnant markets and established brands resulted in the company growing more slowly than its rivals, Nestlé and Unilever.

Kraft, with an operating profit margin of 30 per cent, double that of Unilever, saw the merger as offering opportunities to cut costs. The attraction of the deal had been boosted by the fall in the value of sterling following the 2016 Brexit referendum, which reduced the cost to foreign firms of buying assets in the UK. Kraft immediately encountered fierce resistance from Unilever and withdrew its bid.

Takeovers by food firms usually involve one firm taking over a competitor. They are an external form of growth, sometimes referred to as inorganic growth. Such a takeover strategy allows firms to:

- grow in mature, saturated markets where trying to increase the market share of existing brands could involve costly advertising and sales promotion campaigns and could provoke fierce competitive retaliation from rivals;
- enter growing emerging markets, not by developing their own brands from scratch, which could be expensive, but by taking over the target company's brands; and
- gain a foothold in other market segments—examples being Danone who acquired Whitewave in 2016 for $10 billion to enter the lucrative US organic market, and UK's Reckitt-Benckiser's move into infant nutrition through its acquisition of Mead, the US manufacturer of baby milk.

Given the adverse forces in the external environment, the trend towards mergers in packaged food is likely to continue.

Sources: Euromonitor (2016a); Euromonitor (2017); *Financial Times* 9 January 2012, 11, 18, and 20 February 2017; Trend View (2014)

Introduction

In this chapter we develop the knowledge and skills necessary to carry out analyses of industries. We start off by examining the concepts of the market and the industry. In line with other authors, we see the terms 'market' and 'industry' as being interchangeable. Various market structures are then explored, along with their implications for the nature and intensity of competition and company performance. We go on to look at **market concentration**, how it is measured, and the implications of different levels of concentration for the distribution of market power among firms in the industry. The Five Forces of Porter's model provide a set of tools that allow a systematic and comprehensive analysis of industries. Each force is explained and applied to various industries, along with a sixth force, **complementary products**. Given their increasing global importance, much attention in the chapter is given to giant firms such as Google, Apple, Facebook, and Netflix in tech industries. This is reflected not only in the text but also in the Mini Case Studies, Learning Tasks, and Counterpoint boxes.

The term 'global' is used liberally in this chapter. We use it on occasions where multiple countries are involved. This usage varies from other authors, who interpret the word as meaning 'worldwide'—that is, covering most countries in the world.

The Market and the Industry

Analysing markets and industries involves building up a detailed knowledge of the competing firms in the industry, the goods and services they are selling, and the geographical markets where they compete.

Defining the market involves several steps:

- deciding which goods or services to include;
- identifying the firms competing in the market; and
- indicating the geographical area where those firms are competing.

First, it is important to identify products or services that customers see as very similar. Economists use a concept called the **cross elasticity of demand**, which measures the response of customers when one firm changes its price. If the price of a product increases, and customers switch in large numbers to other, cheaper products, then economists conclude that the products can be classified to the same market. In other words, there is a high cross elasticity of demand because customers see the products as being very good alternatives. One would expect to see this effect were an oil company like BP to raise the price of petrol on the forecourt to a level higher than its competitors, Esso and Shell. This allows us to identify competitors because the firms making products with a high cross elasticity of demand are then defined as being part of the same industry. However, if very few customers transfer their business to the cheaper goods, the products are not seen by consumers as good alternatives and the firms cannot be classified to the same industry.

The concept of cross elasticity, while neat in a theoretical sense, can be difficult to use in practice. Usually, the information required to calculate cross elasticity is not available. In the absence of data on cross elasticity, some observers look for evidence showing businesses reacting regularly to decisions made by other firms. Signs of such interdependence among firms indicate that they see themselves as competitors. For example, if one firm lowers a price or increases spending on advertising and others regularly follow suit, then those firms that end up pursuing similar policies could be seen as members of the same industry. Another approach is to identify firms whose actions as regards, for example, pricing, advertising, and sales promotion are constrained by others. To take the example of low-cost airlines, it would be understandable were firms such as Ryanair and easyJet constrained in their pricing policies by the possible reaction of the other.

Classifying firms to a particular industry may not be as straightforward as it first appears. Car firms are often seen as operating in the same industry, but it would hardly be sensible to view a Rolls Royce as a direct competitor to a Mini or a Fiat Punto. It would make more sense, for our purposes, to consider car manufacturers as producing for a series of markets, from the most basic models to the luxury end of the market.

Diversified firms also complicate the picture. Companies selling a range of goods may end up being classified into several industries. Take domestic appliance manufacturers such as

Whirlpool, Electrolux, or LG, the South Korean multinational. They make various appliances including washing machines, dishwashers, and electric cookers—these products can hardly be seen as close substitutes, so the companies could be seen as competing in various markets, for washing machines, dishwashers, and electric cookers. Of course, the fact that diversified firms such as these can offer customers, like retailers, the ability to source a range of products from a single company may put such firms at a competitive advantage against rivals offering a more limited range.

Companies operating at several stages of production of a product can also complicate the issue of how to classify them. Examples of such **vertically integrated firms** can be found in the oil industry where companies such as Shell, Exxon, and BP drill for oil, refine it, and sell it on the forecourt. They could be classified to three industries: drilling, refining, and retailing. The media sector also provides an illustration with groups like 21st Century Fox producing films and distributing them through their television and satellite broadcasting companies.

Another aspect of the market that needs to be clarified is its geographical boundaries. Firms located in different places could be producing similar products, but not actually competing against each other in the same geographical market place. Geographical distance may mean that the cost of transporting goods from one area to the other is not economic so, in reality, the firms in one area are not competing with firms in the other. There are a variety of factors which keep markets separate, such as geographical distance or poor transport infrastructure. For example, in poor countries in Africa and South East Asia, the lack of road and rail networks may keep markets fragmented, whereas in the developed economies of Northern Europe, improving transport links have integrated previously distinct markets.

Firms may also set out deliberately to keep markets separate. Car producers do this in Western Europe. Traditionally, they have charged significantly higher prices in the UK than in countries like Belgium and the Netherlands. They hope that British customers will not realize that prices are cheaper across the Channel and therefore will not hop across to get their cars from Belgian or Dutch dealers. UK customers who recognize that they can get a lower price on the Continent, and try to buy there, have found that distributors may claim that they are out of supplies or that they do not have access to right-hand drive cars. The EU Commission found Volkswagen guilty of discriminating in price between customers in Southern Germany and those in Northern Italy. German consumers were richer than the Northern Italians so they could afford to pay more. VW, as long as it could keep the two markets separate, increased profits by charging more in Germany than in Italy. Economists identify the geographical boundaries of the market by assessing the extent to which a price increase in one area:

- attracts competition from firms elsewhere. For example, had the high prices charged by VW in Southern Germany attracted many car dealers from Northern Italy lured by the prospect of higher profits, then the two regions could have been classified as one market; or

- drives customers away to cheaper areas. VW's high prices in Germany could have led many German car buyers to go to Italy to get a better deal. The two areas could have been seen as part of the same geographical market had many German consumers taken that route. Such behaviour can be seen in Southern England where consumers get the ferry across to France to buy cheaper alcohol and tobacco. Similarly, French buyers of alcohol and tobacco products flock to the small Spanish towns on the border where the prices of these products are much lower than in France.

Market Structures

There is a variety of market structures ranging from pure monopoly to the perfectly competitive (see Table 3.1). In a pure monopoly, one firm dominates the market and is usually protected from competition by high barriers to entry (barriers to entry are explained in more detail later in this chapter). Such firms control the market and can set prices to extract maximum profit from their customers. Consumers have to pay the price because they have no alternative suppliers. In a globalizing world economy, one rarely encounters pure monopoly outside the pages of basic economics textbooks, although some markets, at times, may come close. For example, Wrigley, owned by Mars, accounts for around one-third of the global market but 89 per cent of the UK chewing gum market, while Microsoft Windows accounts for just less than 90 per cent of the world market for desktop operating software—this drops to around 40 per cent when the market definition expands to include operating systems on tablets and smartphones (Euromonitor 2015 and 2016b; ExtremeTech 3 May 2016; StatCounter.com February 2017; *Forbes* 13 December 2012).

 Learning Task

The European Commission was asked to decide whether a proposed merger between a firm producing instant coffee and one making ground coffee had any implications for competition. To come to a decision, the Commission had to determine whether the firms were competing in the same market. There was no statistical information available to estimate the cross elasticity of demand between instant and ground coffee.

Do you think consumers see these products as good alternatives?

One way to determine this is to compare the prices for both products. A major price difference could indicate that they are not good alternatives. Check prices at your local supermarket. You could also survey your fellow students to find out whether they see the two products as significantly different. An important indication that they are in different markets would be the willingness of the students to pay more for one than the other.

Market structure can be influenced by the costs incurred by business. Very high **fixed costs** can result in the creation of a **natural monopoly.** To survive, firms need to produce on a very large scale relative to the size of the market to generate sufficient revenues to cover their fixed costs. Examples of natural monopolies include gas, water, electricity, and fixed telephone networks where wires go into businesses and residential properties. It is very expensive to build

Table 3.1 Types of market structure

Type of market structure	Number of firms	Barriers to entry	Nature of product
Perfect competition	Very many	None	Homogeneous
Monopoly	One	High	Unique
Monopolistic competition	Many	None	Heterogeneous
Oligopoly	Few	Often high	Homogeneous/differentiated

transmission networks of pipelines for water and gas and electricity and telephone lines. The result is a single producer having an overwhelming cost advantage over potential competitors. Such rivals are deterred from entering the market by the high capital investment involved and the dominant market position of the monopolist.

In perfectly competitive markets, large numbers of firms are completely free to enter and to leave the market, no individual firm can control the market, price is set by the forces of supply and demand, and buyers and sellers have complete knowledge of market conditions. Profit levels are just enough to keep firms in business. Any profits above that level are quickly eroded away by competition from entrants attracted to the market by the prospect of high profits. **Perfect competition**, where many firms supply identical products with no entry barriers, is difficult to find in the real world. In reality, markets are usually imperfect—they can be costly to enter and dominated by a small number of firms which set prices, differentiate their products, earn abnormally high profits, and comprise buyers and sellers who have gaps in their knowledge of market conditions.

Another market structure is **monopolistic competition** with large numbers of firms, no barriers to entry, and only a small degree of product differentiation. The corner shop or convenience store segment of the retail market could be seen as monopolistically competitive with a large number of outlets, ease of entry, and each differentiated by their location.

In reality, most manufacturing and many service sector industries operate in oligopolistic markets where there are few firms, often protected by high entry barriers and able to exercise some control over the market. In oligopolistic markets, firms often try to differentiate their products from those of their competitors in the branding, advertising, packaging, and design of their goods and services. Firms that are successful in convincing consumers that their products are different, such as Apple with its Mac computer, iPod, and iPhone, can charge higher prices and not lose custom. Oligopolists, when formulating their policies, have to take into account that their actions could affect their rivals' sales, market share, and profits, and are therefore likely to provoke a reaction. For example, a price reduction by one player might spark off a price war where competitors try to undercut each other. The end-result could be cut-throat competition with some firms going out of business.

In order to avoid such competition, oligopolists sometimes set up **cartels**. These usually operate in secret and aim to control competition through the firms in the market agreeing to set common prices or to divide the market geographically among cartel members. In the EU, five truck producers (Man, Daimler, DAF, Iveco, and Volvo/Renault) were fined for running a price-fixing cartel that had existed for 14 years (European Commission 2016a; see Table 10.2). Work by Connor (2002: 1) suggests that global cartels are widespread. In the early years of the new century, he found 'a global pandemic' of international cartels and a 'resurgence of global price fixing'. His database records nearly 900 international cartels and he adds 90–100 new entries each year. He calculated that between 1990 and 2016, sales made by cartels totalled $76 trillion (Connor 2016). He argues that, with cartels, crime pays (*The Chronicle of Higher Education* 16 September 2013).

Market structure can influence the behaviour of firms in the industry and the nature and intensity of competition. In perfect competition, firms cannot set their own pricing policy because price is determined by the market, and there would be no point in trying to differentiate one's goods or services in a perfectly competitive market because consumers see the products as identical.

By contrast, a monopolist is free to pursue an independent pricing policy. In addition, monopolists, facing no competition, do not need to try to differentiate their products. On price, oligopolists can usually exercise some influence, although they must take into account the possible reactions of their competitors. Furthermore, in **oligopoly**, especially when selling to the final consumer, firms make strenuous efforts to differentiate the product through, for example, their marketing and sales promotion activities. Automotive firms and companies producing packaged consumer goods are among the biggest spenders on advertising. In 2016, the world's 100 largest advertisers spent $216 billion with the biggest advertiser, Procter & Gamble spending $10.5 billion. By contrast, Apple, with in 2015 an advertising spend of $1.8 billion, spends relatively little on advertising (Adage.com 5 December 2017; *Business Insider* 24 November 2016).

Market structure can also influence company performance. The intensity of competition can affect profitability. In very competitive markets, profits are likely to be lower than they would be were those markets to turn into an oligopoly or a monopoly.

Mini Case Study 3.1 Netflix: the streaming giant

Netflix started in 1997 with a traditional form of distribution, using the postal service to deliver rented VHS and then DVD. In 2007 it launched its streaming service, and in 2008 it set up partnerships with electronics companies, allowing them to stream TV set-top boxes, Apple Mac computers, the Xbox 360 and Blu-ray disc players. Netflix went international in 2010, first in Canada and then into Latin America and Europe. In its 2016 annual report, it claimed to be:

> . . . the world's leading internet television network with over 93 million streaming members in over 190 countries enjoying more than 125 million hours of TV shows and movies per day.

There is no annual contract and the cost of signing up is low, so Netflix customers can switch easily to its few direct competitors like Amazon Prime, Google's Play and YouTube, NowTV, Hulu owned by Walt Disney, 21st Century Fox, and Comcast. Amazon Prime is a major rival to Netflix, with its customers having access in 2018 to 22,971 films and TV series compared with 4,318 through Netflix. Netflix also faces competition with Sky in the UK, Japan's Wuaki.tv, France's Canal Plus, and Star TV in India.

Company strategy has been successful in terms of sales revenues. Between 2003 and 2011 revenues increased 12-fold from just over $270 million to $3.2 billion, and by 2016 they had more than doubled to $8.8 billion. Profits, on the other hand, had fallen from $226 million in 2011 to $187 million in 2016 (Netflix Annual Reports).

Netflix initially relied on others to provide content. Companies such as Dreamworks and Disney supplied Netflix with films while TV channels like the BBC provided series. Then the company decided to get involved in producing its own content such as *House of Cards* and *The Crown*. Netflix claimed to

have produced 600 hours of original programmes in 2016 and intended to increase that to 1,000 hours in 2017. Netflix was reported to have a budget of US$6 billion for the acquisition of content. Rivals responded by increasing their acquisition budgets. Producing original programmes involved Netflix ending some content deals with big studios. Hulu, one of its main competitors, moved quickly to take on some of the content Netflix no longer wanted. The success of streaming companies like Netflix led to restructuring of the film industry. In 2017, Disney made an agreed bid for the film and some television arms of 20th Century Fox (*New York Times* 14 December 2017). In 2018, Comcast, the biggest US cable company and owner of the NBC TV network and Universal Pictures, made a bid for Sky (BBC 27 February 2018).

Netflix also uses the services of cloud computing providers such as Amazon Web Services to stream content to the customer. Partnerships with consumer electronics firms like Samsung are also important to ensure that Netflix programmes are available on the increasing number of devices capable of streaming content.

Questions

1. In which type of market structure does Netflix operate?
2. Netflix produces original content.
   a. What type of integration does this involve?
   b. Give reasons for this strategy.

Sources: BBC 18 January 2017, 27 February 2018; Investopedia 11 January 2016; *Financial Times* 28 November 2016; McNab (2016); *New York Times* 14 December 2017; Netflix Annual Reports 2003–17; Simon et al. (2015).

→

3. Some commentators claim that 20th Century Fox was driven into the arms of Disney by streaming firms like Netflix. Advance reasons for that claim.

4. What are the implications of streaming services like Netflix for cinemas?

See http://www.boxofficemojo.com/yearly or http://www.the-numbers.com/market and http://www.theguardian.com/film/2015/jun/18/netflix-vod-streaming-future-of-cinema; McNab's article in *Sight and Sound* August 2016.

Market Power

The distribution of power among firms in an industry is assessed by the level of market concentration which can be measured by looking at the market share of firms in the industry. Market concentration gives an indication of the competitive pressures in a market. High concentration levels usually indicate that competition will be of low intensity. Big firms in highly concentrated markets will be able to determine prices, the quantity and quality of output they are prepared to supply, and to force policies on reluctant customers.

In search engines, high levels of concentration indicate low intensity competition. Google dwarfs its rivals, holding almost 92 per cent of the global search market while Microsoft's Bing, Yahoo, and China's Baidu trailed far behind with 3, 2, and 1 per cent respectively (Statcounter. com January 2018). More than three-quarters of all web searchers click on the first three links in Google and only a small minority look past the first page of results. Consequently, Google has the power to make or break firms promoting their products on the web. Online travel firms like Expedia claim that Google ensures that its own travel services appear above Expedia in the rankings. Firms, generally having little bargaining power over Google, sometimes complain to the regulatory authorities. In the EU, where Google enjoyed a 90 per cent market share, the Commission forced Google to give its rivals more prominence in specialized search results, such as those for shopping, travel, and local business reviews (European Commission 2017).

Pure monopoly demonstrates the highest level of concentration, with one firm holding 100 per cent of the market. At the other extreme, in perfect competition, power is distributed equally among firms and, as a result, the level of market concentration is low. In oligopoly, a few firms dominate the market and the level of market concentration is usually high. The world smartphone market is a good illustration of this. As can be seen in Table 3.2, the three largest firms (Samsung, Apple, and Huawei) account for more than 40 per cent of the market.

Measuring Market Concentration

There are various ways of measuring market concentration. The most straightforward method is the concentration ratio (CR). This is usually calculated by taking the share of the largest firms in industry sales or output by value or by volume. CR2, CR3, CR10, and so on, indicate the concentration ratio for the two, three, and 10 largest firms in the industry. In 2017, the CR3 for the global smartphone industry was about 47 per cent (Table 3.2). This had changed dramatically compared with 2010 when the top three firms were Nokia, RIM (the makers of Blackberry), and Apple, and the CR3 was 66 per cent (QuirksMode n.d.). The change in concentration was mainly

Table 3.2 Global market share of smartphones Q4 2017 (%)

Apple	19.2
Samsung	18.4
Huawei	10.2
Xiaomi	7.0
Others	45.2

Source: IDC (2018)

due to the great success of Samsung, the marked decline of Nokia and RIM, and aggressive competition from China's Huawei and OPPO.

A second method of calculating market concentration is provided by the **Herfindahl-Hirschman Index** (HHI). The HHI is calculated by summing the squares of the individual market shares of all the firms in the market. The HHI gives proportionately greater weight to the market shares of the larger firms. It gives a more accurate picture than the concentration ratio because it includes all firms in the calculation. There is sometimes a lack of information about the market shares of very small firms; however, this will not be important when such firms do not critically affect the HHI. A market containing five firms with market shares of 40 per cent, 20 per cent, 15 per cent, 15 per cent, and 10 per cent, respectively, has an HHI of 2,550 ($40^2 + 20^2 + 15^2 + 15^2 + 10^2 = 2,550$). The HHI ranges from close to zero in a perfectly competitive market to 10,000 in the case of a pure monopoly.

The European Commission sees an HHI of more than 1,000 in a market as indicating a level of concentration that could have adverse effects on competition. The US Department of Justice sees an HHI of more than 1,800 as an indication of high market concentration. The authorities are especially concerned where firms are also protected by high entry barriers and where their market position faces little threat from innovation. The Commission is also interested when the share of the largest firm in the market—the CR1—exceeds 40 per cent. Consequently, the Commission looks for evidence of firms abusing their market power and examines closely proposed mergers between firms in these markets that would raise concentration to an even higher level.

Concentration figures can also be affected by the geographical focus of the information. In 2017, Apple held only 19.2 per cent of the global market but had around 35 per cent of the US market (TechCrunch 13 October 2017). This shows that a market can appear to be quite highly concentrated at one geographical level but fragmented at another. While AB InBev holds around one-fifth of the world market for beer, the figure is nearer 60 per cent in Brazil (Statista n.d.; Euromonitor 2016c).

 Learning Task

1. Use the information on market shares in Table 3.2 to work out an HHI for the global smartphone market. Assume that the remaining firms in the market only hold tiny shares and that their inclusion would not significantly distort the result.

2. On the basis of your answer to question 1, discuss whether the European Commission would be concerned, on competition grounds, were Samsung to propose a takeover of Huawei. Assume that the market shares in the EU are similar to those in Table 3.2.

Counterpoint Box 3.1 Market power—good or bad?

Firms like to have market power because it reduces competitive risk and gives them more control over price and output decisions.

The traditional case against market power is that it concentrates control in the hands of one or a few firms. Low levels of competition and high barriers to entry allow firms to raise prices above the competitive level in order to reap abnormally high profits. High prices cause customers to buy less of the product, less is produced, firms have excess capacity, and society as a whole is worse off. Furthermore, in facing light competitive pressures, monopolists may become lazy by not innovating or pressing down on costs of production, resulting in resources not being used to maximum efficiency. In short, prices are higher, output lower, and average costs of production greater under monopoly.

On the other hand, the Austrian School argues that dominant firms gain their position through competing better in the market place whether that be through price, new or better products, more effective advertising or distribution channels, or lower costs due to economies of scale. And higher prices, rather than indicating abuse of market power, simply reflect the value that consumers place on the goods and services provided.

Etro (2008) contends that where a firm is dominant, but barriers to entry are low, the leading firm will produce more and at a higher quality, set lower prices, and spend more on R&D.

Schumpeter (1976) and Galbraith (1967) assert that firms need to be large, have a significant market share, and be protected by barriers to entry to induce them to invest in the risky R&D that society needs to advance technologically (also see Threats and Challenges in Chapter 8).

Sources: Stigler (n.d.); Leibenstein (1978); Armentano (2007); Schumpeter (1976); Galbraith (1967); Etro (2008)

Questions

1. In 2017, Google accounted for nearly 80 per cent of the global search engine market (Net Market Share n.d.). The European Commission investigated Google for abusing its dominant position by favouring its own comparison shopping service in its search results, thereby discriminating against competitors (see European Commission 2016 IP16/25/32). Discuss whether the Google case supports the traditional or the Austrian view of market power.

2. Google's Android is the world's dominant operating system in mobile devices. The Commission launched an investigation into Google's imposition of restrictions on Android device manufacturers and mobile network operators (see European Commission 2016 IP16/1492). How dominant is the Android system? Does this case confirm or contradict your answer to question 1?

Analysing Industries—A Framework

Porter provides a useful framework for analysing the competitive environment of an industry (Porter 1979; 2008). His Five Forces model can be used to identify and evaluate the main threats to the firms in an industry (see Figure 3.2).

The Porter model is often used in combination with other complementary tools such as the PESTLE model (see Chapter 4), which focuses on the wider environment, or the resource-based view (RBV). While Porter focuses on the firm's external environment, the RBV tool concentrates on evaluating how the firm's internal resources and capabilities, such as patents and trademarks, or the success of the company in establishing a successful reputation for itself and its brands, can be used to achieve and sustain competitive advantage (see Barney 2007).

Three of the forces are concerned with competition. The first, and most important, is industry rivalry, which involves competition from rivals already established in the industry. Next, there is competition from new entrants to the industry. Third, the industry may have to confront competition from products that carry out the same function for customers but provide

Figure 3.2 Porter's 'Five Forces' model

Source: Porter (2008)

the service in a radically different way. For example, trains and planes both transport customers from points A to B but in a different way, and consumers can get access to music by buying CDs or downloading it from the internet—it is a substitution in use. Porter calls these products, substitutes. The inclusion of this particular force helps get around problems of a precise identification of the industry. For example, in the market for luxury cars we might include firms producing Rolls-Royce, Bentley, and Mercedes cars because we see them as having a high cross elasticity of demand. Such a definition would exclude competition from sailing yachts or motorized vessels, but these could be analysed using the substitution force in the Porter model.

The other forces are concerned with the industry customers and suppliers. We shall now go through each of the forces in turn.

Force 1: Industry Rivalry

Industry rivalry can vary in form and intensity from one industry to another and in particular industries over time. At one point in the 1980s, telecommunications companies such as BT, France Telecom, and Deutsche Telekom in Germany were seen as national flagship companies, with very powerful market positions and protected by the law preventing other firms entering the industry. There was little competition to speak of. This changed in the subsequent 20 years, as legal and technological barriers to entry fell and they faced up to fiercer competition generated by new entrants, such as Vodafone, to the industry.

Competition usually occurs in one or more of the following areas: price, advertising, and sales promotion, distribution, improvements in existing goods and services, or the introduction of completely new products. New and improved products are particularly important in industries such as electronics—as illustrated in the oligopolistic battle between Sony with its PlayStation, Nintendo's Wii, and Microsoft's Xbox in the console market. By the end of 2017, Sony had sold over 70 million PlayStation 4 units, far outstripping Microsoft Xbox One sales of 30–40 million (*Business Insider* 7 December 2017). Nintendo was hoping to reinvigorate its competitive position with the launch of the new Switch game console (venturebeat.com 16 March 2017). Rivalry can also take the form of a struggle for resources. Firms in the oil industry also have to compete for reserves. In 1970, international oil companies controlled 85 per cent of the world's oil reserves. Since then governments have moved to take control of reserves so much so that nowadays, 15 of the world's largest energy companies are state-owned (Investopedia 17 December 2015). The difficulties that big oil firms like BP and Shell confront in their relationships with oil-rich countries like Russia and Venezuela force them to seek out reserves elsewhere. There is also rivalry among business for skilled labour, especially those classified as knowledge workers like scientists, academics, software engineers, and doctors. *Fortune* (29 March 2016) reported that tech companies in Silicon Valley were facing shortages of skilled sales employees. Firms, especially international firms, increasingly strive for competitive advantage through mergers and alliances. In 2017, there were nearly 50,000 mergers worldwide with a total value of $3.6 trillion (Thomson Reuters 2017). Horizontal mergers, which occur between firms at the same stage of production of a product, boost market share and reduce competition. An example of this was Facebook's merger with Instagram and Disney's takeover of Pixar Studios. Such mergers may provoke a response from rivals. The Air France merger with the Dutch carrier, KLM, and its alliance with Delta Air Lines of the USA posed a tough competitive challenge for other transatlantic carriers such as BA. BA, in turn, responded by setting up a joint venture with American Airlines and merging with Spain's Iberia. Horizontal mergers facilitate movement into new geographical markets.

Vertical mergers, where companies move closer to their supplies of raw materials or to their final customers, guarantee supplies of materials or distribution. In the late 1990s, with the internet offering new methods of distributing news, music, and film, media companies in newspaper publishing, TV, radio, and film moved to integrate different levels of production and distribution in order to place their products in the largest possible number of different platforms. The motto appeared to be 'Create Once, Place Everywhere!'. This enabled companies to produce films or music, register them in DVDs or CDs, and distribute them not only through retail outlets but also through the cable, satellite, or mobile telephony networks that they owned. Such vertically integrated companies were in a position to exploit their products at every single level of the supply chain. Thus, Time Warner, the US media giant, merged with internet service provider AOL, and Vivendi got together with Universal. In 2017, Tesco, the UK's largest supermarket, made a bid for Booker, Britain's biggest food wholesaler. While vertical integration may allow firms to make efficiencies in the supply chain, it may also allow them to squeeze rivals where those rivals have to come to them for supplies or for distribution (see Pleatsikas and Teece 2000).

Learning Task

At the time of the proposed takeover of Booker by Tesco, the latter's share of the UK grocery market was around 28 per cent (Kantar World Panel). In 2015, Booker acquired Musgrave, which owned the Budgens and Londis convenience retail stores (*Financial Times* 29 January 2017).

1. How might Tesco's takeover of Booker strengthen its competitive position against:

    a) fellow retailers?

    b) suppliers of packaged food like Nestlé and Unilever?

    (see Pleatsikas and Teece 2000; BBC (2016); *The Guardian* 13 October 2016)

2. Assess Tesco's competitive performance since the acquisition of Booker. (See Tesco Annual Reports.)

Competition intensity can range from cut-throat to weak, and depends on the following:

- The number of competing firms—the larger the number of competitors, the more likely is rivalry to be fierce. Conversely, the lower the number of rivals, the weaker the competition is likely to be.

- The relative size of firms—where rivals are of similar size or have equal market shares, then competition can be expected to be strong. This situation can be found in oligopolies such as cars where a small number of leading firms, including General Motors, Ford, Volkswagen, and Toyota, compete hard for sales. By contrast, in markets where one dominant firm competes with a number of smaller rivals, competition is likely to be less intense.

- **Market growth** rate—when the market is growing slowly, firms wishing to grow faster than the market will try to take market share away from their rivals by competing more fiercely. This is the case in the traditional markets of North America and Western Europe for the packaged food, beer, and car industries. If a beer firm wants to grow in those markets, it has to up its competitive performance or take over a rival. It was therefore no surprise when, in 2016, the US-based AB InBev, the world's largest brewer, acquired a major rival SABMiller with the merged firm holding around one-third of the global market (*Forbes* 10 October 2016).

- The extent of product differentiation—when firms have been successful in persuading customers that their products are different from those of their rivals, then competition is likely to be less intense. In the beer market, Anheuser-Busch InBev has six well-established international brands (Budweiser, Stella Artois, Beck's, Skol, Foster's, and Leffe), and more than 200 local brands, while Heineken manages a large portfolio of beer brands, such as Heineken, Amstel, Cruzcampo, and Tiger. Some firms, such as Hoover, Sellotape, and Google, are so successful that their brand becomes the generic name for the product.

- The importance of fixed costs—these costs do not change with output and include, for example, depreciation, rent, and interest payments. Industries operating with large, expensive pieces of capital equipment often have high fixed costs and relatively low running (or variable) costs. Examples include oil refining, nuclear power generation, and mass car production. In such industries, firms will be under pressure to sell their output in order to generate some contribution to their fixed costs. This pressure will be particularly intense when there is spare capacity in the industry; in other words, where firms are not using the resources to produce to their full potential, a situation faced by the big car producers in the traditional markets of North America and Western Europe.

- Where production capacity needs to be added in large chunks, expansion by firms can add significantly to the industry's ability to supply and could result in supply outstripping demand, leading to more competition. This is a particular problem for the car industry, given that new factories could add significantly to supply in an industry suffering from over-capacity. To be competitive, new factories have to be able to produce several hundred thousand units a year in order to take advantage of economies of scale.

If most or all of the above conditions are met, then competition in an industry will be fierce. Conversely, if none of these conditions prevail, then firms in the industry are unlikely to be competing fiercely against each other.

Often oligopolists, faced with the unpalatable prospect of competition, will make efforts to avoid it. There are various devices they can use to achieve this, such as forming a cartel, which, in many countries, is illegal. The members of the cartel agree to follow certain competition-avoiding policies by, for example, agreeing to set common prices, sharing out the market, or controlling the introduction of new goods or services.

The European Commission found a cross-border price-fixing cartel operating in the market for air conditioning and engine cooling systems in cars involving six companies from Germany, Japan, and France (European Commission IP/17/501). Often, cartels are established by firms producing undifferentiated products where buyers will take their custom to the cheapest supplier. When supply threatens to outstrip demand in such industries, firms fear the outbreak of fierce competition and sometimes set up a cartel to prevent this happening. Alternatively, competitors can avoid competition by resorting to **price leadership**. While cartels bring firms together in an explicit agreement, price leadership can result from implicit understandings within the industry. Under price leadership, one firm raises prices and the others follow suit. Price leadership takes two forms. The first is dominant price leadership, where the biggest firm in the industry changes price and others, either willingly or through fear of the consequences, follow suit. Barometric is the second type of price leadership. This occurs when firms in the industry are of similar size, and the identity of the price leader changes from one period to another.

Mini Case Study 3.2 Consolidation in agrichemicals

Between 2015 and 2017, there was a wave of big mergers in the agrichemical industry. Bayer (Germany) made a bid of US$69 billion for Monsanto (US) while Dow (US) acquired Du Pont (US) for $66 billion. ChemChina (China) proposed a merger costing $47 billion with Syngenta (Switzerland). These compa- nies produce herbicides, pesticides, fertilizers, and seeds, often genetically modified and held under patent. Farmers are the main customers. Figure 3.3 shows the largest players in the industry and their HQs, and Figure 3.4 shows sales revenues of the merged companies. ➔

Figure 3.3 Headquarters of top ten agrichemical companies 2015

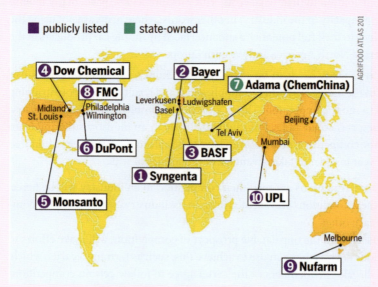

Source: Heinrich Böll Stiftung (2017)

The mergers were being driven by declines in global commodity prices and the consequent falls in farmers' incomes. In addition, the reduced efficiency of genetically modified seeds and evidence of resistance to the vast majority of current crop protection chemicals made farmers increasingly reluctant to buy them. Furthermore, Mammana (2014) says that plants grown from high-yield genetically modified seeds produce seeds with lower yields requiring farmers to buy new seeds each year. Dow, in evidence to a US Senate Committee (2016), also pointed to the rapidly rising costs of developing new crop protection products. In 1995, the R&D and regulatory costs for bringing a new crop protection product to market averaged $152 million. By 2016, the cost had increased to around $286 million. Company profits were being squeezed.

The companies claimed that the merged entities would not harm competition because they operated in different product and geographical markets. Bayer said that it and Monsanto's operations were complementary. Bayer was a leader in crop protection, with a greater presence outside North America, while Monsanto led in seeds with a greater presence inside North America. Syngenta argued that it was an agricultural company and ChemChina a chemical company, so the two companies did not compete.

Farmers feared that the consolidation of the industry would reduce competition, increase prices, reduce choice, stifle innovation, and raise barriers to entry. The National Farmers Union (NFU) in the USA pointed out the significant competition in the 1970s with 30 companies in the seed market was followed in the next 30 years by two major merger waves leaving six big firms. The Dow Du Pont merger combined two of the Big Six firms holding more than 60 per cent of the global seed market and 76 per cent of the global agricultural chemical market. Between 1996 and 2013, the top ten seed companies purchased around 200 seed companies and bought equity stakes in dozens of other seed companies. The top three owned 85 per cent of the corn patents and 70 per cent of the non-corn patents. Seed companies had also established alliances with competitors in R&D and distribution (see Figure 3.5). Furthermore, Mammana (2014) reported that seed companies had taken over distributors. The NFU was also concerned by the possibilities of ➜

→ **Figure 3.4** Expected revenues for seed and pesticide companies in 2017

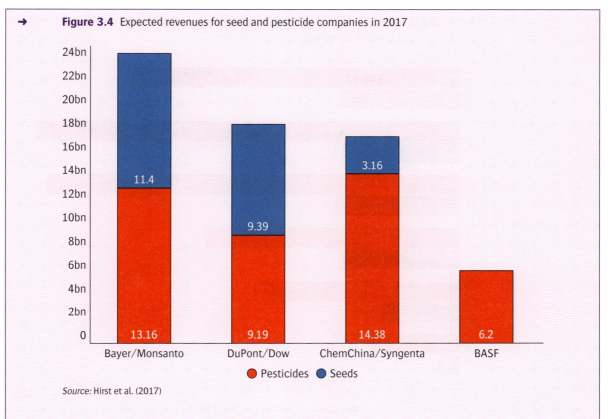

Source: Hirst et al. (2017)

collusion between the leading firms. In addition, there were fears that the merged companies would have a greater influence over industry regulators.

Sources: Euromonitor (2016d); *Financial Times* 4 March 2017; Heinrich Böll Stiftung (2017); Mammana (2014); Senate Committee (2016)

Questions

1. Discuss:
   a. changes in the market structure of agrichemicals; and
   b. how these changes have come about.
2. Identify the major drivers of the latest round of consolidation.
3. Weigh up whether farmers are right to be concerned about the restructuring of the industry.

 Learning Task

Study Figure 3.5 and then answer the following questions:

1. What is a patent?
2. According to Figure 3.5, which agrichemical firms have been most active in seeking patents?
3. Why might firms in this industry be keen to register patents?
4. Discuss the implications for farmers of these firms controlling large numbers of patents.

→

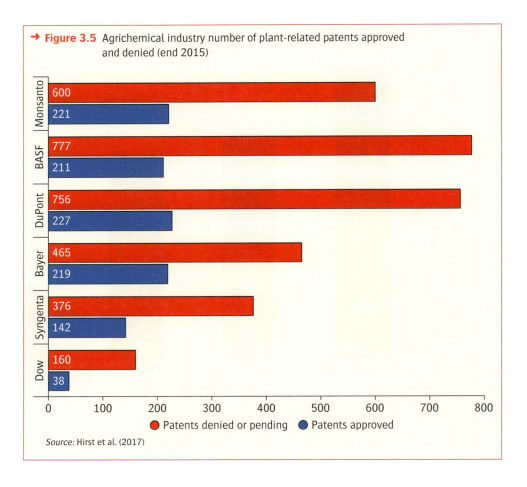

→ **Figure 3.5** Agrichemical industry number of plant-related patents approved and denied (end 2015)

Source: Hirst et al. (2017)

Force 2: Competition from New Entrants

The entry of new firms is another threat to established firms in the industry. New entrants will be attracted into industries by the prospects of high profits and growth. It may be that established firms are not making high profits, but that the entrants can see the potential for profit—this was the case with low-cost entry to the airline industry. Entry increases the number of firms and, if it takes the form of greenfield investment, adds to industry capacity. As a result, competition could become more intense. On the other hand, low growth industries with poor profits are unlikely to be threatened by a rush of new firms. Established firms are likely to leave such industries, looking for more profitable pastures elsewhere.

The probability of new entrants to the industry is dependent on the height of barriers to entry. Industries protected by very high barriers face little threat of new entry. The following are examples of barriers to entry.

- **Absolute cost barriers**—these are advantages which established firms have over newcomers. In the world of five-star hotels, where location is of utmost importance, it would be difficult for a new entrant to find a sufficient number of prime sites to set up an extensive chain of hotels because many of these sites would be already occupied by established hotel chains. Similarly, firms trying to enter the telecommunications, electricity generation, or rail industries could have problems because existing operators control the physical networks.

- Legal barriers—laws and regulations can constitute insurmountable barriers. Before the telecommunications and airline industries were liberalized, the legal and regulatory framework protected existing firms from new entry. In many countries, firms wishing to enter banking usually have to pass a series of legal tests to get permission to set up in business.

- Product differentiation—this can be a major barrier when firms manage to convince customers that their products are significantly different from those of their competitors. Some firms, especially in consumer goods industries such as cars, food, soft drinks, and computer software, spend large amounts of money on advertising, sales promotion, and packaging to differentiate their products. In 2016, Louis Vuitton, the luxury goods firm, allocated $4.4 billion to advertising while Amazon's budget was $3.8 billion (business-review Europe 19 May 2016). Spending on advertising is increasing very fast in countries such as China. Spending is forecast to almost double to $132 billion between 2015 and 2020, with TV and smartphones particularly popular media (Statista n.d.). Promotional expenditure in the pharmaceutical industry is one of its main areas of cost. Some pharma companies spend more on promotion than they do on R&D. Massive promotional expenditures can build up brand loyalty and recognition to such an extent that the brands become very valuable (see Table 3.3). The Apple, Google, Coca-Cola, IBM, and Microsoft brands are each worth more than US$50 billion. Product differentiation can be a significant deterrent to new firms entering an industry.

 Counterpoint Box 3.2 Online advertising: the latest shining object?

Advertising online has grown apace and had become an important competitive tool especially for consumer goods MNCs. Global online advertising spending was $154 billion in 2015 and was forecast to grow to $300 billion by 2021, outstripping advertising expenditure on television (PwC n.d.). The USA is the biggest market for online advertising, but PwC forecast that growing internet access would cause a surge in China and other South East Asian countries.

Online advertising is seen as more cost-efficient than traditional methods because it can provide cheaper access to transnational audiences of millions of potential consumers 24 hours a day. Google offers the possibility of placing such advertisements in multiple locations for a single fee. Targeting and tracking of consumers is also easier on the internet. The technology deployed by Google and Facebook can ensure that only people

likely to be receptive to particular messages will receive those messages. Interactive advertisements placed online can generate feedback, allowing the firm to increase their marketing effectiveness through two-way communication with their target market. In 2012, Procter & Gamble (P&G) announced that it would make $1 billion in savings by targeting consumers through digital and social media. It saw these media as the 'latest shiny objects' (*Marketing Week* 31 January 2017).

However, by 2017 P&G's chief brands officer was complaining of 'an exponential increase in crap . . all too often . . . the outcome has been more crappy advertising accompanied by even crappier viewing experiences'. For him, the rapid adoption of software systems by consumers to block advertisements was no surprise. Another concern for advertisers was an advertising industry investigation suggesting that about one in three →

→ **Figure 3.6** Global internet advertising market (US$bn), by region

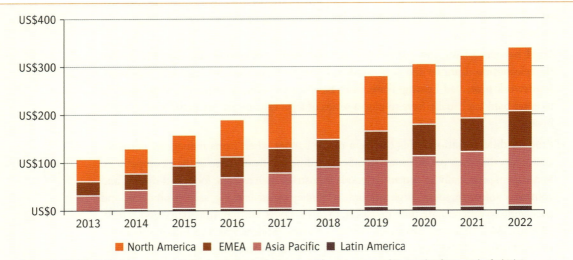

online ads were being seen by bots rather than humans. P&G called for an increase in transparency in the data around online advertising. The P&G executive said, 'We serve ads to consumers through a non-transparent media supply chain with spotty compliance to common standards, unreliable measurement, hidden rebates and new inventions like bot . . . fraud.' The US Association of National Advertisers claimed that advertising fraud on digital media was costing $7 billion annually. P&G said that it had 'come to senses' and would no longer accept publishers reporting their own performance without external verification.

Advertisers face a duopoly in supply of media space comprising the digital giants Google and Facebook, who together hold more than 60 per cent of the market. Edelman (2014, p88) says that advertisers saw non-appearance on Google as a 'death sentence'. In 2017, advertisers like McDonald's, HSBC, Walmart, Marks and Spencer and Starbucks revolted by removing their advertisements from Google's YouTube which was showing

their advertisements alongside extremist videos espousing terrorism and hate. Advertisers were hoping that Snapchat would prove a major rival to Google and Facebook.

Sources: Advertising Age 22 October 2015; Association of National Advertisers 30 March 2017; Edelman (2014); *Financial Times* 14 March 2017; *Marketing Week* 2 February 2017; *Ingram* 31 March 2017; *The Observer* 5 March, 26 March 2017; *Marketing Week* 31 January 2017; PwC (n.d.).

Questions

1. Why would big advertisers like P&G see digital media as the 'latest shiny objects'?

2. Explain why advertisers have become somewhat disillusioned with digital media.

3. Give reasons why advertisers are hopeful that firms like Snapchat will be successful.

- **Economies of scale**—these occur when an increase in the scale of the organization, say from a small factory to a large factory, leads to a fall in unit costs. In some industries, such as cars, firms need to operate on a large scale in order to compete with their rivals. If not, then they will suffer a major competitive disadvantage and some may find it hard to survive. This appears to be happening in China. Car sales in China, the world's largest car market, exceeded 28 million in 2017 (MarkLines 4 January 2018). However, sales are divided up between more than 100 companies, few of whom are anywhere near achieving the economies of scale needed to guarantee long-term survival (*Financial Times* 24 October 2017).

Other factors deterring entry to an industry include **excess capacity**, declining demand, the ability of established firms to freeze out new entrants by controlling supply of materials, and distribution through vertical integration or long-term contracts with suppliers and customers.

The actual or anticipated reaction of established firms can also be an obstacle to entry, especially where those companies are large and powerful. The EU found that French banks used discriminatory prices to block the entry of internet banks and supermarket chains who wished to issue credit cards. Ellison and Ellison (2011) found some evidence that pharmaceutical firms deterred entry of generic rivals through their pricing and advertising policies.

Firms need to be ready to respond to new entrants. In the first decade of the new century, domestic banks in Singapore embarked on a frenzy of mergers when the authorities carried out further liberalization, which was expected to lead to the entry of foreign competitors. The Chinese car industry cut prices when China's membership of the WTO meant that the measures previously protecting them from foreign competition would have to be removed. India's big retailers, such as Reliance Industries, fearful that the Indian government would open up the market completely to foreign firms, expanded very rapidly in order to steal a march on rivals such as Wal-Mart and Tesco. The *Financial Times* (16 February 2017) reported that foreign retailers like H&M, Gap, and Adidas were planning to expand rapidly in India.

Force 3: Substitutes

An industry may face competition from substitutes. In the Porter model, substitutes are goods or services produced by firms in an apparently different industry and delivering a similar service to the consumer but in a different way. In the airline industry, firms sell flights to transport customers from point A to B, say London to Paris. All firms selling flights, such as BA, Air France, Lufthansa, and easyJet, would be seen as part of the same industry competing in the same market. However, trains, ferries, coaches, and private cars could also be used by travellers to get to Paris. If the consumer sees the trains run by Eurostar as being an acceptable alternative to the services provided by airlines, then it would seem sensible to include them in any analysis of an industry's competitive environment.

Table 3.3 Rank and value of international brands 2017

Rank	Brand	Value (US$ bn)
1	Apple (US)	170
2	Google (US)	102
3	Microsoft(US)	87
4	Facebook (US)	74
5	Coca Cola (US)	56
6	Amazon (US)	54
7	Disney (US)	44
8	Toyota (Japan)	41
9	McDonalds	40
10	Samsung (S. Korea)	38

Source: Forbes (2018)

The threat from substitutes will be influenced by the cost and ease with which customers can switch to the substitute product. For example, as oil prices rise, customers with central heating might consider switching to a cheaper form of energy. However, the costs, time, and inconvenience of changing the equipment could deter switching. In addition, switching may be deterred by firms using confusion pricing. This occurs where the deals offered to customers are so complicated that it is virtually impossible to compare the value of one firm's offer against another. Examples can be seen in the competitive struggle in the telecommunications sector between mobile and fixed-line telephones with customers being offered a bewildering variety of tariffs, services, and handsets with different technical capabilities, making it difficult to judge which the best deal is for them.

One problem faced by the industry analyst is that, often, the information is not available to assess whether customers do see different goods or services as being good substitutes; in other words, whether there is a high cross elasticity of demand.

Force 4: Customers

Firms sell their output to customers who could be other businesses or the final consumer. For companies like Intel, business customers will be the main purchasers of its computer chips. On the other hand, supermarkets sell to the final consumer. Some firms, such as Microsoft, sell both to other businesses and to the final consumer. The power relationships that firms have with their customers depend on a combination of factors:

- The number and size of firms: when an industry comprises a small number of large firms facing a large number of small customers, then the industry will be in a powerful position. Losing a customer, in this situation, would not be very costly in terms of sales. This is the position of supermarket chains in Western Europe. They are large, few in number, but have millions of customers. It is also the case for accountancy services in the Asia Pacific region, which includes Australia, China, Japan, India, Singapore, South Korea, and Taiwan. Four major players dominate the market: PwC, KPMG, Deloitte, and Ernst & Young (MarketLine 2016). On the other hand, where many firms in an industry have a small number of large customers, then the power switches to the buyer because loss of a single client could cause much damage to revenues and profits. Firms producing defence equipment, such as BAE in the UK or Mitsubishi and Kawasaki in Japan, are in this position. Usually their domestic governments are, by far, the biggest purchasers of arms and other defence equipment such as tanks, submarines, and aircraft carriers. A situation of only a single customer is called a monopsony.

- The proportion of customer costs constituted by the product: when a product constitutes a large proportion of a business customer's total costs, the more sensitive they will be to price because price increases will have a big impact on their costs and, if they are unable to pass this on, their profits. These buyers, when faced by a variety of sellers, can shop around and play suppliers off against each other in order to get the most favourable prices. Where customers are dealing with only a few suppliers, then their bargaining power is reduced. This is the case in Europe for intensive energy users like steel makers whose energy bills are a large proportion of their total costs. The EU energy sector is highly concentrated, indicating low bargaining power for buyers such as those in the steel industry.

- The extent of product differentiation: the less differentiated the product, the easier it is for customers to switch to a cheaper supplier. Farmers supplying supermarket chains with meat, fruit, and vegetables will be in a much less powerful bargaining position than firms selling branded washing powders.

- The ability of customers to integrate vertically: sellers will be at a disadvantage where customers are big enough to produce their own supplies, either by taking over their suppliers or by setting up new production facilities. Wal-Mart and other supermarket chains built giant warehouses to take over the distribution of supplies direct from the manufacturer thereby cutting out the wholesalers that previously carried out this task. Apple is also vertically integrated because it not only designs and markets Macs, iPhones, and iPads, but also distributes them through its retail outlets. In contrast, buyers will have less power when they are unable to integrate vertically.

Mini Case Study 3.3 Customer power

The technology sector produces graphics processor units (GPUs) for use in PCs, laptops, consoles, and mobile devices such as smartphones. The industry is dominated by three producers. Intel is by far the largest, followed a long way behind by Nvidia and AMD.

Imagination Technologies (IT) is a UK-based technology group employing around 1,700 people operating in 15 countries. It designs graphics processors mainly for Apple. In 2017, Apple announced that it would stop using IT's graphic processors in its iPhone, iPads, iPods, TVs, and watches by 2019. Apple, which owned an 8 per cent stake in IT, had been using its technology under licence for ten years and was its largest customer accounting for half its revenue. In 2016/17, IT expected to earn £65 million from licence fees and royalties from Apple. After the Apple announcement, IT's shares went into freefall, plunging by more than 60 per cent.

Apple, which had been poaching IT employees, claimed that it was independently developing its own graphics design software in order to exercise control over its products and reduce its reliance on IT's technology. IT did not believe that Apple had the ability to design a brand new graphics processor without infringing IT's intellectual property rights. The company therefore asked Apple for the evidence that it could go it alone without using IT's confidential information and violating its patents. Apple refused to provide that information.

Apple, the giant US multinational, operating across the globe, had sales of almost $234 billion in 2015 and directly employed 66,000 in the USA alone. In 2016, Apple had held discussions with IT about taking it over.

Sources: Imagination Technologies press release 3 April 2017; Imagination Technologies Annual Report (2015); SEC 10k Apple Annual Report; *Financial Times* 3 and 8 April 2017; *The Guardian* 4 April 2017

Questions

1. Assess the bargaining power of Imagination Technologies to that of Apple in the case. See the article by ccs insight at http://www.ccsinsight.com/press/company-news/2183-smartphone-sales-to-peak-in-western-markets-in-2017-as-they-enter-new-phase-of-maturity, the report by Mercury Research at http://www.mercuryresearch.com/graphics-pr-2016-q4.pdf, and the John Peddie press release at http://www.jonpeddie.com/press-releases/details/the-cg-market-will-exceed-130-billion-by-2019.

2. CNBC reported that Apple's announcement gave it an opportunity to acquire IT. Discuss. See http://www.cnbc.com/2017/04/04/apple-imagination-technologies-acquisition-share-price.html.

3. Why do you think Apple wanted to develop its own GPUs?

Learning Task

Apple has a history of squeezing suppliers who are dependent on it for business (see Mini Case 3.3 Customer power). An early victim was the audio company PortalPlayer, which depended on Apple for 90 per cent of its sales. Apple switched to another supplier and Portal ended up in the hands of Nvidia. The *Financial Times* (8 April 2017) reported that Apple was pressurizing dependent suppliers for price cuts.

1. Why would Apple pursue these policies towards suppliers?
2. Cirrus Logic, the audio chipmaker, relied on Apple for more than 80 per cent of sales revenue. One analyst recommended the following to suppliers: 'The best thing is to do the deal with Apple anyway ... Even though you are probably going to get throttled in the end, you will have three years of great times you probably would never have had if you hadn't done it' (*Financial Times* 8 April 2017).

What advice would you give to firms like Cirrus? See Imagination Technologies' annual report 2015.

Force 5: Suppliers

'Suppliers' refers to businesses selling inputs, such as fuel, raw materials, and components to the firms in an industry. The position of suppliers can be analysed in a similar way to those of buyers, but in reverse. The only difference, as Grant (2016) points out, is that it is now the firms in the industry that are the customers and the sellers of inputs that are the suppliers. To illustrate, if the supplier industry is dominated by a few large firms, compared to the buying industry, then the ability of suppliers to get away with price increases, reductions in quality, and a worsening of the terms and conditions of sale will be high. Firms producing computers have little bargaining power faced as they are by the world's dominant producer of microprocessors, Intel. Conversely, where the supply side is more fragmented than the buying side, then the advantage will lie in the hands of the customer. This was the case in the European dairy industry where suppliers of milk, cheese, and yoghurt were faced by a smaller number of big, powerful customers like Tesco, Aldi, and Leclerc. The dairy industry responded to this inequality by consolidating. For example, in the UK, Arla took over Express Dairies while Campina, a Dutch firm, took over Germany's Sator (see Food and Drink Europe (2018); Food Navigator (2018)). To see Porter discussing his Five Forces model and its application to the airline industry, go to the video links for Chapter 3 in the **online resources**.

A Sixth Force: Complementary Products

The Porter model pays particular attention to the relationships between competitors' products and also the threat from substitute products. It does not deal with the complementary relationship that can exist between products. Complementary products are those that are used together by customers—in other words, they do not compete with each other but operate in tandem.

There are numerous examples of complementary products: mobile phones need service providers; DVDs need equipment to play them; computers need software; cars need petrol; and printers require ink cartridges. The suppliers of complementary products can play an important role in the competitive environment for firms in an industry, first, because the firms making the products depend on the efforts of the other, for example, in relation to product development. Second, there can be conflict over who gets most of the spoils.

Such a relationship is illustrated in the case of software vendors and the producers of PCs and PC components. Most PC manufacturers want new, exciting software to be developed that requires customers to upgrade to new PCs, but software providers generally prefer to target the larger market of customers with their existing computers. The paradoxical nature of complementarity can be seen in the case of Intel, the maker of computer chips, and Microsoft. According to Casadeus-Masanell and Yoffie (2007: 584), they are 'joined at the hip' because more than four-fifths of the personal computers sold worldwide contain an Intel microprocessor running Microsoft's Windows operating system. The companies are dependent on each other because consumer demand and revenues depend on how well the different software and hardware components work together. This means that the R&D programmes for both players have got to complement each other. Casadeus-Masanell and Yoffie (2007) report that the two companies have been in conflict over pricing, the timing of investments, and who captures the greatest share of the value of the product. An Intel manager puts it thus:

> Intel is always trying to innovate on hardware platforms and thus, always needs software. When software lags, it creates a bottleneck for Intel. Microsoft, on the other hand, wants to serve the installed base of computers in addition to demand for new computers. Therefore, a natural conflict exists between both companies. In addition, the question always remains—Who will get the bigger piece of the pie? The success of one is seen as ultimately taking money away from the other. (Casadeus-Masanell and Yoffie 2007: 584)

Mini Case Study 3.4 Complementary products: sharing the pie

As Koenigsberg (2013) point out, there is no point having a video games console with no games to play on it. Sales of consoles, the hardware, produced by firms such as Sony, Microsoft, and Nintendo therefore depend on the software provided by games developers. Business revenue is generated through the consoles and the games being used together. In 2017, global sales of video games totalled $116 billion. Mobile devices accounted for almost half the revenue, the rest coming from PCs and consoles (Ukie n.d.).

Complementarity can provoke serious tensions between the partner firms in their struggle to get a bigger share of the value generated by the product. Frictions can develop between partner firms in areas such as quality standards, pricing, and royalties. When Sony brings new consoles into production, it decides quality standards. It is dependent on games makers coming up with products complying with Sony's quality requirements. Once the standards have ini-

tially been set, analysts, such as Yalcin et al. (2010), suggest that subsequently, games producers will be tempted to cut corners on quality. Tensions can also arise when one of the partners increases the price of its product in an attempt to get a greater share of sales revenues. If the other partner is not prepared to accept a lower price for its input then the price to the consumer could rise, causing a fall in demand and a reduction in sales revenues. It may be that the partners face different competitive environments, with one partner facing less competition being freer to raise prices, and the other being more constrained. Royalties are a further source of conflict between partners trying to get a larger share of the final value. Console makers charge royalties for the right to publish games for their consoles just as smartphone firms charge makers of the apps appearing on their phones. One partner extracting more of the value can lead the other to skimp on quality.

→

→ Grant (2011) shows how Nintendo managed to keep the upper hand in its relationships with the suppliers of games software for its video games console. It maintained control of its operating system, avoided becoming over-dependent on any single supplier by issuing licences to many developers, and established a firm hold over the manufacture and distribution of games cartridges.

Sources: Koenigsberg (2013); Yalcin et al. (2010); Grant (2011)

Questions

1. Explain the grounds for conflict between console makers and games developers.
2. Why might games developers be tempted to skimp on quality standards?
3. Assess the bargaining power of the thousands of games developers against giants such as Sony, Microsoft, Nintendo, and Apple.

Analysing an industry using the Six Forces: a checklist

- Are there many firms or only a few?
- Are firms a similar size?
- Is the market growing or declining?
- Is product differentiation important?
- How high are fixed costs as a percentage of total costs?
- Do additions to production capacity increase total industry capacity significantly?
- Are there any significant barriers to entry?
- Is there significant excess capacity in the industry?
- Do existing firms have the power to prevent entry?
- Is there any significant competition from substitutes?
- Is there a large number of small buyers/suppliers or a few large buyers/suppliers?
- Does the product constitute a large proportion of customer costs?
- Do input purchases constitute a large proportion of supplier revenues?
- Do customers/suppliers have the ability to take over firms in the industry?
- Are firms in the industry dependent on complementary products?

 Counterpoint Box 3.3 Porter's 'Five Forces' model and its critics

Porter's Five Forces model has become part of the standard toolkit for managers and industrial analysts. However, it has been criticized on several grounds.

Critics claim that economic conditions have changed dramatically since the appearance of the model in the 1980s, when the business environment was much more certain, making it easier for firms to plan ahead. They claim that the model is static only giving a snapshot of the business environment at a point in time when the business environment has become more turbulent and liable to change. Three developments are cited that have made the environment much more dynamic and uncertain for business:

- digitalization and, in particular, the development of the internet and e-business;
- globalization, resulting in firms finding themselves increasingly in a global market where customers can shop around and compare prices, and where rivals, buyers, and suppliers may decide to move production to cheaper locations; and

→

→ • extensive deregulation, which led to a reduction in government influence over industries such as airlines and utilities in the energy, telecoms, and finance sectors, and helped lead to major restructuring in these sectors.

In a dynamic world business needs to be able to identify changes and trends in its environment. It can also be argued that the model ignores the ability of firms, especially big firms, to influence their micro- environment for example through takeovers and cartels and their macro environment through, for instance, lobbying governments.

A further line of criticism holds that a firm cannot be evaluated simply by reference to the five forces in its external environment. These critics, supporting a resource-based view, argue that internal strengths and weaknesses of the firm also need to be taken into account.

Porter's supporters, while accepting the validity of some criticisms, argue that the idea that all firms operate in an environment characterized by rivals, buyers, suppliers, entry barriers, and substitutes remains valid. Some attempts have been made to extend the model. The inclusion of a sixth force, complementary products, has been proposed, while others have suggested adding government (national and regional) and pressure groups as another force.

The message for managers is that, while the model remains a useful tool enabling them to think about the current situation of their industry in a structured, easy-to-understand way, they need to be aware of its limitations when applying it.

Sources: Coyne and Sujit Balakrishnan (1996); Downes (1997); Dulcic et al. *(*2012); Brandenburger and Nalebuff (1996); Porter (2008)

Questions
1. Explain the argument that the Five Forces model is static when firms face a dynamic environment.
2. Why might the Five Forces model might be a more useful analytical tool for small firms selling solely in their domestic market?

● CHAPTER SUMMARY

In this chapter, we set out to explain the concepts and tools that are indispensable to the industry analyst and to show how they can be used to analyse industries. We started off with the concepts of the industry and the market. It was shown that any satisfactory definition of the market needs to specify a set of products and its geographical boundaries. The next issue to be addressed was the various market structures and their implications for business behaviour and industry performance. It was shown that the more highly concentrated is the market, the more power is concentrated in the hands of a few firms able to manipulate prices, the quantity and quality of the good or service, and the terms and conditions of sale. This was followed by an explanation of the Porter Five Forces model and how this could be used to analyse industries. As part of the analysis of Porter's force of rivalry, it was demonstrated how firms sometimes make strenuous efforts to avoid price competition through the establishment of cartels and systems of price leadership. We also revealed the importance of product differentiation as a major element of competitive strategy and as a barrier to entry in certain industries. A sixth force, complementary products, was added to the Porter model to make it an even more effective analytical tool.

● REVIEW QUESTIONS

1. What is a market?
2. Use your response to question 1 to assess whether the market for beer is global, regional, or national.
3. What are entry barriers and how important are they in:

a. the car industry?

b. coffee shops?

4. Explain the concept of market power.

5. Discuss how oligopolists such as Apple can exploit their market power.

● ASSIGNMENT TASKS

1. You are the PA to the CEO of a large MNC considering a move into the food packaging industry, the subject of the opening case. Write a report that:

   a. analyses the structure of the global food packaging industry;

   b. identifies and discusses the major challenges the industry faces in its external environment; and

   c. assesses the success of the industry in responding to these challenges.

2. You are employed in the research department of a technology firm that is considering entering the video streaming market. Your boss asks you to compile a report on Netflix, the major player in the market. Use Porter's Five Forces model to analyse the position of Netflix in the video streaming market.

3. You are a reporter on a web-based business technology magazine. The editor asks you to write an article on the global market for mobile operating systems. In the article, discuss:

   a. the major players in the market;

   b. changes that have occurred in market structure; and

   c. the competitive strategies that have helped bring about changes in market structure.

Case Study 'The tobacco industry should be dead by now'

© iStock.com/Simona Flamigni

The tobacco industry produces a range of products including cigarettes, the main revenue generator, chewing tobacco, snuff, and alternative tobacco products such as electronic cigarettes. In 2015, the industry sold almost 6 trillion cigarettes to a value of US$700 billion to over 1 billion smokers worldwide.

Figure 3.7 shows the big players and their market shares. The biggest tobacco firm is the state-controlled CNTC, which enjoys a virtual monopoly in China.

Smoking rates have been declining generally since the millennium not only in the high-income countries of North America, West Europe, and Japan, but also in Latin America and Asian countries such as China and Bangladesh. On the other hand, rates are rising in low and middle income countries (LMICs) in much of Africa.   →

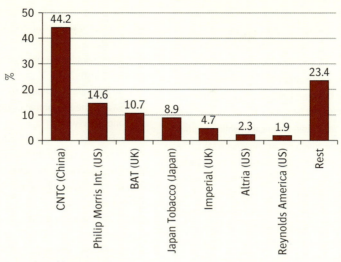

Figure 3.7 Global market shares tobacco industry 2016

Source: http://www.statista.com

The industry has managed to weather multiple challenges in its external environment, including:

- declining markets in the developed world;
- public health campaigns drawing the links between tobacco and cancer;
- lawsuits costing billions;
- heavy restrictions on advertising and sales promotion;
- allegations that its advertising targeted children;
- alleged involvement in illegal smuggling of cigarettes; and
- competition from non-tobacco-based products.

The World Health Organization (WHO) has been a thorn in the side of the industry. In 2005 its Framework Convention on Tobacco Control came into force with the aim of reducing smoking through limits on the advertising, packaging, and sale of tobacco products. In 2017, there were 180 signatories (WHO n.d.a). According to the WHO (2018), 6 million people a year die of smoking and around 80 per cent of the world's one billion smokers live in low and middle income countries. Total deaths are expected to rise to 8 million by 2030, with four-fifths in LMICs. Goodchild et al. (2017) estimated that, globally, 26.8 million years of labour had been lost due to smoking.

The WHO (2015) says that the tobacco industry tries to influence the policies of intergovernmental organizations to portray itself as socially responsible through involvement with those organizations. Philip Morris used the United Nations Environment Programme's (UNEP) logo to advertise its efforts to reduce its impact on the environment, while Japan Tobacco donated money to the International Labour Organization's campaign to eliminate child labour.

Proctor (2008: 17) says that the industry has been opportunistic in the various tactics used against the health lobby in its struggle for survival, '...advertising, duplicitous press releases, the funding of decoy research, establishment of scientific front organizations, manipulation of legislative agendas, organization of "friendly research" for publication in popular magazines'.

The industry has also looked to politicians to support its case. In the UK, Ken Clarke, a former Conservative government minister, was for many years a director on the board of British American Tobacco (BAT), one of the world's largest tobacco firms. In the USA, John Boehner, a former Republican Party speaker in Congress, joined the board of Reynolds American, another giant of the tobacco industry. In 2016, the industry spent almost US$20 million lobbying US politicians, while in 2013, tobacco firms doubled their expenditure to over €8 million (over $9 million) lobbying against the EU Tobacco Products Directive, which aimed to reduce smoking particularly among young people. The industry has also attempted to block →

→ anti-smoking laws by warning countries that such laws breach international trade and investment treaties, and by threatening costly and prolonged legal action which some health activists say is intimidating for poor countries.

The tobacco industry has also responded strategically to external threats through divestments, acquisitions, and changes in target markets. In the USA in the 1990s, and into the new millennium, the industry faced costly cancer-related lawsuits (NOLO 30 December 2015). In response, BAT merged its US Brown and Williams subsidiary with Reynolds American, while another tobacco giant, Altria, spun off Philip Morris International while retaining Philip Morris USA. However, with the US legal situation beginning to stabilize, BAT launched a $50 billion takeover of Reynolds in which it already held a 42 per cent stake (see CNBC 17 January 2017, which includes a video of the chair of Reynolds justifying the merger). The buy-back would make BAT the world's largest listed seller of tobacco products and create a duopoly in the USA, with Altria and BAT holding 85 per cent of the market.

Tobacco companies, facing declining rates of smoking in high-income countries, have focused on LMICs where increases in smoking have more than offset declines elsewhere. These markets are also attractive because their markets will expand with the growth of their economies and their populations. Most of the big tobacco firms have also responded by moving, through takeovers, into non-tobacco products such as electronic cigarettes.

Sources: CNBC 17 January 2017; Euromonitor (2016e); European Commission (2016b); Goodchild (2017); LobbyFacts.eu 1 September 2016 http://lobbyfacts.eu; *Financial Times* 22 October 2016; NCI and WHO (2016); *New York Times* 13 December 2013; NOLO 30 December 2015; OpenSecrets http://www.opensecrets.org; Proctor in Proctor and Schiebinger (2008); Tobacco Asia 1 July 2015 http://www.tobaccoasia.com; Tobacco Atlas http://www.tobaccoatlas.org; World Bank http://blogs.worldbank.org/opendata; see the WHO website for much information on tobacco, for example, http://www.who.int/fctc/en.

Questions

1. Describe the global market structure of the tobacco industry.

2. How does the global market structure compare with that regional/national markets? For information, Google tobacco+national+market+shares; also see the Tobacco Atlas at http://www.tobaccoatlas.org/topic/tobacco-companies.

3. What form would you expect competition to take in the tobacco industry?

4. How did the industry change its advertising strategy when the USA and the EU banned cigarette advertisements on radio and television?

5. How does Porter define a substitute? Discuss whether e-cigarettes are a substitute for cigarettes.

6. Assess how successful the tobacco industry response has been to the major challenges in its external environment in terms of:
   a) growth of sales by value and volume;
   b) profits; and
   c) prevalence of smoking. See WHO (n.d.b)

7. *The Economist* (21 January 2017) points out that restrictions on advertising and sales may not have the effects desired by health campaigners because they lower marketing costs for existing firms and make it more difficult for new firms to enter and get established in the market. Weigh up arguments for the contention by *The Economist* that restrictions on advertising and sales promotion could help existing tobacco firms. See WHO video supporting plain packaging of cigarettes at http://www.who.int/campaigns/no-tobacco-day/2016/en.

8. According to one commentator, the tobacco industry should be 'dead by now'. He argues that the industry has survived by being crafty and resilient (*Financial Times* 17 September 2016). Discuss.

See the case of Boeken v. Philip Morris, Inc. at http://casetext.com/case/boeken-v-philip-morris-inc; 'Tobacco Explained' produced for the pressure group Action on Smoking and Health (ASH) at http://www.who.int/tobacco/media/en/TobaccoExplained.pdf; radio interview with representative of Imperial at http://mpegmedia.abc.net.au/local/melbourne/201106/r784608_6778304.mp3; and article at http://www.ncbi.nlm.nih.gov/pmc/articles/PMC2563590.

● FURTHER READING

For further discussion of global industries, see:

● Dicken, P. (2015) *Global Shift: Mapping the Changing Contours of the World Economy*. London: Sage.

For discussion of the global pharmaceutical industry, see:

● Goldacre, B. (2013) *Bad Pharma: How Medicine is Broken and How We Can Fix It*. London: Fourth Estate.

● Jones, G. (2010) *Beauty Imagined: A History of the Global Beauty Industry*. Oxford: Oxford University Press.

● Katsanis, L. P. (2016) *Global Issues in Pharmaceutical Marketing*. Abingdon: Routledge.

● Pleatsikas, C. and Teece, D. (2001) 'The Analysis of Market Definition and Market Power in the Context of Rapid Innovation'. *International Journal of Industrial Organization* 19 (5).

For discussion and application of Porter's Five Forces model, see:

● Dobbs, M.E. (2014) 'Guidelines for Applying Porter's Five Forces Framework: A Set of Industry Analysis Templates'. *Competitiveness Review* 24 (1).

● Siaw, I. (2004) 'An Analysis of the Impact of the Internet on Competition in the Banking Industry, Using Porter's Five Forces Model'. *International Journal of Management* 21 (4).

● REFERENCES

Armentano, D.T. (2007) *Antitrust: The Case for Repeal*. Auburn: Ludwig von Mises Institute.

Barney J.B. (2007) *Resource-Based Theory: Creating and Sustaining Competitive Advantage*. Oxford: Oxford University Press.

BBC (2016) 'Tesco Removes Marmite and Other Unilever Brands in Price Row'. http://www.bbc.co.uk/news/business-37639518.

Brandenburger, A.M. and Nalebuff, B.J. (1996) *Co-Opetition*. London: Profile Books.

Casadeus-Masanell, R. and Yoffie, D.B. (2007) 'Wintel: Cooperation and Conflict'. *Added Management Science* 53(4).

Connor, J.M. (2002) *The Food and Agricultural Global Cartels of the 1990s: Overview and Update*. Purdue University Staff Paper #02-4, August. Available at http://ageconsearch.umn.edu/bitstream/28631/1/sp02-04.pdf.

Connor, J.M. (2016) 'International Cartel Stats: A Look At The Last 26 Years', 12 August. Available at https://www.law360.com/articles/827868/international-cartel-stats-a-look-at-the-last-26-years.

Coyne, K.P. and Balakrishnan, S. (1996) 'Bringing Discipline to Strategy'. *The McKinsey Quarterly* 4.

Downes, L. (1997) 'Beyond Porter'. *Context Magazine,* Fall.

Dulcic, Z. et al. (2012) 'From Five Competitive Forces to Five Collaborative Forces: Revised View on Industry-structure Firm Interrelationship'. Procedia—*Social and Behavioral Sciences* 58.

Edelman, B. (2014) 'Mastering the Intermediaries; Strategies for Dealing with the Likes of Google, Amazon, and Kayak'. *Harvard Business Review* June.

Ellison, G. and Ellison, S.F. (2011) 'Strategic Entry Deterrence and the Behavior of Pharmaceutical Incumbents Prior to Patent Expiration'. *American Economic Journal, Microeconomics* 3 February.

Etro, F. (2008) 'Stackelberg Competition with Endogenous Entry'. *The Economic Journal* (118:532): 1670–97.

Euromonitor (2015) 'Mondelez aims to breathe life into gum sales with launch of Trident in China'. 15 May.

Euromonitor (2016a) 'Assessing Global Market Suitability for Food'. November.

Euromonitor (2016b) 'Gum in the United Kingdom'. 11 July.

Euromonitor (2016c) 'Beer in Brazil'. 17 June.

Euromonitor (2016d) 'Passport: Will Bayer AG's Monsanto Takeover Pass Regulatory Muster?' 25 October.

Euromonitor (2016e) 'What Is The New Tobacco Data Telling Us?' 20 June.

Euromonitor (2017) 'Passport: Kraft Heinz Co in Packaged Food (World)'. March.

European Commission (2016a) Statement/16/2585 19 July.

European Commission (2016b) IP/16/1762.

European Commission (2017) Memo 14/87, 24 January.

Food and Drink Europe (2018). Available at http://www.FoodandDrinkEurope.com.

Food Navigator (2018). Available at http://www.FoodNavigator.com.

Forbes (2018) 'The World's Most Valuable Brands', available at https://www.forbes.com/powerful-brands/list/#tab:rank.

Galbraith, J.K. (1967) *The New Industrial State.* Woodstock: Princeton University Press.

Goodchild, M. et al. (2017) 'Global economic cost of smoking-attributable diseases'. *Tobacco Control,* 30 January.

Grant, R. (2011) *Cases to Accompany Contemporary Strategy Analysis.* Oxford: Blackwell.

Grant, R. (2016) *Contemporary Strategy Analysis,* 9th edn. Oxford: Blackwell.

Heinrich Böll Stiftung (2017) *Agrifood Atlas; Facts and Figures about the Corporations that Control What We Eat.* October. Available at http://www.boell.de/sites/default/files/agrifoodatlas2017_facts-and-figures-about-the-corporations-that-control-what-we-eat.pdf?dimension1=ds_agrifoodatlas.

Hirst, N., Marks, S., and Smith-Meyer, B. (2017) 'Mega mergers that can tarnish Vestager's ethical legacy'. *Politico Pro* 1 March. Available at http://www.politico.eu/pro/draft-eu-competition- commissioner-margrthevestager-green-challenge/?utm_source=civimail-6311&utm_medium=email&utm_campaign=20170328_EN.

IDC (2018) 'Apple Passes Samsung to Capture the Top Position in the Worldwide Smartphone Market While Overall Shipments Decline 6.3% in the Fourth Quarter, According to IDC', 1 February. Available at https://www.idc.com/getdoc.jsp?containerId=prUS43548018.

Imagination Technologies Annual Report 2015

Koenigsberg, O. (2013) 'Everyone Wins: Never Mind the Complements, Where's the Value?' *Business Strategy Review,* 14 May.

Leibenstein, H. (1978) *General X-Efficiency Theory and Economic Development.* Oxford: Oxford University Press.

Mammana, I. (2014) 'Concentration of Market Power in the EU Seed Market'. The Greens/EFA in the European Parliament. Available at https://www.arche-noah.at/files/seeds-study_uk_28-01v3.pdf.

MarketLine (2016) Industry Profile, 'Accountancy in Asia-Pacific', November.

McNab, G. (2016) 'Ways of Seeing: "The Changing Shape of Cinema Distribution"'. *Sight and Sound* August.

NCI and WHO (2016) *The Economics of Tobacco and Tobacco Control.* National Cancer Institute Tobacco Control Monograph 21. NIH Publication No. 16-CA-8029A.

Net Market Share (n.d.) http://www.netmarketshare.com.

Netflix (2017) 'Netflix Annual Reports 2003–17'.

NOLO (2015) 'Tobacco Litigation: History and Recent Developments', 30 December. Available at http://www.nolo.com/legal-encyclopedia/tobacco-litigation-history-and-development-32202.html.

Pleatsikas, C. and Teece, D. (2000) 'The Competitive Assessment of Vertical Long-term Contracts'. Presented at the Trade Practices Workshop, Business Law Section, Law Council of Australia, Queensland, 12 August.

Pleatsikas, C. and Teece, D. (2001) 'The Analysis of Market Definition and Market Power in the Context of Rapid Innovation'. *International Journal of Industrial Organization* 19(5).

Porter, M.E. (1979) 'How Competitive Forces Shape Strategy'. *Harvard Business Review* March–April.

Porter, M.E. (2008) 'The Five Competitive Forces that Shape Strategy'. *Harvard Business Review* 86(1).

Proctor, R.N. (2008) 'Agnotology: A Missing Term to Describe the Cultural Production of Ignorance (and Its Study)', in Proctor, R.N. and Schiebinger, L. (eds) *Agnotology: The Making and Unmaking Of Ignorance.* Stanford: Stanford University Press.

PwC (n.d.) 'Internet Advertising, Global Entertainment and Media Outlook 2017–2021'. Available at https://www.pwc.com/gx/en/industries/tmt/media/outlook/segment-insights/internet-advertising.html.

QuirksMode (n.d.) http://www.quirksmode.org.

Schumpeter, J. (1976) *Capitalism, Socialism and Democracy.* London: Routledge.

Senate Committee (2016) Judiciary Hearing on 'Competition and Consolidation in the U.S. Seed and Agrochemical Industry', 20 September. Available at http://www.judiciary.senate.gov/imo/media/doc/09-20-16% 20 Collins% 20Testimony.pdf.

Simon, J.P., Benghozi, P.J., and Salvador, E. (2015) 'The New Middlemen of the Digital Age: The Case of Cinema'. *Emerald Insight* Vol. 17 Issue 6.

Statista (n.d.) http://www.statista.com.

Stigler, G.J. (n.d.) 'Monopoly'. *The Concise Encyclopedia of Economics.* Available at http://www.econlib.org/library/Enc/Monopoly.html.

Thomson Reuters (2017) Mergers and Acquisitions Review: Full Year 2017.

Tobacco Asia (2015) http://www.tobacco.asia.com. 1 July.

Trend View (2014) 'Executive Briefing Perspectives'. Available at http://www.tbmcg.co.uk/misc_assets/driving-factors-for-chaos-in-packged-food-markets.pdf.

Ukie (n.d.) http://www.ukie.org.uk.

WHO (2018) 'Tobacco', 9 March. Available at http://www.who.int/news-room/fact-sheets/detail/tobacco.

WHO (n.d.a) http://www.who.int/fctc.

WHO (n.d.b) 'Prevalence of tobacco smoking' at http://www.who.int/gho/tobacco/use/en/.

Yalcin, T. et al. (2010) 'Complementary Goods: Creating and Sharing Value'. Available at https://www0.gsb.columbia.edu/mygsb/faculty/research/pubfiles/5044/complementary%20goods.pdf.

CHAPTER FOUR

The Global Business Environment

LEARNING OUTCOMES

This chapter will enable you to:

- explain the nature of the global business environment;

- understand and apply the PESTLE analytical framework;

- identify organizational stakeholders and construct a stakeholder map; and

- analyse the impact on business of changes in the external environment.

Case Study Apple and the global environment—opportunities and challenges

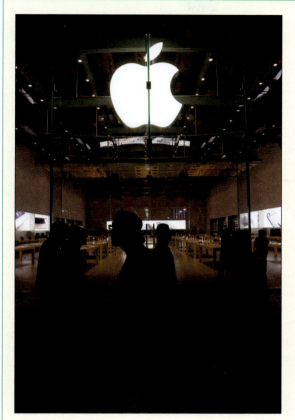

© iStock.com/Joel Carillet

This case examines some of the opportunities and challenges generated for business by the political, legal, economic, social, technological, and environmental forces in the global environment. Apple is the main focus.

Political decisions to liberalize international trade and investment have facilitated the movement of goods, services, capital, and people across borders to the benefit of business and particularly big corporations. Advances in digital technology have allowed the rapid growth of sales of goods and services over the internet both domestically and internationally. Companies like Facebook and Google, providing access to billions of users across the world, earn massive revenues from businesses advertising and promoting their products.

Along with its own software, Apple designs and manufactures iPhones, iPads, Macs, and televisions with devices using the Apple operating system. It sells worldwide online as well as

through more than 450 stores in 18 countries (The Balance 20 November 2017). Globally, the company has successfully marketed digital services from its App Store, iTunes Store, Apple Music Subscriptions, iCloud Storage Costs, and AppleCare (TechCrunch 2 May 2017). In 2017, Apple held almost 15 per cent of the global smartphone market (IDC 13 December 2017).

Apple also operates in financial services with Apple Pay.

Opportunities

Globalization creates great opportunities for corporations like Apple to expand sales and profits by tapping into new markets and signing up new suppliers. Apple takes most of its supplies from outside the USA. Over 700 non-US companies supply Apple with China alone accounting for almost half (Compare Camp 6 December 2017; Figure 4.1).

High economic growth in developing countries and increasing access to mobile technology, particularly in Asia, has created new, fast-growing markets for Apple's products.

Countries increasingly compete with one another to offer ever-lower rates of tax on profits. The ease of moving money internationally has allowed Apple and companies like Google, Amazon, Microsoft, Nike, and Uber to shift profits from high tax countries to those with low taxes or no taxes at all. Apple's reluctance to repatriate profits earned outside the USA because of the relatively high rate of US profit tax, led to the company holding some $252 billion offshore in tax havens such as Ireland (International Consortium of Investigative Journalists [ICIJ] 2017).

Apple adopts strategies allowing it to exploit such opportunities and, in the process, has become the biggest global firm as measured by its stock exchange value, which exceeded $900 billion in 2017 (Bloomberg 3 November 2017). In 2017, Apple recorded profits of $48 billion on sales of more than $229 billion (Apple 2017).

Challenges

Apple also faces challenges in its political and legal environments. Internationally, political pressure is building up to clamp down on tax avoidance (see OECD n.d.). In 2016, the EU introduced measures to reduce tax avoidance by multinationals with member states agreeing to extend their sharing of tax-related information. The Commission, concerned that Apple was aggressively avoiding tax by shifting profits to low tax Ireland, ruled that it pay Ireland some €13 billion (European →

→

Figure 4.1 Number of Apple suppliers by country

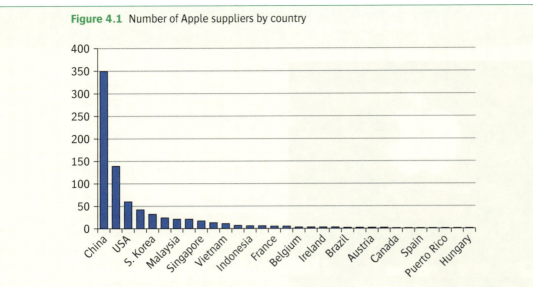

Source: Compare Camp (6 December 2017)

Commission (2016a,b and 2017a,b)) (see Mini Case Study 10.4 Apple versus the European Commission). The company is also under pressure in the USA where a US Senate Committee (US Permanent Subcommittee on Investigations 2013) concluded that it was not paying any tax on its overseas operation. Apple was also targeted by President Trump who threatened to stop the company making iPhones in China and forcing it to build factories in the USA (*Fortune* 19 January 2016; *New York Times* 23 November 2016).

Apple is subject to laws and regulations worldwide which can change and adversely affect the business. For example, there is increasing concern in many countries regarding personal data protection. Apple's multinational operations result in a great deal of customer data being transferred across borders. A new EU

regulation in 2018 on data protection could make the transfer of such data more difficult and costly for the company (European Commission n.d.; see Mini Case Study 4.2 The Law and Personal Data). Breaches of the regulation can result in fines of up to 4 per cent of worldwide turnover, which would amount to $9 billion of Apple's 2017 sales (Moore Stephens UK 2017).

Sources: Apple SEC 2017 10-K filing; The Balance 20 November 2017; Bloomberg 3 November 2017; Compare Camp 6 December 2017; European Commission (2016a) IP 16/2923; European Commission (2017) IP/37/3702; Fortune 19 January 2016; ICIJ (2017); *New York Times* 23 November 2016; Moore Stephens UK (2017); OECD n.d.; TechCrunch 2 May 2017; US Permanent Subcommittee on Investigations 2013. https://techcrunch.com

Introduction

In this chapter, we shall examine the global **macro-environment** and the tools that firms use to analyse it. By macro-environment, we mean the wider external (or general) environment rather than the micro-environment (sometimes referred to as the task environment or industry analysis), the subject of Chapter 3. In this chapter, we will refer to the macro-environment as the 'external environment'. The external environment is changing radically and becoming much less predictable due to:

- the accelerating rate of globalization;
- the information technology revolution;
- the increasing economic and political weight of countries such as China, India, and Russia;

- international institutions like the WTO and the EU becoming increasingly important influences on the global environment; as have **non-governmental organizations (NGOs)** with their vocal opposition to free trade and investment, and their success in getting environmental issues, such as climate change, onto the political agenda of national governments and international agencies.

Firms face great difficulty in monitoring, analysing, and responding to an external environment subject to literally thousands of different forces, both domestic and international. The increasing pace of globalization in recent decades has made the task of monitoring a turbulent external environment much more complex. Firms can find themselves operating in countries with very disparate histories, political and legal institutions and processes, economic, financial, and socio-cultural environments, and physical and technological infrastructures. Firms have to be prepared to cope with various languages, different trading rules and currencies, and volatile exchange rates. Given this complexity, organizations may find it difficult to identify forces that could have a critical impact, as opposed to those that can be safely ignored. This ability to evaluate the external forces is vital because the environment creates opportunities for firms to achieve crucial objectives, such as profits and growth. However, it can also pose dangers to firms that could result, ultimately, in them failing. At the global level, the external environment can force organizations to alter policies on prices, modify products, and adapt promotional policies. It may oblige them to restructure the organization, to change strategies regarding moves into new product or geographical markets, and it can make them vulnerable to take-over.

The External Environment

The external environment of the firm comprises all the external influences that affect its decisions and performance. Such influences can vary from firm to firm and industry to industry and can change, sometimes very rapidly, over time. According to many observers, the environment for international business is changing faster than ever in two particular aspects: complexity and turbulence. Complexity relates to the increasing diversity of customers, rivals, and suppliers, and of socio-cultural, political, legal, and technological elements confronting international business. Complexity is increased by the forces in the external environment continuously interacting with, and affecting, each other. An increasingly complex external environment makes it more difficult for firms to make sense of, and to evaluate, information on changes in the environment, and to anticipate their impact on the business. This, in turn, makes it more of a problem formulating an appropriate response. The problems created by complexity are aggravated by the growing turbulence of the environment. A turbulent environment is one where there is rapid, unexpected change, in contrast to a stable environment where change is slow and predictable. Turbulence has increased with the rapid widening and deepening of the political, economic, socio-cultural, and technological interconnections brought about by globalization and facilitated by advances in telecommunications.

What was a fairly static environment may become turbulent, uncertain and subject to violent change. In 2016, Donald Trump was elected US president while threatening to start a trade war with China, which he claimed was destroying American jobs through unfair competition. This raised fears amongst big merchandise importers like Wal-mart, Nike, and Apple that their ability to import from China would be seriously curtailed. Similarly they were concerned that China might retaliate by restricting their access to the Chinese market and by attacking their production and selling operations there. President Trump's protectionist rhetoric also alarmed foreign MNCs like Korea's Samsung exporting large volumes of goods such as smartphones to the USA (*Financial Times* 31 January 2017; CNBC 7 November 2017).

Business operating on a purely domestic basis is likely to confront a safer environment than its international counterparts. Some firms, like small local retail establishments, face a relatively simple and certain environment whereas multinationals, like Nestlé, operating in almost 100 countries, have to deal with one that is much more dynamic, complex, and, in some cases, dangerous and uncertain.

Growing complexity and turbulence in the environment makes it more difficult for firms to predict demand. It leads to competition becoming more disorderly, shortens the time available to make decisions, increases the risk of product obsolescence, and forces business to speed up the innovation process. Mason (2007) suggests that most managers have not been trained to cope with an environment of complexity, uncertainty, and turbulence and goes on to claim that such an environment is not conducive to traditional authoritarian, top-down, command and control styles of management.

However, it would be unwise to see firms as simply being the subject of the macro-environment. Business, especially big businesses like Microsoft, General Electric, ExxonMobil, JP Morgan, and Deutsche Bank, can exercise influence over their macro-environment. In his election campaign, Donald Trump, vowed to abolish a tax break enjoyed by hedge funds and private equity firms, saying 'They make a fortune, they pay no tax . . . They have to pay taxes.' (*New York Times* 22 December 2017). Yet the tax break remained in the president's first tax reform due to the lobbying power of these financial institutions in Washington (*Financial Times* 23 December 2016). Another example was Apple persuading the US government to intervene on its behalf when the EU imposed a fine of €13 billion (see opening Case Study).

Mini Case Study 4.1 Brexit, uncertainty, and finance

In 2016, the UK vote to leave the EU created great uncertainty both for British and foreign business engaged in trade, investment, and the cross border movement of workers. The UK financial sector (FS) was particularly concerned about Brexit on a number of grounds. Continued barrier-free access to the EU market was regarded as vital because 5,500 UK financial institutions operated freely in the union using the EU passport system. Similarly, more than 8000 EU passport-holding firms could operate freely in the UK (*The Guardian* 22 February 2017). The FS was also concerned about Brexit restricting its ability to recruit finance workers from across the EU (CityUK 2017a; UK Finance 2017).

The consulting firm PwC (2016) concluded that:

- the UK FS would be hit harder by Brexit than the UK economy as a whole;

- its growth would slow down;
- employment would reduce significantly;
- some institutions might move to other locations in the EU to maintain access to the single market; and
- barriers to the EU market might also deter foreign financial institutions from locating in the UK.

The FS, through bodies like CityUK, set out to influence UK government Brexit negotiations with the EU. It highlighted the sector's importance to the UK economy, accounting for around 11 per cent of GDP, employing over 2 million workers, paying the largest tax bill; and being the biggest exporting sector, running an annual surplus of £20 billion (CityUK 2017b; PwC 2016).

The FS argued that after the UK left the EU in March 2019 there should be a clear transitional arrangement between ➡

→ withdrawal and the start of the new trading relationship. Once a new relationship was struck, it wanted time to be given for financial institutions, their customers, and their regulators to adapt their organizations in preparation for the new rules and regulations (CityUK 2017a). In the absence of passporting, CityUK (2017a) argued for equivalent regulations allowing UK institutions to operate freely in the EU. UK Finance, another lobbying body, looked forward to an arrangement where the EU and the UK remained as closely connected as possible, politically, economically and socially.

Sources: CityUK (2017a, 2017b); *The Guardian* 22 February 2017; PwC (2016); UK Finance (2017).

Questions
1. Why are UK and EU financial institutions concerned about Brexit?
2. A report by Global Justice Now and Corporate Europe Observatory reported that banks and big business lobbying were exerting a dominant influence on UK negotiators. Find out:
   a) Who in the financial sector was lobbying the UK government?
   b) How the financial sector went about lobbying the UK government?
   c) To what extent the FS was successful in achieving its objectives as set out in the case study.

See Global Justice (2017); *Independent* (2017)

Opportunities and Threats

Globalization, associated with the increased cross-border movement of goods, services, capital, and people, is creating a more closely interdependent world and has been a major influence in shaping the external environment of business. The widening and deepening of globalization means that local environments are not solely shaped by domestic events. Equally, increased interdependence causes local, regional, or national events, such as the 2007 **credit crunch**, which originated in the USA, the outbreak of Ebola in Africa, and wars in the Middle East and conflict in Myanmar causing massive movements of people across borders, to become global problems. Increasing interconnectedness means that threats and opportunities are magnified, especially for organizations operating internationally.

 Learning Task

Companies such as Google, Uber, Tesla, and big carmakers such as VW are spending much time and money developing self-driving vehicles.

1. What issues do these companies face before being able to launch self-driving vehicles into the market? See: *New York Times* 7 June 2017 and Live Science 14 May 2015.
2. Assuming that self-driving vehicles become the norm, discuss the implications for:
   a) firms providing road transport and taxi services; and
   b) companies selling vehicle insurance. See Actuarial Post (n.d.) and *Harvard Business Review* 5 December 2017.

Opportunities

Globalization generates opportunities for business to enter new markets, take advantage of differences in the costs and quality of labour and other resources, gain economies of scale, and get access to raw materials. Over the last decade, China and India have opened up their economies to foreign trade and investment. Foreign companies, including Tesco, Heineken, Disney, General Motors, and Toyota, have taken advantage of the opportunity to invest in China and India.

Many firms have responded to the new environment by globalizing production and reorganizing their supply chains to take advantage of low-cost labour, cheap international transport, and less regulated operating environments. Wal-mart, the largest retailer in the world, has located its global procurement headquarters in China, and purchases many of its supplies of toys, clothes, and electronic goods there. Other large retail multinationals, like Carrefour and Auchan of France, Metro in Germany, Makro of the Netherlands, UK-based B&Q, IKEA of Sweden, and the US firm Home Depot, have also sourced extensively from China. Zara, the very successful multination Spanish maker and retailer of fashion clothing, originally sourced supplies locally. Subsequently, it purchased its fabrics from more distant suppliers in Morocco, the Middle East, and India (Coe et al. 2007; Jonsson and Tolstoy 2013).

The growth of world trade and the development of international supply chains have been facilitated by the advent of shipping containers, which have significantly reduced the costs of transport. The growth in world trade in goods has resulted, according to the World Bank, in the growth of container trips from around 200 million units per year in 2000 to over 700 million in 2016 (World Bank n.d.). Researchers found that containerization had boosted trade by almost 800 per cent over 20 years (*The Economist* 22 May 2013). According to Harford (2017), the container has been the biggest enabler of global merchandise trade.

Threats

Globalization is also accompanied by threats that can have devastating effects on business, causing long-term damage or even leading to the collapse of the business. In the past, threats for international firms tended to be seen as country-specific, arising from:

- financial risks—for example, currency crises, **inflation**;
- political risks associated with events such as expropriation of assets by foreign governments or unwelcome regulations; and
- natural disasters such as earthquakes and tsunamis.

For example, the 1999 earthquake in Taiwan cut the supply of computer chips to HP, Dell, and Compaq, and the Chinese earthquake in 2008 forced Toyota to halt production there. In 2011 the Japanese earthquake and tsunami restricted the flow of many components to industry around the world, and later that year Thailand, a hub for electronic and car parts, suffered from severe floods. In 2014, riots in Vietnam targeted crucial manufacturing centres owned by Chinese and other foreign companies, disrupting global supply chains. This was in a country viewed as stable and an attractive alternative to China. However, there is now an additional set of cross-border threats—these include terrorism, hacker attacks on computer networks, global warming and global diseases such as Aids, bird flu, and the Ebola virus.

Learning Task

Global warming is forecast to cause unprecedented heat waves, drought, rising sea levels and flooding of coastal cities leading to the displacement of millions of people (see Wuebbles et al. (2017); *The Guardian* 18 January 2018). It is also reported that the number of dead zones in the sea without oxygen has quadrupled since 1950 (Breitburg et al. (2018)).

1. In developing countries, what are the potential implications of:
   a) droughts for farmers and food supplies?
   b) rising sea levels and the increasing numbers of dead zones on the fishing and fish processing industries? For a useful discussion, see the IMF's World Economic Outlook October 2017.
2. Now consider the possible implications of rising sea levels for construction firms in rich countries.

Terrorists are more likely to attack business than other targets, particularly US business. The British Standards Institute (2017) reported that terrorist attacks on supply chains had reached their highest ever and were increasing at an annual rate of 16 per cent. Attacks included the sabotage of oil pipes, hijacking, and the theft of cargoes. Terrorists were also involved in smuggling, extortion and kidnapping schemes. Attacks can impose significant costs on businesses through disruption of supply chains. This could result in shortages or delays in critical inputs, and could cause a threat to their reputations. In addition, governments may adopt policies to deal with terrorism that alter the business environment and the ease with which global commerce takes place, for example at ports and airports. FDI inflows and revenues from tourism may also decline as a result of high rates of global terrorism as observed in Egypt, Libya, Turkey, Latin America, Middle East, and Pakistan (see latest web edition of the Global Terrorism Index).

As firms become more international, they become more vulnerable to threats. For example, with the move towards global sourcing, supply chains can become stretched as they straddle multiple borders and involve more parties (see Khan and Yurt 2011 for a discussion of global sourcing and its risks). This leaves the supply chain more liable to disruption. The 9/11 terrorist attacks led the USA, along with other governments, to tighten up on security at ports. This resulted in a more rigorous inspection of cargoes, which led to increased delivery times. As a result, costs rose for firms that, often facing fiercer competition as a result of globalization, were trying to reduce delivery times and minimize stockholding through the introduction of just-in-time. It also raised costs for shipping firms as it increased the time taken to turn round their vessels.

Another effect of 9/11 was to make it more difficult, and sometimes even impossible, to get insurance cover. Enderwick (2006) reports that Delta Airlines' insurance premium against terrorism in 2002 rose from US$2 million to US$152 million after the attack. In a survey (by Marsh), it was found that more than 60 per cent of US businesses bought insurance cover against terrorism. (You can view The Marsh Report, 2016 Terrorism Risk Insurance through the link in the book's **online resources**.) In 2002 the American government introduced the Terrorism Risk Insurance Act to support the insurance industry providing cover for loss from terrorist acts as losses from terrorism are difficult to predict and quantify and therefore probably uninsurable. This was supposed to be a temporary measure; however, it was extended in 2015 to 2020, even though no claims have been paid.

Increased international sourcing of supplies means that firms need to pay particular attention to the maintenance of quality standards. Boeing, the giant US aircraft maker, decided to out-source 70 per cent of its innovative 787 airliner to local and international suppliers. It hoped that this would make it more competitive against its major competitor Airbus by cutting the time taken to develop the airliner from six to four years and the cost from $10 billion to $6 billion. However, managing such a technologically advanced project would have been challenging sim-ply dealing with domestic never mind foreign suppliers. In the event, the project ran billions of dollars over budget and three years behind schedule. Boeing failed to plan adequately for the potential risks and costs associated with outsourcing such a technically ground-breaking air-craft. The company did not coordinate suppliers well enough, relied on electronic communica-tions with them, and failed to provide suppliers with sufficient on-the-ground technical support. Soon after the launch of the airliner, it ran into problems including battery fires that grounded the whole fleet for three months, cracks in the windshield, fuel leaks, and brake and engine fail-ures (*Forbes* 17 and 21 January 2013).

Threats for some firms and industries can be opportunities for others. In 2005, the US states of Florida and Louisiana, along with the Gulf of Mexico, were devastated by several hurricanes—the city of New Orleans had to be evacuated. Oil firms, operating in the Gulf, suffered extreme losses because of extensive damage to oilrigs and onshore pipelines and refineries. The supply of oil was adversely affected and prices rose, hitting big consumers of oil such as shipping and air-line companies. On the other hand, some firms benefited. With power lines down, and many houses destroyed, producers of portable power generators experienced a surge in demand, as did producers of mobile homes. In 2006, Shell, which had only suffered limited hurricane dam-age, announced its largest profits ever. The Japanese Tsunami in 2011 caused widespread dam-age and estimates are that reconstruction will cost £181 billion over a decade, good news for construction companies. Most nuclear plants have remained closed and some companies are planning safer and cleaner methods of power generation, such as solar plants.

Financial risks have become increasingly important because, over the last 40 years, there have been increasing levels of volatility in financial markets. Unexpected movements in exchange rates, interest rates, and commodity and equity prices are major sources of risk for most MNCs. Surveys show that many large MNCs see the management of foreign exchange risks to be as important as the management of other risks.

Mini Case Study 4.2 **The law and personal data**

Business is subject to the laws and legal regulations of the countries where they operate. The growth of e-commerce has allowed firms to accumulate masses of personal customer data, which is often passed on to other companies. For example, John Lewis, the large UK-based retailer, transfers personal data to a variety of other business organizations, including Google, Facebook, and Adobe Analytics (*Financial Times* 6 January 2018). Scene7, an Adobe subsidiary, helps retailers such as John Lewis attract and retain customers by building customer pro-files, steering customers to the right products, producing per-sonalized, targeted email and print materials, and configuring visual product images for online display. Retail client data pro-files, supplemented by information from social media sites, apps, and search engine queries, can be sold on to other com-panies who use them to target goods and services at particular customers.   ➔

➔   In 2018, business faced a major change in EU law when the General Data Protection Regulation came into force. The new regulation came about because of increasing concern in the EU about breaches of privacy related to the online collection, transfer and use of personal data (European Commission 2015; see Mini Case Study 10.3 Facebook and the Law).

The Regulation:

- gives customers the right to: access their data; deny the right to share their data; compensation if they suffer any damage from businesses breaching the Regulation;
- obliges business to give its customers much more information about which companies are sharing their data, and what is being done with the data;
- compels firms to ensure data is accurate and up to date;
- prohibits firms basing any evaluation of individuals on the basis of the data alone as regards their performance at work, creditworthiness, conduct or reliability;
- requires firms to build in data protection safeguards at the design stage of goods and services; and
- insists that data can only be transferred to non-EU states having an equivalent level of data protection.

Previously, EU data protection law varied from one member state to another, creating administrative burdens for businesses. The EU argued that harmonizing the legal position across the union would establish a single set of rules making it simpler and cheaper to do business with claimed savings of €2.3 billion per year. Business would be dealing with one regulator rather than multiple supervisory bodies. There would be a consistent application and enforcement of the law, legal uncertainty removed, and barriers to trade in the single market reduced (European Commission 2012).

Sources: CX Network 1 November 2017 and 11 August 2017; European Commission (2012); European Commission (2015, 2017a); *Financial Times* 6 January 2018; http://www.adobe.com 19 January 2018

Questions

1. Weigh up the pros and cons of the Regulation from the point of view of:
   a. company costs; and
   b. foreign MNCs like China's Huawei operating in the EU.
2. Surveys show that around one-third of customers are reluctant to share their data (CX Network 11 August 2017). *The Financial Times* (6 January 2018) reported that a large majority of professionals in the retail and advertising technology sectors would not agree to their personal data being shared with other firms. Comment on this and discuss the implications for e-commerce firms.
3. An Aldermore bank 2017 survey showed that nearly half of UK small and medium sized enterprises (SMEs) had not heard of the Regulation, while a survey of UK retail websites found that all would have breached the Regulation requirements (Aldermore 14 September 2017; *Financial Times* 6 January 2018).
   a. Why might UK SMEs be ignorant of the Regulation?
   b. Assess whether these firms need to worry about the Regulation, given the UK's impending withdrawal from the EU.

There are various overlapping risks associated with exchange rate movements that need to be managed. Contractual risk occurs when firms enter into contracts where the revenues or outgoings take place in a foreign currency. A Eurozone firm may agree to buy a good from a US supplier and pay in dollars, or may accept dollars in payment from US customers. If the dollar falls against the euro, then purchasers in the Eurozone benefit because they need to exchange fewer euros to buy the goods. On the other hand, French champagne producers, selling to the USA, will lose out because the dollars they receive will buy fewer euros.

The next risk arises when firms earn money abroad and have to translate that into their domestic currency for the purposes of the reports and accounts. Movements in the exchange rate could have a major impact on the profit and loss account and on the balance sheet value of assets held abroad. Mazda, the Japanese car maker saw, despite a rise in sales, 2016 final quarterly profits fall by 71 per cent largely as a result of the appreciation of the Japanese yen against other currencies (*Automotive News* 2 February 2017). In 2014, China's major state airline suffered big exchange losses because of the weakness of the Renminbi. When buying aircraft they take on finance denominated in US dollars so when their currency declines their debts grow.

Fluctuations in exchange rates make it difficult to evaluate company performance. Some companies get round this by stripping out the effects of movements in rates by translating the current year's turnover and operating profit using the previous year's exchange rate, or stating the sales and profits in the appropriate foreign currencies or, like Unilever, stating how much sales or profits were reduced or increased as a result of exchange rate changes.

Scanning the Environment

Big international firms spend time and resources regularly scanning their environment in order to identify forces that will have a major influence on them. In particular, they will be looking out for changes in the environment that could have an impact on their operations in terms of helping or hindering them to achieve their objectives. These objectives, for industrial and commercial firms, usually include profits and growth; firms may also set themselves targets with regard to market share or becoming the leading brand. Thus, firms will be particularly sensitive to aspects of the external environment that will affect their ability to achieve their objectives.

This scanning of the external environment is part of what is known as 'strategy', that is the process by which firms arrive at decisions about the direction the firm should take. Essential parts of that process are understanding the goals of the organization and analysing the resources and capabilities of the firm and the external environment. Indeed, strategy is the link between these elements.

Thinking about strategic management has gone through several phases. In the fifties and sixties, when the external environment was much more stable, the emphasis was on planning, with detailed operational plans being set typically for five years ahead. Instability in the macro-environment in the seventies made forecasting difficult and so the emphasis changed from planning to positioning the firm in the market to maximize the potential for profit using techniques such as Porter's Five Forces (see Chapter 3). This became known as the industry based view (IBV), emphasizing that a firm's performance was determined by the macro- and micro-environment. In the nineties, the emphasis shifted again from external analysis to internal analysis of resources and capabilities in order to identify what was different about the firm and to look at ways of exploiting those differences—the resource based view (RBV). In the first decade of this century, change, as noted in the Introduction to this chapter, is much less predictable and so there is now increasing emphasis on flexibility and creating short term, rather than sustained, competitive advantage often in alliances with other organizations (see Grant and Jordan 2015: Chapter 1). It could be argued, then, that knowledge of the external environment and identification of the main drivers of change for the organization are more important than ever. Indeed, strategy must start from an understanding of the major trends in society, where your markets are going to be, who your suppliers will be and where, what new technology is on the horizon, and how it will affect products and processes and the way you organize your business (see Figure 4.2).

The role of business in society has also been questioned after corporate scandals such as the Volkswagen emissions case and the impact of business on the natural environment that strategists must consider (see closing Case Study in Chapter 11). This questions whether business exists simply to make profits for owners (or increased shareholder value) or if there should be some wider purpose in serving society. At the heart of this debate is the notion of stakeholders.

Figure 4.2 Strategy

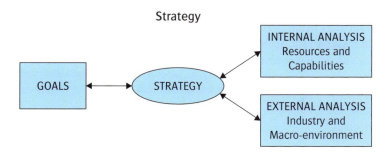

According to Freeman (1984), a stakeholder is any individual, group, or organization that is affected by or can affect the activities of a business (visit the **online resources** for a video of Freeman explaining stakeholder theory). Therefore, they have an interest in the decisions of the business, and equally, it is argued, the determination of strategy should take into account the actions and wishes of stakeholders. This would be true whatever the motivations of the firm. However, for those who argue that firms should have an obligation to society other than their economic role in maximizing shareholder value, the recognition of who and what is affected is fundamental to the realization of that obligation (see Chapter 6 for a much fuller discussion of the debates around corporate social responsibility and Chapter 12 for an analysis of the relationship between business and ecology). Stakeholder analysis, or mapping, aims to identify a firm's stakeholders likely to be affected by the activities and outcomes of the firm's decisions and to assess how those stakeholders are likely to be affected.

Counterpoint Box 4.1 Brexit—hard or soft

The decision by the UK in 2016 to withdraw from the European Union signified major changes in the business environment for both UK and foreign firms. It led to an intense debate between those wishing a 'hard' and those preferring a 'soft' Brexit both of which would have very different consequences for business.

During the referendum, the leave side campaigned on the need for the UK to take back control of immigration, and law making, and on the financial benefits of cutting contributions to the EU budget. They argued that the UK would prosper economically outside the EU. Hard Brexiteers such as Liam Fox, the UK Secretary of State for International Trade who is a passionate believer in free trade, favoured leaving the EU single market and the customs union giving the UK freedom to strike trade deals with fast growing markets in Asia. He envisaged signing 40 new trade deals with non-EU countries the minute after withdrawal in March 2019. Post-Brexit, he foresaw 'an exhilarating, empowering and liberating time' with the UK being enabled to 'liberate global trade' and to resist 'the shadows of protectionism'. Brexiteers further contended that EU members running trade surpluses with the UK, such as Germany, would put pressure on the EU to negotiate a trade deal favourable to Britain. Some Brexit-supporting economists urged the UK, post-Brexit, to remove all trade barriers against the rest of the world, leaving other countries to decide whether to protect their domestic industry from UK exports. They claimed that this would benefit the UK economy to the tune of £135 billion.

Soft Brexiteers wished to maintain close economic ties with the EU by remaining in both the trade barrier-free single market and customs union, allowing the UK to trade freely with fellow members in the UK's biggest export market. Leaving the single market and customs union, they contended, could result in UK exports facing tariff and non-tariff barriers when selling into the EU. This would reduce trade with the EU and, given that less trade is associated with lower productivity, adversely affect →

→ living standards. Complex cross-border EU supply chains set up by, for example the car industry, would be disrupted and investment by foreign MNCs using the UK as a gateway to EU markets deterred They pointed out that the EU did not hinder trade with non-members citing Germany's exporting successes in China as a case in point. Furthermore, negotiating new trade deals with many countries could be a long-drawn-out process, and could result in a lowering of food safety and environmental standards and a deterioration in workers' rights.

Sources: BBC Radio 4 Today, 24 January 2018; *Business Insider,* 2 October 2017; Dhingra et al. (2016); *Financial Times* 27 June (2016); Fox (2016); House of Commons Library (2017); PIIE (2016); Minford (2017).

Questions

1. Some 'hard' Brexiteers want the UK post Brexit to:
   a. remove all trade barriers
   b. cut the flow of low skilled migrant workers from the EU

   Assess the implications of these for British farmers facing tariffs on their exports to the EU and fiercer competition from countries such as Argentina and the USA.

   See: the websites of the National Farmers Union and the CBI on Brexit; House of Commons Library 'Migrant workers in Agriculture' Briefing paper 7987 4 July 2017; information on EU tariffs at http://www.adas.uk/News/agricultural-trade-arrangements-with-eu-and-non-eu-countries; and the EU Meat Market Observatory web site for price comparisons.

2. Assess the likelihood of the UK negotiating and implementing a quick trade deal with the USA. What issues might slow down the process?

   See: Pieterson Institute of International Economics (PIIE) at http://piie.com/blogs/trade-investment-policy-watch/how-long-does-it-take-conclude-trade-agreement-us; Trade Justice Movement's UK_US trade deal at tjm.org.uk/trade-deals/a-uk-us-trade-deal; the article by the head of the British Chambers of Commerce at http://www.theguardian.com/commentisfree/2017/jul/22/rushing-into-trade-deal-with-us-would-harm-uk; *Financial Times* 23 October 2017 at http://www.ft.com/content/2f8c8a8a-b711-11e7-8c12-5661783e5589; CNN at https://edition.cnn.com/specials/politics/congress-capitol-hill; ITV News at http://www.itv.com/news/2018-01-25/theresa-may-donald-trump-davos/; the *Independent* at http://www.independent.co.uk/news/uk/politics/brexit-latest-trade-deal-liam-fox-uk-us-24-july-a7815,751.html.

Post et al. (2002), embracing the concept of the stakeholder, put forward a new strategic approach to managing what they called the 'Extended Enterprise' (see Figure 4.3). They stressed the role of recognizing stakeholder relationships in managing wealth creation in today's complex 'extended enterprise'. This approach recognized the futility of the controversy between those who preached the RBV rather than the IBV approach to strategy and that both of those approaches ignored the socio-political environment. This approach, it is claimed, integrates all three aspects. It recognizes that a network of relationships exists that is not just a matter of contracts, but also needs to be managed through building relationships and that these relationships exist not just between the organization and its stakeholders but also between stakeholders. For this, they put forward a new definition of stakeholders as:

> individuals and constituencies that contribute, either voluntarily or involuntarily, to its wealth-creating capacity and activities, and who are therefore its potential beneficiaries and/or risk bearers.

Stakeholders for each firm will differ, but Post et al. put forward typical groups within each of the three dimensions as demonstrated in Figure 4.3.

This idea of the extended enterprise, along with the industry structure (see Chapter 3), provides a useful framework for assessing the impact of changes in the external macro-environment on the structure of the industry and ultimately on the stakeholders of the organization. This approach

Figure 4.3 The stakeholder view of the corporation

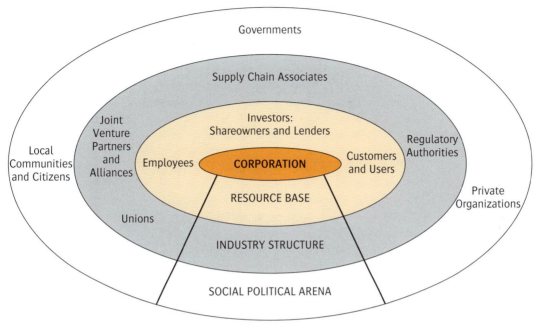

Source: Post, Preston, and Sachs (2002)

could also be used for assessing the impact of particular courses of action or future scenarios. The steps are:

1. Identify the macro-environmental issues.
2. Assess the urgency and likely occurrence of the issues.
3. Analyse the impact on the structure of the industry.
4. Identify the relevant stakeholders.
5. Identify the most important by assessing their impact on the organization.
6. Assess the impact of the issue on each of the stakeholders.

One method of classifying the importance of stakeholders is to map them on to a 2 × 2 matrix according to their power and their interest. Those with the highest level of power and interest are the key stakeholders and need most attention. Others will need to be kept satisfied or informed (see Figure 4.4).

Learning Task

Shell and BP work in the very sensitive area of non-renewable resources and therefore have to be aware of the negative impacts their operations might cause. Choose one of these companies and:

1. Identify their stakeholders, classifying them into the various categories of the extended enterprise.
2. Construct a stakeholder map such as that in Figure 4.4.

Figure 4.4 Stakeholder mapping

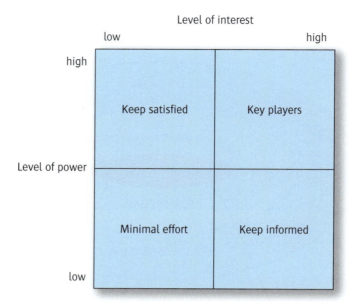

Source: Adapted from A. Mendelow, 'Proceedings of the Second International Conference on Information Systems', Cambridge, MA (1991).

Of course, the situation regarding stakeholders is not a static one, and stakeholder positions change according to the situation. Firms involved in stakeholder engagement keep up a constant dialogue with their stakeholders. Royal Dutch Shell, for example, has incorporated responsibilities to its stakeholders into its Business Principles. Visit the **online resources** for a link to Principle 7, Communication and Engagement, on this topic.

Following embarrassing experiences in the 1990s over the proposed disposal of the Brent Spar Oil storage terminal by sinking it in the sea, and its relationships with the Nigerian government and local communities in Nigeria, Shell now make it a requirement that any new project has a stakeholder engagement plan. Shell, in the decommissioning of the Brent Oil and Gas Field, held a series of meetings with over 140 invited stakeholders and published a series of e-newsletters.

Shell and other organizations make full use of social media to keep in touch with their stakeholders by developing surveys, websites, chat rooms, emails, e-newsletters, bulletin boards, blogs, and podcasts.

This **impact analysis**, when done early enough, allows firms the time to consider a range of responses to exploit the opportunities and defuse the threats. This helps organizations recognize and adapt policies and strategies to their changing regional, national, and global environments. Because of increasing volatility and turbulence in the external environment, firms must expect/prepare for the unexpected. Kotler and Caslione (2009) claim that turbulence, with its consequent chaos, risk, and uncertainty, is now the 'new normality' for industries, markets, and companies. Globalization, together with communications technology, mean the world is now, as we noted in Chapter 1, more interdependent than ever, meaning that change in one country can soon lead to change in many others. According to Kotler and Caslione, the factors that can cause chaos are:

- the **information revolution** and especially cloud technology, which allows instant and flexible access to sophisticated software and data storage, especially useful for new firms;
- disruptive technologies and innovations which quickly render 'old' technologies/products redundant;
- the 'rise of the rest'—a rebalancing of economic power around the world; for example, from the West to China and India;
- hyper-competition—a situation in which competitive advantage is short lived;
- sovereign wealth funds—trillions of US$ owned by states such as China, Singapore, Abu Dhabi, and Kuwait and available for overseas investment purposes, increasing the role of some states in other economies;
- the environment—and especially the need to preserve scarce resources and deal with the effects of climate change; and
- consumer and stakeholder empowerment gained through the information revolution.

Kotler and Caslione state that 'even more unsettling is the harsh recognition that whenever chaos arrives, you'll have little more than a fig leaf to hide behind—unless you can anticipate it and react fast enough to lead your company, your business unit, your region, or your department through it safely' (2009: 11).

Much of the above accords with McKinsey's assessment of the key trends in global forces. They identify five forces, which they label as follows:

- The 'great rebalancing', which, as we have noted, refers to the likelihood that most growth will come from emerging markets that will create a wave of new middle class consumers (as we saw in Chapter 2) and new innovations in product design, market infrastructure, and value chains.
- The productivity imperative—to continue to grow, developed economies will need to generate major gains in productivity.
- The global grid in which the global economy is ever more connected through vast complex networks. Information barriers break down as the walls between private and public information become blurred and economic volatility becomes more likely. The world, more than ever before, is becoming a single market place.
- Pricing the planet arising from the tension between increasing demand for resources and **sustainability**. This will put pressure on using resources more efficiently, cleanly, and in dealing with new regulations.
- The market state in which the role of the state increases rather than withers in protecting individuals from the effect of globalization, intervening to stabilize economies (as in the recent financial crisis), and in bilateral agreements with multilateral agreements becoming more difficult as more becoming demand their say at places such as the WTO and IMF. (Visit the **online resources** for a useful link related to this topic.)

Given that forecasting and prediction become ever more unreliable in turbulent and chaotic times, one way of anticipating or being prepared for change is through what is known as scenario planning. Scenario planning is an approach to thinking about the future, looking at stories relating different possible futures so that strategic responses can be considered and managers better prepared to deal with the issues. Shell has been developing scenarios since the 1970s, initially on a three-year cycle but now, indicative of the pace of change, annually. They have developed a tool called Global Scenario, which is used to explore various scenarios relating to the legal environment, the role and importance of the market and the state, non-governmental organizations in society, forces bringing about global integration, and the factors leading to fragmentation and economic growth. It is also interested in the impact of the growing concerns about environmental issues, such as global warming, on the demand for fossil fuels such as coal, oil, and gas and consequently produces separate energy scenarios.

From an American perspective, an organization busy developing scenarios is the National Intelligence Council of the USA, which issued a report in 2017 looking at global trends to 2035. A link to this report can be found in the **online resources**. From a European perspective, and concerned with the impact on the environment, the European Environment Agency has made its assessment of global megatrends. It has found 11, which it conveniently organizes into five clusters: political, economic, social, technological, and environmental.

The Macro-environment

Macro-environmental forces comprise the wider influences on the business environment and, together with the micro-environment, complete the external environment (see Figure 4.5). For the purpose of analysis, the macro-environment can be classified under the headings of political and legal, economic and financial, socio-cultural, technological, and ecological. Each of these can be examined as independent elements, but often changes in one area of the external environment can have an impact on others. For example, a government may take a policy decision to carry out a big expansion of public spending on infrastructure. This could influence the economic environment by increasing the total demand for goods and services in the economy and boost the rate of economic growth. If the economy is close to operating at full capacity then it could also lead to an increase in inflation and/or suck in more imports or divert exports to the domestic market. The balance of payments might suffer, which could result in a fall in the exchange rate. An instance of the interconnection between the various elements in the external environment occurred when the Chinese and Indian authorities made a decision to open up their economies to foreign trade and investment. These decisions changed the political environment and helped transform the economic environment as their rates of economic growth soared. This, in turn, had an impact on the micro-environment of business because rapid growth of income and demand for goods and services in China and India made them very attractive markets for foreign firms. On the other hand, the micro-environment can lead to changes in the macro-environment—the credit crunch of 2007–08 led to tighter government regulation of financial services. What is important for the individual firm, of course, is not just to identify the relevant external factors but also to analyse what the implications are of any change for their industry environment and their stakeholders.

Figure 4.5 The external environment

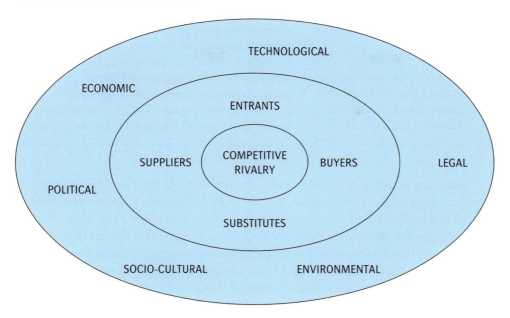

 Mini Case Study 4.3 Brazil—resentment, rage, depression

Brazil's economy is the biggest in Latin America and the world's eighth largest. Although it has a large manufacturing sector exporting substantial quantities of steel, cars, and electronics, the economy is dominated by the service sector. The country has vast natural resources including iron ore, tin, bauxite, manganese, gold, and diamonds, plus one of the world's largest offshore oilfields. Globally, it is a major producer of coffee, fruit, sugar, soya beans, and beef (CIA 2017). While GDP per capita for the population of over 200 million is around $10,000, income inequality, while in decline, is high (Medieros, 2016; IMF 2017). The workforce is highly educated and the financial system is well developed as is the legal system, although the latter is slow-moving (Klotz and Finotti 2016). Brazilian politicians can be reluctant to see foreign firms taking control in certain strategic sectors (*Financial Times* 23 December 2017).

For several years, Brazil has been rocked by corruption scandals involving politicians at the highest levels of the political system. According to Transparency International's 2017 Corruption Perceptions Index, it ranks 79 out of 176. The WEF (2017) reported that corruption was a major factor in doing business in Brazil and that the transparency of government policy making was poor. Directors in Petrobras, the state-owned oil giant, were investigated for accepting billions of dollars-worth of bribes for the award of construction contracts. The former president, Lula Inacio Lula da Silva, was found guilty of accepting an apartment from an engineering firm that had won a Petrobras contract. His political party was accused of using some of the bribes to buy politicians' votes and to fund political campaigns. Michel Temer, who became president in 2016, was charged with receiving money from a large food-processing firm (BBC 2017). However, the constitution requires that politicians and senior officials be tried in the country's higher courts. Their inability to handle the huge number of cases grants corrupt politicians virtual immunity from prosecution (*Financial Times* 2017).

According to Dwyer (2017), corruption has made Brazilians very angry and disillusioned with politicians. This, combined with a deep economic recession has led to the rise of political extremism and to a questioning of the legitimacy of both →

→ the political and legal systems. According to the political scientist, Octavio Neto, 'Brazil today is a country of resentment, rage and depression' (cited in Bloomberg 20 November 2017).

Sources: BBC 12 April, 13 July 2017 http://www.bbc.co.uk; Bloomberg 20 November (2017); CIA 2017; Dwyer (2017); *Financial Times* 23 December 2017; IMF (2017); Klotz and Finotti (2016); Medieros (2016); Transparency International (2017); WEF (2017)

Questions
1. Discuss the attractions of Brazil for foreign MNCs looking for:
   a. markets for their goods and services
   b. production locations
2. Analyse the political, legal, and social factors that might deter those MNCs from engaging with Brazil.
3. In 2017, Boeing was interested taking over Brazil's Embraer, the world's third largest commercial jet maker. Find out what happened and relate it to the case.

Constant monitoring of all external issues might seem desirable, but it would not only be very time consuming but also very expensive. It would probably also result in a mass of information much of which might not be very useful. It is usually sufficient to identify the key drivers of change for an organization and monitor those. We are going to examine each element of the macro-environment in turn, looking in particular at their potential impacts on business. For this, we use PESTLE as an analytical framework. PESTLE is an acronym for the political, economic/financial, social, technological, legal, and ecological factors that fashion the environment within which business operates. This external analysis is often used to identify opportunities (O) and threats (T) which can be combined with an internal analysis of a firm's strengths (S) and weaknesses (W), to produce a SWOT analysis, although internal analysis is not the subject of this book. The second part of this book deals with each section of the PESTLE in much more detail.

Political and Legal Environment

The political and legal environment is made up of the various political and legal systems under which business operates. We treat these together here because political institutions, such as governments and parliaments, pass laws and establish regulations that shape the legal environment within which business operates. The courts, the police, and prisons ensure that the laws are enforced and lawbreakers are punished. Political regimes range from the liberal democratic systems of North America and Europe, to the Communist regimes of China and Vietnam, to military dictatorship in Burma (Chapter 9 deals with political regimes in more depth).

Counterpoint Box 4.2 What's wrong with PESTLE?

It is common to refer to this kind of analysis as a PESTLE (and there are many more acronyms: PEST, PESTEL, EPISTLE, LE PEST C are a few). However, the great danger of this terminology is that the purpose of the analysis is forgotten—that is, to identify key external drivers and their implications for the industry environment and the organization's stakeholders. Too often, the exercise ends up with a long list of external issues with something in each section of the PESTLE, but with no appreciation or analysis of their implications. Moreover, it is often difficult to classify some as say, political, social, legal, or economic. A rise in taxes could be classified in any one of those four categories. The truth is that it does not matter. There does not need to be something →

→ in each section and it does not matter whether issues are political or economic, etc. As long as the main issues are identified and a careful analysis is undertaken of the impact, then that is all that is required. It is also sometimes difficult to classify issues as opportunities or threats as often an issue can be both. Again, it does not matter. Global warming may be a threat in that it is likely to increase energy bills, but it could also be an opportunity in the search for new products and new and more efficient production methods. The same could be said about the classification of internal issues as strengths or weaknesses but that is not the subject of this book.

Question

Identify three external environmental issues and explain how they could be both an opportunity and a threat for business.

Some industries, like oil, need to pay particular attention to their political environment because they operate in a very politically sensitive sector, energy. Politicians and civil servants need to be kept 'on-side' because they are the people who decide whether oil companies are given the opportunity to search for, and exploit, oil reserves. Like other areas of the external environment, the political environment can turn nasty. Countries such as Russia, Venezuela, Bolivia, and Ecuador have been taking back control of their energy reserves from the oil majors. BP is a company with many reasons to nurture relationships with political institutions, and the people within them—it was nationalized in Iran, Iraq, and Nigeria, fined millions of dollars for illegally fixing propane prices in the USA, and for oil spills in Alaska and the Gulf of Mexico. BP reported that the total bill for the 2010 oil spill in the Gulf of Mexico was $62 billion (*Financial Times* 14 July 2016).

Business also often looks to its domestic government to protect it from threats abroad (see next Learning Task). Governments in powerful countries such as the USA can exercise their influence over other countries to provide protection for home-based firms. This is particularly reassuring for MNCs given that the majority of the largest multinationals are based in the USA. However, many see the USA losing position as the dominant world power (WEF 2016; Haass 2008). After the collapse of the Soviet Union, the USA was the dominant economic, political, and military power in the world. However, in the twenty-first century, US dominance is being challenged economically and politically by countries such as China, whose share of the world economy is growing rapidly (for conflicting views of change in the global balance of power, see Wallerstein and Wohlforth (2007)). Going along with this line of reasoning would suggest that the USA will not be able to offer the same degree of protection to its international companies.

Learning Task

Examine Table 4.1, which shows the average level of tariff protection afforded by the authorities in less developed countries (LDCs) and developed economies.

1. Compare and contrast the level of protection given by governments to their domestic producers in developing/emerging economies and developed/rich economies.

2. Discuss the protection given to farmers by developing countries.

   a) Advance reasons for this.

   b) Japan heavily protects its rice farmers. Why should that be the case?   →

→
3. A more detailed breakdown of tariff protection shows that Vietnam provides a very high level of protection to its processed food sector. What are the implications of that level of protection for domestic producers of processed food products in Vietnam, and for foreign food processors wishing to enter the Vietnamese market?

Table 4.1 Average tariffs on imports 2016

	Average tariffs on imports 2016		
	Total	Agriculture	Non-Agriculture
China	9.9	15.5	9.0
India	13.4	32.7	10.2
Japan	4.0	13.4	2.5
Argentina	13.7	10.3	14.3
Nigeria	12.1	15.7	11.5
USA	3.5	3.2	3.2
Vietnam	9.6	16.3	8.5

Source: WTO stat.wto.org/TariffProfile

Firms also have to take account of the increasing importance in the political and legal environment of international institutions like the WTO, the EU, and the substantial number of regional trading blocs that have been established, and bodies such as the International Accounting Standards Board that has the task of setting international accounting standards. Countries get together in the WTO to agree the rules and regulations around international trade and investment. The WTO then acts to ensure respect for the rules. In 2008, a WTO panel ruled, in a case brought by the USA, the EU, and Canada, that China had broken the rules by using tax policy to restrict imports of car parts. In 2016, the WTO found in favour of China in relation to US anti-dumping duties on China's exports of machinery, electronics, and metals (Reuters 19 October 2016).

Saner and Guilherme (2007) point out that the common approach used by the International Monetary Fund and the World Bank towards developing countries included:

- reducing budget deficits by raising taxes and cutting public expenditure;
- giving up control of interest rates;
- reducing barriers to trade and foreign direct investment;
- setting a stable and competitive exchange rate; and
- privatizing public enterprise.

All of these could have significant effects for domestic and foreign firms on the intensity of competition, market shares, prices, costs, and profits. There are signs, though, that the developing world, headed by China, is fighting back. The World Bank 'Doing Business Report' (see Chapter 6) ranks business according to the ease of doing business. China is ranked 78th out of 190 countries (2018) and reflects the fact that a more highly regulated economy scores lowly in the rankings. Critics argue that the rankings have a built-in bias towards deregulation, believing that the private sector is the main driver for growth (see Counterpoint Box 6.1). Opposition to the index comes from China, India, Brazil, and Argentina, among others, and is an indication of the possible shift in power mentioned above (Bretton Woods Project 2017).

Economic and Financial Environment

The economic and financial environment comprises forces that affect large areas of the economy, like the rate of economic growth, interest rates, exchange rates, and inflation, and the policies of domestic and international institutions that influence these economic variables. The rate of economic growth is important for business because it indicates the speed at which the total level of demand for goods and services is changing. In fast-growing economies, income and purchasing power is increasing rapidly, leading to an expansion in demand. By contrast, slow growth means that markets are not expanding so quickly and are therefore not so attractive for business. Institutions like the IMF produce information on the world economy and its component parts. Its figures show that advanced economies have been growing relatively slowly whilst developing countries are expanding at a more rapid rate. Chinese and Indian growth, for example, both topped 6 per cent in 2016, compared with between 2 and 3 per cent for the USA and the Euro area (IMF 2017). The IMF also makes predictions of growth rates that could be of use for business trying to identify which markets will be fastest growing. They estimate that the world economy will grow at an average of over 3 per cent per annum to 2022 but, as we saw in Chapter 2, growth in emerging economies will be faster than growth in advanced economies. China is expected to grow at around 6 per cent per annum and India at more than 7 per cent compared to the USA's 2 per cent (see Figure 4.6). Economic forecasting, however, is a tricky business and figures for future growth are revised regularly.

Figure 4.6 Annual growth rate per cent

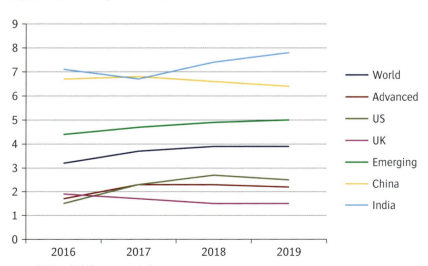

Note: 2018 and 2019 are estimated

Source: IMF World Economic Outlook Database (January 2018)

Learning Task

Using the IMF World Economic Outlook Database, look up the estimated future growth rates for the following countries: Colombia, Indonesia, Vietnam, Egypt, Turkey, and South Africa (the so-called CIVETS countries).

1. Analyse the market implications for foreign producers of telecoms, processed foods, roads, ports, and airports.

Despite the higher rates of economic growth in poorer countries, they still account for a relatively small proportion of world income and purchasing power, indicating that the biggest markets continue to be located in richer regions. IMF data (2017) show that the advanced economies generate 41 per cent of PPP **global income** (down from 69 per cent in 2009). The USA with around 15 per cent of world GDP lags behind China's increasing share of 19 per cent. Japan, Germany, the UK, and France together make up a further 12 per cent of income (see Table 4.2). The biggest economies in Latin America and Africa make up a very small proportion of world income. Brazil and Argentina together account for only around 3 per cent of world income, with Nigeria and South Africa making half of that figure.

Business can also be affected by volatility in the economic and financial environment. In the 20 years after the late 1980s, there were seven periods of turmoil in financial markets, including:

- the US stock market crash of 1987;

- the crisis in the European Monetary System in 1992, when sterling and the Italian lira were removed and several other currencies had to be devalued;

Table 4.2 Total gross domestic product 2017 ($US trillion at current prices)

Ranking	Economy	US$ trillion
1	USA	20.2
2	China	13.1
3	Japan	5.0
4	Germany	3.9
5	France	2.8
6	UK	2.7
7	Brazil	2.2
8	India	2.7
9	Italy	2.1
10	Canada	1.76
	World	79.2
	Advanced	48.6%
	Emerging	31.3%
	sub-Saharan Africa	1.4%

Source: IMF, World Economic Outlook Database (October 2017)

- Russia defaulting on debt repayments and the collapse of Long Term Capital Management in 1998;
- the financial crisis in East Asia of the late 1990s;
- the dotcom crash of 2000;
- the impact of the attacks on the Twin Towers in 2001; and
- the 2007–08 credit crunch.

Such events cause a sudden and, because of globalization, geographically widespread increase in uncertainty in business and finance. Markets become volatile and make the assessment of risk more difficult. As a result, there is a flight from, what are deemed to be, risky to safer assets. Lenders steer away from providing credit to the private sector into lending to governments. It can become more difficult and costly for business and financial institutions to borrow money. Confidence takes a hit, which has a knock-on effect on economic growth because business and consumers become less willing to invest or buy goods and services. The inability to borrow, combined with contracting markets, could result in companies going out of business. These effects can be alleviated, to an extent, when institutions such as central banks, take action to boost confidence by, for instance, reducing interest rates and providing credit to banks, as happened in the USA and the UK during the 2007–08 credit crunch (see Chapter 11 for a more detailed analysis of these events).

Socio-cultural Environment

The socio-cultural environment is concerned with the social organization and structure of society. This includes many social and cultural characteristics, which can vary significantly from one society to another. Social aspects include the distribution of income and wealth, the structures of employment and unemployment, living and working conditions, health, education, population characteristics including size and breakdown by age, gender, and ethnic group, social class, the degree of urbanization, and the provision of welfare for the population in the form of education, health care, unemployment benefits, pensions, and so on. The cultural components cover areas like language, religion, diet, values and norms, attitudes, beliefs and practices, social relationships, how people interact, and lifestyles (for more discussion of the socio-cultural framework see Chapter 7). Responding to cultural differences, whether that is producing packaging in various languages or changing ingredients in food products due to different diets, can incur costs for firms.

Technological Environment

In simple terms, technology refers to the expertise or the pool of ideas or knowledge available to society. Business is particularly interested in advances in knowledge that it can exploit commercially. Technology offers business the prospect of:

- turning new ideas into new or improved products or production techniques;
- entering new markets;
- boosting revenues;

- cutting costs; and

- increasing profits.

However, **technological advance** has been a fundamental force in changing and shaping the patterns of business as regards what it does and how it does it. The advent of microelectronics is a good illustration. In the production process it has cut down the amount of labour and capital required to produce a certain level of output, allowed firms to hold fewer components in stock, improved product quality by increasing the accuracy of production processes and facilitating quality testing, and reduced energy use by replacing machinery with moving parts with microchips (see Chapter 8 for more detailed discussion of the technological framework).

However, technology involves much uncertainty. Firms can pump many resources into research and development, be at the cutting edge of technology with new products that technically excel from those of their competitors, but that does not guarantee success. Big pharmaceutical companies have increased their spending on research and development significantly. In 2017, six of the top 10 R&D spenders were giant ICT companies, four from the USA, one from South Korea, and one from China with the sector spending 18.1 per cent of all R&D spending (European Commission 2017b). The USA is predominant, increasing its share of global R&D from 2007 to 2016 to around 40 per cent, followed by the EU with a stable 26 per cent. Japan's share fell from 24 to 16 per cent while China's rose. The pharmaceutical industry has found it increasingly difficult to make returns on R&D. Deloitte (2017) found that the return on investment had declined from 10.1 per cent in 2010 to 3.2 per cent in 2017, while the cost of launching new medicines had doubled to over from $2 billion and the industry was finding it increasingly difficult to come up with new blockbuster drugs. Deloitte (2017) believes that for the industry to prosper, it must take advantage of the opportunities generated by digital technology such as artificial intelligence and applying advances in automation to clinical trials. (For a more general discussion of the global crisis in R&D, see the Mini Case Study 8.5.)

Mini Case Study 4.4 Technological disruption and the Fang

Digital technology has created opportunities for firms like Facebook, Amazon, Netflix, and Google, sometimes referred to as the Fang, along with companies like Apple, Uber, and Airbnb to offer new services across the globe. This has been facilitated by the increasing international penetration of fixed and mobile broadband, the latter being facilitated by the rising use of smartphones. Figure 4.7 shows the rise in mobile phone subscriptions.

Digital technology has been exploited by the Fang and others. In 2017, Facebook with an app adapted for cheap android smartphones and low bandwidth, had more than 2 billion monthly active users (Zephoria Digital Marketing 21 December 2017). Amazon is the world's 4th biggest in terms of market capitalization and accounts for over 40 per cent of all online sales in the USA (*Business Insider* 7 September 2017). Netflix reported

almost 94 million global subscribers in 2016 (Netflix 2017). Revenues of Google's parent Alphabet rose by almost 40 per cent to over $90 billion between 2014 and 2016 (Alphabet 2017).

Success of the Fang has often been at the expense of traditional business. Through their online distribution systems, they offer vast amounts of content of news, films, music, and goods. The result is a disruption of markets for traditional media and entertainment businesses including newspapers, magazines, books, music, and films. Newspaper and magazine publishers and TV companies have also been hit by Google and Facebook taking a big slice of their advertising revenues. Retailers are particularly vulnerable to competition from companies like Amazon. *The Financial Times* (30 December 2017) reported that at least 50 US retailers had filed for bankruptcy partly due to online ➜

→ competition. The failure of the giant multinational toy retailer, Toys R Us, was the third largest US retail bankruptcy in history. Big UK retailers such as Marks and Spencer and Debenhams are cutting back on the number of high street stores.

Sources: Alphabet (2017); *Business Insider* 7 September 2017, http://uk.businessinsider.com/amazon-size-insane-facts-about-company-2017-9/#75-of-seattles-working-age-population-are-amazon-employees-1; *Financial Times* 30 December 2017;

ITU 2017a; Netflix (2017); Zephoria Digital Marketing 21 December 2017, https://zephoria.com/top-15-valuable-facebook-statistics

Questions

1. Analyse the opportunities created by digital technology for the Fang.
2. Explain how the exploitation of digital technology disrupts traditional business.

Figure 4.7 Percentage mobile penetration by region 2005–17

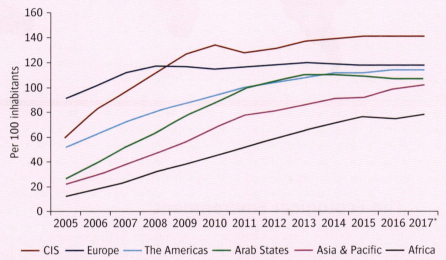

Notes: 2017 is an estimate; numbers sometimes often exceed population size because people have more than one subscription and organizations holding multiple subscriptions.
Source: ITU (2017a)

McKinsey (2013) published a report identifying 12 technologies it describes as 'disruptive' because they have the power to 'transform life, business, and the global economy'. They include, inter alia, cloud technology, mobile technology, advanced robotics, the internet of Things, 3D printing, self-driving vehicles, and energy storage. These transformative technologies make it much more difficult for business to carry out long-range planning.

Learning Task

Online activity is particularly popular among the young. Examine Figure 4.8.

In which continents and countries is internet activity highest/lowest among young people? Analyse the implications of your answer to a) for members of the Fang.

Figure 4.8 Proportion of youth (15–24) using the internet, 2017

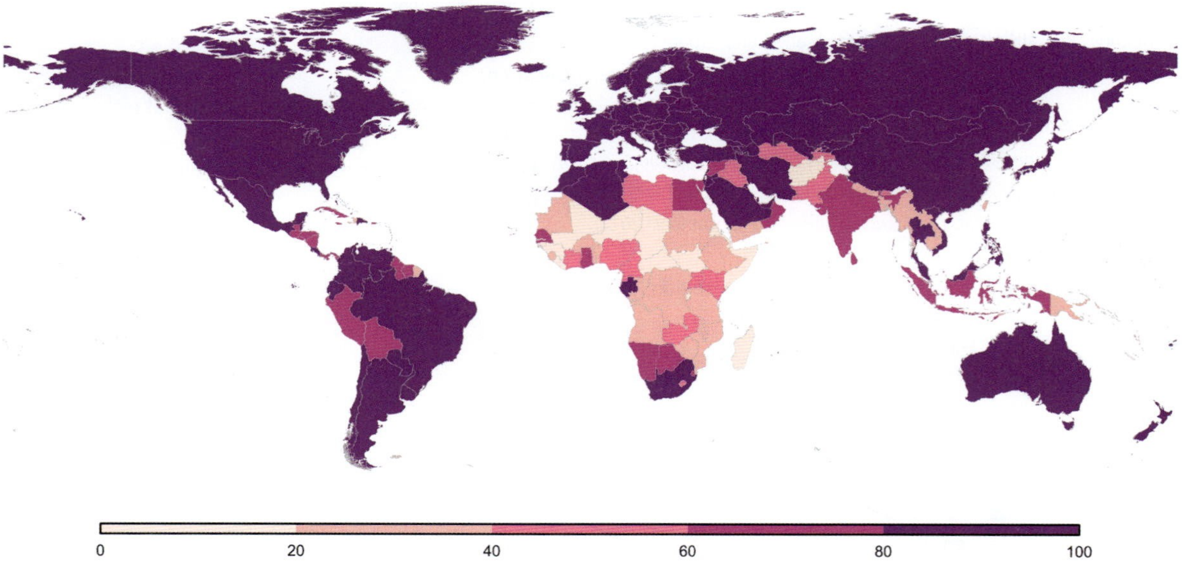

Source: ITU (2017b)

The Ecological Environment

In recent decades, there has been increasing concern, both nationally and globally, about the interaction between human beings, the economic systems they establish, and the earth's natural environment. Business forms a major part of economic systems that affect the environment by using up resources and altering the ecological systems on which the world depends. The damage to the ozone layer, the impact of global warming, and the rise in sea levels due to greenhouse gases emitted by power generation, industrial, transport, and agricultural sectors, have been of growing concern.

Environmental challenges are a global phenomenon. Global warming is not confined within national borders; it affects the whole world. There is widespread recognition that economic growth is harming the environment irrevocably, and that we need to move towards a system that values the natural environment and protects it for future generations.

There is growing pressure on the political authorities to respond to these ecological threats. There are a number of possible policy responses, all of which have implications for business:

- tax the polluter;
- subsidize firms who manage to reduce activities that harm the environment, for example by switching to non-polluting sources of energy;
- use regulations to control the amount of pollution generated by business;
- promote the creation of environmentally friendly technologies.

For more discussion on the ecological environment, see Chapter 12.

● CHAPTER SUMMARY

In this chapter, we examined the global external business environment. The factors in this environment are highly interdependent, but can usefully be analysed in the following categories: political, economic and financial, socio-cultural, technological, legal, and ecological, the various elements that make up the PESTLE model. This environment is increasingly complex, dynamic, uncertain, and can be hostile. Firms need to scan the environment in order to identify opportunities for new markets, for cost reductions, and for new sources of supply. They also need to look out for the many threats, not just from competitors but also from economic and financial volatility, political instability, new technology, and natural disasters. Organizations can assess the impact of external issues by analysing the effect of these issues on the structure of the industry and on the stakeholders of the organization.

● REVIEW QUESTIONS

1. Explain why operating in the international business environment is much more complex than in a firm's domestic business environment.

2. What implications does your answer to question 1 have for planning a firm's strategy?

3. Using the various reports mentioned in the chapter, summarize what you think are the most important issues affecting business in the next 20 years and their consequences for business.

● ASSIGNMENT TASKS

1. Select an organization that operates internationally.

    a. Identify the major external environmental issues.

    b. Analyse the impact on the structure of the industry.

    c. Assess the impact on the organization.

2. Burri (2018), in a study for the European Parliament, showed that digital technology had brought about new patterns of trade and new types of competition.

    a. Discuss, with examples, the opportunities digitization has generated in e-commerce.

    b. Assess to what extent these opportunities have been exploited. Use and update Figure 4.9 to help you answer this question.

    c. See Figure 4.9. Burri (2018) says that countries have responded to digitization by erecting new trade barriers. Identify these barriers and analyse their implications for firms using online platforms.

Figure 4.9 The biggest online platforms have user bases on a par with the populations of the world's biggest countries

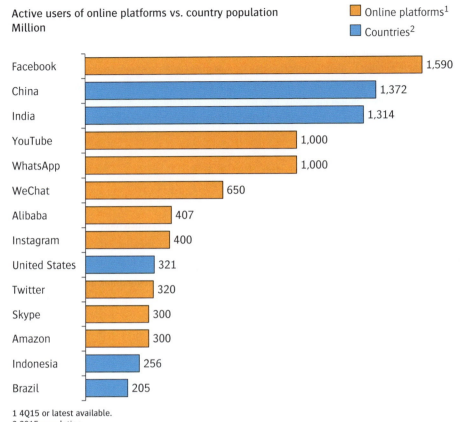

Active users of online platforms vs. country population
Million

Legend:
- Online platforms[1]
- Countries[2]

Facebook	1,590
China	1,372
India	1,314
YouTube	1,000
WhatsApp	1,000
WeChat	650
Alibaba	407
Instagram	400
United States	321
Twitter	320
Skype	300
Amazon	300
Indonesia	256
Brazil	205

1 4Q15 or latest available.
2 2015 population.

Source: Burri (2018)

Case Study Uber, the environment bites back

© Shutterstock.com/Jirapong Manustrong

Uber is a privately owned US start-up company founded in 2009. Technological advances in the internet and mobile devices led Uber to set up a digital platform allowing customers to use a mobile device to book and pay for taxis. It offered lower prices and greater convenience for customers compared to traditional taxi firms. The company grew very rapidly. In 2017, the number of trips taken by customers had increased by 150 per cent compared with the previous year. According to the company, 10 million trips were being made each day worldwide. It operated in 83 countries and 674 cities across the globe. In 2016, it had revenues of $20 billion but losses of $2.8 billion excluding those made from selling its Chinese subsidiary. →

→ Its value was put at anywhere between $50 billion and $68 billion (Uber n.d.; CNBC 23 August 2017; Business of Apps 9 January 2018; TechCrunch 22 June 2017).

In 2017, Uber confronted a plethora of challenges in its external environment both at home and abroad. It was a victim of cybercrime when hackers stole personal data of its 57 million customers and 600,000 drivers. The company, claiming that its security systems had not been breached, stated that the data was held by a third party in the cloud (Uber n.d.). Uber paid the hackers $100,000 on assurances that the data would be destroyed but failed to alert their customers and drivers. Neither did it inform the authorities leaving it open to legal action both at federal and state level in the USA, and in the UK, Australia, and Italy (The Guardian 27 December 2017).

Uber also faced several investigations by the US Department of Justice (DoJ). The company was accused of using technology to deceive authorities in cities where it was breaching local laws (Reuters 5 May 2017). Business Insider (29 August 2017) reported that the company faced allegations that it had bribed foreign officials in violation of the Foreign Corrupt Practices Act in several Asian countries. The FBI opened an investigation into accusations that Uber had spied on drivers working for Lyft, a major rival in the USA. Uber used the information to identify and fill gaps in Lyft's coverage and to find out which drivers were working for both companies (The Verge 8 September 2017). Google's subsidiary Waymo sued Uber for stealing technical information on its self-driving cars. This was followed by the DoJ announcing a criminal probe connected with the Waymo law suit leading some commentators to speculate that Uber had violated the Computer Fraud and Abuse Act (Ars Technica 14 December 2017).

Then the US Federal Trade Commission imposed a £20 million fine on the company for misleading its drivers on how much they could earn using the platform. In 2017, the average monthly income for its drivers in the USA was $364 with the median at $155 (Business of Apps 9 January 2018). When a video of its CEO arguing with one of its drivers over the level of fares appeared on YouTube, the issue went global (YouTube n.d.).

Uber lost its license to operate in London. Transport for London said that the company had not acted responsibly because it had not carried out sufficient background checks on its drivers nor had it reported to the police serious sexual offences that had occurred in its vehicles (The Guardian 23 September 2017).

Uber also faced challenges from its drivers. In India, more than 100,000 drivers went on strike for improved pay and conditions. Similar grievances were expressed by drivers in Brazil, Italy, and Australia. In the UK, the company lost an appeal against a tribunal decision that its drivers were employees and not self-employed as claimed by the company. The decision meant that employees should receive entitlements such as the minimum wage and holiday pay (Financial Times 10 November 2017).

The European Court of Justice landed a further blow ruling that Uber was a transportation company and not simply a digital platform resulting in the company having to abide by the same stricter regulations as a traditional taxi firm (The Guardian 24 February and 27 December 2017).

Uber's image was tarnished when a female engineer at Uber reported to its Human Resources department that she was being sexually harassed by her manager. The HR department responded that her manager was a high performer and that she should transfer to a different team, or stay where she was and get a poor performance appraisal. The engineer wrote a blog post that went global, further damaging Uber's reputation (New York Times 1 October 2017).

The problems faced by Uber in 2017 led to a large number of top executives leaving the company including Travis Kanlanick the founder and CEO, the president, the head of public policy and communications, the top engineer, the chief security officer, the legal director, and the boss of the UK operation.

Sources: Ars Technica 14 December 2017; Business Insider 29 August 2017; Business of Apps 9 January 2018; CNBC 23 August 2017; Financial Times 10 November 2017; The Guardian 23, 24, and 27 December 2017; New York Times 1 October 2017; Reuters 5 May 2017; TechCrunch 22 June 2017; http://www.uber.com press release 21 November 2017; The Verge 8 September 2017

Questions

1. How did the external environment create opportunities for Uber to set up and then expand internationally?

2. What evidence could Uber use to claim that it is a successful company?

3. a. Categorize the main PESTLE challenges Uber faced in 2017 in its external environment.

   b. Analyse the impact of these challenges on Uber's costs and its reputation. When answering this, try to find out the outcomes of the various legal investigations into Uber.

4. It is reported that Uber was making $1 billion a year losses in China (Fortune 7 August 2016). What elements in the external environment contributed to Uber's failure in China?

5. What evidence from its external environment suggests that Uber has been badly managed? Consider whether the company's problems could be related to it being a start-up.

● FURTHER READING

For a very readable view of political, social, economic, and technological developments in the global economy, see:

- Dicken, P. (2015) *Global Shift: Mapping the Changing Contours of the World Economy.* 7th edition. London: Sage.

- Wagner, D and Disparte, D. (2016) *Global Risk Agility and Decision Making: Organizational Resilience in the Era of Man-Made Risk.* London: Palgrave McMillan.

The following article examines the challenges to the global power of the USA:

- Borgman, C. (2017) 'Who's Got the Power?' *Harvard Political Review* 6 October

For discussion of China's growing world power, see:

- Brown, K. (2017) *China's World: What Does China Want?* London: I.B.Tauris.

For an introductory text to strategy, see:

- Johnson, G. et al. (2017) *Exploring Strategy: Text and Cases.* Harlow: Pearson.

● REFERENCES

Actuarial Post (n.d.) 'Driverless cars: How will insurers be affected?' http://www.actuarialpost.co.uk/article/driverless-cars:-how-will-insurers-be-affected-6725.htm.

Aldermore (2017) http://www.aldermore.co.uk, 14 September.

Alphabet (2017) SEC 2017 10-K filing.

Apple (2017) SEC 2017 10-K filing.

Automotive News (2017) 'Mazda Profit Falls 71% on Foreign Exchange Losses', 2 February. http://www.autonews.com/article/20170202/COPY01/302029961/mazda-profit-falls-71-percent-on-foreign-exchange-losses.

Breitburg, D. et al. (2018) 'Declining oxygen in the global ocean and coastal waters' *Science* 5 January: Vol. 359, Issue 6371.

Bretton Woods Project (2017) 'World Bank's Doing Business'. Report 3 July.

The British Standards Institute (2017) 'Impact of supply chain attacks hits highest rate ever' 24 August. Available at http://www.bsigroup.com/en-GB/about-bsi/media-centre/press-releases/2017/august/Impact-of-supply-chain-attacks-hits-highest-rate-ever-.

Burri, M. (2018) 'Current and Emerging Trends in Disruptive Technologies: Implications for the Present and Future of the EU's Trade Policy Directorate-General for External Policies', European Parliament.

CIA (2017) 'The World Factbook'. Available at https://www.cia.gov/library/publications/the-world-factbook.

CityUK (2017a) 'Brexit and UK-based financial and related professional services', 12 January.

CityUK (2017b) 'Key Facts about the UK as an International Financial Centre', December.

Coe, N.M., Kelly, P.F., and Yeung, H.W.C. (2007) *Economic Geography.* Malden: Blackwell.

Deloitte (2017) 'A New Future for R&D: Measuring the Return from Pharmaceutical Innovation 2017'.

Dhingra, S., Ottaviani, G., Sampson, T. and Van Reenen, J. (2016) 'CEP Brexit Analysis No.2', March.

Dwyer, R. (2017) 'Brazil's political risk is very much alive' *Euromoney* March.

Enderwick, P. (2006) 'Managing the Global Threats' *University of Auckland Business Review* 8 (2)

European Commission (2012) 'Impact Assessment', Staff Working Paper: SEC 2012 72 final.

European Commission (2015) 'Agreement on Commission's EU data protection reform will boost Digital Single Market'. IP 15/6321 15 December.

European Commission (2016a) 'State Aid: Ireland Gave Illegal Tax Benefits to Apple Worth Up to €13 Billion', 30 August, Memo 16-2923.

European Commission (2016b) 'State Aid: Commission Refers Ireland to Court for Failure to Recover Illegal Tax Benefits from Apple Worth Up to €13 Billion', 4 October IP/17/3702.

European Commission (2017a) 'Protection of personal data in the European Union' 14 December.

European Commission (2017b) 'The 2017 EU Industrial R&D Investment Scoreboard'.

European Commission (n.d.) http://www.ec.europa.eu/justice/dataprotection.

Fortune (2016) http://fortune.com/2016/08/07/uber-china-didi-chuxing, 7 August.

Fox, L. (2016) 'Liam Fox's Free Trade Speech' Department of International Trade 29 September. Available at http://www.gov.uk/government/speeches/liam-foxs-free-trade-speech.

Freeman, E. (1984) *Strategic Management: A Stakeholder Approach*. Boston: Pitman.

Global Justice (2017) http://www.globaljustice.org.uk/news/2017/dec/13/brexit-lobby-meetings-dominated-big-business-official-figures-reveal.

Grant, R. and Jordan, J. (2015) *Foundations of Strategy* (2nd edn.). Chichester, UK: John Wiley & Sons.

Haas, R. (2008) 'A Political Education for Business: An Interview with the Head of the Council on Foreign Relations'. *McKinsey Quarterly* February.

Harford, T. (2017) *Fifty Things that Made the Modern Economy* London: Little, Brown.

Harvard *Business Review* (2017) 'Driverless cars will change auto insurance'. Available at https://hbr.org/2017/12/driverless-cars-will-change-auto-insurance-hereshow-insurers-can-adapt.

House of Commons Library 'Migrant workers in Agriculture'. Briefing paper 7987 4 July 2017.

ICIJ (2017) 'Leaked Documents Expose Secret Tale of Apple's Offshore Island Hop', 6 November. Available at https://www.icij.org/investigations/paradise-papers/apples-secret-offshore-island-hop-revealed-by-paradise-papers-leak-icij.

IMF (2017) 'World Economic Outlook' October.

Independent (2017) http://www.independent.co.uk/news/uk/politics/brexit-talks-negotiations-david-davis-corporate-banks-eu-lobbying-brussels-a7913131.html, 26 August.

ITU (2017a) 'Measuring the Information Society Report 2017' Vol. 1.

ITU (2017b) 'ICT Facts and Figures 2017'.

Jonsson, A and Tolstoy, D. (2013) 'A thematic analysis of research on global sourcing and international purchasing in retail firms', *International Journal of Retail & Distribution Management*, Vol. 42 Issue 1.

Khan, O. and Yurt, O. (2011) 'Approaches to managing global sourcing risks' *Supply Chain Management: An International Journal* Vol. 16 Issue 2.

Klotz, R. Finotti, A. (2016) 'Brazil—A Complex Land of Opportunity', *The Secured Lender* July/August.

Kotler, P. and Caslione, J. (2009) *Chaotics: The Business of Managing and Marketing in the Age of Turbulence*. New York: American Management Association.

Live Science (2015) 'Future of driverless cars'. Available at http://www. livescience.com/50841-future-of-driverless-cars.html.

Marsh (2016) 'Terrorism Risk Insurance Report'. Marsh Risk Management Research, July.

Mason, R.B. (2007) 'The External Environment's Effects on Management and Strategy: A Complexity Theory Approach'. *Management Decision* 45(1).

Minford, P. (2017) 'From Project Fear to Prospect Prosperity' Economists for Free Trade, August.

McKinsey (2013) 'Disruptive Technologies: Advances that will Transform Life, Business, and the Global Economy'. McKinsey Global Institute. Available at http://www.mckinsey.com/insights/business_technology/disruptive_technologies.

Medieros, M. (2016) 'Income Inequality in Brazil: New Evidence from Combined Tax and Survey Data'. *World Social Science Report 2016*.

Moore Stephens UK (2017) 'GDPR: The Impact on Technology Businesses'. Available 14 June at http://www.moorestephens.co.uk/news-views/january-2017/gdpr-the-impact-on-technology-businesses.

National Intelligence Council (2017) Global Trends: Paradox of Progress. July.

Netflix (2017) SEC 2017 10-K filing.

New York Times (2017) 'Autonomous car technology challenges'. Available at http://www.nytimes.com/2017/06/07/technology/ autonomous-car-technology-challenges.html.

PIIE (2016) 'How long Does It Take To Conclude a Trade Agreement with the US?' 21 July. Available at http://piie.com/blogs/trade-investment-policy-watch/how-long-does-it-take-conclude-trade-agreement-us.

Post, J.E., Preston, L.E., and Sachs, S. (2002) 'Managing the Extended Enterprise: The New Stakeholder View'. *California Management Review* 45(1).

PWC (2016) 'Leaving the EU: Implications for the UK Financial Services Sector'.

Saner, R. and Guilherme, R. (2007) 'The International Monetary Fund's Influence on Trade Policies of Low-Income Countries: A Valid Undertaking?'. *Journal of World Trade* 41(5).

Transparency International (2017) 'Corruption Perceptions Index', accessed 22 December 2017.

Uber (n.d.) http://www.uber.com.

UK Finance (2017) 'Supporting Europe's Economies and Citizens' September.

US Permanent Subcommittee on Investigations (2013) 'Offshore Profit Shifting and the U.S. Tax Code—Part 2 (Apple Inc.)', 21 May.

Wallerstein, I. (2007) 'Precipitate Decline'. *Harvard International Review* 29(1).

WEF (2016) 'America's Dominance is Over: By 2030, We'll Have a Handful of Global Powers', 11 November. Available at https://www.weforum.org/agenda/2016/11/america-s-dominance-is-over.

WEF (2017) 'Global Competitiveness Report 2017–2018'.

Wohlforth, W. (2007) 'Unipolar Stability'. *Harvard International Review* 29(1).

World Bank (n.d.) http://www.data.worldbank.org.

Wuebbles, D.J. et al. (2017) *Climate Science Special Report: Fourth National Climate Assessment*, Volume I.

YouTube (n.d.) https://www.youtube.com/watch?v=9F0IzbXPpnA.

CHAPTER FIVE

Corporate Social Responsibility

LEARNING OUTCOMES

At the end of this chapter, you will be able to:

- define corporate social responsibility;

- assess the free market case against corporate social responsibility;

- explain the business and moral cases for corporate social responsibility;

- identify corporate social responsibility issues in the global economy; and

- discuss the implications of corporate social responsibility for business.

Case Study Can you afford an iPhone?

© Shutterstock/Ym Yik/EPA/REX

In Chapter 1 we defined globalization as a process in which barriers separating different regions of the world are reduced or removed, thereby stimulating greater exchange and linkages between nations. As globalization progresses, business is confronted by important new challenges. Some of these challenges relate to the way business is done. This case looks at Apple's supply chain and some of the working conditions found there, and raises the question of responsibility. It also looks at Apple's alleged tax avoidance.

Apple's iPhone X costs around £1,000 but sold out in less than ten minutes when it was released for pre-order in the UK in October 2017. Demand was obviously high but, allegedly, there were also supply problems (see *Nikkei Asian Review*, 24 October 2017). Apple, like many other multinationals, has a supply chain that crosses the world, and thus aims to reduce cost at each step of the production process. iPhones are designed in the USA, but they are assembled in other countries with parts sourced from lots of different suppliers from across the world. This complex web of suppliers can bring problems, particularly as each country of operation will have different cultures, labour regulations, legal and financial systems, environmental standards, and political systems.

To manage the supply chain and to meet the responsibilities of employing millions of people around the world, Apple have a code of conduct that requires suppliers to adhere to safe working conditions, fair treatment of workers, and environmentally safe manufacturing. To ensure the code is being adhered to, Apple undertakes supplier assessments. In 2016 they under-

took 705 of these assessments. They also say they 'partnered with suppliers to train more than 2.4 million workers on their rights as employees' (Apple n.d.).

In spite of this, Apple has received much criticism for the standards in the factories that produce their goods. The largest of these is a factory in Zhengzhou in China, which is capable of producing up to half a million iPhones per day. The factory is owned by Foxconn, a Taiwanese company. According to the *New York Times* (2016), the facility was built with billions of dollars of 'sweeteners and incentives' from the local government. A total of 1.5 billion dollars was put into the construction of large sections of the factory, and there is continuing help with energy and transportation costs, recruitment of workers, and bonuses paid for meeting export targets.

In 2010, Foxconn hit the headlines when 18 of its employees, because of the working conditions in the factory, tried to commit suicide by jumping off its roof. Fourteen succeeded and one who didn't, but ended up paralysed from the waist down, described her life in the Foxconn factory as being like a 'human battery hen, working over 12 hours a day, six days a week, swapped between day and night shifts and housed in an eight person dorm room' (*The Guardian* 2016a). Foxconn's response was to put up safety nets and to make new employees sign an anti-suicide pledge and confirm that if they did kill themselves, the company would not be blamed or pursued for compensation (CBS News 2013).

Following this, Apple published a set of standards on how workers should be treated. In 2014, a BBC *Panorama* programme sent undercover investigators into another of Apple's Chinese suppliers, Pegatron. They filmed workers falling asleep trying to complete 12-hour shifts. Apple's standards on ID cards, dormitories, work meetings, and juvenile workers were all being breached.

China Labor Watch, based in New York, has been following working conditions at Apple's Chinese suppliers since 2011. They conduct undercover investigations and interviews, and have found that many issues remain in relation to labour rights violations. They found that the major issues were as follows:

1. Weekly working hours surpassing the 60-hour limit claimed by Apple's code of conduct and overtime hours, often far exceeding China's labour law limit of 36 hours per month.

2. In Pegatron, base income in 2016 was less than in 2015. ➔

➜

3. Workers were required to sign an agreement to do overtime voluntarily, opt out of paying social insurance, and opt out of housing funds, all violating China's labour laws.
4. Workers at Pegatron and Green Point were continuously working overtime without pay.

China Labor Watch found that there are serious discrepancies between Apple's sustainability reporting and the reality of working in one of Apple's Chinese suppliers.

Apple has also faced questions about the conditions and the use of child labour in the mines that source the minerals used in the production of the iPhone. Apple's supply chain includes the tin mines of Bolivia, the mud pits in Indonesia, and the 'artisanal' cobalt mines in the Congo (see *LA Times* 2017).

Policing a complex international supply chain is inherently difficult and, as the *LA Times* points out (2017), requires 'serious resources and novel systems-thinking'. The *LA Times* also makes the point that if Apple really wants to live up to its code of conduct, then it, more than any other company, can afford to do so.

That Apple can afford to do so is not in doubt; it is the most profitable company in the world and has managed to amass a cash pot of $252 billion that it keeps in an offshore account in Jersey. Good company governance maintains that companies should try to reduce their tax bill by planning their affairs according to the law. When this becomes aggressive tax avoidance and companies are seen not to be paying their 'fair' share, then it is legitimate to questions these practices. Apple, like many other multinational companies, seeks to avoid paying tax. (See the opening Case Study in Chapter 4.)

Introduction

Multinational corporations are often accused of a number of abuses related to their business activities. Many have appeared in the press accused of, inter alia, bribery and corruption, abusing human rights, sanction busting, dumping, undermining governments, exploiting uneducated consumers, using forced labour, low wages, poor health and safety standards, exploiting natural resources, using child labour, and corruption. One of the many problems for business operating internationally is that standards and 'the way of doing things' differ from country to country. This is not a justification for the abuses listed above, but it does bring into question the very fundamental question of the role of business in society and to what extent business has any responsibility for some of the problems of society. This chapter explores the concept of **corporate social responsibility** (CSR), discusses some examples related to the concept, and looks at the implications for business.

CSR can be defined as the notion that corporations have an obligation to society to take into account not just their economic impact, but also their social and environmental impact. The European Commission defines CSR very simply as 'the responsibility of enterprises for their impacts on society' (European Commission n.d.), and the *Financial Times* defines it as 'a business approach that contributes to sustainable development by delivering economic, social and environmental benefits for all stakeholders' (*Financial Times* n.d.). We shall return to the idea of sustainable development later in the chapter when we discuss the United Nations' Sustainable Development Goals.

We use the term 'corporate social responsibility' throughout this chapter, but it appears that business is not very keen on it. Marks and Spencer refers to its CSR activities as 'Plan A because there is no Plan B when it comes to conserving the earth's finite resources' (Marks and Spencer n.d.). In other words, this is how we do business and we do not need to give it any special label. Others, such as the UK government, have dropped the 'social', which some object to as too narrow, or 'outside our remit', or as a label imposed from outside. Other labels used are 'triple-bottom-line reporting' (i.e. economic, social, and environmental), '**sustainable development**', and the most recent, 'corporate citizenship'. Although there are different interpretations of these terms, they are all essentially about the obligation to society in its widest sense.

Debates about CSR

CSR is not new, and whether business has any social responsibility has been the subject of endless debate.

For some, there is only one social responsibility of business and that is, in the words of Milton Friedman (1970 [1983]), 'to use its resources and engage in activities designed to increase its profits so long as it stays within the rules of the game, which is to say, engages in open and free competition without deception or fraud'. This reflects the view that a free market society is made up of diverse entities, each with a specialist role within society. The role of business is economic and the people who run businesses are expert in that field. Their role is to combine resources to produce some product or service for sale at a profit. They compete with other firms by keeping costs as low as possible and supplying consumers with the goods and services they want at the lowest possible price. Those who are effective at doing this survive and make a profit. Those who fail go out of business. It is the drive to supply consumers with the goods and services they want, and at the same time to make as much profit as possible by driving costs down and selling as much as possible, that makes for a dynamic and efficient economy. If there are social and environmental problems, then this should not be for business people to solve because it would divert them from the role for which they are best equipped and the result would be a less efficient economy. These problems are best left to governments, which can employ experts in those fields.

In this debate, and particularly in the field of international business, we are talking about a particular form of business organization: the 'corporation'. To become a corporation, a business has to go through a legal process which creates a body having a separate legal existence from its owners and from those who work in or manage it. Gap Inc., BP, and Motorola all exist quite separately from the people who work in or manage the organization and from those who own the assets of the business, the shareholders. Shareholders change as shares are bought and sold through various stock exchanges. Managers and other workers change, but the corporation continues in existence. It is said to have perpetual succession.

In Friedman's view, the corporation should act no differently from the single owner business. Corporate managers are employed as the agents of the principals (the owners) and should work in their interest, and that, in his view, is to make as much profit as possible. In that way, both dividends and share value increase. Managers are not experts in social welfare or in dealing with environmental problems, so how would they know how to deploy resources to deal with these problems? Nor, unlike politicians, have they been elected, so the use of funds for some purpose other than profit maximization would be not only wasteful, but also undemocratic, particularly as managers as a group do not tend to be representative of the population at large, usually being more conservative than the general population.

Counterpoint Box 5.1 Executive responsibility—to whom?

The rise in executive pay has been the subject of much public criticism in both the USA and in Western Europe. This intensified following the global financial crisis of 2007–08.

The UK Trade Union Congress reported in September 2016 that the highest paid chief executive in the UK earned £70 million in 2015. The median total pay (excluding pensions) of top FTSE 100 directors increased by 47 per cent in the previous 5 years (to £3.4 million), but average wages for workers rose just 7 per cent and in real terms were still below pre-2008 crash levels. In 2010, the average FTSE 100 boss earned 89 times the average full time salary but by 2015 that had risen to 123 times. An analysis of CEO economic remuneration and economic value creation for FTSE-350 companies (Li and Young 2016) found a negligible link between executive pay and performance. This is not surprising, given that many studies find pay to be less of a motivator than things such as responsibility and status. Indeed, Maslow's hierarchy of needs would suggest such a result.

Bebchuk and Fried (2006) argue that managers use their power to influence their compensation packages. As a result, they end up being paid excessive sums that do not lead to improved company performance and therefore do not serve shareholders' interests. They contend that executive pay is significantly decoupled from company performance. They argue that executives owe their primary duty to shareholders but that corporate governance in the USA disenfranchises the true owners, the shareholders.

Lipton and Savitt (2007) defend multi-million dollar executive pay packages, arguing that highly paid executives have built great firms. They challenge Bebchuk's idea that corporations are the private property of shareholders. They insist that shareholders are merely owners of shares, not of the firm. Their right to exercise control over the company should be limited, but they have the right to share in the profits generated by it. They contend that it is management's prerogative to do what is in the best interest of all the corporation's stakeholders by balancing the interests of shareholders as well as other stakeholders, such as management and employees, creditors, regulators, suppliers, and consumers.

Sources: Hay Group (2011); Bebchuk and Fried (2006); Bebchuk et al. (2010); Lipton and Savitt (2007)

Question

Traditionally, the idea of maximizing shareholder value was supposed to lead to better economic performance. However, if it just leads to increased executive pay what does this say about Milton Friedman's arguments about social responsibility?

Friedman's criticisms of CSR were not that business did not have a social role, but that its role and its obligation to society was to supply goods and services at the lowest price possible. His view was founded in a fundamental belief in the virtues of a free market economy in which each player contributed, without knowing it, to the greater good of society.

A further criticism by Friedman was the notion of a corporation, a legal creation, assuming moral responsibilities. In his words:

> What does it mean to say that 'business' has responsibilities? Only people can have responsibilities. A corporation is an artificial person and in this sense may have artificial responsibilities, but business as a whole cannot be said to have responsibilities, even in this vague sense (Friedman 1970).

There is no argument that the corporation exists as a separate legal entity with legal rights and duties. It is capable of owning and disposing of assets, employing people, entering into contracts, incurring and being owed debts, inflicting and suffering damage, suing and being sued. If it (the corporation) is held responsible for these actions, why then can it not be morally responsible for its other actions? As Goodpaster and Mathews (1982: 135) point out, 'if a group can act like a person in some ways, then we can expect it to behave like a person in other ways.' We have no problem referring to a company's business strategy or its marketing plan. We would not think or refer to these examples as an individual's strategy or plan. This is because corporations have complex internal decision-making structures that arrive at decisions in line with corporate goals (French 1979). The outcome is rarely attributable to any one person, but is usually the result of a series of discussions between directors, managers, and staff. In other words, the corporation acts just like an individual. Examples from legal cases support the difficulty in identifying individuals responsible for corporate decisions. In *P & O European Ferries (Dover) Ltd* ((1991) 93 Cr App R 72), Mr Justice Turner ruled that a company may be properly indicted for manslaughter. That case, however, ended in the acquittal of the defendant company because the Crown could not show that a 'controlling mind' had been grossly negligent. The 'controlling mind' of a company is somebody who can be shown to be in control of the operations of a company and not responsible to another person. In large companies, the 'controlling mind' has proved difficult to identify, but the smaller the company, the easier it is to identify. In *R v Kite and OLL Ltd*, the 'Lyme Bay' disaster, several schoolchildren, who were canoeing across Lyme Bay, died because of the poor safety standards of the company. In this case, it was possible to identify the Managing Director, Peter Kite, as the 'controlling mind' and he was prosecuted successfully for corporate manslaughter. It was because of the difficulty of identifying the 'controlling mind' that the UK strengthened legislation in this area with the introduction of the Corporate Manslaughter and Corporate Homicide Act 2007 (CMA), which came into force throughout the UK on 6 April 2008. A number of charges and convictions, including jail sentences for directors, have been brought under this act.

Another argument supporting the case for assigning moral responsibility to a company is the existence not just of a decision-making structure but also of a set of beliefs and values guiding individual decision-making. This is commonly known as the 'culture' of the organization. Nowadays, this is more often than not enshrined in a written statement such as Google's code of conduct or, as it was initially put, 'don't be evil'. This was intended to convey how employees should approach its users but it was also intended to mean to do the right thing generally, i.e. following the law, acting honourably, and treating co-workers with courtesy and respect.

 Learning Task

On 27 June 2017, the European Commission (EC) announced it was imposing a EUR 2.42 billion fine on Google. The EC claimed that the tech giant abused market dominance by manipulating its search engine results to favour its own comparison shopping service. Part of Google's code points out that 'using Google's size or strength to gain an unfair competitive advantage' may be 'illegal, unfair, or create the appearance of impropriety'. At the time of writing, Google is considering appealing against this decision, but is also facing two other charges of abusing a dominant position (*The Guardian* 2017).

Does this mean that codes of conduct are worthless?

(Note that Google restructured its activities in October 2015 and it is now a subsidiary of Alphabet Inc.)

Some find Friedman's view of the modern corporation to be at odds with reality, and particularly the view that modern capitalism is at all like the classical capitalism of economics textbooks where firms have no economic or political power because they are subject to market forces. As we saw in Chapter 3, most modern markets are oligopolistic in nature, with a few very large and powerful firms dominating many markets. We also see in Chapters 1 and 9 that these players are active politically, using their power to influence policy in their favour—for example, in removing barriers to trade and investment. The idea that the modern corporation is a passive player in the economy is far from the truth. They are powerful players in the world economy whose actions will have an impact both economically and socially, so the modern argument about CSR is not whether corporations should engage in CSR but how they do it and why they do it. In terms of how, as we shall see, there is no universal agreement about what constitutes good CSR.

The Moral Case for CSR

The moral case for CSR is that it is the right thing to do, not because it yields greater financial return (although it might), but as a good corporate citizen with the same social and environmental obligations of any other citizen, i.e. you and me.

The first stage in this argument attributes the status of 'personhood' to the corporation so that they could be considered 'moral agents' and held accountable for their actions. For example, Goodpaster and Mathews (1982) and French (1979) likened the corporation to an individual.

The second strand of the argument emphasizes the social nature of the corporation: it is a creation of society and should therefore serve the needs of society. Some writers (Donaldson 1982: Anshen 1970 [1983]) draw on social contract theory (the view that individuals' moral and/or political obligations are dependent upon an agreement between them to form society) to support these arguments. Anshen (1970 [1983]) argues that the agreement is one that changes as society evolves. In the 1950s, when living conditions were much worse in the West than they are now, society's expectation of business (and so their obligation to society) was to produce the goods required by society. Indeed, it is useful to remember that, from society's point of view, the basic purpose of business is to be the efficient provider of goods and services. Environmental damage, poor working conditions, and inequalities were seen as a fair price to pay for the improving standard of living. As Western societies grew richer, the trade-off between material well-being and the quality of life changed, and the expectations for business to provide safe places to work, not to damage the environment, to respect human rights, and so on, have now become the expectations confronting business.

Stakeholder theory is an offshoot of this theory, which says that business corporations are part of the wider society in which they develop relationships with groups or constituencies (to include biodiversity). These groups are said to have a 'stake' in the organization because the activities of the organization will have an effect on them and, in turn, they can impact on the organization. They are part of a social system and dependent on each other, as opposed to the Friedman view, which sees them as separate entities operating at arm's length.

Other writers, such as De George (2010), reinforce this view of corporations as social institutions by emphasizing that they are indeed creations of society. They are legal creations permitted by the state. They have to go through a process of application to receive their 'charter of incorporation', which brings them into existence; society can then expect these institutions to act for society as a whole. It is the corporation's 'licence to operate' that can, of course, be withdrawn if those expectations are not met. This also underpins the 'corporate citizen' view of corporations in which the corporation is regarded as an institutional citizen with rights and obligations like any other citizen.

Other arguments put forward include the following:

- Large corporations have enormous economic power and are endowed with substantial resources that they should use responsibly for the good of society.

- Business decisions will have social and environmental consequences, so corporations must take responsibility for those decisions.

- Business has been instrumental in causing many of today's problems, such as global warming and resource depletion, and therefore has a responsibility to solve these problems and avoid creating further problems.

The Business Case

The 'Business Case' refers to the underlying reasons business should engage with CSR. In other words, 'What does business get out of it?' The view of the corporation as a private body with an agent(s) acting for a principal(s) is peculiar to the UK and North America. In continental Europe and Japan, corporations are viewed much more as public bodies with obligations to a wider set of groups, investors, employees, suppliers, and customers. These countries regard corporations as social institutions with a strong public interest agenda. In these companies, managers are charged with pursuing the interests of all stakeholders, whereas in the UK and North America, the maximization of shareholder value is the goal. In the UK, the Companies Act 1985 extended the duties of directors to act not just in the interest of its members (shareholders) but also its employees. This has been extended in the Companies Act 2006, which includes the following section:

Duty to promote the success of the company

(1) A director of a company must act in the way he considers, in good faith, would be most likely to promote the success of the company for the benefit of its members as a whole, and in doing so have regard (amongst other matters) to—

(a) the likely consequences of any decision in the long term,

(b) the interests of the company's employees,

(c) the need to foster the company's business relationships with suppliers, customers and others,

(d) the impact of the company's operations on the community and the environment,

(e) the desirability of the company maintaining a reputation for high standards of business conduct, and

(f) the need to act fairly as between members of the company.

Note that this is to 'promote the success of the company'. Rather than driving a new agenda, this is legislation catching up with reality. Most large corporations have already realized that to be successful, or at least not to court disaster, then they must, as a minimum, take into account all of their stakeholders. In the words of the UK government:

> It enshrines in statute the concept of Enlightened Shareholder Value which recognises that directors will be more likely to achieve long term sustainable success for the benefit of their shareholders if their companies pay appropriate regard to wider matters such as the environment and their employees. (Certified Accountants Educational Trust (London) 2011)

For the UK government, the reason for business to undertake CSR is because it makes good business sense, although it would be difficult to sell to business in any other way. In many cases, business has come to accept CSR not because of the positive benefits it might bring but because they have awakened to the risks of ignoring it. Continuing business scandals have undermined public trust in big business. Shell's failure to consult with or to take into account the reaction of Greenpeace to their proposed sinking of a North Sea oil platform led to international protests and a damaged reputation. Nike, Gap, GlaxoSmithKline, Yahoo, BP, HSBC, other banks (see Chapter 10), and many others have suffered damage to their reputations from well-publicized CSR failures. Reputation management is a critical component of corporate success and one of the reasons that, according to Porter and Kramer (2006), 'of the 250 largest multinational corporations, 64 per cent published CSR reports in 2005'. The authors go on to say that much of this was about demonstrating the company's social sensitivity rather than a coherent framework for CSR activities. A KPMG survey in 2017 found that three-quarters of the 4,900 companies surveyed from around the world published CR reports (KPMG 2017). Very often, this activity is lodged in the public relations departments of these companies and is a defensive reaction focused on avoiding the disasters that have struck others. Porter and Kramer have developed their thinking and popularized the concept of shared value. They see capitalism as being under siege, with a common view that business takes a short-term view and is profiting at the expense of communities. They argue that business needs to move beyond CSR to concentrate on activities that create social value, regain trust, and which will in turn create profit and hence shared value (Porter and Kramer 2011). This is not without its critics. Crane et al. (2014) argue that this is not really a novel idea, adding little to the ideas of strategic CSR. They also argue that it ignores the tensions between economic and social goals, is naïve about the challenges of business compliance, and is based on a shallow conception of the corporation's role in society.

Learning Task

1. Read Porter and Kramer's article in the *Harvard Business Review* and explain their ideas of Creating Shared Value.
2. Using the opening case and any other sources you can access, advise Apple how it might create 'shared value'.

From the corporation's point of view, there is good reason for this focus, as the expectations of governments and people have never been higher. Moreover, modern consumers are better and more instantly informed than ever. An oil spill in Alaska, a chemical explosion in India, violation of tribal rights in Nigeria, an explosion on an oil rig in the Gulf, and the collapse of a garment factory all make headline news in the Western media. Consumers want to know where the products they consume come from, under what conditions they were produced, and, more recently, what size the carbon footprint is.

Non-governmental organizations (NGOs), such as Greenpeace, Friends of the Earth, Christian Aid, Oxfam, WWF, and Amnesty International, are also watching (see, for example, http://www.ethicalcorp.com). There are hundreds of thousands, if not millions, of these organizations operating across the world, many of them exceedingly well resourced (see Crane and Matten 2016: Chapter 10 for a discussion of civil society). Greenpeace operates across more than 55 countries and has 2.8 million supporters actively financing its activities as well as receiving money from charitable foundations. Oxfam works in over 90 countries with an income of £408.6 million in the financial year 2016–17.

Mini Case Study 5.1 NGOs and sexual exploitation

Often NGOs have been critical of what they see as socially irresponsible policies pursued by business and governments. They have been important advocates of the need for CSR in relation to issues such as child labour, sweatshops, deforestation of tropical forests, oil pollution, and tribal rights.

However, NGOs themselves face CSR issues within their organizations. Oxfam is a big UK-based charity with total income in 2016 of £409m, of which £176m came from the UK government and other public sector bodies (BBC 12 February 2018). It has around 10,000 staff operating in more than 90 countries with the aim of lifting people out of poverty and rooting out the injustices that cause poverty. Oxfam's mission is to help create a world where 'women and men are valued and treated equally' (Oxfam n.d.a). Two of its goals relate specifically to women:

1. Help people claim their right to a better life
   More women, young people and other poor and marginalised people will be able to exercise their civil and political rights, influence the decisions of people in power and hold them accountable for their actions.
2. Champion equal rights for women
   Women are still massively under-represented and often oppressed. We will help more poor and marginalised women claim their rights, and work to significantly reduce the prevalence of violence against women. (Oxfam n.d.b)

In 2018, it was claimed that Oxfam staff had hired prostitutes in Haiti in the aftermath of the earthquake in 2010 which had killed 220,000, injured 300,000, left over 1 million people needing shelter, and created a food crisis. Oxfam investigated the claims and sacked four workers; three others resigned. That same year it reemployed one of the sacked workers who had also been accused of hiring prostitutes in Chad, and sent him to work in Ethiopia. In 2018, Oxfam came under sustained criticism for its handling of the issue.

Aid organizations had previously been made aware of sexual exploitation by their staff. A report by Save the Children in 2008 found evidence that staff in 23 different humanitarian agencies had been involved in the sexual abuse of minors. The report contended that the problem had been widely known since 2002.

Sources: Arenas et al. (2009); BBC News (2018a and 2018b); Oxfam (n.d.); Save the Children (2008)

Questions
1. Explain how the behaviour of staff in Haiti and Chad breached Oxfam's values.
2. a. Discuss possible effects of the revelations about Oxfam staff on:
      i.   public trust in NGOs like Oxfam;
      ii. donations to Oxfam from the UK government; and
      iii. the willingness of governments to allow humanitarian agencies to operate in their countries.
   b. Google the Oxfam case to find the actual impact on the organization.

Another reason that many large corporations have increased the size of their CSR departments is to deal with NGOs. NGOs, of course, differ in their view of business. Some, such as the World Business Council for Sustainable Business, have a membership made up of some of the world's leading companies. The council has as part of its vision 'to support the business license to operate' by being a 'leading business advocate on sustainable development' (wbscd 2018). Thus, not all NGOs are critical of business, but many are and some, such as Oxfam, have a quite different view of the world and a different set of priorities, especially in the international arena. Sensible companies try to build relationships with relevant NGOs, either through dialogue or in some cases through partnership. The World Food Programme, managed by the United Nations (UN), has a number of corporate partners including Caterpillar, LG, Unilever, and Vodafone.

As we have seen, CSR is definitely on the corporate agenda, but whether business sees this as a duty to society, in the sense implied here, is open to great doubt. The evidence presented earlier paints a picture of business reluctantly taking up CSR as a defensive reaction to protect reputation, possibly leading to a recognition that CSR activities may well improve business performance. Many commentators would contend that the argument is a distraction. In the words of David Grayson (Doughty Chair of Corporate Responsibility, Cranfield School of Management):

> In my experience, business leaders committed to Corporate Responsibility do it for a mixture of 'it just makes business sense and it's the right thing to do'. In practice, those percentages may vary for the same business leader depending on the topic; and certainly will vary even within a business and between businesses. I think we should stop searching for the Holy Grail of precise motivation. We would be much more sensibly employed on improving the practice of management so that whatever the particular motivation, the performance can be commercially viable. ('Sense and Sustainability: Inaugural lecture 2007')

 ## Mini Case Study 5.2 Unilever and sustainability

Unilever is one of the world's largest consumer products companies with over 400 brand names worldwide, such as Persil, Pot Noodle, Bovril, PG Tips, Walls, and Ben & Jerry's. Unilever claims to recognize its responsibility to society. Its corporate purpose is 'to succeed requires the highest standards of corporate behaviour towards everyone we work with, the communities we touch, and the environment on which we have an impact'.

In 2010, Unilever announced a new sustainability initiative aiming by 2020 to:

- halve the environmental impact of their footprint;
- help more than 1 billion people take action to improve their health and well-being; and
- enhance the livelihoods of millions of people as we grow our business.

For example, the Unilever Foundation partners with five leading global organizations—Oxfam, Population Services International,

Save the Children, UNICEF, and the World Food Programme—to tackle some of the world's problems. They are also the primary beneficiaries in times of disaster so that Unilever can channel resources to where they are most needed. In 2013, Unilever launched 'Project Sunlight' a consumer facing campaign aimed at inspiring people to live more sustainably.

All this activity is not entirely altruistic, as Unilever recognizes the business benefits of this type of action. According to Unilever (see https://www.unilever.com/sustainable-living/our-strategy/about-our-strategy), it will:

1. increase growth
2. lower costs
3. reduce risk
4. increase trust.

As Unilever's CEO, Paul Polman, put it: 'consumers want more. They see food shortages, malnutrition and climate change, →

→ and governments are not addressing those problems. Companies that do this will get a competitive advantage. Those that do not will put themselves at risk' (*The Guardian* 15 November 2010).

For others this is all 'greenwash'—advertising that presents an environmentally responsible public image, but which in reality continues to hide 'bad practice' (see, for example, *The Guardian* (2016b), describing a Unilever settlement of a dispute involving mercury poisoning in India) and is simply aimed at promoting the company and its brands in order to increase sales. Unilever has already had to push back its target of halving its products' environmental impact by 2020, to 2030. If companies were serious about saving the environment, goes the argument, then they would be encouraging consumers to buy less. They would not be planning to open new manufacturing plants in the developing world and they

would be actively working to avoid the same consumption patterns as those in the West. Unilever is also the world's largest consumer of palm oil used in the manufacture of many of its products. Palm oil plantations, say the critics, come at the cost of the deforestation of native jungles and their inhabitants, both human and animal.

Sources: http://www.unilever.co.uk; http://www.chinadialogue.net/article/show/single/en/6913-Unilever-and-the-case-for-sustainable-business; http://www.pccnaturalmarkets.com/sc/1403/sustainable-palm-oil.html

Question
Some criticize Unilever's sustainability campaign as just a case of 'greenwash'. If you were a spokesperson for Unilever, how would you deal with this argument?

So why does it make 'sound business sense'?

Leading companies have now moved from the defensive stances of early CSR efforts to explore new ways of engaging with a range of external stakeholders. In 2010, The Doughty Centre for Corporate Responsibility undertook research for Business in the Community. They found 60 business benefits from being a responsible business (Doughty Centre for Corporate Responsibility 2011). They clustered these benefits into the following seven categories:

- **Brand value and reputation**—brand value is strongly influenced by CSR activities. A study by the Reputation Institute in 2013 found that 73 per cent of 55,000 consumers surveyed were willing to recommend companies they perceived to be delivering on CSR, although of the 100 companies included in the study, only five were considered to be delivering on their CSR activities compared to 12 the previous year.

- **Employees and future workforce**—just as prospective employees are put off from what are seen as bad employers, then those seen as leaders in the field of CSR will more easily attract and retain staff. Moreover, they are likely to have a more highly motivated workforce.

- **Operational effectiveness**—more efficient environmental processes can lead to operational efficiency, as can reducing waste. Better-motivated staff can also help companies reduce their operating costs.

- **Risk reduction and management**—i.e. the ability to identify and manage risks better.

- **Direct financial impact**—improved access to capital, reducing costs, and improving shareholder value.

- **Organizational growth**—many surveys show that customers are concerned about the environmental impact of the products they consume, about who made them, and under what conditions they were made. Growth can come from new markets, new product development, lateral expansion, new customers, and new partnerships.

- **Business opportunity**—the opportunities that arise from addressing stakeholder concerns such as poverty, water shortages, and poor health. Food companies, for example, can reduce the salt and fat content of food and thereby reduce costs and the use of resources, and address health concerns of the community.

The Doughty Centre identified two other benefits that were only just beginning to emerge, but were more prominent in those companies already committed to responsible business:

- Responsible leadership—ensuring social and environmental issues are factored into the core business model. Unilever, mentioned above, is seen as a champion of sustainability and has seen growth in sales and profits.

- Macro-level sustainable development—the benefits of contributing to sustained development. The UN Global Compact and the Sustainable Development Goals (see this chapter, Sustainable Development Goals) are good examples of corporations engaging with macro-level issues. Therefore, improving health care or education in a supplier country may have long-term benefits for the organization.

 Learning Task

Access the report 'Combing Profit and Purpose: A New Dialogue on the Role of Business in Society', available at https://www.cranfield.ac.uk/som/research-centres/doughty-centre-for-corporate-responsibility/publications/occasional-papers. Use this report and any other appropriate resources to answer the following questions:

1. Should business have a social purpose?
2. Is this simply CSR in a different wrapper?

Global CSR

Is global CSR any different from domestic CSR? Not in principle, but the implementation is far more complex. Take the argument above that modern CSR reflects the changed expectations of society and that the trade-off between growth and the negative impacts of that growth is no longer acceptable. China has often been criticized for lax regulations on working conditions and the environment. It could justifiably argue that the country has been going through a stage in its growth where the cost of improved living standards, in terms of damage to the environment, was acceptable. As China moves into the next stage of growth, it is devoting more effort to deal with air and water pollution; however, as we saw in the opening case study, working conditions remain questionable (see Climate Change News (2016) and News.com.au (2017)).

But what does this mean for the global corporations operating in China and other economies with differing regulatory standards? Should they be able to operate under the less stringent legislation that exists in that country, or should they be working to the same standards that they work to in their home economy? Is there an obligation on the West to share new, environmentally friendly technologies with developing countries, as much of the growth of companies in the West took place in an era of less stringent environmental controls?

Countries differ not just in their environmental legislation, but also in the institutions that govern the countries that in some cases are not very effective. They also differ in their customs and their culture (see Chapter 7). Setting up operations overseas because it is cheaper might be very attractive, but why is it cheaper? Wages are lower, working hours are longer, and health and safety regulations are lax and not policed very well. Is this acceptable? Child labour is illegal, but quite common. Would you tolerate this if these were your factories or if it was happening in your supplier's factories? If the answer is no, and an undercover investigator discovers this and reports it to the Western media, how would you react? Would you instantly close down the factory? What effect would this have on the children working there? These are the types of issues facing global companies in their everyday operations, and it is not that there is one domestic set of circumstances and one overseas set of circumstances; every country will have some differences. Shell, for example, is a global group of companies working in more than 70 countries and territories and employing 92,000 people worldwide (Shell n.d.).

Whose Standards?

Global companies have the problem of doing business in many countries in which the 'ways of doing things' differ. They therefore have the difficult task of deciding which standards to adopt. Should they take a principled stand and adopt a universal set of values wherever they operate, or take a different approach in each country and operate according to the appropriate standards of that country? The first approach appears morally attractive in that we have a tendency to assume that our own standards are the 'right' or 'best' standards and we therefore tend to judge others by those standards, but this can result in an **ethnocentric** (believing that the customs and traditions of your own nationality are better than those of others) morality which opens multinational companies to the charge of **cultural imperialism**. It would satisfy critics who accuse MNCs of exploiting cultural differences for their own benefit, but it may offend host cultures whose accepted practices may be very different, or it may well be impossible to operate without adopting host country practices. For example, when Google entered China (an enormous market with over 700 million internet users), it agreed to some censorship of search results to comply with the Chinese government. This offended many in the West, used to freedom of expression, but Google argued that it would be more damaging to pull out of China altogether but it more or less did just that when it moved its operation to Hong Kong in 2010 in an attempt to bypass Chinese censorship. Its share of the Chinese search market fell to as low as 5 per cent, as most users in China now use the Chinese search engine, Baidu. Since 2014 Google has been in talks with Chinese officials to return to China. However, according to the Deputy Director of the Cyberspace Administration of China, 'As for foreign internet companies, as long as they respect China's laws, don't harm the interests of the country, and don't harm the interests of consumers, we welcome them to enter China, where they can together share the benefits of China's developing internet' (*International Business Times* 2016).

The other extreme is termed **cultural relativism** and, put simply, says, 'When in Rome, do as the Romans do.' This approach recognizes that countries and cultures are different and that MNCs operating in different countries should recognize and accommodate those differences. This is often used as a reason by MNCs to adopt practices that enhance their profits, such as the employment of child labour or lax health and safety standards, which would be questionable in the MNC's home country.

These extreme ethical approaches are useful to business decision-makers to the extent that they do serve to highlight the problems. Donaldson (1989) has suggested that there are some universal principles that companies and nations could agree to work towards. This entails respect for, and promotion of, some minimal rights, including:

- freedom of physical movement;
- ownership of property;
- freedom from torture;
- fair trial;
- freedom from discrimination;
- physical security;
- free speech and association;
- education;
- political participation; and
- subsistence.

One might argue about which rights should be included, and this may appear as a peculiarly Western set of rights, but this approach to prescribing minimum standards is the approach that has been developed, albeit in a fragmented fashion. Many companies have responded to the CSR debate by developing their own codes of conduct for their global operations, and many international organizations have developed principles that seek to guide companies to best practice in CSR. The UN Global Compact is one such initiative, in which the UN and several campaigning organizations, such as Oxfam and Amnesty International, came together to agree a set of principles for CSR. There were originally nine principles in the areas of human rights, labour, and the environment, and a tenth, concerning anti-corruption, was added in 2004. This initiative was launched in 2000 and now has over 12,000 participants, including more than 9,000 businesses from 170 countries (UN Global Compact n.d.).

 Learning Task

The opening case to this chapter considered conditions in some of Apple's Chinese suppliers. Discuss the statement that Western companies have no responsibility for the conditions in their supplier factories.

The Ten Principles

The principles are derived from:

- the Universal Declaration of Human Rights;
- the International Labour Organization's Declaration on Fundamental Principles and Rights at Work;
- the Rio Declaration on Environment and Development; and
- the United Nations Convention Against Corruption.

The Global Compact asks companies to embrace, support, and enact, within their sphere of influence, a set of core values in the areas of human rights, labour standards, the environment, and anti-corruption (see Table 5.1).

Learning Task

Use the UN's website on the Global Compact to explain why adherence to these principles is in the best interest of business.

Four of the major weaknesses of these codes are as follows:

1. Not many of the world's MNCs are members; 12,000 sounds like a lot, but is actually only a small proportion of the world's tens of thousands of MNCs. However, many of those who have joined are important in terms of size and reputation.

2. The codes are voluntary and the UN cannot afford to be too selective about who joins the initiative.

Table 5.1 UN Global Compact principles

Human rights	Principle 1: Businesses should support and respect the protection of internationally proclaimed human rights.
	Principle 2: Make sure that they are not complicit in human rights abuses.
Labour standards	Principle 3: Businesses should uphold the freedom of association and the effective recognition of the right to collective bargaining.
	Principle 4: Eliminate all forms of forced and compulsory labour.
	Principle 5: Achieve effective abolition of child labour.
	Principle 6: Eliminate discrimination in respect of employment and occupation.
Environment	Principle 7: Businesses should support a precautionary approach to environmental challenges.
	Principle 8: Undertake initiatives to promote greater environmental responsibility.
	Principle 9: Encourage the development and diffusion of environmentally friendly technologies.
Anti-corruption	Principle 10: Businesses should work against corruption in all its forms, including extortion and bribery.

Source: https://www.unglobalcompact.org/what-is-gc/mission/principles

3. It is difficult to monitor the impact that the Compact is making.

4. No effective sanctions for breaches of the code exist, although over 7,000 companies have been expelled from the Compact for failing to report progress for two consecutive years (UN Global Compact (n.d.)).

Companies that join are simply required to work towards implementation of the principles. They do have to report annually on their activities, through what the Compact refers to as 'Communication on Progress'. This entails a statement of continuing support, a description of practical actions, and a measurement of outcomes. In measuring outcomes, participants are encouraged to use the Global Reporting Initiative (GRI). The GRI is an attempt to produce standard sustainability reporting guidelines and make it as routine for companies as financial reporting. It produces a standard format for companies to report on their economic, environmental, and social performance (see GRI (n.d.)). Over 1,000 organizations, ranging from companies, public bodies, NGOs, and industry groups, use the guidelines, which makes it the most common framework in use. Unilever, for example, assesses progress against three indices: the UN Global Compact, GRI, and Sustainable Development Goals (SDGs).

The picture, then, is of a complex global system in which the ability of the state to look after the public interest, even in relatively developed economies, is diminished. Global companies operate in many states that are weak and often corrupt. There are major world issues, such as climate change, poverty, health issues, human rights, corruption, and ecosystem problems, which are also beyond the powers of national governments and, internationally, there is a lack of effective governance. There is also a growing number of very active NGOs, often campaigning on a single issue, who are demanding action from companies. In turn, the health of companies will, in the long term, depend on the health of the global economic, social and political, and environmental systems. The case for CSR rests on a recognition by companies of this scenario and that they are in a unique position to address these issues. Many have responded, perhaps for defensive reasons, by engaging with their stakeholders and developing codes of conduct for their global activities. International organizations have also added to the drive for CSR by developing their own codes or sets of principles to which they encourage companies to adhere.

Having examined the case for CSR, we now turn to examine in more detail some of the specific issues facing global companies.

Corruption

Corruption is a major issue for international business. Transparency International (TI) an international NGO which works across the world to tackle corruption defines corruption as 'the abuse of entrusted power for private gain'. TI classifies corruption as grand, petty, and political.

Grand corruption depends on the amounts of money lost and the sector where it occurs. It consists of acts committed at a high level of government that distort policies or the central functioning of the state, enabling leaders to benefit at the expense of the public good.

Petty corruption refers to everyday abuse of entrusted power by low- and mid-level public officials in their interactions with ordinary citizens, who are often trying to access basic goods or services in places like hospitals, schools, police departments, and other agencies.

Political corruption is a manipulation of policies, institutions and rules of procedure in the allocation of resources and financing by political decision makers, who abuse their position to sustain their power, status, and wealth. TI has a whole glossary of types of corruption available at https://www.transparency.org/glossary.

Corruption occurs when organizations or individuals profit improperly through their position. It occurs in both the public and the private sectors—for example, when private businesses want public contracts or licences, or when private firms wish to do business with others. Bribery is only one example of corruption. It can also include **extortion** (where threats and violence are used to get someone to act or not act in a certain way), **favouritism**, **nepotism**, **embezzlement**, fraud, and illegal monetary contributions to political parties. In some cultures, corruption is accepted as the norm, and many commentators (and sometimes the law) make a distinction between bribes and so-called 'facilitation payments', which are everyday small payments made to officials to 'ease the wheels of business'. International pressure groups, such as Transparency International, make no such distinction (Transparency International n.d.a).

What's Wrong with Bribery and Corruption?

According to Transparency International, it is impossible to gauge the cost of corruption with complete accuracy because of its very nature but they do present a number of informed estimates (Transparency International n.d.b). Global Financial Integrity (GFI) calculate that in 2013, developing countries lost $1.1 trillion to illicit financial flows, and that over the decade 2004 to 2013, this had been increasing at a rate of 10 per cent per year (GFI n.d.). This, of course, only reflects the direct financial costs and takes no account of other costs. As GFI point out, this also has a damaging subversive effect on governments and society in general.

The cost of bribes falls mainly on the poor, whether it is through the diversion of aid money into corrupt officials' pockets or the hiking of prices when the cost of a bribe is passed on in raised prices to consumers.

- Bribery and corruption undermine the proper workings of a market economy, which can seriously reduce GDP in the poorest countries. It distorts price and cost considerations so that resources are not necessarily used in the most efficient way. Decisions are based on 'who pays the biggest bribes' rather than price, quality, service, and innovation. This raises prices for everyone, but has the greatest impact on the poor.

- Resources are often diverted away from public service projects, such as schools and hospitals, towards more high-profile projects, such as dams and power stations, where there is more scope for improper payments. This again impacts most on the poor who are denied vital public services.

- Corruption is ethically wrong. It is an abuse of power, which undermines the integrity of all concerned.

- Corruption undermines the democratic process and the rule of law. Just as business has to earn its licence to operate, so does government. Politicians, government officers, and institutions all lose their legitimacy in a climate of corruption. Again, the poor are likely to be the biggest losers in such a situation.

- The environment is also likely to suffer in such a regime through the lack of environmental legislation or its non-enforcement as corrupt officials fill their pockets in return for turning a blind eye.

For business, there are several risks:

- Accusations of corruption, whether proved or not, can lead to loss of reputation.

- Bribery and corruption is generally illegal wherever it occurs, but even if not, because of international pressure (the UN convention against corruption) it is becoming increasingly illegal at home (e.g. in the USA and UK) to engage in these practices elsewhere (see Chapter 10).

- In paying bribes, there is no certainty you get what you want and no recourse to any retribution or compensation if you do not.

- If you are known as a bribe payer, repeat demands are likely to be made.

- It adds substantially to the cost of doing business.

- If you cheat, so will your competitors. It makes doing business much more difficult.

- Employees and other stakeholders will lose trust in the business.

Transparency International was founded in 1993 to fight corruption. Each year, Transparency International produces the **Corruption Perceptions Index** (CPI). This index ranks 176 countries according to the level of corruption perceived to exist among public officials and politicians. A score of zero indicates highly corrupt and a score of 10 very clean.

On the map in Figure 5.1, the darker the colour the higher the perceived incidence of corruption, which is generally low in North America, Western Europe, and Australasia and high in Central and South America, Africa, Asia, and Eastern Europe.

Figure 5.1 Corruption Perceptions Index 2017

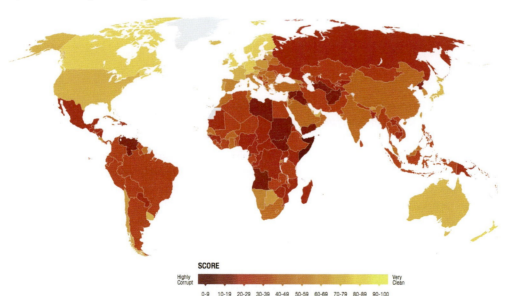

Source: Corruption Perceptions Index 2017 by Transparency International is licensed under CC-BY-ND 4.0, https://www. transparency.org/news/feature/corruption_perceptions_index_2017#resources

Learning Task

Go to the TI website and access the Corruption Perceptions Index, on which the map above is based.

1. Explain what the Corruption Perceptions Index measures.
2. Look up Table 2.1 in Chapter 2. For each of the countries plot on a graph their rank and CPI score against their GDP. What conclusions can you draw from your graph?

Child Labour

Trying to arrive at a clear picture of child work is a difficult task. We are all familiar with the horror pictures of child mineworkers, soldiers, and prostitutes, but most child work takes place within the family in agriculture and domestic work, and in societies where this is often seen as culturally acceptable. The International Labour Office (ILO) divides child work into three categories:

- economically active: a very wide category which refers to any form of productive work, paid or unpaid;
- child labour: work that is done by a child under the specified age for work, which either deprives them of schooling, causes them to leave school early, or requires a combination of schooling and long hours of work; and
- hazardous work: the worst form of child labour, exposing children to conditions which are damaging to their mental, physical, and emotional development, and which the international community has agreed to try to end.

 Counterpoint Box 5.2 Corruption—is it always a bad thing?

Corruption occurs on a large scale and is growing. The IMF, quoting Kaufman (2005), estimate the annual cost of bribery alone at US$1.5–2 trillion or 2 per cent of global GDP (IMF 2016).

According to the IMF (2016), when government functions are impaired, this can adversely affect a number of important determinants of economic performance, including macro financial stability, investment, human capital accumulation, and total factor productivity. Moreover, when systemic corruption affects virtually all state functions, distrust of government can become so pervasive that it can lead to violence, civil strife, and conflict, with devastating social and economic implications.

However, corruption is not always seen as a bad thing. Chang (2008) argues that bribery does not inevitably slow down economic development. For example, where a public servant takes a bribe from a firm and invests that money in a project as productive as the firm would have done, then the act of bribery may have little or no adverse effect on efficiency or growth. He also asserts that a company getting a contract through bribery may be the most efficient contender for the contract. In fact, it is likely that the most efficient firms can afford to pay the highest bribes. Some economists see corruption as rectifying market failure. A government may set a price for a good or service that does not reflect market pressures of supply and demand. A bribe could result in the authorities turning a blind eye to illegal trading on the black market, which could move the price closer to an equilibrium level, thereby bringing about a more efficient allocation of resources. →

→ Corruption, of course, is a broad term covering many different activities, including bribery. Cultural norms differ across the world and in some societies bribes are seen as part of the price paid in order to 'get things done'.

Sources: Chang (2008); Underkuffler (2009); Transparency International, Global Corruption Report 2009; IMF (2016) Corruption: Costs and Mitigating Strategies. IMF Discussion Note. SDN/16/05

Questions

1. Do you think it is possible to differentiate between different forms of corruption and bribery? Explain your answer.
2. Is all bribery bad? Justify your answer.

In 2016 there were 218 million children (down from 306 million in 2008) aged between 5 and 17 in employment, with 152 million (215 million in 2008) involved in child labour and 73 million undertaking hazardous work (45 million boys and 28 million girls). They do it because their survival and that of their families depend on it (International Labour Office 2017).

Not all work done by children is considered harmful, and therefore in policy terms it is not just a case of eliminating all child labour. Work that does not damage health or interfere with schooling may be considered positive in contributing to personal development by developing skills and experience and preparing children for adult life, so-called 'child work'. The ILO has two conventions relating to child labour. Convention 138 allows 'child work' but aims at the abolition of child labour and stipulates that the minimum age for entry into the workforce should not be less than the minimum age for finishing school. Convention 182 calls for elimination of the worst forms of child labour for all under-18s. This includes slavery, forced recruitment for use in armed conflict, prostitution, any illicit activity, and work that is likely to harm the health, safety, and morals of children. These conventions lay down the basic principles to be implemented by ratifying countries and are tools for governments to use, in consultation with employers and workers, to draft legislation to conform with internationally acceptable standards. There are 187 ILO members, of which 181 have ratified convention 182 (including the Ivory Coast—see Mini Case Study 5.3) and 170 have ratified convention 138. However, as the figures given here indicate, child exploitation is still a huge global problem.

Child labour is not simply a problem of the developing world, although most takes place there. The Asian Pacific region has the highest number of child workers, with 62 million representing nearly 7.4 per cent of the age group. This figure had declined by 34 million since 2008. Africa has the highest incidence of child labour at 19.6 per cent. A similar pattern is displayed for children in hazardous work, with 28.5 million in the Asia Pacific region and 31.5 million in the Africa region, which has the highest incidence, indicating nearly 9 per cent children involved (International Labour Office 2017).

Mini Case Study 5.3 Cocoa production in West Africa

The global chocolate market is worth more than US$110 billion per year. Most of that chocolate starts life in West Africa where over 70 per cent of the world's cocoa production is grown. The Ivory Coast is the largest producer with 35 per cent of world production but Ghana, Nigeria and Cameroon are also significant suppliers. In the Ivory Coast, about 1 →

→ million small, family-run farms of less than 4 hectares grow cocoa as a cash crop alongside crops grown for food. More than 6 million rely on these farms for a living. Farms are often remote and as mechanization is not appropriate, production is very labour intensive. Cocoa is a year round crop. When the pods ripen they need to be cut from the trees, usually by machetes. The pods are split open, again with machetes, and the beans extracted from the white milky pulp they sit in. The beans are then fermented, dried, cleaned, and packed. The pods from one tree for a year make about half a kilo of cocoa. Once the beans reach the processors in the Northern hemisphere they are then crushed, the shells removed, roasted, and finally ground. Then the chocolate can be made or the beans can be turned into cocoa butter or cocoa powder.

The global supply chain is quite complex, with many intermediaries before the chocolate reaches the final consumer. Cocoa growers generally sell to a middleman for cash once or twice a year and have to take whatever price they can get. The middleman sells on to processors or exporters. Prices are ultimately determined on the London Cocoa Terminal Market and the New York Cocoa Exchange, but, like many cash crops, the farmer receives a fraction of the world price. The USA and Germany are the biggest consumers.

There is, therefore, great pressure on the farmer to keep costs down; one way of achieving this is to employ child labour. Most of the children are under 14, kept from schooling, work 12-hour days, apply pesticides, and use machetes to clear fields and split harvested cocoa pods to extract the beans. All of this falls into the ILO convention 182 of 'the worst form of child labour'.

In 2000, a British TV documentary claimed that many children were working as slaves in the Ivory Coast. Because the demand for child labour outstrips the supply, children were purchased from the neighbouring states of Burkino Faso, Mali, and Togo. Impoverished parents would receive between £70 and £100 for each child, depending on the age. These children, some as young as six, were forced to endure harsh working conditions and long hours, and many also faced physical abuse by their masters.

An industry protocol (the Harkin-Engel protocol), signed on 19 September 2001, established the International Cocoa Initiative made up of chocolate companies, confectionery trade associations, NGOs, and trade unions to work with governments to end the worst forms of child labour. The initial deadline was 2005, but this has now been pushed back to 2020. The University of Tulane, overseeing the protocol, found that in 2009 there were 820,000 children working in cocoa in the Ivory Coast, only 40 per cent were enrolled in school, and only 5 per cent were paid for their work. Between 2001 and 2009, 8,243 children (about 1 per cent) had been reached as a result of interventions, and Tulane concluded that this was not sufficient in light of commitments under the protocol. They visited again during the 2013 harvest and found that the number of child workers had increased by 46 per cent (from 0.79 million to 1.15 million). There had been a strong growth in cocoa production. The children were less exposed to hazardous work in relation to land clearing but more exposed to agro-chemicals. Access to education had improved, with 71 per cent of children attending school compared to 59 per cent in 2008/09. Tulane concluded that while some progress had been made, the major reduction called for by the Harkin-Engel Protocol 'has not come within reach'.

In 2011 and 2013, as part of their Freedom Project, CNN visited the Ivory Coast to see if conditions were improving. What they found was not very different from the picture painted above. There is a series of videos and other material on what they call 'Cocoa-nomics' CNN (2014).

Sources: http://www.bbc.co.uk/news/world-africa-15681986; Ould et al. (2004); Robson (2010); Schrage and Ewing (2005). The latest University of Tulane report is available at http://www.childlaborcocoa. org/images/Payson_Reports/Tulane%20University%20-%20 Survey%20Research%20on%20Child%20Labor%20in%20the%20 Cocoa%20Sector%20-%2030%20July%202015.pdf.

Questions

1. Why do children work in the cocoa plantations of the Ivory Coast?

2. What efforts are companies making to eradicate this problem? How successful are they?

3. Discuss whether certification is the answer, or whether this is just developed country morals being applied to the less developed world.

Why do Children Work?

Reasons for child work can be divided into push and pull, or supply and demand, factors. On the supply side, the following push children into work:

- Poverty—poverty remains the most important factor which pushes children into work.
- Lack of educational opportunities—poor educational facilities or expensive facilities can exacerbate the problem.
- Family breakdown—divorce, death, or illness can leave the family unit short of income. This has become a major problem in Africa because of the HIV/AIDS epidemic.
- Cultural practices—in many countries it is the practice for young children to help the family by looking after younger brothers and sisters or helping out on the land, by collecting firewood, or tending chickens, for example.

On the demand side, the following pull children into work:

- Cheap labour—employers tend to pay children less than their adult counterparts. Some, especially domestic workers, work unpaid.
- Obedience—even where children are paid the same rate as adults, employers often prefer to employ children as they are much easier to control.
- Skills—the so-called 'nimble fingers' argument, especially in industries such as carpet weaving; probably a mythical argument, but one which is used to justify the employment of children.
- Inadequate laws—or poorly understood and policed laws, enable employers to continue employing children.
- Poor infrastructure—establishing the age of children in some countries can be difficult.

What's Wrong with Child Labour?

- Child labour is a denial of fundamental human rights. The UN has adopted the Convention on the Rights of the Child. Article 32 says that children should not be engaged in work which is hazardous, interferes with education, or is harmful to health.
- It steals their childhood from them.
- It prevents their education.
- Children are exploited by being paid low wages or no wages at all.
- Children often work in poor conditions, which can cause long-term health problems.
- It perpetuates poverty because lack of education limits earning potential.
- It can mean lower wages for everybody, as children swell the labour supply and are usually paid lower wages than adults.
- They replace adult labour because they are cheaper to employ and easier to control.
- It is a long-term cost to society as children are not allowed to fulfil their potential as productive human beings.

Sustainable Development Goals

In 2000, 189 members of the UN adopted the Millennium Development Goals in which they committed to eight goals aimed at alleviating world poverty and achieving general development in areas such as gender equality, primary education, and health. The targets were to be achieved, in the main, by 2015. Have the goals been a success? Unsurprisingly it depends who you listen to. Ban Ki-Moon (then Secretary-General of the UN), in his foreword to the MDGS report of 2015, hailed the MDGs as the 'the most successful anti-poverty movement in history' (UN 2015). The MDGs did help to lift many people out of extreme poverty (halving the number living on less than $1 per day) but it is recognized that much of this was because of the rapid economic prog-ress of China and India and that it focused on the symptoms (a head count measure of poverty) rather than the causes of poverty (lack of education, lack of opportunity, poor health, etc.). Moving a few people from just below the measured poverty level to just above might be easily done and ignore the most deprived. A large proportion of Sub-Saharan Africa (40 per cent) still suffers from extreme poverty, as do many in Southern and Western Asia. The UN also claim that 'The proportion of undernourished people in the developing regions has fallen by almost half since 1990, from 23.3 per cent in 1990–1992 to 12.9 per cent in 2014–2016'.

Others doubt these figures. Hickel (2016) believes that the two key claims of reduced poverty and hunger 'are misleading, and even intentionally inaccurate'. He accuses the UN of having 'used targeted statistical manipulation' to make things seem better than they are. He asserts that poverty and hunger have actually worsened and 4 billion people remain in poverty and about 2 billion remain hungry. He also questions the definitions of poverty and hunger used by the UN, saying that 'they dramatically underestimate the scale likely of these problems'.

The goals themselves have not been without their critics. See, for example, Clemens and Moss (2005: 1), who argued that:

Many poor countries, especially those in Africa, will miss the MDGs by a large margin. But neither African inaction nor a lack of aid will necessarily be the reason. Instead responsibility for near-certain failure lies with the overly-ambitious goals themselves and unrealistic expecta-tion placed on aid.

Others, such as Easterly (2009), criticized the MDGs because they were unfair to Africa whose low starting point made it almost a certainty they would miss the goals. Leo and Barmeier (2010) of the Center for Global Development say that the targets were global and not supposed to be applied to regions or an individual country. Regional reporting tends to mask the fact that some countries are doing well and others not so well. Large African countries such as Nigeria, not doing so well, pull down the regional performance and mask some who had done very well. Many of those not doing well, they noted, had been devastated by conflict.

As well as regional reporting, the targets tended to focus on statistical averages and so ignored inequalities, discrimination, and injustice. As noted below, this left many people still in poverty and lacking basic necessities. The goals have also been criticized for being top-down (i.e. a Western agenda) with a lack of consultation with the 'bottom'. The goals were actually formulated by staff at the UN plus a few other international agencies such as the IMF, World Bank, and OECD.

A more fundamental criticism was the omission of certain key features. The MDGs were built on the UN Millennium Declaration, which considered certain fundamental values to be essen-tial in the twenty-first century: freedom, equality, solidarity, tolerance, respect for nature, and shared responsibility. The Declaration also recognized that to achieve this, progress was needed on several areas: development and poverty eradication, environmental protection, human rights, democracy and good governance. There was no mention in the MDGs of human rights, democracy, and good governance (see Nanda 2016).

Notwithstanding this, the MDGs did focus the world's attention, generated discussion, and gained public support for aid programmes. Significant progress was made in those areas that were targeted and measured; however, as the Millennium Development Goals Report 2015 concludes:

> Despite enormous progress, even today, about 800 million people still live in extreme poverty and suffer from hunger. Over 160 million children under age five have inadequate height for their age due to insufficient food. Currently, 57 million children of primary school age are not in school. Almost half of global workers are still working in vulnerable conditions, rarely enjoying the benefits associated with decent work. About 16,000 children die each day before celebrating their fifth birthday, mostly from preventable causes. The maternal mortality ratio in the developing regions is 14 times higher than in the developed regions. Just half of pregnant women in the developing regions receive the recommended minimum of four antenatal care visits. Only an estimated 36 per cent of the 31.5 million people living with HIV in the developing regions were receiving ART in 2013. In 2015, one in three people (2.4 billion) still use unimproved sanitation facilities, including 946 million people who still practise open defecation. Today over 880 million people are estimated to be living in slum-like conditions in the developing world's cities.

In 2012, the United Nations held a conference in Rio de Janeiro to begin the process of consulting widely (see, for example, the UNDP report, A Million Voices: The World We Want (2013)) to develop a new set of goals to supersede the MDGs. This resulted in the 17 goals set out in Table 5.2.

For each of the SDGs there are specific targets (169 in total for all SDGs), to be met by 2030, and for each goal/target, a list of indicators against which progress can be measured (see UN n.d.). For example, goal 1, 'end poverty in all its forms everywhere', has its first target as 'By 2030, eradicate extreme poverty for all people everywhere, currently measured as people living on less than $1.25 a day'. The first indicator of this is 'Proportion of population below the international poverty line, by sex, age, employment status and geographical location (urban/rural)'.

Unlike the MDGs, which focused mainly on developing countries, the SDGs are universal and apply to all countries equally, recognizing that poverty, inequality, discrimination, etc. exist in developed as well as developing countries (note that goal one refers to 'poverty in all its forms everywhere'). New goals were added on climate change, economic inequality, innovation, sustainable consumption, peace, and justice. It was recognized that the goals are interconnected, and that progress in one often requires progress in other, often systemic, areas. Hence the term 'sustainable' is used, indicating development in the three areas: economic, social, and environmental.

The Sustainable Development Goals and Business

The goals came into effect in January 2016. Governments across the world are expected to integrate the goals into their national development plans although there is no legal obligation for them to do so. Unlike the MDGs, the SDGs explicitly call for all stakeholders, including business, to contribute actively to achieving the agenda. It is, after all, in the interest of business for the

Table 5.2 Sustainable development goals

No.	Goal
1	End poverty in all its forms everywhere.
2	End hunger, achieve food security and improved nutrition, and promote sustainable agriculture.
3	Ensure healthy lives and promote well-being for all at all ages.
4	Ensure inclusive and equitable quality education and promote lifelong learning opportunities for all.
5	Achieve gender equality and empower all women and girls.
6	Ensure availability and sustainable management of water and sanitation for all.
7	Ensure access to affordable, reliable, sustainable and modern energy for all.
8	Promote sustained, inclusive and sustainable economic growth, full and productive employment and decent work for all.
9	Build resilient infrastructure, promote inclusive and sustainable industrialization and foster innovation.
10	Reduce inequality within and among countries.
11	Make cities and human settlements inclusive, safe, resilient, and sustainable.
12	Ensure sustainable consumption and production patterns.
13	Take urgent action to combat climate change and its impacts.*
14	Conserve and sustainably use the oceans, seas, and marine resources for sustainable development.
15	Protect, restore, and promote sustainable use of terrestrial ecosystems, sustainably manage forests, combat desertification, and halt and reverse land degradation and halt biodiversity loss.
16	Promote peaceful and inclusive societies for sustainable development, provide access to justice for all, and build effective, accountable, and inclusive institutions at all levels.
17	Strengthen the means of implementation and revitalize the Global Partnership for Sustainable Development.

* Acknowledging that the United Nations Framework Convention on Climate Change is the primary international, intergovernmental forum for negotiating the global response to climate change.
Source: United Nations

SDGs to succeed. As the SDG Compass developed by the GRI (Global Reporting Initiative) and the UN Global Compact (see Table 5.1) point out,

> the SDGs can help to connect business strategies with global priorities. The SDGs can be used as an overarching framework to shape, steer, communicate and report strategies, goals and activities, allowing capitalization on a range of benefits such as:
>
> • Identifying future business opportunities
>
> • Enhancing the value of corporate sustainability
>
> • Strengthening stakeholder relations and keeping pace with policy developments
>
> • Stabilizing societies and markets
>
> • Using a common language and shared purpose.
>
> (SDG Compass (2015))

These ideas fit well with the business case for CSR made earlier in the chapter and the SDG compass provides a framework for aligning company strategy with the SDGs. A quick internet search will also reveal plenty of private sector agencies presenting grids to enable businesses to map their activities on to the SDG framework. Some, such as Schonherr et al. (2017), argue that the SDGs provide 'a unique opportunity to use the SDGs as a framework for improving CSR engagement of TNCs in line with changing societal expectations'.

Learning Task

Many fear that businesses will cherry-pick the SDGs. and work with those that generate most profit. Does this matter? Is there a risk that some SDGs will be forgotten? How can the UN ensure all SDGs are achieved?

Counterpoint Box 5.3 Are the SDGs the answer to world poverty?

The UN has hailed the SDGs (or as they have become known, 'the Global Goals') as 'an unprecedented opportunity to eliminate extreme poverty and put the world on a sustainable path' (SDG Compass n.d.). However, not all are agreed that this is the best or even the right path to achieve the goals. Hickel (2016) who questioned the UN's claims about the success of the MDGs says the SDGs are simply 'business as usual'; given his criticisms (outlined earlier), they are doomed to failure and are likely to make a bad situation worse. At present, he points out, the strategy for ending poverty and hunger is to promote growth (see goal 8) in the hope that income trickles down from the well-off to the less well-off. However, as he points out, of all the growth in income generated between 1999 and 2008, just 5 per cent went to the poorest 60 per cent. An Oxfam report found that, in 2015, just 62 billionaires (down from 388 in 2010) had the same wealth as the least well-off 50 per cent of humanity (Oxfam n.d.c).

Hickel calls for much stronger redistributive measures and an end to the neo-liberal structuralist agenda proposed by the IMF and the World Bank and supported by the UN. Structural adjustment refers to the policies laid down by these institutions as a condition of receiving loans. They include fiscal austerity (i.e. cutting public spending to reduce budget deficits), deregulation of markets, privatization, devaluation of the currency, and trade liberalization. It is argued that opening up economies to market forces will make them more efficient and that this will lead to improved living standards.

Critics argue that developing countries need the freedom to determine their own policy imperatives. It may be more appropriate for developing countries to protect their industries by raising tariffs rather than reducing them. This would then allow

these economies to diversify away from dependence on price volatile and low value agricultural products. Education, health and infrastructure development are essential to accelerate development, and the free market is unlikely to provide sufficient investment in these areas.

In short, governments in developing countries need to be more active in planning economic activity. Developed economies need to support them by reducing the burden of debt, addressing unfair trading practices, and providing more (condition free) resources.

Questions

1. Explain how the SDGs will lead to reduced poverty and hunger.
2. Critically assess the idea that the SDGs are simply a continuation of the neoliberal agenda.

   Useful resources:

   http://www.globalissues.org/video/727/martin-khor-structural-adjustment-explained: Martin Khor (director of Third World Network) explaining structural adjustment,

   http://www.globalissues.org/video/782/stiglitz-agriculture: Joseph Stiglitz on 'Liberalization & Subsidized Agriculture vs Poor Farmers'.

   Other resources:

   Third World Network (http://www.twn.my/twnintro.htm) and in particular chapter 1 'Reclaiming the public policy space in Spotlight on Sustainable Development' (https://www.2030spotlight.org/en)

   Weber, H. (2017) 'Politics of "Leaving No One Behind": Contesting the 2030 Sustainable Development Goals Agenda'. *Globalizations*, Vol 14 Issue 3.

Mini Case Study 5.4 Rwanda and the Sustainable Development Goals

Rwanda is a landlocked country in east-central Africa with a population of nearly 12 million; it is also the most densely populated country in Africa. Its capital is Kigali. It has a history of ethnic tension, and is perhaps best known for the genocide that took place in 1994 when the majority Hutus slaughtered at least 800,000 Tutsis and moderate Hutus.

It is now a stable but poor country. Its GDP per capita is estimated by the IMF to be $US757 in 2014 ($US2,210 PPP), with the economy growing at an average of between 6 and 8 per cent per annum since 2001. This makes it one of the fastest-growing countries in the whole of Central Africa. Predictions for growth in the next few years are around 7 per cent per annum.

Rwanda's economy is largely dependent on natural resources and commodities. The agricultural sector, although only accounting for 30 per cent of total output, employs around 75 per cent of the workforce. Productivity in this sector is low. The service sector accounts for over 48 per cent of total output and industry 17 per cent. The government is attempting to diversify the economy and industry, and services are growing much faster than the agricultural sector.

Rwanda's relatively fast growth since 2001 has lifted about 1 million people out of poverty, but 63 per cent of the population remain in extreme poverty defined by the World Bank as living on less than US$1.25 per day. Nearly 92 per cent of Rwanda's children now attend primary school; 91 per cent have access to health services, up from 35 per cent in 2006. The rate of infection from HIV/AIDS has been reduced by 50 per cent and maternal mortality has improved greatly from 750 to 540 deaths per 100,000 live births. There is parity between boys and girls in primary and secondary education, and Rwanda has a female majority in Parliament.

Sources: http://www.africaneconomicoutlook.org/en/; http://data.un.org/CountryProfile.aspx?crName=RWANDA; file:///Users/websters/Downloads/Rwanda_EN_2017.pdf

Questions

1. How successful was Rwanda in achieving the MDGs?
2. How do the SDGs differ from the MDGs?
3. How can Rwanda achieve the Sustainable Development Goals?

    See: Africa 2030, How Africa can achieve the Sustainable Development Goals, Report No. 1, 2017, available at https://sdgcafrica.org/wp-content/uploads/2017/03/sdgca-africa-2030-report.pdf.

● CHAPTER SUMMARY

In this chapter, we defined corporate social responsibility as the economic, social, and environmental obligations that firms have to society. Some have a view that the only obligation that business owes to society is to maximize profit; however, many point out that CSR is not necessarily at odds with profit maximization as there is a strong business argument for pursuing CSR. Others argue that companies have a moral duty to pursue a wider set of objectives.

Firms operating in the international business environment face a more complex set of circumstances than those operating only in their own domestic economy, not just because of the different economic and legal context, but because of very different cultural norms. Firms must be wary of what might be seen as cultural imperialism. The UN has established the Global Compact, which seeks to guide companies to best practice in CSR.

Two areas were highlighted to be of particular concern, child labour and corruption, both still common in much of the world. The Global Compact has standards to guide companies in both of these areas. The UN announced in 2000 the Millennium Development Goals, a set of targets for the alleviation of poverty and other development goals to be achieved by 2015. Progress was made, but it was far from uniform across the world or the goals. It was also recognized that there were serious omissions in the MDGs, especially human rights. The MDGs were superseded by the Sustainable Development Goals, launched in 2016, to be achieved by 2030. These recognize many of the deficiencies of the MDGS and call on all stakeholders, including business, to play their part in achieving the goals. Not all are agreed that this is the correct path to reducing world poverty and hunger and achieving the other 'Global Goals' as they have become known.

● REVIEW QUESTIONS

1. Explain what commentators mean when they claim that there is only one responsibility of business and that is to make as much money as possible for their owners.

2. 'Socially responsible business is good business.' Discuss.

3. Explain what is meant by child labour. What might the consequences be for a major Western firm discovered employing young children in overseas factories?

4. Explore the links between the Global Compact and the Sustainable Development Goals. (See UN Global Compact White Paper on the UN Global compact ten principles and the Sustainable Development Goals, available at https://www.unglobalcompact.org/docs/about_the_gc/White_Paper_Principles_SDGs.pdf.)

● ASSIGNMENT TASKS

1. Select an international company of your choice. It should be one that expresses its values on corporate social responsibility in some way. Prepare a report that:

   a. describes the company: name, location, size, main products/services, the market it operates in, main players, and any other information you think is relevant;

   b. outlines the CSR policies of the company; and

   c. analyses the company's activities in relation to its CSR policy.

2. You are working for a large US multinational drinks company wanting to set up a bottling plant overseas. In order to obtain planning permission, you need to make a facilitation payment (bribe) to a local politician, but your company has a strict no-bribes policy. The building of the plant will be subcontracted to a domestic construction company, and one way round this would be to inflate the payment to this company so that they could make the facilitation payment. What would you do? Justify your decision. (Note the US Foreign Corrupt Practices Act—see Chapter 10—and US Dept of Justice (2017).)

Case Study Corruption in Cambodia

© iStock.com/Onfokus

Cambodia ranks 156 out of 176 countries in Transparency International's Corruption Perception's index (2016) alongside the Democratic Republic of the Congo and Uzbekistan. It scored 21 out of 100, showing no improvement over 2015 or 2014.

Cambodia is classified by the World bank as 'lower middle income' (see Chapter 2), although it only just creeps into this bracket with a GNI per head of $1140 (the band is $1026 to $4035) compared to the East Asia pacific average of $9868. On the face of it, Cambodia has done quite well in meeting the MDG of taking people out of absolute poverty with GDP per head rising from $782 in 2010 to $1229 in 2016 (IMF World Economic Database). However, there is widespread poverty and gross inequality. Forty per cent of the population still lives below or close to the poverty line.

Tourism is an important industry in Cambodia with over 5,000,000 international visitors in 2016, according to the Cambodian ministry of Tourism, although the average length of stay is just six days. This is just enough time to see the sights in Phnom Penn and perhaps the Killing Fields at Cheung Ek followed by a trip to Siem Reap to stay in one of the many luxury hotels and spend two or three days visiting the temples of Angkor Wat. Younger tourists can try the delights of 'Pub Street' in the centre of Siem Reap, just like any bar-lined road in Western Europe but hotter and noisier.

While in Sim Reap, tourists might attend a concert by 'Beatocello', the stage name of cellist Dr Beat Richner*, a Swiss national and paediatrician who worked for the Red Cross in Cambodia before the Khmer Rouge reign of terror in the 1970s. In 1991, he was asked by the King of Cambodia to rebuild a children's hospital destroyed during the war. He took up the challenge and now there are five Kantha Bopha children's hospitals providing free care (most families are so poor they could not possibly pay even a small amount for care), funded mainly by private individuals in Switzerland. Beatocello's concerts add to that funding and allow him to spread the word. He is scathing about the World Health Organization's approach to health care in low-income countries, i.e. low-cost/low-technology solutions, and about the corrupt economic and political system so evident in Cambodia. Staff at Kantha Bhopa are paid a 'modest' salary on which they can get by, unlike the usual very low public sector salaries. This seems to have solved the problem of corruption in these hospitals as staff do not need to take, or ask for, a bribe, a problem which is endemic in Cambodia. Nor do they have to take on second 'full-time' jobs unlike many public sector staff who may have had to pay to get their job, and often have two or three 'full-time' jobs in order to make ends meet.

Corruption is an everyday experience for Cambodians. It might be school teachers not fulfilling the curriculum so that they can give extra private lessons, or payment for an alleged motoring offence at a road block erected by the police which seem to pull in every fifth vehicle, or payment for treatment at supposedly 'free' hospitals (not Kantha Bhopa). Worse might be the treatment handed out to the 3,000 poor families who had settled in villages alongside the devastated (as a result of the civil war) railway system. When the Asian Development Bank (ADB) and AusAid (the Australian Aid Agency) combined with the Cambodian Government to fund the reconstruction of the railway system, these families were forcefully evicted by Cambodian developers and moved to inadequate resettlement camps. There they found themselves in appalling conditions and much worse off than they had been previously. AusAid and the ADB found themselves the subject of fierce criticism from NGOs at their failure to manage the resettlement process for which they were responsible. There is no doubt that most Cambodians are poorer than they would be if corruption, and particularly political corruption, was not so widespread.

At the head of this pyramid of corruption is the Prime Minister, Hun Sen. During the civil war, Hun Sen was a Khmer Rouge commander who, in fear for his life from his senior officers, ➡

→ escaped to Vietnam. He later returned with the invading Vietnamese army. He first became Prime Minister in 1985 but lost the election in 1993. He refused to stand down and negotiated to become second prime minister as part of a coalition. In 1997, he seized power in a bloody coup. Although there is the facade of a democracy, Hun Sen has ruled like an autocrat ever since. Whenever he has felt threatened he has resorted to violence, abuse of human rights, corruption, and electoral manipulation.

Having lost ground in local elections in 2016, the Cambodian authorities clamped down on any opposition before elections in 2018. The authorities arrested and jailed the opposition leader, Kem Sokha, on charges of treason, ordered out an American NGO (the National Democratic Institute), and closed down the critical *Cambodia Daily* newspaper by issuing them with a US$6.3 million tax notice, quite out of the blue, with less than a week to pay. All this occurred amid a general clamp-down on all NGOs and civil opposition.

While Prime Minister Hun Sen (or, as he likes to be called, Lord Prime Minister and Supreme Military Commander) has clung on to power, through whatever means he can, his family have become one of the richest, if not the richest, in Cambodia with a combined wealth of between US$500 million and US$1 billion. According to a report by Global Witness (2016), Hun Sen's family 'have amassed vast personal fortunes' through 'a huge network of secret deal-making, corruption and cronyism'. They claim that this probably underestimates the true value, as the data it is based on is limited in scope and the Hun family obscures links by listing friends as nominee owners, or hide their identity behind shell companies. Global Witness accessed original company registration documents for almost 23,000 companies registered in Cambodia to identify holdings of the Hun family members. The family have also populated the ranks of government, military, the courts, and the police with family and friends so they have absolute control over the state and

they can act with impunity, which they do. Such is the justice system that people with wealth are generally able to pay their way out of trouble. The NGOs representing displaced groups as a result of the railways development ended up in the Australian courts, as they knew they would get nowhere in the Cambodian courts. Global Witness concludes that international investors should be wary of investing in Cambodia, as 'the opaque business environment with high-levels of corruption poses major legal, financial and reputational risks for companies'.

Note: *Since this text was written, Dr Beat Richner ('Beatocello') has sadly passed away (9 September 2018).

Sources:

The Situation in 2017, Kantha Bopha Children's Hospitals, available at http://www.beat-richner.ch/Assets/richner_present.html. https://www.centreforpublicimpact.org/case-study/rehabilitation-railway-cambodia

http://devpolicy.org/australian-aid-and-cambodias-troubled-rail-project-20130210

Global Witness (2016) Hostile Takeover, The corporate empire of Cambodia's ruling family. Available at https://www.globalwitness.org/en/reports/hostile-takeover

Questions

1. Assess to what extent Cambodia achieved the MDGs.
2. Explain the process of making the SDGs local, and how this might apply to Cambodia.
3. Explain the terms 'cultural relativism' and 'ethnocentrism'.
4. Using Cambodia as an example, discuss the relevance of these terms for international business.
5. 'The cost of corruption falls mainly on the poor.' Using Cambodia as an example, assess the accuracy of this statement.
6. Global Witness conclude their report by saying the international business should be wary of investing in Cambodia. What are the risks of such an investment?

● FURTHER READING

For a textbook exploring ethics and the CSR agenda within the context of globalization, read:

● Crane, A. and Matten, D. (2016) *Business Ethics: Managing Corporate Citizenship and Sustainability in the Age of Globalisation,* 4th edn. Oxford: Oxford University Press.

They did have a blog at http://craneandmatten.blogspot.co.uk; although this is no longer live, the backfile of articles is still available.

For a view of the case against CSR, see:

- Aneel Karnani in *The Wall Street Journal*. https://www.wsj.com/articles/SB100014240527487033380 04575230112664504890.

- Karnani A. (2011) 'Doing Well by Doing Good: The Grand Illusion'. *California Management Review* 1 February 2011.

For a review of social contract theory and its modern applicability, see:

- Byerly, R. (2013) 'Business in Society: The Social Contract Revisited'. *Journal of Organisational Transformation & Social Change* 10(1): 4–20.

For a book advocating a strategic approach to CSR taking into account global stakeholders, see:

- Werther, B. and Chandler, D. (2013) 'Strategic Corporate Social Responsibility'. *Stakeholders, Globalization, and Sustainable Value Creation,* 3rd edn. London: SAGE Publications.

● REFERENCES

Anshen, M. (1970 [1983]) 'Changing the Social Contract: A Roll for Business'. Reprinted in Beauchamp, T. and Bowie, N. (eds) (1983) *Ethical Theory and Business,* 2nd edn. Prentice Hall.

Apple (n.d.) https://www.apple.com/uk/supplier-responsibility.

Arenas, D., Lozano, J.M., and Albareda, L. (2009) 'Role of NGOs in CSR: Mutual Perceptions Among Stakeholders'. *Journal of Business Ethics* 88.

BBC News (2018a) 'Oxfam scandal: Haiti worker rehired after he was dismissed', 15 February. http://www.bbc.co.uk/news/uk-43079090.

BBC News (2018b) 'Oxfam sex scandal: Director promises justice for victims', 16 February. 2018 http://www.bbc.co.uk/news/uk-43080330.

Bebchuk, L.A. and Fried, J.M. (2006) 'Pay without Performance: Overview of the Issues'. *Academy of Management Perspectives* 20(1).

Bebchuk, L.A., Cohen, A., and Holger, S. (2010) 'The Wages of Failure: Executive Compensation at Bear Stearns and Lehman 2000–2008'. *Yale Journal on Regulation,* 27(2).

CBS News (2013) 'What happened after the Foxconn suicides', 7 August. https://www.cbsnews.com/news/what-happened-after-the-foxconn-suicides.

Certified Accountants Educational Trust (London) (2011) 'Shareholder Primacy in UK Corporate Law: An Exploration of the Rationale and Evidence'. Research Report No. 125.

Chang, H.-J. (2008) *Bad Samaritans: The Myth of Free Trade and the Secret History of Capitalism.* New York: Bloomsbury Press.

Clemens, M. and Moss, T. (2005) *What's Wrong with the Millennium Development Goals.* Centre for Global Development.

Climate Change News (2016) 'China's Five Year Plan to Radically Tighten Air Pollution Targets'. http://www.climatechangenews.com/2016/03/11/chinas-five-yearplan-to-radically-tighten-air-pollution-targets.

CNN (2014), 'Cocao-nomics: Now Can Chocolate Companies Stamp Out Slavery?'. http://thecnnfreedomproject.blogs.cnn.com/2014/02/04/cocoa-nomics-now-can-chocolate-companies-stamp-out-slavery.

Crane, A., Palazzo, G., Spence, L.J., and Matten, D. (2014) 'Contesting the Value of "Creating Shared Value"'. *California Management Review* 56(2): 130–53.

De George, R. (2010) *Business Ethics,* 7th edn. London: Pearson.

Donaldson, T. (1982) *Corporations and Morality.* London: Prentice Hall.

Donaldson, T. (1989) *The Ethics of International Business.* New York: Oxford University Press.

Doughty Centre for Corporate Responsibility (2011) 'The Business Case for being a Responsible Business'. https://www.bitc.org.uk/sites/default/files/kcfinder/files/Business_case_final1.pdf.

Easterly, W. (2009) 'How the Millennium Goals are Unfair to Africa'. *World Development* 37(1): 26.

European Commission (n.d.) http://ec.europa.eu/growth/industry/corporate-social-responsibility_en.

Financial Times (n.d.) http://www.ft.com/lexicon.

French, P. (1979) 'The Corporation as a Moral Person'. *American Philosophical Quarterly*, reprinted in Donaldson, T. and Werhane, P. (1983) *Ethical Issues in Business*. London: Prentice Hall.

Friedman, M. (1970) 'The Social Responsibility of Business Is to Increase its Profits'. Reprinted in Donaldson, T. and Werhane, P. (eds) (1983) *Ethical Issues in Business*. London: Prentice Hall.

GFI (n.d.) http://www.gfintegrity.org/issue/illicit-financial-flows.

Global Witness (2016) 'Hostile Takeover; The Corporate Empire of Cambodia's Ruling Family', July.

Goodpaster, K. and Mathews, J. (1982) 'Can a Corporation have a Conscience?' *Harvard Business Review*, 60(1): 132 reprinted in Beauchamp, T.L. and Bowie, N.E. (1983) *Ethical Theory and Business*, 2nd edn. London: Prentice Hall.

GRI (n.d.). https://www.globalreporting.org/Pages/default.aspx

The Guardian (2016a) 'Your new iPhone's features include oppression, inequality—and vast profit', 19 September. https://www.theguardian.com/commentisfree/2016/sep/19/your-new-iphone-features-oppression-inequality-vast-profit.

The Guardian (2016b) https://www.theguardian.com/environment/2016/mar/09/unilever-settles-dispute-over-mercury-poisoning-in-india.

The Guardian (2017) 'Google fined record €2.4bn by EU over search engine results', 27 June. http://www.theguardian.com/business/2017/jun/27/google-braces-for-record-breaking-1bn-fine-from-eu.

Hay Group (2011) 'Getting the Balance Right: The Ratio of CEO to Average Employee Pay and What It Means for Company Performance'. Available at http://www.haygroup.com/downloads/uk/Getting-the-balance-right.pdf.

Hickel, J. (2016) The true extent of global poverty and hunger: questioning the good news narrative of the Millennium Development Goals. *Third World Quarterly*, Vol. 37, No. 5, 749–67.

International Labour Office (2017) *Global Estimates of Child Labour, Results and Trends, 2012–2016*. Geneva: ILO.

International Business Times (2016) http://www.ibtimes.co.uk/china-would-welcome-facebook-google-return-if-they-play-by-rules-1586235.

International Monetary Fund (IMF) (2016) 'Corruption: Costs and Mitigating Strategies', IMF Discussion Note No. 16/05, 11 May.

KPMG (2017) *The Road Ahead: The KPMG Survey of Corporate Responsibility Reporting 2017*. https://assets.kpmg.com/content/dam/kpmg/xx/pdf/2017/10/kpmg-survey-of-corporate-responsibility-reporting-2017.pdf.

LA Times (2017) 'Were the raw materials in your iPhone mined by children in inhumane conditions?', 23 July.

Leo, B. and Barmeier, J. (2010) 'Who are the MDG Trailblazers? A New MDG Progress Index'. Working Paper No. 222. Center for Global Development.

Li, W. and Young, S. (2016) 'An Analysis of CEO Pay Arrangements and Value Creation for FTSE-350 Companies'. Report commissioned and funded by CFA Society of the United Kingdom (CFA UK).

Lipton, M. and Savitt, W. (2007) 'The Many Myths of Lucian Bebclink'. *Virginia Law Review* 93(3).

Marks and Spencer (n.d.) https://corporate.marksandspencer.com/plan-a/our-approach/delivering-plan-a.

Nanda, Ved P. (2016) 'The Journey from the Millennium Development Goals to the Sustainable Development Goals', *Denver Journal of International Law and Policy* 44, 389.

The New York Times (2016) 'How China Built ''iPhone City'' with Billions in Perks for Apple's Partner', 29 December. https://www.nytimes.com/2016/12/29/technology/apple-iphone-china-foxconn.html.

News.com.au (2017) 'China shuts down tens of thousands of factories in crackdown on pollution'. http://www.news.com.au/world/asia/china-shuts-down-tens-of-thousands-of-factories-in-crackdown-on-pollution/news-story/4d0675471e05d44c5a462c9a4d7f9237.

Oxfam (n.d.a) http://www.oxfam.org/en/about.

Oxfam (n.d.b) http://www.oxfam.org.uk/what-we-do/about-us/how-we-work/our-goals-and-values.

Oxfam (n.d.c) https://www.oxfam.org/sites/www.oxfam.org/files/file_attachments/bp210-economy-one-percent-tax-havens-180116-summ-en_0.pdf.

Ould, D., Jordan, C., Reynolds, R., and Loftin, L. (2004) *The Cocoa Industry in West Africa: A History of Exploitation*. Anti-Slavery International.

Porter, M.E. and Kramer, M.R. (2006) 'Strategy and Society: The Link Between Competitive Advantage and Corporate Social Responsibility'. *Harvard Business Review* 84(12).

Porter, M.E. and Kramer, M.R. (2011) 'The Big Idea, Creating Shared Value'. *Harvard Business Review* January/February.

Reputation Institute (2013) http://www.
    reputationinstitute.com/thought-leadership/
    csr-reptrak-100.

Robson, P. (2010) *Ending Child Trafficking in West Africa,
    Lessons from the Ivorian Cocoa Sector.* Anti-Slavery
    International.

Schonherr, N., Findler, F., and Martinuzzi, M. (2017),
    'Exploring the Interface of CSR and the Sustainable
    Development Goals'. *Transnational Corporations,*
    Volume 24, No. 3.

Schrage, E. and Ewing, A. (2005) 'The Cocoa Industry and
    Child Labour'. *The Journal of Corporate Citizenship*
    2005(18).

SDG Compass (n.d.) https://sdgcompass.org.

SDG Compass (2015) 'The guide for business action on the
    SDGs'. Available at https://sdgcompass.org/
    wp-content/uploads/2015/09/SDG_Compass_Guide_
    Executive_Summary.pdf.

Shell (n.d.) http://www.shell.com/about-us/who-we-are.
    html.

Transparency International (n.d.a) https://www.
    transparency.org/what-is-corruption#define.

Transparency International (n.d.b) http://www.
    transparency.org.uk/corruption/corruption-statistics/#.
    WiaRpRO0PgE.

UN (2015) http://www.un.org/millenniumgoals/2015_
    MDG_Report/pdf/MDG%202015%20rev%20(July%
    201).pdf.

UN (n.d.) https://sustainabledevelopment.un.org/content/
    documents/11803Official-List-of-Proposed-SDG-
    Indicators.pdf.

UN Global Compact (n.d.) https://www.unglobalcompact.
    org/what-is-gc/participants.

UN Global Compact (n.d.), 'Delisted Participants'. https://
    www.unglobalcompact.org/participation/report/cop/
    create-and-submit/expelled.

Underkuffler, L.S. (2009) 'Defining Corruption: Implications
    for Action'. In Rotberg, R.I. (ed), *Corruption, Global
    Security, and World Order.* Cambridge: Brookings
    Institution.

US Dept of Justice (2017) 'Foreign Corrupt Practices Act' at
    https://www.justice.gov/criminal-fraud/foreign-
    corrupt-practices-act.

wbscd (n.d.) http://www.wbcsd.org.

CHAPTER SIX

Assessing Country Attractiveness

LEARNING OUTCOMES

This chapter will enable you to:

- explain the process of internationalization;

- identify reasons for FDI;

- select target markets and sites for exporting and FDI; and

- assess global risks.

Case Study   Netflix and international expansion

© Shutterstock/Kaspars Grinvalds

This case illustrates the rapid and aggressive international expansion of an internet company and some of the issues faced by firms entering overseas markets.

Netflix describes itself as the 'world's leading internet television network' (Netflix 2016). It has 117 million members and operates in over 190 countries. It was founded in 1997 (see Mini Case Study 3.1 Netflix: The Streaming Giant) as a video rental and distribution company by Reed Hastings and Marc Randolph. It operated in its domestic market until 2010, but in just six years it has become truly global.

The year 2007 was something of a watershed moment as Netflix began to offer streaming of on-demand videos which could be viewed from a PC or web-enabled device. The company partnered with various manufacturers of consumer electronics products so the videos could be streamed over an internet connection to those devices. In this way, they hoped to move away from a physical distribution network and reduce costs. This also paved the way for international expansion.

Following slow growth in Netflix's domestic market, the first international expansion was into Canada in September 2010, a market geographically close and not too dissimilar (relatively speaking) to the USA. As Netflix pointed out in its annual report of 2010: 'Operating in international markets requires significant resources and management attention and will subject us to regulatory, economic and political risks that are different from and incremental to those in the United States.' Examples of these risks were the need to take account of cultural and language differences, costs of managing foreign operations, political and social unrest, economic instability, compliance with local laws, different tax regimes, operating in a different currency and exchange rate risk, new and different sources of competition, and reliability of broadband connectivity.

Notwithstanding these additional risks, the move into Canada was followed in 2011 by expansion into 43 countries in Latin America, Central America, and the Caribbean, again with the streaming-only service. There were some problems in the Latin American launch as reliable, fast broadband was limited and unlike in Canada, streaming was new to many. The banking system was also not used to recurrent monthly transactions. Netflix needed more mature markets, with a large middle class, reliable and fast broadband connections, and a well-developed banking system. They found this in the United Kingdom, Ireland, and Scandinavia, their next targets for international expansion in 2012. These countries were relatively easy to enter as English is widely spoken, they have well-developed payments systems, and internet facilities. From there, further European expansion took place in 2013 and 2014, but not always as easily. Germany, for example, had 60–70 good-quality free TV channels and existing streaming rivals. In France and Germany, there are also cultural differences. The Germans like dubbing on English language shows while the French are happy with subtitles. France also has laws that require broadcasters to produce 40 per cent of their content locally and to pay extra taxes to fund the TV and film industry (AdAge 2014). Netflix's strategy for expansion is to make a limited offer, learn quickly from data from the initial subscribers, and then adapt content.

In 2015 Netflix expanded to Australia, New Zealand, Japan, and further in Europe. Japan has well-developed internet services and payments infrastructure, but can be culturally difficult to enter. To overcome this, the company partnered with local agencies to develop 40 per cent more local content, double the usual 20 per cent. In 2016, Netflix announced expansion to the rest of the world with plans to enter 130 new territories. China, because of tight government control of the internet and media, remains a target although a licensing deal with a Baidu (China's leading internet company)-owned company was reached. Other gaps are Crimea, Syria, and North Korea.

In combating Asia, Netflix may face even bigger challenges. There are already many streaming services able to offer local content, and in some markets Netflix is relatively expensive. English is not as widely spoken and payments mechanisms are not as well developed. Government censorship can also be →

→ a big problem. Indonesia (see the Case Study at the end of this chapter) has strict laws on what can be screened, and Netflix ran foul of these. Similar problems were also met in Malaysia and Vietnam. As offerings are expensive in these countries, piracy can also be a problem.

Sources: Netflix company reports; AdAge (2014). Netflix Braves Cultural Barriers for European Expansion. Emma Hall: https://www.digitaltrends.com/home-theater/netflix-launches-in-japan-though-its-doing-things-a-little-differently-there; Reuters (2016).

Introduction

In Chapter 4, we looked at tools that could be used to make sense of the international business environment. In this chapter, we shall explain the internationalization process and why companies would want to invest overseas (FDI). We then show how organizations can assess the attractiveness of countries as markets or production locations.

The Internationalization Process

International business includes firms undertaking imports and exports, producing abroad, or being involved in joint ventures, licensing, or franchising arrangements with a foreign partner. It ranges from firms producing goods and services in a single country and exporting them to another, to firms like Dell with complex global production and distribution networks across dozens of countries.

The traditional view of international business is that firms initially establish a stable domestic base before venturing overseas. Arenius (2005), quoting a Finnish company executive, provides a reason for this:

> it seems easier for a fellow countryman to sell to a fellow countryman . . . It's easier for a Swedish company to do business with a Swedish person, who is located in the nice city of Stockholm and speaks their native language . . . There are cultural differences. You need to have an American to sell to an American company.

Carrefour, a French company, is one of the world's largest retailers with 11,935 stores in over 30 countries. The Carrefour name came into being in 1959, but it was not until 1969 that it took its first venture outside France, and that was in Belgium—a country very similar to France in terms of its business environment. Carrefour's next venture was to Spain and then in 1975 to South America. It was not until 1989, when it entered the Taiwanese market, that it ventured into a very different business environment. However, in 2016, 9,543 of its stores were in Europe, accounting for 73 per cent of turnover (Carrefour n.d.).

Traditionally, companies are seen as internationalizing incrementally in three stages, following the Uppsala model (see Johanson and Vahlne 1977). From their domestic base, firms develop gradually by exporting to another country that is geographically and culturally similar. Initially, exporting takes place either directly through the company's own export department or indirectly via an external export agency. Then, as overseas business expands, and with it the experience and confidence of operating in overseas markets, the firm becomes more committed to

Table 6.1 The traditional model of internationalization

Entry mode	Description
Export from domestic base	Directly through export department or via overseas agent
Licensing/franchising	An agreement to allow a partner to manufacture or sell abroad
Joint venture	An alliance in which an equity investment is made with a partner
Wholly owned subsidiary	Either acquisition of existing firms (brownfield investment) or entirely new facilities (greenfield investment)

foreign activities. This can take the form of exporting to more distant and less culturally similar countries, and perhaps setting up an overseas sales company. Success, combined with the greater knowledge of foreign markets, according to the traditional model, leads ultimately to the setting up of production facilities across the world that can be done with partner firms through joint ventures or totally owned foreign subsidiaries (see Table 6.1). Whatever mode of operations is used, expanding overseas is always challenging.

This traditional model of slow and incremental development of international business has been challenged in a number of ways. Benito et al. (2009) argue that the reality is much 'messier' and that, rather than a simple sequential process, firms may often operate different modes at the same time. Malhotra and Hinings (2010) argue that different types of organization follow different processes of internationalization. The Uppsala model was based on the study of Swedish manufacturing firms, but now many different organizations are internationalizing their operations. Many are consumer and professional service organizations such as hotels, restaurants, accountants, solicitors, retailers, and management consultants, for whom the process is likely to be quite different. Professional service firms often follow clients into new markets, and for consumer services, such as retailing and hotels, the nature of the service demands a physical presence in the host market.

Many empirical studies of the internationalization process, especially in technology-based, knowledge-intensive sectors, contradict the predictions of the three-stage model, and it is now claimed that many firms are 'born global'. A born-global company is one in which foreign sales account for at least 25 per cent of the total within three years of its inception and one that looks to derive significant competitive advantage from operating multinationally (Andersson and Evangelista 2006). Such firms take an international perspective from the outset, with the intention of trading internationally immediately or within a short period of time. 'These firms view the world as their marketplace from the outset and see the domestic market as a support for their international business' (Rennie 1993). They globalize their business rapidly, entering physically distant markets from an early stage in their life cycle (Prashantham 2005). Such companies are usually small, with limited resources but with a global vision (Gabrielson 2005). They tend to be high-technology companies, focused on market niches. Companies in small, open economies, like Denmark, Sweden, and Switzerland, because of the limited size of their domestic market and the pressure of competition, are likely to come under more pressure to enter global markets than are firms based in bigger markets. Andersson and Evangelista (2006) use the example of Rubber, a Swedish company producing advanced cable entries and seals. From the start-up in 1990, the company saw the whole world as its market. It entered around ten new markets each year, and by 2001 it was present in 80 nations. In our opening case study, we could not say that Netflix was 'born global'; however, once it entered the international market in 2011, it became global very rapidly, mostly in response to slow growth in its home market.

The most important macro-trends encouraging the widespread emergence of born-globals are globalization and advanced **information and communications technologies** (ICT). Globalization provides market opportunities and, along with the widespread diffusion of new communications technology and falling transport costs, lowers the costs of entering foreign markets. Born-global firms use technology to achieve competitive advantage and develop a range of alliances and collaborative partnerships with suppliers, distributors, and customers. This helps them to overcome the traditional constraints to internationalization: being too small to gain economies of scale; lack of resources, both financial and knowledge; and an aversion to risk-taking. The financial burden and risk are shared with alliance partners, who provide knowledge about foreign markets (Freeman et al. 2006). Although still small in relation to the total, such firms are taking up an increasing share of world trade (Knight et al. 2004). Fan and Phan (2007) argue that these firms are not such a distinct breed and that they are subject to many of the same influences as in the traditional pattern of internationalization.

 Learning Task

Research the history of an international business organization of your choice. Trace the steps in its growth and see if it fits the traditional path suggested in this chapter.

The Reasons for FDI

Businesses invest abroad for various reasons. The main motives can be summarized as:

- the need to get market access;
- the search for lower production costs; and
- a quest for natural resources and other assets.

Market Access

Business is interested in gaining entry to big markets or markets with the potential for growth and profit. As we saw in Chapter 1, FDI has grown massively in that last 50 years, but it can be very volatile. FDI fell by 16 per cent in 2008 and 37 per cent in 2009 following the global financial crisis. It has since recovered, but is still below pre-crisis levels. In 2017, US$653 billion of FDI flowed into developing countries. Developing Asia was the largest FDI recipient region in the world (China being the major recipient), followed by the European Union and North America (UNCTAD Investment Trends Monitor January 2018).

Emerging markets are particularly attractive markets because of their relatively high rates of economic growth and purchasing power at a time when developed country markets are growing only slowly. As we saw in Chapter 2, emerging markets are estimated to grow at over 5 per cent per annum for the next five years, with China and India estimated to increase by around 7 per cent, whereas the estimate for developed economies is only just above 2 per cent. Looking further into the future, these markets are set to continue to grow and by 2030, 66 per cent of the world's middle class is expected to be in the Asia-Pacific region (see Table 2.3).

A problem confronted by business is that attractive markets are sometimes protected from imports by barriers such as the tariffs the USA levies on imports of steel (*The Economist* 2018), quotas such as those imposed by the EU on Chinese clothing and footwear, and countries such as China and Indonesia trying to ensure that a certain proportion of the cars sold there is manufactured locally. One way of circumventing these barriers is for firms to set up production facilities in the market. Another reason for locating near the market is that, for bulky, low-value goods, transport costs can be prohibitive, and it becomes imperative that firms produce close to their customers. Alternatively, it may be that retail firms like Tesco and Wal-mart, construction companies, or providers of medical or education services have to be in face-to-face contact with their customers. It may also be that important customers can precipitate a decision to invest abroad. When big car firms such as Volkswagen and Fiat moved into Eastern Europe following the collapse of Communism, a large number of car component suppliers felt obliged to follow, given their customers' requirements for just-in-time deliveries (van Tulder and Ruigrok n.d.). Other firms may feel the need to be close enough to respond quickly to alterations in market conditions, such as changes in taste, or to provide speedy after-sales service.

One aspect of modern industrial development is the growth of the digital economy, allowing fast and cheap expansion into other countries without the need for much physical investment in those countries. This means that the investment does not have the same economic impact as conventional FDI in terms of capacity generation or jobs. According to UNCTAD, digital MNEs make about 70 per cent of their sales abroad but only 40 per cent of their assets are based outside of their home country (UNCTAD World Investment Report 2017). As we saw in the opening case study, this growth can be constrained by the so-called 'digital divide' (see Mini Case Study 1.2) in which close to 4 billion people, or three out of every four households, in the developing world lack access to the internet. One of the aims of the SDGs (see Chapter 5) is to 'significantly increase access to information and communications technology and strive to provide universal and affordable access to the internet in least developed countries by 2020'.

Lower Production Costs

Firms are often driven abroad by the need to find cheaper factors of production in order to cut costs. When jobs are transferred abroad, it is referred to as **offshoring**. This has gone on to such an extent that it was estimated that around 40 per cent of US imports are produced by US companies, many of them in China (*Financial Times* 2007). Although this trend has continued, and is much lamented by US workers (it was also a factor in the election of Donald Trump—see Mini Case Study 1.4), some **reshoring** is taking place. Falling labour wage rates in the USA and increasing labour rates in Asia, plus the strengthening of the Chinese currency, have made it more cost-effective to bring production back to the US (Reshoring Initiative 2016).

With the increasing cost of labour in rich countries, industries, particularly labour-intensive industries including textiles, clothing, and footwear, and firms assembling electronic components, have looked abroad for cheaper locations. Financial institutions have also relocated data processing and call centre activities to countries such as India, as have computer manufacturers and internet service providers. Initially, firms transferred low-level, unskilled, or semi-skilled work to countries where labour was cheap, labour market regulation loose, and there was a low level of unionization of the workforce. However, with the passage of time, firms have started to transfer higher-level activities, such as product design and development, as they discovered that developing countries also had pools of highly educated, technically qualified, and relatively cheap labour. In India, there is an abundance of well-trained programming, software-developer, and systems-engineering talent, while China and Taiwan are developing world-class design expertise in specific technologies. Design is one of the most popular subjects at Chinese universities, and hundreds of design consulting firms have sprung up in cities such as Shanghai and Beijing.

The savings in labour costs from offshoring can be substantial. In 2015, a manufacturing worker in the UK cost US\$31.44 per hour, in the USA US\$37.71, and in Germany US\$42.42. (Note: these are compensation costs which include direct labour costs plus any insurance and taxes payable.) A comparable worker in Mexico cost US\$5.90 per hour, in Taiwan US\$9.51 per hour, in Brazil US\$7.97, and in Poland US\$8.53 (The Conference Board International Labor Comparisons (ILC), available at https://www.conference-board.org/ilcprogram.) Data for China and India is not easily available and not directly comparable because of data gaps and for methodological reasons; however, ILC estimates that in 2013, hourly compensation costs in manufacturing in China were US\$4.12 and in India US\$1.59. Labour savings also apply to white-collar work. Project managers, software engineers, and accountants can all be much cheaper in developing countries.

The advantages of cheap labour in developing countries are likely to be offset to an extent by lower levels of **productivity**. Productivity measured in terms of output (GDP) per hour worked is much lower in Mexico than in the USA or UK. In 2016, in Mexico it was US\$18.4, in the UK US\$47.9, and in the USA US\$63.3.

The OECD (2014) states that productivity growth is the key to narrowing the income gap between middle- and high-income countries. However, productivity levels in middle-income countries are low, not rising quickly enough, and in some cases—such as Brazil, Mexico, and Turkey—the productivity gap has widened in recent years.

One effect of these fast-expanding economies is that wages and salaries have been increasing in countries like China, as demand for educated and technically skilled workers starts to outstrip the supply of suitable candidates. Although the productivity of Chinese workers is rising, in many industries it is not keeping pace with wages. Consequently, some MNCs may look elsewhere, like the Philippines, Thailand, and Vietnam, where wages and other costs are much lower than in China. Foxconn, for example, is moving all of its assembly operations for Apple products to Indonesia (China Briefing n.d.). According to *The Economist* (2012), the China 'plus one' strategy (a strategy where Western firms had the bulk of their Asian operations in China but were also active in one other Asian country to hold down costs or reduce over dependence) has widened to a 'China plus' strategy because the options have widened to include Indonesia, Myanmar, Vietnam, Cambodia, the Philippines, and India.

It has also been argued that MNCs, to avoid environmental regulations at home, have intentionally relocated polluting activities to developing countries, including China, where the authorities turn a blind eye to environmental damage (Zheng and Chen 2006). Christmann and Taylor (2001) contend that pollution-intensive MNCs have not taken advantage of lax environmental regulation in China. They found that MNCs were more likely than local firms to comply with local regulations and to adopt internationally recognized environmental standards.

Learning Task

Explain the concept of reshoring. Is it the protectionist policies of Donald Trump driving this or are there good economic reasons?

See the *Financial Times* (24 October 2017, Patti Waldmeir, 'Making Michigan great again, one rung at a time') to help you answer this question.

Natural Resources

Businesses in the primary sector are the principal seekers of deposits of natural resources such as oil, gas, and other minerals. However, deposits of natural resources are not spread evenly across the globe, so resource-seeking firms, such as mining groups like Rio Tinto and BHP Billiton, and oil companies like Shell and Exxon, must locate near deposits of natural resources.

With increasing demand for raw materials from the fast growing economies of China and India pulling up prices, combined with a lack of new deposits, mining companies are also looking to expand their deposits of mineral ores and their capacity to refine them. The main driver of the demand for metals is the growth of urbanization, as this creates a demand for infrastructure projects, and increased wealth also increases demand for consumer durables such as fridges and cars.

The UN (2014) predicts that, by 2050, urban dwellers will likely account for 66 per cent of the population. In 1950 that figure was 30 per cent and in 2014, 54 per cent. Overall, the world urban population is expected to grow from 3.9 billion in 2014 to 6.3 billion in 2050, which would mean that two out of every three people in the world would be living in towns and cities (see Figure 6.1).

Figure 6.1 World urban and rural population

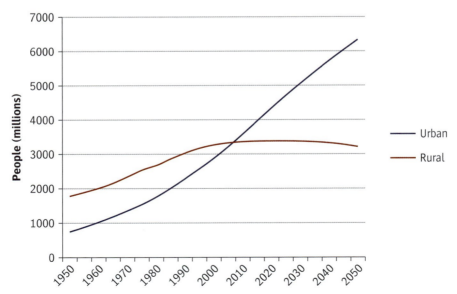

Source: UN (2014) The World Urbanization Prospects: The 2014 revision

To increase production capacity, in 2007 Rio Tinto (one of the world's largest mining companies; mines for coal, copper, iron, bauxite, gold, titanium, lead, zinc, cobalt, nickel, and uranium) put in a successful bid for the Canadian aluminium company, Alcan. This acquisition made it a global leader in aluminium production which, with copper and iron ore, gave it a major role in the key metals associated with growth and urbanization in emerging markets, and especially China. In 2011, it also gained a majority shareholding in an Australian coal mining company, Riversdale. Rio Tinto, in turn, was the subject of an unsuccessful bid by BHP Billiton in 2010.

Competition from Developing Country MNCs

Western and Japanese MNCs not only compete with each other for access to natural resources, but also face increasing competition from companies based in poorer countries. In 2005, the Brazilian mining company Vale S.A. bought Inco of Canada to become the second biggest mining group in the world. The following year, Mittal Steel, whose founder Lakshmi Mittal is of Indian origin, bought Luxembourg rival, Arcelor, for US$34 billion, thereby creating the world's biggest steel maker. Rusal, the Russian minerals company, became the largest aluminium company in the world when it took over another Russian company, SUAL, and the aluminium assets of the Swiss firm, Glencore. In the same year, Tata, one of India's biggest conglomerate firms, took over Corus, the European steel firm (*Financial Times* 2006, 2007).

There is also fierce competition from China for resources. With just over 1.3 billion people, China is the world's most populous country and the second largest consumer of global oil supplies after the USA.

China's oil reserves are limited, and its oil consumption, growing at 7 per cent per annum, is almost double that of its output. By 2020, it is forecast that China will need to import 60 per cent of its energy requirements. By 2030, it is expected to have more cars than the USA, and to be one of the world's largest importers of oil. The Chinese authorities, well aware of their increasing dependence on imported oil, especially from the Middle East, have made aggressive efforts to secure oil and gas supplies all over the globe, in Africa, Latin America, and Central Asia. In 2012, the China National Offshore Oil Co. (CNOOC) paid $15 billion for the Canadian oil company, Nexen, and in 2013 China's top three oil companies spent more than $32 billion on oil and gas acquisitions, mainly in South America, Africa, and the Middle East (*Wall Street Journal* 2014).

Other Assets

Another reason for FDI is to gain other assets, such as technological and managerial knowhow. Firms can set up in other countries to monitor competitor activities more closely, as Kodak did in Japan to learn from their Japanese competitors. They can also enter into joint ventures to learn from others or acquire the assets of another firm, and in so doing acquire access to technology, brand names, local distribution systems, and expertise. A good example of this kind of FDI activity was the acquisition of IBM's personal computer business by Lenovo of China in 2004. Lenovo was able to acquire a foothold in the American market and easier access to Europe (market-seeking activities), but also acquired a famous brand (the 'Think' brand), technological and management expertise, and a distribution network. Similarly, China has the world's largest

Table 6.2 Reasons for investing

Motivation	% of respondents
Access new markets or new customers	87
Lower production costs or establish a new base for exports	51
Coordinate company's value chain, such as being closer to suppliers	39
Acquire another firm that will provide the company with new technologies or brands	15
Access natural resources and raw materials, such as oil, gas, or agricultural products	12

NB. Figures do not add to 100 because respondents are allowed to select multiple motives.
Source: World Bank (2018). Data available under Creative Commons Attribution CC BY 3.0 IGO.

shale-gas reserves, but not the technology to exploit them. The acquisition of Nexen, mentioned above, may have been one way of tapping into Western technology.

The World Bank (2018) surveyed hundreds of executives at multinational companies to find out what drives decisions around MNC foreign direct investment in developing countries. The results in Table 6.2 show that most investors have multiple motivations, but the main one is market-seeking.

Mini Case Study 6.1 China and Brazil—FDI and trade

China has become a major force in FDI. In 2009, with outflows of US$48 billion, it was the sixth largest foreign direct investor and by 2016 had become the second largest with outflows of $US183 billion, after the USA. This has been driven by a search for natural resources and by the opportunities to acquire foreign companies created by global restructuring (UNCTAD 2017). Since 2003, China companies have invested over US$110 billion in Latin America, most of it in the last five years (Avendano et al. 2017).

Brazil, with vast mineral resources and a well-developed agricultural sector, has been a major recipient of Chinese FDI. In 2010, China became the biggest foreign direct investor in Brazil, accounting for about US$17 billion of Brazil's total FDI inflows of US$49 billion. Chinese FDI in Brazil totalled US$60 billion by 2016, more than half of all Chinese FDI in Latin America (Avendano et al. 2017). The biggest transaction was Chinese oil major Sinopec's US$7.1 billion purchase of a 40 per cent stake in Repsol Brazil. The Chinese have also invested in infrastructural projects such as the building of an enormous port complex in the state of Rio de Janeiro. This will allow China to transport iron ore for its fast-expanding steel industry. The complex will include a steel mill, shipyards, an automobile plant, and factories manufacturing oil and gas equipment. Chinese companies have also invested heavily in Brazil's electric power supply business with the purchase of stakes in the country's power grid. Others are looking to buy land in Brazil for the production of soya beans.

From 2011 to 2013, Chinese investment in Brazil fell or projects were put on hold because of the sluggish Brazilian economy, uncertainty about policy on mining laws and foreign ownership of land, and some political and popular backlash against the Chinese. In 2014, with the visit of President Xi Jinping, new commitments were made in both trade and investment. China promised to buy 60 passenger jets from Embraer, invest $7.5 billion in Vale, and promised new investment in infrastructure and a raft of other deals.

China is now also Brazil's main trade partner, accounting for 19 per cent of exports and 16 per cent of imports. It is an ➡

→ example of the growing so-called South–South trade, although it has a flavour of the traditional North–South trade in that Brazil exports commodities to China and imports manufactured products. This causes tensions, because not all see this as a benefit.

Political and economic crises in Brazil in 2015–16 saw the level of FDI fall. However, Chinese firms were expected to invest over US$20 billion in Brazil as, due to the crisis, assets were seen as underpriced (Avendano et al. 2017). Brazil welcomed this investment, as its economic growth was negative in 2016 and very sluggish in 2017.

Sources: UNCTAD (2017); Reuters (2013, 2014); Avendano et al. (2017)

Questions

1. How will Brazil benefit from Chinese investment?
2. How will China benefit from FDI in Brazil?
3. What tensions might the relationship generate?

Screening and Evaluating Foreign Markets

In Chapter 4, we talked about environmental analysis being part of the strategic process. The decision to 'go abroad' is another aspect of strategy that involves a matching of internal resources with external opportunities aimed at achieving the organization's goals. Although the basic principles of strategy apply, the decision-making in international strategy is much more complex because of the 'barriers created by distance' (Ghemawat 2001: 138). Ghemawat identified four dimensions of distance—geographic, cultural, administrative, and economic—all of which, in different ways, add complexity to decision-making. Managers have to decide not just which countries to target, but how they are going to target those countries. They also need some idea of the global systems and structures appropriate for their organization. How companies organize these will depend very much on the type of product/service they produce. For products, such as commercial aircraft, which are transportable, subject to substantial economies of scale, and do not have to accommodate local tastes, then final production is likely to take place in a small number of sites and output exported. Boeing Commercial Airlines, for example, has just three main assembly sites in Renton and Everett in Washington and the most recent, built for the Dreamliner, in North Carolina. Boeing imports many components from manufacturers across the world for final assembly in the USA. It then exports completed planes. For service industries where production and consumption are inseparable, direct investment has to take place in the host economy. This will also be the case where products need to be adapted to local tastes and where there are few economies of scale, such as in packaged foods. Products such as telecommunications equipment, cars, computers, mobile phones, and pharmaceuticals, where some local adaptation is probably necessary, and for which there will be some economies of scale (but which can be produced anywhere and shipped around the world), both direct investment and trade are important. Increasingly, firms try to locate each part of the production chain where resource availability and cost are the lowest, and this global mode of operations is becoming dominant. It is the most complex form of organization, requiring decisions on the most appropriate locations for all aspects of the organization's operations. Whatever method they choose, companies are faced with the complex task of screening and evaluating foreign markets/countries, and this is the subject of this section.

What makes an attractive market or production location? To begin with, there has to be an expectation of profit, but this must be weighed against the risk of operating in the country.

However, there is usually a trade-off to be made between risk and return. High attractiveness and high returns are usually associated with high risk, and low attractiveness and low returns with low risk. Countries differ in terms of their attractiveness as a result of variations in the economic environment, growth rates, disposable income levels, available resources, government incentives, and level of competition. They also differ in the associated risk according to economic and political stability.

In this section we are going to build on the general macro-environmental analysis already established in Chapter 4, together with the industry analysis of Chapter 3, to provide a framework to assess 'attractiveness'. We concentrate here on attractiveness as a market or a production site (or, for many managers in an increasingly globalized world, both) rather than for sourcing or partners. Much of the literature on country evaluation comes from the marketing world and focuses on international market selection (e.g. Cavusgil 1985) rather than production location. Many direct investment decisions are heavily influenced by target market potential (Papadopoulos and Martin 2011), and the sequential process they advocate can also be applied to decisions to locate, albeit with some different considerations. Target market selection will, inter alia, be concerned primarily with indicators such as the size and growth of the market, whereas location decisions will be more concerned with the ease of doing business. Deciding between more than 200 possible country locations is a daunting task, and so the usual process is to carry out a general screening, which narrows down the choice to a group or cluster of countries, possibly a region, against some given criteria for which the data is readily available from public sources (Cavusgil et al. 2004). These selected countries may well be ranked before a more detailed analysis takes place in which those countries are compared with each other. For market selection, information on a range of variables which indicate market size and potential growth will be needed, as well as information about potential competition and the general macro-environment, and how that might affect demand. For site location, information about the competition, resources, infrastructure, and any government incentives will need to be collected. Some information collected will be relevant to both decisions— for example, the ease of doing business and the general attitude of government to business. Infrastructure will also be a common concern, as both will require transport, communications, and power to operate. Once the field has been narrowed down to one or two possibilities, the final stage is to select the market or site. At this stage, site visits and field research will probably be needed to collect more detailed and specific information and to talk to possible partners and/or suppliers and distributors. This can be an expensive process, so thorough initial screening is important. Alongside all of this, managers will also need to undertake a risk analysis to weigh against the possible returns before a decision can be made.

Collecting Data

In order to undertake an assessment of country attractiveness for markets and production sites, companies have to undertake research and analysis, and this can be time-consuming and expensive. Like all research, there has to be a balance between the cost of research and the benefits from the research, as it is impossible to gather all the information and in any case, this may result in information overload. There is a lot of information that can be obtained from the internet and there are many private sector organizations providing country and industry reports at a price.

IMD World Competitiveness Yearbook

The IMD ranks 63 of the most competitive countries according to economic performance, government efficiency, business efficiency, and infrastructure. (A link to the IMD World Competitiveness Yearbook is located in the **online resources**.) Each of these four factors is then broken down into a number of sub-factors (over 340 in all) and scores given to each of these sub-factors. From this, an overall total is calculated. These totals are then formed into indices with the most competitive given a score of 100 and the rest ranked below this with their relative score. Of course, that is only 63 out of over 200 countries, although these countries do account for the bulk of investment and trade. In 2017, Hong Kong topped their list with Switzerland second and Singapore third. Bottom of their 63 countries was Venezuela (IMD n.d.).

According to the IMD, a focus on business friendly regulations, physical and intangible infrastructure, and the promotion of inclusive institutions (i.e. those that include many people in the process of governing) is the key to international competitiveness. Those at the bottom of the list—such as Venezuela, Brazil, and Ukraine—tend to be countries which have suffered political and economic problems (see the IMD's website for a short video explaining the rankings). For the first time in 2017, IMD also produced a report ranking countries' digital competitiveness with Singapore coming top and Venezuela bottom (IMD n.d.).

The Economist Intelligence Unit (EIU)

The EIU ranks 82 countries according to the attractiveness of their business environment. Their model covers ten different factors: political environment, the macroeconomic environment, market opportunities, policy towards free enterprise and competition, policy towards foreign investment, foreign trade and exchange controls, taxes, financing, the labour market, and infrastructure. These categories are then broken down into between five and ten indicators, and assessed for the last five years and the next five years. As with the IMD index, overall scores are calculated and then countries are ranked. As with the IMD table, the top three are Singapore, Switzerland, and Hong Kong; Venezuela is in last place (iberglobal n.d.). As the authors note in the introduction, 'for all the talk of the potential of emerging markets, developed economies in North America, Western Europe, and Asia remain the best places to do business.' The IMD also produce over 200 country reports.

For students trying to collect information, these costly sources are not an option. However, fortunately, there are now many sources of information available free of charge over the internet.

GlobalEDGE

GlobalEDGE is created and maintained by the International Business Centre Michigan State University. (See the **online resources** for a link to this resource.) This is a very extensive resource bank and links to many other sites of interest. In its Global Insights database there are entries for over 200 countries with information on the history, government, and culture of each country as well as a range of statistics on the economy. You can find, for example, that Nigeria has a population of over 185 million people with a GDP per capita (PPP) of $5,867 (2016 current $US). In 2016 the economy actually shrank by 1.54 per cent. It is an oil-based economy, accounting for 20 per cent of GDP, 95 per cent of foreign earnings, and 80 per cent of budgetary revenues coming from oil. Its top three trade partners in 2016 were India, China, and the USA. It is ranked 136 out of 176 countries in Transparency International's Corruptions Perceptions Index (see Chapter 5). It has a high-risk political and economic situation, and an often difficult business environment.

GlobalEDGE also ranks the market potential of 87 markets, albeit from a US business focus, and therefore the USA is excluded. It uses eight factors in its assessment, each with different weights: market size (25), market growth rate (12.5), market intensity (15), market consumption capacity (12.5), commercial infrastructure (10), economic freedom (10), market receptivity (7.5), and country risk (7.5). Countries are scored out of 100. In 2017, China was ranked first with a score of 100, followed by Hong Kong (51) and India (48). There is also an industry database with an overview of each industry, trade statists, main corporations, and links to other resources.

The World Economic Forum (WEF)

The World Economic Forum (WEF) Global Competitiveness Report ranks 137 economies, based on publicly available information and its own survey, according to national competitiveness as well as a detailed profile for each of the economies. (See the **online resources** for a link to this report.) It takes into account the microeconomic and macroeconomic foundations of national competitiveness based on the ideas outlined in Porter's diamond and the stages of development (Porter 1990). The WEF identifies the '12 pillars of competitiveness' as:

1. institutions—the legal framework, government attitudes to markets and freedom, excessive bureaucracy, overregulation, and corruption;

2. infrastructure—quality roads, railroads, ports, airports, electricity supply, and telecommunications;

3. macroeconomy—economic stability;

4. health and primary education—a healthy workforce with a basic education;

5. higher education and training—higher grade skills necessary for the economy to move up the value chain;

6. goods market efficiency—sophisticated customers and competitive domestic and foreign markets;

7. labour market efficiency—flexible labour markets with appropriate reward systems;

8. financial market sophistication—with savings channelled to productive investment;

9. technological readiness—access to ICT;

10. market size—domestic and foreign markets allow economies of scale;

11. business sophistication—quality of business networks and individual firms' operations and strategy; and

12. innovation—high levels of R&D expenditure, collaboration between universities and industry, protection of intellectual property.

According to the WEF, these 12 pillars are the key to national competitiveness (see Figure 6.2). They are interdependent and reinforce each other. For example, the twelfth pillar of innovation is impossible without an advanced higher education system, or without the protection of intellectual property rights.

Figure 6.2 The 12 pillars of competitiveness

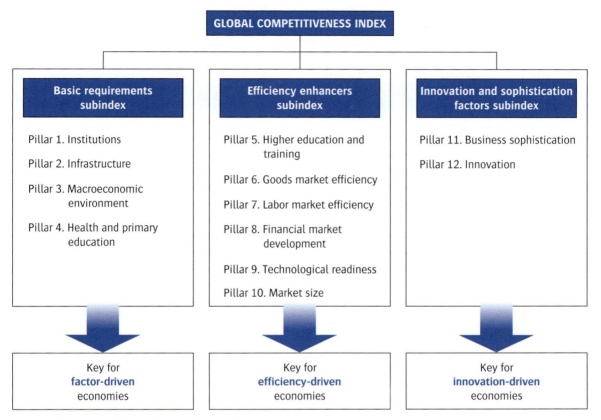

Source: The Global Competitiveness Report 2013–14, WEF

The WEF identifies three stages of development linked to the pillars: the factor-driven stage, the efficiency-driven stage, and the innovation-driven stage. The WEF allocates countries to each stage according to two criteria. The first is the level of GDP per capita (see Table 6.3), and the second is the share of exports of primary goods in total exports with the assumption that countries with a ratio of 70 per cent or more are factor-driven. Those falling in between are said to be 'in transition'. The full list of countries and which stage they are in can be found in the report.

Table 6.3 Income thresholds for establishing stages of development

Stage of development	GDP per capita (in US$)
Stage 1: Factor-driven	<2,000
Transition from stage 1 to stage 2	2,000–2,999
Stage 2: Efficiency-driven	3,000–8,999
Transition from stage 2 to stage 3	9,000–17,000
Stage 3: Innovation-driven	>17,000

Source: The Global Competitiveness Report 2013–14, WEF

Table 6.4 Global Competitiveness Index rankings 2017–18

Country	Rank	Score/7	Country	Rank	Score/7
Switzerland	1	5.86	Vietnam	55	4.36
USA	2	5.85	Botswana	63	4.30
Singapore	3	5.71	Georgia	67	4.28
Germany	5	5.65	Brazil	80	4.14
UK	8	5.51	Kenya	91	3.96
Israel	16	5.31	Ecuador	97	3.91
France	22	5.18	Ethiopia	108	3.78
China	27	5.00	Tanzania	113	3.71
Indonesia	36	4.66	Mali	123	3.33
India	40	4.59	Venezuela	127	3.23
Italy	43	4.54	Malawi	132	3.11
Turkey	53	4.42	Yemen	137	2.87

Source: The Global Competitiveness Report 2017–18, WEF

In 2007–08, the USA topped the overall ranking of the 131 countries included at that time; however, this spot was taken by Switzerland in 2009 and 2010 with the USA relegated to fourth spot behind Sweden. In 2017, Switzerland held the top spot followed by the USA, Singapore, and the Netherlands. What is striking about the table, as with the EIU table, is the top places are dominated by North America, Europe, and Asia. Twenty-seven of the bottom 32 places are from Sub-Saharan Africa (see Table 6.4). The WEF also provides detailed profiles for each of the countries that it assesses.

Doing Business

The World Bank has a very useful website called 'Doing Business' (http://www.doingbusiness. org). Again, this gives basic information for 190 economies, but its major focus is about starting a business in a particular economy and provides answers to such questions as dealing with construction permits, registering property, getting credit, paying taxes, enforcing contracts, and closing a business—as they apply to domestic small and medium-sized enterprises. More detailed information about national and international statistics and trends in the world economy can be found at another World Bank site, http://www.worldbank.org, with information on over 200 countries. The World Bank is particularly interested in the development of countries and so it provides a lot of indicators of development such as figures on health, education, literacy, the environment, and infrastructure, many of which can be good indicators of market potential. For example, the percentage of people using the internet in 2013 was 5.0 in Chad, 26 in Cambodia, 70 for Argentina, but 88.0 in Australia (World Bank n.d.a).

Counterpoint Box 6.1 How useful are competitiveness indices?

Competitiveness is at the top of business and political agendas all over the world. On the basis of the indices, several countries and regions have established policies and institutions devoted to improving competitiveness. Despite its popularity in business and management literature and public policy, the concept of national economic competitiveness remains unclear and the object of criticism.

Critics of the field of competitiveness research argue that there are limitations to the indices. They often fail to include a national economy's unique characteristics, such as geography, culture, and demographics. In addition, the choice of variables and their weight is based on a particular concept of competitiveness and, therefore, a country's competitive rank will be different depending on which index is used. Sabadie and Johansen (2010) specifically contend that indices like that of the WEF pay too little attention to the importance of human capital in national competitiveness indices. They argue that indices risk diverting country attention towards areas with a lesser potential impact on competitiveness, with critical consequences particularly in developing and transition countries because the indexes can have a major impact on policy-making in these countries. This could lead to an inappropriate allocation of resources, an even less competitive economy, and possibly to protectionism.

Krugman (1994) questions the very concept of competitiveness rankings, challenging the basic assumption that countries compete with each other like companies and that a country's prosperity is based on its success in international markets. A firm can go out of business if it is uncompetitive, but an economy does not. This is because all economies produce the bulk of their goods and services for domestic consumption and however uncompetitive an economy may be, most of its business continues, regardless. Furthermore, when two firms compete, one wins and the other loses, but when two economies compete, through trade, both can gain thanks to the law of comparative advantage. Finally, while an uncompetitive firm may be unable to lower its costs, an uncompetitive economy will do so through a deflation of the economy, or a depreciation of the exchange rate, or a combination of both.

Sources: Sabadie and Johansen (2010); Krugman (1994).

Question
The WEF ranks the BRIC countries, China, Russia, India, and Brazil, 20th, 38th, 40th, and 80th, respectively, in its global competitiveness rankings for 2017. In 2013 the countries had been ranked 29th, 64th, 60th, and 56th. Using these rankings and changes in rank, discuss the usefulness of competitive indices.

Mini Case Study 6.2 Investing in Italy

Italy is one of the world's largest economies with a GDP of US$1,807 billion (see Table 2.1, page 49) and a per capita income of US$29,747. It struggles to attract inward investment. In a survey by EY (2014) to establish the most attractive countries to establish operations in Western Europe, Italy came last and did not even appear in the top 15 countries in Europe by FDI projects. Total FDI project numbers in Italy had been declining by 19 per cent per year on average since 2010.

Many tourists will see the Italian towns that retain their traditional shops as quaint, unlike many other European towns and cities which look very much alike with global retail chains and their familiar facades. However, these chains are absent not because they do not want to be there, but because it is made so

difficult to invest there. There is a mass of regulations, selective application, and long drawn-out processes for settling disputes. Italy is ranked 79th in the Heritage Foundation's Index of economic freedom.

The WEF lists tax rates, access to financing, inefficient government bureaucracy, restrictive labour practices, tax regulations, political instability, and corruption (in that order) as the most problematic obstacles to doing business in Italy. In the WEF rankings, Italy comes forty-ninth and scores poorly in institutions, macroeconomic stability, labour market efficiency, and financial market sophistication.

A further EY survey (2017) found investment projects in Italy had risen by 62 per cent between 2015 and 2016, the largest ➜

→ increase among large EU economies with a 92 per cent increase in jobs created. However, it still ranked only 16th in the top 20 destination countries and last in jobs created.

The Financial Times (29 June 2017) pointed out that there is a north-south disparity in Italy with the rich Lombardy region of the north attracting similar amounts of FDI to other rich regions in Europe. It is the poorer south that remains unattractive as an investment location. It points out that Calabria, Basilicata, and Campania are among the 20 regions that have received the least investment in the whole of Western Europe. The main reasons are 'overlapping responsibilities between central and local governments' and the 'poor quality of institutions'.

This means that many organizations feel Italy is not an attractive country in which to invest, with the consequence being economic growth below the European average. According to the IMF, the Italian economy will grow by around 1 per cent per year from 2018 to 2022.

Sources: World Economic Forum; *Financial Times* 29 June 2017; EY (2014 and 2017) European Attractiveness Survey; Heritage Foundation

Questions
1. Access the WEF, GlobalEDGE, and World Bank sites, and build up a picture of 'doing business' in Italy.
2. Research the measures Italy has taken to attract FDI and assess how successful they have been (see http://www. investinitaly.com/en).

Other Useful Sources

The International Monetary Fund has a freely accessible database (http://www.imf.org/external/data.htm) providing data on economic and financial indicators such as GDP, GDP per capita, economic growth, inflation, government finance, balance of payments, and population.

Other useful sources of data from world organizations include:

- OECD (http://www.oecd.org)
- UNCTAD (http://unctad.org/en/Pages/Home.aspx)
- World Trade Organization (http://www.wto.org).

The UK Data Service (formerly the Economic and Social Data Service (ESDS)) is hosted by Manchester and Essex Universities and provides a useful link to many international datasets (http://ukdataservice.ac.uk).

The UK Department for International Trade also has a useful website (https://www.gov.uk/government/organisations/department-for-international-tradeinternational trade department) aimed at supporting UK business to expand internationally through exporting. It offers detailed guides on how to do business in many countries across the world. The USA has a similar site at http://www.export.gov/index.asp.

The Central Intelligence Agency's World Factbook has information on every country recognized by the USA (CIA n.d.). It covers each country's geography, people, system of government, climate, natural resources, infrastructure, and economic conditions. It is a very useful source of information to extract data for country screening, and is updated regularly.

International Data Problems

When collecting international data, it is important to consider some of the problems associated with the data. Using the IMF World Economic Outlook Database as an example, most of the information comes from national datasets and the IMF advises countries on the compilation of the statistics in such areas as analytical frameworks, concepts, definitions, classifications, and valua-tions. Nevertheless, compilation of national statistics is highly complex and not all governments have the same resources to allocate to the process, so governments with limited funds and/or skills at their disposal may not place too high a priority on collecting information. Often, information is not available or is out of date, and sometimes it can be 'managed' for political purposes.

There are also definitional problems. Poverty, literacy, and unemployment, for example, can have very different meanings depending on the context or country. Unemployment in sub-Saharan Africa is not reported in many of the 45 countries included in the IMF database. In any case, many 'unemployed' workers may not be captured by the official employment statistics as they form part of the informal economy or, even if captured, there tends to be considerable underemployment in low-productivity jobs more concerned with survival.

Even where there is common understanding of the terms, capturing the data only takes place in the official recorded economy. Some economies have large, informal economies and some have shadow economies where the production of goods and services is deliberately concealed from the authorities. As we saw in Chapter 2, this can amount to over 60 per cent for some economies.

Difficulties also arise in comparison when converting to a common currency, usually the dol-lar. Again, as we saw in Chapter 2, variations in exchange rates can lead to changes in GDP reported in US dollars when no change has actually taken place. Even when GDPs are converted to PPP terms, comparison is difficult to make and care needs to be taken, especially when trying to estimate market size.

(See Center for Global Development Report (2014) for a discussion of the need for accurate data and the weaknesses of data collection in sub-Saharan Africa.)

The Process of Assessing Country Attractiveness

This section will be divided into the assessment activities shown in Figure 6.3.

Initial Screening

The first stage in any screening process is to eliminate those countries which have little chance of being markets or production sites by assessing if there is a basic demand for the company's

Figure 6.3 Country assessment

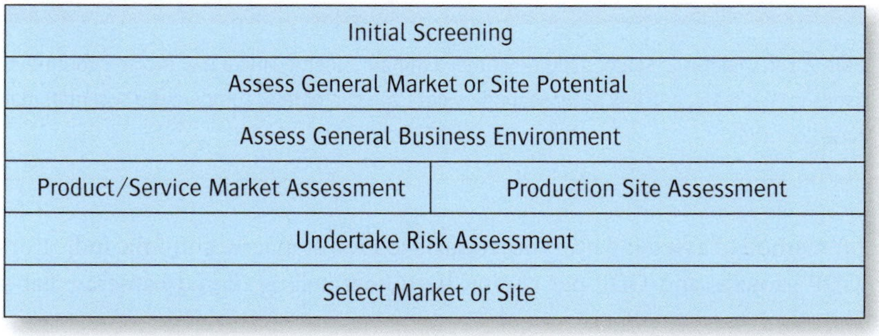

Initial Screening
Assess General Market or Site Potential
Assess General Business Environment
Product/Service Market Assessment / Production Site Assessment
Undertake Risk Assessment
Select Market or Site

products or if the basic resources required are present and the business environment is acceptable. This is a fairly obvious first step that can eliminate many countries from the search. For example, a country's climate can be a significant influence on the pattern of demand. There is no demand for heating in Malaysia, a tropical country with an average year-round temperature above 30°C, but a substantial demand for air conditioning. This makes screening fairly straightforward for specialized goods of this nature, but less so for other, more widely consumed products such as confectionery, computers, and games.

Many businesses, as previously noted, target countries which are close not only geographically but also in language, culture, and business environment, and this can be a simple way of arriving at a handful of countries on which to do more detailed analysis. Of course, this could ignore many potentially good targets, and is no guarantee of success. The USA would be considered to have more in common with the UK than does Thailand; however, Tesco entered Thailand with far fewer problems than it did the USA.

Assessing General Market or Site Potential

Market Potential

At this stage, the objective is to develop a number of indicators which help firms assess the general potential of a market so that further countries can be eliminated. This assessment often uses broad economic, social, or infrastructural indicators as proxy measures. This is intended not to assess the size of markets for particular products, but to be an overall assessment of the market potential of a country. In particular, companies will want an indication of the following:

- Market size—the relative size of the overall economy. Population size can be a useful indicator of the number of potential customers, while GDP per head and disposable income per head indicates whether there is a sufficient level of purchasing power—the overall buying power of those within the economy is referred to as market intensity. The distribution of income tells us about whether purchasing power is evenly spread.

- Market growth—size is important, but the rate at which the market is growing is also important; thus, markets that are large, but shrinking, or growing very slowly, can be avoided and those that are small, but growing rapidly, can be targeted. Growth in population and GDP are often used to assess market growth.

- Quality of demand—refers to the socio-economic profile of the customers within a market.

 Learning Task

Using Table 2.1 in Chapter 2, select a high-income, a middle-income, and a low-income country. Using the statistics in that table, and any other secondary data you can obtain, compare the potential markets of the three countries.

A common method of assessing basic potential is to look at macroeconomic indicators such as GDP, GDP growth, and GDP per capita. If you are selling digital cameras, flat-screen televisions, and DVD recorders, then Australia, with a per capita income in 2017 of US$55,215, is a better starting point than Haiti with a per capita income of only US$719 (IMF World Economic Outlook Database 2017). Other proxy indicators of wealth may also be used to assess market potential, such as the ownership of cars, energy usage, televisions, computers, telephones, and internet usage, usually measured per head of population. These indicators are often associated with an expanding middle class (see Chapter 2), which is often a good indicator of market potential. These types of figures are often used in combination with other indicators, such as demographic changes (population size, growth, and age structure), degree of urbanization, and income distribution. The type of indicator used will depend on the industry. Financial service firms require countries where the population has considerable disposable income.

Another way of targeting countries is to use trade statistics, such as the United Nations' *International Trade Statistics Yearbook*, to look at the goods and services a country is importing from abroad, or to identify to which countries your domestic competitors are exporting. Looking at the domestic output of an economy to see what local producers are selling is another indicator. Many businesses will also follow their customers into new markets.

Site Potential

Similarly, companies intending to produce abroad can do a quick scan of what they consider are essential resources to undertake production. Availability of raw materials is one such consideration, but access to labour and finance are other important considerations. As the reduction in costs is often a major reason for going abroad, then the cost of doing business is also an important factor. This refers not just to labour but also the cost of finance, the price of energy, communications, transport, and tax rates. Against the low cost of labour, the availability, skill level, and productivity must also be considered. A quick consideration of country risk can also eliminate many countries from the equation.

Assess the General Business Environment

Assessing the general business environment can further eliminate some countries and provide useful information to be incorporated into the next steps in the process. In this section, the PESTLE framework from Chapter 4 is a useful framework to use.

Political and Legal Environment

The main factors in any assessment of the political and legal forces are government regulation, government bureaucracy, and law and order.

Most governments impose ownership restrictions which hinder FDI, according to the World Bank (World Bank 2010). In their report, 'Investing Across Borders', the World Bank claim that of the 87 countries surveyed 'almost 90 per cent of countries limit foreign companies' ability to participate in some sectors of their economies' (2010: 8). The removal of such restrictions in the retailing sector by the Thai government in the late 1990s allowed Tesco to enter the country through a joint venture. Governments may also impose trade barriers, so a scan for any barriers can soon eliminate a country. In a globalizing world with countries eager for FDI, a ban is much less likely than a range of incentives trying to attract FDI.

Typical of the type of incentives are:

- financial incentives—investment grants or credit guarantees;
- fiscal incentives—reduced corporation tax;
- regulatory incentives—easing of health and safety or environmental regulations;
- subsidized services—water, electricity, communications;
- market privileges—preferential government contracts; and
- foreign exchange privileges—special exchange rates.

Other features of the regulatory and legal regime to consider are the tax regime, employment laws, health and safety laws, environmental policy, and competition policy.

Government bureaucracy, in relation to business, refers to the difficulties faced by business in day-to-day operations because of the number of regulations with which they have to comply, and the rigidity with which they are enforced, commonly referred to as 'red tape'. For example, how long does it take to obtain licences to operate and how many forms have to be completed and submitted to government, how often, and in how much detail?

The Heritage Foundation in the USA, a libertarian think-tank, assesses countries according to various measures of freedom—business freedom, freedom to trade, freedom from tax, regulation and corruption, the strength of property rights, and labour, financial, and investment freedom. It then ranks countries according to their scores out of 100. Those scoring between 80 and 100 are classified as free, from 70–79.9 mostly free, 60–69.9 moderately free, 50–59.9 mostly unfree, and less than 50 repressed. Hong Kong, with a score of 90.2, was ranked first in 2018. The USA, with a score almost 15 points below Hong Kong, was ranked 18th, and North Korea, with a score of 5.8, was ranked last of 180 ranked countries (see Table 6.5 for the scores of a selection of countries). This is used in several of the country rankings, including the GlobalEDGE rankings.

 Learning Task

1. From Table 6.5, select one country in the top ten and one ranked above 100. Using any secondary data you can obtain, explain the differences in the rankings.

2. How useful is this Economic Freedom Index?

Secondary data is available in World Development Indicators on the World Bank website. The IMF produces country reports and the OECD carries out country surveys, reviews, and guides that are available on their websites. More information is also on the Heritage site under each of the country profiles.

Economic and Financial Environment

The major financial considerations will be rates of inflation, interest rates, exchange rates, credit availability, financial stability, and returns on investment. High and variable rates of inflation might increase earnings in money terms at least, but make forecasting and planning difficult, adding to the risk of operations. Similarly, exchange rate volatility adds to the uncertainty surrounding the value of any repatriated earnings and how much capital is needed for investment. On the other

Table 6.5 Economic Freedom Index 2018 (%)

Country	Rank	Score	Country	Rank	Score
Hong Kong	1	90.2	Poland	45	68.5
Singapore	2	88.8	Hungary	55	66.7
New Zealand	3	84.2	Albania	65	64.5
Switzerland	4	81.7	El Salvador	75	63.2
Australia	5	80.9	Cote d'Ivoire	85	62.0
Ireland	6	80.4	Burkino Faso	95	60.0
Estonia	7	78.8	Moldova	105	58.4
UK	8	78.0	Greece	115	57.3
Canada	9	77.7	Mongolia	125	55.7
UAE	10	77.6	Burma	135	53.9
Taiwan	13	76.6	The Gambia	145	52.3
USA	18	75.7	Maldives	155	51.1
Germany	25	74.2	Ecuador	165	48.5
Japan	30	72.3	Equatorial Guinea	175	42.0
Uruguay	38	69.2	Korea, North	180	5.8

Source: http://www.heritage.org

hand, some firms in the financial sector depend on volatility to make a living. Large industrial and commercial firms quite often have treasury departments that are trying not only to protect earnings, but also to make money out of movements in exchange and interest rates. Equally important are the policies that governments use to attempt to control their economies and how successful they are, since poor economic management can lead to volatility in the above.

Socio-cultural Environment

In assessing countries for markets and industrial locations, socio-cultural factors also have to be taken into account. The cultural elements of language, religion, diet, values and norms, attitudes, beliefs, customs, and social relationships can all be important in terms of employment, and in the acceptability of the product and any adaptations that need to be considered, including labelling and instructions on use of the product. Social factors, such as the distribution of income, modes of employment, living, and working conditions, population characteristics, such as ethnicity, the degree of urbanization, the availability and skill level of labour, the motivational basis of work, levels of pay, working hours, and the level of trade unionization, are all important.

The growth of a 'middle class' in many emerging markets is boosting world demand for mass consumer goods and is making these countries the target for global multinational companies. China is at the forefront of this, although estimates of the growth of its middle class vary. What all seem to agree is that during the next 20 years, a huge middle class with enormous spending power will emerge. Wal-Mart, Carrefour, Tesco, IKEA, and Kingfisher's B&Q are all already well established in China.

Technological Environment

Another key feature of country attractiveness is the development of the infrastructure. An efficient transport and communications network is necessary for markets to function properly. If the intention is to export, a well-developed port infrastructure is also necessary. Key elements to assess in the infrastructure are:

- science and technology infrastructure;
- extent and quality of road network;
- extent and quality of public transport network;
- telephony network;
- internet capacity;
- water supply;
- air transport;
- quality of ports; and
- electricity production and certainty of supply.

Countries with well-developed infrastructures are attractive to business because they facilitate market growth and offer cheaper and better transport and communication networks. Developing countries with poorer infrastructures in Africa, Asia, or Latin America are less appealing.

Ecological Environment

The natural environment is the source not only of essential raw materials, which are part of any basic screening, but also of major but difficult-to-predict risks. Natural catastrophes such as earthquakes, flooding, and hurricanes are all unpredictable, although certain areas are more prone to these occurrences than others.

Mini Case Study 6.3 Doing business in South Africa

South Africa (SA) is located at the southern tip of Africa. There is scrubland in the interior, desert in the north-west and tropics in the south-east. It also has about 1,700 miles of coastline. It has a population of over 55 million made up of predominantly black African (79 per cent) plus a much smaller white (9.6 per cent) and coloured (8.9 per cent) population. Unusually, SA has three capitals. Bloemfontein is the capital of the judiciary, Cape Town is the legislative capital, and Pretoria is the administrative capital. The largest city is Johannesburg. Its currency is the Rand. The most common spoken language in official and commercial life is English, but it only ranks joint fifth as a home language. The state recognizes 11 official languages.

Until 1994, SA had a system of apartheid in which racial discrimination was institutionalized by a white minority ruling over the black majority. Under this system, non-white South Africans were forced to live in separate areas from whites and use separate public facilities. It was not until 1991 that much of the legislation began to be repealed and now a democratic culture has emerged.

SA has one of the continent's largest economies with a GDP of $US318 billion ($US762 billion PPP) and a per capita GDP of US$65,589 (US$13,409 in PPP terms). The economy went into recession in 2009, but since then has been growing at about 3 per cent per annum. The economy has been growing slowly ➡

→ (by African standards), since 2012 at a little over 2 per cent, falling to less than 1 per cent in 2016. It is expected (by the IMF) to rise slowly to 2 per cent per annum by 2020. There remains much poverty, especially in the black population and in the townships. According to STATS SA after a period when poverty was falling it is on the rise with 30.4 million people (55.5 per cent of the population) living in poverty. Public health facilities are poor, as is education and infrastructure services. Job prospects are also poor. SA has one of the highest levels of inequality in the world.

Mining has been the major driving force in the development of the South African economy, especially gold and diamonds, and SA remains an international leader in the mining industry. While those two elements are now not so important, SA (although still the fifth largest producer of gold) is the world's leader in the production of platinum, manganese, vanadium, and chrome, and an important producer of many other minerals. Its main exports are minerals to China, the USA, India, and the UK.

SA was ranked 82 (down from 41 in 2014) in the World Bank's ease of doing business rankings (2017). Starting a business, getting electricity, registering property, trading across borders, and enforcing contracts are categories in the lower half of the rankings.

For market potential, in 2018 GlobalEDGE ranked South Africa 95th out of the 97 countries it ranks; this was down from 70 out of 87 in 2014.

Sources: IMF World Economic Outlook Database, April 2014; GlobalEDGE Country reports; http://www.Statssa.gov.za; World Bank http://www.doingbusiness.org

Question

Assess the market potential and general business environment for South Africa.

Product/Service Market Assessment

Having reduced the number of countries for consideration in the first stage, the next stage is to undertake a more detailed assessment of the potential within each of the selected markets. Initial screening is undertaken using broad indicators, but at this stage much more specific industry indicators are called for in attempting to measure the total market demand in a particular industry and gaining as much information as possible about the market in each of the countries selected after stage 1. Data is more likely to be available for developed economies than for emerging economies, but, again, this information is likely to cost money. A Euromonitor report on alcoholic drinks in Austria, for example, would cost, in 2017, £1,375 (Euromonitor n.d.). It is worth searching your library to see if it has subscriptions to organizations such as Mintel, Datamonitor, and Key Note.

The information that will be needed includes:

- size and growth rate of the market;
- major competitors, products, and market shares;
- prices, marketing, and promotions of competitors;
- distribution networks;
- local standards and regulations, including trade mark rules and product liability;
- value of imports and exports of the product;
- tariffs and other trade regulations; and
- local cultural factors that may require product adaptation.

Information on the size of the market may not be readily available and often it is necessary to look at other indicators. For example, a UK company producing protective coverings for transporting high-value but bulky audio equipment wanted to investigate export markets in

Europe. There was no information available on the products they produced, but a lot on the music industry they supplied, and so comparing this market with the UK market gave them an indication of the potential demand in Europe.

Competitive Forces

As well as information on the size of the market, an analysis of the competitive environment will be required using a model such as Porter's Five (Six) Forces. This was explained in Chapter 3 and a checklist was provided to help in the process (see 'Analysing an industry using the Six Forces: a checklist').

Production Site Assessment

If FDI is taking place, then a more detailed analysis of doing business in each market is required. This will include information on setting up the business, the quality and cost of the resources available, the infrastructure, regulations, taxation, financial reporting, and legal system. In addition, it is important to find information on a whole host of practical issues, as detailed in the following checklist:

- Foreign ownership of enterprises—what are the regulations restricting the ownership of enterprises and what type of businesses are permitted? What regulations exist concerning governance, procedures, and liability?
- Financial system—how developed is the banking system? What currency is used? Are there any foreign exchange controls? Is there a stock exchange?
- Investment—are there any investment guarantees? Are there any incentives? What business registration procedures exist?
- Labour regulations—what regulations are there covering expatriate employees? Are there social, health, and unemployment insurance payments to be made for local and expatriate employees? Is there a minimum wage?
- Disputes—how are disputes settled? Are there any regulations protecting intellectual property rights? Is there any competition law?
- Taxation—what taxes exist and what are the rates?
- Reporting—what are the statutory requirements for financial reporting?
- Expatriate employees—are entry visas and work permits required? What housing, education, and medical facilities are there for expatriate employees?

Counterpoint Box 6.2 Investing in Africa

According to Ha-Joon Chang (2010), the perceived image of Africa is that it is 'destined for underdevelopment'. It has a poor climate, lousy geography, small markets, violent conflicts, corruption, and poor-quality institutions. It is ethnically divided, making people difficult to manage, and has a bad culture in which people do not work hard, do not save, and they cannot cooperate with each other.

These are sweeping generalizations for a group of over 50 countries, but, nevertheless, are probably most people's →

→ image of the prospects for Africa. However, real GDP growth in Africa averaged 4.9 per cent per annum from 2000 to 2008 and this led McKinsey to describe the African economy as 'lions on the move' (McKinsey 2010). Since then, growth has dipped and there are those who suspect that Africa is slipping back into the old ways. It is true that average growth has slowed to around 3.3 per cent per annum; however, this is largely because oil prices have declined and there has been political turmoil in North Africa. Excluding these groups, GDP growth has averaged around 4.4 per cent.

McKinsey (2010) identified four different groups of African economies, including:

1. diversified economies—the most advanced with large manufacturing and services sectors (as a percentage of GDP). The four largest are Egypt, Morocco, South Africa, and Tunisia;
2. the oil exporters such as Angola, Equatorial Guinea, Chad, Libya, and Nigeria—the richest but least diversified;

3. the transition economies, e.g. Ghana, Kenya, and Tanzania, which have begun the process of diversifying, but their income per head remains below the first two groups; and
4. the poorest countries such as the Democratic Republic of the Congo, Ethiopia, Mali, and Sierra Leone, which remain in the pre-transition stage.

Sources: Chang (2010); IMF World (2010)

Question

Select one country from each group and compare their prospects for growth. Use the following resources to help your analysis: 'Lions on the Move II: Realizing the Potential of Africa's Economies'. McKinsey, September 2016, https://www.weforum.org/agenda/2016/05/what-s-the-future-of-economic-growth-in-africa, and http://www.africaneconomicoutlook.org/en/home.

Risk

All of the above must be weighed against the risks of doing business.

Wars, hurricanes, terror attacks, uprisings, crime, earthquakes, and stock market crashes can bring companies to the brink, and sometimes tip them over the edge. The Gulf oil spill in 2010 has cost BP upwards of US$60 billion (*Financial Times* 14 July 2016), and severely damaged its future operations in the USA. Earlier, Hurricanes Katrina and Rita left the global insurance industry with a bill for US$80 billion. The price of insurance and re-insurance cover for areas of the world exposed to US hurricanes has also rocketed. A construction company agreed a contract in Nepal without seriously considering the implications of the uprising by Maoist rebels. Within weeks, a couple of its workers had died at the hands of rebels, and the roads on which the project relied had been blown up. The company was forced to pull out. Worldwide floods have caused major disruption and cost billions of dollars, and it is estimated that climate change combined with rapid population change, economic growth, and land subsidence, could lead to a more than nine-fold increase in the global risk of floods in large port cities between 2018 and 2050. In 2017, insurance losses on natural and man-made disasters amounted to $136 billion, double the 2016 figure and well above the $58 billion ten-year average. Total economic losses from disasters amounted to $306 billion (*Financial Times* 20 December 2017).

In today's more interconnected world, uncertainties can emerge almost anywhere as a result of product innovation, political change, changes in the law, or **market deregulation**. As business becomes more globalized, moving into new markets and transferring production to lower-cost locations, it opens itself up to more risks, especially in countries with political instability and more vulnerability to natural catastrophes. International business needs to weigh up the risk factors when making strategic decisions on FDI.

Country Risk

Country risk refers to the possibility of the business climate changing in a way that negatively affects the way in which business operates. Sources of risk include:

- change in political leadership;
- radical change in philosophy of political leadership;
- civil unrest between ethnic groups, races, and religions;
- corrupt political leadership;
- weak political leadership;
- reliability of the infrastructure;
- supply chain disruption;
- economic risks such as the volatility of the economy and foreign exchange problems;
- organized crime;
- poor relationships with other countries;
- wars;
- terrorism; and
- piracy.

One source of risk is a change in political leadership. Elections take place every four or five years in all of the advanced industrialized economies of the world, and with this can come relatively minor changes in attitude to business. This might result in changes in trade agreements or general changes in policies and regulations towards business. This is risk which is fairly predictable, and should not therefore be a problem. It is unpredictable risk that is the bigger problem. Although past patterns can be analysed to assess the risk, this also has its dangers. Kenya was generally considered as one of Africa's more politically stable countries, with a thriving tourist industry bringing in about US$1 billion per year. However, controversial elections in December 2007 triggered a wave of violent unrest resulting in more than 1,000 deaths and 250,000 forced from their homes. The World Bank was predicting growth in real GDP of 6.5 per cent for Kenya in 2008 (Global Economic Outlook October 2007), but the violence hit the economy by reducing the number of tourists to a trickle. Horticulture was Kenya's other big earner, but this also depended on the tourist industry, as did the many local handicraft sellers. According to the IMF, estimated growth in 2008 was just 1.5 per cent, increasing to 2.4 per cent in 2009. The economy has since recovered and has been one of Africa's best performers growing rapidly at around 5 per cent per annum, but more election problems (although not on the scale of those in 2007) and drought in 2017 have reduced growth prospects by about 1 per cent (IMF World Economic Outlook October 2017).

The other sources of political instability form the biggest risk. The possible consequences are:

- property seizure by:
- confiscation—assets seized by government without compensation,
- expropriation—assets seized with compensation, and
- nationalization—takeover by government of an entire industry;

- property destruction;
- freezing of funds;
- kidnapping of employees;
- market disruption;
- labour unrest;
- supply shortages; and
- racketeering.

Risk Assessments

Again, many commercial organizations provide assessment of risk, but at a price.

The EIU assesses countries for a variety of risks and sells the results to business, although summary information on each of 180 countries is available on their website. Countries are assessed for risk based on ten issues:

1. security;
2. political stability;
3. government effectiveness;
4. legal and regulatory;
5. macroeconomic;
6. foreign trade and payments;
7. financial;
8. tax policy;
9. labour market; and
10. infrastructure.

The least risky countries tend to be the most advanced economies, while poorer countries dominate the ranks of the most risky. Countries with good records on economic policy-making, such as Singapore, Hong Kong, and Chile, tend to do well. Those with poor payment records, institutional failings, and civil violence are the worst rated.

The World Bank has a worldwide governance indicator project that reports governance indicators for 215 economies between 1996 and 2016 for:

- voice and accountability;
- political stability and absence of violence;
- government effectiveness;
- regulatory quality;
- the rule of law; and
- control of corruption.

See World Bank (2017).

The WEF also produces a global risks report (WEF 2018). The 2018 report takes a ten-year view and organizes risks into the PESTE framework (no legal risks considered). It identifies 30

Table 6.6 The ten global risks of highest concern

Rank	Likelihood	Impact
1	Extreme weather events	Weapons of mass destruction
2	Natural disasters	Extreme weather events
3	Cyberattacks	Natural disasters
4	Data fraud or theft	Failure of climate change mitigation and adaptation
5	Failure of climate change mitigation and adaptation	Water crises
6	Large-scale involuntary migration	Cyberattacks
7	Man-made environmental disasters	Food crises
8	Terrorist attacks	Biodiversity loss and ecosystem collapse
9	Illicit trade	Large-scale involuntary migration
10	Asset bubbles in a major economy	Spread of infectious diseases

Source: http://www.weforum.org/issues/global-risks

global risks. The ten global risks of highest concern in terms of likelihood and impact for 2018 are shown in Table 6.6.

Over the next ten years, the WEF sees extreme weather events as the risk most likely to cause significant problems globally, followed by natural disasters, cyberattacks, and data fraud or theft. The most potentially impactful risks it sees as weapons of mass destruction, extreme weather events, natural disasters, and failure of climate change mitigation and adaptation.

Learning Task

Using the sources mentioned prior to Table 6.6, compare the risks of doing business in China and Australia.

According to the World Bank (2018) Global Investment Competitiveness survey, political stability and a business-friendly regulatory environment are most important in MNC investors' decision-making when investing in developing countries. Table 6.7 shows the full results.

Select Market and/or Site

Having reduced the number of countries to a few, and undertaken detailed analysis of the market and business environment in those few countries, a decision has to be made about which country or countries to enter. This decision will require an estimate to be made of the market share the company is likely to gain.

One useful mechanism for comparing countries is to compile a grid using factors judged important to the decision, giving each of them a weight, according to the importance to the company, and then scoring each country. The factors will be different for a company just considering exporting

Table 6.7 Factors affecting investment decisions (% of respondents)

Factor	Critically important	Important	Somewhat important	Not at all important
Political stability and security	50	37	9	2
Legal and regulatory environment	40	46	12	2
Large domestic market size	42	38	14	4
Macroeconomic stability and favourable exchange rate	34	44	16	5
Available talent and skill of labour	28	45	22	5
Good physical infrastructure	25	46	24	5
Low tax rates	19	39	31	9
Low cost of labour and inputs	18	35	35	11
Access to land or real estate	14	31	32	22
Financing in the domestic market	16	28	31	24

Source: World Bank (2018). Data available under Creative Commons Attribution CC BY 3.0 IGO.

from one considering FDI, and will be different for each company. This idea can be used at any stage of the process, with earlier grids using fewer and broader measures of potential. The grid at this stage is likely to be in at least two sections and probably three. One would be for market potential, one for the ease of doing business, and one for potential risk. At its simplest, the grid could be just three rows with a score taken from published ranking tables for each of the above three categories, but this is unlikely to capture all the factors a company might want to take into account. A grid might look like that in Table 6.8, scoring each factor out of five and taking into account the weighting. In the first two categories, higher numbers are preferable, indicating higher potential and greater ease of doing business. In the third category, a low score is preferred.

From this grid, country B and country D would seem to be ruled out, given that their total scores for the first two sections are 19 and 20, respectively, with a risk score of 8 and therefore a net score of 11 and 12. Country A has a net score of 21 (14 + 12 - 5) while country C scores 24 (16 + 14 - 6) and would therefore seem to be the preferred choice, although the risk is slightly higher. At this stage, it is likely that managers would want to undertake field trips to each of the countries in order get a 'feel' for those countries, check the assessments, and meet potential customers, suppliers, and workforce. Only then will the final decision be made and contracts negotiated.

 Learning Task

Carry out a screening of Turkey for firms involved in:

- construction equipment; or
- education services.

Comment on the conditions to be faced by businesses considering setting up operations in Turkey.

Table 6.8 Country attractiveness grid

Factor	Weight	Country A	Country B	Country C	Country D
Market Potential					
Size of market	0.3	4	3	3	2
Growth rate	0.2	2	3	4	2
Market share	0.3	3	1	3	2
Investment required	0.4	3	1	4	2
Tax rates	0.1	2	2	2	2
TOTAL		14	10	16	10
Ease of Doing Business					
Starting a business	0.3	3	3	4	3
Getting credit	0.1	3	2	3	3
Paying taxes	0.1	3	2	3	2
Employing labour	0.3	3	2	4	2
TOTAL		12	9	14	10
Risks					
Political risk	0.4	1	3	2	3
Supply chain disruption	0.2	2	3	2	3
Foreign exchange risks	0.2	2	2	2	2
TOTAL		5	8	6	8

● CHAPTER SUMMARY

In this chapter we examined a process for assessing the attractiveness of countries. We saw that firms tend to follow a gradual process of internationalization, starting by exporting and gradually progressing to the establishment of overseas subsidiaries, although we noted that some firms appear to be 'born global'. Reasons for FDI include market access, lower production costs, and access to resources. China is leading the way in scouring the world for raw materials.

Firms intending to export or invest abroad can systematically screen countries to assess their attractiveness as new markets and/or production locations. This should include an initial assessment of the need for exports or investment before an analysis of the general business environment and the ease of doing business. Many commercial organizations specialize in country and market analysis, but at a price. Once the initial need is established, then a more detailed analysis of industry potential and operations is required before a final decision can be made.

● REVIEW QUESTIONS

1. The internationalization process is normally a gradual transition from exporting to FDI, but some firms may be 'born global'. Explain what this means and why firms should want or need to be 'born global'.

2. Using examples, explain the reasons for FDI.

3. Discuss the problems of collecting international data.

4. Explain what is meant by risk. Use examples to illustrate your answer.

● ASSIGNMENT TASKS

1. You work for a US construction company that has developed a range of eco-friendly building products. It wants to open up export markets and thinks that the UK market might be a good market in which to start. Write a report which investigates the UK construction market and identifies possible opportunities.

2. Your company is looking for investment opportunities abroad and wishes to evaluate various country locations. Select three countries, including one each from South America, Africa, and Asia, and compare the attractiveness of these countries for foreign direct investment.

Case Study **Indonesia**

© 123RF.com/Pavalena

Indonesia is an ex-Dutch colony situated in SE Asia between the Indian Ocean and the South Pacific made up of more than 1,700 islands. The biggest are Java, Kalimantan (part of the island of Borneo), Sumatra, Sulawesi, and New Guinea. Indonesia lies either side of the equator and so has a tropical climate. Its capital is Jakarta, its currency is the Indonesian Rupiah, and the dominant language is Indonesian Bahasa.

With 261 million people, Indonesia has the fourth largest population in the world which is expected (World Bank n.d.b) to rise to 321 million by 2045. It has hundreds of different ethnic groups, brought together as a result of Dutch colonial expan-

sion, although the major ones are the Javanese (41 per cent) and the Sundanese (15 per cent). Eighty per cent of Indonesia's population lives on the two islands of Sumatra and Java. Urbanization is increasing rapidly and it is expected that two-thirds of Indonesia's population will live in urban areas by 2050 (UN). Forty-two per cent of the population is under 25. According to the World Bank (n.d.c), more than 28 million Indonesians (11 per cent of the population) live below the poverty line, and about 40 per cent of the population remains vulnerable as their income hovers just above the national poverty line.

Indonesia seems to suffer from more than its fair share of natural disasters. It is located at one end of what is known as the 'Pacific Ring of Fire'. The Ring is a string of volcanoes and earthquakes. On average a major volcanic eruption (i.e. one with significant loss of life) takes place every 10–15 years. This can be devastating not just for the loss of life but also to the disruption caused to small and medium size enterprises. Earthquakes occur on a daily basis but with a magnitude on the Richter scale of 5 or 6 do little damage. Those above 7, which occur about once a year, can and do cause major casualties and infrastructural damage. The worst was in 2004, when an earth-quake caused a tsunami that killed nearly 300,000 people. A large tsunami occurs about once every five years, mainly in Java and Sumatra. Floods and landslides in the rainy season (December to March), and forest fires caused by the illegal →

→ slash-and-burn activities of farmers and companies are not unusual and can cause billions of dollars of damage.

Indonesia gained its independence from the Dutch in 1949 after years of campaigning and fighting. Its first president following independence was Sukarno, but he faced great difficulty in trying to bring together strong and very different political factions of two big Muslim parties, the nationalists and the Communists. The army was also a significant player and needed to keep many militant movements from across the territories in check. What followed was 40 years of autocratic rule, first by Sukarno and then by General Suharto, after a coup in the mid-1960s. Suharto ruled for more than 30 years. He re-established ties with the West which had been cut by Sukarto and this brought investment and economic development. His 'reign' ended in the late 1990s when the Asian economic crisis hit hardest in Indonesia, undoing much of what had been achieved. This led to mass riots in Jakarta, in which thousands of buildings were destroyed and over 1,000 people were killed. In 1998, Suharto left office and a new era, labelled the reformation, was ushered in promising democracy and decentralization to the regions. Elections have taken place regularly since. The current president is Joko Widodo, who was elected in 2014. Despite the reforms, corruption remains a major problem. Indonesia ranks 90th in the Transparency International Corruption Perceptions Index, scoring only 37 out of 100.

Indonesia has the largest economy in South East Asia and is classified by the World Bank as an emerging middle-income country. From 1990 until the Asian financial crisis in 1997, the economy grew rapidly at an average of 8 per cent per annum. During the crisis, the economy actually shrank but since then has recovered and averaged growth of 5.5 per cent per annum. It was predicted by the IMF (World Economic Outlook Database October 2017) to continue that level of growth until at least 2022. As a result, the country's GDP per capita has also risen, from US$770 (US$2,880 ppp) in 1990 to US$3,858 (US$12,378 ppp) in 2017. It is the world's tenth largest economy in terms of purchasing power parity. It has changed from an economy dependent on agriculture (51 per cent of GDP in 1965) to a more balanced one, with agriculture now only accounting for 15 per cent of GDP, industry 47 per cent, and services 37 per cent. The agricultural sector still accounts for 38 per cent of employment. Indonesia's main exports are palm oil, coal briquettes, petroleum gas, crude petroleum, and jewellery. Its main imports are refined petroleum, crude petroleum, telephones, vehicle parts, and wheat. Its main export destinations are China, the USA, Japan, Singapore, and India; its principal sources of imports are China, Singapore, Japan, Malaysia, and South Korea.

Indonesia is a member of ASEAN, the Association of South East Asian Nations. ASEAN was established in 1967 in Thailand, with the signing of the Bangkok Declaration. The original five members were Indonesia, Malaysia, the Philippines, Singapore, and Thailand. They were later joined by Brunei Darussalam (1984) to make the ASEAN six and then later by Vietnam (1995), Lao PDR and Myanmar in 1997, and Cambodia in 1999 (collectively known as CLMV), making up what are today the ten member states of ASEAN. It is now one of the of the fastest-growing consumer markets in the world. ASEAN established a Free Trade Area in the 1990s, and import and export duties have been all but eradicated. Significant non-tariff barriers remain, such as licences and quotas. The vision is of a region with free movement of goods, services, investment, skilled labour, and freer flow of capital. To this end, the Asian Economic Community (AEC) was formed in 2015 with a view to becoming an Economic Community similar to the European Community. ASEAN have also signed trade agreements with Australia and New Zealand (AANZFA), China (ACFTA), India (AIFTA), Korea (AKFTA), and Japan (AJCEP).

If ASEAN were a single country, it would already be the sixth largest economy in the world (ASEAN 2017); it is projected to be the fourth largest by 2050. By 2030 the population will be about 720 million people, making an enormous market. Three or four of the ASEAN states will be high-income countries, two to four middle-income countries, and three to four becoming upper middle-income countries.

Sources: https://theconversation.com/five-active-volcanoes-on-my-asia-pacific-ring-of-fire-watch-list-right-now-90618; ASEAN Economic Integration Brief, June 2017, available at http://asean.org/storage/2017/06/AEIB_No.01-June-2017_rev.pdf; World Bank, http://www.worldbank.org/en/country/indonesia/overview; https://www.indonesia-investments.com.

Questions

Using this case study, and any other resources mentioned in the chapter, answer the following:

1. Forty-two per cent of Indonesia's population are under 25. Why is this an important factor in the future growth of Indonesia's economy?

2. What are the benefits to business of ASEAN becoming an economic community?   →

→

3. Explain the attraction of the Indonesian economy as an investment location.

4. Investigate how easy it would be for a Western company to establish a new business in Indonesia.

5. What risks would be faced in setting up business in Indonesia?

6. Undertake a country assessment of Indonesia for firms in one of the following sectors:

   a management training;

   b ICT;

   c renewable energy; or

   d defence technology.

● FURTHER READING

For a book about born-globals, see:

● Cavusgil, S.T. and Knight, G. (2009) *Born Global Firms: A New International Enterprise.* New York: Business Expert Press.

For further discussion and ideas about assessing country and market attractiveness see:

● Cavusgil, S.T., Knight, G., and Reisenberger, J.R. (2010) *International Business: The New Realities,* 2nd edn. Harlow: Pearson.

● Daniels, J.D., Radebaugh, L.H., and Sullivan, D.P. (2018) *International Business,* 16th edn. Harlow: Pearson.

For the issues around doing business in China:

● Xiaowen Tian (2015) *Managing International Business in China,* 2nd edn. Cambridge: Cambridge University Press.

● Kroeber, A.R. (2016) *China's Economy, What Everyone Needs to Know.* Oxford: Oxford University Press.

● Wasserstrom, J.N. (2013) *China in the 21st Century: What Everyone Needs to Know,* 2nd edn. Oxford: Oxford University Press.

● REFERENCES

Andersson, S. and Evangelista, F. (2006) 'The Entrepreneur in the Born Global Firm in Australia and Sweden'. *Journal of Small Business and Enterprise Development* 13(4): 642.

Arenius, P. (2005) 'The Psychic Distance Postulate Revised: From Market Selection to Speed of Market Penetration'. *Journal of International Entrepreneurship* 3(2).

Avendano, R. Melguzo, A., and Miner, S. (2017) *Chinese FDI in Latin America: New Trends with Global Implications.* Atlantic Council, OECD Development Centre.

Benito, G.R.G., Peterson, B., and Welch, L.S. (2009) 'Towards More Realistic Conceptualisations of Foreign Operation Modes'. *Journal of International Business Studies* 40: 1455.

Carrefour (n.d.) http://www.carrefour.com.

Cavusgil, S.T. (1985) 'Guidelines for Export Market Research'. *Business Horizons* 28(6): 27.

Cavusgil, S.T., Kiyak, T., and Yeniyurt, S. (2004) 'Complementary Approaches to Preliminary Foreign Market Opportunity Assessment: Country Clustering and Country Ranking'. *Industrial Marketing Management* 33: 607.

Center for Global Development and The African Population and Health Research Center (2014) 'Delivering on the Data Revolution in Sub-Saharan Africa', Final Report of the Data for African Development Working Group. Center for Global Development, Washington, DC.

Chang, Ha-Joon (2010) *23 Things They Don't Tell You About Capitalism*. London: Allen Lane.

China Briefing (n.d.) http://www.china-briefing.com.

Christmann, P. and Taylor, G. (2001) 'Globalization and the Environment: Determinants of Firm Self-Regulation in China'. *Journal of International Business Studies* 32(3).

CIA (n.d.) https://www.cia.gov/library/publications/the-world-factbook/index.html.

Euromonitor (n.d.) http://www.euromonitor.com/alcoholic-drinks.

Fan, T. and Phan, P. (2007) 'International New Ventures: Revisiting the Influences behind the "Born-Global" Firm'. *Journal of International Business Studies* 38: 1113.

Freeman, S., Edwards, R., and Schroder, B. (2006) 'How Smaller Born-Global Firms Use Networks and Alliances to Overcome Constraints to Rapid Internationalization'. *Journal of International Marketing* 14(3):33.

Gabrielson, G. (2005) 'Branding Strategies of Born Globals'. *Journal of International Entrepreneurship* 3(3): 199.

Ghemawat, P. (2001) 'Distance Still Matters: The Hard Reality of Global Expansion'. *Harvard Business Review* September: 137–47.

iberglobal (n.d.) http://www.iberglobal.com/files/business_climate_eiu.pdf.

IMD (n.d.) https://www.imd.org/wcc/world-competitiveness-center-rankings/competitiveness-2017-rankings-results.

IMF (2017) World Economic Outlook Database October 2017. Available at http://www.imf.org/external/pubs/ft/weo/2014/01/weodata/index.aspx.

IMF World (2010) 'What's Driving Africa's Growth'. *McKinsey Quarterly* June.

Johanson, J. and Vahlne, J.E. (1977) 'The Internationalization Process of the Firm—A Model of Knowledge Development and Increasing Foreign Commitments'. *Journal of International Business Studies* 8 (Spring/Summer): 23.

Knight, G., Madsen, T.K., and Servais, P. (2004) 'An Inquiry into Born-global Firms in Europe and the USA'. *International Marketing Review* 21(6): 645.

Krugman, P. (1994) 'Competitiveness: A Dangerous Obsession'. *Foreign Affairs* March/April.

Malhotra, N. and Hinings, C.R. (2010) 'An Organizational Model for Understanding Internalization Processes'. *Journal of International Business Studies* 41: 330.

McKinsey Global Institute (2010) 'Lions on the Move: The Progress and Potential of African Economies', June.

Netflix (2016) 'Annual Report', available at https://s22.q4cdn.com/959853165/files/doc_financials/annual_reports/10K_Final.PDF.

OECD (2014) *Perspectives on Global Development 2014, Boosting Productivity to Meet the Middle-Income-Challenge*. Paris: OECD.

Papadopoulos, N. and Martin, O.M. (2011) 'International Market Selection and Segmentation: Perspectives and Challenges'. *International Marketing Review* Special Issue 28(2).

Porter, M. (1990) *The Competitive Advantage of Nations*. London: Macmillan Press.

Prashantham, S. (2005) 'Toward a Knowledge-based Conceptualization of Internationalization'. *Journal of International Entrepreneurship* 3: 37–52.

Rennie, M.W. (1993) 'Global Competitiveness: Born Global'. *McKinsey Quarterly* 4: 45–52.

Reshoring Initiative (2016) http://reshorenow.org/blog/reshoring-initiative-2016-data-report-the-tide-has-turned.

Sabadie, J.A. and Johansen, J. (2010) 'How Do National Economic Competitiveness Indices View Human Capital?'. *European Journal of Education* 45(2): 236.

The Economist (2018) 'Donald Trump's Difficult Decision on Steel Imports: Being the World's Trade Policeman is Tough Work'. 11 January.

UN (2014) *World Urbanization Prospects: The 2014 Revision*. UN Department of Economics and Social Affairs, Population Division.

UNCTAD (2017) World Investment Report, Investment and the Digital Economy.

UNCTAD (2018) Investment Trends Monitor, Issue 28, January.

WEF (2018) https://www.weforum.org/reports/the-global-risks-report-2018.

World Bank (2010) *Investing Across Borders, Indicators of Foreign Direct Investment Regulation in 87 Economies*. Available at http://iab.worldbank.org.

World Bank (2017) 'World Governance Indicators'. Available at http://info.worldbank.org/governance/wgi/index.aspx#home.

World Bank (2018) *Global Investment Competitiveness Report 2017/2018: Foreign Investor Perspectives and Policy Implications*. Washington, DC: World Bank. doi:10.1596/978-1-4648-1175-3. License: Creative Commons Attribution CC BY 3.0 IGO.

World Bank (n.d.a) http://data.worldbank.org/indicator.

World Bank (n.d.b) http://datatopics.worldbank.org/health/population.

World Bank (n.d.c) http://www.worldbank.org/en/country/indonesia/overview.

Zheng, Y. and Chen, M. (2006) 'China Moves to Enhance Corporate Social Responsibility in Multinational Companies'. *Briefing Series*, Issue 11, August. University of Nottingham: China Policy Institute.

PART TWO
Global Issues

CHAPTER SEVEN

The Socio-cultural Framework

LEARNING OUTCOMES

This chapter will enable you to:

- explain the importance of the social and cultural environment for business;

- apply concepts of cultural theory to international business;

- analyse major social and cultural elements such as demography, youth unemployment, religion, and language and their implications for business; and

- compare and contrast the liberal, conservative, and social democratic social models.

Case Study   Saudi Arabia: women and the labour market

© iStock.com/Zdenka_Simekova

Saudia Arabia is marked by some of the world's greatest gender disparities. Despite some recent advances in the position of Saudi women in the labour market, the participation of women in the labour force and in managerial positions is among the lowest in the world. According to the World Economic Forum (WEF) 2017 Global Gender Gap study, only 21 per cent of women were in the workforce compared with 80 per cent of men. The inequality between men and women is also highlighted by wage levels. Saudi men earned more than four times as much as women (Table 7.1).

The level of education for women has risen, with 62 per cent of women enrolling in the tertiary education sector. Humanities, Islamic Studies, and Social and Behavioural Sciences recruit the largest numbers of female undergraduates (Koyame-Marsh 2017). While the numbers graduating from colleges and universities has increased, the opportunities to enter the world of

work and management remain poor. Koyame-Marsh (2017) notes that in 2015, around 68 per cent of female graduates were unemployed. Most of those managing to get work are employed in traditionally 'feminine' areas of education, the humanities, arts, and health care (Al-Asfour et al. 2016).

Academic research has identified a number of societal barriers to female participation in the labour market, many relating to traditional conservative values and discriminatory gender stereotypes. Barriers include the guardianship system. Women, throughout their lives, are treated as minors. If they wish to travel, work, or study abroad, they need the consent of a male guardian; this can be the father, husband, brother, or teenage son. Until 2018, women were prohibited from driving cars. Arabian society emphasizes the domestic role of women as homemakers, wives, and mothers. In this cultural context, women can find it difficult to strike a balance between work and family life. Hofstede's theory shows that Saudi Arabia is a strongly collectivist society, which means commitment to the group, whether that be the nuclear family, extended family, or tribe, and non-conformists can be shamed (Geert Hofstede n.d.). Al-Asfour et al. (2016) report that women pursuing careers outside the home are often seen as cultural deviants.

There is evidence that women are socialized into believing that they do not have the ability to take on high-level jobs. Researchers found discrimination against women in the workplace with opportunities for promotion being few and far between. Religion also reinforces the difficulties for women wishing to work. The official religion is Islam, which gives women the right to work outside the home. However, in Saudi

Table 7.1 The gender gap in Saudi Arabia

	Female	Male	Female ranking/144 countries
Labour force participation %		80	140
Legislators, senior officials, and managers %	6	94	123
Professional and technical workers %	24	76	120
Estimated earned income (US$, PPP)	17,857	82,164	138
Unemployment %	21	2	NA
Enrolment in tertiary education %	62	64	97

Source: WEF (2016)   ➔

→ Arabia, Wahhabism, the conservative branch of Islam, is dominant and this results in women only being able to work in places where the sexes are segregated.

The Economist (16 March 2017) reported that a rising number of Saudi women, unhappy with their situation, are deserting the country. Some go to Western universities, often financed by the Saudi government, and do not return, others enter into marriages of convenience to men willing to take them out of the country. The untapped potential of women to Saudi society and to the economy is recognized by the authorities who are trying to reduce the country's economic dependence on oil. They set a target of increasing the participation of women in the labour force to 30 per cent by 2030. In 2012, some small steps were taken when they removed the need for guardian approval for a few job categories including assistants in clothes shops, chefs, and amusement park attendants.

Source: BBC 27 September 2017; *The Economist* 16 March 2017; El-Katiri (2016); Koyame-Marsh (2017); World Economic Forum (2017); Al-Asfour et al. (2016)

Introduction

Why do cross-border mergers fail? How is it that mergers such as that between two advertising giants, France's Publicis and Omnicom from the USA, collapse before being finalized? Why do producers of alcoholic drinks, such as Diageo and InBev, flourish in some countries but find it difficult to develop markets in others? Why does KFC have to serve Peking Duck burgers for lunch in Shanghai? Often answers to these questions come down to national differences in social characteristics, cultural attitudes, and values.

This chapter examines the social and cultural environment. This encompasses a vast range of social and cultural characteristics, which can vary significantly both within societies and between one society and another. Social aspects include the distribution of income and wealth, the structures of employment and unemployment, living and working conditions, health, education, population characteristics including size and breakdown by age, gender, ethnic group, and the provision of welfare for the population in the form of education, health care, unemployment benefits, pensions, and so on. The cultural components cover areas like language, religion, diet, values and norms, attitudes, beliefs and practices, social relationships, and how people interact. There are links between certain aspects of culture and social conditions—for example, between diet and certain types of disease, values and norms and the role of women in society, religious beliefs, and attitudes to contraception and their effect on birth rates. To be successful, business has to be aware of socio-cultural differences that could have important implications for levels and patterns of demand, the quality and quantity of labour, and the policies and strategies to be adopted.

There are far too many elements to address comprehensively in a single chapter. Therefore, the chapter focuses on a limited number of social and cultural aspects. We start off by considering culture and then go on to consider some important elements in the social environment.

Culture

Culture can be seen as a system of shared beliefs, values, customs, and behaviours prevalent in a society that are transmitted from generation to generation through a multitude of channels, the family, religion, books, newspapers, television, and the Web (see Bates and Plog 1990). Hofstede, the management scientist, described these elements of culture as the software of the mind, 'the collective programming of the mind which distinguishes the members of one category of people from another' (1994: 5) and which influences how people think and behave. The values in the culture are enforced by a set of norms, which lay down rules of behaviour. These rules are usually supplemented by a set of sanctions to ensure that the norms are respected. Culture comprises a whole variety of different aspects, including religion, language, non-verbal communication, diet, dress, and institutions ensuring that the values and beliefs are transmitted from one generation to another. Culture is dynamic; in other words, it changes over time not least due to the process of globalization with the increasing cross-border movement of goods, services, capital, and the migration of people.

Different cultures can have significantly different attitudes and beliefs on a whole range of issues. As we will see later, when discussing the various social models, there is a significant divide between the USA and Continental Europe on attitudes to social issues such as poverty. In the USA poverty tends to be seen as the fault of the poor, whereas in Europe the poor tend more to be seen as victims of the system. Cultural attitudes can also vary toward issues such as corruption, women at work, sexuality, violence, suicide, and time.

Cultural attitudes can have important implications for business. Some of the most influential research on culture and the workplace was carried out by Hofstede (1991, 2001). He surveyed over 100,000 workers in IBM subsidiaries in 40 countries, looking for cultural explanations of differences in employee attitudes and behaviour. He concluded that the norms and values embedded in national culture were a very powerful influence on the workplace, and that different approaches would be necessary when managing people from different cultural backgrounds. Hofstede (1994) concluded that the workplace can only change people's values to a limited extent. The message for multinational companies was that they would be unwise to assume that an organizational culture that was successful in one cultural context, for example, that of the USA, would be equally successful in a completely different cultural context in, say, China.

Hofstede's work (2007) also contains another message for multinationals. He contends that countries, especially big countries like China, India, Indonesia, and Brazil, do not have a single national culture but rather a variety of cultures that can vary significantly from region to region. A similar point could be made for smaller countries, in Western Europe for instance, where different cultures may be based on ethnic group rather than region.

Mini Case Study 7.1 Can Coca-Cola sell tea to China?

When it comes to culture, even the biggest multinationals can get it wrong. In 1998, Coca-Cola, the US soft beverage giant, launched the 'Heaven and Earth' bottled tea drink in to the Chinese market. The product, popular in the USA, was fruit-flavoured and sugary. The instant tea market in China was a virtual duopoly being dominated by two Taiwanese companies: Uni-President and Master Kong. Coke admitted defeat by withdrawing the product after three years.

Coca-Cola then tried again. In 2001, it launched the Lanfeng honey green tea drink and, in 2002, Sunshine iced fruit tea. In 2004, it got together with Nestlé to launch Nestea, and in 2005 it offered the Tea Research Workshop series, with two versions of tea: one aimed at men and the other at women. They all flopped even though the Chinese instant tea market was tripling in size each year. Coke tried other drinks products in the Chinese market including water, sports beverage and ➜

→ lemonade, and the Simply Orange brand of Minute Maid. With the exception of Minute Maid orange juice, they all failed to make an impact in terms of brand recognition or market share faced with Huiyuan, China's largest juice producer, which is highly regarded by Chinese consumers.

In 2015, Coke acquired Xiamen Culiangwang, a Chinese company primarily selling health-conscious, whole grain and plant-based protein drinks. The market for plant-based beverages was growing at more than 20 per cent per year. However, Xiamen Culiangwang trailed behind Deyufang, Yili and, Mengniu in this market.

Some analysts put Coke's disappointing performance down to its failure to take cultural factors into account. Faced with its inability to crack the market, the company got social scientists to carry out research on Chinese culture to find out why. They found that cultural attitudes to tea in China contrasted sharply with that in the USA. Americans associate tea with indulgence and pleasure so adding fruit flavours went down well with US consumers. Tea consumption in China has a very different cultural meaning bound by a set of rules, some explicit and others implicit. Strong tea might be served to friends or to those with whom one wants to build a closer relationship. It would never be offered to people one has just met. Tea products therefore need to be offered in different strengths. Consuming tea products should remove irritations and distractions like noise. Following the research, Coke eliminated sugar and fruit flavours from 'Heaven and Earth', and gained some success.

Other commentators suggest that Coke's problems in China stem from an over-centralized and bloated, bureaucratic structure which means that decisions have to go through several levels in the organization before being signed off. Coke's brands are centrally managed in the USA, meaning that local managers do not have the authority to adapt brands to local conditions. It is also claimed that Coke's marketing and legal departments act independently leaving it unclear which one the right to make decisions and making coordination difficult.

Sources: Atlantic March 2013; *Financial Times Magazine* 22 April 2017; Madsbjerg (2017); *The World Weekly* 14 May 2015

Questions
1. Why is Coca-Cola so keen to get into the Chinese market?
2. Discuss the reasons for Coke's failures in the Chinese beverages market.
3. Give reasons for Coke's acquisition of Xiamen Culiangwang.

Research has revealed fundamental cultural differences between East and West that have important implications for Western executives trying to do business in the East. Psychologists have shown that Eastern and Western cultures can vary significantly in terms of perception and logic, and how they see the world around them. Apparently, Westerners focus more on detail while Easterners tend to look at things in the round. For example, when American students were asked to look at a picture of a tiger in a forest, they focused on the tiger while Chinese students concentrated more on the background—that is, the context within which the tiger was located.

Researchers attribute this to different social environments. In East Asia, social environments are more complex, collective, and constrained. As a result, Easterners need to pay attention to the social context if they are to operate effectively. On the other hand, Western societies prize individual freedom and there is not the same need to pay heed to the social environment. With their focus on the individual, Westerners tend to view events as the result of specific agents, while those raised in the East set the events in a broader context.

Cultural differences influence the way firms in the East and West do business. For example, when an applicant for a job appears uneasy, Westerners are likely to see that as an undesirable characteristic of the interviewee, which makes them unsuitable for stressful jobs. In the East, they will tend to view the uneasiness in the context of a stressful situation, the interview, and thus be less likely to attribute it to the character of the applicant. Similarly, North Americans, when posing a question, expect a trustworthy person to respond immediately, with any delay inspiring mistrust. In contrast, the Japanese view more favourably those individuals who take time to ponder before giving a reply.

Attitudes toward contracts also vary. Once a contract is signed, Westerners regard them as agreements set in stone, while Easterners, such as the Japanese, take a more flexible view. They are quite happy to renegotiate if circumstances change. They look at the situation of their customers or suppliers in the round and may renegotiate in order to maintain a long-term relationship.

In the East, there is a desire for consensus and harmony. Westerners sometimes perceive Japanese managers as incompetent or indecisive because, in pursuit of consensus, they continually consult their team and are usually reluctant to challenge the decisions made by others. One of the authors came across an example of this in an interview with the Scottish executive put in charge of Mazda the Japanese car company, by the then parent company, Ford. Coming from a Western culture, he was used to debate, discussion, and disagreement when arriving at decisions. In Mazda, he found the reluctance to disagree among his senior managers extremely frustrating.

Hofstede and National Cultures

National cultures can vary significantly from one country to another, and the differences can be reflected by employees in the workplace and by consumers in the market. Such variations in the psychology of work and organizations and in the market place have major implications for management. Managerial systems and approaches that work well in one country may be inappropriate for another.

Geert Hofstede, when working with IBM, noted that while the company promoted an organizational culture in the form of common values, assumptions, and beliefs, there remained differences in attitudes and behaviour among IBM's international subsidiaries. He concluded that organizational culture is less influential than the attitudes and values prevalent in the national culture. In his research, he identified five dimensions of culture:

- **Individualism:** reflects the degree to which people in a country act as individuals rather than as members of a group. Individualistic cultures value the rights of the individual over those of the group. By contrast, cultures low in individualism and high in collectivism emphasize the interests of the group rather than the individual. The USA, the Netherlands, France, and Germany are highly individualistic, while countries in Asia, Africa, and Latin America score low on this dimension.

- **Uncertainty avoidance:** refers to the extent to which people prefer structured to unstructured situations. Societies tolerant of ambiguity, the unknown, and the unfamiliar score highly on avoiding uncertainty. They operate with fewer rules and do not attempt to control all events or outcomes. Cultures with an aversion to uncertainty try to cling to rules and seek ways to control their environment. Latin America, Africa, France, Germany, and Japan have low tolerance levels of uncertainty in contrast to China and the UK; the USA lies somewhere in the middle.

- **Masculinity:** reflects the degree to which masculine values such as competition, assertiveness, a clear role distinction between men and women, money, income, job promotions, and status dominate over feminine values like cooperation, quality of life, and human relationships. In masculine countries, men are favoured for positions of power in organizations. The USA, Japan, and certain South American countries, such as Venezuela, score highly on masculinity, while Nordic countries and Africa score low.

- **Power distance:** shows the degree of inequality accepted as normal in a society. High power-distance cultures accept, and are marked by, significant levels of inequality and hierarchy, such as differences in social class. Low power-distance societies value equality and egalitarianism. In Latin America, Africa, Thailand, and Arab countries, hierarchies are very important and power is distributed very unequally. Less powerful members of organizations, those on the lower rungs of the hierarchy, expect and accept the unequal distribution of power. In the USA and Nordic countries, there is low acceptance of power differences and a greater desire for equality.

- **Long term/short term:** long-term cultures make decisions based on long-term thinking, value perseverance, and thrifty behaviour, such as saving for the future. Short-term losses may be taken to ensure long-term gain. Brazil, India, and China have a long-term orientation. At the other extreme, the USA, Britain, Spain, Nigeria, and Pakistan focus on the short term, while most European countries lie somewhere in the middle.

Subsequently, Hofstede expanded the long-term/short-term dimension and renamed it 'Pragmatic versus Normative'. Pragmatic cultures have long-term characteristics. People do not feel the need to explain everything, and operate on the basis that this is impossible given the complex lives that they lead. Truth is not an absolute but depends on things like context and situation. They can accept contradictions. Indonesia is an example of a pragmatic society. Normative societies have short-term characteristics. Their peoples wish to be able to explain everything and have a desire for the absolute truth. They desire social stability and respect social conventions and traditions. Nigerian society is heavily normative. Hofstede added a sixth dimension to his model: indulgence. In highly indulgent societies, people are free to satisfy their desires to enjoy life and have fun. Societies with low indulgence require people to suppress their desires and enforce that through strict social norms. North America, much of Latin America, the UK, Sweden, the Netherlands, and Australasia score highly on indulgence in comparison with Russia, Eastern Europe, and most of Asia (Hofstede n.d.). Hofstede claimed that his model could be used to predict the behaviour of people, organizations, and institutions.

 Learning Task

According to Hofstede, Brazil scores high on indulgence while China gets a low score.

1. What are the various elements of the indulgence dimension? See Hofstede (2015).
2. Explore the implications for US rock groups trying to promote their music in Brazil and China.

Implications for Business

Cultural characteristics have important implications for international business. According to Hofstede, centralized corporate control is more feasible in societies with large power distances, while decentralization fits better in small power distance cultures. Collectivism is more likely to favour group rewards and family enterprises, while job-hopping and individual remuneration systems are more acceptable in individualistic cultures. Masculine cultures prize competition and survival of the fittest, while feminine cultures favour solidarity and sympathy for the weak. Uncertainty-avoiding cultures are comfortable with strict adherence to rules and principles, while their counterparts are happy to shape policies according to particular circumstances and are more tolerant of deviant behaviour (Hofstede 1994). Studies in many countries show that culture has implications for human resource management, the management of change, entry strategies into foreign markets, the targeting of consumers, and selling to industrial customers.

 ### Counterpoint Box 7.1 Hofstede and his critics

Hofstede's research is widely recognized as a major contribution to the understanding of cross-cultural relationships. He has described his work as paradigm shifting. However, his work has also been subject to many criticisms:

1) Surveys are not a suitable way to measure cultural differences. It is not a good way of measuring phenomena that are subjective and culturally sensitive. Hofstede's response is that methods additional to surveys were also used.

2) Nations are not the best units for studying culture. Hofstede retorts that national identities are the only way of identifying and measuring cultural disparities.

3) Studying the subsidiaries of a single multinational, IBM, is not a valid method of uncovering the secrets of entire national cultures.

4) Critics question Hofstede's claim that his model can be used to predict the behaviour of individuals, organizations and institutions (see Mini Case Study 7.2).

5) Cultures are dynamic and change over time so the data are old and obsolete. Hofstede claims that over 200 other studies have supported his country rankings.

6) Five dimensions are not enough to represent the complexity of culture. Hofstede accepts the criticism that five dimensions are too few and that more should be added. A sixth dimension, indulgence, has been added.

Critics point out that cultures are not limited to the confines of national frontiers, but can straddle national boundaries.

Hofstede's assumption that the population of a country is culturally homogeneous has also drawn criticism on the basis that most countries comprise a variety of different ethnic groups. In his 2007 article, Hofstede went along with this argument but subsequently claimed that the differences between nations tend to be much larger than within them. Some researchers claim that the study data are too old to be of relevance to modern times, particularly given the subsequent changes brought about by the impact of rapid globalization and the collapse of communism. Hofstede refuted this, claiming that cultural change occurs only very slowly and that cross-cultural differences are inherently stable and based on the evolution of societies over centuries.

Sources: Bond (2002); Hofstede and Bond (1998); Hofstede (2001, 2007); Hofstede and Minkov (2011); Jones (2007); McSweeney (2002a, b, 2016); Redpath (1997); Schmitz and Weber (2014)

Questions

1. Choose a country with which you are familiar and consider whether there are cultural differences:
   a. across regions;
   b. between different ethnic groups; and
   c. between different age groups.
2. Advance reasons why a survey of employees in a single US giant technology multinational might not give an accurate picture of national cultures.

Business meetings in North America or Europe have formal agendas setting the order in which items are discussed, and each item is resolved prior to proceeding to the next. The Japanese, rather than deal with agenda items in a rigid sequence, may prefer a more flexible approach that enables them to get a better overview. To Westerners, meetings in Japan may appear unstructured, chaotic, and even threatening. However, Japanese managers are well used to such ambiguity.

Differences in approach can also be seen in negotiations. Westerners expect to focus on contentious issues and try to achieve the most beneficial outcomes for themselves. In contrast, the Japanese prefer to discuss areas of agreement, with the expectation that harmony will lead to the resolution of details. Such differences can lead to bad feeling in negotiations. Lee (2004) quotes a senior South Korean official involved in trade negotiations with Australia. Even though Australia was running a large trade surplus in agricultural products with South Korea, which was of serious concern to the Koreans, 'Australia, nevertheless, continuously puts pressure on Korea to buy more off them . . . they are self-centred, one-sided, only concerned with self-interest, not in considering another's situation or position' (2004: 76).

The upshot is that business has to take cultural differences into account when considering entry to foreign markets through exports, joint ventures, or through takeover or greenfield investment. Similarities between the domestic and foreign cultural norms and values may make entry for a firm easier, whereas large differences may cause major difficulties due to misunderstandings and conflict where social groups do not want to give up valued elements of their culture.

 Mini Case Study 7.2 **Testing Hofstede**

McSweeney et al. (2016) tested the predictive power of Hofstede's generalizations against data on industrial disputes in multiple countries. Hofstede claims that countries ranking highly on masculinity, such as the USA, Ireland, and the UK, should have higher levels of industrial conflict. Therefore in those countries industrial conflict will be resolved by a good fight with the best man winning. Management in very masculine countries are anti-trade union and try to avoid dealings with them, while trade unions behave in a way that justifies that management attitude. Conversely, feminine countries should have fewer industrial disputes. Management and unions resolve their disputes through negotiations and compromise.

Table 7.2 shows data of days lost due to labour disputes per 1,000 employees over a ten-year period (1996–2005, inclusive). The data is divided into two five-year periods (1996–2000, inclusive and 2001–2005, inclusive) in all industries and services for the three 'masculine' countries and the three 'feminine' countries as identified by Hofstede. Column 1 shows the Hofstede's predicted rankings for these countries regarding industrial disputes. The remaining columns show the country rankings in terms of the incidence of industrial conflict measured by working days lost per 1,000 employees in two periods: 1996–2000 and 2001–05. For example, of the countries in Table 7.2, Denmark had the highest incidence of industrial disputes in both time periods.

Table 7.2 Country ranking based on annual averages of working days not worked due to labour disputes, per 1,000 employees in all industries and services

Predicted ranking	1996–2000	2001–05
1. M—Ireland	2	3
2. M—Great Britain	4	4
3. M—United States	3	5
4. F—Denmark	1	1
5. F—Netherlands	6	6
6. F—Sweden	5	2

Note: M=Masculine country; F=Feminine country
Source: McSweeney et al. (2016)

Questions

1. Explain in more detail the characteristics of masculine feminine societies. See http://scholarworks.gvsu.edu/cgi/viewcontent.cgi?article=1014&context=orpc; Hofstede discussing the dimensions in a video: http://www.youtube.com/watch?v=Pyr-XKQG2CM

2. Examine Table 7.2 and discuss the extent to which the masculinity/femininity dimension is a good predictor of industrial conflict.

Mini Case Study 7.3 Hofstede and marketing

Hofstede's findings on culture have implications for the choice of effective marketing strategies. In countries scoring high on individualism, consumers try to distinguish themselves from others, using brands to help them do so. In highly individualistic cultures, people prefer direct communication and expect the sales process to get quickly to the point whereas in collectivist cultures people like indirect communication and firms have to communicate in a way that builds trust. In the former, advertising involves persuading consumers directly through testimonials, demonstrations and comparisons, in the latter creating trust indirectly through drama, entertainment, and symbolism.

Countries with high power-distance stress respect hierarchy, authority, and paternalism, and each person has a specific social status. Particular goods and services are not simply bought for their functional use, but are also a visible reflection of social status. In such cultures, social status must be made evident and this can be done through the ownership of global luxury brands, haute couture products, and the consumption of certain alcoholic drinks.

Members of cultures scoring high on uncertainty avoidance tend to be risk averse and are therefore reluctant to try new products and brands. They like to rely on expert advice and to purchase products they have bought before and trust.

For countries scoring high on masculinity, where the dominant values are success, money, and material wealth, people strive to have more than others and demonstrate their status through the ownership and frequent purchase of particular goods and services—for example, luxury goods—to which they tend to be loyal.

On the time dimension, cultures with a long-term orientation are likely to be more price conscious. Members of such cultures prefer to use cash and debit cards rather than credit cards with implications for the development of e-commerce. They respond positively to promotional activities offering long-term savings opportunities that build a relationship with the retailer or the brand.

Little research has been done on the dimension of indulgence and consumer behaviour. However, people in highly indulgent cultures like to have fun. Since shopping is seen as a fun activity one might expect consumers to be less restrained in their consumption behaviour and to be interested in trying different goods and services and in purchasing luxury products. Bathaee (2014) reports a correlation between high indulgence cultures, junk food, and obesity.

Sources: Bathaee 2014; Watson et al. 1999; Kyoungmi and Shavitt 2006; Güliz and Belk 1996; Hofstede 1980; Hofstede and Bond 1984; de Mooij 2015; de Mooij and Hofstede (2010, 2011); Möller and Eisend 2010

Questions

1. Discuss how maker of luxury goods, like Chanel or Louis Vuitton, should promote its goods in:
   a. China
   b. Argentina.
   To compare countries' cultural dimensions, see Hofstede's website at http://geert-hofstede.com.
2. De Mooij and Hofstede (2011) found that more life insurance policies are sold in individualist cultures than in collectivist cultures. Come up with some explanations for this finding.

Religion

A core element of the culture in many societies is religion. In such societies, religion is a major influence on the attitudes and beliefs that regulate behaviour. Christianity has the Ten Commandments, Islam has five pillars, and Buddhism has eight precepts. Each religion has a system of rewards for those who are good and punishment for those who are evil. Although there are hundreds of religions in the world, five of them, accounting for around 75 per cent of the world population, predominate. In 2015, Christianity with 2.3 billion followers had the greatest number of adherents accounting for nearly one third of world population. The fastest growing religion was Islam with 1.8 billion. Hinduism had 1.1 billion adherents and Buddhism

500 million, followed a long way behind by Judaism with around 10 million (Pew Research Centre 2017a). Christianity and Islam together account for more than half of the world's population and operate in more regions of the world than all the other religions. Western European countries have seen significant rises in their Muslim populations (Table 7.3). Even in China, where religion declined after the Communist revolution, it is estimated that around 400 million Chinese practise some religion, with over 250 million Buddhists, 35 million Muslims, and up to 100 million Christians, and Christian numbers are rising (CIA World Factbook 2017; Council on Foreign Relations 2018).

Some religions lay down rules about which foods can and cannot be eaten, and how they should be prepared. For instance, Muslims are not supposed to consume pork, alcohol, foods that contain animal fats, tinned vegetables that include animal fat, frozen vegetables with sauce, particular margarines, and bread or bread products containing dried yeast. Animals have to be slaughtered in a particular way. In Judaism, meat from cattle, sheep, goats, and deer can be eaten, but not from pigs, and there are rules forbidding the mixing and consumption of dairy products with meats. As in Islam, animals must be slaughtered in a certain way. Only fish with scales and fins can be eaten. Hindus do not eat meat, but dairy products including milk, butter, and yoghurt are considered to enhance spiritual purity, and most Buddhists are vegetarian. There can be differences in dietary rules among faiths of the same religion. Some Christian faiths, such as Protestantism, do not have dietary rules, while others, such as the Mormons, avoid alcohol and caffeinated drinks like coffee, and most Seventh Day Adventists do not eat meat or dairy products. The various rules and rituals around eating help religions reinforce their identity and distinguish them from other religions. These rules have implications for food manufacturers and retailers wishing to operate in countries with large numbers of practising Muslims, Jews, Hindus, and Buddhists.

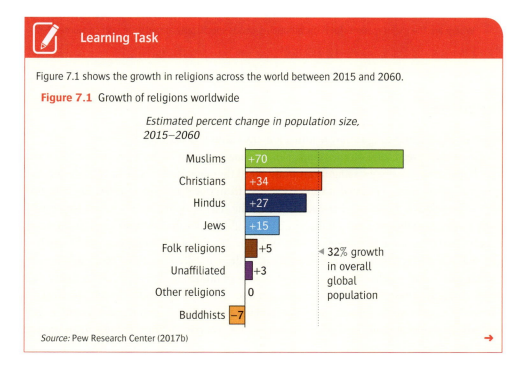

Learning Task

Figure 7.1 shows the growth in religions across the world between 2015 and 2060.

Figure 7.1 Growth of religions worldwide

Estimated percent change in population size, 2015–2060

Muslims +70
Christians +34
Hindus +27
Jews +15
Folk religions +5
Unaffiliated +3
Other religions 0
Buddhists −7

◄ 32% growth in overall global population

Source: Pew Research Center (2017b)

→

Table 7.3 Muslims as a percentage of population in selected Western European countries

	2010	2050
Sweden	4.6	12.4
UK	4.8	11.3
France	7.5	10.9
Germany	5.8	10
Italy	3.7	9.5
Spain	2.1	7.5

Source: Pew Research Center (2015)

1. Which religions are predicted to increase their share of world population between 2010 and 2050?

2. What are the main drivers of change in the religious population? See the Pew Report (2015). at http://www.pewforum.org/2015/04/02/religious-projections-2010-2050.

3. Examine Table 7.3.

   a. Comment on the data in this table.

   b. Discuss the implications for firms in these countries:

      • producing alcoholic drinks; and

      • retailing fast food.

4. Discuss the implications for fast food firms, such as McDonald's or Burger King, of expanding in the Middle East.

5. Where are the major markets for firms producing goods specifically aimed at Jewish consumers?

Language

Another important distinguishing feature for many cultures is language.

There is no agreed total on the number of languages spoken in the world today. Estimates vary, but Ethnologue suggests a figure around 7,000 (Ethnologue n.d.). Estimating the number of speakers is complicated because it can vary widely from one decade to another, due to factors such as population growth and armed conflicts. The Asian population is forecast to grow by more than 700 million to over 5 billion in 2050, while the number of European inhabitants is expected to fall by some 26 million (UN 2017). As a result, the number of speakers of Asian languages like Chinese, Hindi, and Bengali will increase dramatically while those speaking German, French, and Italian will fall. War, civil unrest, abuses of human rights, political instability, and people moving across borders to find work can also cause the figures to change significantly. Climate change could also play an increasing part in causing people to move across borders. It is obvious from the figures given that major changes are occurring in the number and location of speakers of particular languages.

While estimates vary of the most commonly spoken languages, most research identifies Mandarin/Chinese, with around 1 billion speakers, as first in the rankings. Other languages in the top five are Spanish, English, Arabic, and Hindi. The top languages are spoken across many countries. Chinese is spoken in 37 countries, English in 106, and Spanish in 31 mainly Latin American countries (Ethnologue n.d.).

Business will be interested in the speakers of a particular language especially when they congregate together in large enough numbers to constitute a market worth exploiting or present an attractive pool of labour. In the past, language speakers, even where there were lots of them, were not attractive to firms when they were widely dispersed geographically, because of high marketing and distribution costs.

Countries Speaking the Same Language

Even where a single language is the mother tongue in several countries, business may still encounter certain difficulties. English is the mother tongue in the UK, the USA, Australia, and the major part of Canada, but that does not mean that communication is always straightforward. Words used in one country may not be understood in another. The British talk about multi-storey car parks while the Americans refer to a parking garage and the Canadians to a parkade. Similarly, Americans go to a restroom, the British to the toilet, and the Canadians go to a washroom. Australians, like Americans, drive on freeways while the British drive on motorways. And some words have completely different meanings. American cars run on gas, but British vehicles run on petrol. In the UK, a muffler is a scarf that is put round the neck for warmth, but in the USA it is part of the car exhaust system that deadens noise. Similar concerns are likely to arise with Spanish, which is also spoken in many Latin American countries.

Issues also arise in countries where English is an official language, for example, in India, Pakistan, and South Africa, or where it is widely spoken as a second language. Firms would be foolish to assume that they can conduct business effectively in English because levels of proficiency in the language can vary dramatically. Some may have the ability to read the language, but have difficulties speaking or listening to it. Even where people have a good level of proficiency, it does not figure that they can understand it to the required level, especially where the topic of discussion is technical or legal—for instance, around product specifications or patents and copyright.

Facing such difficulties, business will often turn to translators and interpreters. However, according to Crystal (2003), translation always involves some loss of information because it is impossible to get an exact equivalence. The slogan 'Come alive with Pepsi' appeared in a Chinese newspaper as 'Pepsi brings your ancestors back from the grave' (2003: 347). Even big multinational companies can slip up with language. One of the most well-known gaffes was when General Motors sold the Nova model in Spain. Nova, in Spanish, means 'it does not go'. Toyota offered the MR2 in France which, when pronounced, means excrement.

For a long time, British and American firms have come in for much criticism for their linguistic insularity, their assumption that English is the global language of business, and that foreigners will be happy and able to communicate in English. Therefore, for them, building up competence in foreign languages is not a priority. The situation may have improved to a degree, but one US senator said that his country was 'linguistically malnourished' (EricDigests n.d.). International surveys of language skills across Europe tell a consistent tale: the UK is bottom of the league in terms of competence in other languages.

While English is the most widely spoken foreign language throughout Europe, and can be seen as the global language of business, it does seem as if competence in foreign languages is essential for international commerce. Evidence suggests that if companies want to buy anything from anywhere in the world, they can manage with only English; if they want to sell something abroad, they need to learn the language of their customers.

Counterpoint Box 7.2 The problem with English

English is the language for doing global business. Neeley (2012) notes that English is the fastest-spreading language in history and that 1.75 billion people worldwide, that is one in four of the global population, can speak English at a useful level. Therefore companies involved in international trade and investment need employees with the skills in English to deal with foreign customers, suppliers, and employees in the company's foreign subsidiaries. Multinationals such as Airbus, Renault, Samsung, and the Japanese MNC Rakuten have made English the corporate language. Neeley (2012) identifies reasons for the drive to make English the corporate language: increasing competitive pressures as firms strive internationally to meet their corporate goals of profits and growth, the growth of international trade, and the increase in cross-border mergers and acquisitions. From this point of view, in the world of international business, command of the English language is normally seen as an asset.

However, some commentators see it as a recipe for complacency especially on the part of US and UK businesses wishing to do business internationally, complacency bolstered by the reluctance of the British and US citizens to learn foreign languages. Michael Gove, when he was UK education secretary, attacked the 'perverse pride' Britons took in not knowing a foreign tongue. Seldon suggested that 'Great Britain is rapidly becoming little Britain' and should not rely on other countries to learn English to make up for our lack of language skills (*Huffington Post* 5 December 2011). Stein-Smith (2016) reports that US citizens are the least likely to learn a foreign language. Commentators such as Ostler (*The Guardian* 27 February 2017) foresee English, currently at its worldwide peak, coming under challenge from the rise of China.

Kuper (*Financial Times* 14 January 2017) points to the increasing numbers of Russians and Chinese who can speak English. Kuper concludes that US and UK societies are like a glass house because they are transparent to English-speaking foreigners. Foreign firms with their English language capabilities can collect useful business information by tapping into traditional and social media in the USA and UK. This also makes industrial espionage easier for foreign firms through, for example, hacking into the computer systems of British and American rivals. On the other hand, foreign societies and businesses are more opaque to monolingual Britons and Americans, putting US and UK domestic firms at a competitive disadvantage.

Sources: Financial Times 14 January 2017; Neeley (2012); Neeley and Kaplan (2014); *The Guardian* 27 February 2018; Stein-Smith (2016)

Questions

1. Advance reasons why people in the UK and the USA are reluctant to learn foreign languages.
2. Compare and contrast the advantages and disadvantages of a good command of English for UK and US business.
3. Kuper, in his article, discusses Russia, China, and hacking. Why do you think he does this?
4. a. See Neeley (2012) to find the difficulties that non-US and non-UK MNCs encounter when they decide to adopt English as their corporate language.
   b. Now look at Neeley and Kaplan's article at http://hbr.org/2014/09/whats-your-language-strategy. What do the articles recommend that MNCs do to avoid these difficulties?

Time

Different cultures vary in their attitudes to time. In some cultures, the clock directs behaviour; in others, behaviour is determined by the natural course of events in which people find themselves. In cultures where people follow the clock, they are careful to turn up on time for meetings and are likely to be irritated and frustrated if others do not. In other cultures, people behave according to event time, which means that they organize their time around various events, participate in one event until it reaches its natural end, and then begin the next event.

It has been found that the clock directs behaviour in North America, Western Europe, East Asia, Australia, and New Zealand. Event time is often found in South America, South Asia, Mediterranean countries, and in developing economies with big agricultural sectors—in which people operate according to the seasons rather than the clock, and clock time is not yet fully part of people's work habits. North Americans will schedule a meeting for 9 a.m., turn up on time and apologize if they are a few minutes late. In countries like Saudi Arabia, people may turn up 20 minutes late and feel no need to apologize. It may be that, in cultures where status is important, this is demonstrated by the high-status participants turning up late. In event time countries, a higher proportion of time at work is likely to be devoted to social activities such as chatting and having cups of tea or coffee. People from clock time cultures will often get irritated by this behaviour, seeing it as time wasting or an inefficient use of resources. However, these activities could be useful for a business because they may help to build up supportive groups so that when someone comes under pressure, colleagues will be happy to help out on a voluntary basis. In addition, it may be that important business relationships are made during what appears to be aimless social activity.

The Social Environment

In this section, we move on to examine various elements of the social environment. We start off by examining social divisions and then go on to compare three social models that show how the state looks after the welfare of its citizens. Subsequently, we consider demography, and then health and education.

Social Models

In different countries, the state takes on varying degrees of responsibility for the welfare of its citizens. Today, in most developed economies the state spends more on welfare than all other programmes. This spending takes the forms of benefits to the elderly, the disabled, the sick, the unemployed, and the young. It also usually involves spending on health care and education. Welfare policies may vary from country to country in terms of their aims, the amount of money spent on them, the priority given to different programmes, and the identity of the beneficiaries. In some countries, the state intervenes only to provide a limited level of support to those who are regarded as deserving of help. This tends to be the dominant system in Anglo-Saxon countries. In others, such as in Scandinavia, benefits are universal, relatively generous, and open to the entire population. In poor countries, the provision of welfare is often left to the family. Influences on the various approaches are the levels of economic wealth, different attitudes toward poverty, and the proper role of the state.

In the West, there are three social models in operation: the liberal, the corporatist, and the social democratic. Trying to classify different welfare states neatly into separate pigeon-holes is not straightforward because they are continually adjusting to factors like globalization, to demographic change such as the **ageing population**, or to the feminization of the labour force. Sometimes, a country will contain elements of several models. For example, the UK has aspects of both the liberal and the social democratic models. On one hand, as in the USA, unemployment benefits are not tied to incomes and require those out of work actively to seek employment or training, or perform community service. On the other hand, the provision of universally provided social services in the UK, such as the National Health Service, and in-work benefits for those who take low-paid jobs, a policy underpinned by a minimum wage, are more akin to the social democratic model prevalent in countries such as Denmark and the Netherlands.

The Liberal Social Model

The **liberal social model**, found in the USA, Canada, Australia, and also, to an extent, the UK, is based on a clear distinction between the deserving and undeserving poor, with limits on the level of benefit payments. In liberal welfare states such as the USA and the UK, there is a sharp cut-off in unemployment benefits to discourage dependency and to force people back to work.

There is a commitment to keep taxes low and to encourage people to stay in work. While everyone is treated equally, there is a low level of welfare provision as expressed in the level of social expenditure (see Figure 7.2). There is a belief that people can better themselves through their own efforts, and that they may be poor because they do not try hard enough. In the USA, and to a lesser extent in the UK, there is scepticism about the state's effectiveness in tackling poverty. The welfare system, by giving benefits to single parents, is also believed to discourage marriage and to encourage single motherhood.

Even in countries operating the liberal model, there can be major differences in the level and nature of welfare provision. For example, in the UK and Canada, publicly funded health care is provided free to all at the point of delivery. All citizens qualify for health coverage, regardless of medical history, personal income, or standard of living. By contrast, the US system is a combination of private insurance paid for by workers through their employer, publicly provided insurance for the elderly (Medicare), the military, veterans, the poor, and disabled (Medicaid). The implementation of Medicaid varies greatly state by state. In the run-up to the 2010 Obama health care reforms, around 43 million people in the USA did not have private health insurance, which made it the only developed country not providing health care for all of its citizens. Obama's Affordable Health Care Act (2010) required all Americans to have health insurance, offered subsidies to make coverage more affordable, and aimed to reduce the cost of insurance by bringing younger, healthier people into the medical coverage system. Businesses with more than 50 full-time employees were required to provide health insurance. However, in 2016, 9 per cent of the US population remained uninsured. President Trump came into power in 2016 and tried unsuccessfully to repeal the Act.

After 2008, large government budget deficits, brought about by the global financial crisis, led to countries such as the UK back on welfare benefits. See the **online resources** for more details.

We now turn to the corporatist and social democratic models operating in many European countries. They share certain distinctive characteristics. There is a commitment to social justice. Neither system abandons those who fail. They aspire to high levels of employment, universal access to health care and education, adequate social insurance for sickness, disability, unemployment, and old age, and have a well-developed system of workers' rights.

The Corporatist Model

The **corporatist social model** is typical of continental European countries such as Germany, France, Austria, and Italy. Japan and other EU countries, for example, in Southern Europe, also display elements of the corporatist model, but spending is not as generous as in France or Germany (see Figure 7.2). In the past, the Church played an influential role in the model with its commitment to the preservation of the traditional family. Thus, wives who were not working through their husbands while family benefits were paid to those having children. The model emphasizes the importance of work, and benefits are based on individual contributions. Benefits are generous relative to those provided in countries operating under the liberal model. In contrast to the liberal model, poverty is viewed as either inevitable or as a result of social injustice. This is why, in Germany and the Netherlands, political parties of both the right and the left support an extensive welfare state.

In corporatist systems, there is a belief in the value of partnership and dialogue between the government and the various interest groups in society (sometimes called the social partners) such as trade unions and employers' associations. This is seen as a way of avoiding and reconciling conflicts over economic and social policy. It emphasizes solidarity between the various social groups and gives an important role to voluntary organizations such as churches and charities. In Germany, for example, church bodies are important providers of welfare services to groups such as migrants and young people.

The Social Democratic Model

The **social democratic model**, found in Scandinavian countries, has several defining characteristics. Sweden, where social expenditure in 2016 made up 27 per cent of the economy, spends considerably more than the USA at 19 per cent. Britain falls between the low-spending USA and the high-spending continental European countries (Figure 7.2).

Figure 7.2 Social expenditure, percentage of GDP 1960, 1990, and 2016

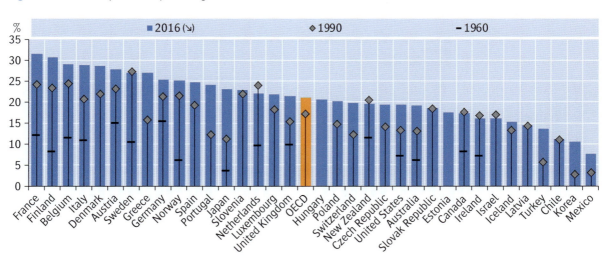

Source: Data from OECD (2016)

There are much lower levels of child poverty in Scandinavia compared to the UK and the USA. According to the OECD (2016), around 7 per cent of Swedish children live in poverty while almost one in five are in that position in the USA.

Support is provided through generous welfare benefits for all those who are poor, old, young, disabled, and unemployed, and there is universal access to education and health care. There is a heavy commitment to helping families and to mothers wishing to work. This is financed by high levels of taxation. Also, unlike the liberal model, governments usually commit themselves to generating and maintaining high levels of employment and low levels of unemployment. There is an emphasis on taxation and spending policies that redistribute income from the rich to the poor and an active approach is taken to finding jobs for the citizens. As in the corporatist model, dialogue between the social partners is valued.

Latin America

Social expenditure has been rising gradually in Latin America. Social security systems in Latin America tend to be funded by payroll taxes, so the amount of funding available is determined by the number of people officially in work; this in a region with the lowest rates of salaried work and the lowest minimum wages in the world. Government-supported health care programmes depend on social security funding and a patchwork of health insurance packages put together by various, and sometimes unregulated, private providers. As a result, citizens requiring health care often have to pay, which, given the high levels of poverty, they can rarely afford. Efforts have been made to extend health insurance to protect low- to middle-income households from financial disaster. Governments have also been improving rudimentary employment services to connect workers to jobs, training, and social services. They are of particular importance in Latin America where the public listing of jobs is not widespread, so large numbers of disadvantaged workers are left to seek work inefficiently through informal contacts. Pension systems are limited and benefits are low which contributes to poverty in old age. Figure 7.3 shows that countries like Cuba and Brazil are spending as much if not more their income on social policies than rich counterparts such as the USA, Canada, and Australia.

Figure 7.3 Social expenditure by policy area as percentage of GDP 2015

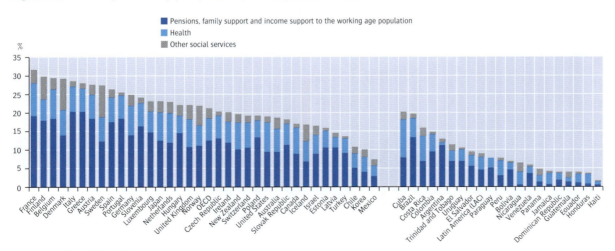

Source: Data from OECD (2017a)

Counterpoint Box 7.3 The clash of social models

Critics have launched bitter attacks on the social democratic and corporatist social models of Western Europe and blame them for the inferior economic performance of Europe compared with the USA—for example, as regards economic growth.

They attribute high and persistent unemployment in France and Germany, declining productivity growth, growing fiscal strains, and the mediocre and inflexible services provided by the state to high tax and spend policies and over-zealous interference with market forces—for example, the setting of a minimum wage. The essence of the argument is that high taxes and benefits discourage people from seeking employment and working hard and discourage businesses from taking risks. The result is mediocrity: people who do well are penalized by high taxes while nobody is allowed to fail. The answer is to move toward a liberal regime where market forces are allowed much freer rein. Critics accept that the free market can result in undesirable outcomes, but argue that it leads to a more creative, flexible, and productive economy. In their view, people should take responsibility for their lives and not be protected by the state from the consequences of their own decisions. Thus, if individuals decide not to buy health insurance then they, not the state, must bear the consequences when they become ill.

Defenders of the social democratic model challenge claims of superior US performance. They argue that growth of GDP per head has grown at roughly the same rate in the USA and the majority of European countries, and that a European country like Sweden is richer than the USA as measured by per capita income, even though its economy is more highly regulated and has a larger welfare state. They also claim that French and German productivity levels are higher than in the USA and that inequality, poverty, and crime rates are much lower. They point to the 28 million Americans not covered by private health insurance despite President Obama's Affordable Care Act.

Sources: Green (1999); Navarro and Schmitt (2005); Pierson et al. (2014); National Center for Health Statistics (n.d.).

Questions

Graham (*The Guardian* 20 June 2017) argues that, in the USA, the costs of being poor are high. She says that there is a lack of safety nets and vocational training for the socially disadvantaged and those experiencing bad luck.

1. Respond to Graham from the point of view of:
   a. a supporter of the US social model; and
   b. a supporter of the European social democratic model.

Asia

Asian countries spend much less as a proportion of their **national income** and government expenditure on social programmes (see Figure 7.4).

Some authors have noted that several East Asian societies do not fit in with any of the models outlined above. In Japan and the four 'tiger' economies of Hong Kong, Singapore, South Korea, and Taiwan, priority has been given to economic growth, and welfare policies have been subordinated to that. They do engage in social policy, but only after attending to their main objective of growth, and social policies are often geared to the achievement of economic objectives. While welfare arrangements do vary in each of these countries, there are some common elements. In these societies, there is hostility towards the concept of the welfare state, public expenditure on social welfare is low, social rights and benefits tend to be limited, and the family is expected to play a central role in social support.

The Japanese Constitution accords its citizens a minimum standard of healthy civilized life. They have a right to basic health care, and pensions are almost universal. However, benefits are limited and the family is expected to play a role. Compared with other OECD

Figure 7.4 Social protection spending as a percentage of total government expenditure, 2015

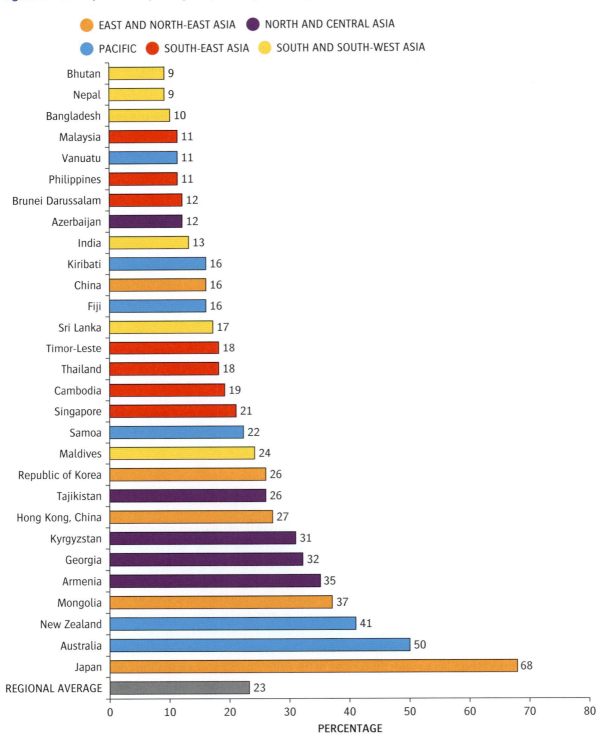

Source: UN ESCAP (2015) © United Nations. Reprinted with the permission of the United Nations.

members, Japan ranks just above average in the level of social assistance it provides (see Figure 7.3) and high relative to other Asian countries. The level of income inequality and child poverty in Japan is high compared with other rich countries (UNICEF 2016). In Hong Kong, around half the population live in rented housing provided by the authorities, and rights to health care and education are universal but limited. The state does not provide pensions, unemployment benefit, or child benefit. In Taiwan, the bulk of welfare spending predominantly goes to groups in the armed forces, state bureaucrats, and teachers, while the less fortunate, the poor, the handicapped, the old, and the young receive almost nothing. A lot of resources have been put into the education system in pursuit of the country's economic objectives. The approach, like the liberal model, is based on the premise that social problems are the result of individual inadequacy like lack of motivation to work or poor skills levels. These countries continue to focus on improving productivity, competitiveness and growth (Chan 2012).

Welfare policy in China prioritizes three aspects: high growth at the expense of other public goods such as health care, education, and environmental protection; the favouring of those in occupations and sectors that are better off than average, such as civil servants and high-ranking military veterans; and a large proportion of expenditures on pensions compared to health care and unemployment. UNESCAP (2015) reported that China has been rapidly expanding health provision in efforts to provide health care for all although it still only accounted for 1.8 per cent of GDP in 2016.

In India, social programmes include the provision of education, housing schemes, income and employment-oriented programmes, and schemes for providing jobs in government and places in higher educational institutions for lower castes. Social protection takes the form of primary health care through government health care centres, nutrition schemes, and old age pensions for the destitute, widows, physically disabled, and informal sector workers. Kapur and Nagia (2015) say that spending on social protection has increased rapidly while basic public services like primary education, health, water, and sanitation have been neglected. The approach is based on dealing with problems as they arise rather than prevention. According to the International Labour Organization (ILO 2014), only 27 per cent of the world's population have access to a comprehensive system of social protection, whereas 73 per cent are partially covered or not at all. Nearly 40 per cent of the world's population has no legal access to health care.

Learning Task

Examine Table 7.4, which shows some health indicators.

1. Rank each country in the table for each health indicator. Compare and contrast the indicators of health between the USA, Sweden, China, and Nigeria.

2. Use your knowledge of the different social models to come up with explanations for your findings.

3. What other explanations might be advanced?   ➔

→ **Table 7.4** Health indicators 2015

	Healthy life expectancy at birth (years)*	Infant mortality per 1,000 live births	Maternal mortality per 100,000 live births
Australia	71.9	2.2	9
Brazil	65.5	8.9	44
China	68.5	5.5	27
Nigeria	47.7	34.3	814
Saudi Arabia	64.5	7.9	12
Sweden	72	1.6	4
UK	71.4	2.4	9
US	69.1	3.6	14

*Healthy life expectancy is the average number of years of full health that a newborn baby could expect to live. Life expectancy is influenced by both positive and negative biological and social factors. Negative biological factors tend to show up quite early after birth so that death rates tend to be higher during the first year of life. Social factors are the main determinants of life expectancy. Positive elements include shelter, health care, educational provision, and working conditions. Malnutrition, poverty, armed conflict, stress, and depression are examples of negative social aspects.

Source: WHO (2016)

Demography

Demography is the study of population. It looks, among other things, at the size of the population, its rate of growth, the breakdown by age, gender, and ethnic group, and the geographical distribution of the population.

Table 7.5 World population 1950, 1975, 2017, 2030

Area	Population (million)			
	1950	1975	2017	2030
World	2,535	4,076	7,550	8,551
Africa	224	416	1,256	1,704
Asia	1,411	2,394	4,504	4,974
Europe	548	676	742	739
Latin America and the Caribbean	168	325	646	718
Northern America	172	243	361	395
Oceania	13	21	41	48

Sources: UN (2015, 2017)

Table 7.6 The ten most populous countries (millions)

1. China	1,410	6. Pakistan	197
2. India	1,339	7. Nigeria	191
3. United States	324	8. Bangladesh	165
4. Indonesia	264	9. Russia	144
5. Brazil	209	10. Mexico	129

Source: UN (2017)

The number of people and their geographical location are of interest to business. Large populations may indicate that markets are there to be exploited. However, to be attractive to business, incomes in such populous areas need to be high enough for consumers to be able to afford to buy goods and services.

The most highly populated countries tend to be found in the less developed regions of the world (Table 7.5). China and India are the most populous, each with over 1 billion people. Together, they account for more than one-fifth of the world population. The USA and Japan are the only rich countries to make the top 10 in terms of population (see Table 7.6).

Changes in Population Size

Population size is affected by the death rate, the birth rate, and net migration.

With increasing prosperity and advances in sanitation, diet, and medical knowledge, death rates have been declining, not only in the richer countries of the developed world, but also in Asia, Latin America, and the Caribbean. Birth rates at a world level have fallen to 2.47 children per woman—less than half the level they were in the 1950s. Women in the least developed countries have more than three times the number of children as their counterparts in the rich world (UN 2017). Birth rates tend to fall as countries become richer. In poor countries, where incomes are low and there is minimal or no welfare provision, people have large families to support them in their old age. Increasing incomes in these countries reduces the need for large families. The changing role of women also has a big influence on the number of children they have. As the level of education of women increases, along with their greater participation in the workforce, so the birth rate declines. The attitudes of women, especially in the developed world, are moving away from their traditional role as bearers and nurturers of children. Even in supposedly Catholic countries such as Argentina, Poland, Italy, and Spain, where the Church condemns contraception, there have been significant declines in the birth rate.

As regards international migration, it has been increasing since the 1970s, with the vast majority going to richer countries, particularly the USA, more prosperous regions in Europe and Oceania. The main senders are Africa, Asia and Latin America and the Caribbean. This movement has led to a significant growth in the labour force of the developed economies. In Europe, Northern America, and Oceania, net migration increased population growth from 1950, while natural increase became less important. The UN sees migration as an important source of population growth in many high-income countries (UN 2015).

Learning Task

In 2015 and 2016, there was a massive flow of refugees with an estimated total of 1.2 million people arriving in Germany to ask for asylum. They started to enter the labour market. An OECD report (2017) said that integration into the labour market takes some time.

1. What caused the increase in the flow of asylum seekers?

2. Look at Figure 7.5. Which countries have experienced the highest and lowest rates of asylum seekers?

3. Why are countries like Germany a popular destination for asylum seekers?

4. What problems do asylum seekers encounter in the German labour market? See OECD Report (2017b).

Figure 7.5 Inflows of asylum seekers into European countries, per 1,000 population 2015/16

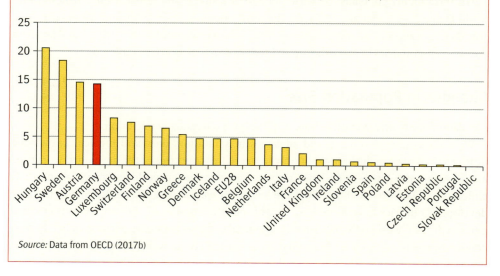

Source: Data from OECD (2017b)

The Ageing Population

Increased life expectancy and falling birth rates mean that the average age of the population in many countries will rise, and this has become a major demographic concern. In 2017 worldwide there were more than 900 million aged 60 or older making up 13 per cent of the global population. By 2050 this is forecast to double to around 2 billion, or more than one-fifth. This phenomenon will particularly affect high income countries in Europe. In some countries, these trends will lead to stagnation and even decline in the population. Europe is the first region in the world to experience demographic ageing. By 2050, in Germany, it is expected that the population share of those older than 60 will increase from less than 30 per cent to almost 40 per cent. Populations in Africa, the Middle East, and Asia, excepting Japan, will start to age later because their populations are much younger.

The OECD (2005) believes that the ageing populations could lead to shortages of labour, wage inflation, increased pressures on taxation and public expenditures, and a fall in the rate of economic growth. Unless something is done to alleviate the problem, taxes will have to rise to meet the increasing cost of pensions and health care, or public expenditure and benefits will have to be cut. Global growth could fall to less than 2 per cent per year, which is almost one-third less than for the period 1970–2000. Possible responses could involve encouraging older people to work longer, getting more women to enter the labour force, and attracting more young immigrants. This could be accompanied by a rise in the age of retirement, as has occurred in the public services in the UK. However, employers would need to change their negative attitudes to the employment of older workers. There would need to be more opportunities for flexible working and retraining for older people to help them develop new skills.

Learning Task

Examine the map in Figure 7.6.

1. Which continents and countries have the highest/lowest proportion of their population over the age of 60?

2. Discuss the likely implications of an ageing population on demand for the following sectors:

   a. pharmaceuticals;

   b. colleges training school teachers; and

   c. travel companies specializing in cruises.

3. In countries with young populations, what are the likely demand prospects for:

   a. retailers specializing in clothing and toys for babies and young children;

   b. amusement parks; and

   c. providers of nursing homes for the old?

Figure 7.6 Percentage of population aged 60 or older in 2050

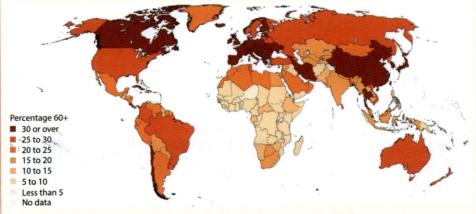

Percentage 60+
- 30 or over
- 25 to 30
- 20 to 25
- 15 to 20
- 10 to 15
- 5 to 10
- Less than 5
- No data

Source: UN (2015). © United Nations. Reprinted with the permission of the United Nations.

Youth Employment and Unemployment—The Lost Generation

The International Labour Organization (ILO 2016) estimated that 71 million young people were unemployed across the globe, a rate of just over 13 per cent (Figure 7.7). High youth unemployment rates were suffered by countries like Egypt (42 per cent) and Greece (50 per cent), while Japan had a rate of just 6 per cent (Assidmi and Wolgamuth 2017; Eurostat 2017).

Although unemployment rates are sometimes higher in richer countries, lower rates in poorer regions do not necessarily indicate a healthier labour market for those young people who have to work in low-quality, poorly paid jobs, often in the informal economy, in order to survive. Young women are often in a worse position than men, experiencing higher unemployment and lower employment rates. Even young people in richer economies who find work can face a proliferation of precarious jobs that are low paid, part time, and temporary. Young people who are unemployed for a long time suffer long-term debilitating effects, called scarring (ILO 2016; see Mini Case Study 7.4 Youth unemployment—A Social Time Bomb).

Figure 7.7 World and regional youth unemployment rates (15–24 years)

Region	Unemployment rate, 2007–17 (percentages)				Unemployed youth, 2015–17 (millions)		
	2007–14	2015	2016	2017	2015	2016	2017
World		12.9	13.1	13.1	70.5	71.0	71.0
Africa							
Northern Africa		29.4	29.3	29.2	3.7	3.7	3.7
Sub-Saharan Africa		10.9	10.9	10.8	11.1	11.3	11.6
Americas							
Latin America and the Caribbean		15.7	16.8	17.1	8.5	9.2	9.3
Northern America		11.8	11.5	11.7	3.0	2.9	2.9
Arab States		30.6	30.6	29.7	2.6	2.7	2.6
Asia							
Eastern Asia		10.6	10.7	10.9	11.9	11.4	11.0
South-Eastern Asia and the Pacific		12.4	13.0	13.6	7.4	7.7	8.0
Southern Asia		10.9	10.9	10.9	13.7	13.8	13.9
Europe and Central Asia							
Central and Western Asia		16.6	17.1	17.5	2.1	2.1	2.2
Eastern Europe		17.1	16.6	16.2	2.0	1.8	1.7
Northern, Southern and Western Europe		20.6	19.7	18.9	4.5	4.3	4.1

Source: ILO (2016)

Mini Case Study 7.4 Youth unemployment—a social time bomb

Unemployment for young people is a global epidemic that has many negative effects. Those who experience unemployment early in their life are more likely to be unemployed again in later years. Moreover, they are likely to earn less over their working life than those finding jobs more easily. The difference in earnings can amount to as much as 20 per cent, and this ➜

→ deficit can last for as long as 20 years. It has also been found that unemployment can have long-term effects on mental and physical health and levels of job satisfaction. Blanchflower (2009) says that unemployment tends to be associated with malnutrition, illness, mental stress, depression, increases in the suicide rate, poor physical health in later life, and reductions in life expectancy. Marmot, a professor of public health, described persistent high youth unemployment as 'a public health time bomb waiting to explode' (The Lancet 9 November 2013).

Young, long-term unemployed may find it difficult to get work because some employers do not see them as productive. Morsy (2012) argues that unemployment can lead to social exclusion, poverty, violence, crime, and social unrest. The young unemployed may also be tempted to take illegal jobs in the black economy. The ILO (2016) reports that on a regional basis youth unemployment at around 29 per cent is highest in Arab states and the countries of North Africa. Standing (2014) attributes the increase in precarious jobs in both young and older people to the spread of neo-liberal policies pursued across the world and the adoption of policies of austerity. He sounds a warning that the jobs situation makes the young ready to listen to dangerous extremist political views. Reports by the National Institute of Economic and Social Research show that, in the UK, underemployment, that is workers wanting to work more hours than employers will give, is particularly concentrated among the young and that pay for young people after 2008 had fallen (Bell and Blanchflower 2013). The World Economic Forum (2017) reported that young people in the USA, the UK, and Japan were the first in modern history to be worse off than their parents.

Countries suffering high youth unemployment are likely to experience increased rates of emigration, particularly of young educated people, which some characterize as a brain drain.

Sources: Bell and Blanchflower (2013); Blanchflower (2009); Hoffman and Jamal (2012); ILO (2016); Morsy (2012); Standing (2014)

Questions

In 2017, almost one-fifth of young people in the EU were unemployed. The figures were 46 per cent in Greece, 42 per cent in Spain, and 38 per cent in Italy (Eurostat 2017).

1. Unemployment, particularly of young people, is very high in Greece and Spain. Find out whether there is any evidence of a brain drain from Greece and Spain.

   See: the paper by Ramos and Royuela (2016); Bloomberg 28 September 2015; *The Guardian* 3 July 2016; *Greek Reporter* 8 March 2017; video of Harvard Spain Annual Conference at https://www.youtube.com/watch?v=AtzFNOS3rWg.

2. Discuss whether large outflows of highly educated young people from Greece and Spain would be good for their economies. Now consider the economic impact of inflows of young people from Greece and Spain to Germany and the UK.

● CHAPTER SUMMARY

We can see from our analysis that the international social and cultural environment offers major opportunities, but also poses many threats and challenges to business.

One conclusion to be drawn is that business ignores cultural differences at its peril. Hofstede has pointed out that, for companies, culture more often leads to conflict than synergy and that cultural differences can be a nuisance at best and are frequently a disaster. Firms need, as a matter of course, to take into account the varying national attitudes to such factors as hierarchy and power distance when considering entry to foreign markets through exports, joint ventures, takeover, or when setting up completely new production facilities. To be successful abroad, firms need to be aware of the impact of culture on the conduct of business meetings, how negotiations are carried out, and on attitudes to contracts. Different national cultures may require business to respond to the local culture by changing their approach to the management of personnel, to the products they produce, and to the methods used to market their products. Failure to do so can lead to higher costs, lower levels of productivity, and poor sales and profits.

Our examination of the social environment demonstrated how social models vary from one country to another, from the less generous liberal approach in the USA to the more generous Swedish social democratic model. The debate continues to rage between the supporters of these models as to which model provides the best environment for business and which promotes economic performance and social cohesion. We have seen how changes in the social environment can be of importance for business. Demographic changes, for example, population growth in Asia and Africa, an ageing population in Europe, youth unemployment and underemployment, and different national levels of health and education, all have implications for the quantity and quality of the labour supply as well as for the economic growth rate and the pattern of demand for goods and services.

● REVIEW QUESTIONS

1. The March 2013 issue of the *Atlantic* magazine reported that companies like General Motors and Dell employ anthropologists—social scientists who research cultural issues. Microsoft is said to be the second-largest employer of anthropologists in the world, behind the US government.

Table 7.7 Public social expenditure (as a percentage of GDP)

	1990	2000	2005	2010	2016
Australia	13.2	17.3	16.5	17.9	19.1
Canada	18.1	16.5	16.9	18.7	17.2*
Chile	9.9	12.8	10.1	10.8	11.2*
Czech Republic	15.3	19.1	18.7	20.8	19.4
Denmark	25.1	26.4	27.7	30.6	28.7
Finland	24.1	24.2	26.2	29.6	30.8
France	25.1	28.6	30.1	32.4	31.5
Germany	21.7	26.6	27.3	27.1	25.3
Greece	16.6	19.3	21.1	23.3	27
Hungary	–	20.0	22.5	22.9	20.6
Ireland	17.3	13.4	16.0	23.7	16.1
Italy	19.9	23.1	24.9	27.7	28.9
Japan	11.1	16.3	18.6	22.3	–
Korea	2.8	4.8	6.5	9.2	10.4
Mexico	3.3	5.3	6.9	8.1	–
Poland	14.9	20.5	21.0	21.8	20.2
Portugal	12.5	18.9	23.0	25.4	24.1
Spain	19.9	20.2	21.1	23.6	24.6
Sweden	30.2	28.4	29.1	28.3	27.1
Turkey	5.7	–	9.9	12.8	–
United Kingdom	16.7	18.6	20.5	23.8	21.5
United States	13.6	14.5	16.0	19.8	19.3
OECD average	17.6	18.9	19.7	22.1	21

Notes: – = data not available.
*2015
Source: OECD StatExtracts http://stats.oecd.org

a. What is culture?

b. Why are multinationals like Microsoft so interested in culture?

2. Identify, and illustrate with evidence, the current major drivers of changes in population. Discuss the challenges of an ageing population for international business.

3. Table 7.7 shows social spending as a percentage of GDP from 1990 to 2016.

a. What are the main components of social spending?

b. What is the trend in social spending over the period from 1990 to 2016? To answer this, look first at the OECD average. Do any countries buck the trend?

c. Discuss some implications of the trend for suppliers to schools and hospitals.

d. Group the countries into continents, North America, South America, Europe, Asia, and Australia, and compare spending in each. Comment on your findings.

e. How would you explain Sweden's high levels of expenditures compared to those of the USA?

● ASSIGNMENT TASKS

1. You are employed as researcher by a non-governmental organization whose aim is to promote equality between men and women. The United Nations body, UN Women, is preparing an international conference on gender equality. Your organization wishes to highlight the unequal treatment of women in Saudi Arabia.

   It asks you to produce a report comparing and contrasting the economic position of women in Saudi Arabia with Swedish women.

   A useful starting point in your research would be the opening case in this chapter.

2. You are employed in the communications department of a multinational producer of alcoholic drinks. Your boss has come across an article in the *Financial Times* referring to Hofstede's work on national cultures. The company is considering entering the market in Nigeria. He asks you to write a report explaining how Hofstede's research could help the firm succeed in Nigeria.

3. You are the PA to a top executive in a large pharmaceutical company under pressure from governments and pressure groups, like Oxfam, to come up with new antibiotics to deal with the proliferation of drug resistant infections in populous countries like India, China and Nigeria. Your boss has been asked to write an article for a quality newspaper on the topic.

   You must prepare a report that:

   a. explains the slowdown in antibiotic development over the previous 50 or so years;

   b. describes the growth of drug resistant infections in lower- and middle-income countries; and

   c. outlines what the pharmaceutical industry is doing to combat the increase in such infections.

   Start off your research by re-reading the following case study.
   Illustrate the report with charts and tables where appropriate.

Case Study Superbugs

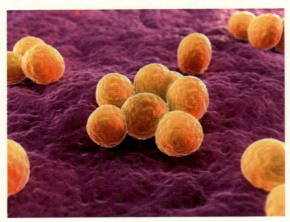

© Science Photo Library/Alamy Stock Photo

There has been growing global concern about antimicrobial resistance (AMR). Superbugs (bacteria, viruses, and parasites) that cause a proliferation of infections that have become increasingly resistant to antibiotics fundamental in the treatment of many human infections like pneumonia and tuberculosis. Superbugs are seen by governments, medical professionals, food scientists, and the pharmaceutical industry as a major global health threat. They cause failures in medical treatments which result in diseases lasting longer and being more severe, increasing lengths of stays in hospital and in the number of deaths, and an adverse effect on productivity. The O'Neil Report (2014) contained estimates showing that a continuing rise in resistance would result in an annual toll of 10 million deaths, and a fall in GDP of 2–3.5 per cent by 2050 below what it would have been, at a global cost of up to $100 trillion.

The main cause of rising AMR is the rapid increase in consumption of antibiotics, particularly in countries like Brazil, India, Russia, China, and South Africa. In some countries, antibiotics are over-prescribed; in others, the same drugs are sold over the counter with no medical prescription required. O'Neil says that the unnecessary use of antibiotics in agriculture also plays a part. His report observes that 70 per cent of drugs medically important for humans are sold for use on animals. Antibiotics are used to prevent or treat diseases and to promote growth in farm animals. Cecchini et al. (2015) report that, in the

USA, around 80 per cent of the antibiotics consumed are taken by livestock and that consumption is forecast to increase significantly. Overuse on farms facilitates the creation of superbugs that can be passed to humans through the food-chain or through contact with animal waste in the soil or water supply.

Globalization facilitates the global spread of AMR (see Figure 7.8). The increasing and rapid cross-border movements of people and food products mean that superbugs can spread rapidly from one country to another. A bug from one region encountering another can share genetic material and mutate into a superbug.

The concern is so serious that, in 2016, all 193 members of the United Nations agreed to tackle the proliferation of drug-resistant infections. The UN General Secretary said:

> If we fail to address this problem quickly and comprehensively, antimicrobial resistance will make providing high-quality universal healthcare coverage more difficult if not impossible . . . It will undermine sustainable food production. And it will put the sustainable development goals in jeopardy.

Why does the pharma industry not create super drugs to kill off the superbugs? The rate of new drug development has slowed since what some have called the 'golden age' of the second half of the 20th century. Only two new classes of antibiotics have been launched in the last 50 years. The industry has identified scientific as well as commercial barriers to the development of new drugs (IFPMA 2016).

The WEF argues that current business models operated by the pharma industry are not conducive to the development of new drug because R&D costs are high and the investment is difficult to recoup because the drugs cannot be sold at high prices, or in large volumes because they have to be used sparingly to avoid bugs becoming resistant to them. The US pharma giant Merck (2015) says bringing a new drug to market takes ten years and costs $3 billion, and only one in five receives regulatory approval. O'Neill (2014) notes that annual sales of antibiotics is about $40 billion, but patented antibiotics only make up $4.7 billion of that total—a possible reason for the lack of corporate investment in research and development. Nonetheless, the pharma industry has committed to the fight against AMR and to ask for more government funding in the battle.   →

→ **Figure 7.8** Annual deaths attributable to AMR by 2050

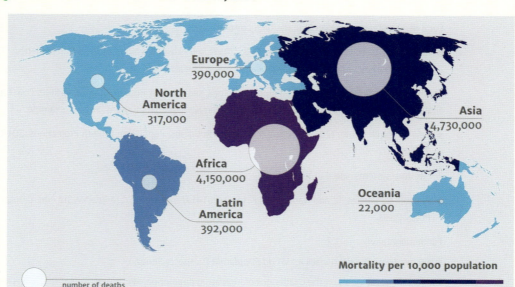

Source: O'Neill (2014)

O'Neill (2016) recommends:

- using existing antibiotics prudently;
- more effective control of infections through education on hygiene;
- improving sanitation systems;
- investment in basic health services in low- and middle-income countries;
- reducing unnecessary use in agriculture;
- increased cross-border coordination via the G20 and the UN;
- increased public and private investment in R&D; and
- $1 billion reward fund for development of new effective drugs.

He puts the cost of taking global action at $40 billion over ten years. Within that total, about $16 billion would go on rewards to promote research and development of new antibiotics and tuberculosis treatments. The costs are based on the idea that 15 new antibiotics decade will emerge. Other proposals were to impose a charge on pharmaceutical companies that do not invest in research in AMR and to put a tax on antibiotics.

Sources: O'Neill (2014, 2016); MarketWatch 19 May 2016; Landers et al. (2012); Merck (2015); IFPMA (2016); Cecchini et al. (2015).

Questions

1. Why is AMR important to societies?
2. Which areas of the world will suffer most deaths due from AMR? Why should that be the case?
3. Explore the implications for the worst hit areas were no effective steps be taken to deal with AMR in terms of:
   a. health care costs; and
   b. tourism in those areas most affected by AMR.
4. Discuss the implications of the increase in drug resistant infections for the pharma industry as regards:
   a. its existing range of antibiotic products; and
   b. its R&D strategy.
5. Why is the pharma industry not developing new antibiotics to deal with drug-resistant infections?
6. What would the effects be on farmers if governments legislated against overuse of antibiotics or imposed substantial taxes on these drugs?

● FURTHER READING

For a review of recent research on national cultures, see:

- Kirkman, B. L., Lowe, K.B., and Gibson, C. B. (2017) 'A Retrospective on Culture's Consequences: The 35-year Journey'. *Journal of International Business Studies* 48(1).

For regularly updated information on global religions, see the Pew Research Center with its Pew-Templeton Global Religious Futures Project which monitors changes in global religions. See, for example:

- Pew Research Center (2015) The Future of World Religions: Population Growth Projections, 2010–2050, 2 April.

For welfare systems, see:

- Pierson, C., Castles, F., and Naumann, I.K. (eds) (2014) *The Welfare State Reader*, 3rd edn. Cambridge: Polity Press.

For demography:

Every two years the UN revises its *World Population Prospects Series.*

For very different views on the challenges of increasing population, see:

- Dorling, D. (2013) *Population 10 Billion.* London: Constable & Robinson.

- Emmott, S. (2013) *10 Billion.* London: Penguin Books.

For health, the World Health Organization publishes statistics and a review of health issues every year:

- World Health Organization *World Health Report,* annual.

● REFERENCES

Al-Asfour, A., Tlaiss, H., Khan, S., Rajasekar, J. (2016) 'Saudi Women's Work Challenges and Barriers to Career Advancement', *Career Development International* 22(2).

Assidmi, L.M. and Wolgamuth, E. (2017) 'Uncovering the Dynamics of the Saudi Youth Unemployment Crisis'. *Systemic Practice and Action Research* April Vol 30 Issue 2.

Bates, D. and Plog, F. (1990) *Cultural Anthropology.* Maidenhead: McGraw-Hill.

Bathaee, A. (2014) *Consumer Culture and Purchase Behaviors: Analyses of Anticipated Regret, Variety-seeking and Quality-consciousness in Germany and Iran.* 6 May.

Bell, D. and Blanchflower, D. (2013) 'Underemployment in the UK Revisited'. *National Institute Economic Review* No. 224 (May).

Blanchflower, D. (2009) 'What Should be Done about Rising Unemployment in the UK?'. Lecture presented at The University of Stirling, 25 February 2009. Available at http://www.bankofengland.co.uk.

Bond, M.H. (2002) 'Reclaiming the Individual From Hofstede's Ecological Analysis—A 20-year Odyssey: Comment on Oyserman et al.'. *Psychological Bulletin* 128(1).

Cecchini, M., Langer, J., and Salwormirski, L. (2015) 'Resistance in G7 Countries and Beyond: Economic Issues, Policies and Options for Action'. September, OECD.

Chan, K.W. (2012) 'Rethinking Flexible Welfare Strategy in Hong Kong: A New Direction for the East Asian Welfare Model?'. *Journal of Asian Public Policy* 5(1).

Council on Foreign Relations (2018) Available at https://www.cfr.org/backgrounder/christianity-china. 9 March.

Crystal, D. (2003) *The Cambridge Encyclopedia of Language.* Cambridge: Cambridge University Press.

de Mooij, M. and Hofstede, G. (2010) 'The Hofstede Model: Applications to Global Branding and Advertising Strategy and Research'. *International Journal of Advertising* 29(1).

de Mooij, M. and Hofstede, G. (2011) 'Cross-cultural Consumer Behavior: A Review of Research Findings'. *Journal of International Consumer Marketing* 23.

de Mooij (2015) 'Cultural Marketing: Maximising Business Effectiveness in a Multicultural World'. *Journal of Cultural Marketing Strategy* 1(1).

El-Katiri, L. (2016) 'Saudi Arabia's Labor Market Challenge'. *Harvard Business Review* 6 July.

EricDigests (n.d.) http://www.ericdigests.org.

Ethnologue (n.d.) http://www.ethnologue.org.

Eurostat (2017) 'News Release Indicators'. 34/2017 2 March.

Geert Hofstede (n.d.) http://geert-hofstede.com.

Green, D.G. (1999) *Benefit Dependency: How Welfare Undermines Independence*. London: Civitas.

Güliz, G. and Belk, R.W. (1996) 'Cross-cultural Differences in Materialism'. *Journal of Economic Psychology* 17(1).

Hoffman, M. and Jamal, A. (2012) 'The Youth and the Arab Spring: Cohort Differences and Similarities'. *Middle East Law and Governance* 4(1).

Hofstede, G. (1980) *Culture's Consequences: International Differences in Work-Related Values*. Beverly Hills, CA: SAGE Publications.

Hofstede, G. (1991) *Cultures and Organizations: Software of the Mind*. New York: McGraw-Hill.

Hofstede, G. (1994) 'Business Cultures: Every Organization has its Symbols, Rituals and Heroes'. *UNESCO Courier* 47(4).

Hofstede, G. (2001) *Culture's Consequences: Comparing Values, Behaviors, Institutions and Organizations Across Nations*. Thousand Oaks, CA: SAGE Publications.

Hofstede, G. (2003) *Culture's Consequences. Comparing Values, Behaviors, Institutions*. London: SAGE Publications.

Hofstede, G. (2007) 'A European in Asia'. *Asian Journal of Social Psychology* 10.

Hofstede, G. (2015) 'Google Indulgence Versus Restraint in 10 minutes' (online)

Hofstede, G. and Bond, M.H. (1984) 'Hofstede's Culture Dimensions: An Independent Validation Using Rokeach's Value Survey'. *Journal of Cross-Cultural Psychology* 15(4).

Hofstede, G. and Bond, M.H. (1998) 'The Confucius Connection: From Cultural Roots to Economic Growth'. *Organizational Dynamics* 16(4).

Hofstede, G. and Minkov, M. (2011) 'Is National Culture a Meaningful Concept? Cultural Values Delineate Homogeneous National Clusters of In-country Regions'. *Cross-Cultural Research* Vol. 46 No. 2.

IFPMA (2016) 'Declaration by the Pharmaceutical, Biotechnology and Diagnostics Industries on Combating Antimicrobial Resistance'. January.

ILO (2014) *World Social Protection Report 2014/15*.

ILO (2016) *World Employment and Social Outlook: Trends for Youth 2016*.

Jones, M.L. (2007) 'Hofstede—Culturally Questionable'. Oxford Business & Economics Conference, Oxford, UK, 24–26 June.

Koyame-Marsh, R.O. (2017) 'The Dichotomy between the Saudi Women's Education and Economic Participation'. *The Journal of Developing Areas* 51(1) Winter.

Kapur, D. and Nagia, P. (2015) 'Social Protection in India: A Welfare State Sans Public Goods?'. *India Review* 14:1.

Kyoungmi, L. and Shavitt, S. (2006) 'The Use of Cues Depends on Goals: Store Reputation Affects Product Judgments when Social Identity Goals Are Salient'. *Journal of Consumer Psychology* 16(3).

Landers, T.F., Cohen, B., Wittum, T.E., and Larson, E.L. (2012) 'A Review of Antibiotic Use in Food Animals: Perspective, Policy, and Potential'. *Public Health Reports* January–February v127(1).

Lee, H.-S. (2004) 'Outstanding Issues in Bilateral Economic Relations between Australia and South Korea'. *Australian Journal of International Affairs* 58 (March).

Madsbjerg, C. (2017) *Sensemaking: The Power of the Humanities In the Age of the Algorithm*. London: Little, Brown.

McSweeney, B. (2002a) 'Hofstede's Model of National Cultural Differences and their Consequences: A Triumph of Faith—A Failure of Analysis'. *Human Relations* 55(1).

McSweeney, B. (2002b) 'The Essentials of Scholarship: A Reply to Geert Hofstede'. *Human Relations* 55: 11.

McSweeney, B., Brown, D., and Iliopoulou, S. (2016) 'Claiming Too Much, Delivering Too Little: Testing Some of Hofstede's Generalisations'. *Irish Journal of Management* 35(1).

Merck (2015) 'Public Policy Statement: Antibiotic Resistance'. July.

Möller, J. and Eisend, M. (2010) 'A Global Investigation into the Cultural and Individual Antecedents of Banner Advertising Effectiveness', *Journal of International Marketing* 18(2).

Morsy, H. (2012) 'Scarred Generation'. *Finance & Development* 49(1).

National Center for Health Statistics (n.d.) Available at http://www.cdc.gov/nchs/fastats/health-insurance.htm.

Navarro, V. and Schmitt, J. (2005) 'Economic Efficiency versus Social Equality? The US Liberal Model versus the European Social Model'. *International Journal of Health Services* 35(4).

Neeley, T. (2012) 'Global Business Speaks English'. *Harvard Business Review,* May 2012.

Neeley, T. and Kaplan, R.S. (2014), 'What's your Language Strategy?'. *Harvard Business Review* September.

OECD (2005) 'Ageing Populations: High Time for Action', 10–11 March. Paris: OECD Publishing.

OECD (2016) Family Database. Available at http://www.oecd.org/els/family/database.htm.

OECD (2017a) 'Enhancing Social Inclusion in Latin America', 16 November. Paris: OECD Publishing.

OECD (2017b) 'Finding their Way: Labour Market Integration of Refugees in Germany', March. Paris: OECD Publishing.

O'Neill, J. (2014) 'The Review on Antimicrobial Resistance'. December.

O'Neill, J. (2016) 'Review on Antimicrobial Resistance: Tackling Drug-resistant Infections Globally: Final Report and Recommendations'. May.

Pew Forum (2015). Available at http://www.pewforum.org/2015/04/02/religious-projections-2010-2050.

Pew Research Center (2015) 'The Future of World Religions: Population Growth Projections, 2010–2050'. 2 April.

Pew Research Center (2017a) 'Christians are the Largest Religious Group in 2015'. 31 March.

Pew Research Center (2017b) 'Why Muslims are the World's Fastest-growing Religious Group', 6 April.

Pierson, C., Castles, F., and Naumann, I.K. (eds) (2014) *The Welfare State Reader,* 3rd edn. Cambridge: Polity Press.

Ramos, R. and Royuela, V. (2016). 'Young educated Greeks'. Available at http://www.ub.edu/irea/

working_papers/2016/201608.pdf; http://www.dw.com/en/greece-central-bank-reports-brain-drain-of-427000-youngeducated-greeks-since-2008/a-19373527.

Redpath, L. (1997) 'A Comparison of Native Culture, Non-native Culture and New Management Ideology'. *Revue Canadienne des Sciences de l'Administration* 14(3).

Schmitz, L. and Weber, W. (2014) 'Are Hofstede's Dimensions Valid? A Test for Measurement Invariance of Uncertainty Avoidance'. *Interculture Journal* 13/22.

Standing, G. (2014) *The Precariat,* 2nd edn. London: Bloomsbury.

Stein-Smith, K. (2016) *The US Foreign Language Deficit: Strategies for Maintaining a Competitive Edge in a Globalized World.* Palgrave Macmillan (ebook, https://www.palgrave.com/gb/book/9783319341583).

UN (2015) 'World Population Ageing [Highlights] 2015'.

UN (2017) 'World Population Prospects; The 2017 Revision'.

UN ESCAP (2015) 'Time for Equality; The Role of Social Protection in Reducing Inequalities in Asia and the Pacific'.

UNICEF (2016) 'Fairness for Children: A League Table of Inequality in Child Well-being in Rich Countries', April.

Watson, J.J., Rayner, R.S., Lysonski, S., and Durvasula, S. (1999) 'Vanity and Advertising: A Study of the Impact of Appearance-related, Sex, and Achievement Appeals'. *Advances in Consumer Research* 26.

WEF (2017) 'Global Gender Gap 2017'.

WHO World Health Statistics (2016) 'Monitoring Health for the SDGs WHO Table of Health Statistics by Country, WHO Region and Globally, Annex B'.

World Economic Forum (2016) 'Global Gender Report 2016'.

World Economic Forum (2017) 'Wages Have Fallen for 43% of Millennials: No Wonder They Have Lost Hope', 15 January.

CHAPTER EIGHT

The Technological Framework

LEARNING OUTCOMES

This chapter will enable you to:

- explain the meaning of technology and associated concepts;

- identify and explain the sources of technology and how firms go about innovating;

- explain why the intensity of technological activity varies by firm size, sector, and country base;

- analyse the importance of the technological environment, both domestic and foreign, for business decisions and performance; and

- explain how the external environment allows business to protect its technology in an international context.

Case Study The Rise of the 'Internet of Things'

© Shutterstock.com/Zapp2Photo

The introduction of Web 1.0 in the early 1990's brought the novelty of being able to instantly search and retrieve web-based data. Web 2.0 later saw this capability develop into technology designed to connect people and take account of social interactions—the rise of social media. With future iterations of Web 3.0 and beyond, applications are becoming smaller, more refined and sophisticated in their ability to connect and capture data and intelligence through our everyday interactions and lives. This concept has become known as the 'Internet of Things'

(IoT) (refer also to this chapter's closing case study). The IoT is ubiquitous and moves beyond traditional computer operating systems. It takes account of complex techno-social systems, and includes all physical objects that contain sensory technology enabling these objects to collect and exchange data continually. As can be seen in Figure 8.1, the global number of connected devices that collectively comprise the IoT is projected to exceed 75 billion by 2025.

The idea that 'big brother is watching' has indeed become a reality. Consider the rise of 'smart' technology, in particular smartphones, which provide convenient mobile internet access, and mobile applications, which continually monitor our whereabouts and share data on local amenities. By 2020, over a third of the world's population is projected to own a smartphone, meaning that there will be an estimated total of almost 2.87 billion smartphone users in the world (see Figure 8.2).

But smart technology is not confined to phones. It includes, among other things, watches designed to enable personal mastery of one's physical health through monitoring heart rate and calorie intake, smart houses that enable us to control appliances such as heating, cooking and lighting remotely, and even smart cities where technology is present everywhere, for example, in CCTV and traffic control sensors.

Figure 8.1 IoT connected devices installed base worldwide from 2015 to 2025 (in billions)

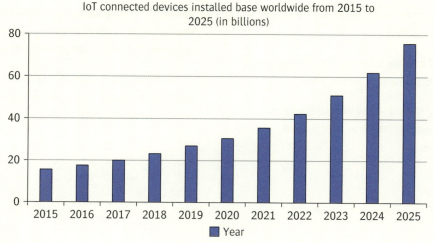

Source: Statista (n.d., a)

→ **Figure 8.2** Number of smartphone users worldwide from 2014 to 2020 (billions)

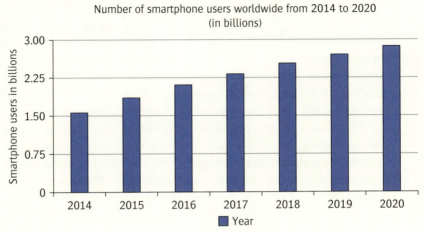

Number of smartphone users worldwide from 2014 to 2020
(in billions)

Source: Statista (n.d., b)

The notion that the IoT involves 24 hour covert monitoring, and the capture and sharing of data that can be used to manipulate our choices and control the world around us, raises a number of philosophical and ethical concerns (Greenfield 2017). The IoT cultivates a worldview of an objective world that is perfectly knowable, free from subjective interpretation and bias, and able to be understood and controlled algorithmically. The danger of this worldview is that it assumes the existence of one correct solution to every problem or need. Consider the concept of the 'smart city', built around complex, often subjective, social and political systems, with divergent cultural norms and expectations. To what extent can decision makers, for example policy makers or town planners, rely on objective data? It is also important to bear in mind that data can be easily manipulated and skewed to suit one's own need, for example, by employers using data to usher in new forms of surveillance and monitoring of employees' performance quotas and targets.

The contemporaneous development and adoption of smart devices, and the type of intelligence they generate, also raises ethical issues in the interactions between business and consumer. Smart technology has become pervasive in targeted advertising for commercial, and sometimes exploitative, purposes. The fairly recent introduction of 'virtual assistant' technology, for instance Apple's Siri, Amazon's Alexa, or Microsoft's Cortana, are powered by language and speech recognition sensors, providing an efficient and integrated way of interacting with technology simply as part of our contemporary lifestyles. The choices presented to users through modern devices are not necessarily benign, however. They are based on a series of inbuilt covert assumptions, with the aim of enabling people to carry out commercial transactions with minimal conscious thought and effort, while simultaneously returning data to the company. From a business perspective, the continual growth of the data-driven economy calls for employees to be increasingly digitally skilled and competent in the capture, interrogation, and reporting of 'big data'; skill sets that are often considered to be in short supply.

Sources: Greenfield (2017); Statista (n.d. a, n.d. b)

Introduction

Technology has been the engine of modernity (Brey 2003). The Industrial Revolution in Britain in the 18th century was inspired by European Enlightenment seeking to explore the force of reason. Philosophers and inventors alike converged on Britain, whose institutions, openness, and tolerance made it an innovation hub (Hutton and Adonis 2018). Technological innovation has shaped modern capitalism, propelling economic reorganization, the creation of new industries, increased productivity, and decades of high growth (Michaelson 2017). In the early twenty-first century, a combination of new information and communication technology (ICT), neoliberal globalization policies, and climate change, are the key drivers of transformative economic and social change (Friedman 2016). The emergence of the information society comes from innovations in ICT and human creativity. The exponential growth in computer power and information technology since 2007 has become the distinguishing technology of our time. New ICT is most visible in, for example, personal laptops, tablets, smart phones and TVs. Smart machines with artificial intelligence (AI) can do tasks that were once the exclusive preserve of humans (Elliott 2018). New technology can also be seen in the products of energy renewables, such as wind turbines, and other high-tech industries, such as pharmaceuticals and **biotechnology**. Technology has become internationalized through economic globalization, migration, and digitization. Thus, consumer goods like smartphones, tablets, and high specification cars can be seen on the streets of Mumbai as well as those of Berlin and Tokyo. Network technologies, such as Facebook and Twitter, usher in new social paradigms and, arguably, are moving us towards a 'post-capitalist' economy (Mason 2016). A parallel explosion of economic globalization and economic interdependency has led multinational companies, such as Microsoft, General Motors, and Sony, to transfer production technologies from their domestic base to foreign, low-wage operations and many, like Samsung and Alcatel-Lucent, take opportunities offered by the international environment to develop global research strategies, carrying out research and development both at home and abroad.

Change in economic and social systems is driven by applications of new technologies. However, technology is a double-edged sword for both capital and labour, offering many opportunities but also challenges. For capital, it opens up a variety of opportunities in terms of new products, processes, services, and markets. On the other hand, it leaves firms more open to a range of competitive threats, such as takeover, increased competition, and even to the theft of their technologies. The rapid internationalization of smart technology means that Sony, for example, has to position data and artificial intelligence 'at the centre of its survival strategy' (Inagaki 2018). For many industries, therefore, technology is of the utmost importance and can determine whether firms prosper or fail.

For labour, advancing technology opens up new forms of employment, for example, designing computer games, such as the immensely popular Grand Theft Auto. On the other hand, technology now has the capacity to do a wide range of non-routine cognitive tasks, thereby putting at risk jobs currently undertaken by professional and skilled labour (Beckett 2018; Elliott 2018; Wood 2018). Thus, any assessment of technology's effect on business and labour is replete with paradox.

The Nature of Technology

Technology is a term that is used rather loosely in everyday discourse to mean computers, robots, and machines. However, defining technology so narrowly neglects the capacity of human capital and accumulated knowledge available to society. Some knowledge is codifiable, meaning it can be written down, captured and transferred easily to others, which accounts for the development of knowledge management (Castells 1996). However, there is also tacit knowledge, which is carried about in the heads of a firm's employees, and therefore not easy to transfer. Over 40 years ago, Alan Fox (1971) made a distinction between material technology and social technology. Material technology is the physical object that can be 'seen, touched and heard'. Social technology, on the other hand, is the human processing arrangements that 'seek to order the behaviour and relationships of people' (p. 13). Social technology includes job boundaries, decision-making procedures, remuneration and other workplace rules, which seek 'to govern what work is done, how it is done, and the relationships that prevail between those doing it' (p. 1).

Recognizing the central role of human agency and 'ideas' in economic growth theory, the U.S. economist Paul Romer (1990: 72) defined technological change as 'an improvement in the instructions for mixing together raw materials.' In the context of business, we define technology as the means by which a firm transforms resources, including information, into products or services, and the social organization of work, which takes such forms as teams, governance rules, and work procedures.

Among some writers, there is an assumption that technological advances will lead to changes in how businesses are configured and behave. The 'boundaryless organization' is associated with radical changes in how goods and services are produced, how production processes are managed, how products are distributed and marketed, and the use of outsourcing to emerging economies, where labour is considerably cheaper (*Anand and Daft 2007*). Technical change can refer to ground-breaking advances in knowledge, or simply to minor modifications of products and processes. Christensen (2013) observes that it is important to make the distinction between 'sustaining' and 'disruptive' technologies. What sustaining technologies have in common is that they improve the performance of established products or processes. Disruptive technologies, on the other hand, create products that are typically cheaper, simpler, smaller and, frequently, more convenient to use. The electronics that build automated telephone exchanges is an example of sustaining technology, whereas silicon chip technology, which produced smartphones, is an example of disruptive technology.

There are a number of other terms associated with technology, and it is useful to have an understanding of these. **Research and Development** (R&D) refers to the discovery of new knowledge (research) about products, processes, and services, and the application of that knowledge to create new and improved products, processes, and services that fill market needs (development).

Basic research is the pursuit of knowledge for the sake of it. In other words, it is carried out to push back the frontiers of knowledge, with no thought of its commercial application. Such research can be very expensive, take an inordinate length of time to yield results, and may produce no results at all. It is therefore commonly funded by governments, and is most often undertaken in universities or research institutes.

An example of basic research was that carried out by Crick and Watson at Cambridge University. In 1953, they announced the most important biological discovery of the twentieth century, the structure of deoxyribonucleic acid, DNA, the chemical of life. Crick and Watson's discovery of DNA spawned the biotechnology industry, producing new treatments for genetic diseases such as cancer, multiple sclerosis, and cystic fibrosis. It led to numerous scientific discoveries that have changed our lives, from the food we eat to the seeds that farmers use in their fields, and to the DNA testing used by the police to help identify criminals.

While there are businesses, for example in the electronics and pharmaceuticals industries, helping to fund basic research in the hope that some commercially exploitable ideas will be generated, firms, as a rule, do not usually get involved. Companies are normally more interested in applied research; that is, activities intended to lead to new or improved products and processes, with clear and more immediate commercial uses. Even in applied research, there is no guarantee that results will be exploitable commercially. Scientists at General Electric (GE)—one of the biggest companies in the world, with interests ranging from jet engines to nuclear power stations to financial services—estimate that around 20 per cent of the company's research projects are scrapped each year. Some authors have observed that a large number of firms compete by continuously changing their products or services (see, for example, Hammer 1997). For instance, Apple is constantly introducing newer features into their iPhone. The ability to make changes that are often ground breaking draws attention to the importance of creativity and innovation.

Creativity is the act of using one's knowledge to come up with novel ideas that are potentially useful to the firm. Creativity forms the central premise of the 'core competence' thesis, which suggests that firms need to build and manage their intellectual human capital (Hamel and Prahalad 1994). Creativity refers to a novel, potentially useful idea; however, not all the ideas generated are adopted.

Innovation is the commercial exploitation of new ideas into products and production processes, and selling them on to customers. The late management guru, Peter Drucker, asserts that it is 'the act that endows resources with a new capacity to create wealth' (1985: 28). Innovation is often measured by R&D spending, or by the number of patents—a patent gives its owner the exclusive right to exploit the idea, and gives the legal right to stop others from using it. But innovation can also arise through investment in new technology, market development, skills, new ways of working, new business processes, and linkages with other organizations. It can involve the implementation of major advances in technical knowledge, such as the digitization of electronic equipment, or small incremental changes, such as a minor improvement in a production process. This spectrum of activity can be referred to as 'breakthrough', and 'incremental' innovation (Bessant 2003). Breakthrough innovations enable firms to 'do things different' by introducing a wholly new process, product or service: the social networking website Facebook, for example. Incremental innovations, on the other hand, improve existing products, processes, or services; enabling firms to 'do things better'. Most innovation follows a pattern of occasional breakthrough (for example, Research in Motion's BlackBerry), followed by long periods of cumulative improvement (for example, Apple's iPhone).

The spread of innovation from one firm and industry to another, nationally and internationally, is known as technological diffusion. Diffusion has been growing at a rapid pace, as is shown by the growth of high-technology exports, foreign licensing agreements, and the foreign ownership of patents. After 1990, high-technology exports worldwide grew very rapidly, with Chinese manufacturing industries performing particularly well. By 2013, China accounted for more than one-third of such exports, with the contribution of Hong Kong taking the share to around 50 per cent, far outstripping the USA's 10 per cent, Japan's 7 per cent, and Germany at 4 per cent (*Financial Times* 18 March 2014).

The intensity of cross-border technological diffusion has been increasing, but appears to have tailed off since 2005, as measured by the foreign ownership of new inventions (OECD

StatExtracts n.d.). Nonetheless, in the USA, foreigners accounted for more than half the patents granted in 2013, compared with 46 per cent before 2000. However, foreign ownership as a proportion of all US patents remains low, as it does for Japan, South Korea, and China, whereas it is high in Belgium, Ireland, and Hungary. Less than 5 per cent of patents in Japan and South Korea are foreign-owned. Foreign owners, predominantly MNCs based in the USA, the EU, or Japan, have a tendency to own patents in countries with close historical and cultural links, as well as geographical proximity, to their home country.

The degree of internationalization varies across different technologies. R&D in pharmaceuticals, motor vehicles, chemicals, and the manufacturing of information and communication technologies are more internationalized than other sectors. Furthermore, some countries are dependent on foreign companies for their R&D capabilities. Foreign MNCs account for a significant proportion of R&D spending in Ireland, Sweden, Spain, Canada, and the UK, as compared with the USA and Japan. The R&D activities of US MNCs are much more internationalized than Japanese companies. Dachs and Zahradnik (2014) identify MNC motives for foreign R&D as a desire to adapt products to foreign markets, and to take advantage of high quality R&D resources based in, for example, research institutes or universities.

Economic globalization in general, and multinational companies in particular, are important vehicles for the international diffusion of new knowledge through their trading, investment, and competitive strategies. Their influence is illustrated by the international spread of lean manufacturing in the car industry. This sets out to reduce labour costs, eliminate waste, and to decrease the time between receipt of a customer order and delivery. It was pioneered by car-maker Toyota in Japan, and subsequently adopted by Western companies, such as GM, Ford, and VW, as a result of the fierce competition they faced from their more efficient Japanese rivals.

Capitalism and Disruptive Waves of Innovation

Industrial capitalism has gone through long cycles driven by major innovations. The Russian, Nikolai Kondratieff, was the first economist to demonstrate the existence of long waves in economic history. He observed that, beyond short-term business cycles, a 50-year pattern existed, the turning points of which coincided with major technological changes and conflicts within capitalism. In Kondratieff's 'wave-theory', each long cycles has an upswing lasting about 25 years, fuelled by investment in new technology, then a downswing of around the same length, usually ending with a depression. In Business Cycles, the Austrian-born American economist Josef Schumpeter (1939) described each of Kondratieff's waves as an 'innovation cycle', and argued that industrial capitalism is shaped by interlocking wave-cycles.

For the waves to occur, there have to be people willing to take the risk of exploiting new ideas commercially. Schumpeter saw the entrepreneur as playing this vital role, which made his wave-theory highly attractive to mainstream academia and capitalists. Industrial capitalism has experienced four long cycles:

- **1790–1848** is the first long cycle discernible in British data. Commonly referred to as the Industrial Revolution, it was driven by a cluster of innovations in the factory system involving water-powered, and then later, steam-powered textile machinery. The start of the downswing is observable in the 1820s.

- **1848–1890s** is the second long wave or cycle observable across Western Europe, the U.S. and Japan. The new technological-economic paradigm was based around railways, ocean-going steamers, the telegraph, machine-produced machinery, and stable currencies. The wave peaks in the mid-1870s, with a financial crisis in Europe and the US leading to two decades (1873–96) of economic depression.

- **1890–1945** is the third long wave, driven by the introduction of assembly-line mass production, expansion in chemical industries, and the introduction of synthetic dyestuffs and high explosives, telephone communications, electrical engineering and scientific management. The break point is 1918, at the end of World War One, which is followed by the depression in the 1930s, and the widespread destruction of capital across Europe and in Japan in World War Two, which ends the downswing.

- **1948–2008** is the fourth and longest wave/cycle. The new technological-economic paradigm is built around a cluster of innovations including oil extraction and application, synthetic materials, transistors, automation, nuclear power, the silicon chip, and robotics. The downward turning point is 1973, caused by a spike in oil prices and President Nixon's unilaterally ending of the policy to exchange dollars for gold, followed by a long period of instability.

Each of the four long cycles have start and end points, a cluster of innovations at the start of each wave-cycle, and significant crises. For Carlota Perez (2003), the primary focus of long-wave theory is the irruption and assimilation of each technological innovation, simultaneously supported by a recognizable new social paradigm—for example, new ways of managing the firm and/or new forms of state intervention. The different versions of wave-theory have been criticized for its explicit determinist hypothesis.

Technological determinism is the view that technology is the prime driver, or determinant, of developments in firms, economic growth, or even society itself. Technological determinism contains a partial truth: that technology matters to firms (MacKenzie and Wajcman 1999). But the key analytical limitations of this simple cause-and-effect approach are, first, the inconsistency in establishing the direction of causation, and second, the mediating effects of other key variables, not least human action, economics and politics, and, notably, the state. This means that a simple linear cause-and-effect technological determinant is not an adequate theory of business behaviour or economic growth.

Some commentators, like Wonglimpiyarat (2005), suggest that a fifth wave could be sparked by nanotechnology, the science of the ultra-small. Nanotechnology is the ability to manipulate and manufacture things using individual particles of materials, the dimensions of which are 100 nanometres or less. Today's business IT systems are built on platforms dating from the 1980s and 1990s. These systems are now costly to operate, prone to catastrophic crashes, and unable to ensure data security from cyber-attacks. These limits, it is predicted, will result in a new 'supercycle' of disruptive technological innovation (Michaelson 2017). The British economist, Paul Mason (2016), suggests that a fifth long cycle is discernible from the late 1990s, driven by information and communications technology (ICT) and artificial intelligence, which allows firms and institutions to create a global network and market place; however, the upswing has stalled because of neoliberalism and the technology itself. See Counterpoint Box 8.1.

Counterpoint Box 8.1 Is technology shaped by social factors?

The key technologies of modernism, which are said to have defined the first, second, third, and fourth long cycles—that is, steam, electricity and computers—have seen fascinating and complex pathways to application in business. These 'general-purpose technologies' emerged, not out of some inventor's mind as much as from the push and pull of the forces of economic and political struggle. The details of the emergence and diffusion of innovations provide important clues to the actual nature of technology as a phenomenon. Is technology a 'thing', or is it a social process? Lazonick (1993: 194) suggests the latter in his discussion of the meaning of 'technological transfer':

> Insofar as the utilization of technology requires complementary human inputs with specific cognitive capabilities and behavioural responses, the transferred technology will have to be developed in the new national environment before it can be utilized there. As a result, when 'transferred' technology is ultimately developed so that it can be productively utilized in a new national environment, it is in effect a new technology.

This type of description is aligned with the notion of configurations (as opposed to 'technologies' as such). Configurations are defined as complex mixes of standardized, and locally customized, elements that are highly specific to a firm. Scholars tend to suggest that technology is not a particular tool, artefact or machine, and neither is it a general-purpose technology such as steam, electricity or computers. Rather, it is 'the way we do things around here' (Franklin 1990), 'an improvement in the instructions for mixing together raw materials' (Romer 1990), 'society made durable' (Latour 2000), and so on. But new technologies are not neutral facilitators: they embody our values and politics (Bridle 2018). Students of business, technology, and society gain the potential for valuable leadership when they break the bonds of conventional wisdom to explore the concept of technology critically. In this chapter, we suggest that we must approach the technology framework as a thoroughly social phenomenon.

Sources: Bratton (2015); Latour (2000); Lazonick (1993)

Question

What do different narratives about technologies obscure, hide or ignore? What does the statement 'technology is a social phenomenon' mean?

The Info-tech Revolution

Information and communications technology (ICT) has become increasingly important in the business world. ICT is a term that encompasses all forms of microcomputer-based technology used to create, store, exchange, and use information in its various forms, whether that be business data, voice conversations, still images, motion pictures, or multimedia presentations. It involves the use of machines such as computers, telephone exchanges, robots, satellites, automatic cash dispensers, AI and cable TV, along with the software installed in them. ICT is all-pervasive, affecting the home, the office, and the factory. It has major implications for business, both large and small; from the small shop, with its computerized accounts, to supermarket chains such as Wal-Mart and Tesco, who use electronic links with their suppliers to ensure that their shelves are always stocked with sufficient quantities of the appropriate goods.

The pace of change in ICT has been extraordinary, due to a variety of factors. The needs of the military have been a major impetus for developing computers to solve problems related to encryption, decoding, and missile trajectory. The development of microelectronic technologies owes much to the space race between the USA and the USSR. US rockets were smaller than Soviet rockets, so they could not carry as much computer equipment. Miniaturization provided the solution and led to the computer chip.

With the power and speed of computer chips doubling every 18 months, and their cost falling by 50 per cent, many new products have emerged, like laptop computers, mobile phones, global positioning systems, and satellite TV. An important development has been the internet, which is an enormous international computer network, initially developed in the US defence sector. It links a vast number of pages of information on the World Wide Web, which is expanding at an exponential rate. It has led to the emergence of auction companies like eBay, search engines such as Google, and social networking sites like Facebook, Instagram, and Snapchat. In 2002, it was estimated that about 10 per cent of the world population was using the internet. By 2017, at over three billion people, this has risen to 49.6 per cent. The highest number of users was in Asia, with well over 1.8 billion, followed by Europe with 636 million, North America with 320 million, Latin America with 385 million, and Africa with 345 million (Internet World Stats n.d.).

Web 2.0

There have been a number of important technological developments on the World Wide Web known as Web 2.0 (see O'Reilly 2005; also see video on this topic by visiting the **online resources**). These rely on user collaboration, and include peer-to-peer networking, blogs, podcasts, wikis, video sharing, and social platforms like Facebook, WhatsApp, YouTube, Instagram, and Twitter. Web 2.0 created global systems that make it much easier for business-to-business, and business-to-customer, interaction. One place to see the application of these advances in action is in the mobile phone market, where manufacturers and service providers are creating 'apps', which users can download to their smartphones. These allow users to play games, locate nearby restaurants or friends, listen to music, find the best deals online, and access countless sources of specific information. Apple claims more than 140 billion app downloads between 2008 and 2016. As of April 2017, Facebook had more than 1.86 billion active users, which is a 17 per cent increase year over year (Statista n.d.). That year around 2.32 billion people in the world were using smartphones (Statista n.d.).

Mini Case Study 8.1 Data are the new oil

Internet usage has grown explosively, and has led to the faster and cheaper accumulation of masses of data, now commonly known as 'big data'. Some firms recognized the potential benefits of such a treasure trove, but the volume of data was so vast that it outstripped the ability of existing software programs to analyse it. This led to the development of new processing technologies, such as Hadoop, used by Yahoo and Facebook. Microsoft, IBM, Amazon, and Oracle all now offer database management services.

The new database technologies analyse the data, looking for statistical relationships; that is, correlations between different data which can be quantitative, text, images, and moving images. Big data analysts are not interested in finding out why the relationships exist.

UK finance firms, like Lloyds Bank, found that customers who are careful with cash are less likely to have car accidents, and it therefore offers them a lower insurance premium. Amazon uses its huge database to predict what its customers will buy, whether that be books, shoes, music, tablets, or smartphones. Reportedly, FedEx can identify which customers are likely to defect to a competitor.

McKinsey (2013) estimated that the use of big data could generate $3 trillion to $5 trillion of benefits, in seven sectors of the US economy, through raising productivity, improving products and services, introducing new products, and increasing cost and price transparency.

Sources: Mayer-Schönberger and Cukier (2014); *InformationWeek* 30 January 2014; *Financial Times* 28 March, 12 July 2014; McKinsey (2013); Hayashi (2013)

Question

1. Some commentators are concerned about the hyping of big data. Explain why.

McKinsey (2013) reported that 82 per cent of surveyed companies were using Facebook, Twitter, Instagram, and other social networks, with two-thirds using mobile networks. Companies can use these technologies to communicate with employees, and also invite customers to rate products and recommend improvements. Social media gives companies powerful new insights into how to position products, create new ones, and decide on pricing strategies. More than 40 per cent of firms surveyed were using video conferencing, social networking, collaborative document editing, video sharing, and blogs. Tools like wikis and podcasts were less popular. McKinsey found that, after years of rapid growth, use of social technology had plateaued.

The Cloud

The cloud is the central metaphor of the internet: a global system of immense energy and power (Bridle 2018). It offers business the possibility of using software from the internet. This means that firms do not need to have software, such as Windows, installed on their own computers. Company data can also be stored in the cloud. Companies like Apple, Google, and Microsoft provide cloud services. Cloud computing reduces the amount of money firms need to spend on IT personnel and infrastructure, such as air-conditioned rooms to store servers, and upgrades on software and hardware. This makes it easier for small and medium-sized firms to compete, because they only need to pay for the IT services they need, when they need them, and they can access the same IT services as their larger competitors. Commentators, such as Kotler and Caslione (2009), argue that cloud computing could make it easier for developing countries to compete with richer economies.

A potential drawback is that firms could become dependent on the cloud company to hold their confidential data, and for the provision of IT services. Problems could arise were the service provider to have a breakdown (as happened with Google and Amazon—*The Observer* 1 March 2009), leak confidential information due to illegal hacking, or go out of business.

Investment in Innovation

The EU R&D Scoreboard 2016 found that corporate R&D spending for the world's top 2,500 companies was about €696 billion, an increase of 6.6 per cent over the previous year. Research intensity, that is R&D as a percentage of sales, varies from sector to sector, industry to industry, by size of firm, and by geographical location. The Scoreboard found that in the USA, the EU, and Japan, the most research-intensive sectors were technology hardware and equipment, pharmaceuticals and biotechnology, and automobiles, involving big companies like Merck, Sony, and Volkswagen. Sectors with low research intensity include oil and gas, tobacco, and mining. In the high-tech sector, the catalyst for much of the rise of corporate R&D was the development of software. In terms of firm size, the larger the firm, the more likely it is to do R&D, even in low-tech industries.

Mini Case Study 8.2 **China and the internet**

Figure 8.3 China—number of users of digital platforms

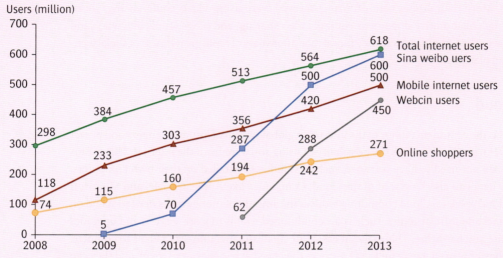

Source: Boston Consulting Group (2014).

Between 2000 and 2014, the number of internet users in China increased 30-fold to 642 million. By 2017, the figure had increased to 731 million, with 95 per cent of these accessing the internet from smartphones. The Chinese have also embraced internet shopping with a passion. In 2013, 271 million Chinese were shopping online, and this figure rose to more than 466 million in 2016 (see Figure 8.3).

A Boston Consulting Group study (2014) found that a majority of online shoppers use the internet as the main source of information on products, brands, and prices, with a significant proportion depending on both online and offline sources. But they shy away from getting that information from actual company websites, preferring to obtain that information elsewhere on the Web; for example, from e-commerce sites like Alibaba, with huge stocks and low prices, blogs, and social networking sites. The study found that most consumers spend up to 80 per cent of their time on a few sites like Youku, a local video-streaming website, Sina.com, a news portal, QQ, an instant messaging service, Taobao, an e-commerce site, and Baidu. Internet users in China also like to follow celebrities on Weibo, a microblogging service with more than half a billion users. However, consumers are sceptical of heavily commercialized blogs and those purporting to represent a celebrity promoting

shoddy products. Product recommendations from grass roots bloggers are seen as more genuine, and can help product sales.

Consumer purchasing behaviour varies from one product category to another. Clothing tends to be bought on impulse. With small appliances and packaged foods, consumers are likely to research online, but make most purchases offline. Skin care products are compared online and offline, but purchased online only if a lower price is on offer and the product is not counterfeit.

Daily peak times for online purchases are 10am, 2pm, and 9pm. The Boston survey points to Uniqlo, the Japanese clothing retailer, as an example of good practice to foreign MNCs in China. It promotes its products in a coordinated way, both online and offline, through activities like interactive games.

Sources: http://www.internetlivestats.com; Boston Consulting Group, The Chinese Digital Consumer in a Multichannel World, http://www.bcg.perspectives 17 April 2014; *Forbes* 28 April 2014; Statista (2017)

Question

What advice would you give to a foreign MNC wishing to sell online in China?

Counterpoint Box 8.2 Does technology kill and deskill jobs?

We have mentioned that any evaluation of technology's effect on labour is replete with paradox. With this in mind, here we examine two important debates: technological unemployment and technological deskilling. Mainstream economists have reassured society that technology creates rather than destroys jobs. This argument is predicated on the assumption that, while technology is replacing workers, the higher productivity can reduce the price of products, which causes a rise in real income, and an increase in demand for other goods and services. This demand creates new jobs for workers displaced by technology. Technological change since the first wave-cycle is used as evidence that technology creates employment. Brynjolfsson and McAfee (2011) partially go along with this view, but they go on to argue that technologies like robotics have replaced jobs involving routine tasks, causing a reduction in demand for semi-skilled labour. Studies by Frey and Osborne (2013) and Meltzer (2014) suggest, also, that it is not simply routine manual work in jeopardy. 47 per cent of US jobs in white-collar occupations are at high risk of being automated, and Meltzer observes that ICT is threatening knowledge-based professions in architecture, law, and medicine (refer also to Mini Case Study 8.4 Automation and Commercial Aviation).

Marx's analysis of machinery has strongly influenced twentieth-century research on technological deskilling (Bratton and Denham 2014). Examining the impact of factory technology, Marx observed: 'Along with the tool, the skill of the workman in handling it passes over to the machine' (1887/1970: 420). Braverman's (1974) highly influential thesis argued that managers' impulse is to control labour, which leads them to pursue systematic strategies of deskilling labour. Mirroring Marx's observations, Braverman writes: 'An automatic system of machinery opens up the possibility of the true control' (1974: 230–2). Braverman's thesis has attracted criticisms (see, for example, Wood 1982) and support (see Thompson 1989).

Sources: Brynjolfsson and McAfee (2011); Frey and Osborne (2013); Braverman (1974)

Questions

1. Can ICT deskill professional occupations or make them obsolete? To help answer this, see Meltzer's (2014) study of the impact of ICT on skilled knowledge-based professions in architecture, law and medicine.
2. Do smartphones increase an organization's control over their employees? To help answer this, see Cavazotte et al.'s (2014) study of the impact of smartphones in law firms.

Unsurprisingly, large manufacturing firms spend a much larger proportion of their turnover on innovation activities than small firms. Table 8.1 shows the top global 10 innovators by sector in 2016. The sector ranked in the top three was the aerospace and defence industry. In terms of industry classification, it is reported that hardware and electronics saw the largest growth in 2016. The growth in this sector reflects the ubiquitous and growing influence of semiconductors and computing hardware across wide areas of activity, including aerospace, automation, displays, and intelligent transportation.

Research activity is not confined to large-sized firms. Using measures of innovation other than R&D and patents shows that small and medium-sized firms can also be important innovators. Historically, manufacturing firms have carried out most R&D. However, research activity in the service sector is on the increase, particularly in telecommunications, information technology, networking, and consultancy.

Industries are not all equally affected by the competition arising from technological change, and the opportunities and threats that it poses. Firms operating in industries where technology evolves and diffuses rapidly need to stay very aware of their technological environment. Such high-technology industries include aerospace, computers and office equipment, communications and media equipment, and pharmaceuticals. A firm in these industries failing to respond effectively to its technological environment runs the risk of falling sales, market share, and profits, and even takeover or bankruptcy. This is particularly so in markets where, due to customer preference, only the latest product sells. There are some industries that are less sensitive to technological change. These are classified as medium technology industries, and include motor vehicles, electrical (other than communications equipment) and non-electrical machines, chemicals excluding drugs, cars, rubber and plastics products, and shipbuilding and repairing. The high and medium-high-tech sectors together usually account for most R&D, and contribute a disproportionately large share of sales of new and improved products.

Finally, there are the low-tech industries that are relatively unaffected by competition in the area of technology, such as paper products, textiles, non-fashion clothes and leather goods, food, beverages and tobacco, wood products, and furniture.

 Learning Task

Globally, it is the largest companies, in the richest countries, in a limited number of sectors that account for the vast majority of the money spent on R&D. Examine Table 8.1 and answer the questions below to test the validity of this claim.

1. Are the 10 companies among the biggest multinationals in the world? To answer this, go to the latest World Investment Report at http://www.unctad.org.

2. Which countries dominate the ranking? Explain why.

3. In which sectors do these firms operate? Why should R&D spending be high in these sectors?

Table 8.1 Top 10 global innovators in 2016, by sector

Firm	Country	Industry
Boeing	USA	Aerospace & Defence
Lockheed Martin	USA	Aerospace & Defence
Safran	France	Aerospace & Defence
Thales	France	Aerospace & Defence
Aisin Seiki	Japan	Automotive
Bridgestone	Japan	Automotive
Delphi	USA	Automotive
Honda Motor	Japan	Automotive
JTEKT	Japan	Automotive
Nissan	Japan	Automotive

Source: Clarivate Analytics (2016)

Geographical Location of R&D

Much of the R&D growth in a country is driven by that country's economic growth, which is measured by the change in gross domestic product (GDP) (see Chapter 2). It is forecast that global R&D investments will increase by 3.5 per cent in 2016, to a total of around £1.519 trillion. As noted in Table 8.2, European countries account for only slightly more than 20 per cent of all global R&D investments and, with United States investments now just 26 per cent, the USA (with Europe) continues to lose global R&D share values on a yearly basis. Asian countries (including China and Japan), on the other hand, account for more than 40 per cent of all global R&D investments.

Sources of Innovation and Technological Advance

As we suggest above, innovation and advances in technology are a thoroughly social phenomenon. Innovation and technological change can usefully be studied as a process of 'learning', at the organizational, group, or individual levels (Bratton 2015: 447). To understand the force of this argument, it is necessary to recognize that new ideas for commercial exploitation do not largely stem from a 'great inventor' working in a university or research centre, but are a matter of the incremental modification of existing technology (Hughes 1989). Scientists at Manchester University discovered how to extract graphene from graphite. It is one molecule thick, 200 times stronger and six times lighter than steel, and is a better electricity conductor than copper. It can be used to make folding mobile phones, and batteries that charge up in minutes, and is added to paints, plastics, and lubricants. Technologists at the University of Oxford invented a direct-drive engine allowing car manufacturers to reduce weight and improve the range of electric and hybrid vehicles by removing heavy gearbox components from the transmission (Oxford University Innovation n.d.). Sometimes businesses establish research links with universities to give them first call on new ideas generated by the university. Huawei, the giant Chinese telecoms company, financially supports six UK universities for research in areas such as advanced multimedia, optical technology, and 5G technologies.

Table 8.2 Share of total global R&D spending 2014–16

Region/Country	Share of total global spending (Percentage)		
	2014	2015	2016*
Americas (21)	29.2	28.5	28.4
USA	26.9	26.4	26.4
Asia (20)	40.2	41.2	41.8
China	19.1	19.8	20.4
Europe (34)	21.5	21.3	21.0
Rest of world (36)	9.1	9.0	8.8
Total	100.0%	100.0%	100.0%

Note: Number in brackets = number of countries. *Forecast
Source: R&D Magazine (Winter, 2016)

Large firms, in industries such as pharmaceuticals and electronics, have their own R&D facilities that generate ideas for new goods and services. GE spends billions of dollars annually on R&D in the USA, India, China, and Germany. As part of its research effort, it runs a Global Research Centre employing thousands of researchers in the USA, India, China, Germany, and Brazil. The centre pioneered very successful breakthroughs in lasers, optical lenses, and digital X-rays, which allowed doctors a more accurate view of organs and bones, and did away with the need for film and light boxes.

Business can also look to the more immediate environment as a way of facilitating the innovation process. For example, firms may cooperate with domestic or foreign rivals when the costs of innovation are high, or to improve their ability to innovate. Collaboration can help lower the costs and risks of innovation, as well as facilitating the commercialization of new scientific and technical knowledge, and can, therefore, be an attractive strategy for small- and medium-sized firms. The Italian furniture and textile industries, comprising mainly small firms, have formed networks of producers, allowing them to cooperate on technology and ensuring that they maintain their competitive edge in the market place. Examples of cross-border collaboration can be seen in the car industry where even financially powerful big car producers feel obliged to cooperate to develop costly new models and components; for example, GM's joint venture with DaimlerChrysler to develop new transmission systems, and Peugeot's joint venture with BMW to develop parts for electric cars. Technology, particularly the internet, facilitates the process of collaboration—it is easy, speedy, and cheap for R&D units based in different countries to exchange information in the form of text, graphics, design drawings, video images, and so on.

Firms often try to involve suppliers, distributors, and customers (the supply chain in other words) in the innovation process to develop and share innovative ideas, or to share in the development of new products or processes. In the aerospace sector, Supply Chain Relationships in Aerospace (SCRIA) is an example of such networking.

Some companies, particularly Japanese firms such as Nissan and Toyota, look to stakeholders such as their employees to come up with ideas for improving products and processes. Every year, Toyota, the world's largest car company, receives literally thousands of suggestions from assembly line workers about how it could do things even better. Workers are encouraged to find ways of shaving as little as one-tenth of a second off routine tasks. Most suggestions involve tiny modifications to existing practices, for example performing a particular task while standing up rather than sitting down. If the modifications work, they are adopted throughout Toyota's factories. Behavioural research underscores the value of problem-centric models of workplace learning, such as action learning (Gold et al. 2013), and employee engagement in successful technological change (Johnstone and Ackers 2015). Finally, the acquisition of new machinery and equipment can be an important source of product or process innovation for small and medium-sized enterprises. The new equipment may require the business to change the way it produces the product or to produce new or improved products.

Learning Task

Advance reasons why firms involved in expensive, risky, or complex research projects, such as those in the pharmaceutical industry, would seek cooperation in R&D with other organizations.

 Visit the **online resources** for a useful link to Hagedorn's paper to help with this task.

Why Business Invests in R&D and Innovation

In Kondratieff's wave-theory, each economic upswing is fuelled by investment in innovation, but what motivates business to invest in R&D and new technology? Critical scholars argue that profit incentivizes firms to invest in innovation. The motive force of profit is the unifying, quantitative objective of corporate strategies, including investment strategy, the touchstone of firm rationality and the measure of corporate success (Baran and Sweezy 1968). Thus, arguably, the purpose of R&D is to create intellectual property rights, such as patients, in order to increase or maintain profit. For example, the drive behind patenting the advanced HIV drug, Darunavir, enables its price to be maintained at $1,095 a year (Mason 2016: 132). In broad terms, innovation is driven by a complex combination of factors in the firm's external and internal environment: the intensity of competition, relationships with customers and suppliers, and government policies.

The Intensity of Competition

Since the mid-1980s, the pace of globalization in the world economy has accelerated. The reduction in the barriers to the movement of goods, services, and capital across borders has meant that markets have become increasingly integrated, innovation has diffused much more quickly, and technological competition has grown more intense. Increasing competition from low-wage economies, such as China and India, has also contributed to the process. Competition means that when one firm innovates, competitors may be forced to react, often in creative ways. This could involve major ground-breaking advances or, more likely, improvements and innovations around the first innovator's design; for example, 'me-too' drugs in the pharmaceutical industry. Technological competition may drive firms to launch new products and at a faster rate, add features, enter, or even create, new markets. In this way, technological competition begets more innovation and more competition. The increase in technological competition makes life more risky for business because one of the persistent characteristics of innovation is that most attempts to innovate fail in the market place. When the rate of innovation accelerates, it has the effect of shortening the length of the product life cycle. The period of time from conception to the death of the product is reduced, and this increases pressure on business to innovate to stay ahead of the competition and meet profit targets.

Customers and Suppliers

Some industries may find that the pressure to innovate comes from customers or suppliers. Car components producers, hoping for contracts with big manufacturers like Nissan, get business on condition that they change their mode of operation to meet Nissan's cost and quality requirements. Nissan advises suppliers on how to go about changing their production processes in order to increase efficiency. In the North East of England, where Nissan manufactures cars, it has set up a high-tech learning centre, which suppliers use to develop their skills and to improve their productivity. For example, through the centre, suppliers can find out about Kaizen, a Japanese management technique embracing the concept of continuous improvement.

Suppliers can also be the instigators of innovation. Taking health care as an example, we can see that advances in body imaging has led to new, and much more sophisticated, scanning techniques being used in hospitals, which has implications for the treatments offered, and also for the training of staff.

Government Policy

Government support for innovation has been a constant feature of modernity. Carlota Perez's version of the wave-theory emphasizes the response of governments at critical points, with innovation and technology driven by governments (Mason 2016: 47). Governments have long been aware of the importance of R&D and technological advancement to the performance of their economies. To this end, they can pursue policies that remove or mitigate the effects of some of the barriers, or give a positive impetus to R&D and innovation. Some innovations never get started, or suffer serious delays, because of their cost, or the inability to secure finance for what financial institutions view as too risky projects. This is a particular problem for small firms, who may also suffer because they are often unaware of the information that is being generated, for example in universities and research institutes, that could be commercially exploited. Lack of qualified scientific and technical personnel can be another barrier to the development and exploitation of new ideas, as can the high cost of protecting intellectual property rights (IPRs), or where the degree of protection awarded to intellectual property is low. However, the regulatory framework can also be a positive influence. For example, stringent environmental and consumer regulation, as found in several EU countries, can force firms to raise their game regarding innovation. Post-Brexit, it remains uncertain whether the UK government will maintain these EU environmental and consumer regulations. Employment laws making it difficult to dismiss employees may cause firms, when they innovate, to search for less labour-intensive production methods. On the other hand, low-regulations and low-wages can act as a barrier to innovation as it discourages investment in new technologies.

In 2000, the EU embarked on its Lisbon Strategy, a 10-year plan to improve competitiveness, with innovation and the knowledge economy as two of its central planks. Member states agreed to pursue policies that would help reduce some of the important barriers to innovation, with the aim of making the EU the most competitive economy in the world. To that end, the EU agreed to aim for an increase in R&D spending to 3 per cent of GDP per year, with two-thirds of that coming from private sector firms, and to coordinate R&D programmes across the members of the union. However, a review by the EU Commission in 2010 found that it had failed to reach the 3 per cent target for R&D as a percentage of GDP. The EU's Europe 2020 Strategy once again prioritized an increase in R&D to boost competitiveness and economic growth (European Commission n.d.).

Businesses operating in developed economies are likely to be at an advantage because of the well-developed school, higher education, and training systems that mean that a high proportion of the population is literate and numerate. Conversely, firms operating in developing countries will be at a disadvantage. However, countries like China and India are producing increasing numbers of highly skilled and technically qualified graduates.

Governments can pursue tax, subsidy, and equity support regimes that make finance more easily available, and cut the costs of R&D and the risks associated with innovation. Almost all developed countries provide tax incentives and subsidies for innovation, although the focus is usually on promoting research, which tends to favour big business and to discriminate against SMEs. Governments, following the prescriptions of Michael Porter (2008) for improved competitiveness, promote the emergence of industrial clusters of associated firms, including suppliers, customers, and competitors, to allow firms to boost their competitiveness by taking advantage of the knowledge of, and interaction with, other businesses located in the cluster. These are visible in countries like, for example, Italy, where a textile cluster comprising of garment manufacture, textile machinery and design are all located within a compact 200–300 square kilometres. In Andhra Pradesh, in India, the state has, through public-private partnerships, encouraged the creation of clusters in the IT, biotechnology, pharmaceutical, and textile sectors.

Why Technology is Important for Business

Technology opens up all sorts of domestic and foreign opportunities for businesses, but it can also pose many threats to firms who are unaware of, and unprepared for, technological change. Significantly, it can, as we will see from the example of the internet, erode boundaries between markets and industries.

Technology can be a principal factor determining the organization of production, the size and growth of firms, the structure of industry on a global scale, its location and ownership. According to Held et al. (1999), technology has played a part in the global restructuring of production. It has helped MNCs slice up the value chain, by facilitating the location of segments of the production process to low-wage countries, or to subcontract production activities to cheaper suppliers in Asia or Latin America.

Competitive advantage regarding productivity, costs, and products can all be heavily influenced by new ideas and innovation. Those ideas and innovation can result in new inventions, trademarks, literary, and artistic works. These are the firm's IP. As noted above, in reality, not many companies invent wholly new products; most of them adapt and extend ideas that others have already tried. Apple's iPod was not the first MP3 player, but the company added enough to make its version innovative. Similarly, drugs companies often build on each other's breakthroughs to produce 'me-too' drugs.

Opportunities

Technology can be a principal factor shaping the firm's system of production. Increased productivity is recorded in firms that invest in new technology. For example, US companies have invested more in ICT than their European counterparts and, consequently, have experienced particularly strong productivity growth in sectors that make intensive use of ICT. Relatedly, innovation and new technologies reduce costs. Telecommunication operators, such as BT or France Telecom, have also been major beneficiaries of automated exchanges, and the replacement of mechanical by electronic parts in communications equipment, thereby saving labour and replacement and maintenance costs. One can also see this in the driverless metros in cities such as Hong Kong, and in airport trains like those in Stansted airport in the UK. Another advantage is that technology can help firms deal with labour shortages. John Smedley, a medium-sized British manufacturer of luxury knitwear, had a costly labour-intensive production process and faced a shortage of skilled textile workers. The company could have cut costs and dealt with its labour shortage by getting its sweaters made in South East Asia. It was reluctant to do this because it would mean sacrificing the 'Made in England' label, the hallmark of John Smedley knitwear, and the reason why the company could demand high margins on its products. The company solution was to invest in new, technologically advanced knitting machinery that made some job occupations obsolete, while enabling more of its workers to focus on pattern designs and hand finishing of its products, which permitted the firm to exploit new markets.

Mini Case Study 8.3 GPS technology: a threat to minds and safety?

With technology rapidly replacing mechanical and, by extension, basic cognitive function, the now ubiquitous nature of technology pervades our everyday lives and shapes the ways in which people receive and manage information to make decisions. This raises the question of the extent to which people rely on and trust technology in their day to day decision making processes. An insightful example is our growing reliance on global positioning system (GPS) or satellite navigation (satnav) systems. By 2015, global sales of navigation systems had exceeded 34 million (see Figure 8.4).

A study by University College London (McKinlay 2016) found that participants who navigated the streets of London from memory had greater spikes of activity in their brain than those who relied on satnavs for guidance. This is important as, according to McKinlay (2016), our natural sense of navigation is a 'use-it-or-lose-it' ability, and over-reliance on GPS devices can therefore have a negative impact on the cognitive skills needed for planned decision making. This principle, of course, can be applied to other forms of technology that reduce the need for brain power, for example, the use of smartphones to conduct basic arithmetic. While technology is generally intended to make our lives easier, over-reliance on it can have a diminishing effect on brain power and skills that were traditionally developed and refined through one's need to cope, before the ubiquitous availability of technology.

A study of 2,000 motorists commissioned by black cab app, mytaxi, found that a quarter of respondents admitted to now relying on satnav for journeys that they would previously have made without the aid of technology, and half of respondents said that they zone out and barely even notice road signs when using satnav. Concurring with McKinlay's (2016) findings, 26% of the respondents reflected that their navigational skills have declined as a consequence of relying on GPS devices (GloucestershireLive 2017). According to McKinlay (2016), when it comes to selecting the most appropriate routes, human judgement continues to outwit technology. But there are a number of high profile instances of people trusting GPS technology over basic judgement and common sense. On some occasions drivers have continued to trust their satnav instructions even when prompted otherwise by their human passengers, and this has led to numerous instances of drivers ending up in fields, rivers, and even in the wrong country. More seriously, in 2011 a judge ruled that over-reliance on satnav, and its effect on a driver's thinking, contributed to the death of a motorcyclist. The judge commented that insufficient attention was paid to the reality of the road ahead and that the driver's manoeuvre was 'fraught with danger' (*Daily Mail* 2011).

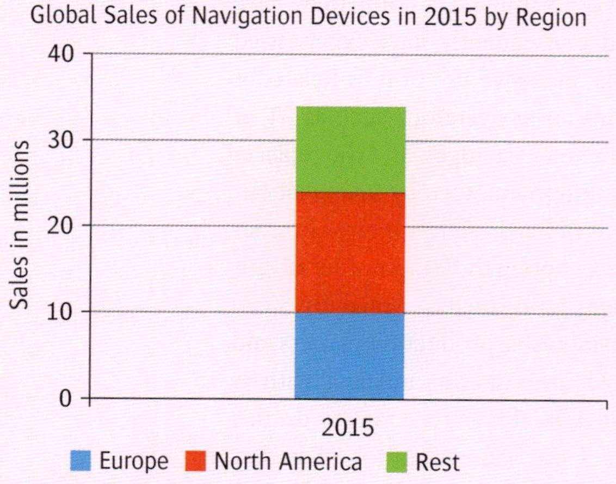

Figure 8.4 Global sales of navigation devices in 2015 by region

Global Sales of Navigation Devices in 2015 by Region

Questions

1. How is advancing technology affecting employees' cognitive skills?

2. Do employees now rely so heavily on workplace technologies that this affects their ability to carry out jobs that once would have been easily achievable through brain power alone?

3. How can employees ensure that they maintain a sense of reality and common sense while at the same time embracing the technology available to them?

Source: Statista (n.d. c)

Technology can facilitate job redesign and change the pattern of skills required by business (see Counterpoint 8.2). ICT in the newspaper industry has led to a disappearance of the traditional skills of the printer and a reduction in labour costs. Printing was a job traditionally done by a highly unionized workforce with skills being built up over a period of five or more years. These days, news information is keyed in by the journalist via the computer, while photographs and advertisements are input by less skilled workers, which means that employers do not have to pay the same levels of wages and salaries. ICT also enhances the ability of business to monitor and control what is going in the workplace. Take for example call centres. Management can monitor the number of calls workers take, how long it takes to deal with customers, what is said in the conversation with clients, and the outcomes; for example, how successfully staff exploit sales opportunities and the length of time staff are logged off on breaks. They can use the data to evaluate the performance of individual employees, or teams, and also for the call centre as a whole. Similarly, such technology can make it easier for firms to monitor employees who are working from home, or workers whose job entails them moving from one location to another, such as salesmen or lorry drivers.

ICT can be used to improve internal communications. E-mail, wikis, and blogs (a blog is an online diary or journal) can be used cheaply and easily to reach thousands of employees simultaneously. Investment banks like Dresdner Kleinwort, and law firms such as Allen & Overy, introduced blogging to facilitate communication, and to allow online collaboration. In firms such as Motorola and Apple, workers are encouraged to use computers to exchange information and engage in problem-solving, which is a feature of a so-called 'learning organization' (Pedler et al. 1988).

Technology can improve existing products or create new goods and services, and consequently enable the firm to expand or penetrate new markets. Danish firm, Lego, is a good example of a firm using technology to revive a flagging product: the toy building brick. The brick is now sold with electronic technology allowing customers to build a range of moving robots. In addition, a firm with a powerful technological position in one product may be able to oblige purchasers of that product to buy related products, thus generating additional income. For example, Microsoft consumers can only use Microsoft games in their Microsoft Xbox, and these games cannot be used in a Sony PlayStation (such behaviour could be seen as anti-competitive and attract the interest of the regulatory authorities—see Chapter 10, Competition Law).

Technology makes it increasingly easy to build a global organization to integrate economic activity in many widely separated locations. Technology has thus facilitated the rapid growth of the multinational corporation with subsidiaries in many countries, but with business strategies, production, and distribution still being determined and controlled by head office in a single nation. Therefore, MNCs like Unilever are able to employ more than 160,000 people and sell its products in 170 countries (Unilever n.d.).

Learning Task

This task requires you to examine links between R&D expenditure and company performance.

Improved performance arising from technology can enhance a company's share performance. The R&D Scoreboard suggests that share prices (and sales growth) in companies with the highest R&D ➡

→ intensity perform better than the average. The list below, taken from the 2013 EU Scoreboard, shows R&D expenditure in large UK-based firms as a percentage of sales revenue.

• Vodafone (telecoms)	0.7 per cent
• AstraZeneca (pharmaceuticals and biotech)	15.9 per cent
• Delphi (automobiles)	7.7 per cent
• MISYS (software)	26.1 per cent
• Royal Dutch Shell (energy)	0.3 per cent

1. Choose a high spending and a low spending company from this list. Construct a graph of changes in their share prices over the last five years.

2. Comment on the relative share performance of the two companies. Identify a range of technological and other factors that could have influenced their share price.

Technology can make it easier for small firms to compete with large. The internet, for example, enables all firms to market their goods and services nationally and internationally. Small companies can design their own websites at relatively low cost. SMEs producing for niche markets can use the Web to reach customers who are of little interest to titan distributors such as Wal-Mart. eBay, for example, provides opportunities for small firms to compete with larger firms. In the United States, the biggest music retailer is Wal-Mart but it is only interested in carrying the biggest hits and cannot afford to carry a CD or DVD that sells only a handful of copies a year. The Web offers firms the opportunity to tap into customers interested in the 'non-hits'; and, in some areas, non-hits can often be a bigger market than the best sellers.

Exclusive control of technology can give firms the ability to freeze out competitors by excluding them from using the same knowledge or techniques. That is why, in industries such as pharmaceuticals, IT hardware, and software, firms readily apply for patents that, if granted, will give them control of a technology. Microsoft, in 2013, filed for around 3,000 patents when in 1990 it received a mere five (US Patents and Trademark Office 2014). To secure profits companies may deliberately set out to hoard patents purely to frustrate rivals by preventing them from getting access to new technology. Apple was particularly effective in freezing out competition when it set up iTunes. The company made it technically impossible for songs bought on iTunes to be played on competitors' equipment. Both iTunes and the iPod won a market share of about 80 per cent in the USA and the UK, as well as a substantial market share in many European countries. The iPod's strong market position gave Apple the bargaining power to strike a deal with the four biggest record companies to sell songs through iTunes for around 54 pence each. The agreement was widely seen as a defeat for record companies.

Another tactic used by large corporations to exclude rivals is to get their technical standards accepted as the norm. Microsoft has done this very successfully by managing to get Windows accepted as the standard computer operating system, and then bundling in additional software such as Internet Explorer, which makes it very difficult for rival browsers to get a foothold in the market. Microsoft's dominance in operating systems has been subject to intense scrutiny by regulatory bodies, particularly in the EU and the USA. Licensing can also be used to control the diffusion of a firm's technology. For example, Microsoft went in for extensive licensing of its patented technology when growth in its core products started to slow down, and the US wireless technology firm, Qualcomm, earned around US$2 billion in licensing revenues in 2013 (SEC 10K filing).

Threats and Challenges

While technology offers many opportunities for business, it can also pose many threats and challenges. Firms have to prepare for, and learn to cope with, new technologies. They must also take advantage of the opportunities offered by technology to devise new forms of industrial organization, new consumer goods, and to exploit new markets. If firms are not properly prepared, then new technologies can cause them to go out of business. Schumpeter (1976) called this the process of creative destruction. He argued that innovation over a period of time, by bringing in new products, new sources of supply, and new types of organization, could create a form of competition that strikes not simply at profits and market shares, but also at their very existence.

Schumpeter's notion of creative destruction is neatly encapsulated by the chief executive of Procter & Gamble, who said: 'People ask me what I lose sleep over. If somebody announced an alternative to solution chemistry (i.e. washing powder) for laundry, all of a sudden I've got an US$11 billion business that's at risk' (*Financial Times* 22 December 2005). HMV, the UK music retailer, underestimated the threat from online competition, both in terms of physical CDs and in music downloading. Sales fell sharply, its share price was undermined, and in 2013 it went into administration. A classic case of creative destruction was Kodak, which was severely punished for reacting too late to important advances in digital photographic technology. It was a very profitable global leader in the production of traditional cameras, film, and photographic paper. In the 2000s, disruptive digital technology began to wreak havoc on Kodak's business. As sales of digital cameras zoomed, Kodak's sales plummeted. It took until 2003 for Kodak to recognize the problem and embark on a digital strategy. In the process, it closed several factories, cutting tens of thousands of jobs.

Even firms sitting on comfortable monopoly positions can find such positions threatened by new technology. The telecommunications industry is a case in point, where national monopolists such as BT, Deutsche Telekom, and France Telecom, who owned networks of telephone lines, found themselves under severe attack from mobile phone companies and from firms using satellite systems. As in telecommunications, competitive threats may not arise from within the existing boundaries of an industry. Companies like Amazon, using the Web as a new business model, have made a significant impact on traditional book retailers, like UK-based Waterstones.

In the travel industry, the internet has pitted travel agents and established airlines against online providers. Skyscanner and Expedia, for example, have shaken up the travel booking business, while low cost airlines such as Ryanair has used the internet to cut the costs of their reservation system, which has made the company more price competitive, and has forced their established rivals, such as British Airways, to extend their online reservation service. But technological advancement for airlines is not confirmed to the travel booking business. Sophisticated technology and automation has also transformed the job of airline pilots, with both positive and negative consequences.

Mini Case Study 8.4 Automation and commercial aviation

Figure 8.5 Annual growth in global air traffic passenger demand from 2007 to 2017

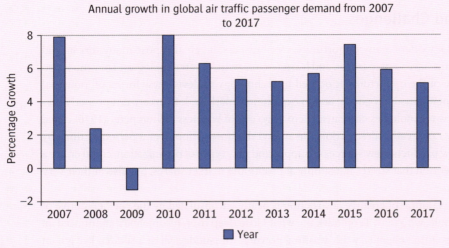

Source: Statista (n.d. d)

The airline industry continues to be transformed by competition and technological change. The exponential growth of low cost carriers, in particular, has forced airlines to reduce operating costs to remain competitive. Since the crash of 2008, there has been a growth in passenger demand for air travel (see Figure 8.5).

Alongside competition and cost pressures, technological advancement has also impacted on the skills needed by professionals to carry out their jobs (refer to Counterpoint Box 8.2). A notable example is that of commercial airline pilots. Modern aircraft are now equipped with highly sophisticated technology which, on the one hand, greatly increases their efficiency and safety. On the other hand, however, pilots reported through a series of 28 in-depth interviews (Maxwell and Grant 2016) that technology is impacting both positively and negatively on their jobs. For example: 'with the technology that's now available in a jet aircraft we generally don't need to worry much about manual flying skills in respect of the fact that we can simply programme the autopilot. We have all these tools available to us to just simply make aircraft fly the way that we want them to', according to a pilot. Indeed, pilots reflected that most airlines are now insistent on the use of autopilot, and while in efficiency and safety terms this is beneficial, there are corresponding implications for pilots' work and skills. According to one pilot:

'soon we will have an electronic flight bag where you have a laptop, and everything that's on the flight deck now will be on the laptop or tablet'. This raises interesting concerns about the changing skills requirements for trainee pilots, and their subsequent ability to fly without the aid of technology should the need arise. An experienced pilot suggested that: 'the new recruits tend to have more of an X-box, Nintendo mentality, it's all about computers and they're up close with automation, not real flying'.

From a work psychology perspective, this increasing use of technology and automation brings additional challenges in the form of repetition and boredom for pilots while on the flight deck. For instance, a pilot commented that: 'long hours of doing nothing other than checking instruments is a constant challenge . . . when you have an hour or two of boredom, sitting doing virtually nothing other than monitoring systems, you're not physically working your brain'. According to Pekrun et al. (2010), boredom arises from monotonous and repetitive job activities which require minimal thought and attention. Linking boredom to pilots' concentration, another pilot highlighted that: 'complacency and monotonous repetitive flights can lull you into a false sense of security, and you don't notice changes quickly enough'. Therefore, it is important to also consider potentially negative aspects ➔

→ of technological advancement. While automation increases efficiency and technical safety, and reduces the job demands placed on pilots, it also has a crucial impact on pilots' subjective concentration and critical decision-making ability. Boredom was highlighted by most pilots as a: 'downside of the job that we have to put up with if we want aircraft to be flown automatically'.

Questions

1. To what extent has automation de-professionalised the work of airline pilots?
2. How might deskilling and boredom through technology and automation be reduced?
3. What advice could be given to other professional occupational groups that may be at risk of deskilling through advancing technology?

Is R&D a Guarantee of Success?

Conventional wisdom assumes that company spending on R&D is a good thing, with the implied assumption that it will lead to innovative success. According to this view, the more a company spends on research the better the result is. But Burton Malkiel, an economics professor at Princeton and a company director in the biotechnology industry, described the risks rather colourfully, calling biotechnology a 'crapshoot' and going on to say that: 'Even biotech companies themselves don't know which one is going to make it' (*Financial Times* 3 July 2007).

However, R&D is an input and its impact, like any other input, such as labour and machinery, depends on how efficiently it is deployed. The productivity of R&D expenditure in terms of new products and processes is determined by the quality of the inputs, and those who are managing it. Consequently, there is no automatic correlation between high R&D spending and company performance.

In a study of nearly 70,000 US firms, Ehie and Olibe (2010) found that R&D expenditures had a persistently positive effect on market value for both manufacturing and service firms, with a more pronounced effect on manufacturing. By contrast, a survey of the world's top 1,000 R&D companies by Jaruzelski and Dehoff (2010) failed to find any significant relationship between R&D spending and business success, as measured by growth in sales, profit, the value of the firm on the stock market, or total shareholder return. The top 10 per cent of R&D spenders enjoyed no consistent performance advantage over companies that spent less on R&D. However, the survey did find that companies spending relatively little on R&D significantly underperformed compared with their competitors. Jaruzelski similarly reported in 2013 that business performance of the top R&D spenders did not match that of companies like Apple, with its iMac, iPod, iTunes, and iBook, who spent less but were classed as more innovative. Pantagakis et al. (2012) found that the market value of EU computer companies was maximized when they spent 41 per cent of their revenues on R&D. The market value of firms decreased when R&D exceeded that figure.

Mini Case Study 8.5 The global crisis and R&D

The 2008 global financial crisis caused a decline in global investment. A modest recovery in investment can been seen in 2017, with digital development in particular now providing a major challenge and impacting heavily on global patterns of investment (UNCTAD 2017) (refer also to Table 8.3 which lists the Top 10 global companies by R&D expenditure). →

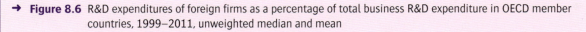

→ **Figure 8.6** R&D expenditures of foreign firms as a percentage of total business R&D expenditure in OECD member countries, 1999–2011, unweighted median and mean

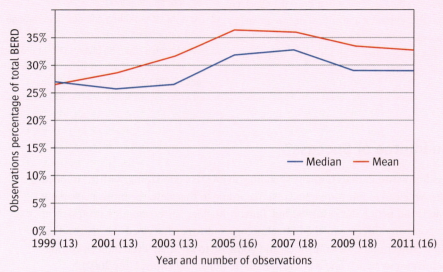

Sources: Dachs and Zahradnik (2014); NCTAD (2017)

Dachs and Zahradnik (2014) reported that the global crisis, after three decades of increasing spending on foreign R&D, led MNCs, the driving force for diffusion, to cut back. The increasing share of foreign firms in total R&D expenditure in almost all countries was brought to a halt by the global financial crisis starting in 2007. They report that foreign firms' R&D was more affected by the crisis than the research spending of domestic firms, and that the downward trend continued until 2010, but then started to recover (see Figure 8.6). US MNCs, the largest overseas investors in R&D, saw a drop in expenditure abroad from about $42 billion to $39 billion between 2008 and 2009, but bounced back to $46 billion in 2010. The main losers from the fall in US R&D were EU countries, but not Asia. Belgium, Sweden, the Czech Republic, and Spain were particularly affected by the fall in inward R&D. By contrast, France, Poland, and the UK bucked the trend. The World Intellectual Property Organization (WIPO) (2013) reported that, with the global crisis, patent filings worldwide fell by about 4 per cent in 2009.

Reasons for the cutbacks in foreign R&D were probably due to MNCs being more dependent on exports than domestic firms. During the crisis, exports and FDI contracted more rapidly than domestic markets. This is likely to have caused MNCs to be pessimistic about future market growth and led to a reduction in R&D expenditure. The OECD (2012) reports that innovative and high-tech businesses suffered particularly badly with the drop in demand for higher quality innovative products, which is characteristic of recessions. It also suggested that the crisis in the banking system could have affected the ability of innovative business to raise external finance. Since MNCs also tend to operate their main R&D activities at home, they may be more reluctant to retrench there.

Question

Explain why US MNCs cut back their R&D hard in EU countries, but not Asia.

Learning Task

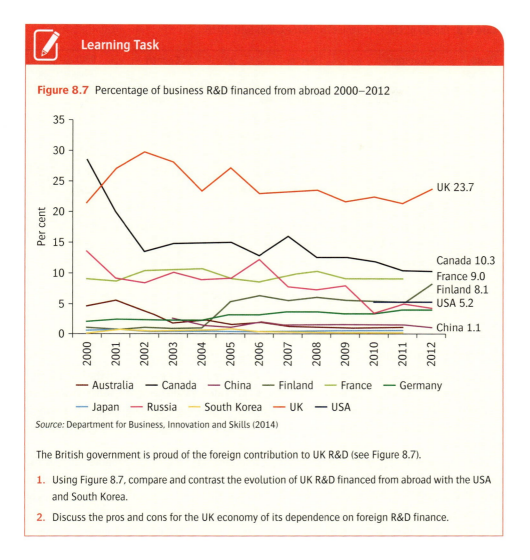

Figure 8.7 Percentage of business R&D financed from abroad 2000–2012

Source: Department for Business, Innovation and Skills (2014)

The British government is proud of the foreign contribution to UK R&D (see Figure 8.7).

1. Using Figure 8.7, compare and contrast the evolution of UK R&D financed from abroad with the USA and South Korea.

2. Discuss the pros and cons for the UK economy of its dependence on foreign R&D finance.

Protecting Technology

Bill Gates underpins the importance of technology on corporate success when he claims that: 'it has become imperative for chief executives to have not just a general understanding of the intellectual property issues facing their business and their industry, but to have quite a refined expertise relating to those issues' (*Financial Times* 12 November 2004). The globalization of markets means that firms have to look for protection not just at home but also abroad. In an economy where technology is so important to company performance the titans of info-capitalism spends much time and effort in protecting its IP and in pursuing those who infringe it. The external environment offers organizations the possibility of protecting their codifiable technology.

Table 8.3 Top 10 global companies by R&D expenditure, 2016

Rank (2016)	Company	Sector	Country	R&D ()Bn
1	Volkswagen	Automobiles	Germany	13.2
2	Samsung	Electronics	S. Korea	12.7
3	Amazon	Software and internet	USA	12.5
4	Alphabet	Software and internet	USA	12.3
5	Intel Co	Electronics	USA	12.1
6	Microsoft	Software and internet	USA	12.0
7	Roche	Health care	Switzerland	10.0
8	Novartis	Health care	Switzerland	9.5
9	Johnson & Johnson	Health care	USA	9.0
10	Toyota	Automobiles	Japan	8.8

Source: The 2017 Global Innovation 1000 Study, https://www.strategyand.pwc.com/innovation1000#GlobalKey FindingsTabs3

Methods of Protection

In richer countries, the owners of IPRs are normally accorded the protection of the law. Legally, the IP system covers five areas (see below), aims to provide legal protection against counterfeiters and copiers, and is vital in many fields, such as music, film, biotechnology, and nanotechnology, and in consumer goods where branding is important in gaining and retaining competitive advantage.

When firms come up with a commercially exploitable idea for a new product, such as the iPod, they will often apply for a patent. Patents can be granted on new inventions for a period of up to 20 years in the UK, Germany, Japan, and the USA. Designs comprise the characteristics of the product, such as the shape, pattern, and colour, and the law allows companies to prevent others using their designs. Trademarks comprise any signs capable of being represented graphically, particularly words, designs, letters, numerals, the shape of goods, or of their packaging, provided that such signs are capable of distinguishing the goods or services of one firm from those of other businesses. Thus, brand names like Perrier or Persil, or logos such as the Nike swish, can be protected.

To protect the intellectual property contained in this textbook, the publisher has taken out a copyright on the text. As well as book publishers, film, television, and music companies can take out a copyright on original dramatic, musical, artistic works, sound recordings, films, and television broadcasts that they have produced and, more controversially, firms can also copyright information on genetic data. So, music by Shakira or Coldplay, and television programmes such as *Game of Thrones* or *Breaking Bad* can be protected, as can cartoon characters such as Disney's Buzz Lightyear and Mickey Mouse.

Industrial espionage involves the theft of a firm's secret information, which is normally protected by the law. A striking example of attempted espionage concerned Coca-Cola, which treats its product formulae as closely guarded secrets. An employee at its headquarters tried to steal a sample of a secret new product with the intention of selling it to Coke's bitter rival, Pepsi. Pepsi, refusing to take advantage of this, reported the approach to Coke, who called in the police. The employee was charged with unlawfully stealing and selling trade secrets. WIPO (2013) reports a steady growth in patenting activity particularly in the areas of computer technology, digital communications, nanotechnology, electrical machinery, and energy, especially relating to green technology.

Problems in Protecting Technology

Even though large firms in developed economies usually enjoy a degree of legal protection for their technology, SMEs may still encounter problems in protecting their IPRs. The cost of filing a patent can be high and can vary considerably from one country to another. It is, for example, more expensive to obtain patent protection across Europe than in the USA. The EU Commission calculated that obtaining a patent across the EU cost €36,000. However, the unitary patent system, agreed in 2012, reduces the cost to around €5,000, compared with €2,000 in the USA and €500 in China.

Multiple applications must be made in different countries to get legal protection. Patent applications usually have to be translated into the language of the country where the patent is to be registered. Getting highly technical application documents translated into various languages, such as Standard Chinese, can be a costly exercise. In 2013, the Global Patent Prosecution Highway pilot scheme was announced, giving multinational protection for patents across 30 countries including North America, several European countries, Australia, Japan, and South Korea (WIPO 1 June 2014). A further complication is differing protection periods in countries. In Japan, for example, designs are protected for 15 years, but in the USA, owners of copyright are given 95 years, while the period in the EU is 70 years. The application time from applying to granting a patent will generally take more than 12 months, and that time period may be further extended where the law provides for other parties to oppose the granting of the patent. Enforcement problems can also exist. In the event that firms have to pursue infringements through various national courts, this can be time-consuming and expensive, and can vary country by country. In the USA, enforcing a patent through the courts can cost millions of dollars. In some countries, the level of legal protection is either low, or non-existent, or the authorities do not enforce the law. China is a particular source of concern in this regard, and is berated regularly by the US authorities for its lax enforcement of IPRs.

While the issues outlined above can pose challenges for corporations, it can make it virtually impossible for SMEs to protect their technology. The consequence of all these issues is that the system excludes small businesses because they cannot afford to defend their IP in court.

Counterpoint Box 8.3 Is info-technology compatible with capitalism?

Economist and journalist Paul Mason (2016) examines the cyclical pattern of capitalism and how it generally adapts to new clusters of technological innovations. Combining political economy and classical social theory, he sketches the emergence of a new economic paradigm—postcapitalism—partly instigated by innovations in ICT. His central argument is that info-technology not only challenges traditional classical economics but, moreover, that capitalism, which he characterizes as a complex, learning organism, has reached the limits of its capacity to adapt and mutate.

The basic logic of capitalism, argues Mason, is to drive technological innovation. In wave-theory, each economic upswing is fuelled by investment in new technologies—steam-power, electricity, computers—but the technological innovation of today's society, info-tech, is different from previous technologies and is not compatible with capitalism. Information has a spontaneous tendency to dissolve markets, destroy ownership and breakdown the relationship between paid work and wages. In classical economics markets are based on scarcity. However, because information is

abundant it 'destroys the normal price mechanism' (p. 118). For example, the largest information product globally is Wikipedia, which is produced and maintained by 27,000 volunteers, for free labour, depriving the advertising industry of billions of pounds a year in revenue and destroying the encyclopaedia business. Thus, ICT has 'robbed market forces of their ability to create dynamism' (p. 30). Mason argues that clusters of info-tech offer the possibility of forging a more socially just and sustainable economy. Critics argue that this scenario is overly optimistic (see Horton 2015).

Sources: Mason, P. (2016) *Postcapitalism: A Guide to our Future*, London: Penguin; Horton, S. (2015) Murray, D. (2015)

Questions

1. What do you think of Mason's central argument? If Mason is correct, what is the impact on business?
2. How is the use of info-technology different, and what definitions of technology covered in this chapter help us explain these potential differences?

● CHAPTER SUMMARY

In this chapter we have suggested that advances in technology are a thoroughly social phenomenon. We have shown how business can commercially exploit technology. The sources of new ideas on which companies can call are many and varied, ranging from universities and research institutes to competitors, customers and suppliers, and employees.

We have explained that industrial capitalism has gone through long cycles driven by technological innovations. The Russian economist Nikolai Kondratieff observed that beyond short-term business cycles, a 50-year pattern whose turning points coincide with major technological changes—steam-power, electricity, computers—and conflicts within capitalism.

Globalization and technology make foreign sources of new ideas more accessible and have made it easier for business to tap in to foreign sources through, for example, cross-border R&D partnerships.

Innovations tend to be concentrated in big firms operating in the high-tech manufacturing sector. The rate of innovation varies from firm to firm, sector by sector, and country to country. Firms are motivated to innovate by increasingly fierce competition from rivals, both domestic and foreign, other elements in the supply chain, developments in the ICT sector, and the policies pursued by governments.

Technology offers opportunities to business organizations to increase their profits and growth, through the introduction of new and improved goods and services, and through changes to their production processes. Technology also helps firms to restructure their global patterns of production through investment in low cost locations, or by sub-contracting to cheaper suppliers. However, as we have seen with Kodak, technology can also pose threats and challenges for firms, particularly if they allow themselves to fall behind their competitors. Technological advance, because it involves change in products or production processes, is a risky business, particularly for firms that do not manage change well.

Finally, the external environment offers business the means to protect its IP, although the degree and cost of protection can vary significantly from one country to another. In countries like China, and some other South East Asian countries, where the level of protection is low, there are significant problems with the theft of IPRs, the counterfeiting of goods, and the piracy of films, music, and books. Attempts to provide protection internationally have been slow to progress and are relatively underdeveloped. Industries and firms differ in the extent to which they protect their IP, with companies in the IT and electronic sectors having a high propensity to protect their technology compared with firms in the car industry.

● REVIEW QUESTIONS

1. Explain the difference between material technology and social technology. Why is it important to make the distinction between 'sustaining' and 'disruptive' technologies?

2. What is the substance of the claims by economists since the 1930s, such as Kondratieff, Schumpeter, Perez and others, regarding technology and cycles of economic growth?

3. 'If we do not understand how complex technologies function then their potential is more easily captured by selfish elites and corporations' (Bridle 2018: 3). Explain.

4. Discuss how multinational companies could contribute to the global diffusion of technology. Illustrate your answer with examples.

● ASSIGNMENT TASKS

1. It is claimed that big data can generate lots of benefits for business.

   a. What is big data?

   b. Explain how mobile telecoms companies like China Telecom are in a strong position to benefit from big data. Illustrate your answer with examples.

   c. Explain how large, global retailers can take advantage of big data. Consider the types of data that are most beneficial to global retailers.

   d. Discuss the issues around privacy and data security faced by competitive organizations and how they might deal with them.

2. You are working as a researcher for a white-collar union. Prepare a research paper analyzing the extent to which technological advancement may be deprofessionalizing jobs and deskilling the contemporary workforce?

Case Study: The rise of Apple and fall of RIM

© Shutterstock.com/JS14

In wave-theory each long business cycle is fueled by investment in new technology. It is plausible to argue that ICT technology is the prime driver of firm performance and, indeed, macro-economic growth in the early 21st century. Indeed, since 2007 the exponential growth in ICT technology has become the distinguishing technology of our time.

However, as explained in this chapter, there are key analytical limitations of this simple cause- and-effect approach to technological change. First of all, the inconsistency in establishing the direction of causation, and second, the mediating effects of other key variables, not least human action, economics and, notably, the state. The 2008 global financial crisis compelled firms to innovate to survive, and wiped out those that failed to adapt or made wrong strategic decisions. Once unassailable firms can become vulnerable. That a simple linear cause-and-effect technological determinant is not an adequate theory of firm behaviour is illustrated by examining the performance of two North American technology companies: Apple, and Research in Motion (BlackBerry).

Apple, the giant US IT company headquartered in California, was founded by a trio of young entrepreneurs, Steve Jobs, Steve Wozniak, and Ronald Wayne, in April 1976, and was incorporated as Apple Computer, Inc. in 1977. Apple develops, manufactures, and markets mobile communication and media devices, personal computers, and portable digital music players, and sells related software and services. Apple's hardware products include the Mac personal computer, the iPad tablet computer, the iPod portable media player, the Apple smartwatch, and the iPhone smartphone. The company's software includes the iOS operating systems, the MacOS, the Safari web browser, and iTunes media player.

In 2007, Apple's net income was US$3.5 billion. In 2015, it was US$53.4 billion, and it became the first trillion-dollar

Table 8.4 Apple's performance 2005–2016

	2005	2006	2007	2008	2009	2010	2011	2012	2013	2014	2015	2016
Net income (US$B)	1.3	2.0	3.5	6.1	8.2	14.0	25.9	41.7	37.0	39.5	53.4	45.7
R&D expenditure ($B)	0.5	0.7	0.8	1.1	1.3	1.8	2.4	3.4	4.4	6.0	7.9	10.4
R&D/ Sales (%)	3.8	3.7	3.2	3.0	3.6	2.7	2.2	2.0	2.6	3.3	3.4	3.7
iPhone unit sales (m)			1.0	12	21	40	72	125	150	169	231	216

Pre iPhone

Post iPhone

Source: Statista (n.d. d); https://www.apple.com/newsroom/pdfs/Q4FY16DataSummary.pdf   ➜

→ corporation in August 2018. The company operates 496 retail stores, in 21 countries, and employs 116,000 full-time employees, as of March 2017. In 2016, Apple's worldwide annual revenue totalled US$215.6 billion. Table 8.4 shows Apple's performance before and after the launch of iPhone in 2007.

With the exception of two years, 2013 and 2014, Apple has seen significant rates of net income over the period. In 2015, iPhone sales generated US$155 billion in revenue, and had become the most important product in Apple's portfolio. In fact, if Apple were only selling iPhones, it would be in the top ten companies in the Fortune 500 list of companies.

Many see Apple as a technological pioneer. An IT journalist put it like this:

> While all the other technology firms were churning out products with all the wow factor of a tumble dryer, Apple set out to change the world with innovative computers and gadgets, again and again and again ... Apple products have revolutionized the way we work and play and listen to music. (techradar.computing 10 March 2013)

The author illustrated his claim by identifying innovative products that had changed human behaviour, including the iMac personal computer, first introduced in 1998, the iPhone (2007), iPod + iTunes (2003), the Apps Store (2008), and iPad (2010). Apple sees itself as operating in highly competitive global markets characterized by aggressive price cutting and downward pressure on gross margins, frequent introduction of new products, short product life cycles, changing industry standards, continual improvement in product price/performance characteristics, rapid adoption of technological and product advancements by competitors, and price sensitivity on the part of consumers.

To remain competitive, Apple needs to develop and market innovative new hardware, software, and service technologies. As a result, it claims to give great importance to investment in R&D and to the need to protect its IP with numerous patents, copyrights, and trademarks, and also through litigation against rivals both in the USA and internationally. In 2015, Apple was awarded 1,938 US patents, placing it 11th overall in newly earned inventions. There is an apparent paradox here because Apple does not spend as much as some of its main competitors on R&D. While Apple spent 2.6 cent of sales revenue in 2013, the figure for Google was 13.2 per cent (see Table 8.5). In 2016, however Apple spent $10.39 billion on R&D in 2016, a 32 per cent increase from 2015, which was 3.7 per cent of sales revenue.

Nevertheless, Apple is still seen by some as the world's most innovative company (strategy& 2017). In 2017, Tim Cook, Apple's CEO, attempted to counter claims that Apple was not being sufficiently innovative by giving detailed comments about Apple's top-secret driverless car project. Cook disclosed in a TV interview that:

> We're focusing on autonomous systems (self-driving cars). We sort of see it as the mother of all AI (artificial intelligence) projects. (Davies and Hern 2017)

Table 8.5 The ten biggest R&D spenders, 2013

	(US$bn)	% of revenue
Volkswagen (Germany)	13.5	5.2
Samsung (South Korea)	13.4	6.4
Intel (US)	10.6	20.1
Microsoft (US)	10.4	13.4
Roche (Swiss)	10.0	19.0
Novartis (Swiss)	9.9	16.8
Toyota (Japan)	9.1	3.5
Johnson & Johnson (US)	8.2	11.5
Google (US)	8.0	13.2
Merck (US)	7.5	17.0

Source: Fortune (2013)

→ The mediating effect of other key variables, notably, the state, has contributed to the global success of Apple. Mazzucato (2013), for instance, argues that Apple would not have been a global success without the investment and intervention of governments. In support of her claim, she points to the equity investment put in by a US federal agency in the early stages of Apple's development. Second, she highlights Apple's access to technology resulting from government research programmes in publicly funded institutions—the iPod, with its tiny but enormous capacity hard drives, owes its existence to the invention, by two European research scientists, of giant magnetoresistance (GMR). She claims that this allowed Apple to take on Sony, and to recover from a long period of stagnant growth. Multi-touch screens were developed at the publicly funded University of Delaware. Mazzucato also identifies military projects and state purchases of goods and services as being important factors in Apple's success. Lastly, she says that the US government played a critical role in protecting the IP of US tech companies against foreign violations, and in ensuring their access to foreign consumer markets. Mazzucato concludes that Apple's success is mainly because of its ability to: 'ride the wave of massive State investments in the 'revolutionary' technologies that underpinned the iPhone, and iPad: the internet, GPS, touch-screen displays and communication technologies' (2013: 88).

In contrast to Apple's phenomenal success, the Canadian technology company Research in Motion (RIM) became a casualty of the new supercycle of innovation. BlackBerry Limited is a Canadian based information technology company, specializing in enterprise software and the 'internet of things'. Two engineering students, Mike Lazaridis and Douglas Fregin, founded BlackBerry as Research In Motion (RIM) in 1984. In 1988, RIM became the first wireless data technology developer in North America. The company is best known to the general public as the former designer and manufacturer of the BlackBerry smartphones and tablets. In 1994, RIM received the Emmy Award for Technical Innovation and the KPMG High Technology Award. However, following the collapse of sales, it transitioned to an enterprise software and services company in the 2000s. Its software products are used worldwide by various businesses, carmakers, and government agencies.

The arrival of Apple's iPhone caused a dramatic slowdown in RIM growth and a decline in sales, most notably in the US. This led to negative media and analyst sentiment over the company's ability to continue as an independent company. Sales of the BlackBerry peaked in 2011, when almost 70 million subscribers were using the device. By 2015, only 46 million of the 198.9 million US smartphone users were using BlackBerry, compared to 87.32 million or 43.9 per cent on Apple's iPhone.

Table 8.6 RIM/BlackBerry's performance 2005–15

	2005	2006	2007	2008	2009	2010	2011	2012	2013	2014	2015	2016
Global sales (US$M)*	1.4	2.1	3.0	6.0	11.0	15.0	20.0	18.4	11.0	6.8	3.3	
Net income (US$M)	n/a	n/a	907	1731	2722	3507	4739	1497	(1235)	(7163)	(423)	
Blackberry users (M)	2.5	4.9	8.0	14.0	25.0	41.0	70.0	77.0	79.0	69.0	46.0	
R&D expenditure (US$M)	n/a	n/a	n/a	n/a	685	965	1351	1556	1509	1286	711	
R&D/Sales (%)	n/a	n/a	n/a	n/a	6.3	6.4	6.5	8.3	13.6	17.1	23.3	

Pre iPhone

Post iPhone

* Note when contrasting Apple's performance, these figures are in millions, not billions

Source: Statista (n.d., e)   →

→ RIM's net income peaked in 2011, at US$4,739 million. The company sustained losses in 2013, 2014, and 2015 of US$1,235, US$7,163, and US$423, respectively. While Apple spent 2.6 cent of sales revenue on R&D in 2013, the figure for BlackBerry was 13.6 per cent, which is close to Google's expenditure on R&D. Table 8.6 shows Blackberry's performance since the introduction of Apple's iPhone.

In 2011, slowing growth prompted Blackberry to make 2,000 employees redundant, and the company restructured, changed its top executives, and changed its business strategy. In 2013, the company reported its first net loss, which resulted in a further lay-off of 5,000 employees and the delay of the new BlackBerry 10 model. The company announced that it was open to being purchased in 2013. In 2016, BlackBerry ceased in-house hardware development, and sub-contracted these roles to third-party partners in order to focus more on its software development.

BlackBerry Limited, once a symbol of Canadian IT innovation, had allowed Apple's iPhone to corner the rapidly developing apps market. There has been much analysis of Blackberry's rise and fall. First, the company faced criticism that its hardware and operating system were out-dated and unappealing compared to its main competitors. For example, it was tardy to recognize the appeal to consumers of incorporating a camera into a mobile phone. Second, analysts have criticized BlackBerry's early dual management structure. Under the original organizational configuration, Jim Balsillie oversaw marketing functions, while Mike Lazaridis oversaw technical functions. This arrangement was arguably dysfunctional, with BlackBerry operating as two companies (Marlow 2013).

Questions

1. Working as a group or on your own, prepare a report which:
   a. includes figures that chart Apple's and RIM's performance in terms of growth rates in sales and net income between 2005 and 2016.
   b. examines the unit sales performance of the Apple's and BlackBerry's iPhones.
   c. compares Apple's spending on R&D with RIM's and its other competitors.
   In the light of these comparisons, provides some explanation for Apple's success and RIM's relative demise.
2. Apple, like many of its competitors, uses litigation like a tool of competition. Research the litigation between Apple and Motorola, owned by Google. What was the issue at stake and the outcome? See Apple Inc. v. Motorola, Inc. Justia (2014).
3. Finally, discuss the importance of the mediating effects of human action, in particular the role of the state, on the rise of Apple and the fall of RIM. [Hint: compare US and Canadian R&D expenditure on military and intelligence related projects.]

● FURTHER READING

● Cavazotte, F., Heloisa, L., and Villadsen, K. (2014) 'Corporate Smart Phone: Professionals' Conscious Engagement in Escalating Work Connectivity'. *New Technology, Work and Employment* 29 (1): 72–87.

● Christensen, C. M. (2013) The Innovator's Dilemma: When New Technologies Cause Great Firms to Fail. Boston, MA: Harvard Business Review Press.

● Davies, R. and Hern, A. (2017) 'Apple Confirms Work on Self-driving Cars', *The Guardian*, 14 June, p. 23.

● Friend, D. (2013) 'RIM's Rise and Fall: A Short History of Research in Motion,' Tech Talk, 28 February. http://www.globalnews.ca/news/384832/rims-rise-and-fall-a-short-history-of-research-in-motion.

● Mazzucato, M. (2013) Innovation Union: A Europe 2000 Initiative, EU Commission; http://www. kantarworldpanel.com 27 January 2014; Apple SEC 10-K filings; http://www.uspto.gov.

- Marlow, I. (2013) 'RIM's long road to reinvent the BlackBerry', *The Globe and Mail*. Toronto, January 27th. Available at: https://www.theglobeandmail.com/globe-investor/rims-long-road-to-reinvent-the-blackberry/article7901031.

- Perlow, L.A (2012) *Sleeping with Your Smartphone: How to Break the 24/87 Habit and Change the Way You Work*. Boston, MA: Harvard Business Review Press.

● REFERENCES

Anand, N. and Daft, R.L. (2007) 'What is the Right Organization Design?'. *Organizational Dynamics*, 36(4), pp. 329–44.

Baran, P.A. and Sweezy, P.M. (1968) *Monopoly Capital: An Essay on the American Economy and Social Order*. Harmondsworth: Penguin Books.

Beckett, A. (2018) 'Post-work: Is the Job Finished?' *The Guardian*, 19 January, pp. 9–11.

Bessant, J. (2003) 'Challenges in innovation management'. In Shavinina, L.V. (ed.). *The International Handbook on Innovation* (761–74), Amsterdam: Elsevier.

Bratton, J. (2015) *Work and Organizational Behaviour* (3rd edn), London: Palgrave.

Bratton, J. and Denham, D. (2014) *Capitalism and Classical Social Theory* (2nd edn), Toronto: OTP.

Braverman, H. (1974) *Labor and Monopoly Capitalism: The Degradation of Work in the Twentieth Century*, New York: Monthly Review Press.

Brey, P. (2003) 'Theorizing Technology and Modernity'. In T. Misa, P. Brey, and A. Feenberg (eds), *Modernity and Technology*, MIT Press, 33–71.

Bridle, J. (2018) *New Dark Age: Technology and the End of the Future*, London: Verso.

Brynjolfsson, E. and McAfee, A. (2011) 'Race against the Machine'. Digital Frontier, Lexington, MA. http://b1ca250e5ed661ccf2f1da4c182123f5956a3d22aa43eb816232.r10.cf1.rackcdn.com/contentItem-5422867-40675649.

Castells, M. (1996) *The Rise of the Network Society*, Volume 1, Oxford: Blackwell.

Christensen, C.M. (2013) *The Innovator's Dilemma: When New Technologies Cause Great Firms to Fail*. Harvard, MA: Harvard Business Review Press.

Clarivate Analytics (2016) 'The Top 100 Global Innovators Report'. http://top100innovators.stateofinnovation.com/sites/default/files/content/top100/L178_Cvt_Top_100_Innovators_Report_008.pdf.

Dachs, B., Stehrer, R., and Zahradnik, G. (2014) *The Internationalisation of Business R&D*. Cheltenham: Edward Elgar Publishing.

Daily Mail (2011) 'Driver "Had Too Much Faith in Satnav" in Run Up to Death of Biker in Appalling Weather, Says Judge'. http://www.dailymail.co.uk/news/article-2080456/Judge-blames-drivers-reliance-sat-nav-jails-killing-motorcyclist.html.

Drucker, P.F. (1985) *Innovation and Entrepreneurship Practices and Principles*. New York: AMACON.

Ehie, I.C. and Olibe, K. (2010) 'The Effect of R&D Investment on Firm Value: An Examination of US Manufacturing and Service Industries'. *International Journal of Production Economics,* 128(1), 127–35.

Elliott, L. (2018) 'Robots Will Take Our Jobs: Plan Now, Before It's Too Late'. *The Guardian,* 1 February, p. 3.

European Commission (n.d.) http://ec.europa.eu/europe2020/index_en.htm.

Fortune (2013). Available at http://fortune.com/2014/11/17/top-10-research-development/.

Fox, A. (1971) *The Sociology of Work in Industry*. London: Collier Macmillan.

Franklin, U. (1990) *The Real World of Technology*. Toronto: CBC Enterprises.

Friedman, M. (2016) *A Theory of the Consumption Function*. San Francisco, CA: Pickle Partners Publishing.

GloucestershireLive (2017) 'Ridiculous Sat Nav Mishap from Gloucester Named in Nation's "most favourite"'. http://www.gloucestershirelive.co.uk/news/gloucester-news/ridiculous-sat-nav-mishap-gloucester-80671.

Gold, J., Holden, R., Stewart, J., Iles, P. and Beardwell, J. (2013) *Human Resource Development: Theory and Practice* (2nd edn.), Basingstoke: Palgrave.

Greenfield (2017) 'Rise of the machines: who is the "Internet of things" good for?' retrieved from https://

www.theguardian.com/technology/2017/jun/06/
Internet-of-things-smart-home-smart-city.

Hamel, G. and Prahalad, C.K. (1994) *Competing for the Future*. Boston, MA: Harvard Business School Press.

Hammer, M. (1997) *Beyond Reengineering*. New York: Harper Business.

Held, D., McGrew, A., Goldblatt, D., & Perraton, J. (1999). 'Global transformations'. *ReVision*, 22(2), 7-7.

Horton, S. (2015) 'Book Review: Postcapitalism'. Available at http://blogs.lse.ac.uk/lsereviewofbooks/2015/12/16/book-review-postcapitalism-a-guide-to-our-future-by-paul-mason.

Hughes, T.P. (1989) *American Genesis: A Century of Invention and Technological Enthusiasm, 1870–1970*. New York: Penguin Books.

Hutton, W. and Adonis, A. (2018) *Saving Britain*, London: Abacus.

Inagaki, K. (2018) 'Sony puts data and AI at heart of survival plan', *The Financial Times*, 24 May, p. 17.

Internet World Stats (n.d.) http://www.internetworldstats.com.

Jaruzelski, B. and Dehoff, K. (2010) 'How the Top Innovators Keep Winning'. *Strategy and Business* 61: 48.

Johnstone, S. and Ackers, P. (2015) *Finding a Voice at Work? New Perspectives on Employment Relations*. Oxford: OUP.

Justia Law (2014) 'Apple v Motorola' http://docs.justia.com/cases/federal/appellate-courts/cafc/12-1548/12-1548-2014-04-25.pdf.

Kotler, P. and Caslione, J.A. (2009) 'Chaotics: The Business of Managing and Marketing in the Age of Turbulence'. AMACOM Div American Mgmt Assn.

Latour, B. (2000) 'Technology is society made durable', pp. 41–53 in K. Grint (ed.), *Work and Society: A Reader*, Cambridge: Polity Press.

Lazonick, W. (1993) 'Learning and the dynamics of international competitive advantage', pp. 172–97 in R. Thomson (ed.), *Learning and Technological Change*, New York: St Martin's Press.

Marx, K. (1887/1970) *Capital, Volume I*. London: Lawrence & Wishart.

Mason, P. (2016) *Postcapitalism: A Guide to Our Future*. London: Penguin.

Mayer-Schönberger, V. and Cukier, K. (2014) *Learning with Big Data: The Future of Education*. Houghton Mifflin Harcourt.

Michaelson, J. (2017) 'Prepare for a New Supercycle of Innovation', *The Wall Street Journal*, 10 May, p. A19.

Maxwell, G.A. and Grant, K. (2016) 'Doors to manual and cross-check: professional and precarious aspects of commercial pilots' employment', paper presented at 34th International Labour Process Conference, 4–6 April, Berlin.

McKinlay, R. (2016) 'Technology: Use or Lose Our Navigation Skills', *Nature*, 531(7596), pp. 573–75.

MacKenzie, D. and Wajcman, J. (eds.) (1999) *The Social Shaping of Technology*, 2nd edn. Milton Keynes: OUP.

McKinsey (2013) 'Disruptive Technologies: Advances that will Transform Life, Business, and the Global Economy'. McKinsey Global Institute. Available at http://www.mckinsey.com/insights/business_technology/disruptive_technologies.

Meltzer, T. (2014) 'Computers Say Go', *The Guardian*, 16 June, p. 11.

Murray, D. (2015) 'Paul Mason's Postcapitalism is proof that the left is out of ideas'. Available at https://www.spectator.co.uk/2015/8/there-will-always-be-a-market-for-books-saying-capitalism-is-doomed.

OECD StatExtracts (n.d.) http://stats.oecd.org.

O'Reilly, T. (2005) 'What is Web 2.0?' Available at https://www.oreilly.com/pub/a/web2/archive/what-is-web-20.html.

Oxford University Innovation (n.d.) http://www.isis-innovation.com.

Pantagakis, E., Terzakis, D., and Arvanitis, S. (2012) 'R&D Investments and Firm Performance: An Empirical Investigation of the High Technology Sector (Software and Hardware) in the EU'. Working Paper, University of Crete, 21 November.

Pedler, M., Boydell, T., and Burgoyne, J. (1988) The Learning Company Project Report, Sheffield: Employment Department.

Pekrun, R., Goetz, T., Daniels, L.M., Stupnisky, R.H., and Perry, R.P. (2010) 'Boredom in Achievement Settings: Exploring Control-value Antecedents and Performance Outcomes of a Neglected Emotion'. *Journal of Educational Psychology*, 102(3), 531–49.

Perez, C. (2003) *Technological Revolutions and Financial Capital*. London: Edward Elgar Publishing.

Porter, M.E. (2008). *On Competition*. Boston, MA: Harvard Business Press.

R&D Magazine (2016) 'Global R&D Funding Forecast' https://www.iriweb.org/sites/default/files/2016GlobalR%26DFundingForecast_2.pdf.

Romer, P.M. (1990) 'Endogenous Technological Change'. *Journal of Political Economy*, 98(5, Part 2), S71–S102.

Schumpeter, J. (1939) *Business Cycles: A Theoretical. Historical, and Statistical Analysis of the Capitalist Process.* New York and London: McGraw-Hill Book Company Inc.

Statista (n.d.) http://www.statista.com.

UNCTAD (2017) World investment report 2017: investment and the digital economy, retrieved from http://unctad.org/en/PublicationsLibrary/wir2017_en.pdf.

Schumpeter, J.A. (1976 [1942]) *Capitalism, Socialism and Democracy.* Illinois: University of Illinois.

Statista (n.d., a) https://www.statista.com/statistics/471264/iot-number-of-connected-devices-worldwide.

Statista (n.d., b) https://www.statista.com/statistics/330695/number-of-smartphone-users-worldwide.

Statista (n.d., c) https://www.statista.com/statistics/276049/global-sales-of-navigation-systems-by-region.

Statista (n.d., d) https://www.statista.com/statistics/193533/growth-of-global-air-traffic-passenger-demand.

Statista (n.d., e) https://www.statista.com/statistics/267728/apples-net-income-since-2005.

Statista (2017) 'Number of Mobile Phone Users Worldwide 2013–2019'.

strategy& (2017) 'The 2017 Global Innovation 1000 Study'. http://www.strategyand.pwc.com/global/home/what-we-think/multimedia/video/mm-video_display/global-Innovation-1000-2013.

Thompson, P. (1989) *The Nature of Work: An Introduction to Debates on the Labour Process.* London: Macmillan.

Unilever (n.d.) http://www.unilever.co.uk

Wood, Z. (2018) 'How rise of robot technology threatens to terminate the British call-centre workforce.' *The Observer,* 13 May, pp. 61–2.

Wood, S. (ed.) (1982) *The Degradation of Work? Skill, De-skilling and the Labour Process,* London: Hutchinson.

Wonglimpiyarat, J. (2005). 'The Nano-revolution of Schumpeter's Kondratieff cycle'. *Technovation* 25(11), 1349–54.

CHAPTER NINE

The Political Environment

LEARNING OUTCOMES

This chapter will enable you to:

- identify and explain the functions performed by the institutions of the state;

- analyse the characteristics of different political systems and understand their importance for business;

- evaluate the arguments regarding the demise of the nation state;

- assess the importance of the state for business; and

- analyse how business can influence the state.

Case Study: Fake news, technology, and the electoral process

© 123RF.com/georgejmclittle

In 2016, Oxford dictionaries declared that their 'word of the year' was 'post-truth', defined as an adjective: 'relating to or denoting circumstances in which objective facts are less influential in shaping public opinion than appeals to emotion and personal belief'. Use of the word spiked during the referendum in the United Kingdom on membership of the European Union, and the Presidential election in the United States, and has its roots in a growing lack of trust in politicians and mainstream media. In 2016, Americans' trust in news fell to 33 per cent, according to the Reuters Institute.

The US Presidential election campaign of 2016 saw accusations of 'Fake News' made by the two main candidates. Donald Trump sought to portray the mainstream media—most TV news outlets and national newspapers—as peddling 'fake news' about him. He carried this stance on into his Presidency, characterizing them as 'enemies of the people'. However, 'fake news' stories generated and circulated largely via social media, including Facebook and Twitter, have been the main focus of growing concern. Much of the activity has been spread through memes shared on blogs and Facebook, through Twitter bots, and through YouTube channels, and has been traced to originators in several countries, including Macedonia and Russia. One notorious example was 'Pizzagate', which resulted in a man entering a Washington pizza restaurant he believed to be at the centre of a conspiracy, brandishing a firearm. This arose from a baseless rumour, which was spread online, that the pizzeria was the base of a child sex ring, involving senior members of Hillary Clinton's campaign team. The origin of the rumour was in turn a baseless belief about the contents of emails, following the hacking and leaking of the email account of John Podesta, Hillary Clinton's campaign chairman.

In the US, an influential provider of 'alternative' news stories has been Breitbart News, an online source and strong supporter of the Trump campaign. Breitbart had 45m unique followers over 31 days during the election period, but its stories were shared many times over on social media. Its founder, Steve Bannon, went on to be named as Chief Strategist in Trump's administration. In addition, questions have been raised about Russian government involvement in the generation of these stories. Valery Gerasimov, chief of the Russian general staff, described in 2013 a new doctrine (often termed 'hybrid warfare') involving 'information conflict', alongside diplomacy and military force, to achieve geopolitical aims. Stories in favour of the National Front's Marine Le Pen, and opposing the campaign of Emmanuel Macron, in the French Presidential election of 2017 were linked to Russian sources, and this raised concerns about possible interference in the German elections of that year.

Some have pointed out, however, that: 'Hoax news, propaganda and misinformation have been around for as long as people have communicated' (*The Guardian*, 17 April 2017), and that Europeans have more confidence in traditional media—54 per cent of Dutch citizens, and 52 per cent of Germans, trust the news, according to the Reuters study.

It is clear that social media is now a powerful force in the communication of political messages, and this raises questions about its effects on elections and democracy. This has in turn put the focus on social media platforms and search engines, and led to their self-regulation being questioned. The European Union established the East StratCom Task Force, specifically to counter perceived Russian dis-information campaigns, whilst Germany introduced plans in April 2016 to fine social media companies up to 53m Euro for failing to remove hate speech and fake news posts quickly. In the UK, the Information Commissioner commenced an investigation into the way political parties target voters through social media, and the Culture, Media and Sport Parliamentary Select Committee set up an Inquiry into Fake News.

Threatened with tighter regulation, social media providers began to volunteer more self-regulation; however, the →

→ monitoring of content can be costly and time-consuming; Facebook broadened its campaign to raise awareness about fake news, by publishing adverts in the UK press listing 10 things to look out for when deciding if a story is genuine, stepping up efforts to remove fake accounts, and introducing a fact-checking tool alerting users to 'disputed content'. Google has started displaying fact-checking labels in its search results to highlight news and information that has been vetted. Whilst there are concerns about costs and the possible effects on advertising revenue, critics of tighter regulation raise concerns about limitations on free speech and point out that the costs will fall disproportionately on smaller firms, thus stifling innovation.

Sources: Reuters and University of Oxford (2016): *The Guardian,* 22 March and 17 April 2017; *The Economist,* 15 April 2017.

Introduction

> Few relationships are as critical to the business enterprise itself as the relationship to government. The manager has responsibility for this relationship as part of his responsibility to the enterprise itself. (Drucker 1999: 283)

This quote from Drucker, seen by some as the inventor of modern management, indicates the importance of the political environment to business. It is no surprise, in the light of Drucker's comment, that firms spend so much time and money trying to influence governments, and politicians like the US President, the UK Prime Minister, the President of the USA, the General Secretary of the Communist Party of China, the Russian President, and the Prime Minister of India. Knowledge of where decision-making power lies is very important for business, whether that be a firm wishing to influence the process of formulating laws or regulations, to get permission to drill for oil, or seeking a contract for building roads and airports.

The political environment has major implications for both the macro and micro environments of business, establishing and enforcing the legal and regulatory framework within which business operates, and having a significant influence on a whole range of business decisions. As we have seen in the opening case study, business activity can have a huge impact on politics, and in turn business faces controls and regulations from governments and international bodies.

What is the Political Environment?

The political environment consists, firstly, of a range of formal institutions at a variety of geographical scales, ranging from the global, like the United Nations, the supranational, for example, the EU, and the national, sub-national, regional and local levels. These together comprise a multitiered system of governance. The primary focus of the political environment for business remains the nation-state, and its institutions of government: the ability of the state to wage wars, pursue diplomacy, agree treaties and alliances, establish policies as regards migration, taxation, interest rates, the exchange rate, the balance of payments, inflation, education, health, the environment, maintaining law and order, and guaranteeing the right to buy and sell private property, all have important implications for business. However, as globalization has proceeded, geo-political and supranational issues have become more important for business, which finds itself increasingly affected by political events outside its home base. Therefore, the political environment now consists of a sometimes complex web of decision-making bodies, in policy areas which bring several of them into play, with climate change being a good example. Whilst the main focus in this chapter is the nation-state, it is important for business to recognize the ways in which these systems of governance interact, where the decisions are being made, and the need to build up an understanding of a diversity of political systems.

The political environment also includes activity outside formal institutions but in the public realm, in groups and organizations that represent often conflicting interests and points of view, which are part and parcel of the political culture—business groupings, trades unions, and pressure groups—and which seek to influence decisions of governing bodies and public opinion. The presence and vibrancy of these groups will depend on the type of political system in place. This wider political culture also includes the media and other forums for debate over issues of public concern, and the political processes by which formal government interacts with broader society. Political parties both represent interests, and aim to hold government office, and therefore, in this sense, hold a position within formal structures of government whilst being extra-governmental with respect to their wider membership.

In this chapter, we examine the different types of political system, the size of the state, and the value of political institutions to business. We also consider the impact the political environment can have on business and, in the final section, we look at how firms go about influencing their political environment.

Different Political Systems

If we take membership of the United Nations (UN) as an indicator of the number of independent countries in the world, then there are 193. These nations operate under a variety of political systems; in some, power is concentrated in the hands of one person or an elite, while, in others, power is spread over a large number of different groups—these systems are more pluralistic.

No two countries have identical political regimes. We examine briefly below four different types of political system, liberal democracy, authoritarian and absolutist, communist, and theocratic, before going on to look at the differences between unitary states and federal states. Whilst these may not exist in reality in 'pure' form, the ideas associated with each underpin the political culture in which business operates. Together with the institutions of government, these systems form the 'enabling environment' for business, which is key, as seen in Porter's model, to the relative attractiveness of countries as business locations (see Chapter 6).

Liberal Democracy

In liberal democracies, citizens elect governments to represent their interests, and have the right to individual freedom. Government is based on majority rule, within a system of representative democracy, with political parties winning their positions through free elections. This occurs, for example, in the countries of Western Europe, North America, Latin American countries such as Argentina and Brazil, and Asian countries like India and Japan. State institutions are constrained in their powers by other institutions. For example, in the USA, this is reflected in the separation of powers, where responsibilities are divided between the legislative branch (the House of

Representatives and the Senate), the executive, and the judges. Each branch acts as a check on, and balance for, the others. However, although the Office of President of the USA is formally the Executive within that system, the President also performs a legislative role by initiating laws, and there is overlap with the Judiciary, as the President appoints senior legal officers and makes appointments to the Supreme Court. (See Counterpoint Box 10.2, Law and politics—the separation of powers.)

Liberal democracies embrace the right to personal freedom and free expression of views. Television, radio, and the press are not under the sole control of the state. There is also the right to assembly, meaning that people can gather peacefully and demonstrate. There is an area of private life and civil society which is outside the domain of the state, and includes a range of groups and voluntary associations. Rights are guaranteed by an independent judiciary, and the rule of law. Government is conducted by a permanent, skilled, and impartial public service (for example), the UK civil service, responsible to the government and, through the government, to the electorate.

Most liberal democracies operate a mixed economy. That is true whether one looks at the countries of North America and Europe, or nations such as Argentina, India, South Africa, and Japan. Indeed, it is often argued that democracy and an open society are necessary pre-conditions for business activity, which depends on free choice by consumers, information being freely available, and the rule of law. However, liberal democracies differ in the extent of state intervention in the economy, ranging from minimal, to more interventionist, social democratic models. Furthermore, liberal democracies, by their nature, have to balance the requirements of business with demands from the electorate. The state can also play an important economic role through taxation and public expenditure, and ownership of, or significant shareholdings in, certain industries. It can also limit the freedom of business to trade and to make profit, through laws and regulation. In general, democracies must balance individual freedoms with restraints deemed to be in the public interest.

 Counterpoint Box 9.1 **Venezuela**

Venezuela, with a population of 31 million, has the largest oil reserves in the world (330 billion barrels in 2017). It is also rich in other raw materials, including natural gas, gold, diamonds, and iron. However, 2017 saw 82 per cent of the population living in poverty, scarcity of food and medicines, a state of emergency, and the country in the midst of a political, social and economic crisis (Watts 2016).

Venezuela has traditionally been viewed as a relatively stable country, compared to others in Latin America. This has been called 'Venezuelan exceptionalism', with the country not experiencing the military dictatorships and political instability which characterized the region in the second half of the twentieth century. In 1958, the Dictator Perez Jimenez was deposed,

and a democracy established, that was to become the longest established democracy in Latin American history. A period of stability was underpinned by oil revenues and a stable, two-party system. Venezuela was named as a 'miracle country'—one of only four Latin American countries identified by the World Bank as an 'upper middle income' economy. In 1970, it was the richest country in Latin America, and one of the 20 richest in the world.

Stability and economic growth broke down in the 1980s as oil prices fell, and foreign debt rose. Following a recession in 1989–93, the country borrowed $45 billion from the IMF. President Carlos Andres Perez instigated a programme of austerity and privatizations, opening the economy to global →

→ markets in response to the IMF's conditions, and the gap between rich and poor grew.

Following accelerating economic decline and social unrest, Hugo Chavez of the United Socialist Party was elected President in 1998. Chavez pursued a Socialist 'Bolivarian' revolution, which involved using oil revenues to re-distribute wealth, the nationalization of private businesses, fixing prices on foodstuffs, paying off the country's foreign debts, and, in 2007, leaving the IMF and World Bank. During this time the oil price exceeded $110 a barrel. By 2010 the country had become the least unequal in Latin America, but was heavily dependent on oil revenues, which had been used to import goods from overseas. Domestic production fell, and foreign debt rose. A looming crisis, inherited by Chavez's successor, President Maduro, in 2013, was compounded by the fall in global oil price. 2016 saw a negative growth rate of 8 per cent and, in 2017, the World Bank's Doing Business Index ranked Venezuela at 186 out of 189; inflation was estimated at 400 per cent. Foreign Investors, including Coca-Cola, left the country.

In elections held in December, 2015, an opposition coalition had won 112 of 167 seats in the National Assembly. That coalition has since found its powers and new laws blocked by the government-controlled Supreme Court. At the same time, opposition leaders were imprisoned, the military used to suppress protests, and Maduro refused to hold a recall referendum.

Sources: Grillo (2016); Transparency International (n.d.)

Questions
1. What factors have influenced the type of political system in Venezuela from around 1958 to the present day?
2. Discuss whether democratic governments should be able to restrict freedoms in times of crisis.

Liberal democracy is more likely to be found in rich, politically stable countries, such as those in North America, Northern and Western Europe, and Japan, making these economies and their markets very attractive. It is no surprise to find that the vast bulk of trade and foreign investment takes place among liberal democracies. Globalization is often held to be a positive force in moving states towards liberal democracy, as increased wealth is held to lead to increased openness to the world and demands for political freedoms.

While there are countries that are clearly liberal democracies, there are others, like Egypt, that have seen recent moves both towards and away from it. Liberal democracy can be difficult to establish where it does not have a foundation in the wider political culture of a country. It is important to note that a state may have elements of democracy, like a system of elections to government, without being fully liberal; it may be an electoral democracy without having the full freedoms which liberal democracies have. An authoritarian regime may allow for some limited types of election for certain positions, and a democracy may have authoritarian elements—like restricting the rights of some minorities to freedom of expression.

Authoritarian and Absolutist Systems

A relatively small number of countries operate under authoritarian or absolutist regimes. These are forms of government in which one person, or one group of people, exercise power unrestrained by laws or opposition. It may be that only one political party is allowed to operate, as in China and Cuba. There is an absence of checks and balances on the power of the rulers. In Saudi Arabia, the royal family holds power with little constraint from parliament or the judiciary. In such systems, support for the ruler is based on **patronage**, or **clientelism**, which occurs where favours, in the form of money, jobs in government offices, or public contracts, are given in return for political support. Alternatively, the system could be based on inheritance, where power and privilege is passed on in the ruling family—once again, Saudi Arabia is a good example.

Of course, patronage can also occur in some liberal democracies. In the USA, the slang expression 'pork barrel politics' is used to describe members of Congress lobbying to get publicly funding for projects that bring money and jobs to their own districts. In Italy, there has been a history of Christian Democrat governments distributing state jobs, tax relief, and preferential pension treatment, to blocs of reliable supporters.

Countries operating under authoritarian or absolutist regimes only constitute a small proportion of the world's population and income, and their markets are not that important for business. However, firms may be interested in these countries because resources like labour are often cheap, and some of these countries are vital because they are rich in natural resources. For example, several countries in the Middle East have vast reserves of oil. Saudi Arabia is the world's single largest oil producer. This makes it attractive to the big multinational oil companies, such as Exxon, Shell, and BP.

Communist Regimes

In Communist regimes, the production of most goods and services is owned and controlled by the state. In China, even though companies such as VW and General Motors have been allowed to invest there, the state continues to exercise a very significant degree of economic control over what, and how much, is produced, where it is produced, and who will produce it. The system is dominated by one political party. Vietnam is another example of a one-party state where the Communist Party has tight control. The ruling Party also controls the legislative, executive, and judicial branches of the state, as well as trade unions and the media. In North Korea, for example, the Communist Party controls television and the press.

Globalization has, however, led to most of these states becoming more open to the rest of the world; China and Vietnam have both seen rapid growth in global trade. Cuba has increasingly encouraged tourism, and in 2015 the United States re-opened its Embassy in the country. North Korea, however, remains quite isolated from international trade. As we saw above, there are arguments as to whether globalization leads inevitably towards a more open political system, and tensions can rise as a result. China, for example, benefits from cross-border internet trade, but continues to clamp down on search engines like Google and its domestic users.

 Counterpoint Box 9.2 Liberal democracy—global convergence?

The number of democracies in the world has grown since the fall of the Berlin Wall in 1989: now 123 out of 193 countries in the United Nations are democracies. For commentators such as Fukuyama (1993), capitalism and economic growth are inevitably linked with democracy, as they require freedom of choice and of information. Deudney and Ikenberry (2009) claim that internal pressures in autocratic countries like China will cause them to move towards liberal democracy. These include: the growth of a middle class with a growing interest in political accountability; high levels of inequality, illustrated by the many landless peasants, marginalized migrants, and underpaid workers, leading to the rise of political parties to represent them; and undemocratic →

→ systems being prone to pursue bad policies, which will consequently undermine their political legitimacy.

Others disagree; Wright (2006) found that public demands for democracy in China fell as the economy prospered, and Reinicki (2013) sees the continuance of the Chinese model as a reflection of the weakness of its major competitor, liberal democracy, wracked as it is by crises of increasing inequality, poverty, and the environment. These, along with the global financial crisis, have undermined faith in the ability of liberal democracies to deliver sustainable social and economic benefits. In addition, Rodrick (2016) points to the differing varieties of democracy, with *illiberal democracies* being those which have elections, but where the regime displays autocratic elements—examples being Hungary, Mexico, and Turkey. The

Economist's Global Democracy Index shows that it is too simplistic to divide states into democratic and non-democratic categories, and uses the classifications full democracies, flawed democracies, hybrid regimes, and authoritarian regimes.

Sources: Fukuyama (1993); Wright (2006); Reinicki (2013); Deudney and Ikenberry (2009); Rodrick, (2016); The Economist Global Democracy Index.

Question

Using the characteristics of liberal democracy in the discussion above, assess the extent to which China, Cuba, Turkey, and Ecuador are, or are moving towards becoming, liberal democracies.

Theocratic Regimes

In **theocratic regimes** religion or faith plays a dominant role in the government; rulers are normally leaders of the dominant religion. Policies pursued by government are either identical with, or strongly influenced by religious faith, and, typically, the government claims to rule on behalf of God, or a higher power.

The rulers in government are normally the same people who lead the dominant religion. There are only a handful of theocratic states. Iran is one example, where the political process is heavily influenced by Islam. The policies of the Islamic political parties are founded on the Koran, and the ayatollahs and mullahs, the religious leaders. They, along with Islamic lawyers, sit on a council that has the power of veto over laws proposed by parliament. A priority in Iran is to resist what is seen as the corruption inherent in Western materialism, which makes it difficult for big Western MNCs to operate there.

Mini Case Study 9.1 **Hungary**

From 1949 until 1989, Hungary was a Communist country belonging to the 'Eastern Bloc' of European countries under the influence of the Soviet Union. Throughout this period its economy was relatively open to the outside world. Hungary joined both the International Monetary Fund and the World Bank in 1982, and was considered to be the most advanced of the economies in the Eastern Bloc. After the collapse of communism in 1989, Hungary became a democracy.

The immediate economic effects were drastic; between 1990 and 1992, GDP fell by more than 20 per cent and inflation was over 160 per cent. In this early post-communist period, 'shock therapy'—rapid movement to free markets and capitalism—was advocated by many in the west. In Hungary, there was a more gradual approach and the economy began to recover. By 1998, 70 per cent of GDP came from the private sector. The early 2000s saw relative economic success, and Hungary joined →

→ the EU in 2004, following 83 per cent support for membership in a referendum. However, the country was hit badly by the global recession of 2008, and required a loan from the IMF.

Hungary is now classed by the World Bank as an upper-middle income economy (9.9m pop.), with GDP per capita of $12,730. However, support for the free market has steadily fallen since 1990; support for the SZDSZ, a free-market supporting party, fell from 21.4 per cent in 1990, to 6.3 per cent in 2006, to them not being represented in the 2010 parliament. The anticipated 'inevitable' transition towards liberal democracy has not been straightforward. 2010 saw the election of Victor Orban, of the conservative centre right. Orban is committed to creating an 'illiberal' state, encouraging nationalism and anti-EU sentiment. Orban's government has centralized power, and suppressed the media and civil society groups. A new Fundamental Law, in 2012, weakened the Constitutional Court, and undermined judicial independence; between 2010 and 2011 a series of laws were passed which were damned by Amnesty International. In October 2016, the main opposition newspaper, *Nepszabadsag*, was closed down under government pressure. It could be said that, whilst democracy is flourishing, liberalism is not.

Sources: CIA World Factbook (2016)

Question

What is the likely impact of Hungary's move towards an 'illiberal democracy' on domestic and international business?

Unitary and Federal Systems

Political regimes may also be classified according to the distribution of power at different levels. The regime may be unitary, where most decision-making power is held by the central government, and where the regions and localities have little or no autonomy. Here, central governments normally are responsible for important policy decisions, for the majority of public expenditure, and for the raising of taxes. The great majority of countries in the world have a unitary system. France, Italy, Japan, the UK, and China are examples of unitary states.

On the other hand, federal systems see power shared between the centre and the component regions, which may have significant autonomy in relation to areas such as spending and taxation. Friction between the centre and the regions in federations is not unusual, the tension between Catalonia, the Basque country, and the Spanish central government being a particular example. More than 2 billion people live in federal states, and they comprise half the world's land area. Examples of federations are the USA, Germany, Brazil, and India. In Unitary systems, firms wishing to influence government have to direct their attention towards the centre: in federal systems they will deal more with the various regions.

To sum up, outright classifications of political systems can be misleading, as can the assumption of trends towards one system or another. According to the Economist's Global Democracy Index (2016), there are now, for the first time, more democracies in the world than authoritarian states, but only 20 (12 per cent of the countries, and 8.9 per cent of the population) are deemed to be 'full' democracies; 59 are flawed democracies, 37 are hybrid regimes, and 51 are authoritarian. There is a spectrum of types of political system. Looking at which type of political system is 'best' for business activity, it seems that liberal democracy, with its guarantees of rights, an open system of government, freedom of information etc. should be most suited. However, some non-democratic states, especially China, have also become increasingly attractive to business.

Research has called into question a straightforward relationship between type of system and economic success. Pereira and Teles (2010) found that the establishing of new democracies in poorer countries had a large economic impact, and also that the more federal and plural/open the system, the better. They also found that the longer autocracies hold power, in general, the worse the economic impact will be. Prezeworski et al. (2000), however, found no direct relationship between economic growth and type of political regime. In turn, Acemolgu et al. (2014) indicated that the global rise in democracy over the past 50 years has produced 6 per cent higher global GDP. As we have noted, there are no 'pure' forms of political system, and so it is not so straightforward to read off types against economic success. As Pereira and Teles point out, also important are the types of institutions in each country—autocracies can differ between each other in terms of business protections, whilst democracies may be 'captured' by particular groups who have more power than others, so it is necessary to look at each case.

Learning Task

In federal systems, national governments often run into conflict with the regions.

1. Come up with reasons for possible conflict between central government and the regions.

2. In one of his first actions on election as President, Donald Trump issued an Executive Order imposing a ban on people from certain named countries from entering the United States. Research and discuss the reaction of various US states to this. What does this tell us about the system of government?

Institutions and the 'Enabling Environment' for Business

Business operates in a framework of governmental institutions, which underpin its activities. This political, legal, and administrative context underpins business operations, ideally enabling trade and ensuring it is conducted in a predictable and secure way. This includes the core organizing structures of government, and the legal and institutional frameworks which lay down the procedures for the rule and enforcement of law, along with the mechanisms for regulating the economy and ensuring financial stability.

National governments are an important part of this environment, but they are only one element of a much broader concept called the state. The state comprises institutions, such as the civil service and the judiciary, as well as governments. Governments come and go, but the other elements of the state tend to be more permanent.

State institutions have the legal power, ultimately backed up by coercion, to make governmental decisions for a specific geographical area and the population living there. States are said to have sovereignty to the extent that they can do these things within their own boundaries. The following are the core branches of the state:

- The legislative branch, which makes the laws, e.g. Parliament in the UK, Congress in the USA, and the Diet in Japan. An important role in such bodies is played by the leading politician—the President in the USA, France, and Russia, the Prime Minister in the UK, Japan, Italy, and Spain, and the Chancellor in Germany—along with cabinet members, ministers, and senior bureaucrats. In many states, there are also elected regional or local authorities, which can also make laws and regulations that apply to their areas. The European Parliament is an example of a legislative body at supra-national level. Global organisations are not usually legislatures in this sense, although UN resolutions do become binding on nation-states in international law.

- The **executive branch** puts the laws into effect and tries to ensure the desired outcomes. At the highest levels, such as the higher civil service in the UK, and the European Commission in the EU, it offers policy advice to ministers. Uniquely, the European Commission has the power to initiate policy. The majority of executive staff are, however, engaged in day-to-day administration of government business. Regulatory agencies also form part of the executive branch—examples include the Federal Communications Commission in the USA, the Office of the Communications Regulator (OFCOM) in the UK, and NERSA, the energy regulator in South Africa. In developed countries, the executive branch is usually large, running to thousands of people. Also, depending on the political system, there may be a range of sub-national authorities responsible for implementing and delivering services at local and regional levels; for example, local councils, and health authorities.

- The **judicial branch** interprets and applies the laws—this branch comprises the judiciary, the police, and the armed forces, which give the state its capacity to enforce the laws that it makes. Businesses operating in the geographical area are required to accept that the state has the authority to make decisions and to maintain order. At the EU level, the Court of First Instance, and the European Court of Justice (ECJ), interpret and apply the laws of the Union (for more discussion of EU law see Chapter 10).

Especially important for business and economic activity is the establishment of property rights: the right to own, buy, and sell goods and services. The law of contract, which underpins the conditions relating to transactions around the buying and selling of goods and services, ensures that customers can be pursued for payment, were that to be necessary. Similarly, a firm contracting to buy a certain quantity and quality of goods can use the law to remedy any shortfalls or deficiencies on the part of the supplier. Business will be reluctant to operate in countries where it is not able to enforce the terms of its contracts. A good example of such a country is the Congo in Africa, which the big oil multinational, Shell, classifies as a country where state institutions are ineffective. The absence of an effective judicial system makes it virtually impossible for firms to enforce the law of contract (for more on contract law, see Chapter 10).

Another function of the state is to protect its geographical area from both external and internal threats. The intelligence services manage both categories of threat. The army, navy, and air force deal with external threats, for example military threats from other countries. The police, courts, and prisons help maintain law and order within the geographical frontiers of the state. States that can effectively protect themselves from external threat, and maintain law and order internally, provide a more stable and attractive operating environment. In turn, security issues raise questions about the extent and balance of state activity; terrorist acts have led to increased powers for governments to monitor the on-line activities of individuals, raising in turn questions about individual rights to privacy.

Other Functions of the State and their Importance for Business

The boundaries of the state are not always clear-cut and, as we now discover, they can extend much further than the narrow description given above. Modern governments perform many functions besides the traditional ones of maintaining law and order, and protecting the country from external attack. We are now going to look in more detail at other functions that can have a significant impact on the environment of business, in which state and other institutions both constrain the ability of business to meet its objectives, and also provide opportunities which firms are able to exploit for commercial gain.

Negotiator

The state acts as a negotiator with other states. Negotiations can be bilateral, where two countries are involved, or multilateral, where more than two participate. The WTO is a multilateral body where important negotiations take place on reductions in barriers to trade, and to the movement of capital across borders. Such negotiations can be very good for business, particularly when they open up new markets. On the other hand, they can remove barriers that protect domestic firms from foreign competition (see Costs for Business, Chapter 1).

Regulator

Regulation can affect a very wide range of business activities. For instance, regulations could constrain the ability of a firm to take out patents, or set its own prices, for example in the telecommunications and water industries in the UK. Regulations could increase a firm's costs, by stipulating requirements relating to consumer health and safety, to employment contracts, and to the natural environment, or by requiring companies to meet certain administrative formalities (for more discussion of the impact of regulations on business see Chapter 10).

In its role as a regulator, the state can take the power to grant or refuse a firm a licence to operate, or to guarantee it a monopoly. In the developed world, banks and other financial institutions usually need to get a licence to sell financial services. Tighter regulation, following the global financial crisis, means that compliance costs for banks have increased. Regulations can also affect the level of competition and market entry, and determine whether or not firms can merge—the US Justice Department moved to block a merger between American Airlines and US Airways. Firms may also find that regulations lay down the technical specifications to which their products must conform. There are examples of drugs regulators, concerned about safety, demanding more rigorous testing, prohibiting the launch of a new drug, or ordering pharmaceutical companies to withdraw products from the market place.

The main forms of regulation are at the national level, but supranational regulation is becoming increasingly important, through bodies such as the WTO and the EU. Again there is a balance to be struck. Whilst regulation can add costs and restrict business, it also provides consumers with assurances over standards. It can also deliver public policy goals for governments in markets which are deemed to be of public interest; for example in the financial sector, to prevent the mis-selling of products such as pensions.

Deregulator

Just as the state can regulate so can it deregulate, or liberalize. The USA and EU liberalized their civil aviation sectors. Now EU airlines have the freedom to set their own prices, to fly over the territory of member states, to operate flights within those countries, and to set up routes between them. As a result, numerous low cost airlines emerged, such as easyJet and Ryanair, causing all sorts of competitive problems for the established national carriers, like British Airways and Lufthansa. The extent of regulation can be seen as an indicator of the size of the state, or its willingness to intervene in business activity. As such, it is often politically controversial, with Donald Trump, for example, promising to reduce bank regulation during his Presidential campaign (see section on regulation in Chapter 11). At the global level, Western governments and the WTO, through measures like the General Agreement on Trade in Services (GATS), have encouraged developing countries to open up their markets in services such as telecommunications and banking.

Arbitrator

The state also acts as an arbitrator, or referee, between firms. Thus, business may look to the courts, or other regulatory agencies, to resolve disputes with other firms or to take action against them. Such disputes could relate to a whole range of issues, such as breach of contract, abuse of market power, or patent infringement.

Microsoft's competitors have complained on numerous occasions to the competition authorities in both the USA and the EU about Microsoft abusing its market power, making it very difficult for them to compete in the software market. Between 2004 and 2013, the software giant paid fines to the EU of over $3 billion (Neowin 2013), and 2017 saw it subject to an antitrust complaint to the EU by Kaspersky Lab.

Financial Guarantor

A crucial role for the state is the preservation of the economic and financial system. A striking example of this occurred during the global credit crunch in 2008–09, when the US and European banking systems were in turmoil. Financial institutions, unable to borrow money, went bust or, like Northern Rock in the UK, were taken into public ownership. In the USA, several major financial institutions failed, including Bear Stearns, Indy Mac, Washington Mutual, and Lehman Brothers. Stock markets gyrated wildly, and the dollar plunged against other currencies. Governments could not allow the global financial system to crash, because the money and credit provided by banks is a vital lubricant for business in a modern economy. The IMF (2014) reported that the financial sector in 10 advanced economies was supported to the tune of around $2 trillion, with the US government alone disbursing more than $400 billion to stem the panic and stabilize the financial system (see US Dept of the Treasury 2013; see also Chapter 11).

Learning Task

Take a look at the World Economic Forum's *Global Competitiveness Report* at http://reports.weforum. org/global-competitiveness-index-2017-2018/#topic=about.

What is included in their measure for 'Institutions'? Is there a link between country's rank on this measure and their overall ranking? What might explain the differences in the assessment of the strength of institutions in each country?

Overall, this political, legal, and economic enabling environment provides the fundamental context in which a business will operate. MNC's will, of course, find themselves working in several institutional contexts, and one of their strengths is having the expertise to do this. As we shall see later, business may also be in a strong position to influence this context towards its own interests. The governmental and institutional context also provides a key element in a country's competitive position when seeking to attract business, as as shown in Michael Porter's Competitive Advantage of Nations model in Chapter 2.

Rodrick (2007) has argued that the quality of institutions, including property rights, regulatory structures, independence of the judiciary, and administrative capacity, is key in explaining the economic success of a country. Similarly, Ketterer and Rodríguez-Pose (2016) argue that strong government institutions in preventing corruption, are a key determinant of economic growth in the EU. However, as Rodrick (2007) also points out, there is no one pattern of governmental arrangement which will be successful everywhere—what brings success is context-specific, and there are many differing 'recipes'. Also, changing political systems and institutions will not be enough in themselves, unless actual or de facto power also changes. Despite the formalities of a country's governance system, what matters is how it actually impacts in practice; powerful groups, as we shall see, may continue to hold power.

The Size of the State

In this section we examine the size of the state relative to the economy, by looking at the amount of money the state is spending, and what it takes in tax as a proportion of the total income generated in the country, i.e. gross domestic product. For business, state spending can be a burden, in the imposition of various forms of taxation, or a support, in that it provides infrastructure, and welfare services, which contribute to a healthy and educated workforce. The size and importance of the state varies from one country to another, and over time. Some states that previously owned public assets/industries have sold them off to the private sector in a process of privatization, reducing the size of the state, which can fluctuate according to changes in the political environment. For example, in the UK in 2017, a majority of people supported the renationalization of railways which had previously been privatized.

Spending and Taxation

Economically, the state has enormous influence, due to its tax and spending powers, and its influence over interest rates and the supply of money. Governments spend money on buying goods and services, paying the wages of state employees, and providing welfare benefits. Taxation takes the form of direct taxes, on incomes, and indirect taxes, levied on expenditure. These powers allow states to influence the level of total demand for goods and services. When the economy is going into recession, the state can increase demand by raising its own spending on goods and services, or it can cut taxes or lower interest rates to encourage consumers and business to increase their spending. Alternatively, when the economy is booming, and there is a danger of inflation getting out of control, the state can cut spending, or raise taxes and interest rates, to reduce consumer spending and relieve inflationary pressures.

Such decisions can have major implications for business. For example, a decision to raise interest rates increases the cost of borrowing for firms. The higher cost of borrowing may also cause consumers to cut back on spending on goods, such as consumer durables, which they would normally buy on credit. On the other hand, organizations such as the retail banks may welcome such an increase in rates because it allows them to charge their customers more for loans.

Public Expenditure

The three decades after the end of the Second World War in 1945 saw the biggest increase, historically, in public spending, as governments took responsibility for maintaining high levels of employment and adequate living standards, and a major expansion of the welfare state. Spending also increased significantly on defence, due to the Cold War between the West and the Communist Bloc. By 1980, in developed economies, the state's average slice of the economy had leapt to 43 per cent (in the US the percentage topped 30 per cent; in many small European countries it breached 50 per cent). Up to the mid-1980s, it continued to grow, but then levelled off. Towards the end of the first decade of the twenty-first century, the financial crisis caused OECD countries to increase spending to around 40 per cent of GDP. In the EU, it was just over half of GDP, and more than 40 per cent in the US and Japan (see Table 9.1).

Where Does the Money Go?

The largest amounts of public spending go on subsidies and transfers, for example, pensions, social security, and unemployment benefits. This is followed by spending on defence, law and order, education, and health, often referred to as public, or government, consumption.

How the Money is Raised—Taxation and Borrowing

A clear trend since the mid-1970s was a steady increase in the proportion of total income taken by taxes. The tax-to-GDP ratio across most of the developed economies rose, despite many countries cutting tax rates on personal and company income. Some countries have tried to offset the effects of cuts in tax rates by drawing more sectors and people into the tax net, and reducing the degree of tax evasion and tax avoidance. However, tax evasion continues to be a global political issue, and one which requires multi-national and multi-level co-operation. (See Mini Case Study 11.2 Panama Papers and the banks). Tax revenues fell in most countries as a result of the financial crisis, but started to recover after 2010 (see Table 9.2).

Table 9.1 General government expenditures as a percentage of GDP

	2000	2005	2010	2015
Australia	35.2	33.4	34.5	..
Austria	50.8	51.4	53.1	51.6
Belgium	49.1	51.4	53.3	53.9
Czech Republic	40.4	41.8	43.0	42.0
Denmark	52.7	51.2	56.7	54.8
Estonia	36.4	34.0	40.5	40.3
Finland	48.0	49.3	54.8	57.0
France	51.1	52.9	56.4	56.6
Germany	44.7	42.6	47.3	44.0
Greece	46.4	45.6	52.5	55.4
Hungary	47.2	49.5	49.5	50.0.
Iceland	..	..	..	42.9
Ireland	30.9	33.3	65.3	29.4
Israel	48.0	45.9	41.1	39.7
Italy	45.5	47.1	49.9	50.3
Japan	38.8	35.5	39.6	39.5
Korea	24.7	29.5	31.0	..
Luxembourg	37.8	43.6	44.1	41.2
Netherlands	41.8	42.3	48.2	45.1
Norway	42.0	42.1	45.0	48.8
Poland	..	44.3	45.7	41.5
Portugal	42.6	46.7	51.8	48.4
Slovak Republic	52.0	39.8	42.1	45.6
Slovenia	46.1	44.9	49.3	48.1
Spain	39.1	38.3	45.6	43.8
Sweden	53.6	52.7	51.2	50.2
Switzerland	35.7	34.0	32.9	33.9
United Kingdom	36.4	40.8	48.0	42.8
United States	33.7	36.4	42.9	37.7

Source: OECD Factbook (2016)

The tax take tends to be higher in Western European countries. In Austria, Denmark, Sweden, Finland, and France it is greater than 40 per cent of GDP. Chile and Mexico have the lowest tax ratio at around 20 per cent, somewhat below countries like South Korea, the USA, and Japan (see Table 9.2).

Table 9.2 Tax revenue as a percentage of GDP

	2002	2007	2010	2014
Australia	29.8	29.7	25.6	n/a
Austria	42.5	40.5	40.8	43.0
Belgium	43.6	42.6	42.4	44.7
Canada	32.8	32.3	30.4	30.8
Chile	19	22.8	19.5	19.8
Czech Republic	33.5	34.3	32.5	33.5
Denmark	45.4	46.4	45.3	50.9
Estonia	31.1	31.1	33.2	32.9
Finland	43.3	41.5	40.8	43.9
France	42.1	42.4	41.6	45.2
Germany	34.4	34.9	35.0	36.1
Greece	32.5	31.2	32.0	35.9
Hungary	37.4	39.6	37.3	38.5
Iceland	34.3	38.7	33.3	38.7
Ireland	27.4	30.4	27.5	29.9
Israel	34.2	34.3	30.4	31.1
Italy	39.7	41.7	41.8	43.6
Japan	25.8	24.8	27.6	n/a
Korea	22.0	24.6	23.4	24.6
Luxembourg	38.0	36.6	38.1	37.8
Mexico	16.2	17.6	18.5	19.5
Netherlands	35.2	36.1	36.2	n/a
New Zealand	33.2	34.0	30.6	32.4
Norway	42.3	42.1	41.9	39.1
Poland	33.2	34.8	31.4	n/a
Portugal	31.4	32.0	30.6	34.4
Slovak Republic	32.7	29.2	28.1	31.0
Slovenia	37.2	37.6	36.9	36.6
Spain	33.4	36.5	29.9	33.2
Sweden	45.2	45.0	43.2	42.7
Switzerland	27.5	26.1	26.5	26.6
Turkey	24.6	24.1	26.2	28.7
United Kingdom	33.3	34.1	32.8	32.6
United States	24.9	26.7	23.2	26.0
OECD Total	33.5	34.1	32.8	34.4

Source: OECD (2015)

Figure 9.1 Average corporate tax rates

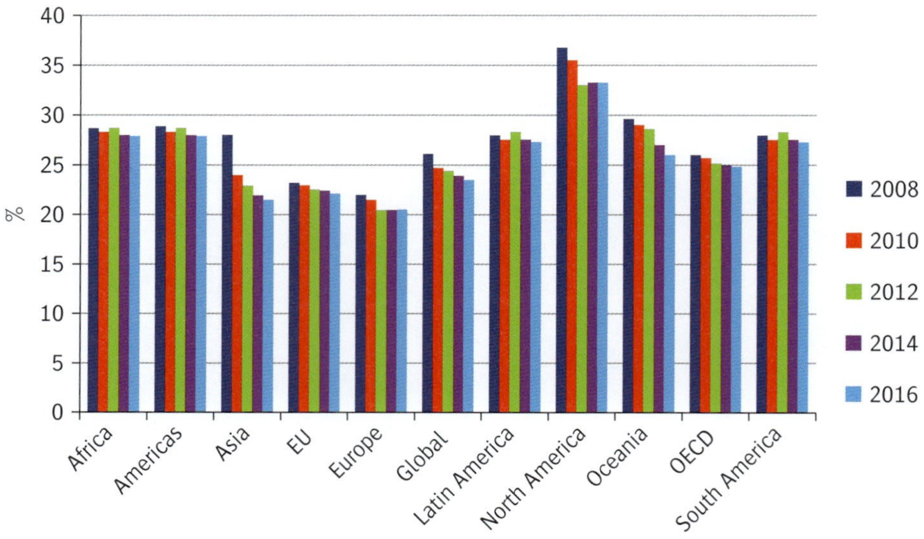

Source: KPMG, (2018)

More than 90 per cent of the tax revenues raised in the developed economies come from three main sources: direct taxes on the income of individuals and business, indirect taxes on goods and services, such as VAT and excise duties on the likes of tobacco and alcohol, and social security contributions—another form of direct tax.

Businesses pay tax on their net income, i.e. their profits. There has been a widespread tendency for tax rates on profits to drop, in the advanced economies. In 1982, 15 countries had tax rates in excess of 40 per cent. In Germany, Sweden, Finland, and Austria, the rate was around 60 per cent (Devereux and Sørenson, 2005). By 2010, rates had fallen significantly across many countries (see Figure 9.1). This trend may be due to the spread of globalization and the wish by countries to attract and retain foreign direct investment. In the UK, the rate has progressively been reduced to 19 per cent. A further reason is that host countries want to encourage those businesses to retain their earnings in the host country. In 2017 the USA had the highest rate, at 39 per cent (which President Trump pledged to reduce in his election campaign), amongst OECD countries, with Hungary the lowest at 9 per cent (OECD n.d.). When spending is greater than the taxes raised, governments usually borrow to cover the deficit. The USA has been running large budget deficits for a number of years. In 2009, in the aftermath of the financial crisis, the deficit in the UK reached a record £154 billion, falling to £52 billion by 2017 (BBC 2017). Of the world's major economies, only Germany was running a surplus (of 0.7 per cent of GDP) in 2016 (CIA n.d.).

The Global Crisis and Government Finances

The global financial crisis and economic downturn caused a dramatic increase in government deficits in developed countries, as tax revenues fell, and massive expenditure on bailing out the banks and on unemployment benefits rose. Most developed countries tried to stimulate their economies through tax and spending policies. Finland, Korea, and the United States cut taxes significantly, while Australia, Denmark, Japan, Korea, and Turkey planned for large increases in spending. China gave a massive fiscal stimulus to its economy, to the tune of 2.5 per cent of GDP, by increasing investment in infrastructure and social welfare. Conversely, the Eurozone, UK, Hungary, and Iceland, trying to cut large budget deficits, pursued austerity programmes, by raising taxes and cutting spending. These programmes have continued to dominate the political environments in these countries, focussing attention on the size of the state, and the effects of the tax increases and spending cuts. They illustrate the complex interconnections of levels of governance amidst globalisation. In Greece, the crisis exposed high levels of government debt, leading to tax rises and dramatic spending cuts, and to the government negotiating loans from the International Monetary Fund and the European Central Bank. As a result of the loan from the ECB, the Greek government was required to make further substantial cuts, despite a popular referendum opposing austerity in 2015. This was seen by many as a substantial loss of sovereignty by the state. (see Counterpoint Box 11.1 the IMF and World Bank).

Learning Task

Examine Tables 9.1 and 9.2 and answer the following questions:

1. Identify and explain changes in the size of the state, in terms of spending and taxation, after 2005.

2. Advance reasons for the high tax rate in Scandinavian countries, and the low tax rates in the USA and Japan.

The Demise of the Nation State?

Commentators, including Ohmae (2005) and, to an extent, Held and McGrew (2007), argue that the state has become increasingly powerless in the face of globalization, leaving national governments no longer able to manage their domestic economies because they are subject to forces outside of their control—for example, business decisions made by powerful MNCs. The state has to be competitive in order to attract and maintain inward investment. So, if an individual government sets profit tax on business at a much higher level than other countries, firms would relocate, or ensure that their profits were earned in countries with a lower profits tax, and tax revenues would fall.

Similarly, if a government wanted to have a relatively low rate of interest, then this would be undermined by investors moving their money out of the country to take advantage of higher rates elsewhere, and this would be facilitated quickly in global financial markets. This would reduce the supply of money available for borrowers, and put upward pressure on interest rates. A government wanting to prohibit dangerous or undesirable working practices might find the affected industries moving abroad or shutting down, because the new regulation would put domestic firms at a disadvantage in competition with foreign producers.

Some commentators supported their arguments with the case of Germany, where welfare benefits were high relative to other countries. Generous benefits meant that, for each worker, employers had to pay a high level of social security tax on top of wages. This pushed up labour costs, and made the German economy less competitive internationally. As a result, Germany, it was claimed, suffered slow growth and high levels of unemployment. It was thus no surprise to the commentators that Germany cut back on the welfare benefit system. They saw the reforms as an indication that countries cannot buck global market forces, and that the market will enforce a convergence of taxation and public expenditure among countries; in other words, there will be a race to the bottom.

In addition, it is argued that the growing influence of supranational organizations, like the WTO and the EU, reduces the sovereignty of the nation state. They set rules on trade and investment through measures such as tariffs, quotas, subsidies, and local content requirements. Some argue that we have seen a move from an international system of nation-states to one of multi-level global governance, where states are but one player in a system including global, supra-national, regional, and local levels; and that political systems need to adapt to this new reality, for example, by making global bodies like the United Nations more democratic. It is, however, more difficult to reach decisions at world and multi-national governing bodies, as evidenced by the WTO's Doha round of trade negotiations. UN Security Council motions can be vetoed by a single member state, and the EU has to get agreement of all member states for its most important decisions.

Others are concerned for the loss of national cultures, seeing the nation-state as a fundamental, emotive basis for political belonging and engagement. In recent years, we have seen these competing sentiments play out, to some extent, in political controversies about the effects of global trade and supra-national co-operation, in the US Presidential election, and the debate about the UK's membership of the EU.

Undoubtedly, there are a range of new actors and organizations which now populate the global environment, and a great variety of institutional forms and types of authority. There is a vast assemblage of groups operating across borders, above, below, and alongside national governments, including not-for profit organizations and social movements operating at a global scale. These include intergovernmental bodies which are part of the UN, the IMF, and the World Bank, and associated bodies like the UNDP and UNCTAD. Also, there are International Non-Government Organizations (INGOs), such as the Red Cross, Greenpeace, Human Rights Watch, and Oxfam. The International Criminal Court was established by a number of INGOs. In addition, some have noted the growing importance of 'private', self-policing, international voluntary agreements, which businesses sign up to. Indeed, May (2015) argues that MNC's should be considered a form of global governance, due to their power and control over international supply chains.

Such diversity has several implications for business. It adds to the complexity of organizations with whom they have to interact—to influence and be influenced by. The global footprint of MNCs, for example, means that the effect of any one national government's institutions and regulations is weakened. With respect to the global governance institutions, it also provides more stages for business to exert influence. A good example where these various types of organizations interact is the WTO, where rounds of negotiations concerning global agreements are the focus of intense interest to business, social movements, nation states, and INGOs. It is often argued that business interests here are the most powerful, exerting influence via international business groups like the Transatlantic Business Council. Other international bodies, which feed into the work of the WTO, are dominated by business, for example the International Organization for Standardization (ISO).

Counterpoint Box 9.3 The nation state—dead or alive?

Many argue that the demise of the nation state is much exaggerated (Dicken, 2015). Hirst and Thompson (2005) pointed out that the actual net flows between major economies were considerably less than a century ago, and contended that the evidence fell far short of any claim for the existence of a single global economy.

Moreover, recent events have seen a resurgence of nationalist sentiment in elections in the USA and across Europe, and in the EU referendum in the UK. Candidates like Donald Trump, Marine Le Pen in France, and supporters of Brexit in the UK, tapped into anti-globalization sentiments. Trump gained votes across the American 'rust belt', where many had felt the effects of job losses as manufacturing moved overseas. As Rodrik (2012a: 4) concludes: 'the nation state refuses to wither away. It has proved remarkably resilient, and remains the main determinant of the global distribution of income, the primary locus of market-supporting institutions, and the chief repository of personal attachments and affiliations'.

Also, the most powerful states, such as the USA and those in Western Europe, continue to dominate decision-making in international financial institutions and forums such as the IMF, World Bank, and G20, with countries like China, Brazil, and India also increasingly making their weight felt. Globalization may have served only to weaken the bargaining positions of smaller and weaker states. Rodrik (2012b) argues that there is a paradox in that, for the benefits of globalisation to be shared by all, national democracies need to be strengthened.

Sources: Dicken (2015); Hirst and Thompson (2005); Held and McGrew (2007); Rodrik (2012a and b).

Question

National identity reflects one's sense of belonging to a state or nation. To what extent is this manifest in your country in international events like the Olympic Games, or the football World Cup?

The Business of the State

The state can also play a vital role as a customer for business. In the UK, the public sector spends around £200 billion on the purchase of goods and services from thousands of suppliers. Some firms, such as MNCs like Serco and G4S, are heavily dependent, in the UK, on such contracts. For industries like pharmaceuticals and armaments, the single most important customer is the state, and the purchasing policies pursued by the state towards those industries is of paramount importance. This can be seen in those countries with ageing populations, where the state is trying to control public expenditure through pressure on pharmaceutical firms to lower prices, and by turning to lower priced generic drugs. Governments are also major customers for firms in the IT sector, and for consultancies such as PwC and McKinsey.

The purchasing strategies pursued by the state can have important implications for suppliers. For example, there are claims in the UK that government procurement policies favour large companies at the expense of small and medium-sized enterprises; this has led to a target of spending 33 per cent of government purchases with SME's by 2020. There is also much evidence that many states pursue nationalistic purchasing policies, favouring domestic producers over their foreign counterparts, even when the foreign firms offer better value.

The state can also be an important client for the financial sector. When governments run budget deficits, they borrow money from financial institutions in exchange for financial instruments such as bonds. This can make governments major customers for lending institutions. In 2016/17, the UK government paid $48.4 billion in interest payments (Keep 2017), while the US government paid out around $266 billion (the balance 2018).

Supplier of Goods and Services

In many countries the state produces and sells goods and services through publicly owned organizations in key sectors like energy, water, sanitation, transport, postal services, and telecommunications.

Governments sometimes take businesses into public ownership because the economic and social impact of them going out of business would be very serious. The global financial meltdown, and the subsequent economic crisis, gave a good illustration of this. Banks were nationalized in the USA, the UK, the Benelux countries, Iceland, and Ireland (see discussion on the global financial crisis in Chapter 11, pages 377–381). In the summer of 2009, General Motors, the giant car maker, went bankrupt and was nationalized by the US government, which, in the process, spent nearly US$60 billion of taxpayers' money. This followed a period in which the general trend had been for states to sell off these kinds of businesses, in a process of privatization, choosing to regulate them rather than own them—a process which has been controversial, especially when it involved basic utilities, like gas, and water. The policies pursued by these state-owned suppliers, as regards pricing and investment, can have a significant impact on the performance of their customers in the private sector. For example, big energy consuming firms in the steel and chemicals industries in France will be very sensitive to the prices charged by the state monopoly suppliers, Electricité de France (EDF) or Gaz de France (GDF), because energy counts for a large proportion of their costs.

The state is usually heavily involved in the provision of welfare services, with health and education services being two prime examples. These services are important for business, since they have implications for the quality of the labour force, in terms of health and education. Again, increasingly, since 1979, there has been a trend towards governments in all types of political system using the private sector to deliver these kinds of services, by means of contracting or commissioning, sometimes labelled as 'New Public Management'. Here Governments effectively purchase the service delivery via long-term contracts with private providers, whilst retaining the responsibility for the service and for monitoring its standards. In Sweden, healthcare is provided for the state by a range of providers, including Capio, which runs Hospitals and medical centres; in China, urban bus services are one of many public services provided in this way. There is now a global market for the delivery of public services. Thus, for example, the US health provider Optum works with the NHS to provide services such as contract negotiation and medication management.

The state supplies some goods and services essential for private sector production, including transport infrastructure in the form of road and rail networks, ports, and airports. Again, New Public Management reforms have led to new infrastructure, government buildings, and capital investment being provided by long term contractual partnerships between government and business. One such method has been the Private Finance Initiative in the UK, which has been used to build and manage hospitals, schools, and prisons.

Financial services may also be provided by state agencies. In the UK, the Export Credit Guarantee Department (ECGD) insures exporters against the risk of not getting paid by their overseas buyer, for reasons such as insolvency, war, or lack of foreign exchange.

Mini Case Study 9.2 Private prisons—the shadow state?

Private companies are involved in running prisons in 11 countries around the world, with the main markets being in the UK and the USA. In the UK, the first privately run prison, HMP Wolds, came into operation in 1992, and 14 per cent of the prison population now resides in privately run prisons, five of them operated by G4S. Three companies dominate the world market—the GEO group, mainly in the American market, Serco, and G4S.

G4S is a multinational company, which provides security related services in 125 countries, employing 585,000 staff, with revenues of £6.8 billion in 2016–17. The company provides a range of services for government in the UK in addition to prisons—including immigration detention centres, operating the welfare to work programme, building and managing the GCHQ communications base, and monitoring tagged offenders. In 2010, it entered into a 10 year contract with the Lincolnshire Police Force to provide a number of support services, including taking routine and emergency calls.

The company's role in these services has proven controversial, and a number of incidents have damaged its public reputation. In 2012 it failed to provide enough trained security staff for the London Olympic Games, meaning that army reserves had to be called in. A prison riot in HMP Wolds in 2016 was attributed to an insufficient number of trained staff. In 2016, five G4S Lincolnshire police control room staff were suspended for making hundreds of 999 calls at quiet times to improve their perceived performance, and the company had to repay £108.9 million after the Serious

Fraud Office found it to have overcharged government for electronic tagging. In its international operations, there have been human rights issues, including accusations of use of electric shock treatment in a South African prison.

In response to adverse publicity, G4S adopted a Human Rights policy in 2013, and a transformation strategy in the same year. The company also stresses its benefits to governments—for example, Lincolnshire Police say the G4S collaboration has improved emergency call response rates, saved time, freeing police to get back on the beat, and cut costs. Evidence with relation to the relative cost efficiency of public and private prisons, both in the UK and the USA, is, however, somewhat inconclusive.

Sources: Hill and Plummer (2013): Panchamia (2012); Pelaez (2016); http://www.politics.co.uk/comment-analysis/2015/07/27/it-s-official-private-prisons-cost-taxpayer-more-than-state

Questions
1. Explain what is meant by the term outsourcing, with reference to public services.
2. From the perspective of the government department involved, what are the pros and cons of outsourcing a service? See http://www.governing.com/topics/mgmt/pros-cons-privatizing-government-functions.html, http://www.bbc.co.uk/news/business-42687032, and http://www.bbc.co.uk/news/business-42666275.

Competitor

State organizations may be important competitors for private sector firms in, for example, energy, transport, and telecommunications, and in areas such as health and education. Often, private sector firms complain that they face unfair competition from their state rivals. This can take several forms. State firms may be subsidized, allowing them to charge artificially low prices. Most of France's electricity is produced by nuclear power, which receives large subsidies from the French government. State firms may be able to raise finance at much lower rates of interest than private sector rivals, simply because they are regarded as less risky by financial markets. Foreign private sector energy companies wishing to enter the French market could face formidable competition from their state-owned rivals, EDF, one of the world's largest electricity companies, and GDF. EDF has entered markets in both Western and Eastern Europe, but foreign energy firms trying to penetrate the French market have run up against barriers to entry put up by the French state, despite EU efforts to liberalize the energy market. State owned companies are also taking advantage of market opportunities and investments in other countries; active in UK public transportation, for example, are Arriva, a German company, Abellio (Dutch), and C2C (Italian).

Learning Task

Research the privatization of the water supply in Bolivia in the late 1990s, looking at the consequences and the outcome. (You could start at https://www.citizen.org/sites/default/files/bolivia_pdf, and also watch https://www.youtube.com/watch?v=hn9wujK0ho4.)

Subsidizer

The state often subsidizes business in the form of grants, tax reliefs, and cheap loans, to maintain or generate employment, or to maintain the production of goods and services regarded as important to the national economy. For example, the US government proposed spending $127 billion on R&D in 2016 (IRI 2016).

Subsidies are not confined to rich countries, but are also often given by poorer countries to domestic producers. From 2015–16 Pakistan introduced a $114 a ton subsidy for sugar producers (US Department of Agriculture 2015).

The Political Power of Business—Pressure and Influence

As trade, overseas investment, and foreign competition have grown in importance, so firms, particularly those with international operations, have perceived the increasing importance of their relationships with states and decision making bodies. To protect themselves against foreign competition, to get trade barriers removed, or to keep them in place, companies often appeal to forces in their political environment that could help. As the chief executive of BP said: 'We've always got to be in a position to turn to the government in power' (*Financial Times* 2 August 2002).

Firms often make big efforts to influence or pressure governing institutions at all levels, and are often prepared to devote very large amounts of resources to ensure a successful outcome. Businesses act as pressure groups to further their own interests, often joining with others to form umbrella groups, which are industry or sector wide. For example, in the UK the Confederation of British Industry (CBI) represents business interests to government. In turn, other interest groups, like Trades Unions, represent alternative views. Business is also the object of pressure by cause groups—for example, environmental campaigners—to exert influence on its decisions. Therefore, the political environment for a business may involve a range of interactions, with a range of interested groupings, around policy areas which affect it.

It is often argued that big business enjoys a privileged position in patterns of influence. Not all pressure groups have equal access to decision-makers; expertise, time, money, and sometimes personal contacts are needed. Some groups do have these, and may be able to offer decision-makers expert advice and help with implementing policies. These are known as insider groups, who often have close and continuing ties to politicians and senior members of the executive.

In the UK, for example, government departments, as a matter of course, consult bodies representing the construction and vehicle industries on draft regulations. The obligation to consult business is written into the Treaty on the Functioning of the European Union. It requires the European Commission to consult firms when preparing proposals, particularly in the areas of social policy such as employment rights, working conditions, and equal opportunities, and in public health legislation relating to fields like biotechnology. The EU intention is for business to play a substantial role, both in drafting and in implementing new measures (see the europa website for examples of business being consulted by the EU). Firms, especially large ones, are often able to get representation on government advisory committees where the concerns of business can be aired. In the EU, business has representation on the European Economic and Social Committee, which is consulted by the various institutions of the union, the Commission, Council, and the Parliament. Over and above these formal structures, big business is also in a good position to get informal access to civil servants and ministers. Such insider group activity is based on an expertise in how and where decisions are made, and the policy process, such that well connected groups will try to influence policy at the initiation and formulation stages, where it is being worked up by senior politicians, civil servants and advisers, and before it is actually formally presented to the legislators for enactment. This can involve seeking to influence political parties as they consider new policies.

Businesses thus have several resources which give them influence. Their decisions can have a major impact on economic prosperity. The need to get them 'on side', and their expertise, gives them bargaining power. They have large financial resources to mount campaigns. MNCs in particular have increased their political power with relation to other actors—trade unions and civil society organizations, and influence on International bodies. Corporate influence, for example, has been seen to have frustrated global attempts to reduce carbon emissions (Civicus, 2017).

Some industries, for example the press or television, are also well positioned to influence the state. This gives the people who run the media the power to influence politicians, especially in the run-up to national elections. The authorities may be reluctant to incur the wrath of firms operating in high technology, high growth industries for fear of losing their contribution to jobs and to economic growth. The pharmaceutical industry is a good example of an industry that is often treated with care by state institutions, such as the UK Medicines and Healthcare Products Regulatory Authority (MHRA). Pharmaceutical firms are major suppliers to the National Health Service (NHS). The NHS depends on the industry, as providers of existing and new medicines that are important in the provision and quality of health care, and thus the UK government is very keen to promote innovation, by encouraging firms to invest in research and development.

Business may enjoy a close relationship with governments and other institutions as a matter of course due to the power they hold, or simply because it is impossible to make laws and policies without them. In democracies in particular, the views of pressure groups, and of business in particular, are difficult to ignore, and indeed their ability to make their views known can be seen as essential to a free and functioning democracy. However, this influence can also be a cause of concern, as most of this influence takes place behind the scenes, and influence is unevenly distributed in favour of the most powerful groups. Research from the United States has found that economic elites, and organized groups representing business interests, have substantial independent impacts on U.S. government policy, while average citizens and mass-based interest groups have little or no independent influence (Gilens and Page, 2014). On the one hand, it can be argued that lobbying enhances the legislative process, as outside groups can provide legislators with important information and expertise, particularly on topics of a more technical and complex nature, which can in turn improve the quality of legislation. However, the extent of this lobbying activity has led to calls for transparency, and the publication of any interactions with lobbyists which may cause conflicts of interest. The EU Transparency Register, the US Lobbying Disclosure Act, 1995, and the UK's Lobbying Act 2014, are all attempts to do this, but each in turn has come in for criticism for failing to adequately deal with the issue.

The Political Power of Business—Pressure, Influence and Lobbying

According to the executive chairman of Google: 'The average American doesn't realize how much of the laws are written by lobbyists' (BrainyQuote n.d.). Businesses try to exert influence by **lobbying** individually, or collectively with other firms. To do this, they set up offices or employ professional lobbyists in the places where public policy decisions are made. A good example is Washington in the USA, where the institutions of the federal government are located. For every dollar spent on lobbying by labour unions and public-interest groups together, large corporations and their associations now spend $34. Of the 100 organizations that spend the most on lobbying, 95 consistently represent business (The Atlantic, 2015). The pharmaceutical industry has more than twice as many lobbyists in Washington as the number of elected representatives in Congress. It wields considerable power over its regulator, the Food and Drugs Administration, and donates millions of dollars each year to members of Congress sitting on important safety committees. In 2016, the industry spent more than US$152 million to influence lawmakers and federal agencies (OpenSecrets n.d.). Where businesses succeed in getting regulatory agencies to serve their interests, rather than those of wider society, they are said to have 'captured' the regulator.

Brussels, as the location for many EU institutions, is another major lobbying focus for business. Hundreds of trade associations have offices there, ranging from the International Federation of Industrial Energy Consumers, to the Liaison Committee of European Bicycle Manufacturers, and the International Confederation of European Beet Growers. Companies such as Google, Siemens, Microsoft, Intel, Procter & Gamble, General Electric, and General Motors have offices in Brussels to lobby the Commission, the European Parliament, and the Council of Ministers. Corporate Europe Observatory estimates that around 37,000 lobbyists compete for the attention of the EU institutions, the vast majority of them representing business (Corporate Europe Observatory n.d.). Google's lobby spending has increased by 240 per cent since 2014, to 4,250,000 euros per year, and it has met with EU Commissioners and their closest advisors 142 times over the last 2.5 years (transparency.eu, 2017).

When deciding how to lobby, businesses have to take a number of factors into account. They must choose whether to act alone or in alliance with others in the industry, the state institutions to be influenced, the nature and amount of pressure to be exerted on the agencies, and the degree of publicity that is advisable.

Big firms are usually powerful enough to lobby on their own account. Boeing, the giant producer of commercial and military aircraft, spends much time and resources lobbying the US government to increase defence spending, to win military contracts, and to protect it from its main European competitor, Airbus (OpenSecrets n.d.).

Small and medium-sized firms, on the other hand, often find it more effective to lobby along with other firms in the same industry through, for example, trade associations, operating either at national or supranational levels. At the national level in Britain, for example, the trade association for the consumer electronics industry is the British Radio and Electronic Equipment Manufacturers' Association (BREMA). BREMA is also associated with the European Association of Consumer Electronics Manufacturers (EACEM), which represents the industry in the EU.

In addition to lobbying on an industry basis, firms can also lobby through national bodies which represent business more generally, like the Confederation of British Industry (CBI) in Britain, the Bundesvereinigung der Deutschen Arbeitgeberverbaende (BDA) in Germany, or the Business Council of Australia, when trying to influence the state at the country level. Or they may subscribe to supranational associations, such as the Union of Industrial and Employers Confederation of Europe (UNICE), or the European Round Table (ERT), at the European level.

Promises or Threats

Occasionally, firms try to influence the state by using promises or threats. Big MNCs are able to offer countries the attractive prospect of large investment projects, generating much income and many jobs. It is no surprise that governments fall over themselves in their attempts to attract such MNC investment, especially in times of high unemployment. When energy companies offer to exploit large oil and gas reserves in poor countries, like Equatorial Guinea or Nigeria, they hold out the promise of vast income from gas and oil revenues, which gives them a deal of bargaining power in negotiations with government.

On the other hand, if business does not like the current or proposed policies of a particular country, it can threaten to cut down investment or relocate production. For example, the chairman of Ford Europe issued such a warning, stating that his company would not hesitate to close down major assembly operations in countries wishing to give workers longer holidays or a shorter working week. Another possibility is for the firm to refuse to supply goods and services. Insurers in the USA threatened to withdraw from certain areas of health insurance if President Obama did not modify his reforms to the US health care system (Consumer Watchdog n.d.).

Employment and Exchange of Personnel

Commentators often refer to the 'revolving door' between industry and the state in terms of personnel. Some companies see major benefits in offering jobs to ex-members of the legislative or executive branches of the state, such as former government ministers and high-ranking civil servants. Such people bring invaluable knowledge when companies are trying to win contracts or influence policy. Others see the jobs as pay-offs for past favours to the company, or an attempt to gain improper advantage for the firm.

Etzion and Davis (2008) did a study of the comings and goings of senior personnel between US government and business during the reign of Presidents Clinton and Bush. They found that employment in government could serve as a way of joining the corporate elite. All but one head of the US armed forces ended up serving on the boards of defence companies like Boeing and Northrop Grumman. Their research also showed a flow of people from business to high-level positions in government service. LaPira and Thomas (2012), in a survey of US lobbyists, found that more than half had held positions in the executive or legislative branches of government.

Learning Task

1. Which types of groups hold most power when trying to influence governments, and why?
2. What is the most effective way, for example, for a defence company to try to influence a policy?

Mini Case Study 9.3 The 'revolving door'

In 2016, Manuel Barroso, head of the European Commission between 2004 and 2014, took up a position advising the US investment bank Goldman Sachs on issues concerning Brexit. In early 2017, George Osborne, former Chancellor of the Exchequer in the UK, became a part-time adviser to Blackrock, the US fund management group. His former adviser at the Treasury, Robert Harrison, had joined the company in 2015. Mr Harrison had been influential in the government's pension reforms and would be helping Blackrock develop its offer in the pensions market. In October, Francis Maude, a former Cabinet Minister, took a job advising international law firm Covington and Burling LLP on the UK's exit from the EU, six months after leaving his government position. In the USA, Marilyn Tavenner was Head of the Centre for Medicare and Medicaid Services from 2011 to 2015, playing a key role in drafting the Obama administration's Affordable Care Act. In 2015, she became CEO of the trade group for health insurers, America's Health Insurance Plans, which had lobbied heavily against the Act.

The door between government and business also revolves in the other direction. Since 2006, Google has been involved in 80 'revolving door' moves with European governments.

15 ex members of staff have been appointed to government positions, including a former Managing Director, Baroness Joanna Shields, being appointed the UK's Minister for Internet Safety and Security; and Google's executive chairman, Eric Schmidt, appointed by Prime Minister David Cameron to his business advisory board. The company has also hired 65 government officials from across the EU since 2005. In the USA, during the administration of President Obama, 258 revolving door moves took place involving Google and related firms. Revolving door activity increasingly overlaps with the work of lobbyists. In the USA, 60 former lobbyists worked in critically important government positions between 2019 and 2011, increasing to 128 in 2011–13.

Sources: Financial Times 12 June 2015; *The Independent,* 21 January 2017; *The Guardian* 12 September 2016; Google Transparency Project https://googletransparencyproject.org; https://www.opensecrets.org

Question

Assess the case for and against the revolving door helping democracies function more effectively.

Giving Money or Gifts

Companies donate money openly to political parties, particularly in the run-up to elections. Firms often justify this support by insisting that they are helping those parties who will create a better environment for the effective functioning of the market economy. Historically, in the

USA, the party traditionally favoured by business has been the Republicans, in the UK the Conservatives, and in Japan the dominant LDP. During the 2016 American presidential elections, the finance and real estate sector donated US$77 million to political parties (OpenSecrets n.d.). Donations and overall expenditure by political parties are often regulated, with restrictions being put on the amount of expenditure during election periods.

Firms may also give money illegally to political parties or state officials. In 2014, an Israeli prime minister was jailed for taking a bribe from real estate developers (BBC 13 May 2014). Pei refers to the 'vast scale of corruption' of Chinese political officials (Project Syndicate n.d.). BAE, Britain's biggest arms manufacturer, has regularly been accused of paying bribes. A BBC investigation revealed that the company had made £60 million in corrupt payments to Saudi officials, including providing prostitutes, Rolls-Royces, and Californian holidays. *The Guardian* (15 September 2005) reported that BAE had been identified as secretly paying more than £1 million through American banks to General Pinochet, the former Chilean dictator, in return for defence contracts. (Chapter 4 examines the issue of corruption in more depth).

● CHAPTER SUMMARY

In this chapter we examined the characteristics of various political systems. We saw how the political organization and institutional configuration of countries can have significant implications for business. We identified and explained the different functions carried out by the state and showed how important they can be, for example, in preventing the collapse of the economic and financial system, and in setting the legal and regulatory rules of the game for business, and how they change over time. We also considered the arguments for and against the thesis that globalization had led to the demise of the nation state. Finally, we considered the variety of methods, from lobbying to the donation of money, that firms use to influence their political environment.

● REVIEW QUESTIONS

1. What is the state? Why is it important for the aerospace industry? Explain with examples.

2. Compare and contrast the characteristics of liberal democratic and communist states. Discuss which of these types of state would be more attractive for a Western MNC.

3. To what extent do you agree that globalization has undermined the power of the nation state? Give evidence to support your arguments.

4. The Economist Intelligence Unit (EIU) produces an Index of Democracy (http://www.eiu.com/topic/democracy-index) that charts the progress of democracy in the world. Its 2016 Report stated that the year had seen the 'Revenge of the deplorables' and also had seen a 'democratic recession'

   a. What is indicated by the term 'Revenge of the deplorables'? Do you agree with the description?

   b. Identify the principal reasons for the 'democratic recession'.

   c. The 2016 Report saw the USA downgraded from 'full democracy' to 'flawed democracy'. Why was this?

   d. What, if any, are the implications of the standstill in democracy for business?

● ASSIGNMENT TASKS

1. You are the PA to an executive in a social media platform which allows sharing of messages and videos, and which generates its income via advertising revenue. Your boss asks you to write a report that:

   a. Sets out the recent issues surrounding fake news;

   b. Analyses the implications of it for your company.

2. You work in the mergers and acquisitions section of a big multinational bank. One of your clients is a large mobile phone company considering moving into India. You are given the task of researching the political environment in India. Your specific remit is to:

   a. examine the experiences of foreign mobile phone companies with the political authorities in India in the decade up to 2018;

   b. outline the attitudes towards foreign business of the political party that took power in the 2014 national elections, and examine possible scenarios for the 2019 elections; and

   c. in the light of your research, assess whether the political environment makes India a good location for your client.

Case Study The Arab Spring and the refugee crisis in Syria

© Shutterstock.com/Istvan Csak

In the spring of 2011, a series of unprecedented popular uprisings took place in several Arab countries, from North Africa to the Middle East, firstly in Tunisia and quickly spreading to Libya, Egypt, Yemen, and Syria.

These societies had significant social and economic inequality, corruption, and abuse of power by the rulers, and repression of political freedom. The media was controlled by the state or the military, and freedom of expression and association was limited. Imprisonment without trial, and torture, were widespread.

In Syria, the protests opposed the rule of President Assad. Assad's use of force against the protests led to a civil war involving multiple factions, and drawing in a range of regional and global players. The Free Syrian Army developed to oppose the Assad regime, and regional players began to take sides—with Turkey and Saudi Arabia supporting the opposition, and Iran sending support to Assad. The war reflected the religious, regional, and global complexity of the issues involved. The opposing factions broadly divided into camps of Sunni (opposition) and Shia (Assad) Muslims. Amidst the fighting, Islamic State (ISIS) personnel entered Syria from Iraq, and Hezbollah from Lebanon. In response to loss of territory, the Assad regime resorted to bombing and chemical attacks, which violated United Nations Human Rights conventions.

The war assumed global political importance, with the Russians providing military support for Assad, with China also in support. The USA and European Union were increasingly concerned but unable to agree on military intervention against Assad. Anti-Assad motions at the UN Security Council were consistently vetoed by Russia. For the Western powers, the growth and military success of ISIS became an equally important issue, following a series of terrorist attacks in Europe.

The effects of the war on the Syrian population have been devastating; by 2016 there had been an estimated half a million ➡

→ casualties, with a tenth of the county's 1.9m population either injured or killed. Life expectancy had fallen by 15 years, and 11 million had fled their homes. In 2016, the United Nations estimated that there were 13.5 million Syrians requiring humanitarian assistance. Economically the cost was estimated at $35bn. On a global scale, the war caused the largest displacement of people since the Second World War. This put great strain on neighbouring countries—there were more than 5 million Syrian refugees in Turkey, Lebanon, and Jordan by March 2017, and over 1 million had entered Europe by 2016. The number seeking asylum in OECD countries rose to a post-war high of 1.65m in 2015.

These influxes of people occurred at a time of what was, for many, a period of hardship. Greece, a country in huge economic difficulties, found itself receiving large numbers of refugees arriving by sea—up to 1,000 a day onto the island of Lesbos in 2016.

In Europe, the issues of Syrians seeking asylum became intertwined with broader issues around immigration and security. Migrants from Syria, and elsewhere, wanting to make their way across Europe, found that borders were increasingly closed—the first ones being those of Macedonia, Croatia and Slovenia. Previously welcoming countries, like Sweden, progressively started to reconsider their degree of openness, as the humanitarian crisis led to raised concerns about pressure on domestic services. These concerns were taken up by nationalist political leaders and parties across the west. The growing strength of ISIS, and its responsibility for terrorist attacks in Paris and Manchester, amongst others, led to a conflation of issues around immigration levels and asylum seeking, which became key in elections in Holland and France in 2017, in the 'Brexit' referendum, and in the campaign of Donald Trump for the US Presidency. Tensions have also surfaced in the EU, due to the differential impacts on member states, and to rising nation-alist sentiment. The EU Commission took legal action against Poland, Hungary and the Czech Republic for refusing to take in any refugees under a relocation plan agreed in 2015. A survey in 2016 found that 76 per cent in Hungary and 71 per cent in Poland were concerned that refugees increased the likelihood of terrorism, and imposed a burden on their countries. Germany's 'open door' policy contrasted with the reluctance of the Visegrad group of Eastern European states, Poland, Hungary, Czech Republic and Slovakia, indicating what may be a fundamental split within the EU.

Sources: Lucas (2016); Reuters (2016); Pew Research Center http://www.pewresearch.org/fact-tank/2016/09/16/european-opinions-of-the-refugee-crisis-in-5-charts; Morillas et al. (2015); UNHCR http://data.unhcr.org/syrianrefugees/regional.php

Questions

1. Which characteristics indicate that the Arab Spring countries were authoritarian?

2. Why has it proven so difficult to establish democracy in a country like Syria?

3. Discuss what the case of Syria tells us about global political institutions like the UN.

4. Looking at examples from Europe, what does this case tell us about the 'demise of the nation state' thesis?

Carry out some further research for these questions:

5. What part, if any, do you think that 'Fake News' has played in the discussion about the impacts of refugees from Syria to European countries?

6. How has the EU tried to collectively resolve the issues resulting from the increase in refugee numbers, and to what extent have they been successful?

● FURTHER READING

This textbook examines a variety of different political systems and concepts:

● Caramani, D. (2014) *Comparative Politics*, 3rd edn. Oxford: Oxford University Press.

For a text on global politics, see:

● Edkins, J. and Zehfuss, M. (2014) *Global Politics: A New Introduction,* 2nd edn. Abingdon: Routledge.

For a useful overview of different political regimes, see:

● 'The Keele Guide to Political Science on the Internet'. http://www.keele.ac.uk/depts/por/psbase.htm. It is wide-ranging, covering the Americas, Europe, Asia, Africa, and Oceania.

● REFERENCES

Acemoglu, D., Naidu, S., Restrepo, P., and Robinson, J.A. (2014) *Democracy Does Cause Growth*. National Bureau of Economic Research Working Paper Series, Working Paper 20004. Available at http://www.nber.org/papers/w20004.

BBC (2017) 'Reality Check: How Big is the UK's Deficit and Debt?' http://www.bbc.co.uk/news/business-39897498.

BrainyQuote (n.d.) http://www.brainyquote.com.

CIA (n.d.) 'World Factbook'. https://www.cia.gov/library/publications/the-world-factbook/fields/2222.html.

Civicus (2017) *State of Civil Society Report*. London: Civicus.

Consumer Watchdog (n.d.) http://www.consumerwatchdog.org.

Corporate Europe Observatory (n.d.) http://www.corporateeurope.org.

Deudney, D. and Ikenberry, G.J. (2009) 'The Myth of the Autocratic Revival: Why Liberal Democracy will Prevail'. *Foreign Affairs* 88(1).

Devereux, M.P. and Sørensen, P.B. (2005) 'The Corporate Income Tax: International Trends and Options for Fundamental Reform', October. Available at http://www.sbs.ox.ac.uk.

Dicken, P (2015) *Global Shift*, 7th edn. London: Sage.

Drucker, P. (1999) *Management: Tasks, Responsibilities, Practices*. Oxford: Butterworth-Heinemann.

Etzion, D. and Davis, G.F. (2008) 'Revolving Doors: A Network Analysis of Corporate Officers and US Government Officials'. *Journal of Management Inquiry* 17(3).

Fukuyama, F. (1993) *The End of History and the Last Man*. London: Penguin.

Gilens, M. and Page, B.I. (2014) 'Testing Theories of American Politics: Elites, Interest Groups, and Average Citizens' *Perspectives on Politics* 12 (3).

Grillo, I. (2016) 'It was once the richest country in Latin America. Now it's falling apart' *Time* 13 August. Available at http://time.com/venezuela-brink.

Held, D. and McGrew, A.G. (2007) *Globalisation Theories: Approaches and Controversies*. Cambridge: Polity Press.

Hill, A. and Plummer, G. (2013) 'G4S: The Inside Story'. *The Financial Times*. 16 November.

Hirst, P. and Thompson, G. (2005) *Globalization in Question: The International Economy and the Possibilities of Governance,* 3rd edn. London: Polity Press.

IMF (2014) 'Fiscal Monitor, Public Expenditure Reform: Making Difficult Choices', April. Available at http://www.imf.org/external/pubs/ft/fm/2014/01/fmindex.htm.

IRI (2016) https://www.iriweb.org/sites/default/files/2016GlobalR%26DFundingForecast_2.pdf.

Keep, M. (2017) 'Government Borrowing, Debt and Debt Interest: Historical Statistics and Forecasts'. House of Commons Library Briefing Paper Number 05745, 21 June.

Ketterer, T.D. and Rodríguez-Pose, A. (2016) *Institutions vs. 'First-nature' Geography: What Drives Economic Growth in Europe's Regions?* Papers in Regional Science. ISSN 1056-8190.

KPMG (2018) 'Corporate Tax Rate Tables' https://home.kpmg.com/xx/en/home/services/tax/tax-tools-and-resources/tax-rates-online/corporate-tax-rates-table.html.

LaPira, T.M. and Thomas, H.F. (2012) 'Revolving Doors: Lobbyists' Government Experience, Expertise and Access in Political Context'. Paper to the American Political Science Association Conference, 12 September.

Lucas, S (2016) 'A Beginner's Guide to Syria's Civil War' *Political Insight* 7 (1).

May, T, (2015) 'Who's in charge? Corporations as institutions of global governance' *Palgrave Communications* 1. Available at https://www.nature.com/articles/palcomms201542.

Morillas, P., Sánchez-Montijano, E., and Soler, E. (2015) *Europe and the refugee crisis: 10 side-effects* Barcelona; CIDOB.

Neowin (2013) http://www.neowin.net, 2013.

OECD (2015) 'Revenue Statistics--provisional data on tax ratios for 2015'. Available at http://www.oecd.org/ctp/tax-policy/revenue-statistics-ratio-change-latest-years.htm.

OECD (2016) *OECD Factbook 2016: Economic, Environmental and Social Statistics*. OECD Publishing.

OECD (n.d.) http://stats.oecd.org.

Ohmae, K. (2005) *The Next Global Stage: The Challenges and Opportunities in Our Borderless World*. New Jersey: Wharton School Publishing.

OpenSecrets (n.d.) http://www.opensecrets.org.

Panchamia, N. (2012) *Competition in Prisons*. London: Institute for Government.

Pelaez, V. (2016) 'The Prison Industry in the United States: Big Business or a New Form of Slavery'? *El Diario-La Prensa*, New York and Global Research 10 March 2008. Available at https://www.globalresearch.ca/the-prison-industry-in-the-united-states-big-business-or-a-new-form-of-slavery/8289.

Pereira, C. and Teles, V. (2010) 'Political Institutions and Substitute for Democracy: A Political Economy Analysis of Economic Growth'. Manuscript presented at the Annual Conference of the European Economic Association.

Project Syndicate (n.d.) http://www.project-syndicate.org.

Przeworski, A., Alvarez, M., Cheibub, J.A., and Limongi, F. (2000) *Democracy and Development: Political Institutions and Well-Being in the World, 1950–1990*. New York: Cambridge University Press.

Reinicki, W.H. (2013) 'Purpose beyond Power'. Brookings, Fall 2013. Available at http://www.brookings.edu/research/articles/2013/10/globalization-liberal-democracy-society-reinicke.

Reuters (2016) 'Economic Costs of Middle East Wars Exceptionally High: IMF Study'. http://www.reuters.com/article/us-imf-conflicts-idUSKCN11M1RR.

Reuters and University of Oxford (2016) *Digital News Report*, Reuters Institute for the Study of Journalism. Available at http://reutersinstitute.politics.ox.ac.uk/sites/default/files/Digital-News-Report-2016.pdf.

Rodrik, D. (2007) *One Economics Many Recipes: Globalization, Institutions, and Economic Growth* Princeton: Princeton University Press.

Rodrik, D. (2012a) 'Who Needs the Nation State?'. Harvard University, May. Available at http://www.hks.harvard. edu/fs/drodrik/Research%20papers/Who%20Needs%20the%20Nation%20State.pdf.

Rodrick, D. (2012b) *The Globalisation Paradox* Oxford: Oxford University Press.

Rodrick, D. (2016) 'Is Liberal Democracy feasible in Developing Countries?' *Studies in Comparative International Development* 51 (1).

the balance (2018) 'Interest on the National Debt and How It Affects You'. https://www.thebalance.com/interest-on-the-national-debt-4119024.

Transparency International (n.d.). Available at https://www.transparency.org/news/pressrelease/venezuela_stop_the_use_of_violence_and_abuse_of_human_rights_to_hold_on_to

US Department of Agriculture (2015) https://gain.fas.usda.gov/Recent%20GAIN%20Publications/Pakistan%20Sugar%20Update_Islamabad_Pakistan_12-15-2015.pdf.

US Department of the Treasury (2013) Monthly 'Report to Congress: Troubled Asset Relief Program', 10 September. Available at http://www.treasury.gov/initiatives/financial-stability/reports/Documents/Monthly%20Report%20to%20Congress%20August%202013.pdf.

Watts, J. (2016) 'Venezuela on the brink: a journey through a country in crisis' *The Guardian* 11th October. Available at https://www.theguardian.com/world/2016/oct/11/venezuela-on-the-brink-a-journey-through-a-country-in-crisis.

Wright, T. (2006) 'Why Hasn't Economic Development Brought Democracy to China?'. Available at http://www.eastwestcenter.org.

CHAPTER TEN

The Legal Environment

LEARNING OUTCOMES

This chapter will enable you to:

- explain the importance of the legal environment for business;

- compare and contrast the different systems of law and their implications for international business;

- assess the importance of contract, tort, and criminal law, for business behaviour;

- demonstrate the significance of international arbitration for firms involved in international trade and investment; and

- recognize the lack of development of the law around the internet, and the growing importance of cybercrime.

Case Study Airbnb and the law

© 123RF.com/Chonlachai Panprommas

This case shows the challenges and opportunities that the law can present to firms, in this case Airbnb. It also illustrates how business can use the law to confront challenges.

The development of the internet has led to the creation of corporations such as Airbnb and Uber, which offer services via on-line platforms, but do not physically provide the services. Their entry has disrupted traditional methods of delivering those services. Airbnb offers holiday accommodation and uses its platform to match supply and demand, in other words it acts as an intermediary between suppliers and customers. It takes a 3 per cent cut from hosts, and anything from 6 per cent to 12 per cent from guests.

Airbnb has grown very rapidly, first in the US and then overseas. In 2009 Airbnb had only 3000 accommodation sites on its platform. This had grown to around 4.5 million by 2017/18. In 2016, the company welcomed its hundred-millionth guest.

Competition from Airbnb was not well received by rivals offering accommodation. Hotel companies complained to the authorities that Airbnb was competing unfairly. For example, in London, one third of the saving on accommodation made by Airbnb users was due to tax advantages. This was a result of the high rates of UK business property taxes and value added tax on hotel stays, combined with generous tax advantages for those renting rooms. Unlike hotel companies, Airbnb hosts are not required to comply with health and safety regulations. However, after cases of guests being injured or dying in the properties, Airbnb guaranteed hosts insurance of up to $1 million.

Airbnb, and the property owners advertising on its platforms, have run up against the law in, for example, the US, Canada, Spain, France, and Germany. New York City passed a law making it unlawful for home owners to advertise whole apartment rentals for periods of less than 30 days, levying fines of $1000 for a first offence, $5000 for a second and $7500 for the third. San Francisco established a registration system for owners offering short-term rentals, proposing fines of $1000 a day for each non-registration. Both cities intended to hold Airbnb responsible for owners not complying with the laws. Airbnb did not take this lying down, filing lawsuits against both New York and San Francisco to prevent fines being levied. It claimed that the actions by the cities breached the right to freedom of speech, as laid down in the First Amendment of the US constitution, and violated the Communications Decency Act, which prevents the authorities holding websites responsible for content posted by users. Airbnb dropped the lawsuits against New York and San Francisco when the city authorities agreed that fines would be paid by home owners and not Airbnb.

Airbnb also encountered legal problems outside the US. In Canada, property owners in Quebec wishing to rent out accommodation need a certificate of approval from the municipality. Those without approval face a daily fine of up to $2,250 and up to $6,750 for a repeat offence. Barcelona, concerned about rising rents and rowdy behaviour by tourists, imposed a fine of €30,000 on Airbnb for breaking tourism laws and, in 2016, fined the company €600,000 for allowing owners to list properties for short-term rental without a licence. In 2017, the city passed a law curbing apartment developments aimed at tourists. Paris levied fines of up to €25,000 on property owners unlawfully offering short-term accommodation. The city did not want whole areas turned into tourist homes, making it more difficult for Parisians to remain in the city. Berlin, where Airbnb was blamed for rising rents, passed a law banning short-term lets, unless approved by the authorities.

The law is not always hostile to Airbnb. Amsterdam passed a law permitting residents to let out their properties whilst, at the national level, France legalised short-term renting for home owners. Official attitudes in Britain were also friendlier to Airbnb, with the government in 2016 offering a tax break of £1000 to those renting out property.

Sources: Bloomberg 7 August 2014 and 11 July 2016; *El País* 7 July 2014; *Financial Times* 24 November 2016 and 7 January 2017; *Forbes* 21 October 2016 and 28 June 2015; *The Guardian* 8 July 2014, 24 February 2018; Investopedia 31 August 2015; *The Observer* 29 January 2017; *The Telegraph* 8 August 2014 and 7 June 2016; *New York Times* 3 December 2016; Refinery 29 November 2015; BBC 30 November 2016; *San Francisco Business Times* 24 May 2016; Santa Clara Law Digital Commons at http://digitalcommons.law.scu.edu

Introduction

In this chapter, we examine the legal environment within which international business operates. We show the importance of the legal framework and how its rules and regulations can impinge on business, literally from the cradle to the grave. The law can have a major influence on business behaviour; for instance, when forming a company or negotiating a contract. It can require firms to compensate those whom they injure.It can forbid business, under the threat of penalty, from undertaking certain types of behaviour, such as mergers and acquisitions, colluding with competitors, and polluting the environment. We go on to consider the major systems of law prevailing across the globe, and we conclude by outlining some important institutions and codes in international law and their implications for the business community. The chapter concludes by examining an attempt to harmonise internet law, and the increasing threats from cybercrime.

Changes in the legal environment can provide businesses with opportunities to make money and grow, but can also generate challenges. A firm may find itself the subject of a claim by a government, a rival, a customer, or a supplier, which could result in a financial loss, and could also result in damage to the company's reputation. Companies may feel that they are legally protected, only to find that judges put a different interpretation on the law, or it may be that the law is not rigorously enforced. Finally, changes in the law could leave the company exposed to a legal suit for actions previously regarded as permissible.

Knowledge of different legal and regulatory systems, operating at national and international levels, is invaluable for business in a world where foreign trade, investment and outsourcing, and international e-commerce are growing rapidly.

The Importance of Law for Business

The legal environment forms a vital element of the external environment for business. Firms producing everything from laptop computers, mobile phones, air flights, toys, cosmetics, financial products, drugs, fertilizers, food, and drink are all subject to requirements laid down by the law. The legal environment sets the rules of the game within which business operates. It can influence a business from its inception, by laying down certain legal steps which must be undertaken to set the business up, to its end, with rules relating to the winding up of the company. When the firm is up and running, the law can not only tell it what to do, but also what not to do. The law is a double-edged sword for business, because it offers both threats and opportunities. On the one hand, it can leave firms open to legal action; on the other, it can help the firm in achieving their objectives by, for example, making it easier to enter markets, or by pursuing others legally to protect and promote their interests.

Business is also subject to regulations. Regulations are not laws, as such, but rules that take their authority from statutes. They are usually issued by governmental agencies at all levels: national, regional, and local. In most developed countries, utilities companies in the energy sector, and in telecoms and water, are regulated. In the UK, OFGEM regulates the energy sector, the China Securities Regulatory Commission deals with the stock market in China, while the US Federal Aviation Administration (FAA) deals with aviation in the USA, and the Federal Trade Commission (FTC) is responsible for protecting the consumer and dealing with monopolies.

The legal environment, both domestic and international, can influence the whole process of production and sale regarding:

- **Production techniques**: how firms produce goods and services can be influenced by laws and regulations. The aerospace industry in the EU is regulated both globally, through the International Civil Aviation Organisation (ICAO), and in Europe, by the European Aviation Safety Agency (EASA). In the EU, passenger safety is of paramount importance, so aircraft and components must meet standards of airworthiness. Increasingly, car makers have been obliged to change their methods of production to meet emissions control regulations introduced by the US, the EU, Japan, China, and India. Africa, facing high rates of population growth, urbanization, and increasing industrialization, suffers from deteriorating urban air quality. Foreign car manufacturers and domestic industries using heavily polluting production techniques such as steel mills and coal-fired power stations in countries producing the largest amounts of greenhouse gases, Nigeria, Egypt, and South Africa, are likely to face increasingly stringent emissions controls.

- **Product characteristics**: the law can determine product characteristics, from the materials used, to the product specifications. Asbestos is used as an insulator in the construction and energy sectors. Large amounts are produced by companies in Russia, China and Brazil. However, many advanced countries, including the USA, the UK, South Korea, and Singapore, along with some emerging economies, such as Saudi Arabia and Turkey, banned asbestos in construction products after it was found to cause lung cancer and other respiratory diseases. Its use is allowed in countries like China, India, and most African countries.

- **Packaging and labels**: most major economies, including the USA, EU, Japan, and China, and many smaller countries have rules relating to the packaging and labelling of products, such as food and hazardous chemicals. Labelling regulations requiring lots of information for the consumer can pose problems for product marketing by taking up too much space on the packaging, or by regulating the type of packaging. In the UK, Australia, and Canada, cigarettes have to be sold in plain packaging.

- **Content and placement of advertising and sales promotion**: tobacco and alcohol are two industries that are heavily regulated in this regard. Tobacco advertising is banned on radio and television in the USA, and the EU, with the EU ban extending to print media and the internet. It is not allowed at all in Canada and New Zealand. South Africa bans advertising and promotion of tobacco, and restricts smoking in public spaces. In order to counter the effects of the advertising bans on sales, tobacco firms, like British American Tobacco and Philip Morris, have had to find other ways of promoting their products. They make more use of billboards and direct mailing, get their products placed in films, and sponsor music-oriented events particularly attractive to young people; for example, festivals, 'raves', and concerts. Squeezed, in rich world markets, by advertising restrictions and bans on smoking in public places, tobacco firms have looked to markets in poorer countries from China and India, to Africa and Latin America. Law makers are becoming increasingly concerned about the push by big tobacco firms into the electronic cigarette market and, worried about the effect on consumer health, are pushing for regulations to be introduced.

- **Treatment of workers**: many countries, including the USA, the UK, China, Japan, Brazil, Colombia, South Africa, and Russia, prescribe a minimum wage. The EU has a longstanding commitment to equal pay for equal work, and lays down the maximum number of hours that can be worked. Both Japan and the EU have laws protecting the security of employment of older people.

- **Terms and conditions of trade with customers and suppliers**: these cover issues such as delivery dates, terms of payment, return policies for defective products, warranties, and so on. Most countries have statutes relating to the sale of goods and services. Usually, the law requires the terms of sale to be clear, consistent, and reasonable. This often appears not to be the case on the internet, where suppliers can hide pro-seller terms in masses of legal jargon, which is incomprehensible to the average consumer. A *Guardian* journalist spent a week reading the terms and conditions (T&Cs) of several products. The T&Cs for Apple iPhone and Sony P both contained at least 20,000 words. Playing video games on the Playstation required him to read three separate sets of T&Cs (*The Guardian* 15 June 2015).

 Learning Task

In California, Google lost a court case relating to its terms and conditions for users of Gmail (Google n.d.).

1. What were the Gmail terms and conditions that broke the law?

2. Which law(s) was Google found to be breaching?

3. What arguments did Google use in its defence?

- **Tools of competition**: this relates to how firms compete with rivals and treat customers. Many developed economies have competition laws regulating business behaviour. In the USA and the EU, for example, the law is hostile to powerful firms exploiting their monopoly power by charging customers high prices, or tying them in through the imposition of exclusive contracts, which force them to buy all their requirements from the same supplier. EU and US law also disapproves of firms squeezing rivals through, for example, artificially low prices. Companies wishing to go in for takeovers can also be affected by the legal environment. Both the USA and the EU prohibit cartels, where firms come to an agreement to avoid competition by agreeing a common price, or by sharing the market out geographically. The OECD has been active in promoting competition policy in Latin American countries such as Brazil, Argentina, and Mexico. Emerging economies tend not to have competition laws, Russia, India, and China being three exceptions. The law may also protect firms from competition from the **grey market**. The grey market refers to trade in goods through distribution channels that have not been authorized by the manufacturer. This often occurs when the price of the product varies from country to country. The good is bought in a country where it is cheap, and sold at below market price in a country where price is high. It is sometimes called parallel importing. The practice is particularly prevalent in cigarettes, pharmaceuticals, cars, music and films, satellite television, and in electronic goods such as cameras and games consoles. Canon, complaining of unfair competition, took US retailers to court for selling imported Canon cameras which they had obtained in Europe and Asia. Most countries have laws against bribery, and these laws can be applied against firms even when the crime has occurred abroad. In 2017, Mondelez, the multinational food manufacturer, paid $13 million to the US authorities for breaching the Foreign Corrupt Practices Act, even though the offences, bribing government officials in India for a license to build a chocolate factory, had been committed outside the US. Similarly Rolls-Royce, the UK aero-engine maker paid a fine of £671 million to regulators in the UK, US and Brazil, settling claims of bribery and corruption relating to 12 countries over a period of 23 years.

- **Ownership of assets**: legal systems usually confer and protect rights of ownership and possession of company assets, both physical, like buildings and machinery, and intellectual assets. For example, the law will often protect intellectual property by giving the holder exclusive rights to exploit the asset for a certain period of time. Protection may also be accorded to holders of copyright covering creative and artistic works, including books, films, music, paintings, photographs, software, product designs, and on trademarks which are signs distinguishing the products or services of firms. Trade secrets may also be protected by the law. Yeh (2016), claims that US companies lose billions of dollars every year through theft of their trade secrets. Cisco, the US-based multinational telecommunications company, successfully sued the Chinese firm, Huawei, for theft of a computer source code. The US court issued a world-wide injunction preventing Huawei using the code (Rowe and Mahfood 2014).

 Learning Task

Legal protection can be obtained for the appearance of a product including, shape, packaging, and colours, if it is a distinctive sign of the product for consumers. Such protection prevents others from copying that particular aspect of appearance.

Nestlé, the giant Swiss-based multinational, has waged long-running battles over intellectual property with Cadbury, which is owned by US multinational Mondelez.

1. Which areas of intellectual property have been disputed by Nestlé and Cadbury?

2. Why do these two companies spend so much time and money trying to get legal protection for their products?

3. Which courts have been involved in adjudicating the disputes?

4. Assess whether either company has won the chocolate war.

See: *The Guardian* 17 September 2015, 12 August 2016, 17 May 2017; ipkitten.blogspot.co.uk/2015/08/a-premature-requiem-proving-acquired.html

- **Financial reporting**: many countries lay down rules and regulations regarding the reporting of the financial state of the company and its performance. There are also moves afoot to establish international reporting standards. Around 150 countries are committed to the International Financial Reporting Standards (IFRS), a single set of global financial standards. These establish a framework for the preparation and presentation of financial statements, so that financial information provided by companies is transparent and comparable. This harmonization of reporting standards has become more important for companies, as they increasingly look overseas, not only for market and investment opportunities, but also to raise finance. Harmonized reporting allows firms to evaluate more easily potential distributors and candidates for joint ventures and takeovers. While the EU, and many other countries around the world, now subscribe to IFRS, the USA stands alone, with its own generally accepted accounting principles (GAAP) (the International Accounting Standards Board is responsible for establishing the IFRS, see http://www.iasb.org).

Counterpoint Box 10.1 How big a role for law?

Neoliberals argue that the law should play a minimalist role in society. According to Buckley (1955):

> It is the job of centralized government (in peacetime) to protect its citizens' lives, liberty and property. All other activities of government tend to diminish freedom and hamper progress.

The law should act as the guarantor of private property. Property, in this sense, refers to assets such as land, housing, company shares, works of art, intellectual property, and so on. The law should protect the rights to property—in other words, the right to own, sell, lend, give away, or bequeath assets—and should enforce contractual agreements. Friedman (2002), referring to the privatization programme in Russia, said:

> Privatization is meaningless if you don't have the rule of law. What does it mean to privatize if you do not have security of property, if you can't use your property as you want to?

Neoliberals argue that the rule of law is vital for the operation of the market by, for example, facilitating transactions between buyers and sellers. They also accept that the law should protect the citizen against violence, theft, and fraud. Friedman (1970) holds that the aim of business is to make as much money as possible, while conforming to society's legal and ethical rules. Neoliberal views draw heavily on the ideas of Hayek, Von Mises, Schumpeter, and Friedman.

Critics of the neoliberal position argue that the law has got to do much more than guarantee private property. According to this school of thought, markets can lead to undesirable outcomes, which domestic and international law should try to prevent; for example, the behaviour of financial institutions that led to the global financial crisis, the creation of monopolies, or damage to the environment. Ownership of an asset should not give the right to do as one pleases; for example, the law should stop owners of coal-fired power stations from polluting the air. Furthermore, the law needs to respond to major disparities in income and wealth, gender inequalities, and to ensure the human right to health and education.

Sources: Buckley (1955); Glinavos (2008); Friedman (1970 and 2002); Stiglitz (2010); Patel (2009); Nozick (1977)

Questions

1. Assess whether the law should respond to residents of Barcelona who complain that the activities of companies like Airbnb are pushing up rents and property prices.

2. Weigh up the case for allowing farmers in Colombia to use their land to cultivate the coca plant used to produce cocaine.

Systems and Sources of Law

In an increasingly globalized world, firms buying, selling, and investing outside their domestic market confront a variety of laws and regulations in the countries where they operate. In this section, we discuss the major systems of law that firms are likely to encounter.

Contrary to a widespread misapprehension, laws are not simply the product of decisions made by governments and parliaments. There are four major legal systems in the world, which are drawn, in large degree, from different sources. They comprise civil law, common law, customary law, and religious law. Civil law and common law systems are predominant in the world and, for that reason, are of most importance to business.

The particular systems operating in countries or regions are the result of the interaction of many historical forces, socio-cultural, political, economic, and technological. One particularly important influence in many countries is the historical legacy of empire. Thus, countries in Africa that were part of the French empire are likely to have laws based on the French system, while former British colonies tend to have systems based on English law. Furthermore, the boundaries between the different systems can break down as the systems evolve over time. Globalization contributes to this blurring of the boundaries, because one country's legal system can end up incorporating elements from others. Thus, the system in Japan has been heavily influenced by the German legal code, and has also been subject to English and American influences. Similarly, the Chinese system reflects, to a degree, Soviet and Continental legal principles.

Business can find that the various legal systems create very different legal environments within which to operate. Laws, regulations, procedures, and outcomes may vary enormously from one system to another.

Civil Law Systems

Most legal systems in the world have their basis in civil law (see Figure 10.1), the primary source of which is legislation. Civil law is a body of laws, and legal concepts, which have their basis in the legal codes of the Roman Empire. Civil law systems give precedence to written law, sometimes called codified law. Judges apply and interpret the law, which is drawn from legal codes and statutes—statutes are written laws passed by legislative bodies, such as national or regional parliaments.

The legal systems in Continental Europe and in Central and South America are largely codified and set out in legislation. In the USA, Louisiana is the sole state having a legal structure based on civil law, with Quebec being in a similar position in Canada. Scottish law is heavily influenced by Roman law, but has not gone in for the extensive codification so prevalent on the continent. Other countries, for example in Scandinavia, while not so influenced by Roman law, have systems akin to civil law because of their heavy dependence on the laws written into statutes.

The procedure in civil law systems is inquisitorial, where judges collect evidence and question witnesses to discover the truth. Rather than orally presenting their case, each side must provide written statements of it to the judge. A consequence of this emphasis on the written word is that lawyers act as advisors, rather than as oral advocates of their client's case to the judge. Judges then decide, on the basis of the evidence, whether the case should go to trial, but trials are relatively rare. Should a trial occur, panels of judges or lay assessors review the written evidence gathered by the judge and come to a decision. Juries are used in some criminal trials. In civil

Figure 10.1 Legal systems across the world

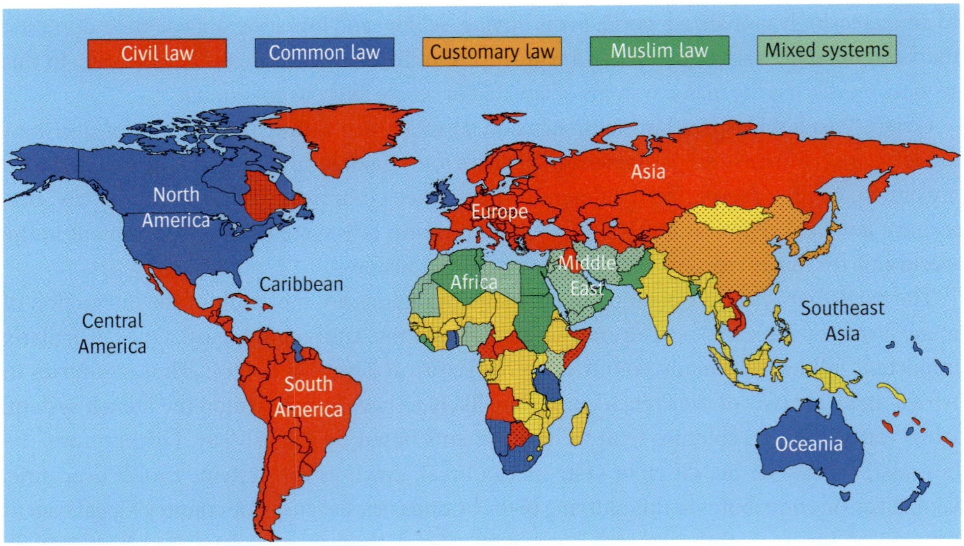

Source: University of Ottawa. Available at http://www.juriglobe.ca/eng

systems, court decisions applying the law may influence subsequent decisions, but do not become binding.

One advantage to business of civil law systems is that, because the law is codified in written form, it is easier to find and to articulate clearly. On the other hand, the emphasis on written evidence means that there must be effective document storage and retrieval systems to handle all the paperwork generated by the system, if the law is to be properly applied. While this may be the case in Continental Europe, many poorer countries, say in Africa or Latin America, do not have efficient bureaucratic systems, and, as a result, are not in a good position to apply the law effectively.

To avoid confusion, it is useful to note that the term civil law is also used to refer to law dealing with the rights and duties of one individual to another, for instance, in relation to the law of contract.

Common Law Systems

Common law is a legal system based on English law that accords greater importance to judgments in court cases than to written codes and statutes. Common law is also known as case law, or judge-made law, inasmuch as legal principles are determined by judgments in court cases (Mayson et al. 2016–17).

Courts, by interpreting and applying the law, determine its meaning and, through their judgments, fill in gaps in the legislative code. Court judgments can set precedents, which are binding on themselves and on lower courts when judging similar cases—in other words, it becomes the law for everyone to follow. Binding precedents are usually made by courts at the higher levels. Judges in lower-level courts cannot usually issue binding precedents.

Mini Case Study 10.1 South Africa

South Africa is a middle-income country with a population of over 54 million. The legal system is well developed, and is based on a combination of Roman-Dutch civil law, English common law, and customary law. This mixed system has come about as a result of the country's history of Dutch colonial government, British imperial rule, and traditional tribal systems.

Judges in the higher courts are appointed by the President, in consultation with a judicial commission, as well as the leaders of political parties represented in the South African parliament. Some commentators are concerned that judges are not sufficiently protected from political influence. Nonetheless, the courts are seen as acting independently and professionally. The World Economic Forum (2018) rates the country high on judicial independence and the efficiency of the legal system, but low on burdensome government regulation. Government officials show favouritism in their decisions, and the reliability of the police service is low.

The World Bank ranks the country 74th out of 190 countries, in terms of the ease of doing business. Where disputes occur over contracts, it takes an average of 600 days to enforce the contract, and the process costs one third of the legal claim. While foreign investors find that their rights are well protected, the country performs poorly on trading across borders regarding the time and costs of procedures around exporting and importing. There are no restrictions when buying property, and investors are free to buy and sell at any time, but investors in assets such as agricultural land face greater risk of expropriation, with the government aiming for a substantial increase in black ownership of land. As regards the protection of intellectual property such as patents, trademarks, and copyrights, foreign companies will find the S. African legal system determined to uphold their rights.

According to the 2017 corruption index, compiled by Transparency International, S. Africa ranks 71 out of 180 states. Although the country compares well with other African states, there remain concerns about the level of corruption. Jacob Zuma, the President who was deposed in 2018, had been accused of accepting bribes from a French arms company, using public money to upgrade his house, and of allowing his son's business associates to influence appointments to the cabinet and the award of public contracts. Analysts claim that public servants often do not declare their business interests, as required by law, and that the ruling African National Congress party charges fees for access to top government officials.

Sources: BBC 22 February 2013; Bloomberg 26 January 2017; CIA Factbook 2017; World Economic Forum 2018; Venter 2012; World Bank 2017; World Economic Forum 2018; Transparency International 2018

Questions

An EU-based consumer goods MNC is seeking a country in Africa where it could sell its goods, but also use as a base for exporting to other African countries.

1. Use the World Bank Doing Business web site and find more information on how S. Africa performs on trading across borders and enforcement of contracts.

2. How does S. Africa compare with African countries like Nigeria on cross-border trading, contract enforcement and corruption?

3. On the basis of your findings to Qs 1 and 2, advance a case to the MNC for either S. Africa or Nigeria as an investment base.

Precedent has a very important role in common law. From the perspective of business, it has the advantage of ensuring certainty, and consistent application of the law. Unlike civil law, precedent allows the law to develop and to respond to changes in society. At the same time, it may be very difficult to find or to state, as it is spread across many cases. It may also give rise to laws based on court decisions in extreme, unusual, or unevenly argued cases—to put it another way, a case may be decided, not on the relative merits of the evidence, but because a lawyer has made an effective presentation of the case in court.

Common law systems are found in countries that have had close ties with Britain, such as the USA, Canada, India, and Australia. In some of these countries, the common law system may sit alongside codes and statutes, but it remains the fundamental basis of the legal system.

Where there is a clash between legislative statutes and common law, statutes take precedence. So, statutes generally have the power to change the established common law, but the common law cannot overrule or change statutes.

Counterpoint Box 10.2 Law and politics—the separation of powers

Under the separation of powers, governmental powers are divided between three branches who all act independently: 1) the legislature, examples being the UK parliament and the US congress; 2) the executive comprising, for example the US president, or the British prime minister, their cabinets, and the civil service; and 3) judicial branches, made up of the courts and the judges. Legislatures pass the laws, government ministers and the civil service administer them, and the courts decide whether the laws have been correctly followed, in cases brought before them.

Originally, separation was seen as necessary to preserve liberty and avoid tyranny. Nowadays, it is held as the best way to ensure the checks and balances necessary for good government. The concept in its pure form requires that no individual should have powers in more than one of these branches, and no branch should have greater power than the others. The separation of powers allows judges and the courts to act independently of the other branches. Democratic countries usually have an independent judiciary, where judges and courts are free to interpret the law. In that way, the law can be applied objectively and impartially without political interference, trials are more likely to be fair, and all can be treated equally before the law.

However, in democratic societies, while there is always some separation of powers, this is never absolute. The powers and responsibilities of the different branches can be blurred, leading to tension and conflict between them. Separation of powers is rare in non-democratic countries. In a one-party state, such as China, the judiciary is under the control of the communist party, with its top judge going so far as to scorn judicial independence, viewing it as part of the West's false ideals (*Financial Times* 17 January 2017).

Politicians sometimes react angrily when the judiciary rules that their policies are not lawful. The politicians often argue that the people elected them and they are carrying out the will of the people. An example of conflict between politicians and the judiciary was seen when a US judge halted President Trump's travel ban on people arriving from 7 mainly Muslim countries in the Middle East. President Trump tweeted:

> The opinion of this so-called judge, which essentially takes law-enforcement away from our country, is ridiculous and will be overturned! (@realDonald Trump 4 February 2017).

The White House, while accepting that the different branches of government were 'co-equal', insisted that the President had broad authority over immigration policy (*The Guardian* 13 February 2017).

Iain Duncan Smith, a former UK government minister, launched an attack on the Supreme Court when it ruled that the parliament had the right to vote on Article 50 of the Lisbon Treaty which would initiate UK withdrawal from the EU:

> They've stepped into new territory where they've actually told Parliament not just that they should do something but actually what they should do . . . I think that leads further down the road to real constitutional issues about who is supreme in this role. (*The Independent* 24 January 2017)

A barrister responded that the Supreme Court was simply informing the Government that the law prevented it triggering Article 50 unilaterally.

Duncan Smith was supported by some British newspapers, which called the judges 'enemies of the people' (*Daily Mail* 4 November 2016), and revealed details of their private lives.

There are examples of politicians trying to take over the powers of the judiciary. In 2014 the president of Turkey passed legislation allowing him to take control of the appointment, promotion, and disciplining of judges (Bipartisan Policy Center 21 April 2014). In 2016, after an unsuccessful coup in Turkey, 3000 judges were sacked, and around 800 judges and prosecutors arrested. Many commentators saw the Turkish president as using the coup as an excuse for silencing opponents, eroding the rule of law, and politicising the judicial system (*Washington Post* 21 July 2016). In Poland, the President of the Supreme Court responding to government attempts to take over judicial appointments said:

> . . . the courts are easily turned into a plaything in the hands of politicians . . . (this) is now becoming a reality (*The Guardian* 27 February 2017)

Sources: Benwell and Gay (2011); Bipartisan Policy Center 21 April 2014; *The Guardian* 13 March 2017; *Financial Times* 17 January 2017; National Conference of State Legislatures; Wells (2006) ➡

→ **Questions**

Ninety-seven tech firms, including Google, Facebook, Airbnb and Netflix, opposed Donald Trump's ban on arrivals from the seven predominantly Muslim countries (Wired 2017). They went to the courts to argue their case (US Court of Appeals 2017).

1. Why did the 97 tech firms challenge the US presidential order?
2. Discuss the legitimacy of business or politicians:
   • being critical of court decisions; and
   • launching personal attacks on the judges making the decisions.
3. Explain why politicians take steps to reduce the independence of the judiciary.

Learning Task

Look at the map in Figure 10.1, which shows the legal systems in the world.

1. Which is the dominant legal system in Latin America?
2. What are the main characteristics of that dominant system?
3. What legal issues might be encountered by a Brazilian firm wishing to use the US courts to sue a customer based in New York?

Common law, in contrast to civil law systems, is adversarial in nature. Thus, both sides are in competition to persuade judge and jury of the legitimacy of their case. In proceedings, lawyers act as the principal advocate of their client's case, and witnesses are called to give oral testimony. Oral argument plays a more important role in common law. In court cases, the judge plays the role of impartial arbiter.

Customary Law Systems

There is no single agreed definition of customary law. It can be seen as a body of rules, values, and traditions based on knowledge gained from life experiences, or on religious or philosophical principles. It establishes standards or procedures to be followed when dealing with social relationships such as marriage, adultery, and divorce, but can also play a part in the ownership and use of land, and issues around fishing rights. Customary law, like common law, is often not written into statutes, and can be fluid and evolutionary. While hardly any countries operate under a legal system which is wholly customary, there are a large number of countries where it plays an important role. This is true in a number of African countries, in some of which it operates in combination with either civil or common law systems, depending on whether the area was colonized by France or Britain. It also plays a part in the legal systems of China and India, as well as islands in the South Pacific.

Islamic Law Systems

Islamic law systems are codes of law mainly based on Sharia law, which is derived from the religious principles contained in the Koran, and in the teachings and example of Mohammed. In some Muslim countries, the law is limited to regulating personal behaviour, while in others its impact is much more wide-ranging. Examples of the latter include countries such as Iran, Saudi Arabia, Sudan, Libya, and parts of Nigeria. In these instances, Islamic Law regulates all aspects of life, both public and private. The law forbids consumption of alcohol and pork as well as gambling, fraud, slander, the making of images of sentient beings, and usury (that is, lending money and charging the borrower interest), especially at an exorbitant or illegally high rate (Britannica Concise Encyclopaedia n.d.). Financial institutions in some Muslim countries operate under Islamic law. Though small on a world scale, they have been growing rapidly internationally with assets valued at nearly $2 trillion (Islamic Financial Services Board 2016).

Mini Case Study 10.2 Saudi Arabia and international business

Saudi Arabia plays an important part in the world economy. Its economy is heavily oil-based, with strong government controls over major economic activities. Holding 16 per cent of proven global petroleum reserves, it ranks second in the world, with around 16 per cent of global proven petroleum reserves. It is the world's largest exporter of oil. The oil sector is of vital importance, accounting for roughly 87 per cent of government revenues, 42 per cent of GDP, and 90 per cent of export earnings. The country is a big importer of arms, machinery, and vehicles. In terms of total GDP, It ranks number 15 in the world. In the first half of this decade, economic growth was adversely affected by the large decline in the price of oil. However, income per head, at over $54,000 (Purchasing Power Parity), is high, and attempts by the government to expand the private sector mean that there are significant opportunities for foreign business.

Shariah law underpins the legal framework of the Kingdom. Shariah law is a set of principles derived from the Koran, the sayings of the Prophet Mohammed, and the works of jurists and Shariah scholars. In addition to Shariah law, the Kingdom's legal framework includes laws promulgated by Royal Orders and Decrees, and various ministerial resolutions and circulars. In particular, royal decrees influence labour, commercial, and corporate law. Tribal and customary law also play an important part in the system.

Shariah law is not codified, and does not have a doctrine of precedent. Each judge has the power to decide the matter that comes before him at his sole discretion, based on his understanding of Shariah law. Furthermore, court reports are not published and the application of Shariah Law is not uniform throughout the court system. According to Clark (2012) there is no public access to court files and no system for reporting cases.

Attempts have been made to modernize the legal system, but progress has been slow. The *Financial Times* (15 January 2015) describes the Saudi legal system as antiquated, with court decisions taking anything up to nine years. Judges have wide discretion to interpret the law, admit or reject evidence, and accept or dismiss lawyers from the courtroom. Members of the highest court, the Supreme Judicial Council, are appointed by the King. The King is the highest court of appeal, and can issue pardons.

Commercial disputes between foreign and Saudi Arabian firms can be referred to international arbitration bodies, and their decisions are binding.

Saudi Arabia is officially a Wahhabi Sunni Muslim country—a highly conservative form of Islam—and the laws and moral standards are considerably stricter than those in the West, as regards dress, alcohol, moral behaviour, and mixing with unrelated members of the opposite sex. Homosexuality, as well as the public practice of any religion other than Islam, is forbidden. Saudi Arabia does not compare well on gender equality. Globally, the World Economic Forum (2016) ranks it second bottom, in terms of economic participation and opportunity for women. Neither did it fare well regarding corruption (Table 10.1). In 2018, Saudi Arabia cracked down on corruption by arresting more than 150 princes, business tycoons and former ministers, and expropriating media companies and company shares.

Questions

1. Using Case Study 10.2 and Table 10.1, assess the attractiveness of Saudi Arabia as a location for multinationals seeking foreign investment opportunities, paying particular attention to the legal environment.
2. Examine human resource management issues raised for foreign MNCs wishing to invest in Saudi Arabia, but committed to equal rights regarding gender and sexuality. ➡

→ **Table 10.1** Saudi Arabia—legal system and business

		Score (7=best)
Property Rights	32/138 countries	5.3/7
Judicial Independence	27/138 countries	5.3/7
Efficiency in settling disputes	24/138 countries	4.8/7
Protection of minority investors	29/138 countries	4.9/7
Strength of investor protection*	86/138 countries	5.2/7
Enforcing contracts ranking	105/190 countries	
Time taken to enforce contract	575 days	
Cost as % of contract claim	27.5	
Quality of judicial processes ranking	6/18 countries	
Corruption	62/176 countries	

Sources: CIA (2017); Clark (2012); *Financial Times* 27 January (2018); Foreign and Commonwealth Office (2013); PwC (2015); Saudilegal (2017); Shearman and Sterling (2016); Transparency International (2017); Washington University Law (2017); World Bank (2017); World Economic Forum (2016, 2018)

Important Aspects of the Law for Business

There are a wide range of laws applicable to business, such as the law of contract, tort, criminal law, and international law. Contract law, and the law of tort, deal with disputes between a business, and the firms and individuals it deals with. Both give rise to actions by the concerned/aggrieved parties through the civil courts. Criminal liability, on the other hand, involves a business committing a crime against the state. Cases are initiated by state bodies, such as the Crown Prosecution Service in the UK, or the Department of Justice in the USA, and are heard in the criminal courts.

Contract Law

When firms do business, they are constantly entering into contracts. Essentially, contracts are struck when a firm buys or sells goods or services from a supplier or a customer, or takes on employees. The contract is a legally binding agreement between the parties concerned, and may be formal, informal, written, or oral. The contract is likely to cover such elements as price, payment terms, contract duration, the consequences of breaching the contract, the process for resolving disputes between the parties, and what will happen if there are unforeseen events such as wars or revolutions (see Hagedoorn and Hesen (2007) for a discussion of contract issues in technology partnerships between firms). The contract obliges those involved to fulfil their side of the agreement. If they fail to do so, then they are in breach of contract, and may be pursued by the aggrieved party through the courts.

Tort Law

Tort is an area of the law concerned with injuries to people, or damage to their assets. The law obliges firms to ensure that their activities do not cause damage, intentional or accidental, to others, and is in addition to any contractual arrangement that may exist. Business activities that involve, for example, negligence leading to injury to a customer, selling defective goods, or counterfeiting another company's product, is a matter for tort law.

A very famous tort case was the McDonald's coffee case in the USA. A customer, called Liebeck, won millions of dollars of damages against McDonald's when she claimed that the company's negligence had caused her to get burned with coffee that was far too hot. A more recent tort case was brought in the US, by Apple against Samsung, for infringing patents, by copying designs of smartphones and tablet computers. After six years of litigation, Apple was finally awarded damages of $120 million. Apple also pursued Samsung in European and Australian courts, while Samsung countersued Apple for patent infringement in S. Korea, Japan, and Europe, both with mixed success (The Verge 6 November 2017).

 Learning Task

Lush, a small company making handmade cosmetics, took the giant, Amazon, to court. Lush did not allow Amazon to sell its products. However, when customers typed the word 'Lush' into Amazon's search facility, they were directed to other products they might like to buy instead. Lush argued that Amazon was infringing its trademark. Lush said that it had cost it £500,000 to defend its intellectual property.

1. On what aspect of the law, contract or tort, is the Lush case based?

2. What issues are small and medium-sized businesses likely to face when considering taking legal action against giants like Amazon?

3. a) Find out the result of the case.

   b) Discuss the implications of the judgement for online retailers such as Amazon.

See *The Guardian* 12 February 2014; Harbottle & Lewis (2014).

Criminal Law

Criminal law applies across many business activities, and has become increasingly important in areas such as financial reporting, the proper description and pricing of goods and services, the safety of goods and services, particularly food, and environmental impacts. In the USA, after several business scandals involving the likes of Enron and WorldCom—both of whom were involved in fraudulent accounting (WorldCom artificially inflated its profits by billions of dollars)—Congress introduced more criminal legislation. This tightened the rules in areas such as financial reporting, tax crimes, foreign currency violations, health and safety in the workplace, and crimes against the environment. The purpose of these legal requirements is usually the protection of life, or health, or the environment, the prevention of deceptive practices, or to ensure the quality of products, the preservation of competition, or the promotion of technological advance.

One country's criminal law can apply even when the offence occurs outside that country, and also when the company involved is not based in the country. Under the US Foreign Corrupt Practices Act, SQM, the Chilean chemicals and mining multinational, agreed to pay the US Department of Justice a fine of around $15 million, for bribing Chilean politicians who had influence over government mining policies (US Department of Justice 2017).

Learning Task

PSA, the owner of Peugeot and Citroen, which is partially owned by the French government, agreed to take over GM's European Opel and Vauxhall operations in 2017. The European car industry is plagued by overcapacity. After the takeover analysts expect PSA to close some of its 24 plants.

1. Discuss whether UK workers at the Ellesmere Port and Luton factories should be more concerned about their security of employment than workers in French and German plants in the light of:

   a) the legal rules around redundancy in the UK, France, and Germany (see Eversheds Sutherland (2018)); and

   b) other factors, like Brexit and trade union strength, which could influence the choice of plants to close (see articles: BBC (2017a), AM online (n.d.) and *The Guardian* 3 March 2017)).

International Law

Usually, when operating in foreign countries, business has to follow the law of the land. However, international law is playing an increasingly important role in the world of international business. As business has become more globalized, so has the law, developing in ways aimed at facilitating international trade and investment. Another development is that international contracts are increasingly being written in English.

International law can reduce the uncertainty, costs, and disputes associated with international commerce when there are doubts about which country's laws apply. In such situations, firms, unsure of their rights, could be less willing to go in for foreign trade and investment. There are a variety of organizations, conventions, codes, and treaties that play a role in international commerce. We now look at some of the most important.

Codes and Conventions

Some national laws have ended up being used by firms involved in international business. One example is the **Uniform Commercial Code** in the USA. It sets down standard rules governing the sale of goods, is in force in many US states, and has been adopted by other countries (see http://www.ilpf.org).

Another element of international contract law is the United Nations **Convention on Contracts for the International Sale of Goods** (CISG) of 1980. It is very similar in content to the Uniform Commercial Code. It aims to make international trade as convenient and economical as trading across state borders in the USA. By 2017, 85 countries, accounting for the vast majority of world trade, had signed up to this convention. The CISG establishes a set of rules governing sales of goods between professional sellers and buyers, who have their places of business in different countries. By adopting it, a country undertakes to treat the Convention's rules as part of its law. The Convention aims to reduce the uncertainty and disagreements that arise when the sales law of one country differs from that of another (see://law.pace.edu).

Given that so many countries have signed up to it, the CISG might seem like a significant advance in the law relating to international trade. However, the reality is that many firms deliberately do not use the convention. In the EU this is true of producers of oils, seeds, fats, and grain, and of most large Dutch companies. This unwillingness to use the agreement appears to be due to some of the terms used in the convention being open to differing interpretations. Also, it may be that firms are ignorant of various elements of the CISG, and are not prepared to invest time and money to find out. Another deterrent factor is that the convention only covers some aspects of the relationship between the buyer and seller so that, in other areas, national laws apply. Finally, countries such as the UK, Nigeria, India, Indonesia, Portugal, and South Africa are not party to the convention (Smits 2005; Unilex n.d.; for discussion of the UK position, see Hofmann 2010 and Moss 2005–06).

An organization trying to facilitate the legal processes around international commerce is the International Institute for the Unification of Private Law (Unidroit), which lays down principles for international commercial contracts. It is an independent, intergovernmental organization, whose purpose is to help modernize, harmonize, and coordinate commercial law between its 63 member states. Only four African countries are members, Egypt, Nigeria, Tunisia, and South Africa. In 1964, a convention was signed relating to the Law on the International Sale of Goods. However, the agreement did not apply to the sale of all products. For example, it did not cover financial products, such as stocks and shares, or sales of electricity. In 2002, a law relating to franchises was agreed (see http://www.unidroit.org).

International Arbitration

Sometimes, disputes arise between firms based in one country, and firms or governments of other countries. For example, there can be disagreement between the firms as to which national law should apply. That such disputes arise is hardly surprising, given the rapid growth of international trade and investment. In these situations, **international arbitration** has become increasingly popular for businesses. There are a number of international agencies who will arbitrate between the warring parties. For example, firms can use commercial arbitration under the **New York Convention,** set up in 1958 under the aegis of the United Nations, and called Uncitral (see United Nations Commission on International Trade Law at http://www.uncitral.org). Uncitral was used in a dispute by BG, a British energy MNC, and the Argentinian government; and by BP in a case against TNK, its Russian partner.

Another international body helping to resolve disputes between governments and foreign business around investment is the **International Centre for the Settlement of Investment Disputes** (ICSID), which is based at the World Bank in Washington DC. It deals with cases such as that involving Eli Lilly, the US pharmaceutical giant, a number of whose drug patents had been invalidated by the Canadian courts. ICSID took the Canadian government to arbitration, claiming that Canada had violated the terms of the NAFTA agreement (Italaw n.d.; for other cases and information about ICSID, go to http://www.worldbank.org/icsid).

The World Trade Organization, when its rules have been broken, also arbitrates in disputes on matters of foreign trade, investment, and intellectual property rights. Firms cannot take a complaint direct to the WTO, for the disputes procedures can only be activated at the request of a member government. This is illustrated by the dispute brought to the WTO by Japan, the US, and the EU, against China, for restricting the export of rare earth minerals used in the production of computer hard drives and mobile phones. China, the world's largest producers of rare earth minerals, argued that controls were necessary to limit the environmental damage caused by mining, but also wanted to promote the expansion of its domestic processing of these minerals. The WTO ruled in favour of the complainants (see dispute DS431 at http://www.wto.org).

When companies agree to insert an international arbitration clause into a contract, it means that disputes between them are dealt with by an independent arbitrator, rather than a court. This has a number of advantages over litigation through national courts. The first advantage is neutrality, because arbitrators have to meet strict independence tests, and can be drawn from countries other than those of the firms concerned. The second is confidentiality. Proceedings, unlike court cases, are normally private, so that there is no public washing of dirty linen. Third, the procedures are flexible, and, lastly, awards made, for instance under the New York Convention, can be widely enforced in almost all trading countries, unlike national court decisions. The disadvantages are that it can be more costly than court litigation, there is normally no right of appeal, it does not work so well when there are more than two companies involved, and, finally, there is no possibility of a quick decision, even when there is no justifiable defence.

International Law and IPRs

Globalization has put an onus on firms to find ways of protecting intellectual property rights abroad. This has become particularly important in certain sectors such as film, music, and software, where the growth of the internet and digitization makes copying much easier. Such protection is relatively well-developed in the rich economies of North America and Europe, but much less so in poorer countries such as China and India—a further deterrent in pursuing cases in China is the corruption of the judiciary, and, in India, the time it takes for the wheels of justice to turn. It is therefore hardly surprising that companies prefer to pursue infringements of their IPRs in countries with well-developed systems of protection, where cases are dealt with in a timely fashion, and where the judiciary is not tainted by corruption. Thus, 3M, the US technology multinational, chose to file an IPR lawsuit with a federal court in Minnesota and the US International Trade Commission, against other producers of laptops, including Sony, Matsushita, Hitachi of Japan, and Lenovo of China. 3M complained that the laptop makers had infringed the technology it used in its lithium-ion batteries.

The costs of taking out protection can vary significantly from one country to another, as can the time taken to get protection, the level of protection given, and the ease with which firms can pursue violators of their property rights.

So, intellectual property laws can vary from country to country—even in the EU, there is still no single system of granting patents. Usually, an application in one country for protection of a firm's IPRs only results in the granting of protection in that country. In the past, firms seeking protection in other countries had to make separate applications in each, which could be very costly in terms of money and time.

However, the situation is changing. Two systems now exist that reduce the need for separate national applications. The Patent Cooperation Treaty allows firms to file a single application indicating in which countries it is seeking protection. The European Patent Convention allows for an application to be filed at the European Patents Office in Munich. The Office can grant separate national patents for specified countries. There have also been some moves towards harmonization of laws as a result of international treaties, including the Agreement on Trade-Related Aspects of Intellectual Property Rights (TRIPS), agreed through the WTO. It aims to establish minimum levels of protection that each government has to give to the intellectual property of other WTO members. Member governments have to ensure that their intellectual property rights systems do not discriminate against foreigners, that they can be enforced in law, and that the penalties for infringement are tough enough to deter further violations. The procedures must not be unnecessarily complicated, costly, or time-consuming (see http://www.wto.org).

Counterpoint Box 10.3 Patents—a necessary evil?

The conventional view is that businesses, without legal protection given by patents which give a monopoly over the commercial exploitation of their intellectual property, would not invest the large amounts of money to develop new products. This would undermine innovation, seen as a driving force in the advances in productivity necessary for economic growth and increases in living standards. An absence of protection would reduce the incentives to innovate, because it would allow others to commercialise the new ideas, thereby cutting revenues and profits for the innovating companies, making it impossible to recoup the millions spent on R&D.

On the other hand, it is argued that the profit motive is only one factor in the generation of ideas for new goods and services. Chang (2008) points out that much research is financed by organisations that are not motivated by profits, such as governments, universities, and charities. He also suggests that patenting may be necessary where copying of products is easy, as is the case in software and pharmaceuticals, but is not required where there is a time lag before imitators can enter the market, thus giving the innovator the time to recoup its investment. Some commentators argue that a strong patent system can actually stifle economic growth, because it prevents companies from modifying the patented ideas and products of others to create new inventions. This particularly affects firms in poorer countries wishing to modify products of MNCs based in rich countries. Boldrin and Levine

(2013) go further, by arguing that there is no empirical evidence that patents promote innovation or increase productivity. They claim that rapid innovation in industries such as cars, chemicals, and personal computers has hardly ever been the result of patent protection, and go on to say that industries look for such protection after their growth has peaked and their markets become less competitive, in other words when they are old and stagnating.

Sources: Boldrin and Levine (2013); Chang (2008); Kapzynski and Kesselheim (2016); Uberi L.J., *Financial Times*, 31 August 2012

Questions
1. Summarise and weigh up the views expressed below in a) and b):
   a. Kapzynski and Kesselheim (2016) argue that pharmaceutical companies are charging excessive prices on patent protected drugs. They urge the US government to use the law to step in and reduce prices (see: http://content.healthaffairs.org/content/35/5/791.full.pdf+html).
   b. Sherkow, in response, contends that pharma companies spend billions of dollars on drug R&D and they would not do that unless they could charge 'supercompetitive' prices (npr 2016).
2. Discuss whether the law around patents should be abolished or strengthened.

European Union

The European Union (EU) comprises 28 members, all of whom are bound by EU laws. The primary source of EU law comes from treaties, such as the Treaty of Rome as modified by the Single European Act, the Treaties of Maastricht, Amsterdam, Nice, and Lisbon. The secondary source of EU law consists of directives that are binding on all member states, who are individually responsible for their implementation, regulations that are binding and implemented consistently across the EU, and, finally, decisions which are made by European institutions like the Commission, the Council of Ministers, and the European Parliament, dealing with specific issues, countries, institutions, or individuals. European law develops through a combination of case law setting precedents, and statutory law. In any clash with national law, EU law takes precedence. The European Court of Justice (ECJ) interprets EU law, and ensures that it is applied consistently across the Union.

 Mini Case Study 10.3 **Facebook and the law**

In 2013 an Austrian law student lodged a complaint against Facebook HQ in Ireland, claiming that the company, by transferring his personal data to the US, was breaching EU privacy law. The EU restricts the ability of business to transfer personal data to countries outside the Union, unless there are adequate privacy protection safeguards in those countries

The transfer of EU personal customer information to the USA by Facebook raised concerns, given the allegations by Edward Snowden, a CIA employee, that the company was passing on data to US intelligence agencies for use in their surveillance programmes (see *The Guardian* 2 December 2013). Initially, Facebook asserted that it complied with the Safe Harbour agreement between the US and the EU, which allowed companies to self-certify that they were protecting the privacy of personal data. The Irish Data Protection Commissioner refused to intervene on the grounds that the Safe harbour system permitted the transfers. The case was referred to the ECJ for an interpretation of EU privacy. It declared invalid the Safe Harbour provision used by Facebook. It also found that the student could not bring a class-action lawsuit involving 25000 Facebook users worldwide against the company, but could pursue the case as an individual.

Facebook then changed its defence from Safe Harbour to Standard Contractual Clauses, claiming that these provided adequate protection for the data transferred to the US. The case then went to the Irish High Court in February 2017.

In 2017, the French authorities fined Facebook €150,000 for collecting massive amounts of personal data on 33 million French Facebook users, while in Holland, Facebook was found guilty of breaching privacy laws. It was also investigated in Belgium, Spain, and Germany.

Sources: The Guardian 6 October 2015; ECJ 6 October 2015 http://curia.europa.eu/; Europe versus Facebook http://www.europe-v-facebook.org; *New York Times* 18 May 2017; Politico 25 January 2018; *SC Magazine* 18 May 2017

Questions

1. Why is it important that personal privacy is protected by the law? See http://www.teachprivacy.com/10-reasons-privacy-matters/

2. Explain why social media companies like Facebook are interested in collecting masses of personal data.

3. The US government was admitted to the Irish case as *amicus curiae*.
   a. Find out what role is played by an amicus curiae.
   b. Why would the US government wish to play that role?

4. What was the result of the Irish High Court case?

Learning Task

See Mini Case Study 10.3. Facebook tangled again with EU law when it was fined €94 million by the Commission in May 2017.

1. Which law was the Commission applying in the case? See Commission documents IP 14/1088 and IP 17/1369.

2. How had Facebook broken the law?

3. Assess Facebook's response to the charges. See BBC (2018b)

Single Market Programme

An essential element of the EU project is the Single Market programme. The programme—by removing internal barriers such as frontier checks, different technical standards for goods and services, and obliging members to recognize academic or vocational qualifications gained in another member state—tries to ensure that goods, services, capital, and people can move freely across borders. The Single Market requires that laws of the various member states do not favour domestic firms over those of other members in areas such as trade, investment, the establishment of businesses on their territory, or the movement of workers.

The EU has seen that different national contract laws can constitute a barrier to the movement of goods and services, so it has passed several directives to deal with this. However, they do not replace national laws by laying down a general law of contract, but only apply to certain types of contract, and to specific areas of contract law, such as that relating to the sale of tour packages and timeshares, on combating late payment in commercial transactions, or in the distance marketing of financial services.

For example, the Consumer Sales Directive does not attempt to harmonize different national laws, nor does it require firms to offer the same product guarantee throughout the EU. However, it does require firms to provide specific information on product guarantees. The information has to be written in plain and intelligible language regarding the consumer's legal rights under the national legislation, and has to make clear that these rights are unaffected by the product guarantee. The guarantee also needs to indicate the duration and territorial scope of the guarantee, and how to make a claim (Schulte-Nölke 2007). The EU is trying to enable consumers to pursue EU-wide claims against firms providing faulty goods or services. As the Commissioner responsible for consumer affairs put it, 'I want a citizen in Birmingham to feel as comfortable shopping for a digital camera from a website in Berlin or Budapest as they would in their high street' (*Financial Times* 14 March 2007). The Commission wants to encourage consumers to buy more abroad.

Smits (2005) points out that EU directives in the field of contract law allow member states to create more stringent rules in the area covered by the directive. In particular, in the area of consumer protection some member states tend to enact rules that are tougher than the directives prescribe. This means that business still has to deal with differences in national legislation among the member states, which may make it less convenient and more costly to do business abroad.

The result is that there remain significant differences in contract law within the EU, with each country in the EU having its own contract law. These can be classified in three main groups. First, England, Ireland, and Cyprus have common law systems that emphasize judge-made law. The second type is the civil law system that holds sway in France, Belgium, Luxembourg, Spain, Portugal, Italy, Malta, Germany, Austria, Greece, and the Netherlands. Civil law is in place in nearly all of the former Communist countries of Eastern Europe that entered the EU in 2004, such as Poland, the Czech Republic, Slovakia, Hungary, Estonia, Lithuania, Latvia, Slovenia, and also Croatia which joined in 2013. Finally, the Scandinavian countries of Denmark, Sweden, and Finland form the third group, which has a number of common statutes relating to contract.

Competition Law

Business operating in the EU is also subject to the competition laws that are important in helping to maintain a barrier-free single market. These laws, which are policed by the Commission, cover four main areas.

First, cartels that prevent or distort competition in the EU are strictly forbidden by Article 101 (ex Article 81) of the Treaty. Cartels are often popular with firms, because they allow them to avoid competition by agreeing to set the same price for their products, or by sharing the market out between them (see Table 10.2). Firms are tempted to set up price-fixing cartels by the significant hike they can make in their prices. It has been calculated that international cartels overcharge their customers by anything from 15 per cent (Boyer and Kotchoni 2015) to 50 per cent (Connor 2014). In 2014, the EU fined Sony, Toshiba, Hitachi, Philips, and 3 other suppliers of optical disk drives €116 million for setting up a cartel to avoid competition for the likes of customers such as Dell and HP (European Commission 2015 IP/15/5885).

Second, Article 102 (ex Article 82) prohibits firms with a strong market position from abusing their dominant position by, for instance, exploiting customers through high prices or squeezing their rivals through artificially low prices. In 2015, Qualcomm, a US technology multinational, was facing a fine of over $2bn for trying to drive a rival out of business. It paid a customer to buy

Table 10.2 The ten highest cartel fines by company

Year	Undertaking	Case	Amount in €m
2016	Daimler	Trucks	1bn
2016	DAF	Trucks	753
2008	Saint Gobain	Car glass	715
2012	Philips	TV and computer monitors	705
2012	LG Electronics	TV and computer monitors	688
2016	Volvo/Renault	Trucks	670
2016	Iveco	Trucks	495
2013	Deutsche Bank	Interest rate derivatives	466
2001	Hoffman-La Roche	Vitamins	462
2007	Siemens	Gas switchgear	397

Source: http://ec.europa.eu/competition/cartels/statistics/statistics.pdf

chipsets only from Qualcomm, and was also accused of predatory pricing by setting prices below cost (European Commission 2015 IP/15/6271; CBR 21 April 2016). The Commission has the power to fine firms up to 10 per cent of their global turnover.

The third area of the law covers mergers. Under the EC Merger Regulation, the Commission has the power to regulate big mergers. Firms have to notify the Commission of proposed mergers. The Commission can wave the merger through, as it did with the takeover of Scottish Power by the Spanish firm Iberdrola, or it can approve the merger subject to certain conditions. When Microsoft made a takeover bid for LinkedIn, the Commission allowed the merger subject to Microsoft agreeing to certain conditions, one of which was to ensure that PC manufacturers and distributors would be free to install LinkedIn on Windows (European Commission 2016 IP/16/4284). The EU, fearful that a merger would lead to reduced competition and increased prices, allowed Unilever to acquire the household and body care products divisions of Sara Lee, on condition that it sell off a number of body care brands. Finally, permission can be refused where the acquisition would reduce competition in the market place. Thus, the attempt by Hong Kong-based CK Hutchison Holdings to buy O2, Telefónica's British mobile operator, was blocked by the commission, concluding that it would have led to less choice, higher prices for UK consumers and slower innovation (European Commission 2016 IP/16/1704).

Finally, Article 107 (ex Article 87) of the Treaty frowns on assistance given by governments to firms that distorts or threatens competition, and impedes the smooth functioning of the Single Market programme. It wants to avoid governments giving aid to domestic firms to the detriment of their foreign rivals. In 2016, the Commission ruled that Spanish football clubs, including Barcelona and Real Madrid, had received illegal State aid not available to other clubs. The aid involved tax advantages, overcompensation for the failure to complete a deal on a transfer, and State guarantees of bank loans (European Commission 2016 IP/16/2401) (see Mini Case Study 10.4 below). To ensure no breach of Article 107, the Commission monitored closely the many government financial support schemes, amounting to a massive €4 trillion, that were put in place across the EU to help the banking sector face up to the damage wreaked by the global financial crisis (European Commission IP/10/623).

Mini Case Study 10.4 Apple versus the European Commission

In 2016 the European Commission, ordered Apple to repay up €13bn plus interest. It ruled that Ireland had been breaking EU rules on state aid by giving Apple illegal tax breaks from 1991. This was judged illegal because it allowed Apple to pay much less tax than other businesses. According to the Commission, Apple was avoiding tax by recording all profits from its European sales in Ireland, and paying virtually no profits tax there. The vast majority of the profits recorded in Ireland were allocated by the company to head office which, according to the Commission, was not based in any country, had no employees or premises, which meant that the allocated profits remained untaxed. It found in 2003, that Apple paid an effective corporate tax rate of 1 per cent on its European profits, and that had fallen to 0.005 per cent in 2014, while corporation tax in Ireland was 12.5 per cent (see Figure 10.2). Ireland was instructed to reclaim the money from Apple.

Apple, along with the Irish government, vowed to fight the case. The company claimed to be a responsible corporate citizen that had followed guidance from the Irish tax authorities, and respected the tax laws wherever it operated. It also claimed to be the largest taxpayer in Ireland, the USA, and the world. The Irish government contended that its tax deal with Apple was founded on the strict application of the law. Both Apple and the Irish Government announced that they would lodge an appeal against the Commission's decision.   ➜

→ **Figure 10.2** Apple: tax avoidance and state aid

Source: European Commission (2016)

In 2015, the US President Barack Obama, concerned about US MNCs avoiding tax by hoarding profits abroad, suggested that these companies should pay a minimum of 19 per cent tax on their future foreign earnings, and 14 per cent of profits which had been stockpiled outside the US. Apple held $232 billion in cash, with about $214 billion of that overseas. This followed a US senate committee (2013) concluding that Apple's overseas operation was not paying tax in any country. Despite this, the US government gave its support to Apple in the EU case, arguing that the decision was unfair, impinged on the freedom of individual member states to set their own tax regimes, threatened to undermine foreign investment in the EU, and endangered US-EU economic cooperation.

The Commission, concerned about aggressive tax avoidance by multinationals, had more than Apple in its sights. It ordered the Netherlands and Luxembourg to recover as much as €30 million euros each in back taxes from Starbucks and Fiat Chrysler, and investigated Amazon and McDonald's operations in Luxembourg.

It declared that tax breaks given by Belgium to 35 MNCs were illegal, and also indicated a willingness to probe Google parent Alphabet's £130 million-pound tax deal with the U.K.

Sources: Apple (2016); BBC 30 August 2016; Bloomberg 1 February 2015 and 30 August 2016; European Commission (2016); *The Guardian* 19 December 2016; US Senate Committee (2013) (includes video).

Questions

1. How does Apple go about minimizing its global tax bill?
2. a. Is tax avoidance illegal?
   b. Why is the Commission using the state aid rules to get Apple to repay the money?
3. a. Give reasons for the EU and the US concerns about tax avoidance.
   b. The fine of €13bn was equivalent to Ireland's national spending on health care (BBC 30 August 2016). Why then did the Irish government not wish to recover the money?

Cybercrime

There has been a massive growth of e-commerce and a rapid growth in cybercrime. The opportunities for cybercrime are forecast to expand exponentially, with rapid increases in the amount of data on the web, and in the number of everyday products such as cars and smart meters connected to the internet of things. Sectors such as health care and financial services, along with government agencies, are a particular target for cybercriminals. Cybersecurity Ventures (2016) reported that three quarters of the software systems of the top 20 US banks were infected with malware, and estimated that global cybercrime would double to $6 trillion between 2015 and 2021. Firms in the Ponemon Institute global survey (2016) reported that, on average, they suffered two successful cyber-attacks each week involving, for example, the theft of intellectual property, the taking over of online bank accounts, infection through computer viruses, or the posting of confidential business information on the internet.

There is much evidence that illegal downloading of copyrighted software, music, and films costs the respective industries billions of pounds. Pirate Bay, the Swedish-based website, is one of the world's most popular file sharing sites, allowing users to share films, television programmes, and music. The Swedish courts imprisoned and fined four people associated with the site for promoting the distribution of illegal content. Many countries such as Argentina, Germany, Malaysia and Australia blocked the site, only to find other sites springing up offering similar services (see Endgadget 2014).

Governments find it difficult enough to control cybercrime within their own territory, never mind transnational cybercrime. A bank in one country, say the USA, finding their computer hacked by a perpetrator thousands of miles away in another, say Russia, is likely to look in vain to the US legal authorities to pursue the perpetrator. Clough (2014) argues that the law needs to be comprehensive and harmonised at the international level. To that end, an International Convention on Cybercrime came into effect in 2004. By 2017, only 52 countries had ratified the Convention—that is, approved in accordance with domestic law and thus rendered enforceable—while 4 had signed, but not ratified. The majority of signatories are European, but countries, like the USA, Canada, Japan, and South Africa, have also signed up. The Convention requires countries to include a range of internet-related activities in their domestic laws, for example, relating to computer hacking, child pornography, computer-related fraud, and infringements of copyright (see http://www.coe.int). But it does not cover areas like identity theft or cyber terrorism. This, along with the limited number of signatories to the convention and the non-membership of countries such as Russia and China, results in a globally fragmented and less than comprehensive approach to cybercrime.

● CHAPTER SUMMARY

As we have seen, the law constitutes a very important element of the environment within which firms must operate. Every aspect of a business operation can be affected by the law, from its inception to its demise. The law can have a major influence on what firms produce, the production processes used, the prices they charge, where they sell, and how they go about advertising and promoting their goods and services. The strategies and policies that firms pursue to boost revenues, cut costs, and increase profits, are shaped by the legal environments within which they operate. However, the law should not be seen solely as a constraint on business activities. It acts as a protection to firms, and offers opportunities, as we saw, with easier access to markets created by the removal of barriers within the EU Single Market.

Companies wishing to get involved in international trade and investment find very different legal environments across the world. The principles on which the systems are based, and the procedures under which they operate, can vary widely, depending on the prevailing legal system. Business can find that what is acceptable in common or civil law systems may not be permissible in countries where the system of Sharia law prevails. Even where countries have a similar legal tradition, firms may encounter very different experiences in each. For example, Germany, Italy, and Colombia all have civil law systems, but the time taken to enforce a contract through the local courts varies enormously. Some of the problems of dealing with different national legal frameworks are being eased by the development of international laws and arbitration procedures, under the auspices of institutions such as the WTO, the EU, and the World Bank.

The law relating to the internet is seriously underdeveloped at both national and international level. There is no code of generally accepted internationally agreed laws to which business can have recourse, and the mixture of laws which do seem to apply are complex. As a result, firms involved in e-commerce face much risk and uncertainty when wishing to have recourse to the law, or when they themselves are being pursued through the courts.

Business operating internationally, whether through trade or investment, has to be aware of the national and international systems of law. It needs to monitor how the law is changing, and must be prepared to deal effectively with the constraints and opportunities generated by the legal environment.

● REVIEW QUESTIONS

1. Why is the legal environment important for international business?
2. Explain why knowledge of different legal systems would be useful for firms involved in international trade and investment.
3. Explain why firms involved in international trade might use international arbitration bodies to settle disputes.
4. a. What is cybercrime?
   b. Why is cybercrime important for business?
   c. Assess the legal protection available to businesses suffering transnational cybercrime.

● ASSIGNMENT TASKS

1. In 2016, Google was accused by the European Commission of abusing its dominant position in the market for mobile operating systems (see European Commission IP/16/1492 and European Commission (2018)).
   a. Which article of EU law was being applied in the case? What types of business behaviour does the article prohibit?
   b. What measure in terms of market share does the European Commission use to decide whether a firm is dominant?
   c. Find out the maximum penalty in US dollars Google could pay if found guilty.

d. How dominant was Google in the market for mobile operating systems?

e. According to the Commission, how was Google abusing its market position?

f. Summarise Google's response to the accusations (see Google (2016) and Ars Technica (2016)).

g. You are employed in the media office of a smartphone manufacturer unhappy with the behaviour of Google The CEO asks you to write a memo that identifies the main arguments the company could use in response to Google. Use the results of your research on a. to f. to help write the memo.

2. You are the PA to the legal director of a giant energy company, which is in a legal dispute with the authorities in a country in Latin America. Your boss is considering going to arbitration to resolve the dispute. As an aid to the decision, your boss asks you to research the dispute between BG, the British energy company, and the Argentine government, which went to arbitration.

Write a report that:

a. Gives a summary of the case.

b. Describes Uncitral and how it works.

c. Explains why BG went to arbitration under Uncitral rather than using the Argentinian courts.

d. Outlines the final result of the case.

e. Recommends whether or not your firm should use international arbitration.

(For information on the case, see http://www.scotusblog.com/2014/03/opinion-analysis- clear-state-ment-ruling-in-investor-state-arbitration-case-leaves-open-question-on-u-s-bilateral-treaties; and for more detail https://www.italaw.com/cases/143.)

(For a summary of the economic and political situation in Argentina around the turn of the century, see http://www.reuters.com/article/us-argentina-debt-chronology-idUSKBN0FZ23N20140730 and for a more detailed and technical report, see https://www.brookings.edu/wp-content/uploads/2016/06/11_argentina_kiguel.pdf.)

Case Study A tale of two regulators

© Shutterstock.com/villorejo

In 2015, the US Environmental Protection Agency (EPA) declared that Volkswagen (VW), then the world's largest car maker, had broken the Clean Air Act by installing software devices in the engines of some of its diesel models that could detect when they were being tested for emissions of NOx gases, nitrogen monoxide and nitrogen dioxide. Emissions were much higher under normal driving conditions. VW ended up agreeing to pay $15bn, remove half a million vehicles from US roads, compensate car owners, and finance pollution-reducing and clean technology programmes. In addition, VW faced further lawsuits from several US States and VW dealers (Bloomberg 28 June 2016). In 2017, VW agreed to pay a fine of $4.3bn to US regulators, and plead guilty to charges of criminal misconduct, including ➜

→ conspiracy to defraud the US (Reuters 11 January 2017). Shortly afterwards, the EPA announced that Fiat Chrysler faced a fine of up to $4.6bn for the violation of the Clean Air Act by its diesel models (*Financial Times* 14 January 2017). Diesel models have a very small share of the US car market, whereas in the EU, governments, and companies like VW, promoted diesels as cleaner for the environment (BBC 23 September 2015).

In contrast to the US, emission regulation in the EU appears to be lax, despite the claim by The European Environment Agency (2016) that high levels of NOx emissions lead each year to 72000 premature deaths in the EU. In 2016 the environmental campaign group, Transport & Environment (T&E), reported that no penalties had been imposed on VW, nor had any compensation been paid to customers, and the company was claiming that it had not done anything illegal. The Transport & Environment researchers found that in road tests VW models were far from the worst offenders, with two thirds of diesel cars breaching EU emission limits set down by the Euro 6 regulations. The poorest performers were Fiat and Suzuki, emitting more than 15 times the permitted level of NOx, followed closely by Renault-Nissan (14 times), and the Opel Vauxhall brands produced by General Motors (10 times) (see Figure 10.3) (Transport & Environment 2016).

Car makers responded by claiming that their emissions complied with EU regulations. They were able to say this because, in the EU, emissions tests are carried out in each member state in laboratories, not on the road. Campaigners had long warned that the lab test results did not reflect the emissions produced by diesels when driven under road conditions. One commentator claimed that 'Gaming and optimising the test is ubiquitous across the industry' (The Guardian 1 October 2015). Another alleged that, 'All car companies cheat on emissions tests—it's just that most do it legally' (qz.com).

Before the VW rigging became public, the EU decided to introduce road testing to get a realistic measure of emissions, the tests to come into force in 2017 (European Commission 2015). At the height of the scandal, the UK, French, German, and Spanish governments, along with big car producers, successfully called for a relaxation of the requirement to meet legal emissions limits. The car makers claimed that they could not possibly meet the proposed emissions targets by 2020. The result was that new cars could exceed emissions of NOx gases by up to twice the legal limit until 2020, and then by 50 per cent afterwards (*The Guardian* 30 October 2015; *Auto Express* 3 October 2015.)

Corporate Europe Observatory (2015) claims that the car industry lobby is one of the most powerful in the EU, and has a

Figure 10.3 Above and beyond the legal NO$_x$ limits

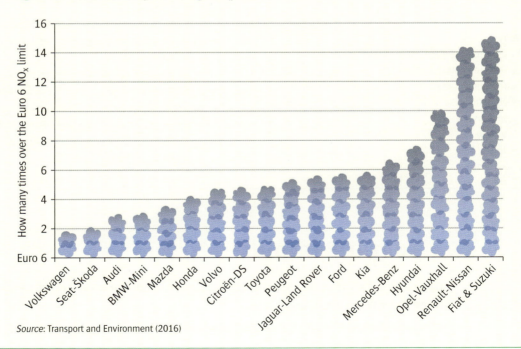

Source: Transport and Environment (2016)

→ successful history of resisting binding emissions targets. Campaigners like T&E conclude that regulators have been captured by the car makers, with regulators prioritising the interests of the industry over that of the wider society (see the section on Lobbying in Ch 9). Manufacturers shop around to find the most lenient national regulators who compete for their business. It argues that governments in France, Germany, and Italy protect their national car makers by not subjecting them to rigorous scrutiny.

T&E argues for a more rigorous implementation of the EU regulations, through a stronger more independent regulatory system, which would oversee the performance of regulators in each member state, car makers being required to submit their models for on-the-road testing by independent laboratories.

An indication that the regulatory environment within EU member states might be changing came with the report that French judges had launched an investigation into suspected cheating on emissions by Renault (*Financial Times* 14 January 2017).

Sources: Auto Express 3 October 2015; BBC 23 September 2015 at http://www.bbc.co.uk; Bloomberg 28 June 2016; Corporate Europe Observatory (2015); *Financial Times* 14 January 2017; European Commission (2015): European Environment Agency (2016); House of Commons Transport Committee (2016); *The Guardian* 1 and 30 October 2015; Reuters 11 January 2017; Transport & Environment (2016); Quartz (2015).

Questions

1. Why did car firms make such efforts to cheat the emissions regulatory systems?
2. Identify which of the following areas of law are being applied to the case in the USA:
   - common law
   - civil law
   - criminal law.
Justify your answer.

3. Discuss reasons why:
   a. the US regulatory authorities have adopted a harsher approach to the cheating of emissions regulation; and
   b. the EU and some of its member states adopted a laxer approach to the case.
4. 'The gaming of defeat device regulations has gone on for far too long in the EU. It is time for the charade to stop' (German, J. International Council on Clean Transportation, blog 10 February 2017). In the light of the number of premature deaths caused by NOx emissions, advance a case for a more rigorous system of emission regulation in the EU.
5. In 2016, the House of Commons Transport Committee concluded that VW had acted with, 'a cynical disregard for emissions limits . . . undermined consumer confidence in vehicle standards . . . (and) brought its own integrity into disrepute' (p. 3).
   a. Assess the impact of the scandal on VW's:
      - sales
      - profits
      - customers
      - share price
      - top executives.
   b. In the light of your answers to a), and bearing in mind your answer to Q4, assess whether the punishment levied on VW by the US fits the crime.

Refer to the following websites: VW's website https://www.volkswagenag.com/en/InvestorRelations/news-and-publications.html; *Forbes*; *The Guardian*; Fortune.

For videos of evidence to the transport committee, see: http://www.parliament.uk/business/committees/committees-a-z/commons-select/transport-committee/news-parliament-2015/volkswagen-emissions-ev2-15-16; and MD of VW UK plus others giving evidence: http://parliamentlive.tv/Event/Index/205c2a9a-37c5-404f-9d32-0ecdc8d31ed6

● FURTHER READING

Goode and Kronke is a standard text on international commercial law. It examines the legal framework and its application to commercial cases.

● Goode, R. and Kronke, H. (2015) *Transnational Commercial Law: Text, Cases and Materials,* 2nd edn. Oxford: Oxford University Press.

Wheater and McCardle produce regular coverage (three times per year) of developments in business law across the globe.

- Wheater, J. and McCardle, W. (eds.), *Business Law International*. London: International Bar Association.

For sources of EU law see Europa, the official website of the EU, and the Cornell University site at http://library.lawschool.cornell.edu.

Carr and Sundaram give up-to-date coverage of the statutes, statutory instruments, and conventions around international trade. It includes some coverage of the law around the internet.

- Carr, I. and Sundaram, J. (2017) *International Trade Law Statutes and Conventions 2016–2018*, Abingdon: Routledge-Cavendish.

Shaw covers internet law and cases in the US, the Americas, the EU, and Asia:

- Shaw, T.J. (2016) *Information and Internet Law—Global Practice*. Online: CreateSpace Independent Publisher.

Siems argues that the law cannot be left to lawyers. He uses an interdisciplinary approach to compare and contrast various legal systems.

- Siems, M. (2014) *Comparative Law*. Cambridge: Cambridge University Press.

REFERENCES

AM online (n.d.). Available at http://www.am-online.com/news/car-manufacturer-news/2017/02/16/psa-has-little-choice-but-to-close-vauxhallplants-if-buyout-goes-ahead.

Apple (2016) Letter to European customers 30 August. Available at http://www.apple.com/uk/customer-letter.

Ars Technica (2016) 'Google responds in EU antitrust case: 'Android hasn't hurt competition'. Available at https://arstechnica.co.uk/techpolicy/2016/11/google-rebuffs-eu-antitrust-charge-against-android.

BBC (2016) 30 August. Available at http://www.bbc.co.uk/news/uk-northern-ireland-37219372.

BBC (2017b) 'EU fines Facebook over "misleading" WhatsApp data claim' http://www.bbc.co.uk/news/business-39958630.

BBC (2017a) 'Vauxhall-Opel sold by GM to Peugeot-Citroen' http://www.bbc.co.uk/news/business-39175740.

Benwell, R. and Gay, O. (2011) The Separation of Powers, House of Commons Library, Standard Note SN/PC/06053.

Bipartisan Policy Center (2014) 21 April http://bipartisanpolicy.org/blog/separation-powers-turkey.

Boldrin, M. and Levine, D.K. (2013) 'The Case Against Patents'. *Journal of Economic Perspectives*, Vol 27, No. 1, Winter.

Boyer, M. and Kotchoni, R. (2015) 'How Much Do Cartels Overcharge?', *Review of Industrial Organization*, 47 (2).

Britannica Concise Encyclopedia (n.d.) http://www.britannica.com.

Brookings (2016) 'Argentina's 2001 Economic and Financial Crisis: Lessons for Europe'. Available at https://www.brookings.edu/wp-content/uploads/2016/06/11_argentina_kiguel.pdf.

Buckley, W. (1955) National Review 19 November. Available at http://www.nationalreview.com/article/223549/our-mission-statement-william-f-buckley-jr.

Chang, H.-J. (2008) *Bad Samaritans*, London: Bloomsbury.

CIA (2017) The World Factbook. Available at http://www.cia.gov/library/publications/the-world-factbook.

Clark, R. (ed.) (2012) 'The Dispute Resolution Review', *Law Business Research*, April.

Connor, J. M. (2014) 'Price-fixing overcharges', *The Law and Economics of Class Actions: Research in Law and Economics*, 26.

Corporate Europe Observatory 2015. Available at://
corporateeurope.org/power-lobbies/2015/09/
power-car-industry-lobby-makes- scandal-inevitable.

Council of Europe//conventions.coe.int/Treaty/EN/
Treaties/html/185.htm.

Clough, J. (2014) A World of Difference: 'The Budapest
Convention on Cybercrime and the Challenges of
Harmonisation', *Monash University Law Review* Vol. 40, No. 3.

Cybersecurity Ventures (2016) Available at http://
cybersecurityventures.com/hackerpocalypse-
cybercrime-report-2016.

Endgadget (2014) 16 December. Available at http://www.
engadget.com/2014/12/16/pirate-bay-shutdown-
explainer.

European Commission (2015) FAQ—Air pollutant
emissions standards, 25 September. MEMO-15-5705.

European Commission (2016) State aid: Ireland gave
illegal tax benefits to Apple worth up to €13 billion,
30 August, Memo 16-2923.

European Commission (2018) 'Antitrust/cartel cases'.
Available at http://ec.europa.eu/competition/elojade/
isef/case_details.cfm?proc_code=1_40099.

European Environment Agency 2016, Premature Deaths
Attributable to Air Pollution.

Eversheds Sutherland (2018) http://www.
evershedssutherland.com/documents/services/
employment/HRPG-wall-charts_Collective%20
redundancies.

Foreign and Commonwealth Office (2013) Living in Saudi
Arabia, 25 March.

Friedman, M. (1970) 'The Social Responsibility of Business
is to Increase its Profits', *New York Times Magazine*
13 September.

Friedman, M. (2002) 'Preface'. *Economic Freedom of the
World: 2002 Annual Report*. Cato Institute. Available
at http://www.cato.org/pubs/efw/efw2002/
efw02-intro.pdf.

Glinavos, I. (2008) 'Neoliberal Law: Unintended
Consequences of Market-Friendly Law Reforms'. *Third
World Quarterly* 29(6).

Google (n.d.). Available at http://www.americanbar.org/
publications/landslide/2015-16/september-october/
terms_of_use_case_update.html).

Google (2016) Available at https://blog.google/topics/
googleeurope/android-choice-competition-response-
europe.

Guardian (2017). Available at http://www.theguardian.
com/business/2017/mar/03/brexit-uk-car-industry-
mini-britain-eu.

Hagedoorn, J. and Hesen, G. (2007) 'Contract Law and the
Governance of Inter-Firm Technology Partnerships: An
Analysis of Different Modes of Partnering and Their
Contractual Implications'. *Journal of Management
Studies* 44: 3. Available at http://core.kmi.open.ac.uk/
download/pdf/6460436.pdf.

Harbottle & Lewis (2014) http://www.harbottle.com/
keywords-ethics-lush-v-amazon.

Hofmann, N. (2010) 'Interpretation Rules and Good Faith
as Obstacles to the UK's Ratification of the CISG and to
the Harmonization of Contract Law in Europe'. *Pace
International Law Review* (Winter).

House of Commons Transport Committee (2016)
Volkswagen emissions scandal and vehicle type
approval, Third report of Session 2016–17, July.

Islamic Financial Services Board (2016) Islamic Financial
Services Stability Report 2016.

Italaw (n.d.) Eli Lilly and Company v. The Government of
Canada, UNCITRAL, ICSID Case No. UNCT/14/2.
Available at http://www.italaw.com/cases/1625.

Kapzynski, A. and Kesselheim, A.S. (2016) 'Government
Patent Use: A Legal Approach to Reducing Drug
Spending', *Health Affairs* 35(5).

Mayson, S., French, D., and Ryan, C. (2016–17) *Mayson,
French and Ryan on Company Law*, 33rd edn. Oxford:
Oxford University Press.

Moss, S. (2005–06) 'Why the United Kingdom Has Not
Ratified the CISG'. *Journal of Law and Commerce* 25(1).
Available at http://www.uncitral.org/pdf/english/
CISG25/Moss.pdf.

National Conference of State Legislatures (n.d.) http://
www.ncsl.org/research/about-state-legislatures/
separation-of-powers-an-overview.aspx.

Nozick, R. (1977) *Anarchy, State, and Utopia*. New York:
Basic Books.

npr (2016) http://www.npr.org/sections/health-
shots/2016/08/23/491053523/tighter-patent-
rules-could-help-lower-drug-prices-study-shows,
23 August.

Patel, R. (2009) *The Value of Nothing*. London: Portobello
Books.

Ponemon Institute (2016) '2013 Cost of Cybercrime Study
and the Risk of Innovation', October. Available at
http://www.ponemon.org/local/upload/file/2016%
20HPE% 20CCC% 20GLOBAL%20REPORT%20
FINAL%203.pdf.

PwC (2015) Doing Business in the Kingdom of Saudi
Arabia: A tax and legal guide, September

Quartz (2015) Available at http://qz.com/511064/all-car-companies-cheat-on-emissions-tests-its-just-that-most-do-it-legally.

Reuters (2014) 'Chronology: Argentina's turbulent history of economic crises'. Available at https://www.reuters.com/article/us-argentina-debt-chronology-idUSKBN0FZ23N20140730.

Rowe, E.A. and Mahfood, D.M. (2014) *Trade Secrets, Trade, and Extraterritoriality*, 66 Ala. L. Rev. 63, available at http://scholarship.law.ufl.edu/facultypub/735.

Saudilegal (2017) http://www.saudilegal.com.

Schulte-Nölke, H. (ed) (2007) 'EC Consumer Law Compendium—Comparative Analysis', December. Available at http://ec.europa.eu/consumers/archive/cons_int/safe_shop/acquis/comp_analysis_en.pdf.

Scotus (2014) 'Clear statement ruling in investor-state arbitration case leaves open question on U.S. bilateral treaties'. Available at http://www.scotusblog.com/2014/03/opinion-analysis-clear-statement-ruling-in-investor-state-arbitration-case-leaves-open-question-on-u-s-bilateral-treaties/.

Shearman & Sterling (2016) Introduction to the Legal System of the Kingdom of Saudi Arabia, September

Smits, J.M. (2005) 'Diversity of Contract Law and the European Internal Market'. Maastricht Faculty of Law Working Paper 2005/9. Available at http://www.unimaas.nl.

Stiglitz, J. (2010) *Freefall: Free Markets and the Sinking of the Global Economy*. London: Penguin.

Transparency International (2017) Corruption Perceptions Index 2016.

Transparency International (2018) Global Corruption Perceptions Index, 21 February.

Transport and Environment (2016) *Diesel Gate: Who? What? How?* September. Available at https://www.transportenvironment.org/sites/te/files/publications/2016_09_Dieselgate_report_who_what_how_FINAL_0.pdf.

Unilex (n.d.) http://www.unilex.info.

US Court of Appeals (2017). Available at https://assets.documentcloud.org/documents/3453410/17-35105-Documents-1.pdf.

US Senate (2013) US Senate Committee on Homeland Security and Governmental Affairs (2013), Offshore Profit Shifting and the U.S. Tax Code—Part 2 (Apple Inc.).

US Department of Justice (2017) 'Chilean Chemicals and Mining Company Agrees to Pay More Than $15 Million to Resolve Foreign Corrupt Practices Act Charges'. 13 January. Available at http://www.justice.gov/opa/pr/chilean-chemicals-and-mining-company-agrees-pay-more-15-million-resolve-foreign-corrupt.

Venter, F. (2012) 'South Africa: A Diceyan Rechtstaat?' *McGill Law Journal* 57(4).

Washington University Law (2017) http://law.wustl.edu/GSLR/CitationManual/countries/saudiarabia.pdf.

Wells, D. (2006) 'Current Challenges for the Doctrine of the Separation of Powers: The Ghosts in the Machinery of Government', *Queensland University of Technology, Law and Justice Journal,* Vol. 6 No.1.

Wired (2017) http://www.wired.co.uk/article/trump-ban-immigration-tech-apple-google-facebook-response-order, 6 February.

World Bank (2017) 'Doing Business 2017'.

World Economic Forum (2016) The Global Gender Gap Report 2016.

World Economic Forum (2018) Global Competitivenes Report 2017–18.

Yeh, B.T. (2016) Protection of Trade Secrets: Overview of Current Law and Legislation, Congressional Research Service, 22 April.

CHAPTER ELEVEN

The Financial Framework

LEARNING OUTCOMES

This chapter will enable you to:

- explain what money is and its importance for business;

- assess the significance of inflation and interest rates for the business environment;

- analyse the role and importance of international financial institutions and markets;

- explain the restructuring and the increasing integration of the international financial system;

- explain the characteristics and impact of the global financial crisis; and

- assess the challenges faced by financial regulators.

Case Study Deutsche Bank—too big to fail

© 123RF.com/joeppoulssen

This case looks at Germany's biggest bank, Deutsche Bank (DB), the problems it faces, and the potential threat it poses to the global financial system. DB is a big global investment bank with more than 20 million clients, and about 100,000 employees in around 3,000 branches in more than 70 countries, from the Americas across Europe, Africa, and Asia to Australia. It provides financial services to private individuals, large and small businesses, institutional investors, and governments. In 2016, measured by asset value, it was ranked 11 in the world's biggest banks. It was Germany's biggest bank and held assets equivalent in value to half the size of the German economy.

In 2016, the bank was wrestling with a string of problems. In the USA, it was charged with mis-selling mortgage bonds in the run up to the 2007/08 financial crisis. At one point it looked as if it would have to pay a $14 billion fine levied by the US Department of Justice. In 2015, it paid a penalty of $2.5 billion for rigging LIBOR, which determines interest rates on trillions of financial contracts around the world. Regulations put in place after the financial crisis made it tougher for Deutsche Bank to make profits and, furthermore, the bank's costs were too high.

The bank set about restructuring the business, especially the investment bank, which generated 85 per cent of the bank's income, and the major cause of its problems. It wanted to cut the workforce by a quarter and raise capital by selling off its Chinese operation and the retail banking business, Postbank.

Low interest rates, which had been in place since the financial crisis, also made it more difficult for Deutsche Bank to earn income.

Deutsche Bank's situation was important, not only to the German economy, but also to the world financial system. Deutsche Bank was closely interlinked with financial institutions in the German insurance sector, and also heavily interconnected globally, so much so that the IMF (2016: 42) gave a stark warning, seeing it as 'a major source of systemic risk in the global financial system'. Figure 11.1 shows the interconnections between DB and other big, globally important banks. The IMF found that volatility in Deutsche Bank's share price had a bigger effect on those of its financial rivals than any other big bank. In the IMF's view, a collapse of the German bank would have a domino effect, endangering the global financial system. In other words, Deutsche Bank was too big to allow it to fail.

Deutsche Bank's assets were the major source of concern. Analysts questioned whether they were worth the £1.5 trillion declared in its balance sheet. Of particular concern was the valuation of Deutsche Bank's illiquid assets; illiquid, because they could not be turned quickly into cash without losing value. According to the *Financial Times* (1 October 2016), these were valued at €28.8 billion using models relying on 'unobservable' inputs. These models were also used to put a value of €10.9 billion on liabilities not traded in any market, and consequently having no market price. This created great uncertainty around DB's balance sheet. In addition, illiquid assets amounted to more than half of Deutsche's shareholders' equity, and retained earnings, of €56 billion. Derivative products and asset backed securities were the main components of Deutsche Bank's illiquid asset and liability exposure. Martin Wolf of the *Financial Times* (4 October 2016) described the bank as, 'a highly-leveraged bank with a doubtful business and opaque assets.'

In 2015 DB made a loss of €6.8 billion. In 2016, hedge funds started to cut down on business with the bank, and revenues fell by 10 per cent. Uncertainty around the bank's assets and the looming threat of a big fine in the USA caused its share price to plummet. The CEO felt obliged to email staff reassuring them that the business was sound.   →

→ **Figure 11.1** Deutsche Bank cross-border interconnections

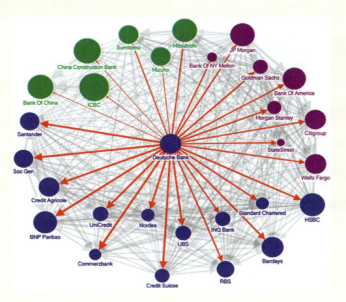

Source: IMF (2016)

Note: The blue, purple, and green denote European, US, and Asian banks, respectively. The thickness of the arrow reflects total linkages. The arrowhead shows the direction of net spillover. The size of the circles shows asset size.

Sources: CNN Money 2 February 2017; *The Guardian* 27 September 2016; Deutsche Bank website http://www.db.com; email from CEO to Deutsche staff 30 September 2016 http://www.db.com/ newsroom; *Financial Times* 1 and 4 October 2016; IMF (2016); Relbanks http://www.relbanks.com/worlds-top-banks/assets; Reuters Profile Deutsche Bank at http://www.reuters.com

Introduction

In this chapter we are going to look at the international financial environment, that part of the international economy concerned with money, interest rates, and financial assets such as deposits, company shares, bonds, **derivatives**, and foreign currencies. We examine the major private financial institutions, the markets where they operate, and the extraordinarily fast rate at which these institutions and markets have grown, both at home and abroad. We also look at the operation of organizations such as the Bank for International Settlements, the International Monetary Fund, the World Bank, and the European Central Bank.

We go on to examine the characteristics of the 2007/08 global financial crisis, which shook the international monetary system. Finally, we consider how the financial system is regulated, and the effectiveness of regulation in maintaining stability in the international financial system.

Money

Money is an essential element of the international financial environment, playing, as it does, a number of vitally important roles for business:

- A medium of exchange—money allows businesses to receive payment from customers, both at home and abroad, and to pay their suppliers.

- A common measure of value—money enables firms to place a value on the goods and services that they buy and sell.

- Divisibility—money can be broken down into different units of value, such as cents and dollars or pence and pounds, facilitating the process of exchange.

- A store of wealth—money gives business the ability to store wealth. Businesses can build up reserves of money now, which can be used later to buy goods and services, or to invest.

The Importance of Confidence

Underpinning the idea of money is an agreement to accept something that, in itself, may have no fundamental use to us.

Normally, we have confidence that it can be exchanged in the market for something that does have use: goods and services. Were that confidence to melt away, the whole financial and economic system would be under threat. In such a situation, neither individuals nor businesses would be prepared to accept money in exchange for goods and services, and the system of monetary exchange would collapse, with drastic consequences for the economy in general, and business in particular.

Money takes various forms, moving from the more to the less liquid. Liquidity refers to how quickly and cheaply an asset can be converted into cash. Thus, paper money or cash is the most liquid asset, because it can be exchanged very easily for goods and services. Current bank accounts are another example of high liquidity, insofar as the money in them is quickly and easily accessible, and also because it can be easily transferred by cheque or electronic means. Less liquid are savings accounts and deposits that need notice before money can be withdrawn. Even less liquid are a variety of financial assets, such as stocks and bonds, which may not be turned into cash so easily.

 Mini Case Study 11.1 **Bitcoin**

The bitcoin is a digital currency in which transactions can be performed without the need for a central bank—the unit of account is the bitcoin. Transactions take place between individuals, but bitcoins are also accepted by some e-businesses including some operating illegally, partly because transactions can be carried out anonymously and partly because the fees are lower than those charged by credit card companies, which can be anything from 2.5 per cent to 5 per cent. Transactions are recorded in a public digital ledger. Firms accepting bitcoin include Microsoft, Subway, PwC, Expedia, and PayPal.

Many individuals and companies buy and sell bitcoins, and such transactions occur in a variety of different currencies. The supply of bitcoins is determined by an algorithm; that is, a mathematical equation. New bitcoins are created every 10 →

→ minutes in batches of 25. The value of the bitcoin varies quite dramatically. It topped $1,000 in 2013, $19,000 in 2017, but slumped to $6,000 in 2018 (*Financial Times* 24 February 2018). Some businesses quickly saw that security could be a major barrier to the growth of bitcoins, so they set up what were claimed to be secure online wallet services where users could deposit their bitcoins. This reassured individual users that their bitcoins were safe with a trusted third party, at the same time allowing payments to be made easily, and lowering the technical know-how required to get and store the currency. However, online wallet providers, like Inputsio and MtGox, became the target of hackers, with the latter filing for bankruptcy, claiming that 750,000 bitcoins had been stolen.

Some national authorities are concerned about bitcoins, one reason being the threat it poses to their control of the money supply. *The Economist* (12 April 2014) reported that China was the 'promised land' for bitcoin, with the country estimated to account for half of the world trade in the currency in 2013. The Chinese market collapsed when China's central bank declared that bitcoins were not a currency, and banned commercial banks from dealing with bitcoin cyber-exchange companies.

The Bank of England (McLeay et al. 2014) does not see the bitcoin as money, because it is not accepted on the high street, and its popularity derives from its ability to act as an asset, like gold. The Governor of the Bank went further by claiming that the digital currency market had 'all the hallmarks of a bubble', claiming that digital currencies like Bitcoin were associated with money laundering and terrorist financing, and called for greater regulation.

Sources: Business Insider 2 March 2018; *Financial Times* 24 February 2018; *The Guardian* 5 and 18 March 2014; MarketWatch 22 May 2017; McLeay et al. (2014); useBitcoins http://www.usebitcoins.info

Questions

1. Reread the section above on money. Assess whether bitcoins are money. In your answer, consider the extent to which bitcoins are:
   a. a good medium of exchange and store of wealth;
   b. divisible into smaller units.
2. Why do the hackers ask for payment in bitcoin?
3. Discuss whether the authorities should ban bitcoin.

 Learning Task

The website 99Bitcoins reported that firms such as Microsoft, Subway, and Expedia were accepting bitcoins in exchange for goods and services (99Bitcoins, 19 June 2016). Weigh up the advantages and disadvantages for these companies in accepting bitcoin.

Inflation and Interest Rates

Inflation

Inflation can be defined as an increase in the overall price level of goods and services in an economy over a particular period of time, or as a reduction in the value of money. It is usually measured by collecting price information on a representative sample of goods and services, and using the information to calculate a Price Index that shows the change in the general price level. Businesses operating in countries with relatively high rates of inflation can find their international competitiveness undermined, as the rising costs of goods and services feed higher costs of production. This process may be exacerbated when workers respond to rising prices by demanding higher wages. On the other hand, this can open up selling opportunities for firms operating out of low inflation economies. They are likely to find it easier to compete with firms operating in countries suffering from high inflation.

The rate of inflation in rich countries started to pick up after 2004, with vigorous growth in the global economy. Rapid growth, particularly in countries like China, led to increases in demand for commodities such as oil, and other raw materials, which pushed up their prices. Up to then, low import prices had helped to hold down inflation rates in rich countries. The Federal Reserve estimated that falling import prices had reduced US inflation by between 0.5 and 1 percentage point a year from the mid-1990s. The onset of the global financial crisis in 2007 led to a slow-down in inflation globally, to the point where, in 2009, price levels were deflating, i.e. dropping, in the USA, the UK, Japan, and Switzerland. Commodity prices, with the exception of oil, dropped by around one-fifth during 2008. Figure 11.2 shows world inflation peaking in 2011 at around 5 per cent, and then, with falls in commodity and food prices, declining to about 2 per cent in 2016.

Inflation generally runs at a higher rate in emerging economies. In 2016, inflation in Nigeria was running at nearly 16 per cent, and in Brazil at just above 6 per cent. This compares with the UK and the USA with rates of less than 2 per cent. High inflation rates are not unusual in coun-tries like Nigeria and Brazil, where economies are growing fast, wages are increasing, and the public may be more accepting of rising prices. Another reason could be that governments in poor countries, like Angola, finance their activities by simply printing more and more money, causing demand for goods and services to outstrip supply.

Interest Rates

An interest rate is the price paid for the temporary use of someone else's money. Interest is a cost to borrowers, but income to lenders. When interest rates rise in a country, this increases the cost of borrowing to business. Business could, given the removal of barriers to the movement of capital, shop around in other countries for cheaper rates. A hike in interest rates may also depress demand for goods and services, as consumers find it more expensive to borrow to buy consumer durables such as cars, computers, plasma TVs, and so forth. On the other hand, rising interest rates could benefit financial institutions that lend money, because they can charge more for their loans.

Figure 11.2 World inflation rate—consumer prices (%)

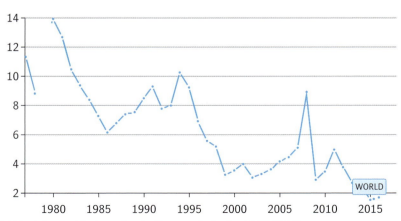

Source: World Bank data.worldbank.org. Creative Commons Attribution 4.0 (CC-BY 4.0)

All the world's leading central banks, concerned about rising inflation after 2004, increased interest rates. However, the global financial crisis raised fears of a collapse of the international financial system, and caused them to reverse the policy. Even by 2017, ten years after the crisis started, with growth in high income economies remaining sluggish, central banks in the Eurozone and Japan had interest rates set at 0 per cent. Rates were 1 per cent in the USA, and 0.25 per cent in the UK. By contrast the rate in Brazil was 11.25 per cent, and in Russia, 9.25 per cent (global-rates.com n.d.).

✏️ Learning Task

1. Examine Figure 11.3 and comment on the evolution of interest rates after 2005.

2. Advance reasons for interest rates being higher in emerging economies than in advanced economies.

3. Discuss the implications of low interest rates for business and consumers.

Figure 11.3 Interest rates advanced and emerging economies (%)

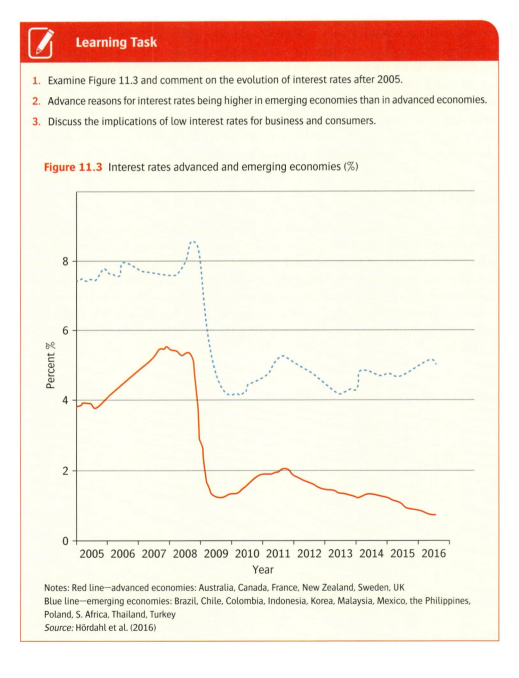

Notes: Red line—advanced economies: Australia, Canada, France, New Zealand, Sweden, UK
Blue line—emerging economies: Brazil, Chile, Colombia, Indonesia, Korea, Malaysia, Mexico, the Philippines, Poland, S. Africa, Thailand, Turkey
Source: Hördahl et al. (2016)

Financial Institutions—Who Are They and What Do They Do?

The functioning of the international economy, and the production, trading, and investment activities of the organizations and individuals within it, are dependent on the effective operation of a variety of financial institutions, both public and private. We look first at several international financial institutions and their functions, and then we examine an array of other organizations in the financial sector.

International Financial Institutions

There are several international financial institutions whose main aim is to facilitate the effective operation of the international payments mechanism, and to ensure stability in the international financial system.

Bank for International Settlements

The Bank for International Settlements (BIS) has 60 members, 59 of which are countries represented at the BIS by their central banks, the other being the European Central Bank. The BIS fosters international monetary and financial cooperation and stability. It serves as an international central bank for national central banks, such as the Federal Reserve, the European Central Bank, and the Bank of China. It acts as a forum to promote discussion and policy analysis among central banks, and in the international financial community.

The BIS deals with the central banks on a daily basis and, by buying and selling foreign currencies and gold, helps them manage their foreign currency and gold reserves. It also advises the central banks, and other international institutions, on how to prevent financial fraud. In times of financial crisis, the BIS offers short-term credits to central banks, and may also coordinate emergency short-term lending to countries.

The Bank played a key role in establishing BASEL I, II, III, and IV, which recommended levels of capital that banks should hold, to guard against the risk of collapse. The BIS hosts the Financial Stability Board (FSB), set up in 2009 in the aftermath of the global financial crisis. The FSB promotes international financial stability by monitoring the world financial system and advising on effective regulation.

International Monetary Fund

The International Monetary Fund (IMF), which has 189 members, was established to preserve international financial stability; in other words, to avoid financial crises that could threaten the international financial system. Member countries contribute funds to a pool from which they can borrow on a temporary basis when running balance of payments deficits. Applicants for loans in the past have faced IMF demands for changes in government policy, such as cutting public expenditures on social programmes, reducing subsidies on basic necessities, increasing taxes, eliminating import tariffs, and the privatization of publicly owned assets.

It has some very ambitious aims: to promote global monetary cooperation, secure financial stability, facilitate international trade, promote high employment and sustainable economic growth, and reduce poverty. The IMF differs from the BIS insofar as it can provide temporary financial assistance to members to enable them to correct international payment imbalances. The idea is that such assistance discourages countries from trying to rectify their balance of payments deficits by resorting to policies such as competitive currency devaluations, which could have disruptive effects on the international trading and financial systems, exchange controls, or trade protection.

During the latest global financial crisis, the IMF came to the rescue of countries with large amounts of financial assistance. For example, Greece was given a loan of US$30 billion, Hungary and Ukraine each got support of around US$16 billion, while Latvia secured an IMF stand-by arrangement, worth more than US$2.3 billion (http://www.imf.org). These loans came with conditions forcing countries to implement austerity measures. In 2009, in the aftermath of the crisis, IMF members agreed to double the resources available to the IMF, to US$1 trillion. While this represented a significant increase in resources, they remained minuscule compared with the cost to banks of the financial crisis. The Fund estimated that for the USA alone, banks had to write down loans and make provisions for losses to the sum of US$588 billion as a result of the financial crisis. The figure for Eurozone banks was US$442 billion (IMF 2010).

While the ability of the IMF to deal with global financial crises has been strengthened, it is difficult to envisage it making a significant difference were there to be another full-blown financial crisis of global dimensions, such as that starting in autumn 2007.

World Bank

The World Bank, with 189 member countries, was set up to reduce global poverty and to improve standards of living. Currently, its specific aims are to reduce extreme poverty to no more than 3 per cent of the world population, and to promote income growth for the bottom 40 per cent of each country's population.

It provides low cost loans and interest-free credit to developing countries for education, health, and for the development of infrastructure projects in water supply, transport, and communications. World Bank projects can be a source of lucrative contracts for businesses, such as water, energy, and telecommunications utilities, as well as construction companies.

In 2016 it provided $49 billion to developing countries (World Bank 2016). Like the IMF, the Bank may have the capacity to bring about change in individual countries, but its budget does not equip it to have a major impact on the billions of people who continue to live in poverty.

European Central Bank

The European Central Bank (ECB) is the central bank for countries that are members of the Eurozone (19 in 2017). Its main job is the control of inflation using the tools of monetary policy, in other words the money supply, and interest rates, to achieve price stability. The ECB conducts foreign exchange operations on behalf of member states, manages their foreign reserves, and promotes the smooth operation of payments systems within the zone. It carries out the tasks typically associated with national central banks.

Counterpoint Box 11.1 The IMF and World Bank

The World Bank and the IMF have come in for criticism. The critics claim that both institutions work in the best interests of rich economies, in that they provide assistance to debt-ridden or near-bankrupt developing countries that are powerless to resist their demands for the introduction of reforms. These reforms remove barriers to private business in advanced economies, wishing to export goods or services to those poor countries, import raw materials from them, or to invest there. In addition, poor countries are pressurized to cut public expenditure, remove state monopolies, and prioritize repayment of debt to foreign banks and investors. This hits the poor in those countries as jobs are cut, health and education budgets reduced, price supports removed, and food and natural resources exported abroad.

Supporters argue that the removal of barriers to trade, public monopolies, and subsidies increases competition, leading to a more efficient allocation of resources and economic growth. They claim that these countries would be in an even worse state were they not forced to adopt responsible budgetary policies. The IMF has made efforts to protect the vulnerable during the latest crisis by inclusion of a commitment to strengthen the provision of social safety nets. Supporters also argue that the institution has moderated its belief in free markets by accepting that, in some cases, inflows of private capital need to be controlled, because they can fuel credit booms and inflation, and harm competitiveness.

Critics have hit back, claiming that even after IMF and World Bank rhetoric about protecting the poor, reform programmes have insisted on weakening labour rights, reducing unemployment benefits, and freezing salaries in places like Tunisia and Morocco. The UN Human Rights Council (2016) concluded that the reforms imposed on Greece by the IMF and others deepened the economic crisis, and forced more than 1 million people into extreme poverty.

Sources: *Bretton Woods Observer* Spring 2017; Stiglitz (2002); Harrigan (2010); Muuka (1998); http://www.imf.org; Moschella 2014; UN Human Rights Council (2016 and 2017)

Questions

1. What reforms did the IMF, the European Commission and the ECB propose for Greece?

2. a. Argue a case for those reforms.
   b. Now argue the case against the reforms.

   See ODS (n.d.) and GlobalResearch (2017).

Private Financial Institutions

There is a whole range of other financial institutions carrying out an array of functions invaluable for business. Banks, insurance companies, pension funds, investment trusts, and unit trusts all act as intermediaries between those who wish to borrow money and those who wish to lend. Retail banks take deposits from private individuals, firms, and other bodies. Insurance companies, pension funds, and unit trusts collect longer-term savings, which they then invest in a variety of stocks and shares. By not being dependent on the shares of a single company, they offer savers the possibility of spreading risk. Investment banks (also called merchant banks) provide a range of financial services to business. They give advice in areas such as mergers and acquisitions, the disposal of businesses, arrange issues of new shares, and buy and sell assets on behalf of clients or, increasingly, on their own account.

Private equity funds, including venture capital companies, are another source of funding for business. These firms gather funds from private and public pension funds, charitable foundations, business, and wealthy individuals, and often use them to finance smaller, sometimes start-up, companies. They usually do this in return for a share in the ownership of the company.

Functions of Financial Institutions

We now look in more detail at some of the important functions performed by financial institutions for business.

Mobilizing Savings and Providing Credit

The mobilization and pooling of savings is one of the most obvious and important functions of the financial sector. Savings facilities, such as bank accounts, enable businesses and households to store their money in a secure place. In countries where secure facilities for savings are lacking, or where there is a lack of confidence in the stability of the financial sector, for example in some developing economies, people often opt to save in physical assets such as gold or jewellery, or store their savings at home. In such situations, business can find it difficult to raise finance, and may have to rely on internally generated profits. By offering such facilities, the financial sector pools savings, and channels them to businesses to be used productively in the economy. Interest paid on savings may increase the amount saved, giving a boost to the funds available for businesses to invest.

Financial intermediaries, by pooling the savings of firms and individuals and lending them on to business, can make it easier and cheaper for business to export and import, and to finance investment for expansion or for the introduction of new technology. Thus, the sector can help business service new foreign markets and sources of supply, and can also make it easier for firms to improve competitiveness by increasing productivity or by introducing new products.

Payment Facilities

Financial intermediaries facilitate the exchange of goods and services, both in terms of domestic and cross-border transactions, by providing mechanisms to make and receive payments. To be effective, payments systems need to be readily available for both domestic and foreign buyers and sellers, through bank branches or electronically, and they also need to be affordable, fast, and safe from fraud.

Good payments mechanisms free up firms to concentrate on what they do best, that is to make goods and provide services, and this ability to specialize makes it easier for them to innovate and to increase productivity. Anything that reduces transaction costs and better facilitates the exchange of goods and services—whether that be faster payments systems, more bank branches, or improved remittance services—will help to promote business growth.

Normally, payments systems are more highly developed in advanced economies than in poorer countries, but systems can vary from one rich country to another. The existence of multiple payments systems can raise problems of inter-operability, that is the ability of the various systems to accept payments from others. Inter-operability may be made more diffi-cult when systems are using incompatible hardware or software systems. While this may not be such an important issue for big multinational companies, whose subsidiaries are trading with each other and where payments systems are internal to the company, it does have major implications for firms dependent on making or receiving cross-border payments from third parties.

There are various systems which operate internationally and facilitate cross-border payment:

- SWIFT has been adopted by more than 150 financial institutions worldwide, in 220 coun-tries, dealing daily with over $100 billion of payments (SWIFT 2018). Its services are used by over 11,000 banks, central banks, and other financial institutions, such as securities brokers and dealers, investment management institutions, and money brokers, along with big MNCs such as Microsoft, GE, and DuPont.

- Continuous Linked Settlement (CLS) claims to be the world's largest multicurrency cash payments system. Its members comprise the world's largest banks, and more than 23,000 other clients, including non-bank financial institutions and multinational corporations. It deals in the 18 main currencies used in global trade. Daily, around 800,000 transactions are carried out, reaching a peak of some $11 trillion in 2017 (CLS Interim Financial Report 30 June 2017).

- Visa International and MasterCard are other international organizations offering a range of cashless payment services in 160 currencies in more than 200 countries. Visa has 16,300 financial institution customers and 45 million merchants worldwide. It handles more than 65,000 transactions per second, totalling $10.2 trillion in 2017 (Visa 2017). In the third quarter of 2016, Mastercard dealt with 14.5 bn transactions, to a value of $1.2 trillion (Mastercard n.d.).

- PayPal, and China's Alibaba, are two online payments companies offering secure methods of payment for goods and services on the Web, on sites such as eBay. They are not regis-tered as banks, and therefore need the support of existing financial institutions to offer their services. PayPal operates in multiple currencies in more than 200 countries, with 197 million account holders making over 6 billion payments totalling $354 billion annually (SEC Filing 13 April 2017).

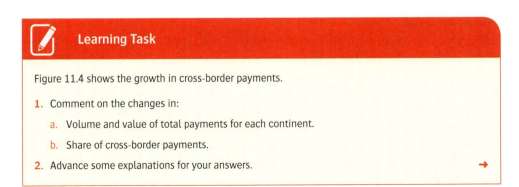

Learning Task

Figure 11.4 shows the growth in cross-border payments.

1. Comment on the changes in:
    a. Volume and value of total payments for each continent.
    b. Share of cross-border payments.
2. Advance some explanations for your answers. →

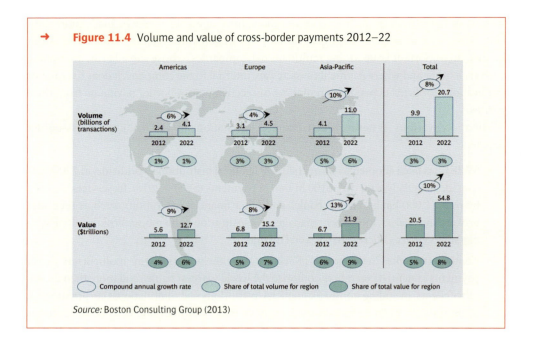

→   **Figure 11.4** Volume and value of cross-border payments 2012–22

Source: Boston Consulting Group (2013)

Electronic payments systems have become more widely available internationally, and this has enabled firms to move their business-to-business (B2B), and business-to-consumer (B2C), activities on to the Web. Electronic payments across the European Union are now fast and cheap, and are generally more efficient than payments within the USA. In Japan, cash is used extensively compared with other industrial countries. However, Japanese businesses and consumers do also use direct debits, credit transfers, credit cards, debit cards, and cheques. Electronic payments have been increasing, partly reflecting the development of a variety of access channels, such as Automatic Teller Machines (ATMs), the internet, and mobile phones. In China, online business is growing rapidly.

By contrast, in Russia, the population continues to prefer payment in cash. This is the major payment means used for retail payments for goods and services. Cash is also used for paying salaries, pensions, welfare allowances, and grants. However, the use of ATMs is growing very rapidly, as is the use of 'plastic' as a means of payment, with Visa and MasterCard the main players. Compared to richer countries, the Russian payments system is underdeveloped.

In Africa, only 15–20 per cent of people have bank accounts, but almost half have mobile phones, with an additional 250 million subscribers expected by 2020 (GSMA 2016). Although the majority of sub-Saharan African countries, including Nigeria, Sierra Leone, and Tanzania, still have largely cash and cheque-based economies, significant progress is being made in the regional development of electronic payment systems. East African countries, like Kenya, have moved rapidly to develop the use of mobiles for money transfers. While Latin American countries do have growing electronic payments systems, in many, because more than half of the population have no bank accounts, payments are made in cash. However, the use of debit and credit cards there is increasing quickly.

Learning Task

Examine Figure 11.5 which shows the proportion of people worldwide who have bank accounts.

1. Which countries and continents have the highest and lowest proportions of people with bank accounts?

2. Advance reasons for the different rates of bank account penetration.

3. Explore the implications of the different penetration rates for business.

Figure 11.5 Bank account penetration worldwide 2014

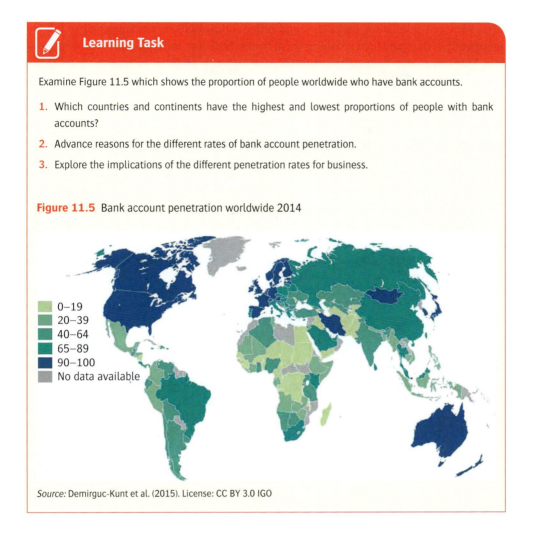

- 0–19
- 20–39
- 40–64
- 65–89
- 90–100
- No data available

Source: Demirguc-Kunt et al. (2015). License: CC BY 3.0 IGO

Reconciling Liquidity and Long-term Finance Needs

Business investment projects often require a medium- to long-term commitment of capital, whereas many savers prefer to have ready access to their savings. In other words, they like their savings to be 'liquid'. Banks and other financial intermediaries can offer finance to business for medium and long-term investment because they combine the savings of many households and businesses. Experience shows that savers do not usually all want to withdraw their money at the same time. As a result, financial institutions need only keep a proportion of their assets in a liquid form to meet the demands of those savers wishing to withdraw money while, at the same time, being able to provide medium to long-term capital for business investment.

Spreading the Risk

Savers are usually averse to risk and generally reluctant to invest all their money in a single project. They much prefer to spread the risk by investing in a range of projects. Financial intermediaries, such as banks, stock exchanges, and hedge funds, facilitate the spreading of risk by aggregating savings and then spreading them among both low and high-risk investment projects. This can enable business to get finance for high-risk projects, such as those involving ground-breaking technology.

Industry Restructuring and Diversification

Financial institutions have similar objectives to other private sector commercial organizations: at the most basic level they wish to survive, but they also aim to make profits and grow. Profits are made from the commissions, charges, and interest rates levied on the financial services offered, both domestically and, increasingly, abroad. They also benefit from arbitrage, which involves taking advantage of price differences between markets; for example, when a financial product can be bought cheaply in, say, Tokyo and sold for a higher price in Amsterdam.

Domestic Consolidation and International Expansion

In pursuit of their objectives, financial institutions have been getting bigger through mergers and acquisitions, and also through organic growth—in other words, increasing their own output and sales. This has led to industry restructuring. The global banking system now comprises a small number of large banks operating in highly concentrated markets with relatively low rates of entry and exit.

Weiss et al. (2014) report that there were 440 global bank mergers between 1991 and 2009, the majority of which were domestic mergers within North America and Western Europe in the period 2004–07. With the onset of the financial crisis, the appetite for mergers fell away (Figure 11.6).

Fifty years ago, banks and other financial institutions tended to confine their operations to their domestic markets. Increasingly, they have expanded their operations abroad—the big German bank, Deutsche Bank, offers a wide range of financial services to private and business clients in over 70 countries.

Figure 11.6 Number and value of mergers ($m) pre- and post-crisis

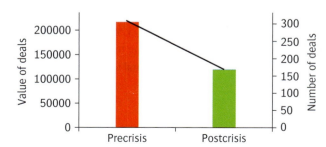

Source: Rao-Nicholson and Salaber (2016)

US banks, such as Citigroup, and European banks, like Royal Bank of Scotland (RBS), have also gone in for mergers, both at home and abroad, to get round the problem of slow-growing domestic markets. The fast-growing Chinese economy has attracted the interest of foreign banks, such as Citigroup and RBS. KPMG (2017) reported that total assets of foreign banks in China had increased at an annual compound rate of 20 per cent between 2006 and 2016. The strategies pursued by financial institutions have led to a restructuring of the sector, and have resulted in the creation of large financial conglomerates, selling a range of products in a variety of countries.

Product Diversification

Financial institutions have also grown by expanding their product range. Traditionally, banks borrowed and lent money, but did not sell insurance or trade in shares. Building societies made long-term loans on the security of private houses, but did not provide banking services such as current accounts. In their quest for profits and growth, they have diversified, and consequently have become less specialized. Big retail banks, for example, have increasingly seen their future as financial supermarkets, selling a range of financial products and services. As a result, the various institutions now compete with each other over a wider product range.

Product Innovation

The financial sector has been very inventive in devising new financial products. A major development has been the growth of the hedge fund. Hedging implies action to reduce risk. While hedge funds do attempt to reduce risk, they also trade in a range of financial assets, from equities to bonds to commodities, and strive to take advantage of arbitrage opportunities. So, for example, if a currency or commodity is selling for one price in London and a higher price in New York, then hedge funds will buy in London and sell in New York. Hedge funds often use complex mathematical models to make predictions of future price movements of financial assets to determine their trading strategies. Their aim is to produce good performance, regardless of the underlying trends in the financial markets.

Derivatives, Swaps, and Options

In financial markets, stock prices, bond prices, currency rates, interest rates, and dividends go up and down, creating risk. Derivatives are financial products whose value is based on the value of other products like shares, bonds, currencies, and commodities such as cocoa and zinc. Derivatives give the right to buy or sell these existing products in the future at an agreed price. Firms such as airlines buy them to insure against increases in fuel prices. Others use them to gamble on future price changes.

Swaps are derivatives which firms can use to cover themselves against adverse movements in interest rates, inflation, exchange rates, and the possibility of borrowers defaulting on their loans. Thus, pension funds can use inflation swaps to protect the value of their assets against increases in inflation, while lenders, concerned about defaulting loans, can use credit default swaps. They work like this: two banks, one of whom has lent to General Motors and one to VW, can diversify their risk by agreeing to exchange a part of the loan potential default. Both would then be less exposed to a default by their original borrower. This ability to spread risks may make financial institutions more willing to lend, consequently making it easier for non-financial firms to borrow.

Much of the trade in derivative products does not take place through financial markets, but between individual institutions. Such trade is called over-the-counter (OTC) trading, and is massive. The value outstanding in OTC derivatives was $554 trillion in the first half of 2016, which was around eight times greater than global output (BIS 2017). Policy makers, fearing the effects a meltdown in the OTC market resulting in another global financial crisis, have been trying to centralize the trading in organized exchanges.

An option is a derivative allowing the buying or selling of a specific amount of, for example a loan, a commodity, a currency or a company share, at a specified price over a certain period of time. The buyer pays an amount of money for the option, and the potential loss is limited to the price paid. When an option is not exercised, the money spent to purchase the option is lost. So, a firm could take out an option to borrow money at a specific rate of interest of, say, 8 per cent over a certain time, for example six months. If the interest rate rises above 8 per cent, the firm can exercise its option. If the interest rate falls below 8 per cent, then the firm borrows at the lower rate and loses the price it paid for the option.

Motives for Industry Restructuring and Diversification

Economies of scale—financial organizations hope to gain scale economies in the purchasing of supplies and savings by getting rid of duplication (a merged bank does not need more than one HQ building, one marketing department, and so on). This proclivity to merge has continued, despite research literature showing that economies of scale can be exhausted by the time a bank reaches a relatively modest size. However, Hughes and Mester (2013) concluded that smaller banks benefit from large scale economies, but bigger banks experience even greater scale economies. Anderson and Joever (2012) find evidence of economies of scale particularly among the biggest banks, but note that the benefits accrue more to bankers than to investors.

Economies of scope—the idea here is that the extra costs of selling additional products alongside the old ones are small compared to the increase in revenues. So, a bank can diversify into credit cards or insurance and apply its traditional skills of selling loans to the marketing of these products. The logic is that selling extra financial products through established branch networks to existing customers offers a low cost, high productivity method of distribution.

Market share—when a bank takes over a competitor, this increases its market share, reduces competition, and may, because the take-over makes it bigger, reduce its own vulnerability to take-over.

Restructuring was also a response to the external environment:

- The global financial crisis caused banks to merge. For example, a number of Spanish savings banks were forced to merge by their government. In the USA, Bank of America merged with Merrill Lynch, and in the UK Lloyds TSB took over HBOS. The crisis has led to increased regulatory costs and stronger capital requirements, which could force a new round of bank mergers.

- To finance the increase in international trade and investment which grew at unprecedented rates after the Second World War.

- Economic expansion in developing nations in South East Asia led to an increased demand for financial services.

- In order to avoid regulation by the monetary authorities, financial institutions have been very clever in developing business outside regulated areas, where there are profits to be made. Austrian banks, for example, faced lighter regulation than their German counterparts regarding the amount of information they had to provide on their borrowers. The Austrians attracted German clients by advertising their lax rules, leading to complaints of unfair competition by German banks.

- High prices for oil, especially in the 1970s, led to oil-producing countries having very big trade surpluses. International syndicates of banks were formed to channel the enormous sums of money from those countries to borrowers in other nations.

- Opportunities offered by the progressive deregulation of financial markets, which took place from the early 1970s. Deregulation involves the removal or reduction of certain governmental controls on financial institutions, allowing them to move into other product areas, and also into other countries.

The product and geographical diversification strategies followed by the financial sector have increased the international integration of financial institutions and markets. This has been facilitated by the falling cost, and the cross-border diffusion, of information and communications technologies. Institutions can move funds around the world to markets in different time zones easily, cheaply, and quickly. Even in the 1990s, technology was helping financial institutions 'bypass international frontiers and create a global whirligig of money and securities' (*The Economist* 3 October 1992).

Learning Task

Table 11.1 shows the assets of 10 of the biggest banks. Examine the table and carry out the tasks below.

1. Comment on the rate of growth in the value of total assets between:
   - 1995 and 2007
   - 2007 and 2016
2. Advance possible explanations for your answers to question 1.
3. Identify changes in the nationality of the biggest banks and give some reasons for the changes. →

→ **Table 11.1** World's top ten banks by assets

Bank	Assets 1995 ($bn)	Bank	Assets 2007 ($tn)	Bank	Assets 2016 ($tn)
HSBC	352	HSBC	2.4	Industrial and Commercial Bank of China	3.5
Crédit Agricole	386	Citigroup	2.2	China Construction Bank Corporation	3
Union Bank of Switzerland	336	Royal Bank of Scotland	3.8	Agricultural Bank of China	2.8
Citicorp	257	JP Morgan Chase & Co	1.6	Bank of China	2.6
Dai-Ichi Kangyo Bank	499	Bank of America Corp	1.7	Mitsubishi	2.6
Deutsche Bank	503	Mitsubishi	1.8	JP Morgan Chase	2.5
Sumitomo Bank	500	Crédit Agricole	2.3	HSBC	2.4
Sanwa Bank	501	Industrial and Commercial Bank of China	1.2	BNP Paribas	2.2
Mitsubishi Bank	475	Banco Santander	1.3	Bank of America	2.2
Sakura Bank	478	Bank of China	0.8	Wells Fargo	1.9
Total assets $ trillion	**$4.3**		**$19.1**		**$25.7**

Source: The Banker (2017); *Business Insider* 21 April 2017

Financial Markets

Financial institutions usually operate through markets. Markets are mechanisms for bringing together borrowers and lenders, and buyers and sellers of financial products. For example, capital markets, such as the bond and stock markets, bring together organizations, both public and private, wishing to borrow and lend long-term funds in exchange for shares and bonds. The issue of new bonds and shares to raise money takes place in the **primary market**. Stock exchanges also enable shareholders to buy and sell existing shares in the **secondary market**. Non-financial organizations also purchase bonds or shares in the secondary market. Money markets, on the other hand, enable organizations to borrow and lend short term for anything up to, or just over, a year, trading in such instruments as derivatives and **certificates of deposits (CDs).** Companies with surplus cash that is not needed for a short period of time, can earn a return on that cash by lending it into the money market.

Other financial markets include the foreign exchange market, which facilitates trading between those, such as importers, exporters, and speculators, who wish to trade in currencies. A variety of institutions trade in foreign currencies: non-financial companies wishing to buy goods and services abroad, central banks trying to influence the exchange rate, commercial banks trading on their own account, financial institutions wishing to buy foreign securities and bonds, hedge funds, governments financing their military bases abroad, and so on. In fact, importers and exporters account for only a very small proportion of this trading, as foreign currencies have increasingly been seen as assets in their own right. The amount of foreign exchange traded is enormous. BIS (2016) figures show that daily turnover more than doubled, from almost US$2 trillion in 2004, to US$5.1 trillion in 2016, dwarfing the value of international trade in goods and services. Currency trading is dominated by the US dollar, with the euro and the yen lagging well behind. Trading in China's renminbi is growing rapidly, while some Asian currencies, the Korean won, the Indian rupee and the Thai baht are also increasing market share. Financial markets in five countries, the UK, the USA, Singapore, Hong Kong, and Japan, account for the vast majority of currency trading.

Mini Case Study 11.2 Panama Papers and the banks

In 2015, over 11 million documents belonging to the Panamanian law firm Mossack Fonseca were leaked, showing how billions of dollars were hidden in shell companies and in offshore accounts. The leaks, known as the Panama Papers, revealed how shell companies are used to transfer funds across borders, for both legitimate and illegitimate reasons. Mossack Fonseca specialized in concealing the identity of the owners of these companies, some of them criminals, allowing them to avoid paying taxes, and to launder the proceeds of crime (Figure 11.7). The Papers named individuals and companies involved with Mexican drug lords, terrorist organizations, and 'rogue nations' like N. Korea.

According to the International Consortium of Investigative Journalists (ICIJ 2016), the documents showed 'how major global banks work hand-in-glove with other players in an offshore industry that helps the superrich, politicians and criminals keep their assets under wraps'. More than 500 banks, their subsidiaries, and branches, had registered nearly 15,600 shell companies with Mossack Fonseca. The most active banks setting up offshore companies are shown in Figure 11.8. Shell company owners need the services of licensed banks if they wish to carry out international financial transactions.

Figure 11.7 How the system works

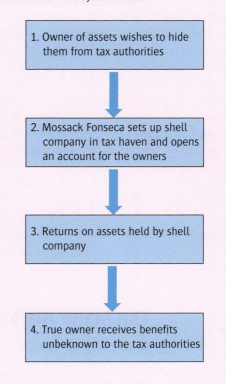

1. Owner of assets wishes to hide them from tax authorities

2. Mossack Fonseca sets up shell company in tax haven and opens an account for the owners

3. Returns on assets held by shell company

4. True owner receives benefits unbeknown to the tax authorities

→

→ **Figure 11.8** The ten banks that requested most offshore companies for clients

Source: ICIJ (2016)

Other international banks involved included France's Société Générale, Commerzbank from Germany, and the Royal Bank of Canada.

According to the ICIJ, HSBC registered more than 2,300, and Credit Suisse 1,105 companies through Mossack Fonseca. Tax havens such as the British Virgin Islands, Panama, and the Bahamas, were the most popular locations for registering shell companies, with the UK tenth in the popularity league.

Some of these banks have a history of tax avoidance and evasion. In 2015, Swiss authorities raided HSBC offices in Switzerland on suspicion that the bank was shielding accounts worth more than $100 billion. In the USA, Credit Suisse pleaded guilty, in 2014, to illegally allowing some American clients to evade taxes, and was fined $2.6 billion. In 2009, UBS paid fines of $780 million for helping US taxpayers hide money abroad. At least 80 Swiss banks have been fined by the US authorities.

While avoiding tax is not illegal it is ethically questionable. The European Parliament PANA Committee (2017a and b) estimated tax losses to EU member states associated with the Panama Papers schemes and, others like it, at between 109 billion and 237 billion euros. Such losses, said the studies, left less money for public services such as health and education, transport infrastructure, and job creation.

O'Donovan et al. (2017) found that publicly quoted firms were using offshore shell companies to finance corruption and aggressively avoid tax. They also reported that the leaks caused the value of shares in those companies to fall.

Sources: CNN Wire 5 April 2016; European Parliament PANA Committee (2017a and b); *The Guardian* 1 December 2016; ICIJ (2016); O'Donovan et al. (2017)

Questions

1. a. Who were the super-rich, politicians and criminals exposed by the Papers?
      See *The Guardian* 3 April 2016 and 6 April 2016.
   b. Discuss the pros and cons for banks of setting up shell companies for the super-rich, politicians, and criminals.
2. Governments tightened up regulation after the Panama Papers leak. What are the implications of this for banks? See (PwC, 2016).

The Major Markets

Modern communications and information technology allow financial institutions to operate from virtually anywhere, yet the financial sector prefers to cluster in certain locations. London and New York are the two leading global financial centres, and appear to act as a magnet for finance companies. London is pre-eminent in international bond trading and leads the way in OTC derivatives, marine insurance, and trading in currencies and foreign equities. It is also the most popular place for foreign banks to locate, with over 250 foreign banks operating there (CityUK 2016). Tokyo, Chicago, Frankfurt, Singapore, and Hong Kong are other important centres.

Financial Crises

Shiller defines financial crises, so-called bubbles, as:

> A situation in which news of price increases spurs investor enthusiasm which spreads by psychological contagion from person to person, in the process amplifying stories that might justify the price increase and bringing in a larger and larger class of investors, who, despite doubts about the real value of the investment, are drawn to it partly through envy of others (*The Guardian* 19 July 2013).

There is no generally accepted theory to explain the causes of financial crises, but one thing is sure, they are a recurring phenomenon. They involve bouts of speculation when assets are bought, in the hope that the price will rise, or sold in the expectation of a fall in price. If the price rises, those who purchased the asset can sell and make a profit. If the price falls, sellers can profit by buying the asset back at a lower price. The objects of speculation can be financial assets such as shares, bonds, currencies, or physical assets such as land, property, or works of art. Crises occur when the speculation destabilizes the market, causing prices to rise or fall dramatically.

Galbraith (1990), Stiglitz (2002), and Minsky (2008), examine how destabilizing speculative episodes develop. When an asset is increasing in price, it attracts new buyers who assume that prices will continue to rise. This boosts demand for the asset and its price goes up. With prices soaring, investors charge in to take advantage of the easy profits to be made. Speculative euphoria develops as market participants come to believe that the upward movement in prices will go on indefinitely. Asset prices part company with the income they generate, whether that be rents from property or dividends on shares. As the value of the asset rises, investors are able to use it as security to borrow money from the banks to buy more of the asset. However, inevitably, there comes a tipping point, the causes of which are much debated, where some participants decide to withdraw from the market, perhaps due to an external shock, bad news, or even a rumour. Borrowers and lenders realize that debts will never be paid off; this is called the 'Minsky moment'. It has been likened to the point when a cartoon character runs off a cliff and realizes it is running on thin air. The resulting fall in price sparks off panic in the market, with investors rushing to off-load their assets, leading to a market collapse. Stiglitz (2002) makes the point that the excessive optimism or euphoria generated by bubbles is often followed by periods of excessive pessimism. Financial crises are contagious domestically and internationally. For example, a banking crisis can make borrowing more difficult and costly for firms and consumers. This could cause them to reduce their demand for goods and services, leading to spare capacity, bankruptcies, and increasing unemployment. In an increasingly interconnected world, a financial crisis in one country can very quickly spread to others, as happened during the South East Asian crisis of the late 1990s and the credit crunch of 2007/08.

In summary, financial crises are characterized by:

- bouts of speculative activity, market euphoria, and rapidly rising prices;
- a tipping point which leads to panic selling, excessive pessimism, and plummeting prices;
- contagion of domestic and foreign economies.

Research by Reinhart and Rogoff (2008) shows that full-blown financial crises are regular occurrences and are deep and prolonged. House prices in real terms decline by an average of 35 per cent, and share prices by 55 per cent. Output drops by over 9 per cent from the peak to the trough of the bubble, unemployment increases by over 9 per cent, while the real value of government debt explodes by 86 per cent. And problems remain after the crisis subsides. Reinhart found that growth in real incomes tended to be much lower during the decade following crises, and that unemployment rates were higher, with the most extreme increases occurring in the richest advanced economies (*Financial Times* 31 August 2010). Reinhart and Rogoff (2008a) contend that financial crises have repeatedly been the result of high international capital mobility, and often follow when countries experience large inflows of capital.

Counterpoint Box 11.2 The financial meltdown and the free market

Alan Greenspan, head of the Federal Reserve for 18 years up to 2006, was a great advocate of the free market. Even with the onset of the global financial crisis in 2007, he stuck to his position, 'free, competitive markets are by far the unrivaled way to organize economies' (Greenspan 2008a). Leaving financial markets free from government intervention enables them to gather resources from savers and allocate them swiftly and efficiently to borrowers. Countries letting financial markets operate freely can grasp market opportunities more quickly and benefit from higher levels of competitiveness and growth. New financial products, such as pricing options and derivatives, help to spread risks and to create 'a far more flexible, efficient, and hence resilient financial system' (Greenspan 2005). Therefore, governments should not regulate financial markets tightly because those markets are best able to withstand and recover from shocks when provided with maximum flexibility.

Greenspan's critics assert that his free market ideology led to excessive risk-taking in the finance industry, creating an enormous bubble and ultimately resulting in a devastating financial crisis and recession.

In the USA, by March 2009, the stock market had fallen by 40 per cent in seven months and over 4 million jobs had disappeared. World output was falling for the first time since the Second World War, and global unemployment had increased by 30 million between 2007 and 2009, three-quarters of which had occurred in the advanced economies. New financial products, rather than spread risk, had made economies and the global financial system much more unstable. Long before the onset of the crisis, credit derivatives were described by Warren Buffett (2002), one of the world's most influential investors, as 'time bombs' and 'financial weapons of mass destruction', while the head of the UK Financial Services Authority referred to an 'explosion of exotic product development', and described many activities of the finance industry as 'socially useless' (*Prospect Magazine* 27 August 2009; *The Guardian* 22 September 2010).

Critics, like Johnson and Kwak (2010), argue that the finance industry in the USA is far too powerful—a financial oligarchy that has captured the institutions of US government by convincing them that 'more finance is good, more unfettered finance is better, and completely unregulated finance is best' (2010: 160). Supporters of tighter regulation of the finance industry point out that Greenspan, in an appearance before a Congressional committee in 2008, accepted that, in the face of 'a once-in-a-century credit tsunami', his belief in the self-correcting powers of the free market had been misplaced. (Visit the accompanying **online resources** for a video link on this topic.) Critics →

→ argue that much tighter regulation of the finance industry is required if another global financial crisis is to be
avoided.

Sources: Buffett (2002); Greenspan (2005, 2008a and b); *The
Guardian* 22 September 2010; Johnson and Kwak (2010); Johnson
(2009); IMF/ILO (2010); *Prospect Magazine* 27 August 2009

Questions

1. Compare and contrast the arguments advanced by
   Greenspan and his critics.
2. In the light of the financial crisis, should banks be left to
   operate freely, without government intervention?

Anatomy of the Financial Crisis 2007/08

Easy Credit, Bad Loans, and Euphoria

The main elements of the crisis can be summarized as follows. Low interest rates drove bankers
to engage in a ferocious search for higher returns and the resulting higher bonuses (Financial
Services Authority 2009). More than a trillion dollars was channelled into the US mortgage market, lent to the poorest, high-risk borrowers with low or uncertain incomes, high ratios of debt
to income, and poor credit histories (Reinhart and Rogoff 2008). Borrowers took the loans to
cash in on the boom in US house prices. These became known as **subprime loans**. Borrowers
were led into taking loans by what Feldstein (2007) called 'teaser rates', unrealistically low interest rates at the start of the loan which, when they subsequently rose, became too expensive for
customers to pay. Initially, borrowers only needed to pay back a minimum amount each month,
which neither covered the interest nor paid back any of the capital sum. The result, in many
cases, was that the size of the debt increased. This was not a great problem when interest rates
were low and house prices were rising. In the five years up to 2005, house prices in the USA rose
by more than half. In addition, large amounts of savings from trade surplus countries like China
were being recycled into US finance markets.

Complex Financial Products and Subprime Mortgages

The boom in subprime loans was accompanied by explosive growth and complexity in financial
products, such as derivatives, credit default swaps, and collateralized debt obligations, many
based on subprime mortgages. Lenders repackaged poor quality mortgages with more traditional
and less risky financial products, like bonds, and sold them on to US and foreign financial institutions, a process called **securitization** (Figure 11.9 shows the rapid growth in these securities in the
run-up to the crisis). Ratings agencies, such as Moody's and S&P, gave top rating to many subprime backed securities. Buyers then used the securities as collateral to borrow more money.

Financiers seeking higher returns on their investments, and driven by the prospect of massive
bonuses, were misled by mathematical models indicating that the new products would diversify
risk and reduce the possibility of a collapse in the financial system. Because risk was reduced, banks
needed to hold less capital (Financial Services Authority 2009). Finance companies did not need to
show these securities on their balance sheets, leading to a lack of information and transparency on
levels of risk, and on which institutions were carrying most risk. Lax regulatory systems and weak
supervision of complex financial products allowed this dangerous process to develop (Naudé 2009).

Figure 11.9 Value of asset-backed securities 1999–2009 (€billion)

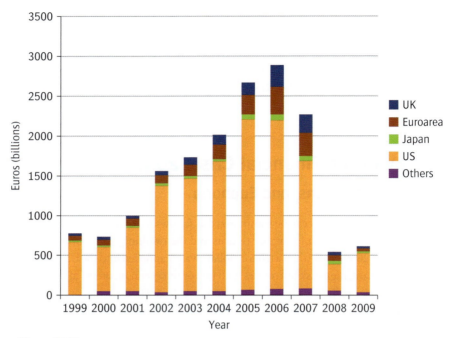

Source: Liikanen (2012)

Tipping Point, Impact, and Government Response

By the summer of 2007, house prices in the USA were falling and teaser rates began to expire. The rate of default on loans by subprime borrowers ballooned, and the value of the assets held by the institutions plummeted. There was widespread panic and a flight from risk. This led to a credit crunch, with institutions refusing to lend money to other finance firms, fearing that they were carrying large amounts of subprime assets off their balance sheets. Facing a severe shortage of liquidity, institutions started a mass sell-off of their financial assets, which was difficult, given the lack of credibility and trust in the finance industry.

In the USA, bad subprime debts and the drying up of liquidity led to the shock collapse of the giant multinational investment bank, Lehman Brothers. The US government forced a fire sale of Bear Stearns to JP Morgan, and a take-over of Wachovia by Wells Fargo. It also bailed out institutions such as AIG, Goldman Sachs, and Morgan Stanley, to the tune of US$700 billion, through its Troubled Asset Relief Programme (TARP), and nationalized Fanny Mae and Freddie Mac, two of the biggest operators in the mortgage market.

The crisis was not confined to the USA. The interconnectedness of financial markets, especially among the developed countries, meant that panic was contagious, spreading rapidly across borders. Acharya and Schnabl (2010) found that the main foreign traders of subprime securities were based in the UK, Germany, the Netherlands, and Japan. Banks had to be taken into public ownership not only in the USA but also in the UK, the Netherlands, France, Iceland,

and Portugal. The Irish and Icelandic economies went into meltdown, with the former, along with Greece and Portugal, forced to accept a bail-out by the IMF and the EU, and the latter obliged to go to the IMF. The EU set up the €750 billion European Financial Stability Fund (http://www.efsf.europa.eu) to secure stability by providing assistance to struggling Eurozone members. Share prices on stock markets in New York, London, Paris, Frankfurt, and Tokyo plunged, and financial markets became extremely volatile, with share prices and currencies fluctuating violently.

The crisis meant that the value of bank assets had to be written down by US$2.3 trillion. It helped create the deepest recession in developed economies since the 1930s, led to an increase in unemployment of 30 million, and to a massive increase in government deficits (IMF 2010). The Basel Committee estimated that the crisis had cost its member states $76 trillion in economic output by 2015 (Ingves 2016).

Stiglitz (2010) sums up the crisis:

> A deregulated market awash in liquidity and low interest rates, a global real estate bubble, and skyrocketing subprime lending were a toxic combination. (2010: 1)

Central banks in the USA, Europe, and Japan went on the offensive, pumping massive amounts of financial assistance into the financial system. Allesandri and Haldane (2009) estimated total assistance at US$14 trillion, or one-quarter of global GDP. Central banks also reduced interest rates, on account of fears of sharp falls in consumption and investment in their economies as a result of the crisis. Anxious to avoid a collapse in the global economy, the G20 met in 2009, and agreed to a significant increase in resources for the IMF. They committed themselves to a US$5 trillion fiscal expansion promoting growth and jobs. (Visit the supporting **online resources** to access videos of G20 leaders commenting on the outcome of the summit.)

Counterpoint Box 11.3 Quantitative easing

In 2008 central banks, trying to avoid a collapse of the global financial system, cut interest rates significantly (see Figure 11.3), and embarked on quantitative easing (QE). They increased liquidity in their economies by buying large quantities of assets, usually government bonds, typically from banks, insurance companies, and pension funds, with money created out of thin air. Subsequently they also started purchasing corporate bonds. QE increases demand for bonds, pushing up their prices, and lowers the interest rate paid on them. In 2015, the 4 biggest central banks, the US Federal Reserve, the ECB, the Bank of England, and the central bank of Japan, bought $1.2 trillion of bonds. Ten years on from the crisis, and faced with sluggish economic growth, QE continues.

Supporters of QE argue that it averted the worst global economic downturn since the Great Depression of the 1930s, increased the availability of credit, and lowered the cost of borrowing for firms and households. It helped boost confidence in the economy, stimulated demand for goods and services, and increased investment, which should boost productivity. Furthermore, lower interest rates caused investors to move funds abroad, which lowered the exchange rates and made exports more competitive.

Critics saw the injection of money and low interest rates as not so much boosting economic growth, but directly fuelling a boom in stock markets and housing prices. They were concerned that another bubble was being created. They argued that QE increased inequality because the rich, the principal owners of assets ➜

→ such as shares and expensive property, saw their values rising, while non-owners lost out. Low interest rates made investors look for higher returns in riskier assets, further boosting equity and property prices. Firms, rather than using cheap money to invest, used it to buy back shares in their companies. Cheap money meant that inefficient firms stayed in business, putting a drag on productivity. The Bank of England found that low interest rates resulting from QE had increased company pension deficits, causing some firms to cut back investment and dividends (Bunn et al. 2018). Households in high income economies, given increases in life expectancy and uncertainties around pensions, might respond to lower income on their savings, by saving more and spending less on goods and services.

Sources: Bunn et al. (2018); Carney (2016); *The Economist* 14 January (2014); IMF 2014; *Financial Times* 13 August and 18 October 2016; *Daily Telegraph* 18 October 2016.

Questions

1. Explain the link between QE and:
   a. interest rates
   b. company pension deficits
   c. house prices.
2. Examine the evidence on the effects of QE on house prices. See the BIS findings at http://www.bis.org/statistics/pp_residential_lt_1705.pdf.
3. Assess whether the evidence supports the critics of QE.

Mini Case Study 11.3 Day of reckoning for the bankers?

In the years after 2007, the US authorities set out to investigate the possible mis-selling of securities which bundled various assets together with subprime mortgages. The US Department of Justice (DoJ) pursued banks whom they judged had falsely assured investors that the securities being sold were backed by sound mortgages, when they knew that they held many mortgages likely to fail. The Attorney for Eastern California claimed:

> Abuses in the mortgage-backed securities industry helped turn a crisis in the housing market into an international financial crisis . . . The impacts were staggering. (CNN 23 December 2016)

By 2013, the Department of Justice (DoJ) had reached 27 civil law financial settlements with US banks, including Goldman Sachs, Bank of America, Wells Fargo, Citigroup, and JPMorgan. The DoJ, along with several US states, agreed a $13 billion settlement with JPMorgan, the largest settlement in American history. The fines in total were equivalent to the GDP of a medium-sized country, such as Hungary. Ratings agencies that had assured investors that the securities were safe also took a hit. Moody's agreed to pay $864 million to the DoJ while Standard and Poors paid out $1.5 billion. By early 2017, cases involving UBS, RBS, and Barclays, were ongoing, and these banks had set aside money to settle their cases (Figure 11.10).

Barclays, accused of selling $31 billion of toxic mortgage-backed securities, was one of the few banks vowing to fight the DoJ, case even though one of its own bankers was quoted as saying that one set of Barclays' loans 'scares the sh*t out of me' (*The Times* 26 December 2016).

Despite paying very large penalties, some banks neither admitted nor denied guilt. Others continued to plead their innocence. JP Morgan Chase admitted that it had seriously misrepresented the safety of the securities to their customers but, following the settlement, claimed that it had not broken US law. The CEO retained his post, and in 2010 was awarded a 51 per cent pay rise and a $5 million cash bonus.

Some commentators lamented the fact that hardly any bankers went to jail for their subprime misdemeanours.

Sources: Bloomberg 13 January 2017; CNN 23 December 2016; DoJ http://www.justice.gov; *Financial Times* 23 December 2016, 13 and 26 January 2017; *Forbes* 11 April 2016

Questions

1. Go to the DoJ website and summarize the judgement and results of the UBS, RBS, and Barclays cases.
   a. How do they compare with other fines levied by the DoJ?

→

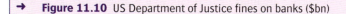

Figure 11.10 US Department of Justice fines on banks ($bn)

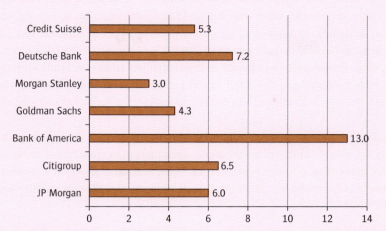

*Still awaiting settlement—amounts set aside by banks; in 2017 RBS paid £4.3 billion to the Federal Housing Finance Agency for selling subprime mortgage bonds.
Source: Carletti (2017)

2. The purpose of fines is to punish offenders and deter them, and others, from repeating the offence.
   a. How many bankers went to jail as a result of the subprime scandal? Why was that the case?
   b. Discuss whether the penalties levied on the banks would be effective.

   See:

   Slate – http://www.slate.com/articles/business/the_edgy_optimist/2014/07/citigroup_and_bank_of_america_settlements_punishing_banks_is_beside_the.html

   History and Policy – http://www.historyandpolicy.org/policy-papers/papers/why-have-no-bankers-gone-to-jail

   New York Times – http://www.nytimes.com/2014/05/04/magazine/only-one-top-banker-jail-financial-crisis.html?_r=0;

   The Atlantic – http://www.theatlantic.com/magazine/archive/2015/09/how-wall-streets-bankers-stayed-out-of-jail/399368/

   The Economist – http://www.economist.com/blogs/economist-explains/2013/05/economist-explains-why-few-bankers-gone-to-jail.

Financial Regulation

Regulation plays an important role at both a domestic and an international level. It is a big element in the financial sector's external environment, because of the effect it can have on their sales turnover, costs, and profits.

Effective regulation is also important for non-financial firms. Businesses and individuals dealing with financial institutions have an interest in those institutions being effectively regulated and supervised. Regulation can avoid hiccups in payments systems, protect customers against financial fraud, ensure financial institutions are prudent in weighing up risks, and make sure that they have enough cash and other liquid assets on hand, so that they do not go bankrupt when things go wrong.

Another major reason for regulation is the failure of countries and financiers to learn the lessons of history. Reinhart and Rogoff (2008a) recorded a widespread view that 'this time it is different', because countries and financiers claim to have learned from the mistakes made in previous crises (2008a: 53). Major crises are unlikely to occur, so it is argued, thanks to wiser macro-economic policies, sophisticated mathematical models, and more discriminating lending practices. In response, Reinhart and Rogoff (2008) comment, 'the ability of governments and investors to delude themselves, giving rise to periodic bouts of euphoria that usually end in tears, seems to have remained a constant' (2008: 53). Galbraith (1990) talks about 'the extreme brevity of the financial memory [which means that] financial disaster is quickly forgotten' (1990: 13). Reinhart, Rogoff, and Galbraith would not be surprised that, following the election of President Trump, banks lobbied successfully to weaken regulations introduced after the financial crisis (*New York Times* 3 February 2017).

Regulation is necessary to avoid financial crises that would threaten not only global financial stability but also the ability of business and consumers to borrow, invest and make payments. Evidence shows that effective regulation can have a positive effect on a country's economic income and output, which could be good news for business seeking expanding markets (Levine et al. 2000; OECD 2006).

Different Systems of Regulation

Regulatory systems can vary quite considerably from one country to another. The authorities face a number of dilemmas regarding regulation. Too much regulation could reduce the attractiveness of their financial centres to banks, while too little regulation could frighten customers away.

At one extreme is a state-owned banking system, in which banks are an arm of government and are never allowed to go bust, at the other is a lightly regulated system of private banks without an explicit safety-net, in which bank failures are common. Either extreme faces certain dangers. Banking systems where no bank can be allowed to fail, and depositors face no risk of loss, may breed management and depositor recklessness. At the other extreme, systems which rely only on market discipline run the risk of unnecessary bank and, possibly, systemic failure, and great loss to depositors.

In many countries, the state has a major presence in the financial sector. State intervention plays an important role in both the developing and the developed world, taking various forms of intervention, from explicit intervention in the banking system in China and Germany to implicit government-sponsored enterprises in the USA. A large swathe of German, French, and Austrian banks are publicly owned, while in many countries, banks are in private hands, including Canada, Japan, New Zealand, the UK, and the USA—at least they were up to the financial meltdown in 2008. In India, liberalization has taken place only very slowly but, like Italy, it continues to restrict foreign ownership. State intervention can also extend to insurance schemes and pension funds, but, generally, these are subject to less systematic regulation than the banks.

 Mini Case Study 11.4 **Shadow banking and the next crisis?**

Shadow banks include financial institutions, some regulated and some not, offering a 'vast array' of new, high risk, complex financial products that do not appear in their balance sheets.

Vítor Constâncio (2016), vice chair of the European Central Bank, notes that the shadow banking system expanded rapidly in the run-up to the global financial crisis, forming a new market-based credit system which helped cause the crisis. He says that international financial regulators have focussed on traditional banks, and have been slow in devising appropriate methods of regulating shadow banking. The chair of the US central bank, ➔

→ **Figure 11.11** Global shadow banking assets

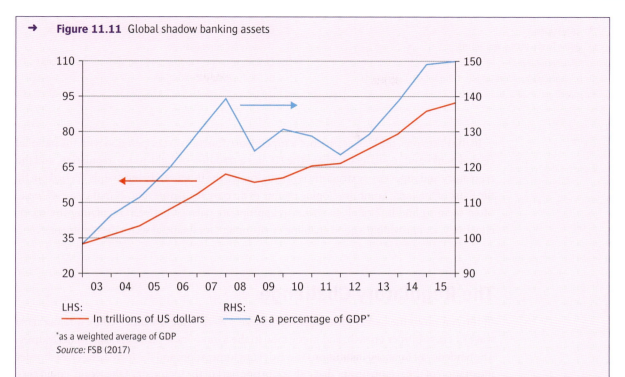

LHS:
── In trillions of US dollars

RHS:
── As a percentage of GDP*

*as a weighted average of GDP
Source: FSB (2017)

the Federal Reserve, also expressed concerns about the shadow banking system, declaring it is a: '"huge challenge" to the stability of the world financial system' (*Wall Street Journal* 2 July 2014).

The shadow banking system includes institutions like insurance companies, pension funds, hedge funds, investment trusts, money lenders, and peer-to-peer lending websites. It also includes unregulated financial products offered by banks. The Financial Stability Board (2017), which monitors developments in the shadow banking system, estimated the size of global shadow banking assets at $92 trillion, and noted that they were growing faster than world GDP, and were worth more than half of the world's financial assets. It pointed out that shadow system assets were the equivalent of 150 per cent of global GDP, compared to 139 per cent prior to the financial crash (Figure 11.11). Shadow sector asset value was more than double GDP in Ireland, the Netherlands, Switzerland, and the UK. For the Cayman Islands, the offshore tax haven, these assets were the equivalent of 170,000 per cent of GDP.

The FSB (2017) sees shadow banking as providing healthy competition for banks, by offering alternative sources of finance for business. However, it foresees risks to the global financial system, given the proclivity of shadow banking institutions to operate with very high levels of leverage, to borrow short and to lend long, and through their interconnectedness with traditional banks. The

FSB (2017) also identified cross-border links between financial institutions that could lead to contagion during periods of financial stress, with spillovers from one country to another. Most directly affected would be the Eurozone, the USA, and the UK, where 70 per cent of shadow bank assets are held (Figure 11.12).

Figure 11.12 Share of global shadow banking assets 2015 (%)

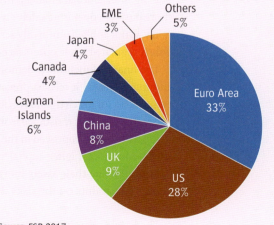

Source: FSB 2017

Sources: Constância (2016); *The Economist* 2 February 2016; Financial Stability Board 2017; *Wall Street Journal* 2 July 2014 →

→ **Questions**
1. What is meant by the terms:
   a. leverage
   b. borrowing short and lending long?

2. Comment on the growth and geographical share of shadow banking assets.
3. Explain why the shadow banking system is a concern to the financial authorities.

In the Eurozone, the ECB carries out a supervisory function in cooperation with the national central banks and regulatory bodies. The UK has a tradition of 'light-touch' regulation, and the regulatory and supervisory structure is much simpler, the functions being mainly carried out by the Bank of England. Some developing countries do have regulators, but, as in the case of India, often seem to find it difficult to strike an appropriate balance between regulating the sector effectively, and providing a good enabling environment for financial sector development.

The Regulatory Challenge

In the run up to the global crisis, financial markets were being transformed by a remarkable wave of cross-border growth, and innovation in the form of new products such as derivatives. The tendency of financial institutions towards conglomeration, and the increasing cross-border integration of the sector, meant that a shock in one part of the sector, or of the world, could very quickly spread. This could turn into a big threat to the system as a whole, as illustrated by the credit crunch of 2007/08. Furthermore, regulatory systems in some countries were very loose (see OECD 2006). There was also a danger that some regulators had been captured by the financial institutions they were supposed to regulate. This was reflected in their willingness to take on trust what the financial institutions told them, rather than subjecting them to intensive scrutiny. Furthermore, many countries lacked any real regulation to speak of—the British Virgin Islands and the Cayman Islands being two examples. However, it was not just small island territories. The big international financial markets, London, New York, and Tokyo, all had a thriving off-shore business operating safely away from the eyes of the regulator. A final issue was that regulation was not applied uniformly across the range of financial products, with some products being tightly regulated while others faced hardly any regulation at all.

The financial meltdown demonstrated the inability of existing regulation, both at national and international levels, to prevent crises. This was widely recognized during the crisis, but enthusiasm for much tighter regulation began to wane with the recovery of the financial system, and faced ferocious resistance from the finance sector.

Regulation has improved in the aftermath of the global financial crisis. In the major industrialized countries, higher capital requirements have been imposed; financial institutions are obliged to value their assets more conservatively, and to hold more liquid assets. Banks face greater constraints on the risks they can take, and must make greater provisions against bad loans.

The Basel Committee on Banking Supervision agreed a package of measures called Basel III. This nearly trebled to 7 per cent, the minimum amount of equity capital banks had to hold against losses, 2.5 per cent of which was to be held as a buffer. Banks straying into the buffer zone would be subject to restrictions on share dividends and discretionary bonuses if regulators felt that they were extending credit too freely. The new rules were to be phased in from 2013 to 2019. Basel IV proposed higher holdings of capital, a standardized method of assessing risk, and greater financial disclosure.

The USA, in order to avert future financial crises, imposed tighter regulations on financial firms, which would have the effect of reducing their profits. It boosted consumer protection, forced banks to be more transparent and to reduce risky trading and investing activities. The transparency around derivatives was increased by obliging them to be traded on exchanges, rather than over the counter. A new, more orderly process for liquidating troubled financial firms was established (Schoenholtz and Wachtel 2010). Critics argued, however, that the regulations had been watered down due to intense lobbying by the financial sector, and that another financial crisis could occur before the regulations took full effect (Helleiner 2010; *Financial Times* 20 August 2010).

The EU established three new financial supervisory bodies for the banking, securities markets, and insurance and occupational pensions sectors, and set up the European Systemic Risk Board (ESRB). The Commission proposed new capital requirements for the financial sector, rules governing banker pay and bonuses, and stronger rules on disclosure of financial information. It was also looking for ways to regulate credit rating agencies and auditing firms. While responsibility for financial supervision remains at national level, a new body, the European Supervisory Authorities, will act as coordinator. Measures, such as the Markets in Financial Instruments Directive (MiFID), and the Market Abuse Directive (MAD), were brought forward to promote efficiency, stability, and transparency, in financial markets (see European Commission Memo/13/774 10/09/2013).

In 2014, the IMF praised efforts to make banks more secure by obliging them to hold more capital, and through rules restricting risky lending. However, Turk-Ariss (2017) identified concerns about banks being allowed to assess the riskiness of their balance sheets and exploiting the lack of coordinated, cross-border regulations by establishing operations where regulation was weak. In 2017, the BIS warned of a steep rise in risky bank lending, which could threaten the global financial system. Policy makers have also been criticized for lack of progress in failing to deal with the problem of banks that were too big to fail. Since the crash, banks have grown even bigger, and therefore remain a threat to the stability of the global financial system.

● CHAPTER SUMMARY

In this chapter we have examined the importance of the financial environment for business, whether that be in the provision of money and credit, the operation of systems of payment, providing protection against risk by the financial sector, or the impact of monetary phenomena such as inflation, interest rates, or exchange rates. We have also seen how the big financial institutions, and the increasingly integrated financial markets of London, New York, and Tokyo, are vital for the effective functioning of business, and the economies in which it operates.

In the advanced economies, business has relatively easy access to finance through a variety of financial institutions offering a wide range of financial products. As we have seen, access to finance in developing countries is much more difficult, making it harder for businesses to start up and grow.

The financial sector has grown rapidly in terms of output and employment, and has become highly internationalized. The industry has come to be dominated by a small number of very large and diversified companies operating across the globe. These big financial institutions have become very powerful actors on the world stage.

Because of their size, the extent of their diversification and internationalization, and their ability to invent new financial products, they continue to pose great challenges to the regulatory authorities. The regulation of the financial sector is fragmented within and between different countries, and can vary considerably from one state to another. Financial crises occur regularly in the system, affecting not only the country where they started, but also moving at terrifying speed across continents and markets and threatening major parts of the global economy, as we saw with the global crisis of 2007/08. While improvements in regulation have occurred, many critics argue that they remain inadequate, and that the stability of the international finance system cannot be taken for granted.

● REVIEW QUESTIONS

1. Why is it vital for business to have confidence in the international payments system?

2. Explain the increasing internationalization of the banking system. What factors have made it easier for banks to internationalize their operations?

3. Analyse the need for effective regulation of the financial system. Explain why bankers resist the tightening of regulation.

● ASSIGNMENT TASKS

1. You work in the office of a financial regulator. A local university has invited you to give a talk on the causes of the global financial crisis 2007/08, paying particular attention to the culture in investment banks. Prepare your speech.

   See:

   a. Discussion of bank culture by Lo at http://alo.mit.edu/wp-content/uploads/2015/08/culture_9.pdf.

   b. Interview with Karen Ho author of *Liquidated: An Ethnography of Wall Street*, at http://content.time.com/time/business/article/0,8599,1912085,00.html; and the video at https://www.youtube.com/watch?v=h9rUzLoKpfs.

   c. Personal history by Michael Lewis at https://pdfs.semanticscholar.org/f668/a1f64bca460e747caf4aad71ee03c42bb4ed.pdf.

2. You are a journalist on a web site producing material for a business audience. The editor wishes to produce a series of articles on financial crises. You are asked to write an article on the prerequisites of good bank regulation. Your research discovers that banks need to be solvent, liquid, and not so big as to threaten the financial system if they fail. In the article:

   a. Explain what is meant by bank solvency, liquidity, and being too big to fail.

   b. Show why it is important for non-financial businesses that banks are well regulated.

● FURTHER READING

On bank solvency and liquidity, see:

- Vickers on banking reforms at University of Oxford (2012)

- Chapters 2, 3, and 4 of the Vickers Report (2012) at Internet Archive (2014) and HMT (n.d.).

- Chapter 4 of the Liikanen report at European Commission (2012).

On banks too big to fail, see:

- CNN (2015), the G20 list at FSB (2015). and US Congress report at US Congress (2016).

On bank regulation, see:

- University of Warwick (n.d.) and Economics (2017).

Case Study US banks and the financial crisis

© 123RF.com/serts

The financial crisis, which started in the autumn of 2007, left the global financial system on the brink of collapse. Banks went out of business or were taken into public ownership. Governments pumped billions of dollars into financial institutions to keep them afloat. The financial crisis caused an economic crisis, the long-term effects of which were felt worldwide.

Deregulation

US banks played a major role in the generation of the financial crash. In the decade before the crisis they lobbied hard for financial deregulation. In 2004, investment banks persuaded the Securities and Exchange Commission (SEC) to ease the amount of capital they needed to hold as a proportion of their loan book. Instead of holding 10 cents for every $1 of loans, the new rules allowed them to hold 5 cents, and even less for top rated mortgage loans. Banks could increase their leverage ratios of loans to capital from 10:1 to 20:1 and more.

Banks, spurred on by the desire for higher returns and bigger bonuses, responded by piling into the mortgage market, leading to huge increase in mortgage-related risk, some of which did not appear on their balance sheets (Figure 11.13). They combined mortgages and other assets carrying varying risks and sold them as bonds, a process called securitization. As a result, risks were transferred, both domestically within the USA and to non-US banks. It was thought that this would spread risk but it had the opposite effect. Financial institutions wanted to increase their leverage, that is to become more indebted, to 'spice up' their short-term profits so they bought each →

➜ **Figure 11.13** Commercial banks and market-based holdings of US home mortgages

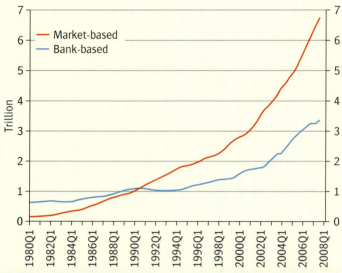

Note: Market-based holdings refer to mortgage loans held by financial institutions other than banks
Source: Adrian and Shin (2009)

other's bonds with borrowed money, concentrating the risks within the banking system (Adrian and Shin 2009: 11). Trading in these bonds was more attractive than lending to business for investment because they promised high returns and the risks could be hidden.

This trade was boosted by ratings agencies, like Standards and Poor, and Moody's, classifying many of these bonds as low risk and awarding them triple A, the highest rating. In reality, many were high risk, or 'subprime', as they ended up being called. Financial institutions, trusting the ratings agencies, snapped up the supposedly safe bonds. But as *The Economist* (7 September 2013) pointed out, there was a conflict of interest at play because the ratings agencies were paid by, and bound to, the banks, the creators of the bonds, and consequently were far too generous with their ratings.

By 2008, non-commercial financial institutions ended up holding two thirds of the 11 trillion dollars total of home mortgages. Bholat et al. (2016) report that in 2007–09, the US financial institutions had devoted about three quarters of their total loan portfolios to real estate lending, peaking at about $14.8 trillion in the second quarter of 2008.

The insurance industry entered the fray by selling insurance policies covering losses arising from mortgage holder defaults. There was a massive expansion in these policies, known as credit default swaps (CDS). They ended up being bought and sold, as financial institutions speculated on the possibilities of mortgage default. AIG, the US insurance giant, sold around $500 billion of this insurance to financial institutions.

The Crisis Breaks

Between 2004 and 2006, interest rates started to rise causing the US housing market to weaken. In 2007, the number of defaults on mortgages rose, and the value of subprime assets plunged. Blind panic ensued not only in the USA, but internationally. Lending between financial institutions seized up, because they did not know which banks were carrying most risk on their balance sheets.

The crisis led to the demise of some giant financial institutions like Lehman Brothers. Merrill Lynch was taken over by Bank of America and the US authorities pumped $85 billion into America's biggest insurance company AIG. The crunch also had repercussions outside the USA, particularly in Western Europe. In the UK, RBS and Lloyds TSB were taken into public ownership. The Dexia and Fortis banks were rescued by Benelux governments, while Germany rescued a number of regional ➜

→ state-owned banks, and put almost $11 billion of capital into Commerzbank. There was a massive write-down of the value of financial institution assets—it was estimated that write-downs totalled nearly $4 trillion, including $2.7 trillion for the USA, $1.2 trillion for Europe, and £131 billion for Japan (IMF 2009). Citigroup in the USA alone accounted for $55 billion of write-downs, UBS $44 billion and HSBC $27 billion (Bloomberg 12 August 2008). Icelandic banks went into meltdown. Table 11.2 shows countries where the crisis threatened to bring down the financial system.

Table 11.2 Bank rescues 2007/08

Country	Start date	Extensive liquidity support	Significant restructuring costs	Significant guarantees or liabilities	Significant nationalizations
Systemic cases					
Austria	2008	X		X	X
Belgium	2008	X	X	X	X
Denmark	2008	X		X	X
Germany	2008	X		X	X
Iceland	2008	X	X	X	X
Ireland	2008	X	X	X	X
Latvia	2008	X		X	X
Luxembourg	2008	X	X	X	X
Mongolia	2008	X	X	X	X
Netherlands	2008	X	X	X	X
Ukraine	2008	X	X		X
United Kingdom	2007	X	X	X	X
United States	2007	X	X	X	X
Borderline cases					
France	2008	X		X	
Greece	2008	X		X	
Hungary	2008	X		X	
Kazakhstan	2008	X	X		
Portugal	2008	X		X	
Russia	2008	X		X	
Slovenia	2008	X		X	
Spain	2008	X		X	
Sweden	2008	X		X	
Switzerland	2008	X			

Note: Borderline countries are those coming near to a collapse of their financial system
Source: Rao-Nicholson and Salaber (2016)

Sources: Admati and Hellwig (2013); Adrian and Shin (2009); Bholat et al. (2016); Bloomberg 12 August 2008; Havemann n.d.; CNBC 2 October 2008; *New York Times* 3 October 2008; BBC 7 August 2009, available at http://news.bbc.co.uk/1/hi/business/7521250.stml; *The Economist* 7 September 2013.   →

→ **Questions**

1. a. Review your understanding of the term leverage?
   b. Why did banks lobby for rules on leverage to be relaxed?
2. Explain why trading in bonds was more attractive for banks than lending to business.
3. What factors brought about the tipping point in the subprime bond market?
4. a. Explain the term contagion.
   c. How did the crisis spread internationally from the US?

d. Which countries' financial systems were more/less endangered? Advance reasons for your answer.
5. Discuss the results of the subprime crisis for:
   a. Banks
   b. Governments and central banks
6. Andy Haldane (2015), chief economist at the Bank of England asserts that, 'The historical evolution of the financial system has been a game of cat and mouse between the state and the banking system.' Discuss in the light of the global financial crisis.

● FURTHER READING

For a non-technical discussion of banking, its problems and what needs to be done, see:

● Admati, A & Hellwig, M. (2013) *The Bankers' New Clothes: What's Wrong with Banking and What to Do about It.* Woodstock: Princeton University Press.

For a more technical approach, see:

● El-Erian, M. (2016) *The Only Game in Town: Central Banks, Instability, and Avoiding the Next Collapse.* London: Yale University Press.

For analyses of financial crises, refer to:

● Kindelberger, C.P. and Aliber, R. Z. (2015) *Manias, Panics and Crashes: A History of Financial Crises,* 7th edn. Hoboken: John Wiley & Sons.

● Reinhart, C. and Rogoff, K. (2008a) 'This Time is Different: A Panoramic View of Eight Centuries of Financial Crises', March. Available at http://www.nber.org/papers/w13882.

For the 2007 crisis, see:

● Stiglitz, J.E. (2010) *Freefall: Free Markets and the Sinking of the Global Economy.* London: Allen Lane.

● Tett, G. (2010) *Fool's Gold: How Unrestrained Greed Corrupted a Dream.* London: Abacus.

● Wolf, M. (2014) *The Shifts and Shocks: What We've Learned—And Have Still to Learn—From the Financial Crisis.* New York: Penguin.

● REFERENCES

Acharya, V. and Schnabl, P. (2010) 'Do Global Banks Spread Global Imbalances? Asset-Backed Commercial Paper during the Financial Crisis of 2007–09'. *IMF Economic Review* 58(1).

Admati, A. and Hellwig, M. (2013) *The Bankers' New Clothes: What's Wrong with Banking and What to Do about It.* Woodstock: Princeton University Press.

Adrian, T. and Shin, H.S. (2009) The Shadow Banking System: Implications for Financial Regulation. Federal Reserve Bank of New York, Staff Reports, July.

Allesandri, P. and Haldane, A.G. (2009) *Banking on the State*. Bank of England, November. Available at http://www.bankofengland.co.uk/archive/Documents/historicpubs/speeches/2009/speech409.pdf.

Anderson, R.W. and Joever, K. (2012) 'Bankers and Bank Investors: Reconsidering the Economies of Scale in Banking', *Financial Markets Discussion Group Paper* 712, September.

The Banker (2017). Available at http://www.thebanker.com/Top-1000-World-Banks.

Bholat, D. et al. (2016) 'Non-performing loans: regulatory and accounting treatments of assets', Bank of England Staff Working Paper No.594.

BIS (2017) *Statistical Bulletin* March BIS (2016) 'Triennial Central Bank Survey: Foreign Exchange Turnover in April 2016'. September.

BIS (2017) *87th Annual Report 1 April 2016–31 March 2017*, June.

Boston Consulting Group (2013) 'Global Payments 2013: Getting Business Models and Execution Right'. Available at https://www.bcgperspectives.com/content/articles/financial_institutions_digital_economy_global_payments_2013/?chapter=2.

Buffett, W. (2002) *Berkshire Hathaway Annual Report 2002*.

Bunn, P. et al. (2018) *Growing pensions deficits and the expenditure decisions of UK companies*. Staff Working Paper 714, Bank of England.

Business Insider (2018) 'CRYPTO INSIDER: Digital Currencies Fall—But Not as Much as stocks'. 2 March.

Business Insider (2017) 'These are the 23 biggest global banks—all with more than $1 trillion of assets' 21 April.

Carletti, E. (2017) 'Fines for Misconduct in the Banking Sector—What is the Situation in the EU?' Directorate General for Internal Policies, European Parliament, March.

CityUK (2016) *Key Facts About The UK As An International Financial Centre*, November.

CNN (2015) 'The No. 1 "too big to fail" bank is . . .', https://money.cnn.com/2015/11/03/investing/too-big-to-fail-banks-jpmorgan-hsbc/index.html.

Constancio, V. (2016) 'Challenges for the European Banking Industry' Conference. 'European Banking Industry: What's Next?' University of Navarra, 7 July. Available at https://www.bis.org/review/r1607014b.pdf.

Demirguc-Kunt, A., Klapper, L., Singer, D., Van Oudheusden, P. (2015) 'The Global Findex Database 2014: Measuring Financial Inclusion around the World'.

Policy Research Working Paper; No. 7255. World Bank, Washington, DC. © World Bank. https://openknowledge.worldbank.org/handle/10986/21865.

Economics (2017) 'Impact of a banking crisis', at https://www.economicshelp.org/blog/16958/economics/impact-of-a-banking-crisis/.

EU Commission (2012) 'High-level Expert Group on reforming the structure of the EU banking sector' at http://ec.europa.eu/internal_market/bank/docs/high-level_expert_group/report_en.pdf.

European Parliament PANA Committee (2017a) 'The Impact of Schemes revealed by the Panama Papers on the Economy and Finances of a Sample of Member States', PE 572.717, April.

European Parliament PANA Committee (2017b) 'Role of Advisors and Intermediaries in the Schemes Revealed in the Panama Papers', PE 602.030, April.

Feldstein, M. (2007) 'Housing, Housing Finance and Monetary Policy', Federal Reserve Bank of Kansas City, 1 September. Available at http://www.kc.frb.org.

Financial Services Authority (2009) 'The Turner Review: A Regulatory Response to the Global Banking Crisis', March.

Financial Stability Board (2015). Available at http://www.fsb.org/wp-content/uploads/2015-update-of-list-of-global-systemicallyimportant-banks-G-SIBs.pdf.

Financial Stability Board (2017) Global Shadow Banking Monitoring Report 2017, 5 March 2018.

Galbraith, J.K. (1990) *A Short History of Financial Euphoria*. London: Pelican.

global-rates.com (n.d.) http://www.global-rates.com.

Global Research (2015) 'The Greek Economic Crisis, The Social Impacts of Austerity. Debunking the Myths'. Available at https://www.globalresearch.ca/the-greek-economic-crisis-the-social-impacts-of-austerity-debunking-the-myths/5431010.

Greenspan, A. (2005) 'Economic Flexibility', Remarks to the National Association for Business Economics Annual Meeting, Chicago, Illinois, 27 September.

Greenspan, A. (2008a) 'A Response to My Critics'. The Economists' Forum, FT.com, 6 April.

Greenspan, A. (2008b) *The Age of Turbulence: Adventures in a New World*. London: Penguin Books.

GSMA 2016 *The Mobile Economy: Africa 2016*. Available at http://www.gsmaintelligence.com/research/?file=3bc21ea879a5b217b64d62fa24c55bdf&download.

Guardian (2016a) 'The Panama Papers: how the world's rich and famous hide their money offshore'. Available at https://www.theguardian.com/news/2016/apr/03/

the-panama-papers-how-the-worlds-rich-and-famous-hide-their-money-offshore.

Guardian (2016b). 'From Kubrick to Cowell: Panama Papers expose offshore dealings of the stars'. Available at http://www.theguardian.com/news/2016/apr/06/panama-papers-reveal-offshore-dealings-stars.

Haldane, A. (2015) 'Who Owns a Company?' Speech to University of Edinburgh Corporate Finance Conference, 22 May.

Harrigan, J. (2010) Globalisation, Democratisation and Radicalisation in the Arab World. Basingstoke: Palgrave Macmillan.

Havemann, J. (n.d.) 'The Financial Crisis of 2008: Year In Review 2008' Britannica. Available at http://www.britannica.com/topic/financial-crisis-of-2008-the-1484264.

Helleiner, E. (2010) 'Filling a Hole in Global Financial Governance? The Politics of Regulating Sovereign Debt Restructuring'. In Mattli, W. and Woods, N. (eds), The Politics of Global Regulation. Princeton: Princeton University Press.

HMT (n.d.). Available at https://hmt-sanctions.s3.amazonaws.com.

Hördahl, P., Sobrun, J. and Turner, P. (2016) 'Low long-term interest rates as a global phenomenon', BIS Working Papers No. 574 August.

Hughes, J.P. and Mester, L.J. (2013) 'Who Said Large Banks Don't Experience Scale Economies? Evidence from a Risk-return-driven Cost Function', Working Paper No. 13-13/R, Federal Bank of Philadelphia.

ICIJ (2016) 'Global Banks Team with Law Firms to help the Wealthy Hide Assets' 4 April. Available at http://panamapapers.icij.org/20160404-banks-lawyers-hide-assets.html.

IMF (2009) 'Annual Report 2009'.

IMF (2010) 'Global Financial Stability Report: Meeting New Challenges to Stability and Building a Safer System', April.

IMF (2016) Germany: Financial Sector Assessment Program: Stress Testing The Banking and Insurance Sectors—Technical Note IMF Country Report, No. 16/191.

IMF/ILO (2010) 'The Challenges of Growth, Employment and Social Cohesion'. Discussion Document, Oslo Conference.

Ingves, S. (2016) 'Finalising Basel III: Coherence, Calibration and Complexity', speech at the second Conference on Banking Development, Stability and Sustainability, Santiago, 2 December.

Internet Archive (2014) https://web.archive.org/.

Johnson, S. (2009) 'Financial Oligarchy and the Crisis'. The Atlantic May; and Brown Journal of World Affairs (2010) XVI(II Spring/Summer).

Johnson, S. and Kwak, J. (2010) 13 Bankers: The Wall Street Takeover and the Next Financial Meltdown. New York: Pantheon Books.

KPMG (2017) Mainland China Banking Survey 2017. August.

Levine, R., Loayza, N., and Beck, T. (2000) 'Financial Intermediation and Growth: Causality and Causes'. Journal of Monetary Economics 46(1).

Liikanen, E. (2012) High-level Expert Group on reforming the structure of the EU banking sector. Final Report 2 October.

Mastercard (n.d.) http://investor.mastercard.com.

McLeay, M., Radia, A., and Thomas, R. (2014) 'Money in the Modern Economy: An Introduction', Bank of England Quarterly Bulletin Q1.

Moschella, M. (2014) 'The Institutional Roots of Incremental Ideational Change: The IMF and Capital Controls after the Global Financial Crisis'. British Journal of Politics and International Relations June.

Muuka, G.N. (1998) 'In Defense of World Bank and IMF Conditionality in Structural Adjustment Programs'. Journal of Business in Developing Nations 2.

Minsky, H.P. (2008) Stablizing an Unstable Economy. New York: McGraw-Hill.

Naudé, W. (2009) 'The Financial Crisis of 2008 and the Developing Countries', Discussion Paper No 2009/01, United Nations University, January.

O'Donovan, J, Wagner, H.S., and Zeuma, S. (2017) 'The Value of Offshore Secrets: Evidence from the Panama Papers'. Available at https://editorialexpress.com/cgi-bin/conference/download.cgi?db_name=AFA2018&paper_id=1045.

ODS (n.d.). Available at http://documents-dds-ny.un.org/doc/UNDOC/GEN/G16/441/36/PDF/G1644136.pdf?OpenElement.

OECD (2006) 'Regulation of Financial Systems and Economic Growth', Working Paper 34.

PwC (2016) 'Global Economic Crime Survey 2016'. Available at https://www.pwc.com/gx/en/economic-crime-survey/pdf/GlobalEconomicCrimeSurvey2016.pdf.

Rao-Nicholson, R, and Salaber, J. (2016) 'Impact of the Financial Crisis on Cross-Border Mergers and Acquisitions and Concentration in the Global Banking Industry', Thunderbird International Business Review, Vol 58 No 2 March/April.

Reinhart, C. and Rogoff, K. (2008) 'The Aftermath of Financial Crises', paper presented at the American Economic Association meeting, 3 January 2009.

Reinhart, C. and Rogoff, K. (2008a) 'This Time is Different: A Panoramic View of Eight Centuries of Financial Crises', The National Bureau of Economic Research, March. Available at http://www.nber.org/papers/w13882.

Schoenholtz, K. and Wachtel, P. (2010) The Architecture of Financial Regulation: July 2010 Archives: Dodd-Frank and the Fed. Available at http://www.stern.nyu.edu.

Stiglitz, J.E. (2002) *Globalization and its Discontents.* London: Penguin.

Stiglitz, J.E. (2010) *Freefall: Free Markets and the Sinking of the Global Economy.* London: Allen Lane.

SWIFT (2018) http://www.swift.com, 28 February.

Turk-Ariss, R. (2017) 'Heterogeneity of Bank Risk Weights in the EU: Evidence by Asset Class and Country of Counterparty Exposure', June, IMF Working Paper WP/17/137.

UN Human Rights Council (2016) 'Report of the Independent Expert on the Effects of Foreign Debt and Other Related International Financial Obligations of States on the Full Enjoyment of All Human Rights, Particularly Economic, Social and Cultural Rights on His Mission to Greece', 29 February, 31st session.

UN Human Rights Council (2017) 'Promotion and Protection of All Human Rights, Civil, Political, Economic, Social and Cultural Rights, Including the Right to Development', 27 February–24 March, 34th session.

University of Oxford (2012) 'Some Economics of Banking Reform' at https://www.economics.ox.ac.uk/materials/papers/12467/paper632.pdf.

University of Warwick (n.d.) 'Why Regulate?' at https://warwick.ac.uk/research/warwickcommission/financialreform/report/chapter_1.pdf.

US Congress (2016) 'Too Big to Jail' https://financialservices.house.gov/uploadedfiles/07072016_oi_tbtj_sr.pdf

Vickers, J. (2012) 'Some Economics of Banking Reform', department of economics discussion paper series Number 632 November.

Visa (2017) 'Annual Report 2017'.

Weiss, G.N.F., Neumann, S., and Bostandzic, D. (2014) 'Systemic Risk and Bank Consolidation: International Evidence'. *Journal of Banking and Finance* 40.

World Bank (2016) 'Annual Report 2016'.

CHAPTER TWELVE

The Ecological Environment

LEARNING OUTCOMES

This chapter will enable you to:

- examine the ecological impacts of business activity;

- describe the range of global initiatives designed to address ecological problems;

- engage in the debate as to the role of business in causing, preventing, and curing ecological damage; and

- analyse the problems posed by global climate change.

Case Study The air that we breathe

© Shutterstock.com/Nickolay Khoroshkov

Across the world urgent attention is being paid by policy makers to the health problems caused by ambient air pollution. In 2015, in a documentary entitled 'Under the Dome', a Chinese journalist, Chai Jin, profiled the increasing pollution problems that China was experiencing, and the prevalence of smog that was enveloping so many Chinese cities. The documentary was watched by over 300 million concerned Chinese citizens, but her criticisms of the lack of effective state regulation were too much for the authorities, and the documentary was banned in China (it is still available on YouTube at https://www.youtube.com/watch?v=T6X2uwlQGQM).

This, though, should not imply that the Chinese government is burying its head in the sand over the environmental challenge that China is facing. In fact, for its leader, Xi Jin Ping, if China is to achieve what he has labelled 'The Chinese Dream', an urgent priority has to be to restore what is seen as a new 'harmony' in the relationship between humans and the environment (see http://www.xinhuanet.com/english/special/chinesedream). China is not alone in the developing world in facing up to the environmental challenges of economic growth (as we will see in the end of chapter case study), and the problems of pollution caused by transport are, of course, not confined to the developing world.

In 2012 the World Health Organization estimated that, globally, 12.6 million deaths were attributable to modifiable environmental factors; representing 23% of all lives lost in that year. The total loss of years of healthy life, as a result of death and disability (measured in Disability Adjusted Life Years or DALY) caused by environmental factors, was 590 million years; which was 22% of the total DALY for 2012 (Prüss-Ustün et al. 2016).

Approximately 8.2 million of the 12.6 million deaths were caused by non-communicable diseases (NCDs). Air pollution from transport is associated with rises in deaths and disability due to a range of NCDs such as heart disease, strokes, asthma and other respiratory diseases. According to *The Lancet*, big reductions in NCDs caused by environmental factors can be achieved:

> through modifiable risks in the environment. Much of the burden is linked to fossil fuel combustion, and production and consumption patterns. (Watts et al. 2016)

While the *Lancet* report is primarily concerned with effects of global climate change that we will consider later in the chapter, it also highlights the specific health effects of transportation systems as a major source, not only of the greenhouse gases that cause climate change, but also of particulate matter, nitrogen oxide, sulphur dioxide, carbon monoxide and volatile organic compounds that impact directly on human health.

From the mid-1990s onwards, policy makers, especially in Europe, began to try to encourage a shift from petrol based vehicles to diesel, on the basis that diesel engines were far more fuel efficient and produced less carbon dioxide, the major source of greenhouse gases. This pattern of shifting to diesel was not mirrored in the USA, where sales of diesel vehicles remained very small.

Since the turn of the millennium, research has cast doubt on the claims that diesel is the cleaner alternative. Some of the worst problems caused by transport pollution, in relation to a direct impact on health, come from emissions of nitrogen dioxide, and of fine particulate matter, of which PM 2.5 is the most injurious to health. Recent evidence has shown that, in terms of these pollutants, diesel is now the worst fuel, and there are calls to either phase out diesel powered vehicles, or for car companies to invest in technologies that improve fuel →

→ efficiency and filter out the worst of the damaging particles. In response to this, car companies have been seeking to fit Diesel Particulate Filters, as well as developing new fuel injection systems to reduce nitrogen dioxide emissions. However, attempts to reduce the pollutants have compromised the fuel efficiency of diesel vehicles.

In the last few years, many European car companies, including VW, have been trying to boost sales of diesel vehicles in the USA. In 2015 the US Environmental Protection Agency (EPA) found that VW had been guilty of deliberately trying to manipulate the declared emissions levels on many of its diesel vehicles. The company had installed 'a defeat device', which was able to detect when the vehicle was being tested for emissions levels. The device was able to reduce nitrogen oxide emissions during the tests, but under normal conditions was switched off. In some cases actual levels of nitrogen oxide were 40 times greater than under test conditions.

The scale of the ecological challenge is daunting. Policy makers must seek to ensure that businesses operate in such a way as not to compromise environmental standards. For business there are clear threats posed by failing to comply with environmental standards. In the case of VW, there was the PR disaster with which they had to contend after the discovery of their having cheated; as well as the huge financial cost of having to recall vehicles, deal with compensation claims of angry customers, and the fines imposed by the Environmental Protection Agency (EPA) of the USA. We, as consumers, also have a challenge in addressing environmental issues. Here the challenge is one of knowing, or facing up to, the environmental impact of our purchasing decisions, and the way in which we might perceive the balance between private and social cost.

However, in relation to the car industry there is also a huge potential opportunity. There is clearly a need to develop new technologies to increase fuel efficiency, but increasingly there is a recognition that the age of a transport system reliant on fossil fuels may well be over. The hunt is on for alternative ways of powering vehicles, holding out the prospect that we might one day be able to have environmentally friendly transport systems.

Sources: Hotten (2015), Neate (2015), Gates et al. (2017).

Introduction

This chapter examines the relationship between business activity and the global ecological environment, the debates as to the responsibility of business and consumers in terms of their contribution to global ecological problems, and the possible responses to dealing with these challenges.

The Ecological Problem

It is simple to outline the basic ecological problem in the context of business. We need to extract the resources that we need for production from the ecological environment. If we exploit the sources of these materials without replacing what we have taken, then we face a long-term certain problem of resource depletion. Not all resources can be replaced, especially the fossil fuels on which so much of the world's energy supplies currently depend. It is also clear that the nature of many of our productive processes result in pollution, or other forms of ecological damage.

Nature itself can provide ways of neutralizing these harmful by-products in the form of 'sinks', such as the oceans, forests, and plants that can absorb the pollutants; however, the rising acidification of seas, deforestation, and loss of biodiversity are all undermining this. The debate provoked by attempts to quantify the 'state of the world' in terms of the rate of resource depletion and its effects on food supplies, water availability, and energy, or the 'carrying capacity' of the planet, is hotly contested.

The Economic Approach to Explaining the Ecological Problem

Economic analysis has been very influential in explaining why there is a conflict between our rational desire to increase our incomes, and our ability to increase our quality of life.

While free markets, in theory, bring about consumer satisfaction and profits for producers, there are dangers of market failure. In relation to the external ecological environment, it may well be the case that, while markets ensure that private benefits accrue to consumers and producers, social costs may be incurred. Social costs, or negative externalities, are costs which occur as the result of the production or consumption of goods and services, but for which no individual or organization pays. They will, therefore, need to be identified, and mechanisms devised to either reduce or eradicate them, or at least allow them to be paid for.

Consider the external environmental problems caused by motor transport, profiled in the opening case study. Drivers and their passengers, or the customers for whom they are driving, derive enormous benefit from this activity and are prepared to pay for the initial costs of the vehicle itself, and the substantial running costs, including the cost of the (fossil) fuels needed to power the vehicles. However, these private costs are not the only costs, as there are substantial external environmental costs. Motor vehicles produce pollutants damaging to the environment, not least of which is the production of greenhouse gases (GHGs). This is especially the case when cars are used on congested roads. The costs of lost output through time delays to transport of people and goods due to congestion are also considerable. It is argued that it is only fair that motorists sitting inside the relative comfort of their vehicles should pay for the external costs that they are imposing on society through higher road taxes, petrol duties, or even paying to use the road through 'road pricing' schemes, such as the electronic road congestion charge in London and Singapore. Of course, it might well be that the better environmental solution would be to switch away from using cars powered by petrol or diesel to greener forms of transport such as electric cars, buses, trains, cycles, and, yes, even walking.

This market-based analysis of the externalities of production and consumption can point the way to 'correct' the environmental market failures. The simplest solution might be to devise a way whereby the agents who are responsible for the pollution pay for this. This process of 'internalizing the externality' ensures that the 'polluter pays principle' is implemented. This can be seen as being fair, in terms of forcing those responsible for environmental damage to at least pay for it and, of course, the revenue raised could be used to invest in measures to clean up the environment or 'compensate' those affected. It might also have the effect of discouraging environmentally damaging behaviour. Along the same lines, regulation could be put in place to 'permit' pollution to take place, but only in return for compensation payments.

However, critics of this approach argue that levying environmental charges may encourage the belief that the problem is solved, even though the environmentally damaging behaviour still continues. Robert Goodin sees this as the 'selling of environmental indulgences', and argues that we should simply not cause the pollution in the first place (Goodin 2007).

Furthermore, there are equity implications. Is it 'fair' to charge green taxes if more prosperous members of society or businesses can afford to pay, while the poor are unfairly penalized? On a global level, there is an inherent inequity in resource use, and a potential inequity in the solutions being designed to deal with environmental problems. The developed world became wealthy by being able to industrialize at a time when the environment was effectively ignored. Now that policies are being implemented to deal with environmental issues, it would not be fair if the developing world were asked to adhere to the same levels of environmental protection. It is argued that the richer countries can afford to pay for the cost of the environmental harm they have largely caused, and developing countries should not be asked to adopt environmental regulations at their early stage in the development process.

The analysis of ecological problems as the negative externalities of market failure has become commonly accepted, but what is contested is where the responsibility for such externalities should fall, and the range of policy measures we should adopt to address these problems.

Business as Usual

One of the biggest fears for those concerned about the environmental impact of business is that, even where businesses recognize potential problems, all too often they continue with 'business as usual' (BAU) behaviour. Indeed, some argue that businesses will actively seek to resist change, in order to preserve their profits. Others argue that, given the right incentives, businesses will choose to 'go green'. Furthermore, they argue, there is very often a 'business case' to be made for sustainable business practices as this will boost profitability, either through the enhanced reputation that being seen to be green brings, or through the reduction in costs resulting from a better use of resources.

There is increasing awareness of the need for businesses to be ecologically sustainable among a range of pressure groups across the business, environmental, and academic communities that seek to promote and profile responsible behaviour, such as: the World Business Council for Sustainable Development, the World Economic Forum (WEF), Forum for the Future, Net Impact, The Ethical Corporation, and the Globally Responsible Leadership Initiative (see WBCSD (2018), Forum For the Future (2018, Net Impact (2018), Ethical Corp (2018), and GRLI (2018)). Visiting these websites will give you a good idea of the range of initiatives that are being undertaken in relation to sustainable business practices. In relation to fossil fuels, one of the fastest-growing sectors in energy production is the renewable sector and, in this regard, broad swathes of business have embraced the need for change.

The WEF is the leading policy body that represents the interests of the world's biggest corporations and most wealthy individuals. In its 2017 assessment of the greatest risks for global business, the WEF puts the ecological threats to water supply, failure to adapt to or mitigate against climate change, food security, and unexpected weather events, as having increased prominence in the threats facing the global business environment (WEF 2017).

Mini Case Study 12.1 Assessing the risks

According to the Global Facility for Disaster Relief and Recovery (GFDDR), global disaster risks have been increasing rapidly. Between 1976 and 1985, the annual average loss as a result of disasters was $14 billion, and the number of people affected annually was 60 million. In the period 2005–2014, these figures had risen to $140 billion and 170 million people. Disaster risk depends on three factors: the hazard, the nature of the exposure to the hazard, and finally the vulnerability of exposure to the hazard. In terms of hazards (as the WEF also warns), environmental problems have risen up the agenda; and of these, it is global climate change that is now the most important. As we will see, global climate change is predicted to lead to: a rise in sea levels of up to 0.6 metres by the end of the century, an increase in the intensity and frequency of storms, increases in extremes of temperature, and alterations to global rainfall patterns. There is thus a clear link between human induced climate change (anthropogenic causes) and what might appear to be 'natural disasters'. In terms of exposure, changes in climate cause population movements. This results in more and more people living in vulnerable areas, especially in flood plain areas

or in marginal areas prone to landslides. Increasing urbanization has caused an expansion in the area of impermeable surfaces, as more and more land is covered in concrete. This increases the prospects of flooding, as well as leading to falls in water tables and increasing subsidence.

What is needed is a response from policy makers in assessing the likely risks, and then action by business to both mitigate (prevent), and adapt to, likely future environmental problems, and ensure that future communities can build resilience to these challenges.

Source: GFDRR (2016)

Questions

1. What role might the private business sector play in mitigating and adapting to the increase in environmental threats of the future? Which sectors, in particular, can play an important role in this?

2. In what ways might the public sector be involved, both in anticipating environmental risk, and ensuring that the effects are minimised?

Learning Task

Look at cases which are profiled as examples of responsible business practice in relation to the ecological environment (see, for example, http://www.bitc.org.uk or http://www.wbcsd.org).

1. What are the problems that businesses face in addressing environmentally responsible business practice?

2. How convincing do you think the case for this is?

Perspectives on the Role of Business

Business activity is essentially the conversion of natural resources into goods and services to satisfy the needs, wants, and desires of human beings. This generates economic growth, but also creates environmental problems. Industries such as steel, cement, oil, power generation, chemicals, and transport are heavy polluters in a range of ways, but all businesses have an environmental impact. There are competing perspectives about ways in which businesses should respond to the environmental challenges.

Views from the Right

For free market liberals, it is the ability of private businesses to operate in markets free from government regulation that will drive economic progress. While the indirect cost of growth might be environmental damage, there is a trade-off to be made between this and growth in living standards, and business plays a vital role in developing 'environmentally friendly' technologies—given the right incentives. Where this is not realistic, then the negative costs can be measured and businesses can be charged for the environmental damage, according to the 'polluter pays principle'.

Views from the Left

There are, however, objections to this version of the secret for economic success.

Critics of business see it as being primarily interested in maximizing profits and cutting costs, and believe it will treat the environment as a free 'sink' for pollution. Businesses have a vested interest in encouraging consumers to buy more and more, and so are indirectly responsible for rampant consumerism. While it could be argued that businesses are simply responding to the wishes of consumers, it is clear that a business in pursuit of profit has every interest in fuelling consumer demand.

A major source of disquiet is the belief that the distribution of income and wealth that results from free markets is highly unequal, and that the immediate problem facing the world is not that there is not enough to go around, but that the fruits of economic growth are enjoyed by the richer members of society while the poor lose out. The biggest global problem is the gap between the living standards of the 'Global North' as opposed to the 'Global South' and that those consumers in the former are responsible for far more global environmental damage than those in the latter.

Governments need to ensure that businesses do not develop positions of monopoly power, but they frequently struggle to enforce environmental controls over powerful 'Big Business', especially when, increasingly, globalization means that corporations operate across national boundaries and, therefore, different regulatory regimes.

Green Views

The development of the modern 'Green' movement can be traced to the publication of *The Silent Spring* by Rachel Carson in 1962. A biologist, Carson became very concerned about the use of pesticides in agriculture and their effects on human beings, through links with cancers, and on wildlife—hence the emotive title of the book, which looks to a future where birdsong is absent (Carson 1962). Her books and articles had a huge influence on the grass roots environmental movement in the USA and resulted in the eventual ban of the pesticide DDT (Dichlorodiphenyltrichloroethane) in the USA. *The Silent Spring* also attracted a large volume of criticism from the chemical industry. This theme of environmental claim and business counterclaim will be seen again in this chapter.

Counterpoint Box 12.1 'The Tragedy of the Commons'

In 1968, Garrett Hardin provided a critique of what he saw as an essential problem for the future of humanity. 'The Tragedy of the Commons', published in the journal *Science*, argued that when human beings have access to commonly owned resources for which they do not have to pay, we each, as an individual, seek to get as much as we can from this shared resource, but, collectively, the result of this action will be that we will soon exhaust the resource, and so all lose out.

Hardin used the example of feudal agricultural societies where farmers/peasants worked mostly on land owned by landlords, but where there might be some limited common land available for grazing livestock. A rational farmer would seek not to overgraze land if s/he had private ownership of it, and would see the benefit in having fallow periods to allow the land to recover from potential overgrazing. The 'Tragedy of the Commons' is where, if land is not privately owned, or, in economic terms, property rights are not clearly defined, then each farmer will end up overusing the land in the fear that if they keep their animals off the land others will not.

Source: Hardin (1968)

Question

Discuss examples of ecological or environmental problems that might arise from 'Tragedy of the Commons' type situations in relation to your own living or working environment, or in relation to the impact of business in general.

The Limits to Growth, another key text, focused on the key areas of population—food production, industrialization, pollution, and consumption of non-renewable resources—and predicted that growth trends would, within the next 100 years, cause sudden falls in population and industrial production unless action was taken to create ecological and economic stability based on a more equitable sharing out of the products of economic prosperity (Meadows et al. 1972). Other influential books include *The Costs of Economic Growth* (Mishan 1969), *The Affluent Society* (Galbraith 1958), and *Small is Beautiful* (Schumacher 1973). Mishan's work was one of the first economics books to outline the costs of economic growth and the methods of cost benefit analysis that are needed when judging economic decisions, and Schumacher's focus is clear in its subtitle: *Economics as if People Mattered*. For Galbraith, writing at a time when the American postwar consumer boom was beginning to take off, the focus of economics had to be on analyzing why people keep consuming even when their needs are met.

Otter (2017) shows that there is a problem in relation to defining a distinctive 'green approach to business'. Across the political spectrum, it is possible for people to argue that environmental issues are an important aspect of their thinking and policy approaches. Green territory is contested from a range of different ideological perspectives, and there exist recognized branches of thinking about the ecological environment, ranging from Green Conservatism, Eco-Socialism, and Eco-fascism, to Socialist Ecology and Eco-Feminism.

Many commentators draw a distinction between 'Shallow' and 'Deep' Ecology. Shallow Ecology treats environmental issues as being important, but capable of being able to be addressed within existing ideological frameworks. Otherwise, they tend to treat environmental issues as single issues, capable of being dealt without reference to wider considerations.

Dobson argues that single issue environmental campaigning needs to be distinguished from true Green thinking, which he terms 'Ecologism' (Dobson 1991). At the heart of 'Green thinking' is the belief that we need to move away from an **anthropocentric** view of the world, which sees human beings as the driving force of nature and the sole beneficiaries of the resources that are there to be exploited, to an ecocentric view of the world, which recognizes our interdependence with nature. While there is an enormous range of opinion within this deeper Green movement, it is commonly accepted that our lives would be improved by not abusing nature, and recognizing that we need to alter the prevailing economic model of growth by accounting for environmental costs. In order for this to happen, there would need to be the development of a new form of ecological consciousness, and corresponding changes in the way in which environmental policy is enacted, allowing much more space for local democratic participation rather than 'top-down' hierarchical control. The philosopher and eco-activist Arne Naess developed what he called an 'eco-sophy' based on the principles of 'Deep Ecology' (Naess 1989).

However, it is recognized that there is potentially a conflict for the Green movement between this idealized Green value theory, which seeks to de-emphasize the primacy of human beings, and the need to accept compromises with those who, while not prepared to immerse themselves in Deep Green thinking and action are nevertheless sympathetic to dealing with environmental problems (Goodin 1992).

Recent developments in a distinctive Green business policy have focused on the need to challenge conventional growth models, and have built on the 'Steady State' ideas of Herman Daly (Daly 1991), as well as Galbraith's criticisms of consumerism. Jackson argues that conventional growth models imply that as we grow there can be a 'relative decoupling' between resource use and growth. Relative decoupling occurs when growth is accompanied by an increase in resource efficiency, but this still means that environmental damage is occurring. The only way forward is to have prosperity without growth in which there is an 'an absolute decoupling' in which environmentally harmful effects fall. This therefore implies that we need to question the imperative of growth (Jackson 2009). Such 'de-growth' ideas can be seen in the work of Dietz and O'Neill (2013), Coyle (2012), Sheehan (2010), and Skidelski and Skidelski (2012).

Environmental Regulation

There have always been voices raised to challenge the view that economic growth represented human progress. Even at the beginning of the industrial revolution in Europe, a range of people, from poets to social activists and politicians, were anxious about the costs of economic growth. These criticisms were often centred on what they saw as the destruction of the natural environment, and the effect on traditional ways of life, as a result of industrialization.

The dramatic success of the industrial revolution clearly had a severely damaging impact on a range of environmental factors, such as public health, pollution, and sanitation, and it was clear that there was an urgent need for governments, both local and national, to clean up the mess that was the by-product of economic growth.

In the twentieth century, it became accepted that business activity needed to be regulated in order to protect the natural environment, and that the government would have to take direct control over a range of environmental areas to deal with these externalities. Environmental legislation was seen as the responsibility of national governments, although as global trade increased, and with the rise of the multinational corporations, it has become clear that not all countries have the same levels of governance, nor the ability or willingness to enforce environmental regulations.

It has been increasingly acknowledged that if trade was to be free and fair between nations then it was important that all countries played by the same rules in terms of environmental protection, to stop certain countries gaining from cheaper costs because of looser environmental compliance. Within formally agreed common markets, such as the European Union, there is an insistence that all member states adhere to the same environmental rules, so environmental legislation is determined at the EU level. However, in the absence of the sort of political and legal structures that bind the members of the EU together and form the basis of the Single Market, it is difficult for nation states to reconcile the rush to liberalize trade and investment across borders with the need to have commonly agreed environmental standards. Trying to develop common international environmental standards that are legally binding and enforceable is very difficult.

The World Trade Organization claims that 'Sustainable development and the protection and preservation of the environment are fundamental goals of the WTO' (WTO n.d.).

Lack of international environmental rules can lead to trade disputes and claims of double standards. Developing countries will point to the developed world's hypocrisy in insisting on levels of environmental protection that they themselves did not have to implement as they were developing, and claim that this is simply being used as an artificial restraint on trade. Developed countries cry foul of what they perceive to be relatively poorer environmental standards in developing countries' exports, with the developing countries gaining an unfair advantage in relation to trade. Equally, there are accusations that multinational businesses are able to exploit their ability to work across boundaries, behaving in less environmentally responsible ways in developing countries than they would if operating in more tightly regulated developed markets. However, this is contentious territory. The impact of business on the ecological environment is explicitly recognized in the environmental regulations with which businesses have to comply.

At the global level, as a result of the 1992 Rio Declaration (discussed below in The Notion of Sustainable Development), the international standard, ISO 14001, was developed to provide a framework for the development of an environmental management system and supporting audit programme (see http://www.iso-14001.org.uk for details of how businesses can seek accreditation for this).

Binding environmental legislation is only possible at the international level if nation states agree to pool sovereignty in order to participate in customs unions, such as the EU. Various attempts have been made to enforce international environmental standards, through measures such as ISO 14001, and through initiatives such as the UN Global Compact, which is an attempt to provide an enabling framework in which businesses can address issues concerning human rights, labour standards, the environment, and measures to combat corruption (see Chapter 11 for a fuller examination of this).

ISO 14001 sets out the steps that a business can take to establish an environmental management system. Successful implementation of this system means that businesses can then apply for ISO certification. To be eligible for the standard, businesses must show that they not only comply with legislation, but also that they have looked at all areas where there is an environmental impact. The underlying philosophy of the standard is that there is a clear 'business case', through a systematic ISO 14001 approach. According to the ISO, this can encompass benefits such as:

- reduced cost of waste management;
- savings in consumption of energy and materials;

- lower distribution costs;

- improved corporate image among regulators, customers, and the public; and

- a framework for continual improvement of environmental performance (ISO n.d.).

In relation to the three principles that relate to the environment, the UN Global Compact is keen to impress on businesses that there need not be a conflict between preserving the environment and business success.

This could best be seen in terms of a continuum, in that if businesses do not take action now to reduce their environmental impact, their profits will suffer in the future. This short-term action is seen as an investment to prevent longer term costs, and is referred to as mitigation. It is argued that some changes as a result of ecological damage are already upon us, so businesses will need to play their part in adapting to these changes now to save the need for greater adaptation changes in the future.

Businesses are now urged to show their commitment to change by going beyond simply reporting their financial bottom line. It is argued that they should also report on their 'social' and 'environmental' impacts, and this has in turn produced a variety of systems to account for the environment. In 1994, John Elkington developed the concept of 'triple bottom line accounting' as a way of highlighting the responsibility of businesses in relation to social and environmental performance, as well as financial performance, and this is commonly referred to as the trio of 'People, Planet and Profit' (Elkington 1994).

Mini Case Study 12.2 Plan A or Plan B?

Marks and Spencer launched its Plan A in 2007, which mapped out a five-year programme of environmental change with 100 commitments. In March 2010, it reported that it had achieved 62 of these commitments and, in recognition of this, extended its commitments to 180 targets. This plan was supported with what they called the five pillars—Climate Change, Waste, Sustainable Raw Materials, Health, and being a Fair Partner—with a range of targets for each of these pillars.

Its 2014 Plan A Report reflects on progress, and what it sees as the obstacles to Plan A forming the basis for transforming the company into a genuinely sustainable business. It is argued that Plan A, in its original conception, was an improvement from the narrow CSR focus on philanthropy and compliance in building a genuine business case for sustainable business practice. In 2014 the company launched Plan A 2020. At the heart of this plan is the belief that there was a need to move away from specifying sustainability as a range of targets to be hit, and simply have sustainability as being justified so long as there was a bottom line business case. The five pillars have gone as specific target areas, and sustainability is now seen as being integrated across the value chain of the business, by embedding it in the core strategic values of the company, and by engaging all the company's stakeholders from employees, shareholders, suppliers, and customers into buying into the fact that sustainable practice will be at the heart of the business. For Marks and Spencer, one clear lesson from the experience of developing Plan A is that, in order for targets to be achieved, there needs to be acceptance of these goals from its wider stakeholders, and that one business alone cannot change the world. For critics, this could be seen as Marks and Spencer simply aiming for easy wins, like using low energy light bulbs or aiming for better fuel efficiency, and stopping short when the commitments begin to alienate shareholder support, especially in tough economic times. In 2016 the company was able to report significant achievements in relation to energy and water efficiency, but acknowledged that there was some way to go in relation to its integrated marketing strategy (Marks and Spencer 2016). However, Plan A continues to attract much praise from within the sustainable business community (Zwick 2017). ➔

→ We have seen that some environmental activists are cynical about the genuine commitment of businesses to move beyond 'green washing'. Even where such cynicism does not exist, environmentalists such as Lester Brown (2009) argue that, in order for real change to occur, it is not businesses alone that can effect such change. We have seen that the Marks and Spencer report acknowledged the need for this wider engagement. Since 1974, when he founded the Worldwatch Institute, Brown has been an influential figure in the world environment movement. In 2001, he established the Earth Policy Institute to act as a more direct campaigning organization, which translates research into policy proposals. For Brown, there has to be an alternative to what he terms 'Plan A' (not related to the Plan A of M&S) or the belief that, despite this range of problems, there is no alternative than to follow the 'Business as Usual' (BAU) model.

For Brown, there needs to be a 'Plan B' which identifies the fundamental challenges facing us and the policies that need to be developed to combat these challenges.

The central question that needs to be posed is: to what extent does the response of businesses address the ecological challenges?

Sources: Marks and Spencer (2016); Brown (2009); Zwick (2017).

Questions
1. In the case of a company like Marks and Spencer, what would be the business case for embarking on a programme such as Plan A?
2. Why might environmental campaigners argue that regarding sustainable business practice as simply complying with a set of environmental targets will not bring about genuine sustainability?

However, there is no commonly agreed set of procedures for doing this; instead there is a hotchpotch of approaches developed by some businesses eager to publicize their social credentials. While many leading businesses have been undertaking a range of environmental initiatives, there remains an unwillingness to be subject to government regulation to enforce compliance. Critics question the ability of self-regulation to achieve real benefits, and see this desire to be 'seen to be green' as sitting uneasily with the temptation to trumpet this as a way of securing competitive advantage through 'green washing' (see Chapter 11).

 Learning Task

1. In what ways do businesses potentially have a negative impact on the ecological environment?
2. In what sense do ecological problems represent a 'global Tragedy of the Commons'?

Global Cooperation—Establishing Effective Environmental Regimes

There is a growing recognition of the global nature of environmental problems.

What is the point of one country or area having stringent environmental safeguards if others do not, since ecological systems overlap? In other words, environmental problems are often **'trans-boundary'**. National policies alone are not sufficient, and put businesses at a severe competitive disadvantage if such policies are not universally applied. In the field of international relations this is a recurrent theme: how can international cooperation be achieved in a world of 'anarchy', or, in other words, one in which there is no overall global authority which all countries must obey.

There are a number of global commons issues that require international cooperation, if they are to be addressed. The following are examples that have been the focus of attempts to develop a global response:

- desertification;
- deforestation;
- loss of biodiversity;
- whaling;
- protection of fisheries and the marine environment;
- acid rain;
- protection of the ozone layer; and
- climate change.

In 1972, the Stockholm conference explored the causes of 'acid rain' and its effects on lakes and forests in Northern Europe, and this led to the formation of the United Nations Environment Programme. The notion that pollution does not respect national borders was given direct expression when radioactivity from the Chernobyl nuclear explosion in 1984 covered most of Western Europe, and in recognition of the effect of chloro-fluoro carbon (CFC) gases on the ozone layer (see Mini Case 12.3 Ozone depletion).

For effective action to be undertaken, it is important to devise a system of international cooperation, and this is referred to in international relations literature as a 'regime'. To establish such regimes, multilateral treaties are required, and these may be regulated either through a committee of organization or through what is referred to as the convention/protocol process, or a combination of both. The International Convention for the Regulation of Whaling makes annual schedules of catch regulations, and the Convention on International Trade in Endangered Species of Wild Fauna and Flora regulates which species are to be controlled.

In the convention/protocol process, states come together and agree an initial 'framework convention' to identify the problems and ways of dealing with them, but which at first may not contain specific obligations. Once agreement is made for the convention, this is then followed by a series of meetings at which 'protocols' are negotiated which then do require member states to sign up to specific actions. The Montreal Protocol (1987) was the first global agreement to phase out those chemicals held responsible for ozone depletion. The Kyoto Protocol (1997) was the first step in developing a regime to tackle climate change, and we will return to this later.

Mini Case Study 12.3 Ozone depletion

Ozone in the upper atmosphere is important as it acts as a barrier to prevent ultraviolet radiation getting through to the earth. Consequently, depletion of the ozone layer can lead to increases in skin cancers, immune disorders for humans and other species, and crop damage. In the 1970s, it became clear that the release of CFC gases into the atmosphere was indeed causing depletion of the ozone layer. CFCs were primarily used for refrigeration and air conditioning and were also commonly found in aerosols and fire extinguishers.

What has been remarkable is the speed with which action was taken to curb the use of CFCs and other ozone depleting substances. Initially, the industries involved in the ➡

→ manufacture of CFCs, such as DuPont, were resistant to changing their behaviour, arguing that it was not feasible to develop substitutes for CFCs. However, a combination of consumer pressure and US government determination to take a lead in regulating against their use, once the scientific evidence became clear, was vital. At the global level, the signing of the Montreal Protocol in 1987 established a very effective international regime for cooperation to phase out CFCs. Since customers would now be obliged to use substitutes to CFCs, even if these were more expensive, and once it became clear that the market for these was now a global one, there was a real incentive for chemical companies, such as DuPont, to spend the required research and development funds in developing substitutes.

Sources: De Sombre (2007); http://www.undp.org/ozone; http://ozone.unep.org/new_site/en/montreal_protocol.php

Questions

1. To what extent was there the creation of an effective international regime of cooperation to reduce the emissions of CFCs?

2. Why might such agreements be more difficult to achieve in the case of deforestation, or global fisheries and the protection of the global marine environment?

The fact that states have the right to exert their own sovereignty over their own resources makes the process of environmental regime creation a complex, and at times very slow, process, with conflicts between the interests of states and, of course, differences in their respective power and influence.

As well as the problems of establishing such global cooperation there are also specific problems that relate to the nature of environmental issues.

Risk and Uncertainty

The main obstacle when examining environmental problems is that, often, these problems are not immediately obvious. Environmental policy requires people and organizations to change their behaviour in relation to resource use. It requires them to recognize that the ecological environment is not a free good, and seeks to make them fully aware of the social costs of environmental damage. It is clear that across many parts of the world there has been an increase in environmental awareness, and in areas such as recycling this has changed behaviour. However, a major barrier to effecting more widespread environmental improvements lies in our lack of knowledge of exactly what our ecological impact is, and indeed the measures we should take to minimize this.

Environmental policies involve a 'trade-off' in that there is a conflict between short-term production and the immediate gratification of consumption, and longer term well-being. While people may well be more aware of the costs of motoring and air travel, the predicted rises in the uses of these modes of transport shows that people are not prepared to alter their behaviour voluntarily.

For both consumers and producers, the costs of adapting to ecological change may appear to be too great, and the task for environmental policy lies both in how to deal with this resistance, and in persuading us all that the long-term benefits of preventing ecological damage are greater than the costs of taking action now to minimize it.

The Role of Science

In order for risks to be quantified, we need careful research and analysis, and this entails further problems. Scientific surveys are often very complex and contradictory, and most people lack the understanding to unravel the findings. Faced with this lack of understanding, it is easy for people to simply ignore the debates and carry on as usual.

The Notion of Sustainable Development

In 1987, *Our Common Future*, a report from the United Nations World Commission on the Environment and Development (WCED), was published (commonly referred to as the Brundtland Report). This built on the work of the Stockholm Conference, which also looked at environmental concerns more widely. The publication of *Our Common Future*, and the work of the WCED, led to the 1992 Conference at Rio de Janeiro and the adoption of Agenda 21, the Rio Declaration, and the establishment of the Commission of Sustainable Development.

At the heart of the debate about the nature of the ecological environment lies the concept of sustainable development. The commonly accepted definition of this was outlined in the Brundtland Report:

> Sustainable Development is development that meets the needs of the present without compromising the ability of future generations to meet their own needs (WCED 1987).

This part of the statement is the bit which is most quoted, and clearly shows the commitment that is made here to ensuring **inter-generational equity**; in other words that our actions today should not undermine the standards of living of the future. However, what is often left out is the full version, which goes on to say:

> it contains within it two key concepts: the concept of 'needs', in particular the essential needs of the world's poor, to which overriding priority should be given; and the idea of limitations imposed by the state of technology and social organization on the environment's ability to meet present and future needs (WCED 1987: 43).

This second statement directly argues that growth is needed if it is to ensure that **intra-generational equity** is achieved (helping the poor in the world today).

The 1992 Earth Summit, held in Rio de Janeiro, Brazil, was pivotal in that it formulated Agenda 21, a comprehensive programme to be adopted globally, nationally, and locally, to promote sustainable development in the twenty-first century. The Rio Declaration outlined 27 key principles concerning the actions that states should take in order to safeguard the environment, and these were adopted by the 178 countries that took part in the Earth Summit (United Nations 1992).

It established the United Nations Framework Convention on Climate Change (UNFCCC), an international environmental treaty to deal with climate change. Every year, there is a Conference of the Parties to the Convention (COP) to monitor progress on actions to combat climate change (see this chapter, The Progress on Climate Change Action).

While the Brundtland definition of **sustainability** has become widely accepted, there is still wide disagreement as to its implications (see Kates et al. 2005). For advocates of the free market approach to dealing with ecological problems, BAU models using market prices, and, where necessary, techniques such as **cost benefit analysis** or **environmental impact analysis** to reflect environmental market failures, should normally be sufficient to allow public/private sector businesses to incorporate their environmental responsibilities into their corporate strategies. The emphasis in the free market approach is that, as far as possible, where market policies are not sufficient, businesses should be encouraged to minimise their environmental impact, but on a voluntary basis that will best be achieved only when there is a clear business case to be made. But, as we have seen, those on the left side, or green side, of politics, argue that markets will not be in themselves guarantors of sustainability, and that there needs to be more stringent regulation and control of business. For such critics there may well be many areas where the private interests of the business to make profits do conflict with their responsibilities to people and the planet and that, therefore, they cannot be left alone to make sustainable business decisions.

Learning Task

In terms of importance what do you think should take precedence? The needs of people in the present or the needs of future generations? What are the problems and challenges that face us when making this decision?

Global Climate Change

There is a clear consensus that the most pressing ecological problem of our age is global climate change, and that the causes of climate change are anthropogenic (that is, caused by human activity) and the result of our dependence on systems of production and consumption that rely heavily on fossil fuels, in particular. Since the industrial revolution, we have continued to emit ever more GHGs into the atmosphere. This has led to an increase in global average surface temperatures, which in turn create a whole series of interrelated risks for people, economies, and ecosystems. The Intergovernmental Panel on Climate Change (IPCC) was established in 1989 by the World Meteorological Office and the United Nations Environment Programme (UNEP), to provide an objective source of information about climate change. This information has been published in a series of assessment reports (AR), beginning in 1990 with AR 1 (with a supplement in 1992), and further reports in 1995, 2001, and 2007 (AR4). These reports are important as they represent the views of a multinational and comprehensive range of experts, assembled by UNEP, about the precise role of human beings in creating climate change, and its associated risks.

The fifth assessment report was published in October 2014 and in terms of the physical science, AR5 was clear:

> Warming of the climate system is unequivocal, and since the 1950s, many of the observed changes are unprecedented over decades to millennia. The atmosphere and ocean have warmed, the amounts of snow and ice have diminished, sea level has risen and the amount of greenhouse gases have increased (Stocker et al. 2013: 4).

GHG emissions are problematic because, once emitted into the atmosphere, they stay there for many, many years. They help create the 'greenhouse effect' in that they prevent the solar rays that penetrate the earth's atmosphere from getting back out again, leading to a gradual warming of the planet's surface.

Meyer illustrates the problem by using a 'bath-tap' analogy (Meyer 2007). The dominant greenhouse gas from anthropogenic sources is carbon dioxide (CO_2). Just as a bath will fill if the tap is left running, so the atmosphere fills up as emissions flow from sources such as the burning of fossil fuels for energy use. If there is no outflow from the bath, over time the constant flow will mean that the stock of water will rise. If there is a plughole with no plug, then this stock need not rise so fast, as some of the water is drained away. In relation to our CO_2 emissions, this means that if we have 'sinks' to absorb the carbon such as forests or the oceans, then not all the carbon will be added to the total stock. If, for example, the flow of water is twice the rate at which it drains away, then the net increase in the stock of water will be 50 per cent of the flow.

During the last 200 years, there has been a rise in CO_2 concentration from 280 ppmv to a level of 406.17 ppmv, as of April 2017 (see NASA (2018)). AR5 confirmed that CO_2 emissions have increased by 40 per cent since pre-industrial times and that, while the ocean has absorbed 30 per cent of the increase, this has led to ocean acidification. As more and more concentrations of GHGs occur, there is a warming of overall average global earth temperatures, and AR5 confirms that, '[i]t is *extremely likely* that human influence has been the dominant cause of the observed warming since the mid-20th-century' (IPCC 2013: 17 [my emphasis]). It also shows that the last three decades are *likely* to have been the warmest 30-year period of the last 1,400 years. Figure 12.1 shows the trend in CO_2 emissions.

As emissions increase, the sinks' ability to absorb them are decreasing. This is due to warming and acidification of the oceans, and the burning of forests to increase land availability. This 'aggravated accumulation' will mean that the level of the 'bathwater' will rise more quickly, and is in serious danger of overflowing.

In order to stop the long term rises in global temperatures, it is argued that, in the short run, the rate of growth of emissions of GHGs will have to slow, and that in the long run there will have to be significant cuts in the amount released into the atmosphere.

Figure 12.1 Rising CO_2 levels

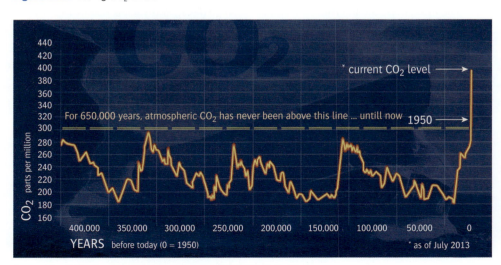

Source: http://climate.nasa.gov/evidence (Courtesy NASA/JPL-Caltech)

Figure 12.2 Global air temperature

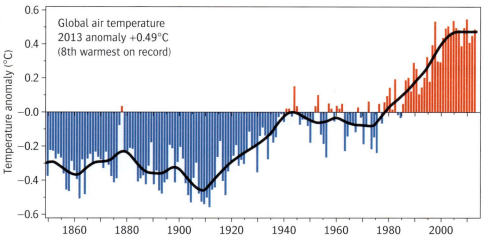

Source: Climatic Research Unit © Climatic Research Unit, University of East Anglia

Figure 12.2 shows the evidence about temperature rises on the basis of the methodology used by the Climatic Research Unit (CRU) at the University of East Anglia in the UK, whose work directly informs the IPCC.

This chart is drawn by taking the average global and marine temperatures in the period 1961–90 and then, using time series analysis from a variety of temperature monitoring methods, showing the variation (or anomaly) from this norm from 1850–2016.

Commenting on this data, the CRU states:

The time series shows the combined global land and marine surface temperature record from 1850 to 2016. This year was the warmest on record . . . The period 2001–2010 (0.49°C above the 1961–90 average) was 0.22°C warmer than the 1991–2000 decade (0.27°C above the 1961–90 average). 2015 and 2016 are clearly the warmest years (0.76°C and 0.77°C respectively) with 2014 (0.58°C) third, slightly warmer than 2010 (0.56°C), 2005 (0.54°C) and 1998 (also 0.54°C). The coldest year of the 21st century (2008 with a value of 0.39°C) was warmer than all years in the 20th century with the exception of 1998. The average of the first six years of the present decade (2011–2016) is 0.10°C warmer than the average for 2001–2010.

 Counterpoint Box 12.2 Is the sky the limit for you?

The proportion of the total GHGs emitted by aviation in the EU is only 3% of its overall total, but if global aviation was classified as a country it would be in the top 10 of global emitters. It has been estimated that an individual taking 1 return flight from London to New York emits more carbon that the average EU citizen creates with their annual heating needs. By 2020, global aviation emissions are projected to be 70% higher than in 2005, and the International Civil Aviation Organization fore-

casts that by 2050 they could grow anywhere between 300% and 700%. Since 2012 emissions from aviation have been in the European Emissions scheme (see Mini Case Study 12.4), and since 2014 there has been a proposal to have a voluntary global Carbon Off-setting and Reduction Scheme for International Aviation (CORSIA). In 2013, in response to the 5th Assessment Report's worst predictions of what is likely to happen as a result of unchecked rises in global temperatures, →

→ an American meteorologist posted on social media that he would now be reluctant to fly again unless there was an emergency. This provoked a fierce backlash from individuals resistant to the idea of global warming, and the American news network, Fox News, labelled him a 'kook' (Goldenberg 2013). The British climate change journalist, author and climate campaigner George Monbiot argued that the rational response of concerned individuals was indeed to limit the amount flights that they take, and that personally he had decided that this should be one return flight every three years. Despite the huge advances made by airlines in building more fuel efficient planes, and attempts to change away from fossil fuels to biofuels, Monbiot argues that demand for air travel will vastly outstrip these reductions and that reliance on carbon offsetting (whereby airlines finance other economic activities which are reducing carbon) is simply not sufficient; therefore, the only solution is drastic reductions in demand. For Monbiot the decision by the UK government to build a third runway at Heathrow is a 'flight from reason', and shows that, in the minds of policy makers, it is the imperative of economic growth that must come first (Monbiot 2016).

Questions
1. Who has the responsibility for curbing the emissions of GHG's from aviation? The airlines? The Government? The International Aviation Authority? You as an individual?
2. Can the projected increase in air travel ever be seen as being sustainable?

The Effects of Climate Change

The Fifth Assessment Report reaffirmed the five areas of concern that had been highlighted in the Third and Fourth Assessment Reports. AR5 lists these as five integrative reasons for concern (RFCs), which act as a starting point to analyse the dangerous effects of anthropogenic interference with the climate system on people, economies, and ecosystems. These risks range from the immediate loss of life due to flooding, storms, or heat exhaustion, through to rising food and water insecurity and destruction of biodiversity.

- **Unique and threatened systems**—There is high confidence that there are already some ecosystems and cultures that are at risk because of climate change, and this risk grows with each 1°C increase in warming. If there is 2°C warming, then there are very high risks in relation to coral reef damage and Arctic sea ice.

- **Extreme weather events**—The risk of projected increases in droughts, heat waves, and floods, as well as their adverse consequences, is already moderate and will become progressively higher with each additional 1 °C rise in warming.

- **Distribution of impacts**—The most vulnerable people will be people in the weakest economic position, especially the poor and the elderly in both developing and developed countries.

- **Global aggregate impacts**—AR4 attempted to counter an often-expressed view that, while global warming may well cause problems for some, it will equally bring benefits to others. It is easy to see how people living in cold northern climates might welcome warmer conditions. However, if global warming were to increase, AR5 confirmed that aggregate damaging impacts increase as warming increases. There will be many more losers than winners.

- **Large scale singular events**—The main concerns about abrupt and irreversible changes, which may endanger some physical systems and ecosystems, are focused on coral reefs and the effect of sea level rises as a result of ice melting.

The IPCC emphasizes that adaptation (preparing now for the future problems that climate change will bring) and mitigation measures (trying to reduce the amount of GHGs and so lower potential risks) are unlikely to stop all climate change effects, but combined, they can significantly reduce the risks. Conversely, delays in reducing emissions will significantly constrain the opportunities to lower stabilization levels, and will increase the risk of severe climate change impacts. Technology, both that which is presently available and that which is likely to become commercially available, is seen as offering a realistic hope that stabilization levels can be achieved.

In 2006, the UK government asked the respected economist, Nicholas Stern, to look at the economics of climate change. For Stern, 'Climate change presents a unique challenge for economics; it is the greatest and widest ranging market failure ever seen' (Stern 2006).

The Stern Review highlighted four main policy areas that needed to be addressed if we are to be able to mitigate the worst effects of climate change, and adapt to those that will occur:

- reduce demand for emissions-intensive goods and services;
- increase resource efficiency;
- take action on non-energy emissions, such as avoiding deforestation; and
- switch to low-carbon technologies for power, heat, and transport.

Stern was keen to emphasize that, while this may be seen to be a threat to BAU behaviour, in practice these changes may well provide opportunities to create markets for low-carbon energy products, and to reduce costs through developing new low energy systems.

The Sceptical Environmentalists

There is a small, but highly vocal, minority of critics who argue that the earth has been subject to variations in temperature before, and that this is the result of natural factors such as solar and volcanic activity. Some go further and dispute the accuracy of the data, arguing that there is now too much of a vested interest in the scientific community to prove the existence of anthropogenic climate change, which sometimes leads them to misrepresent the data. Such views are especially prevalent among many groups in the USA.

Bjorn Lomborg, in his book *The Skeptical Environmentalist*, argues that the risks of global warming are overestimated. He argues that, even where such risks can be proven, it is important for us not to prevent the present generations from reaping the fruits of economic growth on the basis of the uncertain prediction that unspecified groups in the future might suffer as a result of environmental damage (Lomborg 2001). In similar vein, the Nobel Prize winning economist Solow has argued, 'those who are so urgent about not inflicting poverty on the future have to explain why they do not attach even higher priority to reducing poverty today' (Solow in Rao 2000: 86). Lomborg is by no means the only critic to dispute the scientific evidence (see Booker 2009; Lawson 2008; Singer and Avery 2007).

This academic debate can often be clouded by mutual accusations of 'dirty tricks' across the spectrum of the debate. Climate change campaigners argue that there is a 'business of climate denial', with powerful business groups spending large amounts of money to lobby hard against legislation, and spread disinformation to undermine the strength of the climate change evidence.

In a widely reported study, which reviewed all global peer reviewed literature into the existence of Anthropogenic Global Warming (AGW), it was concluded that:

> The number of papers rejecting AGW is a miniscule [sic] proportion of the published research, with the percentage slightly decreasing over time. Among papers expressing a position on AGW, an overwhelming percentage (97.2% based on self-ratings, 97.1% based on abstract ratings) endorses the scientific consensus on AGW. (Cook et al. 2013)

The Progress on Climate Change Action

As outlined above, the UNFCC arose out of the Rio Earth Summit, and entered into force in 1994. Since 1995, there have been annual meetings of the Conference of the Parties (COP) who participate in the UNFCCC. COP 3, in 1997, established the Kyoto Protocol, which attempted to set binding agreements in terms of carbon reduction targets, and other measures discussed above. These targets applied only up to 2012, and mainly on developed countries, so it was always acknowledged that further agreements would be needed. It was argued that, since the developed countries were principally responsible for the current high levels of GHG emissions in the atmosphere as a result of more than 200 years of industrial activity, the Protocol should place a heavier burden on developed nations. This principle was stated as one of 'common but differentiated responsibilities'.

However, there were also objections from key parties such as the USA and Australia, who initially did not sign up to the protocols. Powerful business lobby groups in these countries not only question the science on which climate change predictions are based, but argue in the vein of Lomborg that, in the long run, the costs of mitigating climate change will outweigh the benefits. It would, they argue, be far better to allocate resources, intended to help developing countries mitigate and adapt to climate change in the future, to the very real and proven development problems of poverty and disease today. Many also fundamentally question the principle of common and differentiated responsibility, arguing that many developing countries are now a real competitive threat to the developed world, and that to place more of a burden for global climate change alleviation on the developed world now puts their businesses at a competitive disadvantage.

Under the Kyoto Protocol, countries agreed to identify and quantify the sources of GHG emissions. At the heart of the UNFCCC and Kyoto Protocol were three mechanisms designed to reduce global GHGs:

- Developed countries were set assigned amounts of GHGs for a given time period and, through International Emissions trading, could trade any unused amounts with other countries.

- The Clean Development Mechanism allowed developed countries to fund carbon reducing projects in less developed countries in return for carbon credits.

- Joint implementation allowed cooperation between developed countries, where one country can help another by investing in emissions reduction projects and earn credits.

At the global political level, the acceptance of climate change as being real and anthropogenic, as a result of the growing scientific evidence, and a change in the stance of the Australian and American governments, gave hope that real progress on climate change was possible. Despite clear divergences of opinion between many of the Parties at the Copenhagen Climate Conference in December 2009 (COP 15), there began to be optimism that a comprehensive global climate change treaty, binding on all the parties, could be achieved.

In December 2015 the COP 21 resulted in the first ever universal legally binding global climate deal. In the run up to the Paris talks, all the Parties submitted their Intended Nationally Determined Contributions (INDCs), which declared the reductions in GHGs that they would commit to achieve up to 2030. On the basis of the evidence presented by AR5, the aim of the Paris agreement is to create a platform of global action, based on the INDCS, to reduce GHGs, so that the rise in global temperature this century will be 'well below' 2 degrees Celsius above pre-industrial levels, and ideally to limit this to a rise of 1.5 degrees. In order to achieve this, on the basis of present evidence, growth in emissions needs to stop by 2020, and then there will need to be a global reduction in GHGs of 60% by 2050, compared to 2010. If no action were to be taken, global temperatures might rise on average by 5%, and it is argued this would give rise to catastrophic effects.

The agreement explicitly recognizes that there needs to be the provision of adaptation assistance for many developing countries. In 2018 there is to be a global stock take of the progress that countries have made in relation to achieving their targets, and this then is to continue every five years up to 2030.

In 2017, President Trump overturned the executive decision of his predecessor, Barack Obama, and the USA pulled out of the Paris Agreement. While this was seen as a blow to the intended universal agreement, there was a determination from the other parties, and indeed from states and a range of leading and environmentally conscious businesses and pressure groups in the USA, that this would not undermine the attempt to achieve the global temperature reduction targets (for more details on the UNFCC and progress, see UNFCC (2018)).

Learning Task

The UNFCCC was one of three conventions that arose out the 'Rio Earth Summit' in 1992. The other two were the UN Convention on Biological Diversity (see CBD (2018)), and the Convention to Combat Desertification (see http://www2.unccd.int). The three conventions were seen as being linked and, as a result, a joint liaison committee was established to co-ordinate action between the three. This now also incorporates the Ramsar Convention on Wetlands (see http://www.ramsar.org).

By looking at the websites of the Conventions above, identify why there is a need for co-ordination between these global conventions.

Mini Case Study 12.4 The EU's climate change strategy

The EU sees itself as a key Party to the Convention on climate change, and has signed up to the second phase of the Kyoto protocol from 2013 to 2020. By 2020 it aims to have achieved a:

- 20% cut in greenhouse gas emissions compared with 1990;
- 20% of total energy consumption from renewable energy; and
- 20% increase in energy efficiency.

→

→ And by 2030:

- at least 40% cut in greenhouse gas emissions compared with 1990;
- at least 27% of total energy consumption from renewable energy; and
- at least 27% increase in energy efficiency.

By 2050 the aim is to have reduced its emissions by 80–85% compared to 1990 levels.

In order to achieve this, there are a number of policies that the EU has adopted. At least 20% of the total EU budget is now earmarked for climate change policies, and this is in addition to the climate change budgets in the individual member countries. In terms of regulations, individual member states are required to support renewable energy sources, to reach designated green energy targets, to reduce energy use of buildings and industries, and improve energy efficiency of equipment and household appliances.

While it is hoped that such measures will mitigate against climate change, there is also an acknowledgement that there is a need for adaptation strategies in terms of:

- using less water;
- adapting building regulations;
- building flood defences; and
- developing crops that cope better in drought conditions.

In relation to reducing GHGs, the cornerstone of EU policy is the European Emissions Trading Scheme (ETS). This is a *cap and trade* system, which was established in 2005, and is a vital cornerstone in how the EU intends to reduce its emissions of GHGs. Having agreed to the national target of emissions, each country then allocates individual targets across businesses that are responsible for high levels of GHGs.

These allowances must then be adhered to, and if a firm exceeds them then they either pay a fine or else they seek to purchase allowances from a firm that has not used all its allowances. In this way, a market for carbon is established and there will be an incentive for firms to cut back on emissions, and invest in non-polluting technologies In principle, if the cap is set at progressively lower levels, this should produce reductions in GHGs. Even if, initially, this is not achieved, revenues raised from the scheme can be used to develop renewables, act against deforestation, undertake forest plantation, fund research into, and development of, carbon capture and storage facilities, and undertake extensive energy efficiency programmes.

Under the ETS, businesses are obliged to declare their emissions and submit to certificated verification procedures. The first phase was not so successful, as it is now acknowledged that initial caps were far too generous and so the prices of carbon collapsed. However, phase II worked better, and there has been a concerted attempt to harmonize rules across all EU members in phase III, which started in 2013, and this will run until 2020.

Sources: https://ec.europa.eu/clima/citizens/eu_en; https://ec.europa.eu/clima/policies/ets_en

Questions
Look at the details of the EU policies to deal with climate change and the ETS scheme on the websites listed above.

1. Review the range of policies, and categorise them is relation to whether they are mitigation or adaptation measures.
2. Which businesses are at the forefront of achieving reductions in GHGs?
3. What are the threats and the opportunities that face businesses in responding to climate change?

Learning Task

1. How aware are you of the science behind the debate about global warming?
2. What changes have you made, if any, to minimize your own 'ecological footprint'?
3. Have a go at measuring your own ecological footprint (see, for example, http://www.footprint.wwf.org.uk).
4. What reactions do you have to this footprint exercise?

The 2030 Sustainable Development Agenda

The Paris Climate Agreement was not the only major global agreement in 2015. In September 2015, the Sustainable Development Goals (SDGs) were also agreed by heads of state at the UN General Assembly. Prior to 2015, the philosophy that underpinned the publication of 'Our Common Future' could be seen to have been pursued via a multifaceted approach, with various conventions dealing with global environmental commons issues, and a separate approach to dealing with problems of poverty and lack of development through the Millennium Development Goals, which were agreed in 2000. The 17 goals of the SDGs are an attempt to bring together the agendas of development and sustainability, and reflect the belief that there is a need for a holistic approach, which addresses both inequality and environmental challenges. In the preamble to the 2030 Agenda for Sustainable Development, the emphasis is on developing an action plan for 'People, Planet and Prosperity' and it argues that the 17 goals and 169 targets are:

> integrated and indivisible and balance the three dimensions of sustainable development: the economic, social and environmental (UN 2015).

As with the battles over securing agreement in relation to climate change, there is a similar tension behind such an apparently optimistic agreement. Critics from the right argue that such 'green' thinking will inevitably conflict with the need to ensure economic growth, and critics from the left argue that, despite the warm words, essentially it will be BAU models that will win out. Inevitably, while environmentalists may take comfort from the recognition of sustainability at the heart of the development agenda, there is a conflict between those who see commitments made as progress, and those who will only be satisfied if all targets are achieved.

● CHAPTER SUMMARY

The nature of many environmental problems is that they are trans-boundary, and if we are to avoid potential tragedies of the global commons, then there needs to be concerted action at the global level, which is then translated into national and local environmental action.

It is clear that businesses have a big role to play. As converters of resources into products, attention has to be focused on their roles as sustainable businesses, not just in relation to the 'bottom line' of profit, but also in relation to their impact on people and the environment. The Rio Declaration and Agenda 21 established a comprehensive set of ambitious principles for states to promote in relation to environmental policy. The UN Global Compact then translated these principles into the prescriptions for responsible business behaviour.

It is evident that there are obstacles to environmental policies. Businesses have to balance the risks of incurring the costs of environmental compliance with the risks of doing nothing. Here, there is a clear role for science and economics to specify these risks. For businesses with the short-term goal of maximizing shareholder value, it is all too easy to maintain 'business as usual', but the increasing recognition of the range of global environmental problems means that this is not a realistic possibility. Across the spectrum of business there are many examples of how individual businesses are seeking to address these concerns, but, especially in relation to climate change, it is argued that the response has not been enough. It is clear that, unless businesses rise to the challenge, there will be calls for tougher environmental regulation. It is equally clear that, in order to make these changes, businesses do need external help and advice, and there is a need to embed global responsibility into the overall business strategy.

● REVIEW QUESTIONS

1. What is the meaning of the term 'the tragedy of the commons' and how does this relate to ecological damage?

2. Explain how it is argued that market-based measures such as the 'polluter pays principle' address ecological problems.

3. Why do 'green' thinkers and left-wing activists argue that market-based measures are not, on their own, adequate to tackle the ecological problem?

● ASSIGNMENT TASKS

1. You have applied for, and been successful in obtaining, an internship for a leading newspaper. You will be working in the research team supporting the Global Environment news team. You have been asked to update the web content on its popular online pages, and, in particular, the Frequently Asked Questions section of the Climate Change web pages, for which this team is responsible. At the briefing meeting, the web editor has asked you to do the background research that would enable you to provide copy to answer the following questions:

    a. What are the problems that climate change poses for the global community?

    b. Which businesses will be most affected by current and future policies to reduce emissions of greenhouse gases?

    c. In what ways will policies to reduce global GHG emissions impact on business behaviour?

(For an example of a successful environment online presence from a newspaper, see http://www.the-guardian.com, the website of *The Guardian* newspaper in the UK.) The web editor would like this in the form of a 2,000-word report, together with all the references that you consulted to support your findings.

2. The UK Government has announced that, under the Companies Act 2006 (Strategic and Directors' Reports) Regulations 2013, quoted companies are required to report their annual greenhouse gas (GHG) emissions in their directors' report. All quoted companies have to measure and report greenhouse gas (GHG) emissions. Quoted companies are those that are UK incorporated and whose equity share capital is officially listed on the main market of the London Stock Exchange; or is officially listed in a European Economic Area; or is admitted to dealing on either the New York Stock Exchange or NASDAQ' (Carbon Trust n.d.).

Select three companies that will be affected by the reporting requirement above, and compare and contrast their approaches to responding to the challenges of reducing their GHG emissions. Comment in particular on the extent to which they have identified a business case for this.

Case Study Economic growth and environmental risks

© iStock.com/Marcus Lindstrom

While across the world levels of absolute poverty are falling, and average incomes are rising, there are serious social and environmental problems associated with rapid economic growth. In countries such as China, India, and Brazil, the pace of change has been extremely fast; although rates of growth have slowed since 2008, compared to those experienced in the first decade of the twenty-first century. A major feature of this economic transformation has been the speed of urbanization, and all are struggling to cope with the environmental consequences of such rapid change on housing, transport, water quality and quantity, and airborne pollution.

However, average income per capita in these countries is still low and, especially in the case of Brazil and India, a major feature of this urbanization has been the creation of vast slums. The Millennium Development Goals of the United Nations explicitly recognized that it was the poor who often suffer the most from the environmental degradation brought about through rapid economic growth. These goals explicitly targeted the need for sustainable development to be central to growth strategies, as well as focusing attention on the need to improve the lives of slum dwellers, and improve sustainable access to water. As we have seen the SDGs agreed in 2015 explicitly try to square the circle between attaining economic development and ensuring environmental sustainability.

As countries develop, it is argued that entrepreneurs need to be allowed to pursue their own interests, and that their pursuit of profits will encourage them to be responsive to market needs. Simon Kuznets argued that, as countries develop, it is inevitable that the gap between high-income earners will grow relative to the poor, but that, as countries mature, this gap will close. If you plotted the relationship between inequality and income on a diagram, as incomes rise at first so does the level of inequality, but over time this gap begins to fall. This is referred to as the 'Kuznets Curve'. As economic growth increases, more and more people will be employed, and governments will be able to use greater tax revenues from the higher incomes to engage in education and health programmes, raising general well-being. This is the basis of what has become called 'Trickle Down Economics'. In similar vein, it is argued that there is an environmental Kuznets Curve in that, as countries develop rapidly, it is inevitable that the environmental costs will increase, but that as they become richer, people can afford higher levels of protection and/or invest in new and environmentally friendly technologies.

However, the pace of change in developing countries, coupled with the realization that global environmental problems impact more on the most vulnerable in the developing world, has led many to question this belief in the infallibility of the market. The WEF has highlighted water security as one the major risks for business in the future (WEF 2012). These risks can stem from too much water, as in the case of flooding, or too little, as the result of droughts and desertification. While events such as droughts and flooding are often local in their effects and it falls to the local or national authorities to try to deal with them, they can have severe global effects as well. In 2010, drought in Russia led to falls in wheat production, which led to soaring food prices across North Africa and the Middle East, and for many political commentators, this in turn provided the spark for the political upheavals of the Arab Spring.

Water quantity and quality directly affect business operations from agriculture to industry and, of course, is essential for maintenance of health and well-being in our households. Across the world there are problems with access to adequate water supplies, and this is exacerbated by the global differences in terms of access to water, as well as large income inequalities in water scarce regions, which mean that poor people are always at a disadvantage. This, then, means that there needs to be attention paid to investing in the infrastructure vital for water purification and distribution. There is intense debate as to who should pay for this, and the degree to which water should be bought and sold as a commodity or seen as a public good. ➔

→ Inevitably, the struggle to get adequate access to such a valuable resource, if not solved through an effective production and distribution system, has the potential to cause local and global conflicts.

Questions

1. In what ways might there be a conflict between the goals of economic growth and the concept of sustainable development?

2. Why do developing countries face particular problems in relation to environmental problems?

3. What are the main risks that face business in relation to water security?

4. If there are water security issues in relation to quantity and quality, who should take the lead in ensuring that there is universal access to adequate supplies of safe and clean water?

● FURTHER READING

For an introduction to the range of thinking about the environment, see:

- Otter, D. (2017) 'Environmentalism' in Wetherly P. (ed) *Political Ideologies,* Oxford: Oxford University Press.

This chapter provides a good introduction to the issues surrounding the relationship between business and sustainable development:

- Judge, E. (2018) 'The Natural Environment Global Warming, Pollution, Resource Depletion and Sustainable Development'. In Wetherly, P. and Otter, D., *The Business Environment—Themes and Issues in a Globalizing World*. Oxford: Oxford University Press.

This is the synthesis report of the UN Intergovernmental Panel on Climate Change, and contains all the established academic evidence regarding climate change and its effects:

- IPPC (2015) Fifth Assessment Report. Available at http://www.ipcc.ch/report/ar5.

This report outlines the responses that the World Bank feels are needed to prevent catastrophic climate change:

- World Bank (2012) 'Turn Down the Heat: Why a 4°C Warmer World Must be Avoided'. Available at http://documents.worldbank.org/curated/en/2012/11/17097815/turn-down-heat-4%C2%B0c-warmer-world-must-avoided.

● REFERENCES

Booker, C. (2009) *The Real Global Warming Disaster: Is the Obsession with 'Climate Change' Turning Out to be the Most Costly Scientific Blunder in History?* London: Continuum.

Brown, L. (2009) *Plan B 4.0—Mobilizing to Save Civilization*. Washington, DC: Earth Policy Institute.

Carbon Trust (n.d.) https://www.carbontrust.com/resources/guides/carbon-footprinting-and-reporting/mandatory-carbon-reporting.

Carson, R. (1962) *The Silent Spring*. Boston: Houghton Mifflin.

Climate Research Unit, Information Sheets, http://www.cru.uea.ac.uk/information-sheets.

Convention on Biological Diversity (UN)(2018) https://www.cbd.int/convention/.

Cook, J., Nuccitelli, D., Green, S.A., Richardson, M., Winkler, B., Painting, R., Way, R., Jacobs, P., and Skuce, A. (2013) *Quantifying the Consensus on Anthropogenic Global Warming in the Scientific Literature*, Environ. Research.

Letters. 8 024024 (http://iopscience.iop.org/article/10.1088/1748-9326/8/2/024024/pdf).

Coyle, D. (2012) *The Economics of Enough: How to Run the Economy as if the Future Matters.* Princeton University Press.

Daly, H. (1991) *Steady State Economics.* Washington: Island Press.

De Sombre, E. (2007) *The Global Environment and World Politics.* London: Continuum.

Dietz, R. and O'Neill, D.W. (2013) *Enough is Enough—Building a Sustainable Economy in a World of Finite Resources.* San Francisco, CA: Berrett Koehler Publishers.

Dobson, A. (1991) *The Green Reader,* London: Andre Deutsch.

Elkington, J. (1994) 'Towards the Sustainable Corporation—Win-Win-Win Business Strategies for Sustainable Development'. *California Management Review* 36(2).

Ethical Corp (2018) http://www.ethicalcorp.com.

Forum For the Future (2018) http://www.forumforthefuture.org.

Galbraith, J.K. (1958) *The Affluent Society.* New York: Houghton Mifflin Company.

Gates, G., Ewind, J., Russell, K., and Watkins, D. (2017) 'How Volkswagen's Defeat Devices Worked' (https://www.nytimes.com/interactive/2015/business/international/vw-diesel-emissions-scandal-explained.html?_r=0).

GFDRR (2016) The Making of a Riskier Future: How our decisions are shaping future disaster risk: Washington D.C: Global Facility for Disaster Reduction and Recovery (https://www.gfdrr.org/sites/default/files/publication/Riskier%20Future.pdf).

Goldenberg, S. (2013) IPPC report makes US meteorologist cry and give up flying, *The Guardian* 3 October (https://www.theguardian.com/environment/2013/oct/03/ipcc-climate-report-eric-holthaus).

Goodin, R.E. (1992) *Green Political Theory,* Cambridge: Polity Press.

Goodin, R. (2007) 'Selling Environmental Indulgences'. In Dryzek, J.S. and, Schlosberg, D. (eds) *Debating the Earth—The Environmental Politics Reader.* Oxford: Oxford University Press.

GRLI (2018) http://www.grli.org.

Hardin, G. (1968) 'The Tragedy of the Commons'. *Science* 162(December), American Association for the Advancement of Science.

Hotten R (2015) 'Volkswagen: The Scandal Explained' (http://www.bbc.co.uk/news/business-34324772).

IPCC (2013) 'Climate Change 2013—The Physical Science Basis, Summary for Policy Makers, Technical Summary and Frequently Asked Questions. Working Group 1 Contribution to the Fifth Assessment Report of the Intergovernmental Panel on Climate Change'. Available at http://www.climatechange2013.org/images/report/WG1AR5_SummaryVolume_FINAL.pdf.

ISO (n.d.) http://www.iso.org.

Jackson, T. (2009) *Prosperity without Growth: Economics for a Finite Planet,* London: Earthscan.

Kates, R., Parris, T., and Leiserowitz, A. (2005) 'What is Sustainable Development? Goals, Indicators, Values and Practice?'. *Environment: Science and Policy for Sustainable Development* 47(3): 8–21. Available at http://www.hks.harvard.edu/sustsci/ists/docs/whatisSD_env_kates_0504.pdf.

Lawson, N. (2008) *An Appeal To Reason: A Cool Look At Global Warming.* London: Duckworth.

Lomborg, B. (2001) *The Skeptical Environmentalist.* Cambridge: Cambridge University Press.

Marks and Spencer (2016) Plan A Report 2016 (http://planareport.marksandspencer.com/M&S_PlanA_Report_2016_Overview.pdf).

Meadows, D.H., Meadows, G., Randers, J., and Behrens, W.W. III (1972) *The Limits to Growth.* New York: Universe Books.

Meyer, A. (2007) 'The Case for Contraction and Convergence'. In D. Cromwell and M. Levene (eds), *Surviving Climate Change—The Struggle to Avert Climate Catastrophe.* London: Pluto Press.

Mishan, E. (1969) *The Costs of Economic Growth.* London: Penguin.

Monbiot G (2016) 'The Flight of Reason', *The Guardian* 19 October (http://www.monbiot.com/2016/10/19/the-flight-of-reason).

Naess, A. (1989) *Ecology, Community and Lifestyle: An Outline of an Ecosophy,* Cambridge: Cambridge University Press.

NASA (2018) 'Carbon dioxide' https://climate.nasa.gov/vital-signs/carbon-dioxide/.

Neate, R. (2015) 'Volkswagen under Investigation over Illegal Software that Masks Emissions' (https://www.theguardian.com/business/2015/sep/18/epa-california-investigate-volkswagen-clean-air-violations).

Net Impact (2018) http://www.netimpact.org.

Prüss-Ustün A., Wolf, J., Corvalán, C., Bos, R., and Neira, M. (2016) 'Preventing Disease through Healthy Environments—A Global Assessment of the Burden of Disease from Environmental Risks'. Geneva: World

Health Organization (http://apps.who.int/iris/bitstream/10665/204585/1/9789241565196_eng.pdf).

Rao, P.K. (2000) *Sustainable Development—Economics and Policy*. Oxford: Blackwell.

Schumacher, E.F. (1973) *Small is Beautiful—Economics as if People Mattered*. New York: Harper and Row.

Sheehan, B. (2010) *The Economics of Abundance: Affluent Consumption and the Global Economy*. Cheltenham: Edward Elgar.

Singer, S.F. and Avery, D.T. (2007) *Unstoppable Global Warming Every 1,500 Years*. Plymouth: Rowman and Littlefield.

Skidelski, R. and Skidelski, E. (2012) *How Much is Enough?: Money and the Good Life*. New York: Other Press.

Stern, N. (2006) 'The Stern Review, Executive Summary—the Economics of Climate Change'. HM Treasury. Available at http://www.hm-treasury.gov.uk.

Stocker, T.F., Qin, D., Plattner, G.-K., Tignor, M., Allen, S.K., Boschung, J., Nauels, A., Xia, Y., Bex, V., and Midgley, P.M. (eds) (2013) 'Summary for Policymakers in Climate Change 2013: The Physical Science Basis: Contribution of Working Group 1 to the Fifth Assessment Report of the Intergovernmental Panel on Climate Change', IPCC, Cambridge, UK; New York, NY: Cambridge University Press.

United Nations (1992) http://sustainabledevelopment.un.org/content/documents/Agenda21.pdf.

United Nations (2015) Transforming Our World: the 2030 Agenda for Sustainable Development (https://sustainabledevelopment.un.org/post2015/transformingourworld).

United Nations Convention to Combat Desertification (2018) https://www.unccd.int/.

United Nations Framework Convention on Climate Change (2018) https://unfccc.int/2860.php.

Watts, N. et al. (2016) The *Lancet* Countdown: tracking progress on health and climate change, http://www.thelancet.com. Published online 14 November 2016 http://dx.doi.org/10.1016/S0140-6736(16)32124-9.

WBCSD (2018) http://www.wbcsd.org.

WCED (1987) *Our Common Future*. Oxford: Oxford University Press (commonly known as the Brundtland Report).

WEF (2012) 'Global Agenda Council on Water Security'. Available at http://www.weforum.org/reports/global-agenda-council-water-security-2012-2014.

WEF (2017) 'The Global Risks Report 2017'. (12th edn.) Available at http://www3.weforum.org/docs/GRR17_Report_web.pdf.

WTO (n.d.) http://www.wto.org/english/tratop_e/envir_e/envir_e.htm.

Zwick S. (2017) Plan A Made Marks and Spencer a Leader in Sustainability—Now Comes the Hard Part (http://www.ecosystemmarketplace.com/articles/plan-made-marks-spencer-sustainable-company-now-comes-hard-part).

Glossary

Absolute cost barriers obstacles deterring entry of new firms because the capital costs of entering are huge or where the existing firms control a vital resource, e.g. oil reserves—the company Aramco controls 98 per cent of Saudi Arabian oil reserves

Accountability the idea that organizations and people should take responsibility for their actions and their outcomes

Acquisition one firm takes over or merges with another; some authors use this term when a deal is contested

Advanced economy a country whose per capita income is high by world standards

Ageing population an increase in the average age of the population

Agrichemical industry firms producing chemicals, used in agriculture such as fertilizers, pesticides, fungicides, or soil treatment, that improves the production of crops

Anthropocentric a view of the world that sees humans as being the most important species on earth

Applied research research specifically seeking knowledge that can be exploited commercially

Arbitration a process to resolve disputes that avoids using the courts

Authoritarian system one person or a group of people exercise power unrestrained by laws or opposition

Barriers to entry obstacles that prevent new firms from entering an industry and competing with existing firms on an equal basis

Basic research the pursuit of knowledge for the sake of it with no explicit aim to exploit the results commercially

Biodiversity the variety of life forms which exist on Earth. There is clear evidence that ecological changes can lead to a reduction in this

Biotechnology the use of biological systems or living organisms to make or modify products or processes

Born global refers to firms who get involved in international activities immediately after their birth

Bribery the offer of inducements in return for illegal favours

BRIC refers to Brazil, Russia, India, and China. Countries whose economies have been growing relatively rapidly in the first years of the twenty-first century and are seen as becoming major economic powers in the future

Brownfield investment where a firm expands by taking over existing production or service assets—most FDI is brownfield investment

Bubble refers to a situation where speculation causes the price of an asset to rise very rapidly, way above its intrinsic value, and then to plunge

Capital intensive where production of a good or service relies more heavily on capital, in the form of plant and equipment, than labour

Capital markets physical and electronic markets that bring together savers and investors, e.g. the stock market

Cartel firms come together to agree on a common price or to divide the market between them

Cash crop crops grown to sell in the market for money rather than for the consumption of the producer

Centrally planned economy major economic decisions, e.g. on production, prices, and investment are made directly by government rather than being left to market forces

Certificate of deposit (CD) low risk and low return; issued by a bank to those depositing money for a specified length of time at a specified rate of interest

Civil law system based on statutes and written codes

Clientelism politicians confer favours on members of the electorate in order to obtain votes—sometimes referred to as patronage

Collectivized where the means of production are owned by the people collectively or by the state on their behalf

Common law system accords more importance to court judgments than to written codes and statutes

Common market a customs union, but with the addition that member states agree to allow free movement of goods, services, capital, and labour

Communist system usually a one-party system where the party controls the institutions of the state, and owns and controls most of the production of goods and services

Comparative advantage the ability of a country to produce a good at lower cost, relative to other goods, compared to another country; even if a country is not the most efficient at producing the good, it can still benefit from specializing in producing and exporting that good

Competitive advantage strategies, skills, knowledge, or resources that allow firms to compete more effectively

Complementary product a product that is manufactured or used with another product, e.g. computers and computer software

Concentration ratio (CR) a way of measuring market concentration that takes the proportion of industry sales or output accounted for by the largest firms. A CR5 shows the share of the five largest firms in the market

Contract a legally binding agreement between a buyer and a seller

Convention on Contracts for the International Sale of Goods (CISG) UN rules governing the sale of goods between professional buyers and sellers in different countries

Copyright the holder has the exclusive right to publish and sell literary, musical, or artistic works

Corporate social responsibility (CSR) organizations take responsibility for the impact of their activities on society including customers, suppliers, employees, shareholders, and communities, as well as the environment

Corporatist social model welfare system offering relatively generous benefits and where work is seen as very important—found in countries such as Germany and Japan

Corruption where people misuse their power to enrich themselves

Corruption Perceptions Index (CPI) a ranking of countries by level of corruption carried out by Transparency International

Cost benefit analysis a technique used by economists when assessing the viability of investments (usually involving large-scale investments) that seeks to measure the negative and positive externalities of these

Creative capitalism the notion that business needs to generate profits and to solve the world's problems, e.g. use market forces to better address global poverty

Creative destruction the process by which radical new products, processes, transportation systems, and markets transform industry by destroying the old ways of doing things

Credit crunch a sudden and sharp reduction in the availability of money or credit from banks and other financial institutions

Credit default swap (CDS) a type of credit derivative, which seeks to protect a lender in the event that the borrower defaults by swapping the risk of default. It is a derivative because its value is based on the value of the underlying asset—for example, a mortgage

Cross elasticity of demand a measure of the extent to which customers change their purchasing patterns when one firm changes its price

Cross-border merger when a firm based in one country merges with a firm based in another

Cultural imperialism the imposition of one country's culture on another country

Cultural relativism understanding other cultures and not judging them according to one's own cultural norms and values

Culture shared beliefs, values, customs, and behaviours prevalent in a society that are transmitted from generation to generation

Customary law body of rules, values, and traditions based on knowledge gained from life experiences or on religious or philosophical principles

Customs union a free trade area, but with the addition that members agree to levy a common tariff on imports of goods from non-members

Cybercrime crime committed using computers and the internet

DDT Dichlorodiphenyltrichloroethane, a pesticide that was widely used in agriculture in the 1950s

Deforestation the destruction of forests either because of logging for timber or as people seek to clear forests so that they can farm the land

Demography the study of population in its various aspects—size, age, gender, ethnic group, and so on

Derivative in financial markets, an asset whose value derives from some other asset. Buying an equity derivative does not mean buying shares, but involves taking out a contract linked to the level of share price. The contract can offer protection against adverse movements in the price of the share

Desertification the process by which once-fertile areas of land become deserts. This is seen as a consequence of ecological damage

Devaluation a fall in the value of one currency against others

Developed countries see Advanced economy

Developing countries countries whose incomes are low by world standards

Directive (EU) laws that bind member states but are their responsibility to implement

Disposable income income remaining net of taxes and benefit payments available for spending or saving

Distribution of income the division of income among social groups in an economy or among countries

Diversified firm a business that operates in more than one industry or one market

Dumping selling goods in a foreign market at below their costs of production or below the price in the domestic market

Ecocentric a view of the world that stresses that all species are important and that the health of the planet depends on our recognition of the mutual inter-dependence between all species

Economic growth the rate of change in GDP

Economic nationalism the state protects domestic business firms from foreign competition. They become richer and more powerful and this, in turn, increases the power of the state; same as mercantilism

Economies of scale reduction in unit costs associated with large-scale production

Economies of scope cost savings resulting from increasing the number of different goods or services produced

Embezzlement refers to the stealing of money or other assets

Emerging economy/market an economy with low-to-middle per capita income; originally it referred to economies emerging from communism

Environmental impact analysis the use of cost benefit analysis in the form of a report undertaken by businesses when considering an investment to ensure that all the environmental costs are considered

Equity support regime government support for innovation by buying shares and taking a stake in the ownership

Ethnocentric a belief that the values of your own race or nation are better than those of others

Eurozone members of the EU having the euro as their currency

Excess capacity where demand is not sufficient to keep all resources in a firm or industry fully occupied

Exchange rates the price of one currency expressed in terms of another, e.g. £1 = US$2

Executive branch implements laws, regulations, and policies and gives policy advice to government ministers

Export credits loans offered by countries, often at low cost, to buyers of exports

Export guarantees where exporters are guaranteed by governments that they will receive payment for their goods or services

Export processing zone (EPZ) an area where MNCs can invest, produce, and trade under favourable conditions such as being allowed to import and produce without paying tax

External factors components of the micro- and/or macro-environments of business

Extortion obtaining money or other benefits by the use of violence or the threat of violence

Factors of production inputs combined by organizations to produce goods and services; the main categories are land, labour, and capital

Favouritism where a person is favoured unfairly over others, e.g. in the award of contracts

Federal system there is a sharing of significant decision-making powers between central and regional governments

Feminine society one which values highly the quality of life and human relationships

Financial markets these are mechanisms for bringing together buyers and sellers of financial assets—they can be located in one place or be dispersed

Fixed costs costs that do not vary with the level of output and are incurred whether output is produced or not

Fixed exchange rate when the exchange rate of a currency is fixed against others—in reality, a completely fixed rate is difficult to achieve

Floating exchange rate when the exchange is allowed to float freely against other currencies

Foreign direct investment (FDI) the establishment, acquisition, or increase in production facilities in a foreign country

Foreign indirect investment (FII) the purchase of financial assets in a foreign country

Franchising granting the right to an individual or firm to market a company's goods or services within a certain territory or location; McDonald's, Subway, and Domino's Pizza are examples of companies granting franchises to others

Fraud deception by those aiming to make an illegal gain

Free trade goods and services are completely free to move across frontiers—i.e. there are no tariffs or non-tariff barriers

Free trade area member states agree to remove tariffs and quotas on goods from other members of the area. Members have the freedom to set the level of tariff imposed on imports of goods from non-members of the area

GATT an international organization set up to remove barriers, particularly tariffs and quotas, to international trade; was subsumed into the WTO

GHGs greenhouse gases of which the most serious for climate change are carbon dioxide, methane, and nitrous oxide

Global income the total value of world income generated by the production of goods and services

Global integration the interconnections between countries, which increase with the reduction in barriers to the movement of goods, services, capital, and people

Global supply chains the sequence of steps that a good goes through to get from the producer of the raw materials to the final product

Globalization the creation of linkages or interconnections between nations. It is usually understood as a process in which barriers (physical, political, economic, cultural) separating different regions of the world are reduced or removed, thereby stimulating exchanges in goods, services, money, and people

Governance the structures and procedures countries and companies use to manage their affairs

Greenfield investment where a firm sets up completely new production or service facilities

Greenhouse gases see GHGs

Grey market goods sold at a lower price than that intended by the maker; the goods are often bought cheaply in one national market, exported, and sold at a higher price in another

Gross domestic product the value of all goods and services produced within the geographical boundaries of a country

Guanxi the reciprocal exchange of favours and mutual obligations among participants in a social network in China

Hedge funds financial institutions selling financial products that allow clients to reduce financial risk or to speculate in equities, commodities, interest rates, and exchange rates; they also operate on their own account

Herfindahl-Hirschman Index (HHI) gives a measure of market concentration that includes all firms in the market. The more competitive the market, the closer the value of the index is to zero. The value of the index for pure monopoly is 10,000

Horizontal merger where a firm takes over a competitor, i.e. the merging firms are operating at the same stage of production

Human Development Indicators (HDI) used by the UN to measure human development; they include life expectancy, adult literacy rates, and GDP per capita

ICSID agency based at the World Bank that resolves international commercial disputes between businesses

Impact analysis the process of identifying the impact on business of a change in its external environment

Income inelastic when the quantity demanded of a good or services changes proportionately less than national income, i.e. the value of income elasticity is less than one

Industrial revolution a transformation from an agricultural economy to an industrialized economy with large-scale mass production carried out in factories in towns

Industry comprises all those firms who are competing directly with each other

Industry based view an organization's performance is determined by its position in relation to the external environment

Infant mortality the death rate of children in the first year of life, expressed as the number of deaths per 1,000 live births

Inflation a rise in the general price level or an increase in the average of all prices of goods and services over a period of time

Information and communications technologies (ICT) technology that is relevant to communications, the internet, satellite communications, mobile telephony, and digital television

Information revolution the increasing importance of information and the increasing ease with which information can be accessed

Innovation the commercial exploitation of new knowledge

Intellectual property rights (IPRs) legal protection of ideas and knowledge embodied in new goods, services, and production processes

Interest rate the price paid to borrow someone else's money, sometimes called the price of money

Inter-generational equity the belief that our actions today should not undermine the standards of living of future generations

Internal factors the internal strengths and weaknesses of the organization

International arbitration companies in different countries who are in dispute can ask that their case be resolved under the New York Convention or by referring it to ICSID at the World Bank

International Centre for the Settlement of Investment Disputes (ICSID) an international body based at the World Bank in Washington that helps to resolve disputes between governments and foreign business around investment

International Comparison Program a World Bank programme that is developing ways of comparing relative standards of living

International Labour Organization (ILO) a UN agency promoting social justice in the workplace

International Monetary Fund (IMF) an international agency promoting monetary cooperation and stability

Inter-operability the ability of systems such as IT systems to work together

Intra-generational equity the belief that it is important that rich producers and consumers today do not impose environmental costs on the poor members of the present generation

ISIC the UN industrial classification system

Judicial branch institutions such as the police, courts, prison system, and armed forces responsible for enforcing the law

Labour intensive where production of a good or service relies more heavily on labour than on capital, i.e. plant and equipment

Legislative branch political institutions like parliaments with the power to make laws, regulations, and policies

Liberal democracy a system in which citizens have the right to elect their government and to individual freedom

Liberal social model a form of welfare system offering relatively low welfare benefits and distinguishing between those deserving welfare support and those who do not—found in North America and Australia

Liberalization the reduction of barriers to trade or of entry into a market

Licensing where a firm grants permission for another to use its assets, e.g. to produce its product, use its production processes, or its brand name

Life expectancy the average number of years that a person can expect to live from birth, which varies significantly between countries

Liquidity the ease with which assets can be turned into cash

Lisbon strategy EU 10-year plan to improve competitiveness

Lobbying attempt to influence the decisions taken by others, e.g. state institutions

Macro-environment comprises all the political, economic and financial, socio-cultural, technological, and ecological elements in the wider environment of business

Maquiladora a factory set up in Mexico close to the US border as a result of the establishment of NAFTA

Market comprises competing goods and services, the firms producing those goods/services, and the geographical area where the firms compete

Market concentration measures the distribution of market power by market share

Market deregulation the reduction of barriers of entry into a market

Market economy an economy where prices and output are determined by the decisions of consumers and private firms interacting through markets

Market growth the change over time in the demand for a good or service

Market ideology a set of beliefs asserting that economic decisions are best left to private individuals and firms through the market; government intervention in the market is abhorred

Market size measured by the sales turnover of a good or service in a market: the relative size of the overall economy

Masculine society one where money, incomes, promotion, and status are highly valued

Mercantilism the idea that international trade should primarily serve to increase a country's financial wealth, especially of gold and foreign currency—in this view, exports are good and imports are bad

Merger occurs where two or more companies combine their assets into a single company; some authors use the term only when all parties are happy to conclude the deal

Micro-environment the components of the firm's immediate environment: rivals, customers, suppliers, potential competitors, and substitutes

Migrant the UN defines migrants as people currently residing for more than a year in a country other than where they were born

Migration the movement of people across national borders from one country to another

Millennium Development Goals (MDGs) eight goals adopted by the United Nations concerning world poverty and general development

Monarchy refers to a country where the monarch is the head of state

Monetary policy attempts by the authorities to influence monetary variables such as money supply, interest rates, and exchange rates

Money an accepted medium of exchange for goods and services

Money laundering making illegally acquired money appear to come from a legitimate source

Money supply there are various definitions—all include the quantity of currency in circulation and then add various other financial assets such as bank current and deposit accounts

Monopolistic competition a market structure where there are many sellers producing differentiated products

Monopoly a market structure where there is only one seller

Multinational corporations (MNCs) companies who own and control operations in more than one country

NACE the EU system of industrial classification

NAFTA (North Atlantic Free Trade Area) a free trade area comprising the USA, Canada, and Mexico

NAICS the system of industrial classification used by members of NAFTA, the USA, Canada, and Mexico

Nanotechnology the science of the ultra-small

National income income generated by a country's production of goods and services—the same as GDP

Natural monopoly occurs where the market can be supplied more cheaply by a single firm rather than by a number of competitors, e.g. in the supply of water where it would not be economical to build more than one supply network

Negative externalities are the costs of either the production or consumption of goods and services that are not borne by the direct producers or consumers, but which affect society in general, e.g. exhaust fumes from vehicles pollute the air that we all have to breathe

Neoliberals believe in a minimal role for the state in the economy and society and letting market forces prevail

Neo-mercantilism government policies to encourage exports, discourage imports, and control outflows of money with the aim of building up reserves of foreign exchange

Nepotism conferring favours on the members of one's family

New trade theory models of trade that incorporate market imperfections such as monopoly elements and product differentiation into their analysis

New York Convention a commercial body set up under the aegis of the UN to resolve international commercial disputes between companies

Non-governmental organization (NGO) not for profit organizations who try to persuade government and business on a variety of issues such as human rights, the environment, and global poverty

Norms rules in a culture indicating what is acceptable and unacceptable in terms of peoples' behaviour

OECD international organization comprising 30 member countries, mostly advanced: tries to promote sustainable economic development, financial stability, and world trade

Offshoring transfer of jobs abroad

Oligopoly a market structure with few sellers where the decision of one seller can affect and provoke a response from the others

Open economy a completely open economy is one where there are no restrictions on foreign trade, investment, and migration

Opportunities occur where the external environment offers business the possibility of meeting or exceeding its targets

Opportunity cost the sacrifice made by choosing to follow one course of action: the opportunity cost to a country deciding to use resources to manufacture more of a product is the benefit it gives up by not using those resources to make another good

Option the right to buy or sell an asset at an agreed price

Organizational culture comprises the values and assumptions underpinning the operation of the business—for example, regarding how authority is exercised and distributed in the firm and how employees are rewarded and controlled

Outsourcing occurs where business or public bodies award contracts to outside businesses to perform services or produce goods that were previously performed in-house

Patent a patent gives the holder the exclusive right to exploit the invention commercially for a fixed period of time

Patronage see Clientelism

Per capita per head

Perfect competition a market structure with many sellers, homogeneous products, free entry and exit, and where buyers and sellers have perfect knowledge of market conditions

PESTLE a model facilitating analysis of the macro-environment, the acronym standing for Political, Economic and Financial, Socio-cultural, Technological, Legal, Ecological

Piracy the unauthorized duplication of goods such as software or films protected by patent or copyright; robbery committed at sea usually through the illegal capture of a ship

Planned economy a system where the means of production are owned by the state on behalf of the people, and where the state plans and controls the economy

Poverty occurs where people do not have enough resources to meet their needs in absolute terms and relative to others; the World Bank uses income of US$1/US$2 a day to measure global poverty

Power distance the extent to which a society accepts hierarchical differences, e.g. inequality in the workplace

Precedent when the decision of a court binds others in subsequent cases when similar questions of law are addressed

Price leadership a situation where prices and price changes are determined by the dominant firm or a firm accepted by others as a price leader

Primary market a market where the first trading in new issues of stocks and shares occurs

Product differentiation where firms try to convince consumers that their products are different from those of their competitors through activities such as product design, branding, packaging, and advertising

Product life cycle stages of development through which a product typically moves: introduction; growth; maturity; decline

Productivity the amount of output per unit of resource input, e.g. productivity per worker; used as a measure of efficiency

Public procurement the purchase of goods and services by government departments, nationalized industries, and public utilities in telecommunications, gas, water

Purchasing power parity where the value of, for example, GDP is adjusted to take account of the buying power of income in each economy. It takes account of the relative cost of living

Qualified majority voting (QMV) EU system where any proposal must receive three quarters of the votes to be approved

Quantitative easing central banks deliberately expand the money supply by buying assets, usually government bonds, from private sector companies like pension funds. Bond prices rise and interest rates fall, hopefully promoting increases in demand and boosting economic growth

Quota limitation imposed by governments on the total amount of a good to be imported; the amount of money IMF member countries are required to subscribe to the Fund

Recession a significant decline in the rate of economic growth; technically it can be defined as a fall in GDP over two successive three-month periods

Regional trade area (RTA) barriers to movement such as tariffs and quotas are abolished among the members

Regulation rules that take their authority from statutes

Regulation (EU) laws that must be applied consistently in all member states

Religious law based on religious principles, e.g. Sharia, or Muslim, law is based on the religious principles contained in the Koran

Research and Development (R&D) the discovery of new knowledge (research) about products, processes, and services; the application of that knowledge to create new and improved products, processes, and services that fill market needs (development)

Resource based view an organization's performance is determined by its resources and capabilities

Revenue the income firms generate from their production of goods and services

Risk analysis systematic attempt to assess the likelihood of the occurrence of certain events

Rules of origin laws and regulations determining the origin of a good—this can be an issue in free trade areas where the origin of the good determines whether a tariff is imposed

Scanning a process of identifying issues in the macro-environment that have an impact on the organization

Scenario planning using views of the future to help organizations to plan

Screening a technique to assess whether countries are attractive as a market or as a production location

Secondary market where stocks and shares are traded after their initial offering on the primary market

Securitization a process of taking several financial assets, like mortgages, and repackaging into interest-bearing securities—interest payments and repayments of the loans are received by the purchaser of the security where decision-making powers and responsibilities are divided among the legislative branch, executive branch, and judicial branch

Shadow bank a financial intermediary creating credit across international borders but not subject to regulatory oversight. Regulated financial institutions may also be active in unregulated shadow banking activities

Shadow economy goods and services produced (legally and illegally) but not recorded in official figures—no tax is paid and laws and regulations are ignored

Shell company a company that exists only on paper, often without employees but may have a bank account and be the registered owner of assets such as intellectual property or ships, held on behalf of another entity. Many such companies are registered in tax havens and while not necessarily illegal, some may be used illegitimately to disguise the true ownership of assets, reduce tax liabilities, or launder money from criminal activities

Social democratic model welfare benefits are generous and available to all; the system is committed to maintaining high employment and low unemployment

Social entrepreneurs where entrepreneurial/business approaches are used to deal with social problems, e.g. providing microfinance to help reduce rural poverty in developing countries

Soviet bloc the Soviet Union and its allies in Eastern Europe such as Poland, East Germany, Hungary, and Romania; the bloc started to collapse in the late 1980s

Specialization concentration on certain activities, e.g. the law of comparative advantage suggests that countries should specialize in producing those goods at which they are relatively most efficient/least inefficient

Spot rate/price the current rate or price

Stakeholder individuals or groups who have an interest in an organization and who can affect or be affected by the activities of the organization

Stakeholder map a way of prioritizing stakeholders by comparing their power against their interest

State a set of institutions having the legal power to make decisions in matters of government over a specific geographical area and over the population living there

Statutes laws passed by a legislative body such as a national or regional parliament

Strategy deciding the long-term direction of an organization

Subprime loans a mortgage loan granted to individuals with a poor credit history that renders them unable to access a conventional mortgage

Subsidies financial assistance from governments to business, often to protect it from foreign competition

Superbug bacteria that have become resistant to antibiotic drugs

Supply chain the systems and agencies involved in getting a good from the raw material supplier to the final consumer

Sustainability the ability of productive activities to continue without harm to the ecological system

Sustainable development economic development that does not endanger the incomes, resources, and environment of future generations

Swaps a means of hedging or reducing the risk of adverse price or rate changes

SWOT comprises four factors, Strengths, Weaknesses, Opportunities, and Threats, arising from a structured analysis of their internal operations (SW) and their external environment (OT)

Tariff a tax levied by countries on imports or exports

Tax avoidance exploiting legal loopholes to avoid paying tax

Tax evasion illegally avoiding paying tax

Technological advance new knowledge or additions to the pool of knowledge

Technological diffusion the spreading of new technologies within and between economies

Technology the expertise or pool of ideas or knowledge available to society

Theocratic regime religious principles play a dominant role in government, and those holding political power lead the dominant religion

Threats occur when the external environment threatens the ability of business to meet its targets

Tort an area of law concerned with injuries to people or damage to their assets

Trade surplus when the value of goods exceeds the value of imported goods

Trans-boundary processes which occur across national frontiers. Pollution in one country can often cross over into other countries. Carbon emissions are a prime example of trans-boundary pollution

Transnational Corporation synonym for MNC—a company with operations in more than one country; also used to refer to MNCs who see themselves as a global company and thus not tied to any particular country

Trillion one thousand billion, i.e. a trillion has nine zeros

UNCTAD a UN agency aimed at promoting trade and investment opportunities for developing countries and helping them integrate equitably into the world economy

Unidroit an organization trying to harmonize commercial law between countries

Uniform Commercial Code rules in force in many US states governing the sale of goods

Unitary system major decisions on policy, public expenditure, and tax rest with central government with regions having little power in these areas

Urbanization the increase in the proportion of a population living in towns and cities areas

Vertical merger a merger of firms at different stages of production of a product from raw materials to finished products to distribution. An example would be a steel manufacturer taking over a mining company producing iron ore

Vertically integrated firm a business operating at more than one stage of the production process of a good

World Bank international institution providing financial and technical help to developing countries

World Economic Forum (WEF) a think tank bringing together technical experts and business and political leaders who try to find solutions to major global economic, political, and social problems. It holds an annual meeting in Davos, Switzerland

World system the global system whose countries and regions are interconnected through a network of trade, investment, and migration linkages

World Trade Organization (WTO) international organization aimed at liberalizing world trade and investment; the successor to GATT

Index

V